HEALTH CARE FACILITIES HANDBOOK

Second Edition

HEALTH CARE FACILITIES HANDBOOK

Second Edition

Based on the 1987 Edition of NFPA 99,
Standard for Health Care Facilities

BURTON R. KLEIN, Editor

 National Fire Protection Association
Quincy, Massachusetts

This *Handbook* has *NOT* been processed in accordance with NFPA Regulations Governing Committee Projects. Therefore, the commentary in it is not to be considered the official position of NFPA or any of its committees and is not to be considered or relied upon as a Formal Interpretation of the meaning or intent of any specific provision or provisions of NFPA 99, *Standard for Health Care Facilities*.

NFPA No. 99HB87
ISBN 0-87765-331-3
Library of Congress No. 86-61652
Printed in the United States of America

First Printing, June 1987

Contents

Preface

NFPA 99, *Standard for Health Care Facilities*, is the integration of twelve documents developed by the Health Care Facilities Correlating Committee (formerly the Committee on Hospitals) over a period of forty years (*see Cross-Reference to Previous Individual Documents at the end of this Handbook*). However, it is not the only document applicable to health care facilities; there are some fifty other NFPA documents that either address, in part, health care facilities or can be used by them.

In categorizing fire protection for health care facilities, two general divisions can be identified:

Facility Fire Protection Features: those features built into or around a structure to minimize hazards, such as hydrants, types of structural protection, length of exit travel distances, and detection and extinguishing systems. They generally do not require human intervention to provide safety.

Operational Fire Protection: those practices intended to minimize fire hazards once the health care facility is occupied, such as safe use of inhalation anesthetics, safe use of electricity, safe practices in laboratories, emergency electrical power, and emergency planning. These very definitely rely on human intervention.

Some items, of course, could fit into both divisions (such as portable extinguishers, manual pull stations, performance criteria for grounding systems). Generally, NFPA 99 is concerned with operational fire protection for the many activities occurring in hospitals, ambulatory health care centers, clinics, medical and dental offices, nursing homes, custodial care facilities, and supervisory care facilities. This includes provisions for patient care areas (wards, intensive care units, operating suites, hyperbaric and hypobaric facilities), certain laboratories, several facility-wide systems, and overall emergency planning for a facility in the event of an internal or external disaster.

The effort to combine these twelve health care facility documents began in late 1979 at the suggestion of Marvin J. Fischer, Chairman of the Health Care Facilities Correlating Committee, and Assistant Vice-President for Facilities Planning and Engineering Services, Brookdale Hospital Medical Center, Brooklyn, New York. It was his firm belief that combining these individual documents into one cohesive document would benefit health care personnel and patients, as well as designers, builders, and enforcing authorites. The Correlating Committee agreed, but to assure itself that those affected by the change concurred, it solicited comments on the idea in 1981. With overwhelming support, the Committee proceeded with the first step: publication of a compilation of the latest editions of each of the documents into one bound volume in January 1982. This compilation was designated NFPA 99, *Health Care Facilities Code*, since it was, and still is, the Committee's intent that the document be a Code. The 1984 edition of NFPA 99 was the next step in the process: integration of the previous individual documents into one new document following the NFPA *Manual of Style* (all definitions in one chapter; requirements in the main body of the text; recommendations in the appendixes). The 1987 edition of NFPA 99 completes this integration process.

The idea of a handbook on NFPA 99 was a natural extension of the document once the combining process started. With so much material in one document, assistance, in the form of commentary, seemed the best method for sharing some of the history of this material as well as providing additional information and guidance in applying the standard to present conditions.

Codes and standards by themselves can be difficult to understand for those not involved in their development; however, it is not practical to include everything involving the requirements that are adopted (the reasons behind requirements, the pros and cons, the voting, the compromising, the research, and the discussion). Appendix material can help. Of late, rationales are being stressed. Handbooks present another vehicle for helping readers to better understand the requirements and recommendations of a document.

It is the hope of the editor that this second edition of the *Health Care Facilities Handbook* for the 1987 edition of NFPA 99 adds to the resources on health care firesafety, and is another useful adjunct for all those involved in protecting health care facilities from the hazards of fire.

About the Editor

Burton R. Klein is NFPA's Chief Health Care Fire Protection Engineer and serves in the dual capacity of Secretary for both the Health Care Facilities Technical Committee and Subcommittees and Executive Secretary for the Health Care Section, one of NFPA's most active Sections.

Mr. Klein is a graduate engineer, having received a bachelor of science degree in Electrical Engineering from Tufts University in 1965 and a master's degree in Engineering from The George Washington University in 1970. As a result of his master's thesis, "Automated Patient Histories," he has been constantly associated with the health care field. From 1970 to 1976, he established and directed the Medical Electronics Department at Tufts-New England Medical Center. During that time, he helped coordinate the establishment of the first hospital-affiliated Medical Electronics Technology Program at an associates degree level. It was implemented at the Franklin Institute of Boston and Tufts-New England Medical Center. He designed and taught two courses for that program.

In 1976, Mr. Klein took a position with the Scientific Apparatus Makers Association in Washington, D.C. Initially its staff medical engineer, he became the Association's Technical Affairs Director in 1977. In 1978, he returned to Boston and began his work with the National Fire Protection Association.

Mr. Klein holds a patent for a testing device for blood pressure monitors and is the author of the following books: *Introduction to Medical Electronics for Medical and Technical Personnel* (Copyright 1973, 1975, Tab Books), *Testing Instrumentation for Medical Equipment* (Copyright 1977, Quest Publishing Co.). He also authored the *Health Care Firesafety Compendium* (Copyright 1984, 1987, National Fire Protection Association) as a guide to locating firesafety requirements and recommendations for health care facilities.

Acknowledgments

The editor gratefully acknowledges the following persons for their invaluable contributions:

Saul Aronow, PhD, Newton, MA
John M. Bruner, MD, Massachusetts General Hospital, Boston, MA
Suzanne W. Conner, Childrens Hospital Medical Center, Akron, OH
Yadin David, St. Luke's Episcopal Hospital, Houston, TX
William H. L. Dornette, MD, Armed Forces Institute of Pathology, Washington, DC
James F. Ferguson, Allied Health Products, Inc., St. Louis, MO
Marvin J. Fischer, Brookdale Hospital Medical Center, Brooklyn, NY
George Harlow, Tufts-New England Medical Center, Boston, MA
Jon Jones, University of Massachusetts Medical Center, Worcester, MA
James Kerr, Winter Park, FL
Wes M. Lampe, Post-Glover, Inc., Erlanger, KY
Alan Lipschultz, Waterbury Hospital, Waterbury, CT
Ralph Loeb, Sherlock Smith & Adams, Inc., Montgomery, AL
David A. McWhinnie, Jr., Hickory Hills, IL
Reginald Nease, Medical Gas Services, Inc., Lenexa, KS
Ray J. Nichols, MD, University of Texas Medical Branch, Galveston, TX
Bryan Parker, Montefiore Hospital and Medical Center, Bronx, NY

In addition, the editor wishes to thank the following NFPA staff members:

Kathleen Montana, typing original drafts; Peggy Travers, keying and typesetting; Sharon Summers, composition; Jennifer Evans, Code Project Editor; Pat Donegan, Handbook Project Editor; Elizabeth Carmichael, Production Coordinator; Donald McGonagle, Printing Purchaser; and Jim Linville, Project Manager.

Technical Artist: George Nichols

Photographs: James Pothier, Richard Green

Cover Design: Frank Lucas

Notes:

Further explanatory information on Chapters 1 through 19 can be found in Appendix C.

Information on referenced publications can be found in Chapter 20 and Appendix B.

Sections of Chapter 3 identified by a dagger (†) include text extracted from NFPA 110-1985, *Standard for Emergency and Standby Power Systems*. Requests for interpretations or revisions of the extracted text will be referred to the Technical Committee on Emergency Power Supplies. Sections of Chapter 9 identified by a dagger (†) include figures extracted from NFPA 493-1978, *Standard for Intrinsically Safe Apparatus and Associated Apparatus for Use in Class I, II and III, Division 1 Hazardous Locations*. Requests for interpretations or revisions of the extracted figures will be referred to the Technical Committee on Electrical Equipment in Chemical Atmospheres. Sections of Appendixes A and C identified by a dagger (†) include text extracted from NFPA 30-1984, *Flammable and Combustible Liquids Code*. Requests for interpretations or revisions of the extracted text will be referred to the Technical Committee on General Storage of Flammable Liquids.

The text, illustrations, and photograph captions that make up the commentary on the various sections of the *Health Care Facilities Handbook* are printed in color. The photographs, all of which are part of the commentary, are printed in black for better clarity. The text of the standard itself is printed in black.

An asterisk (*) following the number or letter designating a subdivision indicates explanatory material on that subdivision in Appendix A. Material from Appendix A is integrated with the text and is identified by the letter *A* preceding the subdivision number to which it relates. Text in Appendix A is for informational purposes only and is not part of the requirements of NFPA 99.

"Extracted" text results when one NFPA document prints text from another NFPA document in lieu of merely referencing that other document. It can be considered akin to quoting. However, NFPA documents are dynamic, being revised periodically (at five-year intervals maximum). Thus, identifying such text with a date is necessary to eliminate confusion regarding from which edition such text came. Also, NFPA committees have scopes of responsibilities. Hence, extracted text is naturally outside the scope of the Committee that extracted the text.

Identifying "extracted" text precludes changes being made (however well intentioned) by the Committee that has extracted text.

The NFPA Standards Council developed an Extract Policy in 1983 after many years of differences that developed between text in Article 517 of NFPA 70, *National Electrical Code®*, and three health care documents (which became part of NFPA 99-1984). (By the mid 1970s, much of the text in Article 517 had originated with these three documents.) After scopes of responsibilities were developed for Panel 17 (the Committee responsible for Article 517) and the Health Care Facilities Committees, it became a matter of identifying what material in each Committees' document(s) came from the others' document. The Health Care Facilities Committees removed the few paragraphs that fell within the scope of Panel 17; all other *National Electrical Code* requirements in NFPA 99 are by reference only. The National Electrical Code Committee does not like to reference other documents within NFPA 70. Thus, Article 517 in NFPA 70-1984 had many paragraphs identified as extracted text.

The identification of text extracted from NFPA 110-1985 in this 1987 edition of NFPA 99 occurred because no other document covered this particular material prior to NFPA 110-1985 (i.e., requirements for generator sets used for emergency power). A Technical Committee on Emergency Power Supplies was formed in 1976 and assigned responsibility for emergency power supply systems irrespective of where used. With the adoption of NFPA 110-1985, some requirements for generators in NFPA 99 became "extracted" requirements from NFPA 110. In this 1987 edition of NFPA 99, extracted text is identified with daggers immediately following those paragraph numbers in which some or all of the text in those paragraphs is extracted.

All of the above commentary is for information only, since extracted text does not mean any more or less because it is extracted from another document. For users of this document, identification only means that some or all of the text in a particular paragraph actually comes from another NFPA document.

NOTE: Because of the complete restructuring of NFPA 99 for 1987, the following guide has been prepared (Brunerian style) to assist the many different persons who use this document.

ANESTHESIOLOGISTS might want to pay particular attention to the following sections within NFPA 99-1987:

RISK MANAGERS AND SAFETY/SECURITY OFFICERS might want to pay particular attention to the following sections within NFPA 99-1987:

ARCHITECTS, DESIGNERS, and ENGINEERS might want to pay particular attention to the following sections within NFPA 99-1987:

LABORATORIANS might want to pay particular attention to the following sections within NFPA 99-1987:

1 INTRODUCTION

Prologue

Combining twelve individual Health Care Facilities documents has been an evolving process; although all cover some aspect of health care firesafety, as individually developed documents, they did not readily translate into one integrated document. Some integration was achieved with the 1984 edition of NFPA 99. This 1987 edition of NFPA 99 fully integrates all previous documents and creates a structure should additional areas need to be included.

The former Health Care Facilities Correlating Committee stated its intention to produce a code on numerous occasions. For the 1984 edition of NFPA 99, there were public comments questioning whether, in the purest sense, the simple combination of previous standards (with recommended practices and manuals in appendixes), could legitimately be called a code. Some of the Health Care Facilities standards had been adopted into state law and could meet the test of being a code; the status of other standards was not known. The Correlating Committee accepted the arguments for that edition and titled the document a standard, although the Correlating Committee (now Technical Committee on Health Care Facilities) is still committed to producing a code.

The Health Care Facilities Project is a result of changing needs in the health care field. In 1917, NFPA formed a committee to address the use of gases. The 1930s found explosions in operating rooms occurring more than infrequently, and the Committee on Gases investigated the problem and developed recommendations for the safe use of anesthetic gases. In the 1940s, other problems in hospital operating rooms became evident and a separate Committee on Hospital Operating Rooms was established to address them.

In the 1960s, all aspects of hospital activities involving fire and explosion hazards (including electric shock and emergency electric power) were seen to be in need of some guidelines and/or standards. The name was changed once more to the Committee on Hospitals; and Standing Subcommittees on Anesthetizing Agents, Respiratory Therapy, Laboratories, Essential Electrical Systems, Safe Use of Electricity, Medical-Surgical Vacuum Systems, Safe Use of High-Frequency Electricity, Disaster Planning, and Hyperbaric/Hypobaric Facilities were established.

In 1975, the breadth of the Subcommittees had become so extensive that the role of the Committee on Hospitals shifted again, and its function became that of correlating the diverse activities of the eight Subcommittees under it. Thus, the Health Care Facilities Correlating Committee came into existence, and the Subcommittees were elevated to Technical Committees.

In 1985, it was seen by the Correlating Committee that, to be more effective, the Correlating Committee would have to be able to make technical changes in the documents under its responsibility. Since, under NFPA procedures, Correlating Committees cannot make such technical changes, the Correlating Committee petitioned the Standards Council to discharge the Correlating Committee and Technical Committees under it and establish a new (main) Technical Committee, with standing subcommittees under it. These subcommittees were not to be simply the previous Technical Committees; rather they were to reflect the restructuring of NFPA 99.

This restructured NFPA 99 essentially covers the same material included in the 1984 edition of NFPA 99. The only differences are: 1) material on hypobaric facilities has been separated out into a new document (NFPA 99B) since these facilities are no longer used for medical purposes; 2) material on the home use of respiratory therapy (Appendix F in the 1984 edition of NFPA 99) has been deleted entirely since the Committee felt that its form was no longer useful (though the need for this information is still necessary), and that a simplified brochure was a better way to get this safety information to patients; and 3) the text of NFPA 56F-1983, *Standard on Nonflammable Medical Gas Systems,* has been incorporated essentially as Sections 4-3 to 4-6. (Responsibility for this document was transferred by the Standards Council in October 1985 from the Technical Committee on Industrial and Medical Gases to the Technical Committee on Health Care Facilities.)

The use of the term "(Reserved)" throughout this 1987 edition of NFPA 99 should not be construed as an omission, or imminent inclusion of text. When the Subcommittee on Restructuring was analyzing ways of organizing the material included in NFPA 99-1984, a matrix of function versus location evolved. However, when the text itself of NFPA 99-1984 was rearranged to fit the matrix, some of the boxes in the matrix were found to have no text developed against them. The Subcommittee then had a choice of deleting such empty boxes (and thus paragraph numbers) or just leaving the box empty [i.e. "(reserved)"]. It was decided to retain the "box" so that the "form" of the new structure could be seen.

New text for these empty boxes will be added whenever the Subcommittee responsible for that material feels text is warranted or when public proposals are received recommending text. In either instance, any new text will have to go through the full NFPA adoption procedures.

1-1 Scope. The scope of this document is to establish criteria to minimize the hazards of fire, explosion, and electricity in health care facilities. These criteria include performance, maintenance, testing, and safe practices for facilities, material, equipment, and appliances, and include other hazards associated with the primary hazards.

This scope reflects the scopes of the previous thirteen individual documents from which NFPA 99 was created.

1-2 Application. This document shall apply to all health care facilities. Construction and equipment requirements shall be applied only to new construction and new equipment, except as modified in individual chapters.

Chapters 12 through 18 specify the conditions under which the requirements of Chapters 3 through 11 shall apply in Chapters 12 through 18.

In this and most other standards, requirements are not intended to be retroactive; basically, they apply only to new equipment and construction. Existing facilities should be considered individually. However, this is not meant to authorize or condone clearly hazardous conditions. Minimum requirements for existing equipment and construction are specifically indicated in more than several instances.

Paragraph 2 was added to clearly indicate how Chapters 3 to 11 are linked to 12 to 18 as a result of the new structure of NFPA 99.

1-3 Intended Use. This document is intended for use by those persons involved in the design, construction, inspection, and operation of health care facilities and in the design, manufacture, and testing of appliances and equipment used in patient care areas of health care facilities.

It should not be construed by persons involved in the activities listed that the material in NFPA 99 is required per se. *Required* use will depend on whether and by whom the document is adopted for use.

Because of the wide audience for NFPA 99, the subcommittee that restructured NFPA 99 for this edition took this diversity into consideration to try to meet the needs of each (e.g., system requirements, requirements for the seven major types of health care facilities, and manufacturer requirements have all been addressed separately.)

1-4 Discretionary Powers of Authority Having Jurisdiction. The authority having jurisdiction for the enforcement of this document shall be permitted to grant exceptions to its requirements.

Nothing in this document is intended to prevent the use of systems, methods, or devices of equivalent or superior quality, strength, fire resistance, effectiveness, durability, and safety to those prescribed by this document, providing technical documentation is submitted to the authority having jurisdiction to demonstrate equivalency and the system, method, or device is approved for the intended purpose.

While authorities having jurisdiction can adopt and enforce voluntary standards they consider appropriate (e.g., adopt and enforce requirements as written; issue waivers to specific facilities not meeting certain requirements; adopt a document but change certain requirements), this section, which was previously in three of the twelve Health Care Facilities documents, has been retained and extended to apply to the entire standard as a reminder to authorities that they can grant exemptions.

Paragraph 2 adds the concept of "equivalency" to the previous permission of allowing enforcing authorities (governmental and non-governmental) to grant exceptions to requirements. This wording on equivalency is almost verbatim from Paragraph 1-5.1 in NFPA *101*-1985, *Life Safety Code®*.

1-5 Interpretations. The National Fire Protection Association does not approve, inspect, or certify any installation, procedure, equipment, or material. In determining the acceptability of installations, procedures, or material the authority having jurisdiction may base acceptance on compliance with this document. To promote uniformity of interpretation and application of its standards, NFPA has established interpretation procedures. These procedures are outlined on the inside front cover of this document. Refer to Section 16 of the NFPA *Regulations Governing Committee Projects* for complete details.

1-6 Organization of this Document.

1-6.1 This 1987 edition of NFPA 99 is a complete restructuring of the 1984 edition. Its new organization reflects an attempt to make the document completely integrated and cohesive.

Having been originally developed from 12 previously independent documents, the 1987 edition of NFPA 99 restructures all the existing text in the following way:

Chapter 1 is an introductory chapter.

Chapter 2 lists all definitions.

Chapters 3 to 11 contain requirements but do not state where they are applicable.

Chapters 12 through 18 are "facility" chapters listing requirements from Chapters 3 to 11 that are applicable to specific facilities. These chapters also contain any additional requirements specific to that facility.

Chapter 19 contains safety requirements for hyperbaric facilities (whether freestanding or part of a larger facility).

Chapter 20 lists required references made in Chapters 1 through 19.

Appendix A contains nonmandatory information keyed to the text of Chapters 1 through 19 (e.g., A-5-2.4 is explanatory information on 5-2.4).

Appendix B lists informatory references.

Appendix C contains more explanatory information on Chapters 1 through 19, though not keyed to specific text (i.e., numbering is such that the first number after the letter C indicates the chapter to which material is related, e.g., Appendix C-7 contains information related to Chapter 7).

Finally, two annexes contain guidance on the following subjects: disaster planning (Annex 1) and the use of high-frequency electricity (Annex 2).

As a result of this restructuring, a reader interested in learning, for example, what the electrical system requirements are for a hospital, would begin by first turning to Chapter 12 ("Hospital Requirements"), then to Subsection 12-3.3 ("Electrical System Requirements"). Similarly, electrical system requirements for a nursing home would be found by first turning to Chapter 16 ("Nursing Home Requirements"), then to Subsection 16-3.3 ("Electrical System Requirements").

1-6.2   Each general chapter (3 to 11) has been organized into the following sections:

-1   Scope
-2   Nature of Hazards
-3   Source
-4   Distribution
-5   Performance Criteria and Testing
-6   Administration

The major topics considered in each facility chapter (12 through 18) under "General Requirements" (e.g., 12-3, 13-3, etc.) are arranged in the following order (for consistency with the order of the general chapters):

.3   Electrical Systems
.4   Gas Systems
.5   Environmental Systems
.6   Materials
.7   Electrical Equipment
.8   Gas Equipment

1-6.3 This 1987 edition completes the original goal of combining the 12 previously individual documents under the jurisdiction of the former Correlating Committee on Health Care Facilities, now Technical Committee on Health Care Facilities. Cross-referencing to the previous individual documents is possible but would be complicated because of the major difference between the structure of the previous individual documents and the structure for this 1987 edition of NFPA 99.

> See chart at end of handbook that provides a general scheme of where text from previous documents is now located.

1-7 Metric Units. While it is common practice for medical appliances to use metric units on their dials, gauges, and controls, the components of systems within the scope of this document, which are manufactured and used in the United States, employ nonmetric dimensions. Since these dimensions (such as nominal pipe sizes) are not established by the National Fire Protection Association, the Technical Committee on Health Care Facilities cannot independently change them. Accordingly, this document uses dimensions that are presently in common use by the building trades in the United States. Conversion factors to metric units are included in Appendix C-4.5.

1-8 Effective Date. The effective date of application of any provision of this document is not determined by the National Fire Protection Association. All questions related to applicability shall be directed to the authority having jurisdiction.

1-9 Preface. This document's genesis was a series of explosions in operating rooms during surgery in the 1930s. The problem was traced to static discharges of sufficient energy to ignite the flammable anesthetic agents being used. A series of recommendations to mitigate the hazard were then promulgated. In addition, a Committee on Hospitals was established with responsibility to periodically review and revise recommendations.

Since then, the concerns of this Committee have grown to encompass many other fire and fire-related hazards related to the delivery of health care services. The Committee was also allowed to enlarge its scope to include all health care facilities.

The major concerns of the Committee are those hazards associated with operating a health care facility, treating patients, and operating laboratories. This includes the electrical system (both normal and emergency power), gas systems (both positive and negative pressure), medical equipment (both electrical and gas powered), environmental conditions peculiar to health care facilities operation, and the management of a facility in the event of disasters (e.g., fire, chemical spill) that disrupt normal patient care.

The Committee and its Subcommittees originally developed separate documents as hazards were identified. NFPA 99 is the result of a proposal to combine, organize, and integrate into one document all the material contained in the individual documents. The intent was, and still is, to provide as useful as possible a document to its many and varied users.

2 DEFINITIONS

[Secretary's Note: The letters in parentheses at the end of each definition refer to the Technical Committee Standing Subcommittee responsible for defining the term. The key to identifying responsibility is as follows:

(AS):   Subcommittee on Anesthesia Services
(DIS):   Subcommittee on Disaster Planning
(EE):   Subcommittee on Electrical Equipment
(ES):   Subcommittee on Electrical Systems
(GE):   Subcommittee on Gas Equipment
(HFE):   Subcommittee on Use of High Frequency Electricity
(HHF):   Subcommittee on Hyperbaric and Hypobaric Facilities
(LAB):   Subcommittee on Laboratories
(MGS):   Subcommittee on Nonflammable Piped Gas Systems
(VSE):   Subcommittee on Vacuum Systems and Equipment
(TC):   Technical Committee on Health Care Facilities.]

For the purposes of this document, the following definitions apply as indicated.

2-1 Official NFPA Definitions.

Approved. Acceptable to the "authority having jurisdiction."

NOTE: The National Fire Protection Association does not approve, inspect or certify any installations, procedures, equipment, or materials nor does it approve or evaluate testing laboratories. In determining the acceptability of installations or procedures, equipment or materials, the authority having jurisdiction may base acceptance on compliance with NFPA or other appropriate standards. In the absence of such standards, said authority may require evidence of proper installation, procedure or use. The authority having jurisdiction may also refer to the listings or labeling practices of an organization concerned with product evaluations which is in a position to determine compliance with appropriate standards for the current production of listed items.

Authority Having Jurisdiction. The "authority having jurisdiction" is the organization, office or individual responsible for "approving" equipment, an installation or a procedure.

NOTE: The phrase "authority having jurisdiction" is used in NFPA documents in a broad manner since jurisdictions and "approval" agencies vary as do their responsibilities. Where public safety is primary, the "authority having jurisdiction" may be a federal, state, local or other regional department or individual such as a fire chief, fire marshal, chief of a fire prevention bureau, labor department, health department, building official, electrical inspector, or others having statutory authority. For insurance purposes, an insurance inspection department, rating bureau, or other insurance company representative may be the "authority having jurisdiction." In many circumstances the property owner or his designated agent assumes the role of the "authority having jurisdiction"; at government installations, the commanding officer or departmental official may be the "authority having jurisdiction."

Code. A document containing only mandatory provisions using the word *shall* to indicate requirements and in a form generally suitable for adoption into law. Explanatory material may be included only in the form of "fine print" notes, in footnotes, or in an appendix.

Labeled. Equipment or materials to which has been attached a label, symbol or other identifying mark of an organization acceptable to the "authority having jurisdiction" and concerned with product evaluation, that maintains periodic inspection of production of labeled equipment or materials and by whose labeling the manufacturer indicates compliance with appropriate standards or performance in a specified manner.

Listed. Equipment or materials included in a list published by an organization acceptable to the "authority having jurisdiction" and concerned with product evaluation, that maintains periodic inspection of production of listed equipment or materials and whose listing states either that the equipment or material meets appropriate standards or has been tested and found suitable for use in a specified manner.

NOTE: The means for identifying listed equipment may vary for each organization concerned with product evaluation, some of which do not recognize equipment as listed unless it is also labeled. The "authority having jurisdiction" should utilize the system employed by the listing organization to identify a listed product.

Manual or Guide. A document which is informative in nature and does not contain requirements.

Shall. Indicates a mandatory requirement.

Should. Indicates a recommendation or that which is advised but not required.

Standard. A document containing only mandatory provisions using the word *shall* to indicate requirements. Explanatory material may be included only in the form of "fine print" notes, in footnotes, or in an appendix.

2-2 Definitions of Terms Used in the Standard.

ACFM. Actual cubic feet per minute. The unit used to express the measure of the volume of gas flowing at operating temperature and pressure, as distinct from the volume of a gas flowing at standard temperature and pressure (*see definition of SCFM*). (VSE)

Adiabatic Heating. The heating of a gas caused by its compression. (HHF)

In general thermodynamic terms, adiabatic heating refers to an energy exchange process where there is no external gain or loss of heat energy. As used in this standard, it refers to the special case of the rapid compression of a gas where the mechanical energy input serves to raise the temperature of the gas.

Aerosol. An intimate mixture of a liquid or a solid in a gas; the liquid or solid, called the dispersed phase, is uniformly distributed in a finely divided state throughout the gas, which is the continuous phase or dispersing medium. (GE)

A previous definition did not clearly define how the liquid or solid (dispersed phase) related to the gas (continuous phase or dispersing medium).

Air, Oil-Free, Dry. Air complying, as a minimum, with Grade "D" in CGA Pamphlet G-7.1, *Commodity Specification for Air*, and having a maximum dew point of $-63°F$ ($-52.8°C$). (AS)

Alternate Power Source. One or more generator sets, or battery systems where permitted, intended to provide power during the interruption of the normal electrical service; or the public utility electrical service intended to provide power during interruption of service normally provided by the generating facilities on the premises. (ES)

Ambulatory Care Facility. A facility, not hospital-based, wherein nonflammable inhalation anesthetic agents are administered to ambulatory patients for the production of general anesthesia or relative analgesia. (AS)

Ambulatory Health Care Center. A building or part thereof used to provide services or treatment to four or more patients at the same time and meeting either (1) or (2) below.

(1) Those facilities that provide, on an outpatient basis, treatment for patients that would render them incapable of taking action for self-preservation under emergency conditions without assistance from others, such as hemodialysis units or freestanding emergency medical units.

(2) Those facilities that provide, on an outpatient basis, surgical treatment requiring general anesthesia. (EE)

Ampacity. Current-carrying capacity of electric conductors expressed in amperes. (ES)

Anesthetic. As used in this standard, applies to any inhalation agent used to produce relative analgesia or general anesthesia. (AS)

Anesthetizing Location. Any area of the facility that has been designated to be used for the administration of any flammable or nonflammable inhalation anesthetic agents in the course of examination or treatment, including the use of such agents for relative analgesia (*see definition of relative analgesia*). (AS)

The current definition for this term was extensively discussed before concurrence was reached in 1978. It reflects recent concern that the previous definition might be misinterpreted, leading to consideration of many areas of a facility as "anesthetizing locations," although this was not the intent of the Committee responsible for this definition. The key word is "designated." Any area must be designated by the administrative body as an anesthetizing location before the requirements of Section 12-4.1 or 13-4.1 are applicable.

Designation of a facility is necessary so that it is clear to all what requirements are applicable to a particular location. Regular administration of inhalation anesthetics in a location *not* administratively designated for such practice might be regarded as imprudent.

The anesthetizing locations referenced are those where general anesthesia is administered (i.e., inhalation anesthetics), not where just local anesthetics are administered.

Anoxia. A state of markedly inadequate oxygenation of the tissues and blood, of more marked degree than hypoxia. (HHF)

Antistatic. That class of materials that includes conductive materials and, also, those materials that throughout their stated life meet the requirements of 12-4.1.3.8(f)(3) and (4). (AS)

Apparatus. Furniture, laboratory hoods, centrifuges, refrigerators, and commercial or man-made on-site equipment used in a laboratory. (LAB)

Appliance. Electrical equipment, generally other than industrial, normally built in standardized sizes or types, which is installed or connected as a unit to perform one or more functions. (EE)

The definition used in this document is in general agreement with that listed in NFPA 70, *National Electrical Code.*

The definition here, however, encompasses many kinds of electrical end-use devices, from cord-connected devices — such as a monitor — to hard-wired devices — such as a whirlpool bath or X-ray machine. Larger physical plant equipment, such as pumps, air conditioners and elevators, is generally not included. Thus, the usage of a device must be considered in determining the applicability of the provisions of this standard.

Applicator. A means of applying high-frequency energy to a patient other than by an electrically conductive connection. (HFE)

NOTE: In the above sense, an applicator is not an electrode since it does not use a conductive connection to the patient in order to function. The radio frequency "horn" of a diathermy machine is a typical applicator.

Area of Administration. The room in which oxygen is being administered, except that rooms containing more than two patients shall be designated as patient wards. The area of administration in patient wards shall be any point within 15 ft (4.3 m) of oxygen equipment or an enclosure containing or intended to contain an oxygen-enriched atmosphere. In all cases the area of administration shall include access aisles and immediately adjacent patient beds. (GE)

Atmosphere. The pressure exerted by, and gaseous composition of, an environment. As employed in this standard, atmosphere may refer to the environment within or outside of a hyperbaric facility. When used as a measure of pressure, atmosphere is expressed as a fraction of standard air pressure (14.7 psi) (101.4 kPa). (*See NFPA 99B, Appendix C-3, Pressure Table, Column 1.*) (HHF)

This definition is the technically accurate one for this term. However, the term atmosphere has two distinct meanings. Its general meaning is the space occupied by gases surrounding a particular region. This is usually air at a particular pressure and temperature. The term has another technical meaning, that of a unit of pressure. It is usually obvious from the text which meaning is pertinent.

Atmosphere, Absolute (ATA). (*See definition of atmosphere.*) Two ATA = two atmospheres. (HHF)

Atmosphere, Ambient. The pressure and composition of the environment surrounding a chamber. (HHF)

The Subcommittee on Hyperbaric and Hypobaric Facilites (responsible for this definition) considered it important to be precise in describing the various atmospheres associated with hyperbaric operation (i.e., ambient and chamber). The term "composition" replaced "concentration" since composition includes concentration, and is more technically correct in describing the atmosphere surrounding the chamber.

Atmosphere, Chamber. The environment inside a chamber. (HHF)

Atmosphere of Increased Burning Rate. * Any atmosphere containing a percentage of oxygen, or oxygen and nitrous oxide, greater than the quotient of 23.45 divided by the square root of the total pressure in atmospheres, i.e.,

$$\frac{23.45}{\sqrt{T.P._{atmos.}}} \text{ where } T.P._{atmos.} = \text{total pressure in atmospheres}$$

(See Appendix A-2-2.) (HHF)

A-2-2 Atmosphere of Increased Burning Rate. The degree of fire hazard of an oxygen-enriched atmosphere varies with the concentration of oxygen and diluent gas, and the total pressure. The definition contained in the current edition of NFPA 53M, *Manual on Fire Hazards in Oxygen-Enriched Atmospheres*, and in editions of NFPA 56D, *Standard for Hyperbaric Facilities*, prior to 1982, did not necessarily reflect the increased fire hazard of hyperbaric and hypobaric atmospheres.

The definition of atmosphere of increased burning rate in Chapter 19 and in NFPA 99B, *Standard for Hypobaric Facilities*, defines an oxygen-enriched atmosphere with an increased fire hazard, as it relates to the increased burning rate of material in the atmosphere. It is based upon a 1.2 cm/second burning rate (at 23.5 percent oxygen at 1 atmosphere absolute) as described in Figure A-2-2(a) from Technical Memorandum UCRI-721, *Chamber Fire Safety*, by Schmidt, Dorr & Hamilton (Ocean Systems Inc., Research & Development Lab, Tarrytown, NY 01591). [*See Figure A-2-2(a).*]

The definition accounts for the special atmospheres now in use by military, nonmilitary, and private sector operators of such chambers. It is based on actual test data under hyperbaric and hypobaric conditions.

The ability of an atmosphere to support combustion is sensitive principally to the oxygen percent by volume concentration. This can be seen by reviewing results of another test by Schmidt, Dorr, and Hamilton (*see Figure 1*). Report by Cook, Meierer, and Shields is the original source from which curves in Figure A-2-2(a) were generated.

Automatic. Self-acting, operating by its own mechanism when actuated by some impersonal influence as, for example, a change in current, voltage, pressure, temperature, or mechanical configuration. (ES)

Bends. Decompression sickness, caisson worker's disease. (*See Appendix C-19.1.3.3.2.*) (HHF)

Branch Circuit. The circuit conductors between the final overcurrent device protecting the circuit and the outlet(s). (ES)

This definition conforms to that in NFPA 70, *National Electrical Code*. It refers to the wiring and does not include the overcurrent device or the outlet.

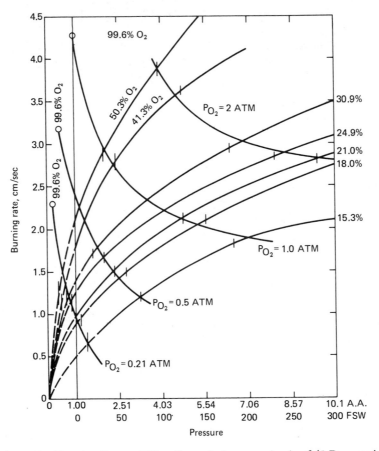

Figure A-2-2(a)   Burning Rates of Filter Paper Strips at an Angle of 45 Degrees in N_2–O_2 mixtures. (From Figure 4, "Technical Memorandum UCRI-721, Chamber Fire Safety," T. C. Schmidt, V. A. Dorr and R. W. Hamilton Jr., Ocean Systems, Inc. Research and Development Laboratory, Tarrytown, New York 10591. Work carried out under U.S. Office of Naval Research, Washington, DC, Contract No. N00014-67-A-0214-0013.) (From Cook, G.A., Meierer, R.E., Shields, B.M. *Screening of Flame-Resistant Materials and Comparison of Helium with Nitrogen for Use in Diving Atmospheres.* First summary report under ONR Contract No. 0014-66-C-0149. Tonawanda, NY: Union Carbide, 31 March 1967. DDC No. AD-651583.)

Bulk Systems:

Bulk Nitrous Oxide System.   An assembly of equipment as described in the definiton of bulk oxygen system that has a storage capacity of more than 3200 lb (1452 kg), approximately 28,000 cu ft (793 m³) (NTP), of nitrous oxide. (MGS)

Bulk Oxygen System.   An assembly of equipment such as oxygen storage containers, pressure regulators, pressure relief devices, vaporizers, manifolds, and interconnecting piping, that has a storage capacity of more than 20,000 cu ft (566 m³) of oxygen (NTP) including unconnected reserves on hand at the site. The bulk oxygen system terminates at the point where oxygen at service pressure first enters the supply line. The oxygen containers may be stationary or movable, and the oxygen may be stored as gas or liquid. (MGS)

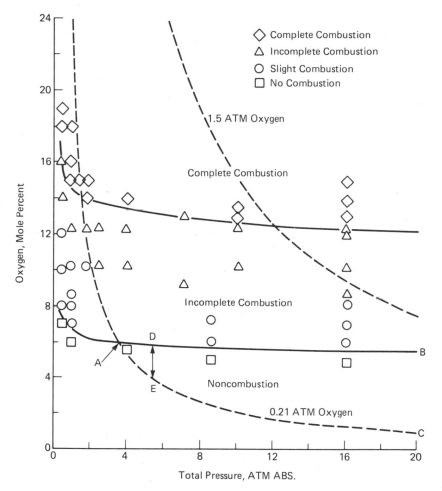

Figure 1 Three combustion zones for vertical paper strips in $N_2 - O_2$ mixtures. (From Figure 7, "Technical Memorandum UCRI-721," Chamber Fire Safety, T. C. Schmidt, V. A. Dorr, and R. W. Hamilton, Jr., Ocean Systems, Inc. Research and Development Laboratory, Tarrytown, New York 10591.)

Cannula, Nasal. Device consisting of two short tubes to be inserted into the nostrils to administer oxygen or other therapeutic gases. (GE)

This term was added to distinguish nasal cannula from nasal catheter, which is a slightly different apparatus for administering oxygen.

Catheter, Nasal. A flexible tube for insertion through the nose into the nasopharynx to administer oxygen or other therapeutic gases. (GE)

Clinic. A health care facility where patients are seen on an ambulatory basis, but where surgery involving general anesthesia is not performed. (TC)

When the Restructuring Subcommittee was developing the new structure for NFPA 99, it first listed the many types of health care facilities, and then analyzed what differences existed between them (vis-a-vis fire, explosion, electrical hazards as covered by NFPA 99). Those facilities that had the same hazards were grouped together. "Clinics" were observed to be sufficiently different to warrant being a separate chapter (14) in NFPA 99.

Cold Room.   A refrigerated area large enough for personnel to enter. (LAB)

Combustible.   A substance that if ignited will react with oxygen and burn. (AS)

Combustible Liquid.   See definition of liquids and Appendix C-10.2.1. (LAB)

The definition used is from NFPA 30, *Flammable and Combustible Liquids Code.*

Combustion.   A chemical process (such as oxidation) accompanied by the rapid evolution of heat and light. (AS)

NOTE: Combustion is not limited to a chemical reaction always involving oxygen. Certain metals, such as calcium and aluminum, will burn in nitrogen; nitrous oxide will support the combustion of phosphorous and carbon; etc. However, this document deals with the more common process of fuels burning in air.

Combustion Products.   The gases, volatilized liquids and solids, particulate matter, and ash generated by combustion. (AS)

See 5-2 for a discussion on the toxicological hazards of combustion products that result from materials subjected to fire. With increased use of novel synthetic and plastic materials, concern for protection against the associated hazards grows. Research is continuing on the subject.

Conductive.   Not only those materials, such as metals, that are commonly considered electrically conductive, but also that class of materials which, when tested in accordance with this document, have a resistance not exceeding 1,000,000 ohms. Such materials are required where electrostatic interconnection is necessary. (AS)

The definition here encompasses more than the traditional definition of materials with very low resistance (less than one ohm, e.g., wire). In flammable anesthetizing locations, "conductivity" values can be up to 1,000,000 ohms, *but* only as it relates to antistatic purposes.

Container.   A low-pressure, vacuum-insulated vessel containing gases in liquid form. (GE)

This term is used in Chapter 8 specifically to refer to oxygen containers. It is now widely accepted for this type of application. The term cylinder is reserved for high-pressure application.

Critical Branch. A subsystem of the emergency system consisting of feeders and branch circuits supplying energy to task illumination, special power circuits, and selected receptacles serving areas and functions related to patient care, and which can be connected to alternate power sources by one or more transfer switches during interruption of normal power source. (ES)

Critical Equipment. That equipment essential to the safety of the occupants of the facility. (HHF)

Critical System. A system of feeders and branch circuits in nursing homes and custodial care facilities arranged for connection to the alternate power source to restore service to certain critical receptacles, task illumination, and equipment. (ES)

Custodial Care Facility. A building, or part thereof, used for the housing, on a 24-hour basis, of four or more persons who are incapable of self-preservation because of age or physical or mental limitation. The following types of facilities, when accommodating persons of the above description, shall be classified as custodial care facilities:

(1) Nursery facilities that provide full-time care for children under six years of age.

(2) Facilities for the care of the mentally retarded that normally provide housing and custodial care on a 24-hour basis in an institutional setting such as a hospital or institution for the mentally retarded.

Facilities housing older persons or mental patients, including the mentally retarded, who are judged to be capable of evacuating the building with staff assistance in an emergency, are covered by other chapters in NFPA *101®, Life Safety Code® (see 12-1.1.1.6 and 12-1.1.1.9 in the Life Safety Code)*.

Facilities that do not provide housing on a 24-hour basis for their occupants are classified as day-care centers, group day-care centers, or family day-care homes. (EE)

The definition coincides with that in NFPA *101-1985, Life Safety Code.*
Definition of the term became necessary when the Restructuring Subcommittee identified custodial care facilities as having some distinct differences from other types of health care facilities (vis-a-vis firesafety hazards addressed by NFPA 99), and included this type of facility as a separate chapter (17).

Cylinder. A supply tank containing high-pressure gases or gas mixtures at pressures that may be in excess of 2000 psig (13.8 kPa gauge). (GE)

See commentary under the definition of Container.

Decompression Sickness. A syndrome due to evolved gas in the tissues resulting from a reduction in ambient pressure. (HHF)

Commonly referred to as "the bends" or "caisson worker's disease," decompression sickness occurs when pressure surrounding a person is reduced too quickly (e.g., when a diver surfaces too quickly).

Detonation. An exothermic reaction wherein the reaction propagates through the unrelated material at a rate exceeding the velocity of sound, hence the explosive noise. (AS)

Direct Electrical Pathway to the Heart. An externalized conductive pathway, insulated except at its ends, one end of which is in direct contact with heart muscle and the other outside the body, and is accessible for inadvertent or intentional contact with grounded objects or energized, ground-referenced sources. Catheters filled with conductive fluids and electrodes, such as may be used for pacing the heart, are examples of direct electrical pathways to the heart. (EE)

Double-Insulated Appliances. Appliances having an insulation system comprising both basic insulation necessary for the functioning of the appliance and for basic protection against electric shock, and supplementary insulation. The supplementary insulation is independent insulation provided in addition to the basic insulation to ensure protection against electric shock in case of failure of the basic insulation. (EE)

This definition is in general agreement with other non-NFPA documents that define the term.

Electrical Life Support Equipment. Electrically powered equipment whose continuous operation is necessary to maintain a patient's life. (ES)

This term is intended to better define which electrical equipment requires continuous electrical power for patient care to ensure that equipment can be relied upon, even if normal electric power is interrupted.

Electrode. A device intended to provide an electrically conductive connection through a cable to a patient. Some electrodes of interest are: (EE)

In the purest sense, an electrode is the terminal where electrical energy is transferred from a device to the patient or vice-versa. Of necessity, however, an electrode must be connected to a cable for the transfer to occur; thus, the reference to a cable in the first sentence.

Active Electrode. An electrode intended to generate a surgical effect at its point of application to the patient. (HFE)

Dispersive Electrode. An electrode intended to complete the electrical path between patient and appliance, and at which no surgical effect is intended. It is often called the "indifferent electrode," the "return electrode," the "patient plate," or the "neutral electrode." (HFE)

The term neutral electrode is used by the International Electrotechnical Commission. However, the term does not imply that it is related to the neutral conductor of the power supply system.

Emergency System. A system of feeders and branch circuits meeting the requirements of Article 700 of NFPA 70, *National Electrical Code*, and intended to supply alternate power to a limited number of prescribed functions vital to the protection of life and safety, with automatic restoration of electrical power within 10 seconds of power interruption. (ES)

See commentary on 3-3.2.1.8 for information on the 10-second restoration time.

Equipment Grounding Bus. A grounding terminal bus in the feeder circuit of the branch circuit distribution panel that serves a particular area. (EE)

This bus should provide a common connection point for all the equipment grounding conductors in a given patient area.

One equipment grounding bus may serve several patients fed from the same branch-circuit distribution panel. It is not intended that an additional grounding bus be installed if an appropriate bus is already present.

Equipment System. A system of feeders and branch circuits arranged for automatic or manual connection to the alternate power source and which serves primarily three-phase power equipment. (ES)

This system serves heavy equipment (e.g., pumps, fans, etc.), which are often three-phase powered. This equipment is necessary for the operation of the hospital, but can be placed back in service after a short delay. Transferring these heavy loads rapidly to the alternate power source could cause large surges that could further disrupt the system.

Essential Electrical System. A system comprised of alternate sources of power and all connected distribution systems and ancillary equipment, designed to assure continuity of electrical power to designated areas and functions of a health care facility during disruption of normal power sources, and also designed to minimize disruption within the internal wiring system. (ES)

Exposed Conductive Surfaces. Those surfaces that are capable of carrying electric current and that are unprotected, uninsulated, unenclosed or unguarded, permitting personal contact. (EE)

Failure. An incident that increases the hazard to personnel or patients or affects the safe functioning of electric appliances or devices. It includes failure of a component, loss of normal protective paths such as grounding, and short circuits or faults between energized conductors and the chassis. (EE)

Fault Current. A current in an accidental connection between an energized and a grounded or other conductive element resulting from a failure of insulation, spacing, or containment of conductors. (ES)

Feeder. All circuit conductors between the service equipment or the source of a separately derived system and the final branch-circuit overcurrent device. (ES)

This definition is similar to that in NFPA 70, National Electrical Code. (See NFPA 70 for definitions of the specific terms used.)

Flame Resistant. Where flame resistance of a material is required by this standard, that material shall pass successfully the small-scale test described in NFPA 701, *Standard Methods of Fire Tests for Flame-Resistant Textiles and Films*, except that the test shall be conducted in the gaseous composition and maximum pressure at which the chamber will be operated. (HHF)

NOTE: A source of ignition alternate to the gas burner specified in NFPA 701 may be required for this test if it is to be performed in 100 percent oxygen at several atmospheres pressure.

This criterion applies to finishes and materials within hyperbaric and hypobaric chambers that must be flame resistant. For interior finishes criteria, see 19-2.2.3.

The test in NFPA 701 was retained, though modified, because the Committee responsible for Chapter 19 felt that the flame-resistant test should account for the gaseous composition and pressure that materials would be subject to if used in hyperbaric chambers.

Flame Retardant. *(See definition of flame resistant.)* (HHF)

Flammable. An adjective describing easy ignition, intense burning, and rapid rate of flame spread during combustion. It may also be used as a noun to mean a flammable substance. Many substances nonflammable in air become flammable if the oxygen content of the gaseous medium is increased above 0.235 ATA. (AS)

This definition goes beyond the normal atmospheric definition of flammable and includes information peculiar to hyperbaric operation.

Flammable Anesthetizing Location. Any area of a facility that has been designated to be used for the administration of any flammable inhalation anesthetic agents in the normal course of examination or treatment. (AS)

Flammable Gas. Any gas that will burn when mixed in any proportion with air, oxygen, or nitrous oxide. (LAB)

Flammable Liquid. See definition of liquids and Appendix C-10.2.1. (LAB)

The definition used is from NFPA 30, *Flammable and Combustible Liquids Code.*

Flash Point. The minimum temperature at which a liquid gives off vapor in sufficient concentration to form an ignitible mixture with air near the surface of the liquid within the vessel, as specified by appropriate test procedures and apparatus. *(See Appendix C-10.2.2.)* (LAB)

Flow-Control Valve. A valve, usually a needle valve, that precisely controls flow of gas. (GE)

Flowmeter. A device for measuring volumetric flow rates of gases and liquids. (GE)

It should be noted that some flowmeters may indicate mean flow rates, in addition to the volumetric flow rate, of a substance being measured.

Flowmeter, Pressure Compensated. A flowmeter indicating accurate flow of gas whether the gas is discharged into ambient pressure or into a system at nonambient pressure. (GE)

Frequency. The number of oscillations, per unit time, of a particular current or voltage waveform. The unit of frequency is the hertz. Formerly the unit of frequency was cycles per second, a terminology no longer preferred.

NOTE: The waveform may consist of components having many different frequencies, in which case it is called a complex or nonsinusoidal waveform. (EE)

Governing Body. The person or persons who have the overall legal responsibility for the operation of a health care facility. (*See the Accreditation Manual for Hospitals, Joint Commission on Accreditation of Hospitals, Chicago, 1985.*) (AS)

Ground-Fault Circuit Interrupter. A device whose function is to interrupt the electric circuit to the load when a fault current to ground exceeds some predetermined value that is less than that required to operate the overcurrent protective device of the supply circuit. (ES)

Grounding. See grounding system.

The history of grounding has been controversial. Grounding, by definition, is a means of providing the least-resistance pathway to ground (the point of relative zero energy level) for metal parts of appliances not intended to carry currents. If a fault should occur within the appliance and induce a voltage between these parts and ground, current would flow through the means rather than some higher resistance path, such as a person (assuming the person was touching the metal part when the fault occurred). The means of providing that low-resistance path has evolved into a third conductor in the power cord of appliances, and a third conductor in the building circuit wiring. Thus, a continuous low-resistance path became possible between the noncurrent-carrying metal parts of appliances and earth ground (*see Figure 2*).

In the health care community, the question of grounding intensified when the number of electrical appliances began to increase in the late 1960s. Instead of one or two devices being involved in any procedure, six or more might be attached to a patient, raising the question of this grounding method's reliability. Some thought even more grounding techniques were necessary; others insisted that existing grounding methodology was adequate, but better quality and maintenance were needed. Equipotential grounding systems were devised in the early 1970s. However, this concept proved too restrictive; consequently, only performance criteria were listed, leaving to designers the methodology by which to achieve the required (minimum) levels of performance. (*See 3-5.2.1.1.*)

Grounding becomes a concern only because most electrical power systems are grounded; that is, the neutral conductor is physically connected to earth. This grounding is not necessary for the operation of the electrical appliance, as long as the voltage difference between the two power conductors is the operating voltage of the appliance. However, it has long been established as a safety measure to ground (and identify) one conductor so that lightning, transformer faults, etc., could not raise both conductors to some high voltage with respect to ground.

While this safety measure solved one problem, it created another hazard. Since many conductors are found in a building (e.g., the structural steel, plumbing), and

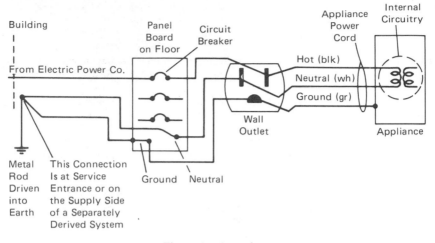

Figure 2   Grounding.

they are physically connected to the earth, they are all effectively electrically connected to one side of the power line. Further, even with a direct conductive connection to a grounded object, a person could be connected to earth via his body capacitance. Thus, everyone could be considered possibly connected to one power conductor, awaiting only an accidental connection to the other power conductor in order to experience a shock.

A case could be made that it would be safer not to have either conductor grounded. For example, for a wiring system of limited size, such as an isolated power system in an operating room, ungrounded systems are practical. However, for a large system, such as an entire building, capacitive coupling and other problems defeat the object of the system.

Grounding System.   A system of conductors that provides a low-impedance return path for leakage and fault currents. It coordinates with, but may be locally more extensive than, the grounding system described in Article 250 of NFPA 70, *National Electrical Code.* (ES)

Hazard Current.   For a given set of connections in an isolated power system, the total current that would flow through a low impedance if it were connected between either isolated conductor and ground. The various hazard currents are: (ES)

Fault Hazard Current.   The hazard current of a given isolated power system with all devices connected except the line isolation monitor. (ES)

Monitor Hazard Current.   The hazard current of the line isolation monitor alone. (ES)

Total Hazard Current.   The hazard current of a given isolated system with all devices, including the line isolation monitor, connected. (ES)

Hazardous Area in a Flammable Anesthetizing Location.*   The space extending 152 cm (5 ft) above the floor in a flammable anesthetizing location. (*See 12-4.1.3 and Appendix A-2-2.*) (AS)

A-2-2 Hazardous Area in a Flammable Anesthetizing Location.   The definition in Chapter 2 of this standard is based upon the following considerations:

(a) Available data and recent investigations indicate that under customary operating procedures, flammable anesthetic mixtures are diluted by air in the anesthetizing area to a nonflammable range before reaching a vertical height of about 30 cm (1 ft) from any source of leakage or spillage involving quantities of anesthetics used in anesthesia procedures. These findings corroborate the premises on which safeguards required in this standard were originally based and do not negate the need for any of the protective measures required; however, they do provide a sound basis for the statement that recirculation of air in ventilating systems serving anesthetizing locations does not increase the hazards of fire and explosions from flammable anesthetic vapors.

(b) The mobile character of the operating table and portable equipment and the variety of the surgeon's techniques and surgical positions that will alter the physical relationship of the anesthesia gas machine, the surgeon, the anesthetist, and the patient's head, and all of these with respect to their relative location within the room, must be considered in the determination of the electrical safeguards to be provided.

(c) The portion of the flammable anesthetizing location extending 152 cm (5 ft) above the floor as defined in Chapter 2 constitutes a "hazardous area." Because persons entering such anesthetizing locations may have accumulated electrostatic charges, the floors of corridors and rooms contiguous to the flammable inhalation anesthetizing location must be conductive and at the same potential as the floor in the flammable anesthetizing location. Patients should not be transported while flammable anesthetics are being administered. Rooms such as sterilizing rooms directly communicating with flammable anesthetizing locations are required by 12-4.1.3.1(c) to be provided with conductive floors to equalize static charges. Such charges, if not used as flammable anesthetizing locations, are not required to be served by explosionproof wiring specified in 3-4.1.2.1(e)(2). Where flammable anesthetizing locations open directly onto a passageway not a part of an operating room or delivery room, the conductive floor should extend 3 m (9.84 ft) from either side of the door frame and out from the frame (into the passageway) for 3 m (9.84 ft). It is desirable to demarcate the hazardous location of such a corridor by a physical barrier (doors) and cautionary signs to check smoking, use of open flame, wearing of improper clothing and shoes, and the application of insulating floor wax.

(d) Designated areas in which the use and handling of flammable anesthetic agents are prohibited by hospital regulations, such as corridors in the surgical suite, rooms adjacent to flammable anesthetizing locations, and nonflammable anesthetizing locations, should be indicated by prominent signs permanently installed [see Appendix A-12-4.1.3.9(b)].

(e) Postoperative recovery units that are not immediately adjacent to flammable anesthetizing locations and in which the use of flammable anesthetic agents is prohibited are not considered to involve explosion hazards and therefore do not require the installation of static-dissipation systems nor explosionproof equipment required for explosive atmospheres. Prohibition of the use of flammable anesthetic agents by hospital regulation and the proper indication of such prohibition by prominent signs, as recommended in subsection (c) above, is recommended.

In recent years, the boundaries for the hazardous area in a flammable anesthetizing location have been heavily criticized by a portion of the health care community. Much has been written about changing the boundary, for example, to "two feet from anesthetizing circuits." The following, taken from the April 1979 issue of "Code Red!" (the news bulletin of NFPA's Health Care Section), is a summary of the position of the then Committee on Anesthesia Agents (now Subcommittee on Anesthesia Services) responsible for the definition:

Anesthesia personnel have a multiplicity of responsibilities in the operating room, many of which must be carried out simultaneously, or almost so. Included are administering the anesthetic, monitoring the vital signs of the patient, administering blood, fluids, and medications other than anesthetic agents, and recording all of these events in a fairly detailed manner. It would be literally impossible to add to this burden the task of monitoring and policing a movable zone of risk, especially since the area in the vicinity of the head of the operating room table and gas anesthesia apparatus is one which visitors to the operating room frequently, but inappropriately use to be able to look over the "ether screen" to view the site of the operation.

The concept of a "moving hazard" makes accidental violation of safe practice more likely than when a fixed "hazardous area" is defined. For example, in the usual operation of some gas scavenging systems, and in a "failure mode" of some others, anesthetic gases are discharged through tubing that vents near the floor. If an explosive agent is being scavenged with such a device, a nonexplosion-proof foot switch could easily be bumped into the zone of discharge of an explosive mixture.

By retaining the "five-foot level," one is able to keep flammable agents in the gaseous, vaporous, or liquid state well away from sources of ignition. The fact that the gas anesthesia apparatus can be moved widely around the operating room to accommodate operative requirements would make the role of a fire or building safety inspector infinitely complicated in any attempt to police a "zone of risks." With the present "five-foot level," hospital inspectors are afforded a standard that is readily subject to inspection. Costs are not increased, since nonexplosion-proof electrical outlets can be installed above the "five-foot level." Finally, anesthesia personnel who utilize flammable agents are afforded much peace of mind.

Committee members opposing this statement have cited various studies, the International Electrotechnical Commission draft standard covering the subject, and 12-4.1.3.8(j) of this standard (formerly 4-5.2 of NFPA 56A-1978). That paragraph has been changed as a result of public comments on this issue. (*See commentary following 12-4.1.3.8(j).*)

Arguments were submitted again during the 1984 revision of NFPA 99 to change the "five-foot level" requirement. The Committee, however, still considered the current requirement necessary. In addition to the above arguments, the Committee noted that the current requirements were necessary in light of the infrequency of use of flammable anesthetics and the concomitant decrease of familiarity with safety requirements involved in such use. The Committee also cited: (1) the lack of control studies for a two-foot zone; (2) the litigious climate prevailing in the US today; and (3) the cessation of teaching in medical schools the use of flammable inhalation anesthetics.

Clearly, the use of flammable inhalation anesthetics has fallen off sharply in the last 10 years. It is estimated that less than 5 percent of hospitals even use flammable anesthetics, and then only infrequently. The Committee established procedures (Section 12-4.1.3), however, because there have been explosions, and these procedures have reduced the hazards associated with the use of flammable anesthetics to an acceptable level. What is currently at issue is the necessity of some of the criteria developed for flammable anesthetizing locations, particularly the "five-foot level."

Hazardous Area in Laboratories.   The area inside fume hoods or enclosures where tests or procedures are being conducted under the conditions listed in 10-7.4.1. (LAB)

Hazardous Chemical.* A chemical with one or more of the following hazard ratings as defined in NFPA 704, *Standard System for the Identificaton of Fire Hazards of Materials*: Health — 2, 3, or 4; Flammability — 2, 3, or 4; Reactivity — 2, 3, or 4. (*See Appendixes A-2-2 and C-10.2.3.*) (LAB)

A-2-2 Hazardous Chemical. For hazard ratings of many chemicals, see NFPA 49, *Hazardous Chemicals Data*, and NFPA 325M, *Fire Hazard Properties of Flammable Liquids, Gases, and Volatile Solids*.

Hazardous Location. An anesthetizing location or any location where flammable agents are used or stored. (AS)

Health Care Facilities. Buildings or portions of buildings that contain, but are not limited to, occupancies such as: hospitals; nursing homes; custodial care; supervisory care; clinics; medical and dental offices; and ambulatory care; whether permanent or movable. (ES)

This definition is consistent with NFPA *101, Life Safety Code.*

Hood, Oxygen. A device encapsulating a patient's head, and used for a purpose similar to that of a mask. (*See definition of mask.*) (HHF)

Hospital-based. In the interpretation and application of this document, physically connected to a hospital. (AS)

"Daytime" health care facilities that include inhalation anesthetizing locations, and that stand alone, can easily be classified as ambulatory care facilities in the context of Section 13-4.1. Those ambulatory care facilities located adjacent to, or forming a portion of, a hospital are more difficult to classify. To determine whether former NFPA 56A or 56G (now 12-4.1 or 13-4.1) applied to an anesthetizing location, the Committee on Anesthetizing Agents (now Subcommittee on Anesthesia Services) extensively debated the best and most practical method of differentiation. The above definition reflects the conclusion that if an ambulatory care facility is physically connected to a hospital and has an anesthetizing location, there is a reasonable chance that inpatients from the hospital will be operated on in the ambulatory care facility. For purposes of Chapter 13 and anesthetizing locations, "physically connected" means that a patient can be wheeled directly from the inpatient portion of the facility to the ambulatory care facility without going outside. The Committee's concern was whether a hospital was able to easily accommodate an overflow of its inpatient surgical patients through the use of operating rooms in the ambulatory care facility.

Hospital Facility. A building or part thereof used for the medical, psychiatric, obstetrical, or surgical care, on a 24-hour basis, of four or more inpatients. *Hospital*, wherever used in this standard, shall include general hospitals, mental hospitals, tuberculosis hospitals, children's hospitals, and any such facilities providing inpatient care. (ES)

The definition is consistent with other NFPA documents (e.g., NFPA *101, Life Safety Code*).

Humidifier. A device used for adding water vapor to inspired gas. (GE)

Hyperbaric. Pressures above atmospheric pressure. (HHF)

Hyperbaric Oxygenation. The application of pure oxygen or an oxygen-enriched gaseous mixture to a subject at elevated pressure. (HHF)

Hypobaric. Pressures below atmospheric pressure. (HHF)

Hypoxia. A state of inadequate oxygenation of the blood and tissue. (HHF)

Immediate Restoration of Service. Automatic restoration of operation with an interruption of not more than 10 seconds. (ES)

Impedance. Impedance is the ratio of the voltage drop across a circuit element to the current flowing through the same circuit element. The circuit element may consist of any combination of resistance, capacitance, or inductance. The unit of impedance is the ohm. (EE)

Impedance is frequency dependent, and is thus stated at some frequency. The symbol for impedance is the letter "Z."

Intermittent Positive Pressure Breathing (IPPB). Ventilation of the lungs by application of intermittent positive pressure to the airway. (GE)

Intrinsically Safe. As applied to equipment and wiring, equipment and wiring that are incapable of releasing sufficient electrical energy under normal or abnormal conditions to cause ignition of a specific hazardous atmospheric mixture. Abnormal conditions may include accidental damage to any part of the equipment or wiring; insulation or other failure of electrical components; application of overvoltage; adjustment and maintenance operations; and other similar conditions. (HHF)

Isolated Patient Lead. A patient lead whose impedance to ground or to a power line is sufficiently high that connecting the lead to ground, or to either conductor of the power line, results in current flow below a hazardous limit in the lead. (EE)

The development of isolated patient leads is a direct result of findings that very low levels of leakage currents in leads can be disruptive to the heart (*see commentary on the definition of Leakage Current*). Conversely, a non-isolated patient lead either is in direct electrical connection with the ground wire or does not have sufficient impedance to keep current flows in the leads below a hazardous limit.

Isolated Power System. A system comprising an isolating transformer or its equivalent, a line isolation monitor and its ungrounded circuit conductors. (*See NFPA 70, National Electrical Code.*) (ES)

With the 1984 edition of NFPA 99, a major change took place as to where isolated power systems (IPSs) are required in health care facilities. When explosions in operating rooms were first addressed in the 1940s, the inclusion of isolated power systems was one of the techniques utilized to reduce the occurences of sparks. (A spark of sufficient energy is able to cause an explosion when flammable gases are present.) In recent years, the use of flammable anesthetics has diminished almost completely, but other factors led many on the Committee on Anesthetic Agents (now Subcommittee on Anestheia Services) to continue to require the installation of these systems in all anesthetizing locations (*see below*). However, others in the mid-1970s began to question the need for IPSs in nonflammable anesthetizing locations (*also see below*). (Note: the requirement for IPSs in flammable anesthetizing locations has never been at issue.)

The following is a brief summary of the reasons put forth in 1984 by proponents and opponents of IPSs in nonflammable anesthetizing locations.

Proponents:
• Surgical techniques and procedures are involving more and more electrically powered devices; patient safety mandates uninterrupted power as much as is reasonably possible.
• The environment of the anesthetizing location, with the proliferation of electrical devices and the frequent spillage of biological and other fluids onto gowns and floors creating wet environments, increases the electrocution hazard.
• Not all health care facilities have trained personnel adequately to conduct preventive maintenance for modern diagnostic and therapeutic equipment now used in anesthetizing locations.
• IPSs sharply limit the maximum ground-seeking current that can flow through any conductor, including a human.
• IPSs are passive systems; they do not depend on activation to provide protection. Alternative measures included in NFPA 70, *National Electrical Code*, are not considered appropriate for anesthetizing locations (i.e., ground fault circuit interrupters).
• Nuisance alarms should be eliminated with the elevation of the alarm level of hazard current from 2 to 5 milliamperes. The increased alarm level also allows the use of larger transformers so that the problem of overloading is ameliorated.
• The lack of published incidents cannot be construed to mean that no electric shocks have occurred. A litigious climate is prevalent in the United States today, particularly involving medical practitioners.
• Equipment in anesthetizing locations can be assembled and disassembled several times a day, thus subjecting it to frequent handling and abuse (unlike equipment in other patient care areas where this type of usage is not common).
• The cost of installing IPS during new construction is a minimal fraction of the total cost of constructing an anesthetizing location.

Opponents:
• Adequate margins of safety against the hazards of fire, explosion, and electric shock can be achieved in nonflammable anesthetizing locations utilizing a conventional grounded system.
• The risk of accidental electrick shock with conventional grounded systems is already so small it is difficult to justify the additional cost of IPS.
• Overloading the IPSs is one of the more common causes of loss of electric power in anesthetizing locations. (Note: this relates to the sizing of the isolation transformer and how many devices are allowed to be connected to it.)
• A significant portion of new anesthetizing locations do not have IPSs, and their record of incidents is little or no different from those anesthetizing locations with IPSs.
• Patients in other areas of a health care facility can be at the same fire risk as those in anesthetizing locations (i.e., helpless, comatose, unresponsive, etc.), and IPSs are not required in these areas.
• Deleting this requirement does not prohibit those who desire IPSs from installing them.

• A primary hazard for which IPSs provide protection is a line-to-ground fault; however, this fault is now rare because of changes in equipment design.

The case for deleting requirements for IPS formally began in 1977 during the revision of the 1973 edition of NFPA 56A, *Standard for Inhalation Anesthetics*. Comments were submitted in the fall of 1977 recommending deletion of mandatory requirements. The then Committee on Anesthetic Agents rejected the comments, but one of the submitters raised the issue at the 1978 NFPA Annual Meeting. The NFPA members present passed an Amendment approving one of these comments (to delete the requirement for IPSs). However, under NFPA "Regulations Governing Committee Projects," Association Amendments to Committee Reports (such as that amendment) have to be upheld by a two-thirds vote of the Committee. This did not occur. The American Hospital Association subsequently appealed the Committee action; first to the Standards Council, which directed the Committee to meet and vote on the matter again (the same Committee action resulted), and then to the NFPA Board of Directors, which directed the Committee to clarify the matter.

The Committee met in February 1980 for two days, and extensively discussed the necessity of ungrounded electrical systems in anesthetizing locations. What emerged was a listing of four conditions in anesthetizing locations under which the Committee believed sufficient hazards were present to warrant the installation of an ungrounded electrical system. These criteria were as follows:
• The possibility of wet conditions being present, including standing fluids on the floor;
• Three or more line-operated electrical devices were to be normally connected to the patient;
• Invasive procedures, which could not be terminated immediately, were to be carried out; or
• Flammable anesthetics were to be used.

These conditions were added to NFPA 56A-1978, in the form of a Tentative Interim Amendment (TIA).

For the 1984 edition of NFPA 99, this TIA was proposed for incorporation into the standard (i.e., all TIAs are automatically proposals for the next edition of a document). However, there again were proposals recommending that IPS be required only in flammable anesthetizing locations. The Committee again rejected them; and again, amendments were passed at the 1983 NFPA Fall Meeting deleting IPS mandatory requirements in nonflammable anesthetizing locations (i.e., the amendments permitted a grounded system). The Committee again did not support the Association Amendments by the ⅔ majority as required by NFPA Regulations. (Note: a simple majority this time did support the amendments.) A complaint was subsequently filed with the Standards Council, recommending acceptance of the Association Amendments. New arguments for the complaint included the following:
• Several enforcement authorities had eliminated the mandatory requirement for IPSs in nonflammable anesthetizing locations;
• A majority of NFPA's Health Care Section, a majority of NFPA members at two Association Meetings, and a majority of the Committee should not be ignored; and
• The four criteria for installing IPSs, as listed in a TIA developed for NFPA 56A-1978, still essentially mandated IPSs in nonflammable anesthetizing locations.

The Council listened to all the previous arguments, and heard some new information: (1) with the combining into one new document of all health care facilities documents under the jurisdiction of the Health Care Facilities Correlating Committee, the responsibility for setting general electrical performance requirements appeared to be with the then Committee on Safe Use of Electricity in Patient Care Areas of Health Care Facilities, which was responsible for then Chapter 9 on the Safe Use of Electricity in Patient Care Areas in Hospitals of NFPA 99-1984 [special considerations, however, could be included in then Chapter 3 (for purposes here, now Section 12-4.1)]; (2) electrical requirements for wet locations were included in then Chapter 9, and were consistent with the requirements in Chapter 3 (*see 3-4.1.2.6 in this 1987 edition of NFPA 99*); and (3) while then Chapter 4 (Inhalation Anesthetics in Ambulatory Care Facilities) of NFPA 99-1984 addressed ambulatory care facilities where only nonmajor procedures were supposed to be carried out, general anesthesia was still being administered, but there was no requirement for IPSs in these facilities.

Under NFPA Regulations, the Standards Council reviews all the material related to the processing and adopting of a document, and issues (or does not issue) a document based on *all* the data. The Council, in this case, voted to issue NFPA 99-1984 with the amendments that deleted the mandatory requirement for IPSs in nonflammable anesthetizing locations; and, in addition, the Council recommended that the Commitee process a Tentative Interim Amendment in the form of a footnote (not a requirement) strongly recommending the installation of IPSs since all parties at the Council Hearing acknowledged that these systems do provide an added level of electrical safety for patients and staff.

Following the Standards Council Action, an appeal was subsequently filed to the NFPA Board of Directors to reverse the decision of the Standards Council. The Board, upon reviewing material and procedures that were followed, denied the appeal (i.e. upheld the Council Action) in April 1984.

The Board did note that the Council recommendation regarding a TIA was not appropriate.

Thus, the issue of IPS in anesthetizing was completed — at least procedurally. It has not, nor did not, mean that the issue was resolved to everyone's satisfaction.

Interestingly enough, in permitting (for anesthesia purposes) a grounded electrical system in nonflammable anesthetizing locations, the subject of "wet locations" requirements surfaced.

Former Chapter 9 of NFPA 99-1984 (on the safe use of electricity in patient care areas in hospitals) required an additional level of safety in wet locations. This safety was to be achieved essentially by either ground fault circuit interrupters (GFCI) or an IPS (depending on whether power interruption could be tolerated).

When all anesthetizing locations were required to have IPSs, this issue of whether anesthetizing locations were wet locations was not considered. However, with the change in 1984, the question now had to be answered for each nonflammable anesthetizing location: Was it a wet location?

For this 1987 edition of NFPA 99, this question was extensively discussed by three subcommittees (Anesthesia Services, Electrical Equipment, and Electrical Systems) and by the Technical Committee on Health Care Facilities. It was noted that for some surgical procedures, operating rooms remained "dry" (e.g., eye surgery, dermatological surgery), while for other procedures, extensive use or spillage of liquids/fluids made conditions very "wet," (e.g., cystoscopy, certain bowel procedures, urological procedures, cardiothoracic surgery). The definition of "wet location" was reviewed, and some changes proposed, including a suggested list of "wet" and "dry" nonflammable anesthetizing locations. However, the Technical Committee on Health Care Facilities, the Committee responsible for coordinating recommendations from all the subcommittees under it, could not agree (by the required ⅔ vote) as to what changes should be made, either in the form of requirements or recommendations. An informatory Note was proposed by the former Technical Committee on Anesthetizing Agents and approved [*see 12-4.1.2.6(a)*]. This Note called readers' attention to the fact that "wet location" provisions could be applied to some anesthetizing locations (since anesthetizing locations were patient care areas). But no other changes (with regard to isolated power systems, electrical requirements for nonflammable anesthetizing locations, or the definition) were made. It is still the responsibility of the individual health care facility to decide on which, if any, anesthetizing locations should be considered wet locations.

Thus, this subject will continue to be discussed, even with this new edition of NFPA 99.

For a discussion on the need for maintaining power ("continuity of power"), see commentary under 3-2.4.2

Isolation Transformer. A transformer of the multiple-winding type, with the primary and secondary windings physically separated, that inductively couples its ungrounded secondary winding to the grounded feeder system that energizes its primary winding. (ES)

Isolation transformers change a grounded electrical system to an ungrounded electrical system (*see Figure 3 below*) and provide an added level of protection with

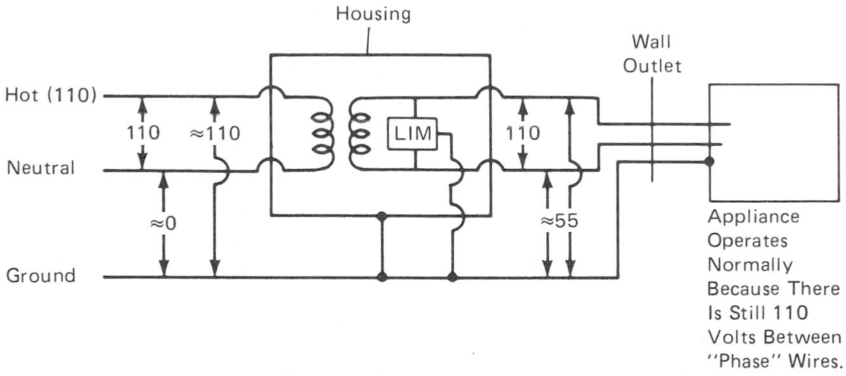

Figure 3   Isolation transformer (schematic).

regard to hazardous electric current flow for *certain* electrical faults within appliances.   Thus, the connection to ground of one conductor of the electrical power system is eliminated (see commentary on the term Grounding), and two gross faults, rather than one, are required in order to cause a severe shock.

A further advantage, where interruption of power is critical, is that certain first faults *within* a device (e.g., line-to-ground) will not interrupt the flow of electricity to that device. (An operating room is an example of a location where constant electricity is most desired.) In a grounded electrical system, a fault, such as the phase (hot) conductor touching the chassis of a properly grounded appliance, would create a short circuit and trip (open) either the appliance's overcurrent protector or the branch circuit breaker, thus removing power from the appliance or from all the appliances on that breaker. In an ungrounded (isolated) electrical system, such a fault would remove only one layer of protection, reducing the system to the equivalent of a conventionally grounded system but allowing the device to continue to be used if absolutely essential. With a monitoring device (i.e. line isolation monitor) to warn that a fault has occurred, the fault can be identified without electrical power being interrupted. (NOTE: A line-to-line fault will trip a circuit breaker, whether appliance is operating from an IPS or a grounded system.)

This added level of protection applies to gross macroshock effects (i.e., in the milliampere and ampere levels of current). It does not apply to microshock effects (i.e., in the microampere levels of current), because electrical systems usually have large enough capacitive couplings at these low-current levels to negate the isolating effects of an isolation transformer.

Isolation transformers are built in various sizes (electrically). The units used in anesthetizing locations, for example, range up to 25 kVA. It is therefore necessary to know the approximate number of devices expected to be used and their power ratings when installing isolation transformers in these locations. Otherwise, the transformer may overload or its overcurrent protection will sense too much current being drawn and thus trip and cut off power to all devices connected to the transformer.

When an isolation transformer is installed in a health care facility, it must be in conjunction with a line isolation monitor (LIM) (see definition of Line Isolation Monitor). LIMs provide visual and audible indications of current flow between the output wires of the isolation transformer and ground as a result of coupling (resistive or capacitive). The LIM will alarm when this current passes above a preset value (now 5 milliamperes).

Laboratory. A building, space, room, or group of contiguous rooms located in any part of a hospital or health care–related facility and intended to serve activities involving procedures for investigation, diagnosis, or treatment in which flammable, combustible, or oxidizing materials are to be used. These laboratories are not intended to include isolated frozen section laboratories; areas in which oxygen is administered; blood donor rooms in which flammable, combustible, or otherwise hazardous materials normally used in laboratory procedures are not present; and clinical service areas not using hazardous materials. (LAB)

Isolated frozen section laboratories are included in this definition if they use flammable liquids. They are not included if they do not use flammable liquids.

Laboratory Equipment. See definition of apparatus. (LAB)

Laboratory Hood. An enclosure designed to transform the suction of an exhaust system into an airflow across the face of the enclosure to prevent the release of hazardous materials back into the laboratory work area. This definition does not include canopy hoods or recirculating laminar flow biological safety cabinets that may not be designed for use with flammable materials. (LAB)

Laboratory Unit. An enclosed space used for experiments or tests. A laboratory unit may or may not include offices, lavatories, other contiguous rooms maintained for or used by laboratory personnel, and corridors within the units. It may contain one or more separate laboratory work areas. It may be an entire building. (LAB)

This term is used only to mean a functional area. The requirements in Chapter 10 apply to the laboratory as a whole, not to the laboratory unit level.

Laboratory Unit Separation. All walls, partitions, floors, and ceilings, including openings in them, that separate a laboratory unit from adjoining areas. (LAB)

Laboratory Work Area.   A room or space for testing, analysis, research, instruction, or similar activities that involve the use of chemicals. This work area may or may not be enclosed. (LAB)

Leakage Current.   Any current, including capacitively coupled current, not intended to be applied to a patient but which may be conveyed from exposed metal parts of an appliance to ground or to other accessible parts of an appliance. (EE)

> Leakage current *is* electric current as governed by Ohms Law: $I = V/Z$, where I = Current, V = Voltage, and Z = Impedance (resistance of the circuit). There needs to be some driving force (voltage) and a closed circuit before current flows. Leakage current is a name given only to those particular currents meeting the definition above, and it is peculiar only in that part of the circuit may be a capacitive coupling or a faulty resistive insulation. A human being may form part of the circuit (though not an intended part), and thus permit the flow of electric current. See A-9-2.1.13.4(c) for an extensive discussion on the leakage current limits contained in Chapters 7 and 9.
>
> Leakage current became of greater concern in the health care community in the 1960s when cardiovascular medicine and surgery began invading the heart with electrical and electromechanical probes. Researchers learned that the heart's pumping action was interruptable with rather small levels of current — particularly at the power distribution frequency of 60 Hz current. Various factors contributed to this phenomenon including the condition and temperature of the heart, the types of drugs being administered, and the location, size, and duration of the electrical contact on or in the heart as well as the variability and shape of the current waveform. The fact that this unintended current was an inevitable byproduct of using electrical equipment, and that relatively low levels of current could be disruptive or even lethal, dramatically altered the design, application, and maintenance of electromedical equipment in health care facilities.

Life Safety Branch.   A subsystem of the emergency system consisting of feeders and branch circuits, meeting the requirements of Article 700 of NFPA 70, *National Electrical Code*, and intended to provide adequate power needs to ensure safety to patients and personnel, and which can be automatically connected to alternate power sources during interruption of the normal power source. (ES)

Limited-Combustible Material.   A material (as defined in NFPA 220, *Standard on Types of Building Construction*) not complying with the definition of noncombustible material that, in the form in which it is used, has a potential heat value not exceeding 3500 Btu per pound (8141 kJ/kg),[1] and complies with one of the following paragraphs (a) or (b). Materials subject to increase in combustibility or flame-spread rating beyond the limits herein established through the effects of age, moisture, or other atmospheric condition shall be considered combustible.

(a) Materials having a structural base of noncombustible material, with a surfacing not exceeding a thickness of ⅛ in. (3.2 mm) and having a flame-spread rating not greater than 50.

(b) Materials, in the form and thickness used, other than as described in (a), having neither a flame-spread rating greater than 25 nor evidence of continued progressive combustion and of such composition that surfaces that would be exposed by cutting through the material on any plane would have neither a flame-spread rating greater than 25 nor evidence of continued progressive combustion. (MGS)

---

[1]See NFPA 259, *Standard Test Method for Potential Heat of Building Materials.*

Line Isolation Monitor. An instrument that continually checks the hazard current from an isolated circuit to ground. (ES)

Liquid. Any material that has a fluidity greater than that of 300 penetration asphalt when tested in accordance with ASTM D571, *Test for Penetration of Bituminous Materials*. When not otherwise identified, the term *liquid* shall include both flammable and combustible liquids. (*See Appendix C-10.2.1.*) (LAB)

mA. Milliampere.

Macroshock. The effect of large electric currents (milliamperes or larger) on the body. (EE)

The effect of large electric currents on the human body is dependent on the current entry and exit points, and the current frequency, duration, and density.

Manifold. A device for connecting the outlets of one or more gas cylinders to the central piping system for that specific gas. (MGS)

Mask. A device that fits over the mouth and nose (oronasal) or nose (nasal), used to administer gases to a patient. (AS)

Mask, Oronasal. A device that fits over the mouth and nose, to deliver therapeutic gases to the user. (HHF)

In hyperbaric facilities, the user can be other than just a patient.

Medical Compressed Air.* For purposes of this standard, medical compressed air is:

(a) Air supplied from cylinders or bulk containers or that has been reconstituted from oxygen U.S.P. and nitrogen N.F. and that complies, as a minimum, with Grade D in ANSI Z86.1, *Commodity Specification for Air* (CGA Pamphlet G-7.1), or

(b) Local outside atmosphere to which no contaminants in the form of particulate matter, odor, oil vapor, or other gases have been added by a compressor system. Local atmosphere air may not be equal in purity or dryness to the commodity specification Grade D reconstituted air. (MGS)

A-2-2 Medical Compressed Air. For fire and safety purposes, air supplied from on-site compressor and air-treatment systems should comply as a minimum with the limiting characteristics of Table A-2-2 at the design conditions.

The quality of local atmospheric air should be determined to assist in establishing the optimum compressor and air-treatment system performance.

Hydrocarbon contamination of compressor supply systems for medical compressed air and the carryover into the pipeline distribution system could be detrimental to the safety of the end user and to the integrity of the system, and be a potential fire hazard. Mixing of medical compressed air with oxygen is a common clinical practice and the hazards of fire are increased if the air is thus contaminated. No quantitive data is readily available concerning specific levels or mixtures that could create this hazard. Therefore, the limit for liquid hydrocarbons is established on the basis of empirical data.

Table A-2-2   Recommended Medical Compressed Air Limiting Characteristics.

Characteristic	Limit Value
Condensed Water	0 (nominal)
Hydrocarbons:	
Liquid	0 PPM (nominal)
Gaseous (as methane)	25 PPM
Carbon Monoxide	20 PPM
Carbon Dioxide	1000 PPM
Permanent Particulates	1 micron nominal @ 98% efficiency
Dew Point	The dew point at line pressure should be at least 10°C (18°F) below the minimum ambient temperature to which any part of the medical air piping system can be exposed.

NOTE: When the air source is reconstituted from oxygen, U.S.P., and nitrogen, N.F., or from liquid air, the oxygen level should be continuously monitored with an alarm and maintained between 19.5 percent and 23.5 percent.

The dew-point temperature at line pressure outlined recognizes that some medical compressed air piping systems may be routed outside buildings. This requirement calls attention to the fact that where colder ambient temperatures are experienced the system design precludes freezing of the air line.

The subject of the "quality of air" may seem to be outside the scope of this document, and perhaps even NFPA. But the subject was brought before the former Medical Gas Application Panel (now Subcommittee on Nonflammable Medical Piped Gas Systems) in 1984 by several members of the Panel. At issue was the subject of oil being introduced into piped air systems by compressors. This poses a fire hazard, in addition to affecting patient medical treatment. As a way of addressing the problem, the Panel decided to list a set of criteria for medical air (i.e., "air quality") that would address the problem without telling manufacturers what or how to build their devices that produced the compressed air.

This proposed list of criteria, which was expanded into criteria for air-treatment systems as well, was constantly changed during deliberations. However, the proposal would have seriously impacted all existing compressed air systems, making more than a few no longer acceptable. And the proposal would have increased the cost of medical air significantly. Because of this controversy (i.e., limits could not be agreed upon by Subcommittee members, justification of costs was difficult), the Subcommittee changed the original proposal to a *recommendation*, and placed material in the Appendix for guidance only.

The Subcommittee, in its deliberations, extensively reviewed the subject of air compressors and concluded that, as a minimum, medical air-compressors were to be oil-free (*see definition of Oil-Free Air Compressor; see 4-3.1.9.1*). Thus, oil-lubricated reciprocating compressors were prohibited and removed from a proposed table (*see Appendix A-4-3.1.9.8, Table A-4-3.1.9.8*).

The definition of medical compressed air is thus the same one that appeared in NFPA 56F-1983.

This subject will definitely be reviewed again during the next revision cycle of NFPA 99.

Medical Laboratory.   As used in this standard, limited suction usage rooms in routine, direct support of patient therapy (as contrasted with laboratories used extensively or exclusively for analysis, research, and teaching). (VSE)

Medical-Surgical Vacuum System. A system consisting of central-vacuum producing equipment with pressure and operating controls, shutoff valves, alarm warning systems, gauges, and a network of piping extending to and terminating with suitable terminals (inlets) at locations where patient suction may be required. (VSE)

Microshock. The effect of small electric currents (as low as 10 microamperes) on the body. To be hazardous, such currents must be applied to a conductor inside or in very close proximity to the heart. (EE)

This term is a descriptor. As such, no specific value should be associated with it because of the many factors that influence the value (e.g., path, density, duration, pathology, etc.). Readers are urged to study the material relating to this subject in A-3-2.2.2 and A-9-2.1.13.4(c).

The term *microshock* consists of two words: *Micro*, a Greek word meaning minute or small, and *shock*, which is taken from French, meaning an extreme stimulation of the nerves and muscles accompanying the passage of electric current through the tissue. For a given electric current, the smaller the contact surface area with a tissue, the greater its current density and therefore the potential for hazardous conditions. For example, leads connected to the heart and leads connected to a finger might cause the same current to flow (and cause microshock to occur); however, the affect on the heart might be to stop (or start) its rhythmic pulsing; the affect on the finger might be just a momentary jerking or twisting of the finger.

Mixed Facility. A facility wherein flammable anesthetizing locations and nonflammable anesthetizing locations coexist within the same building, allowing interchange of personnel or equipment between flammable and nonflammable anesthetizing locations. (AS)

mV. Millivolt.

Nebulizer. A device used for producing an aerosol of water and/or medication within inspired gas supply. (GE)

Negative Pressure. Pressure less than atmospheric. (GE)

This definition can apply to air within the body as well as that in the surrounding environment.

Nitrogen. An element that, at atmospheric temperatures and pressures, exists as a clear, colorless, and tasteless gas; it comprises approximately four-fifths of the earth's atmosphere. (AS)

Nitrogen Narcosis. A condition resembling alcoholic inebriation, which results from breathing nitrogen in the air under significant pressure. (*See C-19.1.3.1.2.*) (HHF)

It is the nitrogen under pressure that causes the condition experienced.

Nitrogen, Oil-Free, Dry. Nitrogen complying, as a minimum, with Grade D in CGA Pamphlet G-10.1, *Commodity Specification for Nitrogen*, as used for cleaning pipelines. (AS)

Nitrous Oxide. An inorganic compound, one of the oxides of nitrogen; it exists as a gas at atmospheric pressure and temperature, possesses a sweetish smell and is capable of inducing the first and second stages of anesthesia when inhaled; the oxygen in the compound will be released under conditions of combustion, creating an oxygen-enriched atmosphere. (AS)

Noncombustible (Hyperbaric). Within the context of Chapter 19, "Hyperbaric Facilities," an adjective describing a substance that will not burn in 95 ± 5 percent oxygen at pressures up to 3 ATA (44.1 psia). (HHF)

A distinction was made between noncombustibility in hyperbaric and hypobaric chambers to reflect the different atmospheric conditions that exist inside these chambers and the conditions in each under which substances are considered noncombustible.

While 100 percent is normally the percentage used, 95 ± 5 percent is considered acceptable because of limitations on measuring techniques.

Noncombustible (Hypobaric). Within the context of NFPA 99B, *Standard for Hypobaric Facilities*, an adjective describing a substance that will not burn in 95 ± 5 percent oxygen at pressures of 760 mmHg. (HHF)

Noncombustible Material. A material (as defined in NFPA 220, *Standard on Types of Building Construction*) that, in the form in that it is used and under the conditions anticipated, will not ignite, burn, support combustion, or release flammable vapors when subjected to fire or heat. Materials reported as noncombustible, when tested in accordance with the *Standard Test Method for Behavior of Materials in a Vertical Tube Furnace at 750°C*, ASTM E136, shall be considered noncombustible materials. (MGS)

Nonflammable. An adjective describing a substance that will not burn under the conditions set forth in the definition of flame resistant. (HHF)

Nonflammable Anesthetic Agent.* Refers to those inhalation agents that, because of their vapor pressure at 98.6°F (37°C) and at atmospheric pressure, cannot attain flammable concentrations when mixed with air, oxygen, or mixtures of oxygen and nitrous oxide. (AS)

A-2-2 Nonflammable Anesthetic Agent. It is possible to halogenate a compound, and render it partially or totally nonflammable by the substitution of one or more halogens (e.g., fluorine, chlorine, bromine) for hydrogen. Thus halothane ($CF_3CHClBr$) is almost completely halogenated and is nonflammable. Methoxyflurane ($CF_2CCl_2OCH_3$) is partially halogenated and is nonflammable in conditions encountered during clinical anesthesia (if it is heated its vapor concentration will increase enough to burn). Fluroxene ($CF_3CH_2OCHCH_2$) is halogenated even less; it is flammable in concentrations of four percent or greater.

The following agents are considered flammable during conditions of clinical use in anesthesia:

cyclopropane
divinyl ether
ethyl chloride

ethylene
ethyl ether

The following agent is flammable during use in clinical anesthesia in higher concentrations:

fluroxene

NOTE: Because fluroxene is flammable under certain conditions of use, it is listed as a flammable agent. Concentrations required for induction of anesthesia generally exceed four percent, and are flammable. Maintenance of fluroxene anesthesia may be accomplished with concentrations of less than four percent, however.

The following agents are nonflammable during conditions of use in clinical anesthesia:

chloroform	nitrous oxide
halothane	trichloroethylene
methoxyflurane	enflurane

Nonflammable Anesthetizing Location. Any anesthetizing location designated for the exclusive use of nonflammable anesthetizing agents. (AS)

Nonflammable Medical Gas System. A system of piped oxygen, nitrous oxide, compressed air or other nonflammable medical gases. (*See Chapter 4, "Gas and Vacuum Systems," Sections 4-3 through 4-6.*) (MGS)

Nursing Home. A building or part thereof used for the housing and nursing care, on a 24-hour basis, of four or more persons who, because of mental or physical incapacity, may be unable to provide for their own needs and safety without the assistance of another person. *Nursing home*, wherever used in this document, shall include nursing and convalescent homes, skilled nursing facilities, intermediate care facilities, and infirmaries in homes for the aged. (EE)

The definition coincides with that in NFPA *101*-1985, *Life Safety Code.*
Definition of the term became necessary when the Restructuring Subcommittee identified nursing homes as having some distinct differences from other types of health care facilities (vis-a-vis fire safety hazards addressed by NFPA 99), and thus included this type of facility as a separate chapter (16).

Oil-Free Air Compressor. An air compressor designed specifically to exclude oil from the air stream and compression chamber. (MGS)

See commentary under term "Medical Compressed Air" for background on this new term.

Oil-Free, Dry Air. Air complying, as a minimum, with Grade D in Compressed Gas Association, Inc., Pamphlet G-7.1, *Commodity Specification for Air,* and having a maximum dew point of $-20°F$ ($-28.9°C$). (MGS)

This air is used for pressure-testing purposes [*see Sections 4-5.1.3.4(a) and (b)*]. It should not be confused with "medical-air" (*see term "Medical Compressed Air" in this chapter*).
The reason for requiring this air to be "oil-free" is its use in piped oxygen lines where particles of oil can be a fire hazard.

Oil-Free, Dry Nitrogen. Nitrogen complying, as a minimum, with Grade D in Compressed Gas Association, Inc., Pamphlet G-10.1, *Commodity Specification for Nitrogen.* (MGS)

This gas is used for pressure-testing purposes [*see Sections 4-5.1.3.4(a) and (b)*]. The reason for requiring this gas to be "oil-free" is its use in piped oxygen lines where particles of oil can be a fire hazard.

Operating Supply. The portion of the supply system that normally supplies the piping systems. The operating supply consists of a primary supply or a primary and secondary supply. (MGS)

Primary Supply. That portion of the equipment that is actually supplying the system. (MGS)

Secondary Supply. When existing, a supply that automatically supplies the system when the primary supply becomes exhausted. This is a normal operating procedure of the equipment. (MGS)

Oxidizing Gas. A gas that supports combustion. Oxygen and nitrous oxide are examples of oxidizing gases. There are many others, including halogens. (HHF)

Oxygen. An element that, at atmospheric temperatures and pressures, exists as a colorless, odorless, tasteless gas. Its outstanding property is its ability to sustain life and to support combustion. Although oxygen is nonflammable, materials that burn in air will burn much more vigorously and create higher temperatures in oxygen or in oxygen-enriched atmospheres. (AS)

Oxygen Delivery Equipment. Any device used to transport and deliver an oxygen-enriched atmosphere to a patient. If an enclosure such as a mask, hood, incubator, canopy, or tent is used to contain the oxygen-enriched atmosphere, then that enclosure is considered to be oxygen delivery equipment. (GE)

This term was added to clarify several different terms used in Chapter 8.
Sentence two was added in this 1987 edition of NFPA 99 to clarify when an "enclosure" would also be part of an oxygen delivery device.

Oxygen-Enriched Atmosphere. An atmosphere in which the concentration of oxygen exceeds 23.5 by volume. (HHF)

The value 23.5 percent is used because the normal percentage of oxygen in air is 21 percent, and an added error factor of 10 percent for reading the meter and for manufacturer tolerance is considered necessary. The oxygen concentration in air itself can vary because of location, altitude, etc. The Committee did not intend that normal atmospheric areas that may be using compressed air cylinders be considered an oxygen-enriched atmosphere.

This definition now agrees with that listed in NFPA 53M, *Manual on Hazards of Oxygen-Enriched Atmospheres*, in which the definition is independent of the atmospheric pressure of the area, and is based solely on the percentage of oxygen. Under normal atmospheric conditions, oxygen concentrations above 23.5 percent will increase the fire hazard level. However, different atmospheric conditions (e.g., pressure), or the presence of gaseous diluents, can actually change the fire hazard level (increase or decrease), even if an oxygen-enriched atmosphere (by definition) exists. Thus, an oxygen-enriched atmosphere in and of itself does not always also mean an increased fire hazard exists.

Oxygen, Gaseous. A colorless, odorless, and tasteless gas; and the physical state of the element at atmospheric temperature and pressure. (GE)

Oxygen Index. The minimum concentration of oxygen, expressed as percent by volume, in a mixture of oxygen and nitrogen which will just support combustion of a material under conditions of ASTM D2863. (HHF)

Oxygen, Liquid. Exists at cryogenic temperature, approximately $-300°F$ ($-184.4°C$) at atmospheric pressure. It retains all of the properties of gaseous oxygen, but, in addition, when allowed to warm to room temperature at atmospheric pressure, it will evaporate and expand to fill a volume 860 times its liquid volume. If spilled, the liquid can cause frostbite on contact with skin. (GE)

Oxygen Toxicity (Hyperbaric). Physical impairment resulting from breathing gaseous mixtures containing oxygen-enriched atmospheres at elevated pressures for extended periods of time. Under the pressures and times of exposure normally encountered in hyperbaric treatments, toxicity is a direct function of concentration and time of exposure. (*See Appendix C-19.1.3.1.3.*) (HHF)

Oxygen Toxicity (Hypobaric). Physical impairment usually resulting from breathing gaseous mixtures containing oxygen-enriched atmospheres at elevated pressures for extended periods of time; it may occur under the pressures and duration of exposure normally encountered in long-duration hypobaric exposures, since toxicity is a direct function of concentration and time of exposure, and involves toxicity of the lung. (HHF)

> While oxygen toxicity is not common in hypobaric facilities, it has been reported to the Committee that subtle changes in red cell mass and respiratory distress have been demonstrated in research hypobaric chambers over long-term exposures.

Patient Care Area. Any portion of a health care facility wherein patients are intended to be examined or treated. (EE)

NOTE: Business offices, corridors, lounges, day rooms, dining rooms, or similar areas typically are not classified as patient care areas.

> This term was added since it is used in Chapter 12, but only quasi-defined by the listing of different categories of patient care areas (i.e., critical care areas, general care areas, and wet locations).

Patient-Care-Related Electrical Appliance. An electrical appliance that is intended to be used for diagnostic, therapeutic, or monitoring purposes in a patient care area. (EE)

Patient Equipment Grounding Point. A jack or terminal that serves as the collection point for redundant grounding of electric appliances serving a patient vicinity or for grounding other items in order to eliminate electromagnetic interference problems. (EE)

> The inclusion of the reference to electromagnetic interference was considered necessary by the Subcommittee on Electrical Equipment (responsible for this definition) since it is a recognized problem, and proper grounding will reduce effects of this problem.

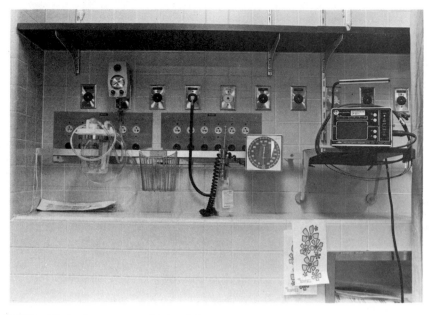

NOTE: All circuits are on essential electrical system.

Figure 4(a)   Recovery room.

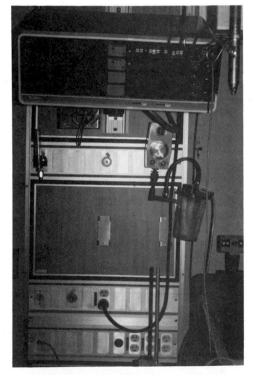

Figure 4(b)   Another recovery room.   Figure 4(c)   An intensive care unit.

Figure 4   Examples of patient care areas and the utilities now necessary to support medical care.

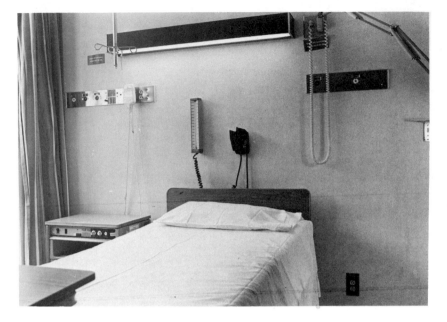

NOTE: Receptacle coverplate (lower right) is red, indicating it is on a circuit that will be re-energized from emergency generator in the event of loss of normal power.

Figure 4(d)   General care patient room.

Patient Lead.   Any deliberate electrical connection that may carry current between an appliance and a patient. This may be a surface contact (e.g., an ECG electrode); an invasive connection (e.g., implanted wire or catheter); or an incidental long-term connection (e.g., conductive tubing). It is not intended to include adventitious or casual contacts such as a push button, bed surface, lamp, hand-held appliance, etc. (EE)

NOTE: Also see definition of isolated patient lead.

Patient Vicinity.   In an area in which patients are normally cared for, the patient vicinity is the space with surfaces likely to be contacted by the patient or an attendant who can touch the patient. Typically in a patient room, this encloses a space within the room 6 ft (1.8 m) beyond the perimeter of the bed in its nominal location and extending vertically within 7 ft 6 in. (2.3 m) of the floor. (EE)

A patient vicinity is within a room; it does not extend through barriers, such as walls, partitions, or floors. A patient vicinity is also fixed; it does not move with a patient through corridors, hallways, or waiting rooms.

The dimensions of a patient vicinity are based on the possible reach of the patient or of an attendant who may be touching the bed with one hand and touching a piece of apparatus with the other. A small safety factor is included for a possible unusual circumstance. Vertically, the dimension provides for the use of an I.V. pole, orthopedic frames, or similar vertically mounted attachments.

Dimensional limits were established so that in large rooms it would not be necessary to treat the entire room as the patient vicinity.

Like many code provisions, this definition is an example of providing a definable baseline — admittedly somewhat arbitrary — for applying safety regulations. This inhibits both extremes: those groups wanting very expansive requirements (e.g., the whole hospital to be a patient vicinity), and those denying any safety problem (e.g., no need to consider any patient vicinity).

Piped Distribution System. A system that consists of a central supply system (manifold, bulk, or compressors) with control equipment and piping extending to points in the facility where nonflammable medical gases may be required, with suitable station outlet valves at each use point. (MGS)

Piping. The tubing or conduit of the vacuum system. There are three general classes of piping, as follows: (VSE)

Branch (Lateral) Lines. Those sections or portions of the vacuum piping system that serve a room or group of rooms on the same story of the facility. (VSE)

Risers. The vertical pipes connecting the vacuum system main line(s) with the branch lines on the various levels of the facility. (VSE)

Main Lines. Those parts of the vacuum system that connect the vacuum source (pumps, receivers, etc.) to the risers or branches, or both. (VSE)

Plug (Attachment Plug, Cap). A device that, by insertion in a receptacle, establishes connection between the conductors of the attached flexible cord and the conductors connected permanently to the receptacle. (EE)

Positive-Negative Pressure Breathing. Ventilation of the lungs by the application of intermittent positive-negative pressure to the airway. (GE)

Positive Pressure. Pressure greater than ambient atmospheric. (GE)

Pressure, Absolute. The total pressure in a system with reference to zero pressure. (HHF)

Pressure, Ambient. Refers to total pressure of the environment referenced. (HHF)

Pressure, Gauge. Refers to total pressure above (or below) atmospheric. (HHF)

Pressure, High. A pressure exceeding 200 psig (1.38 kPa gauge)(215 psia). (GE)

Pressure, Partial. The pressure, in absolute units, exerted by a particular gas in a gas mixture (the pressure contributed by other gases in the mixture is ignored). For example, oxygen is one of the constituents of air; the partial pressure of oxygen in standard air, at a standard air pressure of 14.7 psia, is 3.06 psia or 0.208 ATA or 158 mmHg. (HHF)

Pressure Reducing Regulator. A device that automatically reduces gas under high pressure to a usable lower working pressure. In hospitals, the term *regulator* is frequently used to describe a regulator that incorporates a flow-measuring device. (RT)

Pressure, Working. A pressure not exceeding 200 psig (11.6 kg/cm^2). A pipeline working pressure of 50 to 55 psig (2.9 to 3.2 kg/cm^2) is conventional because medical gas equipment is generally designed and calibrated for use at this pressure. (GE)

Psia. Pounds per square inch absolute, a unit of pressure measurement with zero pressure as the base or reference pressure. (HHF)

Psig. Pounds per square inch gauge, a unit of pressure measurement with atmospheric pressure as the base or reference pressure (under standard conditions, 0 psig is equivalent to 14.7 psia). (HHF)

Quiet Ground. A system of grounding conductors, insulated from portions of the conventional grounding of the power system, that interconnects the grounds of electric appliances for the purpose of improving immunity to electromagnetic noise. (ES)

Reactance. The component of impedance contributed by inductance or capacitance. The unit of reactance is the ohm. (EE)

See commentary under term "Impedance."

Reactive Material. A material that, by itself, is readily capable of detonation, explosive decomposition, or explosive reaction at normal or elevated temperatures and pressures. (*See Appendix C-10-2.3.3 for definitions of Reactivity 3 and Reactivity 4.*) (LAB)

Reference Grounding Point. A terminal bus that is the equipment grounding bus, or an extension of the equipment grounding bus, and is a convenient collection point for installed grounding wires or other bonding wires where used. (EE)

Refrigerating Equipment. Any mechanically operated equipment used for storing, below normal ambient temperature, hazardous materials having flammability ratings of 3 or 4. It includes refrigerators, freezers, and similar equipment. (LAB)

Relative Analgesia. A state of sedation and partial block of pain perception produced in a patient by the inhalation of concentrations of nitrous oxide insufficient to produce loss of consciousness (conscious sedation). (AS)

Remote.* A use point and/or the gas system storage shall be considered remote if it cannot be accessed directly by walking from the front door of the treatment facility through to the use point or storage area without walking out through another exit. A remote use point shall be considered a separate single treatment facility. (MGS)

A-2-2 Remote. A gas storage supply system may be remote from the single treatment facility but all use points must be contiguous within the facility. [*See Figure A-2-2(b).*]

Note that "remoteness" is not a matter of distance; rather, it is based on whether one has to go through an exit to go from the use point treatment facility to the storage area. (*See Appendix A diagrams under paragraphs 4-4.1.1.2(d) and 4-4.2.1.2.1.*)

Reserve Supply. When existing, that portion of the supply equipment that automatically supplies the system in the event of failure of the operating supply. The reserve supply only functions in an emergency and not as a normal operating procedure. (MGS)

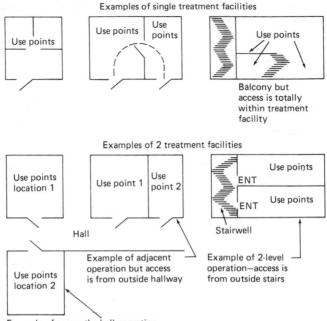

Figure A-2-2(b) Examples of Treatment Facilities.

Safety Can. An approved container, of not more than 5 gal (15.5 L) capacity, having a spring-closing lid and spout cover and so designed that it will safely relieve internal pressure when subjected to fire exposure. (LAB)

The definition used is from NFPA 30, *Flammable and Combustible Liquids Code.*

SCFM. Standard cubic feet per minute. The unit used to express the measure of the volume of a gas flowing at standard conditions — a temperature of 68°F (20°C) and a pressure of one atmosphere (29.92 in. of Hg). (VSE)

Selected Receptacles. A minimal number of receptacles selected by the governing body of a facility as necessary to provide essential patient care and facility services during loss of normal power. (ES)

While no specific number is listed in 3-4.2.2.2(c) or 3-4.2.3.3(b), the Subcommittee on Electrical Systems (responsible for this term) has emphasized the need to be judicious in selecting only the *minimum* number of receptacles for connection to the essential electrical system. While it might be argued that any electrical receptacle might be needed in an emergency, prudent selection, based on need and past experience, is to be used.

The change in definition of this term for the 1987 edition of NFPA 99 emphasizes this point of limiting the number of receptacles on the essential electrical system to limit the load on generator sets. The other change made to the definition clarified that the administration of a facility is responsible (and liable) for determining number and location of receptacles on the essential electrical system.

Self-Extinguishing. A characteristic of a material such that once the source of ignition is removed, the flame is quickly extinguished without the fuel or oxidizer being exhausted. (HHF)

Single Treatment Facility. * A diagnostic or treatment complex under a single management comprising a number of use points but confined to a single contiguous grouping of use points, i.e., do not involve widely separated locations or separate distinct practices. For the purposes of this standard a single treatment facility will be on a single level or one in which a person may get to a second level totally from within the confines of the treatment area. One-, two-, or three-level complexes in which entry to other use points is achieved through an outer foyer or hall entry shall not be considered single treatment facilities. (MGS)

A-2-2 Single Treatment Facility. The definition of single treatment facility was established to take into consideration principally single-level installations or those of a practice that could be two-level, but are reached by open stairs within the confines of the single treatment facility.

Site of Intentional Expulsion. All points within 1 ft (0.3 m) of a point at which an oxygen-enriched atmosphere is intentionally vented to the atmosphere. For example: for a patient receiving oxygen via a nasal cannula or face mask, the site of expulsion normally surrounds the mask or cannula; for a patient receiving oxygen while enclosed in a canopy or incubator, the site of intentional expulsion normally surrounds the openings to the canopy or incubator; for a patient receiving oxygen while on a ventilator, the site of intentional expulsion normally surrounds the venting port on the ventilator.

NOTE: This definition addresses the site of intended expulsion. Actual expulsion may occur at other sites remote from the intended site due to disconnections, leaks, or rupture of gas conduits and connections. Vigilance on the part of patient-care team is essential to assure system integrity. (GE)

Prior to this 1987 edition of NFPA 99, the term "site of administration" was used. It encompassed a volume of one foot around the oxygen delivery equipment. That concept (term and definition) was changed because an oxygen-enriched atmosphere did not necessarily exist to that extent. It did occur within the oxygen delivery equipment, and at the point (or points) where oxygen was vented to the atmosphere. Thus, the new term, "site of intentional expulsion" was adopted.

The Note is to call attention to the unexpected and the unintentional (former being equipment failure, the latter being human error). When these occur, a hazard exists and should be corrected without delay.

See also commentary under 7-6.2.3.1 and 9-2.1.9.3

Slow-Burning. As used in this standard, the term *slow-burning* refers to an Underwriters Laboratories Inc. test procedure. In this small-scale test, conducted in air at atmospheric pressure, a sample 6 in. (15.24 cm) long, ½ in. (1.27 cm) wide, and of ⅛ in. (0.32 cm) nominal thickness is suspended with longitudinal axis horizontal and transverse axis 45 degrees to the horizontal. A Bunsen burner flame is held against one end for 30 seconds and then removed, after which the time is measured for flame to spread along the bottom edge of a 4 in. (10.16 cm) segment between marks 1½ in. (2.54 cm) from each end. If the rate of burning is not more than 1 in. (3.81 cm) per minute, the sample is classified as slow-burning. (GE)

Station Outlet. An outlet point in a piped medical gas distribution system at which the user makes connections and disconnections. (MGS)

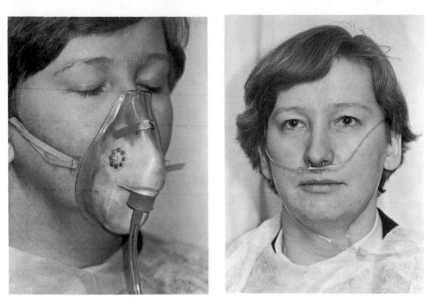

Figure 5(a) Site of intentional expulsion is one foot away from any point on face mask.

Figure 5(b) Site of intentional expulsion is one foot around nostrils.

Storage Cabinet.* A cabinet for the storage of flammable and combustible liquids constructed in accordance with Section 4-2 of NFPA 30, *Flammable and Combustible Liquids Code.* (*See Appendix A-2-2.*) (LAB)

A-2-2 Storage Cabinet. Some local jurisdictions require bottom venting of flammable liquids storage cabinets. While this is not required by NFPA 30, *Flammable and Combustible Liquids Code*, some manufacturers provide a plugged vent connection on one side of the cabinet, close to the base, to accommodate these local jurisdictions.

Storage Location for Flammable Inhalation Anesthetics. Any room within a consuming facility used for the storage of flammable anesthetic or flammable disinfecting agents (*see NFPA 30, Flammable and Combustible Liquids Code*) or inhalation anesthetic apparatus to which cylinders of flammable gases are attached. Such a storage location shall be considered a hazardous area throughout the location. (AS)

Supervisory Care Facility. A building or part thereof used for the housing, on a 24-hour basis, of four or more mental health patients who are capable of self-preservation and who require supervision and who are receiving therapy, training, or other health-related care and who may have imposed upon them security measures not under their control. (EE)

The definition coincides with that in NFPA *101*-1985, *Life Safety Code.*
The definition of this term became necessary when the Restructuring Subcommittee identified supervisory care facilities as having some distinct differences from other types of health care facilities (vis-a-vis fire safety hazards addressed by NFPA 99), and included this type of facility as a separate chapter (18).

Surface-Mounted Medical Gas Rail Systems.* A surface-mounted gas delivery system intended to provide ready access for two or more gases through a common delivery system to provide multiple gas station outlet locations within a single patient room or critical care area. (MGS)

A-2-2 Surface-Mounted Medical Gas Rail Systems. It is the intent that surface-mounted medical gas rail systems would be permitted in individual patient rooms but would not be allowed to go directly through room walls to adjacent patient rooms. However, it is the intent to allow surface-mounted medical gas rails to be used in a given critical care area where there may be a partition separating certain patient care functions, essentially leaving the system within the given critical care area. As an example, two adjacent patient rooms outside of a critical care unit would not be permitted to have a surface-mounted medical gas rail interconnect between the two rooms through the wall. However, in a nursery where there may be one or two segregated areas for isolation, a medical gas rail system supplying more than one isolation room, but within the nursery area, would be permitted to be interconnected with the nursery system.

Task Illumination. Provisions for the minimum lighting required to carry out necessary tasks in the areas described in Chapter 3, including safe access to supplies and equipment, and access to exits. (ES)

Tube, Endotracheal. A tube for insertion through the mouth or nose into the upper portion of the trachea (windpipe). Endotracheal tube may be equipped with an inflatable cuff. (GE)

Tube, Tracheotomy. A curved tube for insertion into the trachea (windpipe) below the larynx (voice box) during the performance of an appropriate operative procedure (tracheotomy). A tracheotomy tube may be equipped with an inflatable cuff. (AS)

Unattended Laboratory Operation. A laboratory procedure or operation at which there is no person present who is knowledgeable regarding the operation and emergency shutdown procedures. Absence for even short periods without coverage by a knowledgeable person constitutes an unattended laboratory operation. (LAB)

The slight difference between this definition and the one found in NFPA 45, *Standard on Fire Protection for Laboratories Using Chemicals*, reflects the Subcommittee on Laboratories' feeling that absence for even short periods constitutes unattended laboratory operation.

Use Point. A room, or area within a room, where medical gases are dispensed to a single patient for medical purposes. A use point may comprise a number of station outlets of different gases. (MGS)

Wet Locations. Those patient care areas that are normally subject to wet conditions, including standing water on the floor, or routine dousing or drenching of the work area. Routine housekeeping procedures and incidental spillage of liquids do not define a wet location. (EE)

The designation of wet locations is restricted to areas where there are long-term significant amounts of water. Many patient areas are wet, in the sense of washing, incontinence, hot packs, etc. However, these are not considered wet locations for the purpose of this document.

This term now appears here in Chapter 2 since the definition, originally developed for hospitals, is applicable to all health care facilities.

3 ELECTRICAL SYSTEMS

NOTE 1: The application of requirements contained in this chapter for specific types of health care facilities can be found in Chapters 12 through 18.

NOTE 2: Sections of Chapter 3 identified by a dagger (†) include text extracted from NFPA 110-1985, *Standard for Emergency and Standby Power Systems*. Requests for interpretations or revisions of the extracted text will be referred to the Technical Committee on Emergency Power Supplies.

Prologue

It should be noted that identifying a paragraph as extracted text does not change its meaning or whether it applies more or less. While "extracted" text may come from another NFPA document, it has the same authority and weight as any other text in Chapters 1 to 19. (*See also Notes at beginning of Handbook.*)

Prior to incorporation into NFPA 99, the material in this chapter relating to emergency power (its generation and distribution) was initially in a separate document designated NFPA 76 (later NFPA 76A). It was the first health-care-related standard concerned solely with electrical supply and distribution problems.

The main features of that standard were (and still are): (1) the designation of areas and equipment in health care facilities where an alternate source of electric power is necessary; (2) the identification of emergency and equipment systems for these areas and equipment; and (3) a method of generating electricity in lieu of the normal supply from electric utility companies. The electric generator had to be able to supply sufficient power to meet the load of the emergency circuits for a period of time. However, since many non-ambulatory patients must remain in a health care facility during most emergencies (the defend-in-place concept), the length of time for "non-exiting" electric power is a matter each health care facility has to determine. (NFPA 101, *Life Safety Code*, contains minimum requirements covering exiting a building.)

The original NFPA 76 document addressed only hospitals. However, over the years, it was expanded to include every type of health care facility except veterinary.

The Chairman of the then Hospital Committee received frequent complaints in the 1960s about compliance with this standard. Following the great Northeast power blackout in 1965, these complaints ceased. It is now standard procedure to provide emergency electric power appropriate to the needs of a facility.

In the late 1970's, NFPA was queried about emergency power generation in other types of facilities (at the time, only health care facilities had a standard on the subject). As a result, a "generic" standard, NFPA 110, *Standard on Emergency and Standby Power Systems*, was developed. It contains performance requirements for alternate electric power sources in the event of normal power-source failure. Some of the material in NFPA 99 came under the Committee responsible for NFPA 110 when NFPA 110 was adopted. This is the reason for the daggers (†) in Chapter 3; they indicate that material in that paragraph (some or all) is now "extracted" from NFPA 110.

3-1 Scope.*

A-3-1 Although complete compliance with this chapter is desirable, variations in existing health care facilities should be considered acceptable in instances where wiring arrangements are in accordance with prior editions of this document, or afford an equivalent degree of performance and reliability. Such variations may occur particularly with certain wiring in separate or common raceways, with certain functions connected to one or another system or branch, or with certain provisions for automatically or manually delayed restoration of power from the alternate (emergency) source of power.

3-1.1 This chapter covers the performance, maintenance, and testing of electrical systems (both normal and essential) used within health care facilities.

The scope of this chapter is not all inclusive. Those responsible for an individual medical facility, or for an individual patient care function within a medical facility, are urged to evaluate the adequacy of this chapter for their individual facility or function. If additional electrical supply features are installed, it is to be done in a manner consistent with the details and philosophy of this chapter.

This chapter should be used in conjunction with NFPA 70, *National Electrical Code*, particularly Article 517, which addresses health care facilities.

3-1.2 Specific requirements for wiring and installation on equipment are covered in NFPA 70, *National Electrical Code*.

3-1.3 Requirements for illumination and identification of means of egress in health care facilities are covered in NFPA *101, Life Safety Code*. The alternate source of emergency power for illumination and identification of means of egress shall be the essential electrical system.

3-1.4 This chapter does not cover the requirements for fire protection signaling systems except that the alternate source of power shall be the essential electrical system.

For requirements of signaling systems, see NFPA *101, Life Safety Code*, and NFPA 72 series documents.

3-1.5 This chapter does not cover the requirements for fire pumps except that the alternate source of power shall be permitted to be the essential electrical system.

For requirements of fire pumps, see NFPA 20, *Standard for Centrifugal Fire Pumps*.

3-1.6 Requirements for the installation of stationary engines and gas turbines are covered in NFPA 37, *Standard on the Installation and Use of Stationary Combustion Engines and Gas Turbines*.

3-2* Nature of Hazards. The hazards attendant to the use of electricity include electrical shock, thermal injury, and interruption of power. (*For further information see Appendix A-3-2.*)

A-3-2 Nature of Hazards. The major concern in this chapter is electric shock resulting from degradation or some type of failure within normally safe electrical appliances or the facility's electrical distribution system. The defect may be in the wiring, a component, or the result of deteriorating insulation. The failure may be caused by mechanical abuse or by improper use of the equipment.

Hospital service presents unusually severe environmental stress to equipment, similar to hard industrial use. Appliances are frequently subjected to large mechanical stresses in the course of being transported around the facility. Patients and staff, particularly those in operating rooms, critical care areas, clinical laboratories, and some physical therapy areas, are frequently surrounded by exposed, electrically grounded conductive surfaces that increase the risk of serious injury in the event of certain types of electrical failure.

As noted above, the hazards addressed in this chapter and Chapter 7 relate primarily to electrical shock, power continuity, and fire. While these are important in any occupancy, the special circumstances of health care facilities (and, in particular, hospitals) require special treatment.

3-2.1 Fire and Explosions. Electrical systems may be subject to the occurrence of electrical fires. Grounding systems, overcurrent protective devices, and other subjects discussed in this standard may be intended for fire prevention, as well as other purposes. This aspect of electrical systems is the primary focus of other NFPA standards, and will not be emphasized herein.

3-2.2 Shock.

3-2.2.1 General.

3-2.2.1.1 The major hazard of concern is electric shock resulting from failure in normally safe electric systems or appliances. The defects may be in wiring, faulty component, deteriorated insulation, or mechanical abuse.

3-2.2.1.2 Electric shock may cause undesired muscular contractions that may cause further injury to the patient or, in the case of health care personnel, may harm others coming under the health care personnel's management; e.g., during surgery. Additionally, anesthetics remove the feeling of pain, including that of electrical shock, and normal reflex action will not take place.

While normal reflex action may not take place in some parts of the body, muscular contraction in other parts can still occur if sufficient external electrical stimuli are applied.

3-2.2.1.3 Electric shock may cause burns by virtue of the electrical energy supplied by the defective system.

3-2.2.1.4 Electric shock may cause cardiac disturbance which may lead to death, i.e., ventricular fibrillation.

3-2.2.1.5 A defective electrical system can cause severe sparks that may serve as a source of ignition.

3-2.2.1.6 Normally the dry skin poses a formidable barrier to the passage of electrical current. Currents must approach ampere strength before the danger of electrical fibrillation of the heart occurs. If a patient has a cardiac pacemaker with externalized conductors, there is a direct conductive pathway to the heart. If stray electrical currents in the microampere range (millionths of an ampere) come in contact with one of these conductors, it is possible that ventricular fibrillation will occur (*see definition of microshock in Section 2-2 of Chapter 2*).

3-2.2.1.7 Patients with externalized pacemakers normally would not be expected to be treated in ambulatory care facilities (*see 7-6.2.2.4*).

3-2.2.2* Control. Control of electric shock hazard requires the limitation of electric current that might flow in an electric circuit involving the patient's body, and is accomplished through a variety of alternative approaches covered in Appendix A-3-2.2.2.

A-3-2.2.2 Shock Prevention. Since electric shock results from the effect of an electric current flowing through a part of the human body, three conditions must be satisfied simultaneously before a patient or staff member can be shocked. [*See Figure A-3-2.2.2(a)*.] There must be:

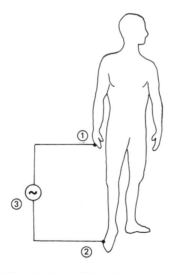

Figure A-3-2.2.2(a)   **The Three Basic Conditions Required to Produce an Electric Shock.**

(a) one part of the body in contact with a conductive surface (Point 1);

(b) a different part of the same body in contact with a second conductive surface (Point 2);

(c) a voltage source that will drive current through the body between those two points of contact (Point 3).

In the general case, six or seven independent and separable factors must combine simultaneously to satisfy these three conditions. [*See Figure A-3-2.2.2(b)*.]

Several separate factors should be analyzed when evaluating a potential electric shock hazard [numbers refer to Points in Figure A-3-2.2.2(b)]:

(1) the likelihood that a piece of line-powered equipment will be within reach of the patient;

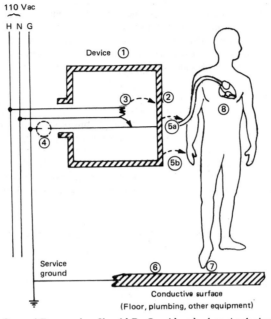

Figure A-3-2.2.2(b)   General Factors that Should Be Considered when Analyzing Electrical Safety.

(2a) the possibility of direct exposure of a "live" 110-volt conductor through a damaged line cord or attachment plug;

(2b) the likelihood that the equipment will have exposed metal parts that through some reasonably credible accident could become "live";

(3) the likelihood that equipment is accidentally damaged or malfunctions in some way and the metal becomes "live," i.e, electrified;

(4) the likelihood of the exposed metal parts not being grounded or accidentally becoming ungrounded;

(5) the likelihood that the patient (or member of staff, or visitor) will make good contact with this exposed, potentially live surface;

(6) the likelihood that a second exposed conductive surface that is, or that could through a reasonably credible event become, grounded is also within reach;

(7) the likelihood that the patient (or member of staff, or visitor) will make good contact with this grounded, or potentially grounded, surface;

(8) the probability that the resultant current flow will be sufficient to cause an injury.

The chance of a patient actually sustaining an electric shock is a product of the likelihood that each of the above events will occur. If the likelihood of occurrence of any one event is very close to zero, then the risk of electric shock will be very close to zero. Put another way, six or seven links in a chain need to be intact in order for a shock to be sustained. If any one link can be made extremely weak, by design or operating procedure, chance of receiving a shock will be minimal.

Working to minimize the occurrence of one factor (i.e., one safety factor) can achieve one "layer of protection." A second layer of protection is achieved by working to make the chance of occurrence of a second factor in the overall chain also very close to zero. However, extending this process to minimize the occurrence of all factors can lead to overdesign, overspecification, and less than cost-effective utilization of resources to control any problem.

Consider briefly each of the component factors. First, more could be done operationally to ensure that the minimum amount of line-powered equipment is within reach of the patient. Second, equipment that does not have a significant amount of exposed metal is to be preferred. Third, the staff should be instructed to report all obviously damaged equipment, even if it is still functional. Fourth, all grounding circuits should be tested frequently. Fifth, minimize the amount of grounded metal that is within reach of the patient. Avoid when possible attaching any grounded leads directly to the patient. Do not deliberately ground any metal part, such as a curtain rail or a metal cabinet, that cannot become accidentally "live." Insulate the patient from ground as much as possible.

In consideration of these objectives, four basic principles can be examined to avoid electric shock:

shock prevention by insulation and enclosure;

shock prevention by grounding;

shock prevention by device design;

shock prevention through user procedures.

Shock Prevention by Insulation and Enclosure. Physical provisions should be made to prevent personal hazardous contact between energized conductors or between an energized conductor and ground.

(a) Noninsulated current-carrying conductors, which could produce hazardous currents, should be protected from contact through suitable enclosure.

(b) Energized conductors, which could produce hazardous currents when not in protective enclosures, should be insulated by materials suitable to the voltage and environment.

In order to minimize the probability of completing a hazardous circuit, exposed conductive surfaces not likely to be energized from internal sources should not be intentionally grounded. Insulated covering of such surfaces is desirable.

NOTE 1: Past measures recommended by earlier editions of NFPA standards and other standards associated with equipotential grounding and bonding of "dead metal" served to increase likelihood that a patient or staff member would complete an undesirable pathway for electric shock.

NOTE 2: This principle does not intend to mandate construction of an insulated environment, but rather to avoid intentional grounding of otherwise dead metal surfaces.

Shock Prevention by Grounding. A grounding system for fault currents should be supplied for two reasons: to minimize the fraction of the fault current that might flow through an individual during the fault condition; and to operate overcurrent devices in order to minimize the possibility of damage and fire. This grounding system should also be utilized to provide a safe path for leakage currents.

(a) Unless doubly insulated, each line-powered electrical appliance within the patient vicinity should have a grounding wire, which normally carries the leakage current directly to ground, in the same power cable as the energized conductors.

(b) Each receptacle for line-powered electrical appliances should provide a low-impedance grounding connection and path.

Shock Prevention by Device Design. Leakage current should be minimized.

New device designs should not intentionally provide a low-impedance path at 60 Hz from patient to ground.

Shock Prevention through User Procedures.

General: A total electrical safety program incorporates the best features of design, manufacture, inspection, maintenance, and operation. The design should be such that limited departures from ideal conditions of maintenance and use will not cause unreasonable risks.

Where existing equipment that does not meet new-equipment requirements is to be used, such use is permissible if procedures of use and maintenance can establish an equivalent level of safety.

User procedures should include:

(a) establishing a policy to prohibit the connection of nonisolated input equipment to externalized intracardiac electrodes,

(b) establishing user educational and training programs, and

(c) establishing a testing and routine maintenance program.

3-2.3 Thermal. (Reserved)

3-2.4 Interruption of Power.

3-2.4.1 General. Medical and nursing sciences are becoming progressively more dependent upon electrical apparatus for the preservation of life of hospitalized patients. For example, year by year, more cardiac operations are performed, in some of which the patient's life depends upon artificial circulation of the blood; in other operations, life is sustained by means of electrical impulses that stimulate and regulate heart action; in still others, suction developed by electrical means is routinely relied upon to remove body fluids and mucus that might otherwise cause suffocation. In another sense, lighting is needed in strategic areas in order that precise procedures may be carried out, and power is needed to safeguard such vital services as refrigerated stores held in tissue, bone, and blood banks.

Interruption of normal electrical service in health care facilities may be caused by catastrophes such as storms, floods, fires, earthquakes, or explosions; by failures of the systems supplying electrical power; or by incidents within the facility. For all such situations, electrical systems should be planned to limit internal disruption and to provide for continuity of vital services at all times. Outages may be corrected in seconds or may require hours for correction. This indicates that the system or protection must be designed to cope with the longest probable outage.

Selecting vital areas and functions considered to be essential, designing safeguards to assure continuity in these circuits, and maintaining the electrical and mechanical components of such essential services so that they will work when called on are complex problems that warrant standardized guidance for regulating agencies, governing boards, and administrators of health care facilities, and architects and engineers concerned with their construction. Such guidance is offered in this chapter.

This chapter is predicated on the basic principle of achieving dependability. It is intended to recognize the different degrees of reliability that can result from varying approaches to electrical design. Therefore, its requirements have been developed to allow the designer the flexibility needed to achieve a reliable electrical system.

This section provides rationale for the need for requirements on emergency power specific to health care facilities. A reliable supply of electricity, consistent with the types of medical procedures performed in, and the nature of activities of, each health care facility is required. In addition to the fire-protection and life-safety features that are similar to those for other occupancies, electricity is essential for vital functions unique to health care facilities. These include special lighting, monitoring systems, and electromedical appliances.

Failures of the normal electrical supply do occur and must be considered unavoidable. Public utility sources and on-premises generation sources are subject to interruption. This chapter provides standardized guidance toward providing and maintaining electrical systems that help minimize the probability of total loss of electricity, and help to ensure a high probability of a reliable supply of electricity to vital functions. It does not guarantee that total loss of electricity will not occur or that vital functions will not be left without a supply of electricity (as has occurred because of unusual situations). But the track record for health care facilities, with respect to emergency power, has been excellent over the past two decades.

For a discussion on the need to maintain power see commentary under 3-2.4.2.

While it may seem obvious, it is worth repeating. Activation of emergency electric generator(s) does *not* occur because of some electrical failure within a facility (e.g., a GFCI trips, or a branch circuit breaker trips, or a cable is cut). If such an event occurs, supplying electricity from generators would not change the status (i.e., electricity would only go as far as the point of interruption). Activation of emergency electric generator(s) occurs in the event of a failure of the *normal* power source at the main switch gear.

3-2.4.2 Need to Maintain Power. Interruption of the supply of electric power in a hospital may be a hazard. Implementation of the requirements of this chapter serves to maintain the required level of continuity and quality of electrical power for patient care electrical appliances.

In Chapter 2, under the definition of "Isolated Power System," extensive commentary is included on the history of these systems as used in anesthetizing locations, and as related to electrical and personnel safety. Under paragraph 3-4.2.1.4(d), there is commentary as to how the time of 10 seconds was arrived at for restoration of electric power in the event of loss of normal power to a health care facility.

In this regard, the subject of "continuity of power" has come under closer scrutiny of late. However, this phrase is a bit of a misnomer since it can have several meanings, depending on the context in which it is used. For some, one meaning refers to the presence of electric power being supplied to a facility, and whether some mechanism is used to switch in a second source in the event the first source stops (either the source itself stops or the wires carrying the power to a facility are accidentally or intentionally cut). For others, this phrase refers to equipment that allows electric power to continue to flow to a device even though one of several types of electrical faults has occured within the device that would normally stop the flow of electricity within the device. Thus, it is necessary to be clear as to which problem (or possibility) is being addressed: the incoming electric power to a facility, or the electric power being supplied to a specific device.

The wording of paragraph 3-2.4.2 originated with the former Technical Committee on Essential Electrical Systems in Health Care Facilities, which was addressing the problem of a facility losing its normal electrical power from the utility company.

In the early 1960s when the then Committee on Hospitals began to address the issue of emergency power, the question of how long facilities could tolerate loss of power until emergency power came on-line was discussed. A brief period of time (up to 10 seconds) was considered acceptable in view of the technology of the day and the medicine/surgery being practiced.

Today, some in medicine do not want any loss of power. They contend that a loss of power for even a fraction of a second, or a power surge, may be damaging because of the use of, and reliance on, computers, or because of some of the medical procedures now being conducted. With respect to *computers*, loss of power would mean a shutdown of the computer, and a reprogramming or resetting when power was restored. Since computers are now used on-line (either alone or as part of a device) to store data as well as control pumps, etc., this recycling could be detrimental to the patient in the middle of a critical surgical procedure. With respect to *medical procedures*, some, such as neuro-microsurgery or cardiac by-pass surgery, involve very intricate movements. A sudden loss of light *could* be harmful to the patient.

Others in medicine, however, do not feel this 10 second "downtime" is serious enough to warrant the installation of equipment to eliminate this interval of no power. They feel that *physicians* take care of patients, and thus are, quite able to continue to take care of patients when there is a short, temporary loss of power. [Note: An electrical feeder fault *within* a facility will not allow power from any source to flow beyond the fault; *and* it will also mean no power to all devices downstream from the fault, irrespective of a system that allows power to continue to flow to appliances for certain appliance faults.]

Thus, it is necessary to know in what context the phrase "continuity of power" is being used. And for purposes of NFPA and this document, that context has to be within the scope (broad, though limited) of fire or electrical safety for people and property. Other concerns may be interrelated (e.g., interruption of medical procedure; efficacy of appliance) but NFPA does not have the collective expertise or authority to make judgements in these other areas.

Anesthetizing locations are areas where debate over isolated power systems (IPSs) has expanded to the issue of "continuous power" because of the way IPSs function. Since IPSs detect *some* types of electrical faults in electrical equipment (which in a grounded electrical system would either trip the equipment's internal fuse or trip a branch circuit breaker), IPSs are, in a sense, allowing power to continue (since only an alarm is activated, and no fuses or current breakers are tripped). But this is distinct from an IPS being a "source" of power, such as a generator set, which actually provides power. In reviewing the literature on isolated power systems, the original intent focussed on safety (electrical and personnel) because of the flammable anesthetics being used, not on the fact that isolated power systems also allowed appliances to continue operating in the event of certain electrical faults within the appliance. However, while the use of flammable anesthetics has practically stopped, the use, and reliance on, more and more electrical appliances in the anesthetizing locations has occurred and requires some addressing, but from the perspective of electrical and personnel safety.

Health care facilities, thus, need to be certain as to their electrical needs and dependency, and how long a power outage in various areas can be tolerated (if at all).

3-2.5 R.F. Interference. (Reserved)

(See Annex 2, "The Safe Use of High-Frequency Electricity in Health Care Facilities," at the end of this document for recommendations.)

3-3 Sources.

3-3.1 Normal (AC). Each appliance of a hospital requiring electrical line power for operation shall be supported by power sources and distribution systems that provide power adequate for each service.

3-3.1.1 Power/Utility Company. (Reserved)

3-3.1.2 On-Site Generator Set. (Reserved)

3-3.2 Alternative.

The wording in the following sections provides for the usual situation in which the normal power source is a public utility and the alternate source is on-site generation. The Exceptions provide for situations when *normal* power is provided by *on-site* generation. However, there must always be at least two independent power sources, and at least one of them must be on-site generation. In certain situations the power source(s) defined as "normal" and "alternate" may change, and even be reversed, under different modes of operation.

The normal source should be made as reliable as possible as dictated by local conditions. When the normal source is a public utility, the greatest reliability and continuity is provided by a properly protected network fed by multiple independent services. The next highest reliability is from multiple independent services with local automatic switching. This chapter does not require multiple services, or network or switching arrangements because of widely varying local conditions and the limited availability of multiple services at certain locations.

The regional blackouts of the past two decades prove that multiple public utility services cannot be considered absolutely reliable, and thus cannot be used as the alternate source in lieu of on-site generation.

When the normal source is on-site generation, it is suggested that its reliability be designed and maintained to at least equal to that of any available public utility.

3-3.2.1 On-Site Generator Set.

Nothing in this section precludes the use of coolants for heat recovery purposes. However, it should be noted that Article 700 of NFPA 70, *National Electrical Code*, does not allow municipal water supplies to be the primary source of coolant.

3-3.2.1.1* Design Considerations. Facilities whose normal source of power is supplied by two or more separate central-station-fed services (dual sources of normal power) experience greater

reliability than those with only a single feed, and shall be considered whenever practical, but such dual source of normal power does not constitute an alternate power source as defined in this chapter (*see Appendix A-3-3.2.1.1*).

Distribution system arrangements shall be designed to minimize interruptions to the electrical systems due to internal failures by the use of adequately rated equipment. Among the factors to be considered are:

(a) Abnormal currents: current-sensing devices, phase and ground, shall be selected to minimize the extent of interruption to the electrical system due to abnormal current caused by overload and/or short circuits.

(b) Abnormal voltages such as single phasing of three-phase utilization equipment, switching and/or lightning surges, voltage reductions, etc.

(c) Capability of achieving the fastest possible restoration of any given circuit(s) after clearing a fault.

(d) Effects of future changes, such as increased loading and/or supply capacity.

(e) Stability and power capability of the prime mover during and after abnormal conditions.

(f) Sequence reconnection of loads to avoid large current inrushes that could trip overcurrent devices or overload the generator(s).

NOTE: Careful consideration should be given to the location of the spaces housing the components of the essential electrical system to minimize interruptions caused by natural forces common to the area (e.g., storms, floods, or earthquakes, or hazards created by adjoining structures or activities). Consideration should also be given to the possible interruption of normal electrical services resulting from similar causes as well as possible disruption of normal electrical service due to internal wiring and equipment failures. Consideration should be given to the physical separation of the main feeders of the essential electrical system from the normal wiring of the facility to prevent possible simultaneous destruction as a result of a local catastrophe.

In selecting electrical distribution arrangements and components for the essential electrical system, high priority should be given to achieving maximum continuity of the electrical supply to the load. Higher consideration should be given to achieving maximum reliability of the alternate power source and its feeders rather than protection of such equipment, provided the protection is not required to prevent a greater threat to human life such as fire, explosion, electrocution, etc., than would be caused by the lack of essential electrical supply.

A-3-3.2.1.1 Design.

(a) *Design Considerations.* Consideration should be given to properly designed and installed bypass arrangements to permit testing and maintenance of system components that could not be otherwise maintained without disruption of important hospital functions.

The former Technical Committee on Essential Electrical Systems has addressed at least once each year for many years, the issue of making mandatory the use of Bypass/Isolation Switches for automatic transfer switches. The use of these switches has never been made a requirement because of their significant cost. Hence, facilities considering installing this type of transfer switch need to carefully evaluate the cost/benefit ratio.

Bypass/isolation switches are very useful in properly maintaining automatic transfer switches.

(b) *Connection to Dual Source of Normal Power.* For the greatest assurance of continuity of electrical service, the normal source should consist of two separate full-capacity services, each independent of the other. Such services should be selected and installed with full recognition of local hazards of interruption, such as icing and flooding.

Where more than one full-capacity service is installed, they should be connected in such a manner that one will pick up the load automatically upon loss of the other, and so arranged that the load of the emergency and equipment systems will be transferred to the alternate source (generator set) only when both utility services are deenergized, unless this arrangement is impractical and waived by the authority having jurisdiction. Such services should be interlocked in such a manner as to prevent paralleling of utility services on either primary or secondary voltage levels.

NOTE: In any installation where it is possible to parallel utility supply circuits, for example, to prevent interruption of service when switching from one utility source to another, it is imperative to consult the power companies affected as to problems of synchronization.

These factors should not be considered the only ones necessary for minimizing power interruption within a facility. External incidents or failures, for example, are obviously beyond the control of a facility but can occur, and will affect the facility.

Essential electrical systems must be designed as complete systems. They are not simply generators and transfer switches appended to normal distribution wiring. The overall goal of providing reliable power for fire protection, life safety, and medical functions must not be forgotten when designing a system.

There is extensive history on the destruction of electrical distribution equipment and resulting outages within facilities caused by internal ground faults. This chapter attempts to mitigate the effects of such outages, and to some degree to minimize their occurence, by requiring segregated distribution systems with multiple transfer switches. Those not familiar with the engineering factors of electrical design are urged to recognize that internal ground faults are a major exposure that must be considered in the design of electrical systems. In addition, the proper engineering technique for coping with the ground fault problem is to divide, limit, and segregate the electrical system and its components. No single component or system can be practically designed to be massive enough to withstand the sudden extremely large currents thay may be imposed when a major ground fault occurs.

This chapter does not require the application of all available technology and techniques that might possibly be used for essential electrical systems. The chapter does require the optimum combination of "real world" reliability, economics, and allowance for human factors in the design of an essential electrical system. The chapter does not prevent the application of additional technology and techniques to individual facilities.

Provisions for the maintenance of main switchgear and supply feeders should be considered when establishing distribution details of the normal and essential electrical systems. Such maintenance is greatly simplified when the main switchgear can be de-energized while essential electrical systems are fed from the alternate source.

(c) *Installation of Generator Sets.* For additional material on diesel engines see *Diesel Engines for Use with Generators to Supply Emergency and Short Term Electric Power*, National Research Council Publication 1132, available as Order No. O.P.52870 from University Microfilms, a Xerox Company, P.O. Box 1366, Ann Arbor, Michigan 48106.

3-3.2.1.2 Essential electrical systems shall have a minimum of two independent sources of power: a normal source generally supplying the entire electrical system, and one or more alternate sources for use when the normal source is interrupted.

It is not the intent of the Subcommittee responsible for this chapter that dual power sources of normal power be used in lieu of an alternate power source. This point was emphasized in 1984 by a change to 3-3.2.1.1 relative to design considerations.

3-3.2.1.3 The alternate source of power shall be a generator(s) driven by some form of prime mover(s), and located on the premises.

Exception: Where the normal source consists of generating units on the premises, the alternate source shall be either another generating set or an external utility service.

Even with the Exception, it should be noted that at least one source of power (normal or alternate) has to be on-site.

Figure 6(a)   A 950-kilowatt generator in a large medical center that starts when normal power is lost.

A Formal Interpretation was issued in 1986 (F.I. 99-84-2) concerning the Exception and a group of adjacent hospitals that had a contractual agreement relative to the acquisition of electric power. While the Exception states that an external utility service can be the alternate power source if the facility has a generator *on site*, in this instance a limited group of adjacent facilities had developed their own electric delivery system in lieu of each facility having their own generator. Because of this restricted access, and because each hospital otherwise met the requirements for an essential electrical system, the Subcommit-

Figure 6(b)   A steam-operated generator used in conjunction with a local utility company (i.e., "cogeneration"). When power from utility company is lost, this generator keeps operating, supplying power to the circuits on the essential electrical system.

tee on Electrical Systems felt that this arrangement met the intent of the Exception, and that an external utility service could serve as the alternate power source.

3-3.2.1.4 General.   Generator sets installed as an alternate source of power for essential electrical systems shall be designed to meet the requirements of such service.

"Utility" or "general purpose" generators are not acceptable if they do not meet the requirements listed in this chapter. The original Committee that developed these criteria spent a lot of time and effort developing these criteria for the generator portion of the essential electrical system to be reliable.

3-3.2.1.5 Exclusive Use for Essential Electrical Systems.   The generating equipment used shall be either reserved exclusively for such service or normally used for other purposes. If normally used for other purposes, two or more sets shall be installed, such that the demand and all other performance requirements of the essential electrical system shall be met with the largest single generator set out of service.

Exception: A single generator set shall be permitted to operate the essential electrical system for (1) peak demand control, (2) internal voltage control, or (3) load relief for the external utility, provided any such use will not decrease the mean period between service overhauls to less than three years.

Controversy exists concerning whether, and to what extent, the emergency generator is to be used for other than standby power. The Exception was developed in the 1970s as an energy control consideration. The likelihood of the emergency generator to function when needed is the major concern. Reliability, in view of safety, must be considered.

To utilize this Exception, the electrical system of the facility would have to be wired and controlled in such a way that, in the event of loss of normal power, the emergency generator would supply power only to the essential electrical load, dropping out all nonessential loads.

3-3.2.1.6† Work Space or Room. Adequate space shall be provided for housing and servicing the generator set and associated equipment used for its starting and control. Service transformers shall not be installed in this area.

The specific size of the space or room for the generator set has been deliberately left undefined because of differences at each facility. However, separation of service transformers from generator sets has been included in the interest of safety (i.e., in an incident that affected the service transformer, the generator set might also be damaged if it were in the same area).

3-3.2.1.7† Capacity and Rating. The generator set(s) shall have sufficient capacity and proper rating to meet the maximum demand of the essential electrical system at any one time.

This requirement should not be misconstrued as requiring that a generator set(s) be able to supply 100 percent of a facility's electrical load; rather, only that load connected to the essential electrical system need be considered for sizing purposes. The load should be the actual electrical load (i.e., amperage of the electrical equipment and devices to be provided emergency power); it is not the circuit breaker ratings in electrical panels. While demand factors are used in calculating loads for normal operation, the same demand factors may not be appropriate when calculating the size of generator set(s) needed. Article 700-5(a) of NFPA 70, *National Electrical Code*, requires an emergency system to be able to supply enough electricity for all loads on the essential electrical system to be operated simultaneously. [NOTE: Loads may be picked up sequentially in order not to load-down generator too quickly.] Also, momentary loads and in-rush currents may account for higher percentage of the load on essential electrical systems than on normal load (e.g., motor loads, X-ray equipment).

Any change in load should be recorded so that the actual load is always known and can be compared to the capacity of the generator. (*See Appendix C-3-2, "Maintenance Guide," for further information.*)

If more than one generator is used to supply electricity for the essential electrical system, load shedding or load shifting (within the essential electrical system) is permitted or may be necessary if one generator fails or becomes overloaded. This section (3-3.2.1.7) states only that the generator set (or sets) be able to meet the essential electrical system load. With a system having only one generator, shedding would have to be done (if the load became too great) to have some emergency power available. The same would hold true for multiple-generator systems.

Should this situation develop (either overload or generator failure) priority would be given to maintaining power to the most essential equipment first (those on the life safety branch), then the next most essential equipment (those on the critical branch).

It should be understood that the above load shedding and shifting applies only to the essential electrical system. It is also another reason why separating circuits on the essential electrical system (life safety, critical, and equipment) is required: to make it more possible to maintain power to the most essential equipment.

3-3.2.1.8 Load Pickup. The generator set(s) shall have sufficient capacity to pick up the load and meet the minimum frequency and voltage stability requirements of the emergency system within 10 seconds after loss of normal power.

Voltage as well as frequency stability of the alternate power source is necessary before connection to the load (i.e. the wiring system) to prevent damage to such items as voltage-sensitive equipment and fluorescent lighting. The operation of transfer switches is thus usually delayed until the voltage and frequency from the generator system are within specified limits. While this standard calls for such stability in 10 seconds (max.) from the time normal power is lost, transfer to alternate power source can be accomplished *whenever* stability of the alternate power source is achieved (10 seconds can seem like an eternity in critical areas such as operating rooms). (*See also commentary under 3-5.1.2.5.*)

3-3.2.1.9† Maintenance of Temperature. Provisions shall be made to maintain the generator room at not less than 50°F (10°C) or the engine water-jacket temperature at not less than 70°F (21.1°C).

The Subcommittee responsible for emergency power requirements has noted from experience that generators required for essential electrical systems may not start or pick up their connected load unless temperatures listed above are maintained.

3-3.2.1.10† Ventilating Air. Provision shall be made to provide adequate air for cooling and to replenish engine combustion air.

Recent incidents suggest that serious consideration should be given to the protection from fire and smoke of the air supply for the generator set(s). Smoke entering the generator air intake has caused generators to shut down.

3-3.2.1.11*† Cranking Batteries. Internal combustion engine starting batteries shall have sufficient capacity to provide 60 seconds of continuous cranking.

A-3-3.2.1.11 Cranking Battery. The engine automatic starting system should have an overcrank device to terminate cranking with enough reserve battery power to permit additional cranking after an investigation into the reason for a failure to start.

3-3.2.1.12† Compressed Air Starting Devices. Internal combustion engine air-starting devices shall have sufficient capacity to supply five 10-second cranking attempts, with not more than a 10-second rest between attempts, with the compressor not operating.

Air starting devices have a shorter cranking time than electric starters, but need rest periods between cranks to prevent overheating.

3-3.2.1.13† Fuel Supply.   The fuel supply for the generator set shall be liquid with on-site fuel storage capacity. The amount of on-site storage shall take into account past outage records and delivery problems due to weather, shortages, and other geographic conditions.

While no actual time is stated, there are other NFPA standards that contain requirements that, in turn, affect fuel supply levels. These standards include:

• NFPA *101, Life Safety Code,* which requires a minimum of 1½ hours for lights used for illuminating exits and exit signs;

• Article 700-12(b)(2) in NFPA 70, *National Electrical Code,* requires a fuel supply of 2 hours minimum for legally required standby emergency generators;

• The NFPA 72 series documents on signaling systems require emergency power systems to supply power to fire alarm systems for 24 to 60 hours, depending on the type of fire alarm signaling system.

If the above requirements are met by a generator system, as opposed to a battery system, then these requirements have to be factored into fuel supplies for the generator. Whatever supply is maintained, consideration should be given to its capability to replenish the fuel supply before it is exhausted. (An essential electrical system might have to function for an extended period in some emergencies.) As an example, if a facility maintains an on-site fuel supply capable of running the generator for three days, then replenishment procedures should not exceed two days.

Exception: The use of other than on-site liquid fuels shall be permitted when there is a low probability of a simultaneous failure of both the off-site fuel delivery system and power from the outside electrical utility company.

Determination of low probability should be made by technical personnel in consultation with such groups as local utility companies, state energy authorities, etc.

3-3.2.1.14† Requirements for Safety Devices.

(a) *Internal Combustion Engines.*   Internal combustion engines serving generator sets shall be equipped with:

(1) A sensor device plus visual warning device to indicate a water-jacket temperature below those required in 3-3.2.1.9.

(2) Sensor devices plus visual prealarm warning device to indicate:

(i) High engine temperature (above manufacturer's recommended safe operating temperature range).

(ii) Low lubricating oil pressure (below manufacturer's recommended safe operating range).

(3) An automatic engine shutdown device plus visual device to indicate that a shutdown took place for:

(i) Overcrank (failed to start).

(ii) Overspeed.

(iii) Low lubricating oil pressure.

(iv) Excessive engine temperature.

(4) A common audible alarm device to warn that any one or more of the prealarm or alarm conditions exist.

NOTE: One method to accomplish both (2) and (3) is to use two sensors for each alarm condition set at different operating points.

The safety devices listed above are specifically for the essential electrical system. They are in addition to any general requirements for internal combustion engines contained in NFPA 37, *Stationary Combustion Engines and Gas Turbines*. Audible as well as visual indicators are considered necessary to help ensure that malfunctions are investigated in a timely manner.

(b) *Other Types of Prime Movers.* Prime movers, other than internal combustion engines, serving generator sets shall have appropriate safety devices plus visual and audible alarms to warn of alarm or approaching alarm conditions.

(c) *Liquid Fuel Supplies.* Liquid fuel supplies for emergency or auxiliary power sources shall be equipped with a sensor device to warn that the main fuel tank contains less than a three-hour operating supply.

Article 700 of NFPA 70, *National Electrical Code*, requires any internal combustion engine used as a prime mover to have sufficient on-site fuel supply to operate for two hours. However, the Subcommittee responsible for emergency power in this document believes, for health care essential electrical eystem purposes, a facility should be alerted when its on-site liquid fuel supply is down to a three-hour operating supply. This is an instance of the "specific" (i.e., health care facility requirements for liquid fuel supply for prime movers) being more stringent than the "general" (i.e., minimum liquid fuel supply for all internal combustion engines used as prime movers).

3-3.2.1.15† Alarm Annunciator. A remote annunciator, storage battery powered, shall be provided to operate outside of the generating room in a location readily observed by operating personnel at a regular work station (*see NFPA 70, National Electrical Code, Section 700-12*).

The annunciator shall indicate alarm conditions of the emergency or auxiliary power source as follows:

(a) Individual visual signals shall indicate:

(1) When the emergency or auxiliary power source is operating to supply power to load.

(2) When the battery charger is malfunctioning.

(b) Individual visual signals plus a common audible signal to warn of an engine-generator alarm condition shall indicate:

(1) Low lubricating oil pressure.

(2) Low water temperature (below those required in 3-3.2.1.9).

(3) Excessive water temperature.

(4) Low fuel — when the main fuel storage tank contains less than a three-hour operating supply.

(5) Overcrank (failed to start).

(6) Overspeed.

Where a regular work station may be unattended periodically, an audible and visual derangement signal, appropriately labeled, shall be established at a continuously monitored location. This derangement signal shall activate when any of the conditions in 3-3.2.1.15(a) and (b) occur, but need not display these conditions individually.

For (a)(1), the usual practice is to provide a visual signal that the generator is producing voltage.

For (b)(1) and (b)(3), the audible/visual signal is a pre-shutdown type (i.e., it provides a warning before shutdown actually occurs). It is not intended that two lights (functions) be provided at the alarm annunciator: one for warning (pre-shutdown) and one for shutdown. An annunciator remote from the generating room is useful only if it indicates impending problems.

An annunciator is normally in one location near the generator(s). A derangement signal, if necessary, is in another location where continuous monitoring (i.e., 24 hours a day) is possible.

3-3.2.2 Battery. Battery systems shall meet all requirements of Article 700 of NFPA 70, *National Electrical Code.*

3-3.2.3 Separate Utility. (Reserved)

3-4 Distribution.

3-4.1 Normal (AC) System.

3-4.1.1 Installation shall be in accordance with NFPA 70, *National Electrical Code.*

3-4.1.2 All Patient Care Areas. (*See Chapter 2 for definition of patient care area.*)

3-4.1.2.1* Wiring, Regular Voltage.

A-3-4.1.2.1 Wiring, Regular Voltage.

Integrity of Insulation on Conductors. At the time of installation, steps should be taken to ensure that the insulation on each conductor intended to be energized, or on quiet grounds, has not been damaged in the process of installation. When disconnected and unenergized the resistance should be at least 20 megohms when measured with an ohmmeter having an open-circuit test voltage of at least 500 volts dc.

Accessibility of Overcurrent Protection Devices. Consideration should be given to providing reasonable accessibility to branch-circuit switching and overcurrent protection devices by the hospital staff in the patient care area. Consideration should also be given to providing labels at each receptacle and on installed equipment as to the location and identity of the distribution panel serving that power outlet or equipment, especially where the location or identity may not be readily apparent.

(a)* *Circuits.* Branch circuits serving a given patient vicinity shall be fed from not more than one normal branch circuit distribution panel and/or one emergency branch circuit distribution panel.

Exception: Branch circuits serving only special-purpose outlets or receptacles (e.g., portable X-ray receptacles) need not conform to the requirements of this section.

A-3-4.1.2.1(a) Circuits. The requirement that branch circuits shall be fed from not more than one distribution panel was introduced for several reasons. A general principle is to minimize possible potential differences between the grounding pins of receptacles in one area by bringing the grounding conductors to a common point. A specific reason is to simplify maintenance by making it easier to find the source for the receptacles in a room. This is particularly a problem in hospitals where emergency conditions may require rapid restoration of power.

A requirement to have only one phase in a patient vicinity was proposed and used for a short period by some designers on the mistaken premise that it would prevent faults involving 208 volts from occurring. This practice was not widely adopted for several reasons:

1. The fault addressed is extremely unlikely, requiring double faults (loss of ground in the appliance plus 110 volts coming in contact with chassis) on two different appliances, in addition to the patient touching both appliances simultaneously.

2. If one phase of power dropped out, most of the power to that patient vicinity could be lost.

3. Since at least one circuit to a patient vicinity has to be on an emergency circuit, single phasing a room was more difficult and costly because of the correlation and extra wiring that became necessary. Thus, this chapter does not contain requirements on this subject.

(b) *Grounding.*

(1) Grounding Circuitry Integrity. Grounding circuits and conductors in patient care areas shall be installed in such a way that the continuity of other parts of those circuits cannot be interrupted nor the resistance raised above an acceptable level by the installation, removal, or replacement of any installed equipment, including power receptacles.

Acceptable limits are listed in 3-5.2 (Performance Critera and Testing of the Electrical Distribution System).

(2)* Reliability of Grounding. In all patient care areas the reliability of an installed grounding circuit to a power receptacle shall be at least equivalent to that provided by an electrically continuous copper conductor of appropriate ampacity run from the receptacle to a

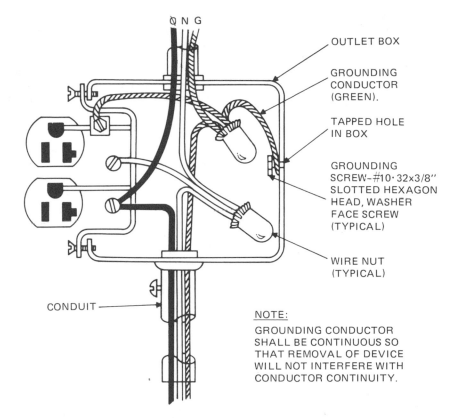

ⵁ N G

OUTLET BOX

GROUNDING
CONDUCTOR
(GREEN).

TAPPED HOLE
IN BOX

GROUNDING
SCREW–#10· 32x3/8″
SLOTTED HEXAGON
HEAD, WASHER
FACE SCREW
(TYPICAL)

WIRE NUT
(TYPICAL)

CONDUIT

NOTE:

GROUNDING CONDUCTOR
SHALL BE CONTINUOUS SO
THAT REMOVAL OF DEVICE
WILL NOT INTERFERE WITH
CONDUCTOR CONTINUITY.

Figure 7 Typical method of wiring a receptacle to meet criteria of paragraph 3-4.1.2.1(b)(1). [For details on wiring installation, see Sections 251-14 and 300-13(b) in NFPA 70, *National Electrical Code.*]

grounding bus in the distribution panel. The grounding conductor shall conform to NFPA 70, *National Electrical Code.*

Exception: Existing construction that does not use a separate grounding conductor shall be permitted to continue in use provided that it meets the performance requirements in 3-5.2.1, "Grounding System in Patient Care Areas."

A-3-4.1.2.1(b)(2) Reliability of Grounding. This requirement is usually met by appropriate mounting hardware, and not by wire jumpers.

The Appendix material was added by the Committee to avoid misinterpretation on wire jumpers, as well as not specify a particular method to meet the requirement.

Where metal receptacle boxes are used, the performance of the connection between the receptacle grounding terminal and the metal box shall be equivalent to the performance provided by copper wire no smaller than No. 12 AWG.

(c)* *Grounding Interconnects.* In patient care areas supplied by the normal distribution system and any branch of the essential electrical system, the grounding system of the normal distribution system and that of the essential electrical system shall be interconnected.

A-3-4.1.2.1(c) Grounding Interconnects. The requirement for grounding interconnection between the normal and essential power systems follows the principle of minimizing possible potential differences between the grounding pins of receptacles in one area by bringing the grounding conductors to a common point.

Since the wiring for the normal electric power system and the essential electric power system are installed in separate conduits, it may be possible to have widely separated grounds. This section emphasizes that the grounding of both systems must be connected together locally to avoid potential differences between local grounds.

(d) *Circuit Breakers, GFCIs, GFIs.*

(1) Circuit breakers, fuses, ground fault circuit interrupters (GFCIs) and ground fault interrupters (GFIs) shall be coordinated so that power interruption in that part of the circuit which precedes the interrupting device closest to a fault shall not occur.

This is good design practice as required by performance criteria listed. It is important to maintain continuity of electrical power as much as possible in health care facilities.

(2) Ground Fault Circuit Interrupters (GFCIs). If used, the GFCIs shall be approved for the purpose.

NOTE: Listed Class A ground fault circuit interrupters trip when a fault current to ground is 6 milliamperes or more.

(e) *Wiring in Anesthetizing Locations.*

(1) All Anesthetizing Locations.

(i) Wiring. Installed wiring shall be in metal raceway or shall be as required in NFPA 70, *National Electrical Code*, Sections 517-100 through 517-104.

(ii) Raceway. Such distribution systems shall be run in metal raceways along with a green grounding wire sized no smaller than the energized conductors.

(iii) Grounding to Raceways. Each device connected to the distribution system shall be effectively grounded to the metal raceway at the device.

This requirement would be exempted for double-insulated appliances.

(iv) Installation. Methods of installation shall conform to Articles 250 and 517 of NFPA 70, *National Electrical Code*.

(2) Flammable Anesthetizing Locations. Electric wiring installed in the hazardous area of a flammable inhalation anesthetizing location shall comply with the requirements of NFPA 70, *National Electrical Code*, Article 501, Class I, Division 1. Equipment installed therein shall be approved for use in Class I, Group C, Division 1 hazardous areas.

3-4.1.2.2 Wiring, Low-Voltage. Fixed systems of 30 volts (dc or ac rms) or less shall be ungrounded, and the insulation between each ungrounded conductor and the primary circuit, which is supplied from a conventionally grounded distribution system, shall provide the same protection as required for the primary voltage.

Exception No. 1: A grounded low-voltage system shall be permitted provided that load currents are not carried in the grounding conductors.

It should not be inferred that low-voltage wiring has to be insulated the same way as 120-volt wiring. It is required only that insulation of low-voltage windings on the transformer be provided with equivalent protection as higher voltage wiring.

Exception No. 2: Wiring for low-voltage control systems and nonemergency communications and signaling systems need not be installed in metal raceways in nonflammable anesthetizing locations, or when outside or above the hazardous area in flammable anesthetizing locations. (See also 12-4.1.3.)

This Exception was added to eliminate some confusion as to whether low-voltage systems were required to be installed in metal raceways in anesthetizing locations.

3-4.1.2.3 Switches.

(a) *Anesthetizing Locations.*

(1) Electric switches shall comply with 3-4.1.2.1(e)(1) and 3-4.1.2.3(a)(2).

(2) Switches controlling ungrounded circuits within or partially within an inhalation anesthetizing location shall have a disconnecting pole for each conductor.

(3) Electric switches installed in hazardous areas of flammable anesthetizing locations shall comply with the requirements of Section 501-6(a) of NFPA 70, *National Electrical Code*.

(4) Electric switches installed in other than hazardous areas of flammable anesthetizing locations shall comply with 3-4.1.2.1(e)(1).

3-4.1.2.4 Receptacles and Attachment Plugs.

(a)* *Types of Receptacles.* Each power receptacle shall provide at least one separate, highly dependable grounding pole capable of maintaining low contact resistance with its mating plug despite electrical and mechanical abuse. Special receptacles (such as four-pole units providing an extra pole for redundant grounding or ground continuity monitoring; or locking-type receptacles; or, where required for reduction of electrical noise on the grounding circuit, receptacles in which the grounding terminals are purposely insulated from the receptacle yoke) shall be permitted.

In NFPA 70-1987, *National Electrical Code*, a change now adds the requirement (new construction only) that receptacles in critical care areas have to be listed "hospital grade." *{See Section 517-84(b) in NFPA 70-1987.}* For receptacle requirements in anesthetizing locations, see Section 3-4.1.2.4(d) below.

A-3-4.1.2.4(a) Types of Receptacles. It is best, if possible, to employ only one type of receptacle (standard three-prong type) for as many receptacles being served by the same line voltage to avoid the inability to connect life-support equipment in emergencies. The straight-blade, three-prong receptacle is now permitted in all locations in a hospital. Previously, special receptacles were specified in operating room locations and have caused compatibility problems.

In the past, only those receptacles listed as "hospital grade" met the criteria of highly dependable and thus were used by installers. These receptacles generally had a green dot stamped on the face of the receptacle to indicate they were hospital grade and listed by testing laboratories. Today, there are a variety of high-grade commercial receptacles that adequately meet the intent of these criteria. However, it is difficult to distinguish from a distance poorer-quality specification grade receptacles from higher-quality specification grade. Thus, hospital personnel need to be sure that only the appropriate quality receptacle is installed in patient care areas.

Some facilities have recently been able to reduce the generally higher priced "hospital grade" receptacles by purchasing large quantities or through group purchasing, thereby eliminating the objection of the lack of the easily verifiable "green dot" on receptacles.

(b) *Minimum Number of Receptacles.* The number of receptacles shall be determined by the intended use of the patient care area. There shall be sufficient receptacles located so as to avoid the need for extension cords or multiple outlet adapters. In any case, there shall be provision for the attachment of at least four separate appliances with a total connected load of at least 20 amperes for each patient vicinity.

Exception No. 1: Receptacles shall not be required in bathrooms or toilet rooms.

Exception No. 2: Receptacles shall not be required in areas where medical requirements mandate otherwise; e.g., certain psychiatric, pediatric, or hydrotherapy areas.

It is stressed that the minimum number of receptacles specified is only a minimum; this performance requirement is not in conflict with NFPA 70, *National Electrical Code.*

Additional receptacles should be considered if the clinical circumstances warrant them.

(c) *Polarity of Receptacles.* Each receptacle shall be wired in accordance with NFPA 70, *National Electrical Code*, to ensure correct polarity.

(d) Receptacles and attachment plugs for use in nonflammable anesthetizing locations and nonhazardous areas of flammable anesthetizing locations shall be listed for the use.

Receptacles or attachment plugs used in anesthetizing locations are to be "listed" as defined by NFPA (*see Section 2-1*). Receptacles and attachment plugs listed as "Hospital grade" would be acceptable. (*See 3-4.1.2.4(a) and 9-2.1.2.1.*)

Figure 8   Receptacles in an anesthetizing location are suitable for the use of flammable anesthetics since receptacles are 5 ft above the floor.

Exception No. 1: Wall-mounted receptacles installed above the hazardous area in flammable anesthetizing locations shall not be required to be totally enclosed or have openings guarded or screened to prevent dispersion of particles.

As with Exception 2 to 3-4.1.2.4(d), the usual type of receptacle seen in facilities would be acceptable above the hazardous area in a flammable anesthetizing location.

Exception No. 2: Receptacles located in nonflammable anesthetizing locations shall not be required to be totally enclosed or have openings guarded or screened to prevent dispersion of particles.

The usual type of receptacles seen in a health care facility would be acceptable in nonflammable anesthetizing locations but must be listed per paragraph 3-4.1.2.4(d).

(e) Plugs and receptacles for use with 250-volt, 50-ampere and 60-ampere ac service shall be designed for use in nonhazardous areas of flammable anesthetizing locations and nonflammable anesthetizing locations and shall be so designed that the 60-ampere receptacle will accept either the 50-ampere or the 60-ampere plug. Fifty-ampere receptacles are to be designed so as not to accept the 60-ampere attachment plug. These plugs shall be of the two-pole, three-wire design with a third contact connecting to the (green or green with yellow stripe) grounding wire of the electric system.

(f) Receptacles provided for other services having different voltages, frequencies, or types on the same premises shall be of such design that attachment plugs and caps used in such receptacles cannot be connected to circuits of a different voltage, frequency, or type, but shall be interchangeable within each classification and rating required for two-wire, 125-volt, single-phase ac service.

(g) Receptacles and attachment plugs in hazardous areas shall comply with the requirements of Section 501-12 of NFPA 70, *National Electrical Code*. They shall be a part of an approved unit device with an interlocking switch arranged so that the plug cannot be withdrawn or inserted when the switch is in the "on" position.

NOTE: It should be recognized that any interruption of the circuit, even of circuits as low as eight volts, either by any switch or loose or defective connections anywhere in the circuit, may produce a spark sufficient to ignite a flammable anesthetic agent.

(h) Nonexplosionproof plugs shall not engage, or be energized by, the poles of Class I, Group C, Division 1 receptacles.

NOTE: It is desirable to promote "one-way" interchangeability by using attachment plugs in hazardous areas that can also mate with the nonexplosionproof receptacles in nonhazardous areas.

3-4.1.2.5 Special Grounding.

(a) *Use of Quiet Grounds.* A quiet ground, if used, shall not defeat the purposes of the safety features of the grounding systems detailed herein.

NOTE: Care should be taken in specifying such a quiet grounding system since the grounding impedance is controlled only by the grounding wires and does not benefit from any conduit or building structure in parallel with it.

Quiet grounds are special grounding systems to reduce electrical noise and interference in communication or instrumentation systems. They may be needed when there are nearby high-power transmission equipment, or when noise-sensitive equipment, such as computers, are used. This section recognizes that such quiet grounds may be needed, and that they may be of peculiar design. This section also points out that the signal protection design must not compromise the electrical safety protection.

(b) *Patient Equipment Grounding Point.* A patient equipment grounding point comprising one or more grounding terminals or jacks shall be permitted in an accessible location in the patient vicinity.

These terminals or jacks can be of assistance in some locations (such as in older buildings with poorer grounds) or when unusual electrical noise is present. However, a properly constructed power system with a grounding conductor and electrical appliances with good third-wire ground connections are normally adequate for grounding purposes as well as for eliminating interference on most physiological monitors.

(c) *Special Grounding in Patient Care Areas.* In addition to the grounding required to meet the performance requirements of 3-5.2.1, additional grounding shall be permitted where special circumstances so dictate. (*See A-3-2, "Nature of Hazards."*)

NOTE: Special grounding methods may be required in patient vicinities immediately adjacent to rooms containing high-power or high-frequency equipment that causes electrical interference with monitors or other electromedical devices. In extreme cases, electromagnetic induction may cause the voltage limits of 3-5.2.1 to be exceeded.

Electromagnetic interference problems may be due to a variety of causes, some simple, others complex. Such problems are best solved one at a time. In some locations, grounding of stretchers, examining tables, or bed frames will be helpful. Where necessary, a patient equipment grounding point should be installed. This can usually be accomplished even after completion of construction by installing a receptacle faceplate fitted with grounding posts. Special grounding wires should not be used unless they are found to be essential for a particular location because they may interfere with patient care procedures or present trip hazards.

As indicated in the Note, the elimination of electrical interference may be difficult because the interference may be generated by various mechanisms: conducted (or power line), radiated, or coupled (via magnetic fields). It is often easier to locate and remove the source of the interference than it is to protect the appliance being disturbed. In any event, simple solutions, such as moving the appliance, should be tried before expensive solutions, such as the installation of special grounding, shielding, etc., are attempted.

3-4.1.2.6 Wet Locations.

(a) Wet Location (Class W) patient care areas shall be provided with special protection against electric shock because the contact resistance of the body may be reduced by moisture, and electrical insulation is more subject to failure. This special protection shall be provided by a power distribution system that inherently limits the possible ground fault current due to a first fault to a low value, without interrupting the power supply; or by a power distribution system in which the power supply is interrupted if the ground fault current does, in fact, exceed a value of 6 milliamperes.

Exception No. 1: Patient beds, toilets, bidets, and wash basins shall not be required to be considered wet locations.

Exception No. 2: In existing construction, the requirements of 3-4.1.2.6(a) may be waived provided that a written inspection procedure, acceptable to the authority having jurisdiction, is continuously enforced by a designated individual at the hospital, to indicate that equipment-grounding conductors for 120-volt, single-phase, 15- and 20-ampere receptacles, equipment connected by cord and plug, and fixed electrical equipment are installed and maintained in accordance with NFPA 70, National Electrical Code, and applicable performance requirements of this chapter. The procedure shall include electrical continuity tests of all required equipment, grounding conductors, and their connections. These tests shall be conducted as follows:
Fixed receptacles, equipment connected by cord and plug, and fixed electrical equipment shall be tested:

(1) when first installed,

(2) where there is evidence of damage,

(3) after any repairs,

(4) at intervals not exceeding six months.

It was brought out at a January, 1984, hearing before the NFPA Standards Council that this requirement can be applied to operating rooms since many meet the definition of wet location as listed in Chapter 2, "Definitions." It thus becomes necessary for a facility to determine what type of procedures will normally take place in each operating room.

See also related commentary under the definition of Isolated Power Systems in Chapter 2.

(b) The use of an isolated power system (IPS) shall be permitted as a protective means capable of limiting ground fault current without power interruption. When installed, such a power system shall conform to the requirements of 3-4.3.

(c) Where power interruption is tolerable, the use of a ground fault circuit interrupter (GFCI) shall be permitted as the protective means that monitors the actual ground fault current and interrupts the power when that current exceeds 6 milliamperes.

3-4.1.2.7 Isolated Power. An isolated power system is not required to be installed in any patient care area except as specified in 12-4.1, "Anesthetizing Locations." The system shall be permitted to be installed, however, and when installed, shall conform to the performance requirements specified in 3-4.3.

> While Section 12-4.1 contains a restriction that an isolated power system, when installed, can serve only one operating room, there are no such restrictions in other patient care areas, (e.g., an isolated power system could serve 2 adjacent patient beds in a patient room, if the transformer were large enough).

3-4.1.3 Laboratories. Power outlets shall be installed in accordance with NCCLS Standard ASI-5, *Power Requirements for Clinical Laboratory Instruments and for Laboratory Power Sources.* Outlets with two to four receptacles, or an equivalent power strip, shall be installed every 1.6 to 3.3 ft (0.5 to 1.0 m) in instrument usage areas, and either installation is to be at least 3.15 in. (8 cm) above the counter top.

> Reference is made to the NCCLS (National Committee for Clinical Laboratory Standards) document because of its growing use in the clinical laboratory field. The document is intended to promote safe installation and operation of electric equipment through the installation of adequate numbers of outlets that have been properly located, thereby eliminating the need for extension cords, cube taps, or other makeshift arrangements. In many existing laboratories, circuits and outlets are inadequate to serve the multitude of modern, line-operated instruments now in common use. (*See Chapter 12 for NCCLS address*).

3-4.1.4 Other Nonpatient Areas. (Reserved)

3-4.2 Essential System.

> NOTE: It must be emphasized that the type of system selected and its area and type of coverage should be appropriate to the medical procedures being performed in the facility. For example, a battery-operated emergency light that switches "on" when normal power is interrupted and an alternate source of power for suction equipment, along with the immediate availability of some portable hand-held lighting, would be advisable where oral and maxillofacial surgery (e.g., extraction of impacted teeth) is performed. On the other hand, in dental offices where simple extraction, restorative, prosthetic, or hygenic procedures are performed, only remote corridor lighting for purposes of egress would be sufficient. Emergency power for equipment would not be necessary. As would oral surgery locations, a surgical clinic requiring use of life support or emergency devices such as suction machines, ventilators, cauterizers, or defibrillators would require both emergency light and power.

> The Note was added to provide guidance on the type of essential electrical system that should be installed, taking into consideration the medical procedures that will be carried out in the facility.

3-4.2.1 General.

3-4.2.1.1† Electrical characteristics of the transfer switches shall be suitable for the operation of all functions and equipment they are intended to supply.

Figure 9   Typical labeling of transfer switches.

3-4.2.1.2† Switch Rating.   The rating of the transfer switches shall be adequate for switching all classes of loads to be served and for withstanding the effects of available fault currents without contact welding.

For requirements on the capacity of switches, refer to Article 517 of NFPA 70, *National Electrical Code.*

3-4.2.1.3 Automatic Transfer Switch Classification.   Each automatic transfer switch shall be approved for emergency electrical service (*see NFPA 70, National Electrical Code, Section 700-3*) as a complete assembly.

3-4.2.1.4† Automatic Transfer Switch Features.

(a) *General.*   Automatic transfer switches shall be electrically operated and mechanically held. The transfer switch shall transfer and retransfer the load automatically.

Exception: In some installations, it may be desirable to program the transfer switch for a manually initiated retransfer to the normal source so as to provide for a planned momentary interruption of the load. If used, this arrangement shall be provided with a bypass feature to permit automatic retransfer in the event that the alternate source fails and the normal source is available.

The term "momentary interruption" indicates the time taken for the transfer switch to move from alternate source contacts to normal source contacts.

Note that consideration has been made for the condition where normal power is available but the *alternate* source has failed.

(b) *Interlocking.* Reliable mechanical interlocking, or an approved alternate method, shall be inherent in the design of transfer switches to prevent the unintended interconnection of the normal and alternate sources of power, or any two separate sources of power.

This paragraph was changed in 1984 to make it clear that co-generation of electrical power is not prohibited. However, such operation must be accomplished very deliberately, and in coordination with local utility companies.

The inadvertent interconnection of the normal and alternate sources of power, or of any two separate sources of power, is very likely to cause major damage to electrical system, as well as danger to personnel. Components will probably be destroyed and require replacement or major repair, resulting in great expense and disruption of the operation of the facility.

The interlocking feature of the transfer switch must be reliable and fail-safe.

Available interlocking schemes vary from simple mechanical means to complex combinations of mechanical, electrical, and electronic means. It is recommended that all interlocking include a reliable stand-alone mechanical means that is completely independent of all electrical and electronic means. Those considering alternate methods are advised to give due recognition to the NFPA definition of "approved." It should also be noted that 3-4.2.1.4(a) requires automatic transfer switches to be electrically operated/mechanically held.

(c)* *Voltage Sensing.* Voltage sensing devices shall be provided to monitor all ungrounded lines of the normal source of power [see *Appendix A-3-4.2.1.4(c)*].

A-3-4.2.1.4(c) Voltage Sensing. Consideration should be given to monitoring all ungrounded lines of the alternate source of power when conditions warrant.

Monitoring only the ungrounded lines is considered satisfactory for essential electrical system purposes.

(d) *Time Delay on Starting of Alternate Power Source.* A time delay device may be provided to delay starting of the alternate source generator. The timer is intended to prevent nuisance starting of the alternate source generator with subsequent load transfer in the event of harmless momentary power dips and interruptions of the normal source. The time range must be short enough so that the generator can start and be on the line within 10 seconds of the onset of failure.

It is the intent of this chapter that essential electrical systems be powered by the alternate source within 10 seconds of failure of the normal source. The 10-second value was set by the Committee as the shortest practical time that could be generally accepted, consistent with technical and economic realities.

The 10-second value consists of: (1) a time delay on commanding the starting of the alternate power source, considered to be an on-site generator set; plus (2) the time for the generator set to start, attain operating voltage and frequency, and be capable of generating the required power; plus (3) time for operation of the transfer switches; plus (4) a factor of design-safety interval.

Interval (1) is considered to be about two seconds, with a range from about one to three seconds. It is the time setting of a field-adjustable timer to be set to meet local needs. The timer starts when normal supply voltage is sensed to drop to less than a predetermined value, also selected to meet local needs.

Interval (2) is considered to be about five seconds, with a range from about three to six seconds. It is a function of the generator set, its controls, and its loading. The interval is actually zero seconds when the alternate source is an external utility service.

Interval (3) is considered to be a small fraction of a second. It is a function of the characteristics of the transfer switches. Time delays may be imposed upon interval (3) as part of an individual design to prevent loading the generator too rapidly.

Interval (4), used in establishing the 10-second value of the chapter, is about three seconds.

The Committee considers the 10-second value to be reasonably attainable on a national and facility-wide basis. It is not based on the established needs of any fire protection, life safety, or medical function.

For equipment that can not tolerate a loss of even a "cycle" of power (e.g., computer-driven equipment), or procedures where 10 seconds of power-outage can not be tolerated, the use of uninterrupted power supplies (UPS) will have to be considered. *(For further discussion on this issue, see commentary under Section 3-2.4.2.)*

Figure 10   Time recordings of voltage at various points in a large medical center where many transfer switches are used.

(e) *Time Delay on Transfer to Alternate Power.*   An adjustable time delay device shall be provided for those transfer switches requiring "delayed automatic" operation. The time delay shall commence when proper alternate source voltage and frequency are achieved. The delay device shall prevent transfer to the alternate power source until after expiration of the preset delay.

(f)* *Time Delay on Retransfer to Normal Power.* An adjustable timer with a bypass shall be provided to delay retransfer from the alternate source of power to the normal. This timer will permit the normal source to stabilize before retransfer to the load and help to avoid unnecessary power interruptions. The bypass shall operate similarly to the bypass in 3-4.2.1.4(a).

A-3-4.2.1.4(f) Time Delay on Retransfer to Normal Power. It is recommended that the timer be set for 30 minutes [*see A-3-5.1.2.3(b)(1)*]. Consideration should also be given to an unloaded engine running time after retransfer to permit the engine to cool down before shutdown.

The 30-minute setting for the running of the generator is recommended, even if normal power is restored within 30 minutes and transfer switches return to their normal settings. This is so that the generator set will be lubricated adequately and/or acids and carbons burned out. The 30 minutes, if for a real run, could also be an acceptable substitute for one of the tests described in 3-5.1.2.3.

It should also be noted that an unloaded engine running timer is recommended.

(g) *Test Switch.* A test switch shall be provided on each automatic transfer switch that will simulate a normal power source failure to the switch.

Test switches are provided to permit appropriate testing of individual components and of the entire essential electrical system without requiring interruption of the normal source.

(h) *Indication of Switch Position.* Two pilot lights, properly identified, shall be provided to indicate the transfer switch position.

One pilot light indicates that the switch is in the normal power position, and the other pilot light indicates that the switch is in the alternate power position. They not only indicate the transfer switch position to the system operator, but they can be useful in troubleshooting operational problems.

(i) *Manual Control of Switch.* A means for the safe manual operation of the automatic transfer switch shall be provided.

Manual control is required to assist in solving operational problems. This can be accomplished by direct manual means, electrical remote manual means, or both. Many operating personnel prefer the positive advantages of direct manual means.

This requirement is an example of this chapter's attention to the safety of operating personnel who may tend to neglect their own personal safety while attempting to troubleshoot malfunctions that have left patients in a hospital without electrical power.

During the revision process for the 1984 edition of NFPA 99, the then Committee on Essential Electrical Systems discussed adding recommendations or requirements with respect to how switching might be affected. The Committee concluded, however, that no guidelines could be suggested without impinging on the design of some one manufacturer's product. In addition, an Appendix Note to 3-4.2.1.6(a) was deleted since the term "external operation" could not be satisfactorily defined.

3-4.2.1.5 Nonautomatic Transfer Device Classification. Nonautomatic transfer devices shall be approved for emergency electrical service (*see NFPA 70, National Electrical Code, Section 700-3*).

3-4.2.1.6† Nonautomatic Transfer Device Features.

(a) *General.* Switching devices shall be mechanically held. Operation shall be by direct manual or electrical remote manual control. Electrically operated switches shall derive their control power from the source to which the load is being transferred. A means for safe manual operation shall be provided.

(b) *Interlocking.* Reliable mechanical interlocking, or an approved alternate method, shall be inherent in the design in order to prevent the unintended interconnection of the normal and alternate sources of power, or of any two separate sources of power.

As in 3-4.2.1.4(b), this paragraph was changed to make it clear that co-generation of electrical power is *not* prohibited.

(c) *Indication of Switch Position.* Pilot lights, properly identified, shall be provided to indicate the switch position.

3-4.2.2 Essential Electrical Distribution Requirements — Type I.

The use of the term "Type I" is simply for identification purposes. In Chapters 12 to 18, the type of essential electrical system (I, II, III) for a particular health care facility (hospital, nursing home, etc.) is stipulated. See Chapter 1, text and commentary, for a complete explanation of how NFPA 99 is now structured and to be used.

3-4.2.2.1* General. Essential electrical systems for Type I facilities are comprised of two separate systems capable of supplying a limited amount of lighting and power service, which is considered essential for life safety and effective hospital operation during the time the normal electrical service is interrupted for any reason. These two systems are the emergency system and the equipment system (*see Appendix C-3.1*).

The emergency system shall be limited to circuits essential to life safety and critical patient care. These are designated the life safety branch and the critical branch.

The equipment system shall supply major electrical equipment necessary for patient care and basic Type I operation.

Both systems shall be arranged for connection, within time limits specified in this chapter, to an alternate source of power following a loss of the normal source.

The concept of separate systems and, thus, separate transfer switches, dates from the late 1960s. The intent was to have a limited number of areas and functions on the essential electrical system and, with various systems having their own transfer switches, provide the maximum protection for each.

After much discussion and various proposals, two major systems evolved: the emergency system and the equipment system.

The *emergency system* was, in turn, subdivided into two branches:
  a. the *life safety branch*, to which only exit lights, corridor lights, and alarm and activating devices are connected. These were related to life safety and were primarily to announce emergencies and to provide sufficient lighting and directions for exiting. There are very few receptacles on this branch, thus reducing the chances of the branch being electrically violated and not operating in an emergency.
  b. the *critical branch*, to which single-phase loads (e.g., receptacles, task illumination) are connected to maintain essential medical care in patient care areas.

The *equipment system* is intended to maintain essential support services such as fans, pumps, elevators, etc.

Restoration of power to loads on the emergency system is to be automatic and should occur within 10 seconds. Restoration of power to loads on the equipment system does not have to be automatic, nor must it occur within 10 seconds; it can be time-delayed or manually operated. (*See Section 3-5.1.2.1.*)

The number of transfer switches to be used shall be based upon reliability, design, and load considerations. Each branch of the essential electrical system shall be permitted to be served by one or more transfer switches. One transfer switch shall be permitted to serve one or more branches or systems in a facility with a maximum demand on the essential electrical system of 150 kVA (120 kW).[1]

A-3-4.2.2.1 Separation of Wiring on Emergency System in Type I Facilities.
In principle, Chapter 3 is designed to seek security of electrical function by protection against both internal disruption and the loss of primary power sources. In keeping therewith, Chapter 3 aims to limit the security deterioration that may occur when poorly maintained and heavy-current-consuming items are connected to the same feeders that supply critical patient care functions.

For greater protection, such segregation of suspect and critical connections is best carried out throughout the length of a feeder system, preferably including the transfer device. This practice gives rise to the phrase *protected feeder*.

While Chapter 3 must leave details of wiring and overcurrent protection to engineering judgment, in view of wide variations of conditions, the Subcommittee on Electrical Systems's consensus is that feeders serving anesthetizing locations, special nursing care units, and special treatment areas where continuity of care may be vital to life should be given security through the segregation of protected feeders and that, to the greatest extent practical, feeders should connect to the alternate source of power by means of separate transfer devices.

As a further protection against internal disruption, it is also recommended that, when practical, critical areas served by the essential electrical system have some portion of lighting and receptacles connected to feeders supplied by the general system.

  • The last sentence of the last paragraph represents extensive discussion to eliminate the previously used term "small facility" to describe the situation when

[1] In new construction, careful consideration should be given to the benefits of multiple transfer switches. However, selection of the number and configuration of transfer switches, and associated switchgear, is to be made with consideration given to the tradeoffs among reliability, transfer switch and generator load characteristics, maintainability, and cost.

a single transfer switch could be used to bring emergency power on-line. The value 120kw was selected based on experience and safety. However, even an essential electrical load of this value may warrant more than one tranfer switch because of the criticalness to restore power. *One* transfer switch means that a loss of that one transfer switch will preclude *any* emergency power from being available in an emergency. For this reason, careful consideration should be given when deciding on the number of transfer switches (as noted in the footnote).

• The Subcommittee responsible for this chapter has reaffirmed its position that, for new facilities, the wiring for the emergency system and the equipment system be kept separate from each other and from the remainder of electrical circuits supplying normal electric power to the various parts of a facility. The major reason given for this separation was concern for reliability.

• A Formal Interpretation was issued in July 1979 after an inquiry was received as to whether a single overcurrent protective device (OPD) on the generator to the distribution board was permissible or whether a minimum of two OPDs were necessary: one for the emergency system and one for the equipment system. The Interpretation Committee believed that one feeder (and thus one OPD at the generator) was permitted to serve a distribution board, which in turn distributed power via transfer switches, etc. It was noted that a single feeder is often used when the generator is remote from the distribution board. A parallel set of feeders was considered unnecessary and costly. No significant differences in safety or reliability were noted in using just one feeder.

3-4.2.2.2 Emergency System.

The further dividing of the emergency system for Type I facilities into two branches is for identification purposes. The life safety branch [3-4.2.2.2(b)] provides power only to those functions or warning systems necessary for safely leaving any building in an emergency: alarm systems, exit signs, lighting of means of egress, communication systems. The critical branch [3-4.2.2.2(c)] includes those functions that maintain essential patient services since health care facility fire response is designed around a defend-in-place concept (i.e., not initially or necessarily leaving the building in an emergency). Paragraph 3-4.2.2.3, "Equipment System," includes those functions which do not have to be restored within 10 seconds since they are not critical in regard to timeliness. In addition, they might overload the alternate power source if they were to come on line within the 10 seconds specified for the emergency system.

(a) *General.* Those functions of patient care depending on lighting or appliances that are permitted to be connected to the emergency system are divided into two mandatory branches, described in 3-4.2.2.2(b) and (c).

(b) *Life Safety Branch.* The life safety branch of the emergency system shall supply power for the following lighting, receptacles, and equipment:

(1) Illumination of means of egress as required in NFPA *101, Life Safety Code.*

Chapter 5 of NFPA *101, Life Safety Code,* lists where and how much illumination is required for means of egress.

(2) Exit signs and exit direction signs required in NFPA *101, Life Safety Code.*

(3) Alarm and alerting systems including:

(i) Fire alarms.

This includes any type of fire alarms, whether for one area or function, or the entire facility. It may, under certain conditions, include interfaces with an engineered smoke-control system.

(ii) Alarms required for systems used for the piping of nonflammable medical gases as specified in Chapter 4, "Gas and Vacuum Systems."

(4)* Hospital communication systems, where used for issuing instruction during emergency conditions.

A-3-4.2.2.2(b)(4) Communication Systems. Departmental installations such as digital dialing systems used for intradepartmental communications may have impaired use during a failure of electrical service to the area. In the event of such failure, those systems that have lighted selector buttons in the base of the telephone instrument or in the desk units known as "director sets" will be out of service to the extent that the lights will not function and that the buzzer used to indicate incoming calls will be silenced. The lack of electrical energy will not prevent the use of telephones for outgoing calls, but incoming calls will not be signaled, nor will intercommunicating calls be signaled. This communication failure should be taken into consideration in planning essential electrical systems.

(5) Task illumination and selected receptacles at the generator set location.

(6) Elevator cab lighting, control, communication, and signal systems.

For the 1984 edition of NFPA 99, item (6) was added to the life safety branch because of concern for persons who might be in elevators when normal power was interrupted. Lack of lighting, etc., could cause panic. Although power for elevator movement might be restored on a delayed or manual basis, it could be a very stressful wait for those in the elevators. The Committee felt that restoring lights and communication within 10 seconds would reduce the possibility of panic.
Item (6) was added as part of the life safety branch because, in a real sense, these functions provide a means of egress for persons in elevators.

No function other than those listed above in items (1) through (6) shall be connected to the life safety branch.

In a fire or other emergency, electricity is automatically interrupted to hold-open devices (generally via any fire-alarm signal) so that smoke and fire doors (that are being held open) will close and stay closed until manually reset. However, if a smoke or fire door requires an electrical motor to have it close, then that motor needs to be connected to the life safety branch of the essential electrical system so that it will close should normal power be lost *and* a fire-alarm signal occur indicating an emergency (e.g., a smoke detector is set off).

(c)* *Critical Branch.* The critical branch of the emergency system shall supply power for task illumination, fixed equipment, selected receptacles, and special power circuits serving the following areas and functions related to patient care. It shall be permitted to subdivide the critical branch into two or more branches.

A-3-4.2.2.2(c) Critical Branch. It is recommended that hospital authorities give consideration to providing and properly maintaining automatic battery-powered lighting units or systems to provide minimal task illumination in operating rooms, delivery rooms, and certain special-procedure radiology rooms where the loss of lighting due to failure of the essential electrical system might cause severe and immediate danger to a patient undergoing surgery or an invasive radiographic procedure.

"Task illumination" will vary depending on the activity in a given area. The criteria is sufficient light to maintain patient care. In surgery, it would mean all the surgical lights; in a general ward, it could be just one overhead light in the room; in a pediatric ward, it would be lighting everywhere youngsters were allowed to go. It does not mean supplying power to lighting used for nonessential purposes, or activities that can be temporarily postponed.

(1) Anesthetizing locations — task illumination, all receptacles, and fixed equipment.

Requirements were altered in 1984 to reflect changes in requirements for isolated power systems (IPSs) in anesthetizing locations. Since IPSs may not be present, the Committee wanted to make sure receptacles, task illumination, and fixed equipment in anesthetizing locations were on the essential electrical system (whether IPSs were present or not).

(2) The isolated power systems in special environments.

This reference to isolated power systems is not to be construed as meaning that this chapter requires the provision of such systems. It is the intent of the Subcommittee on Electrical Systems only that the electrical receptacles on isolated power systems in special environments be served from the critical branch, and thus have power restored in 10 seconds to all receptacles on the isolated power system.

(3) Patient care areas — task illumination and selected receptacles in:

(i) infant nurseries,

(ii) medication preparation areas,

(iii) pharmacy dispensing areas,

(iv) selected acute nursing areas,

(v) psychiatric bed areas (omit receptacles),

(vi) ward treatment rooms, and

(vii) nurses' stations (unless adequately lighted by corridor luminaires).

(4) Additional specialized patient care task illumination and receptacles, where needed.

(5) Nurse call systems.

(6) Blood, bone, and tissue banks.

(7)* Telephone equipment room and closets.

A-3-4.2.2.2(c)(7)   *(See A-3-4.2.2.2(b)(4).)*

(8) Task illumination, receptacles, and special power circuits for:

(i) acute care beds (selected),

(ii) angiographic labs,

(iii) cardiac catheterization labs,

(iv) coronary care units,

(v) hemodialysis rooms or areas,

(vi) emergency room treatment areas (selected),

(vii) human physiology labs,

(viii) intensive care units, and

(ix) postoperative recovery rooms (selected).

(9) Additional task illumination, receptacles, and special power circuits needed for effective facility operation. Single-phase fractional horsepower exhaust fan motors that are interlocked with three-phase motors on the equipment system shall be permitted to be connected to the critical branch.

> This should not be construed as an open-ended option to include anything on the critical branch. Only essential items should be included.
>
> For a discussion on "task illumination," see commentary under 3-4.2.2.2(c).
>
> Exhaust fan motors were added to the critical branch out of practicality. These motors are sometimes located at the end of a wing, making it costly to link up with three-phase motors of the equipment system which could be on the roof. The Subcommittee responsible for emergency power requirements did not feel that these small exhaust motors added significantly to the critical branch load.

NOTE: Care should be taken to analyze the consequences of supplying an area with only critical care branch power when failure occurs between the area and the transfer switch. Some proportion of normal and critical power, or critical power from separate transfer switches, may be appropriate.

> This Note was added to call attention to the possibly undesirable situation of having only critical branch circuitry in an area. While the generator system may be

reliable, malfunctions downstream from the transfer switch can occur. This could mean all power to an area would be jeopardized; therefore, some division was considered appropriate. NFPA 70, *National Electrical Code*, requires both critical branch and normal lighting in anesthetizing locations.

3-4.2.2.3 Equipment System.

(a) *General.* The equipment system shall be connected to equipment described in 3-4.2.2.3(c) and (d). It shall be permitted to be connected to equipment listed in Appendix A-3-4.2.3.4(c).

(b) *Connection to Alternate Power Source.* The equipment system shall be installed and connected to the alternate power source, such that equipment described in 3-4.2.2.3(c) is automatically restored to operation at appropriate time lag intervals following the energizing of the emergency system. Its arrangement shall also provide for the subsequent connection of equipment described in 3-4.2.2.3(d) by either delayed-automatic or manual operation.

The absence of specific time lag intervals is deliberate. These intervals are dependent on the facility and its activities, and on the technical judgment of those designing the essential electrical system.

(c) *Equipment for Delayed Automatic Connection.* The following equipment shall be arranged for delayed automatic connection to the alternate power source:[1]

If everything on the essential electrical system were restored at the same time, the generator could be loaded too quickly, even though it might be capable of carrying the total load if accomplished over a period of time.

(1) Central suction systems serving medical and surgical functions, including controls. It shall be permitted to place such suction systems on the critical branch.

Determination of whether central suction is restored in 10 seconds (critical branch connection) or in some longer interval (delayed automatic connection) will depend on the type(s) of surgery performed in the facility and the resultant condition of patients being treated after surgery.

(2) Sump pumps and other equipment required to operate for the safety of major apparatus, including associated control systems and alarms.

(3) Compressed air systems serving medical and surgical functions, including controls.

(d) *Equipment for Delayed Automatic or Manual Connection.* The following equipment shall be arranged for either delayed automatic or manual connection to the alternate power source [*also see Appendix A-3-4.2.3.4(c)*].

---

[1]The equipment in 3-4.2.2.3(c)(1) through (3) may be arranged for sequential delayed automatic action to the alternate power source to prevent overloading the generator where engineering studies indicate that it is necessary.

(1) Heating equipment to provide heating for operating, delivery, labor, recovery, intensive care, coronary care, nurseries, infection/isolation rooms, emergency treatment spaces, and general patient rooms.

Exception: Heating of general patient rooms during disruption of the normal source shall not be required under any of the following conditions:

(a) The outside design temperature is higher than +20°F (−6.7°C), or

(b) The outside design temperature is lower than +20°F (−6.7°C) and a selected room(s) is provided for the needs of all confined patients {then only such room(s) need be heated}, or

(c) The facility is served by a dual source of normal power as described in 3-3.2.1.1.

NOTE: The outside design temperature is based on the 97½ percent design value as shown in Chapter 24 of the *ASHRAE Handbook of Fundamentals* (1985).

This Exception dates from the early 1960s during the development of an emergency power standard. It was added strictly for economic reasons — to save costs on the system. In the early 1970s, it became, by coincidence, an energy conservation measure. It is also an aid to facilities that use electric heat throughout since, in an emergency, only selected rooms would have to be heated if the facility met this Exception.

(2) Elevator(s) selected to provide service to patient, surgical, obstetrical, and ground floors during interruption of normal power. [*For elevator cab lighting, control and signal system requirements, see 3-4.2.2.2(b)(6)*].

In instances where interruption of normal power would result in other elevators stopping between floors, throw-over facilities shall be provided to allow the temporary operation of any elevator for the release of patients or other persons who may be confined between floors.

(3) Supply, return, and exhaust ventilating systems for surgical and obstetrical delivery suites, intensive care, coronary care, nurseries, infection/isolation rooms, emergency treatment spaces, and exhaust fans for laboratory fume hoods, nuclear medicine areas where radioactive material is used, ethylene oxide evacuation, and anesthesia evacuation.

(4) Hyperbaric facilities.

(5) Hypobaric facilities.

(6) Automatically operated doors.

(7) Autoclaving equipment shall be permitted to be arranged for either automatic or manual connection to the alternate source.

(8) Other selected equipment shall be permitted to be served by the equipment system. [1,2]

---

[1]Consideration should be given to selected equipment in kitchens, laundries, and radiology rooms, and to selected central refrigeration.

[2]It is desirable that, where heavy interruption currents can be anticipated, the transfer load may be reduced by the use of multiple transfer devices. Elevator feeders, for instance, may be less hazardous to electrical continuity if they are fed through an individual transfer device.

As noted previously, this requirement should not be construed as a carte blanche allowance for anything to be connected to the equipment system. Each item should be reviewed as to its effect on patient safety should power to the item be interrupted for an extended period of time.

3-4.2.2.4 Wiring Requirements.

(a) *Separation from Other Circuits.* The life safety branch and critical branch of the emergency system shall be kept entirely independent of all other wiring and equipment. See NFPA 70, *National Electrical Code*, for installation requirements.

In 1977, the Committee responsible for essential electrical systems reaffirmed its position that the wiring for the normal power and the essential electrical system be separated. It considered this to be the only way to ensure against simultaneous damage to both systems. This position has not changed.

(b) *Receptacles.*

(1) The number of receptacles on a single branch circuit for areas described in 3-4.2.2.2(c)(8) shall be minimized to limit the effects of a branch circuit outage. Branch circuit overcurrent devices shall be readily accessible to nursing and other authorized personnel.

The Subcommittee on Electrical Systems's intent here is to limit the number of receptacles on a branch circuit (in this instance, essential electrical systems circuits) to minimize power outages of these circuits due to overloading. Also, it is considered very poor practice to design systems in a manner such that a faulty piece of equipment connected to a circuit could, by opening its branch circuit protective device, cause other essential equipment to become inoperative. Outages of these circuits can be life threatening in many instances because of the condition of patients and their dependency on the electrical equipment used on them (these electrical devices are functioning in a life-support capacity).
Nursing personnel are specifically identified since they are always in a patient care area, and need to be able to reset circuit breakers if assistance is not readily available (e.g., at 3:00 a.m. on a Saturday morning).

(2) The cover plates for the electrical receptacles or the electrical receptacles themselves supplied from the emergency system shall have a distinctive color or marking so as to be readily identifiable.[1]

It is very important that all facility personnel know what the different colors mean so that in an emergency they will know to plug necessary (essential) devices into those outlets on the essential electrical system.
It is good practice to plug life-support devices into receptacles on essential electrical circuits so that these devices will be repowered automatically, and within 10 seconds, when normal power is interrupted.

---

[1]If color is used to identify these receptacles the same color should be used throughout the facility.

(c) *Switches.* Switches installed in the lighting circuits connected to the essential electrical system shall comply with Article 700, Section E, of NFPA 70, *National Electrical Code.*

(d) *Mechanical Protection of the Emergency System.* The wiring of the emergency system of a hospital shall be mechanically protected by raceways, as defined in NFPA 70, *National Electrical Code.*

> Raceways are required in Type I facilities because the highest percentage of nonambulatory patients is found in these types of facilities. [In former NFPA 76A, *Standard on Essential Electrical Systems in Health Care Facilities,* raceways for the essential electrical systems were required in hospitals. In this new 1987 edition of NFPA 99, Type I essential electrical systems are required in Chapter 12, Requirements for Hospitals.] Patients in Type I facilities can be anesthetized, comatose, in traction, connected to electrical life-support equipment, etc. As such, the former Technical Committee on Essential Electrical Systems (now Subcommittee on Electrical Systems), which is responsible for emergency power requirements, considered that these facilities needed the greatest mechanical protection for electrical wiring since evacuation (or even movement) was the action least desired, if at all. Thus, Type I facilities were provided with the most protection.
>
> From this it should not be construed that the patients in other types of facilities were considered any less important. It meant only that it was more possible, in general, to move patients in an emergency, if only horizontally, to another portion of the building.
>
> For the definition of raceway, see Article 100 in NFPA 70, *National Electrical Code.* For reader reference, Type AC cable is listed as a cable, *not* as a raceway.

Exception No. 1: Flexible power cords of appliances or other utilization equipment connected to the emergency system shall not be required to be enclosed in raceways.

Exception No. 2: Secondary circuits of transformer-powered communication or signaling systems shall not be required to be enclosed in raceways unless otherwise specified by Chapter 7 or 8 of NFPA 70, National Electrical Code.

3-4.2.3 Essential Electrical Distribution Requirements — Type II.

3-4.2.3.1 Applicability. The requirements of this section shall apply to Type II facilities.

3-4.2.3.2 General. Essential electrical systems for Type II facilities are comprised of two separate systems capable of supplying a limited amount of lighting and power service, which is considered essential for the protection of life and safety and effective operation of the institution during the time normal electrical service is interrupted for any reason. These two separate systems are the emergency system and the critical system.

The number of transfer switches to be used shall be based upon reliability, design, and load considerations. Each branch of the essential electrical system shall be permitted to be served by one or more transfer switches. One transfer switch shall be permitted to serve one or more branches or systems in a facility with a maximum demand on the essential electrical system of 150 kVA (120 kW).[2] (*Also see Appendix A-3-4.2.2.1.*)

---

[2] In new construction careful consideration should be given to the benefits of multiple transfer switches. However, selection of the number and configuration of transfer switches, and associated switchgear, is to be made with consideration given to the tradeoffs among reliability, transfer switch and generator load characteristics, maintainability, and cost.

See Commentary under 3-4.2.2.1 regarding the subject of using one transfer switch for the essential electrical system.

3-4.2.3.3 Emergency System. The emergency system shall supply power for the following lighting, receptacles, and equipment:

(a) Illumination of means of egress as required in NFPA *101, Life Safety Code.*

(b) Exit signs and exit directional signs required in NFPA *101, Life Safety Code.*

(c) Alarm and alerting system, including:

(1) Fire alarms.

As in 3-4.2.2.2(b)(3)(i), all fire alarms are to be connected to the essential electrical system.

(2) Alarms required for systems used for the piping of nonflammable medical gases as specified in Chapter 4, "Gas and Vacuum Systems."

(d)* Communication systems, where used for issuing instructions during emergency conditions.

A-3-4.2.3.3(d)   *(See A-3-4.2.2.2(b)(4).)*

(e) Sufficient lighting in dining and recreation areas to provide illumination to exit ways of 5 footcandles minimum.

(f) Task illumination and selected receptacles at the generator set location.

(g) Elevator cab lighting, control, communication, and signal systems.

See Commentary under 3-4.2.2.2(b)(6), since the reason for inclusion of elevators is the same.

No function other than those listed above in items (a) through (g) shall be connected to the emergency system.

3-4.2.3.4 Critical System.

(a) *General.* The critical system shall be so installed and connected to the alternate power source that equipment listed in 3-4.2.3.4(b) shall be automatically restored to operation at appropriate time-lag intervals following the restoration of the emergency system to operation. Its arrangement shall also provide for the additional connection of equipment listed in 3-4.2.3.4(c) by either delayed automatic or manual operation.

(b) *Delayed Automatic Connections to Critical System.* The following equipment shall be connected to the critical system and be arranged for delayed automatic connection to the alternate power source:

(1) Patient care areas — task illumination and selected receptacles in:

(i) medication preparation areas,

(ii) pharmacy dispensing areas,

(iii) nurses' stations (unless adequately lighted by corridor luminaires).

(2) Sump pumps and other equipment required to operate for the safety of major apparatus and associated control systems and alarms.

(c)* *Delayed Automatic or Manual Connections to Critical System.* The following equipment shall be connected to the critical system and be arranged for either delayed automatic or manual connection to the alternate power source:

(1) Heating Equipment to Provide Heating for General Patient Rooms. Heating of general patient rooms during disruption of the normal source shall not be required under any of the following conditions:

(i) The outside design temperature is higher than $+20°F$ ($-6.7°C$), or

(ii) The outside design temperature is lower than $+20°F$ ($-6°C$) and, where a selected room(s) is provided for the needs of all confined patients, then only such room(s) need be heated, or

(iii) The facility is served by a dual source of normal power as described in 3-3.2.1.1.

NOTE: The outside design temperature is based on the 97½ percent design value as shown in Chapter 24 of the *ASHRAE Handbook of Fundamentals* (1985).

The same rationale as for the Exception to 3-4.2.2.3(d)(1) applies here: to reduce energy needs by being able to move and group patients as is reasonably practical.

(2) Elevator Service. In instances where interruptions of power would result in elevators stopping between floors, throw-over facilities shall be provided to allow the temporary operation of any elevator for the release of passengers. [*For elevator cab lighting, control and signal system requirements, see 3-4.2.3.3(g)*].

A-3-4.2.3.4(c) Equipment for Automatic or Manual Connection. Other selected equipment may be served by the critical system.

NOTE 1: Consideration should be given to selected equipment in kitchens, laundries, and to selected central refrigeration.

NOTE 2: It is desirable that, where heavy interruption currents can be anticipated, the transfer load may be reduced by the use of multiple transfer devices. Elevator feeders, for instance, may be less hazardous to electrical continuity if they are fed through an individual transfer device.

(d) *Optional Connections to the Critical System.* Additional illumination, receptacles, and equipment shall be permitted to be connected only to the critical system.

3-4.2.3.5 Wiring Requirements.

(a) *Separation from Other Circuits.* The emergency system shall be kept entirely independent of all other wiring and equipment.

NOTE: See NFPA 70, *National Electrical Code*, for installation requirements.

(b) *Receptacles.*   The cover plates for the electrical receptacles or the electrical receptacles themselves supplied from the emergency system shall have a distinctive color or marking so as to be readily identifiable.[1]

3-4.2.4 Essential Electrical Distribution Requirements — Type III.

3-4.2.4.1 General.   The essential electrical system for Type III facilities comprises a system capable of supplying a limited amount of lighting and power service, which is considered essential for life safety and orderly cessation of procedure during the time normal electrical service is interrupted for any reason.

Professional, technical, and medical judgments are required in determining what minimum lighting and power services are required for patient and staff safety. The condition of patients, the types of procedures used, and the location of the facility are some of the factors that need to be considered (*see Note under 3-4.2*).

3-4.2.4.2 Connection to the Essential Electrical System.   The system shall supply power for task illumination that is related to the safety of life and that is necessary for the safe cessation of procedures in progress. The system shall also supply power as follows:

(a) That required for all anesthesia and resuscitative equipment used in areas where inhalation anesthetics are administered to patients, including alarm and alerting devices as required in Chapter 4, "Gas and Vacuum Systems."

(b) That required for all electrical life-support equipment.

3-4.2.4.3 Connections to Alternate Source of Power.

(a) The alternate source of power for the system shall be specifically designed for this purpose and shall be either a generator, battery system, or self-contained battery integral with the equipment.

3-4.2.4.4 Wiring Requirements.

(a) *General.*   The design, arrangement, and installation of the system shall be in accordance with NFPA 70, *National Electrical Code.*

(b) *Receptacles.*   The cover plates for the electrical receptacles or the electrical receptacles themselves supplied from the emergency system shall have a distinctive color or marking so as to be readily identifiable.[1]

3-4.3* Isolated Power Systems.

It should be remembered that, in the new structure of NFPA 99, requirements under 3-4.3 are for the isolated power system itself. *Where* isolated power systems are to be installed (i.e., are required) will be found in Chapters 12 to 19. This includes the performance, maintenance, and testing criteria listed under 3-5.2.5.

---

[1]If color is used to identify these receptacles the same color should be used throughout the facility.

A-3-4.3 Isolated Power. Patient protection is provided primarily by an adequate grounding system. The ungrounded secondary of the isolation transformer reduces the cross-sectional area of grounding conductors necessary to protect the patient against voltage resulting from fault current by reducing the maximum current in case of a single probable fault in the grounding system. The line isolation monitor is used to provide warning when a single fault occurs. Excessive current in the grounding conductors will not result in a hazard to the patient unless a second fault occurs. If the current in the grounding system does not exceed 10 milliamperes, even under fault conditions, the voltage across 3 m (9.84 ft) of No. 12 AWG wire will not exceed 0.2 millivolt, and the voltage across 3 m (9.84 ft) of No. 18 AWG grounding conductor in a flexible cord will not exceed 0.8 millivolt. Allowing 0.1 millivolt across each connector, the voltage between two pieces of patient-connected equipment will not exceed two millivolts.

The reference grounding point is intended to assure that all electrically conductive surfaces of the building structure, which may receive heavy fault currents from ordinary (grounded) circuits, are grounded in a manner to bypass these heavy currents from the operating room.

3-4.3.1 Isolation Transformer.

3-4.3.1.1 The isolation transformer shall be approved for the purpose.

3-4.3.1.2 The primary winding shall be connected to a power source so that it is not energized with more than 600 volts (nominal). The neutral of the primary winding shall be grounded in an approved manner. If an electrostatic shield is present, it shall be connected to the reference grounding point.

The value of the voltage was raised to 600 volts to allow three-phase transformers to supply single-phase power to the same anesthetizing location (correlating with changes to 12-4.1.3.3 and 12-4.1.3.4). This also eliminated the need for two transformers to isolate circuits in those rooms where three-phase power was needed.

3-4.3.1.3 Wiring of isolated power systems shall be in accordance with Article 517-104 of NFPA 70, *National Electrical Code.*

Requirements of Article 517-104 of the 1984 edition of NFPA 70, *National Electrical Code,* were changed to correspond with changes made in 3-3.3.1.2 and 3-3.3.2.2 of the 1984 edition of NFPA 99 (12-4.1.3.3 and 12-4.1.3.4 in this 1987 edition of NFPA 99). Article 517-104 now allows three-phase, three-wire systems, with up to 600 volts possible across the secondary of the transformer.

3-4.3.2 Impedance of Isolated Wiring.

3-4.3.2.1 The impedance (capacitive and resistive) to ground of either conductor of an isolated system shall exceed 200,000 ohms when installed. The installation at this point may include receptacles but not lighting fixtures or components of fixtures. This value shall be determined by energizing the system and connecting a low-impedance ac milliammeter (0 to 1 mA scale) between the reference grounding point and either conductor in sequence. This test may be performed with the line isolation monitor (*see* 3-4.3.3) connected, provided the connection between the line isolation monitor and the reference grounding point is open at the time of the test. After the test is made, the milliammeter shall be removed and the grounding connection of the line isolation monitor shall be restored. When the installation is completed, including permanently connected fixtures, the reading of the meter on the line isolation monitor, which corresponds to the unloaded line condition, shall be made. This meter reading shall be recorded as a reference for subsequent line-impedance evaluation.

NOTE 1:   Before conducting this test it shall be determined in a safe manner that there is no gross fault between either conductor or ground.

NOTE 2:   It is desirable to limit the size of the isolation transformer to 10 kVA or less and to use conductor insulation with low leakage to meet the impedance requirements. Keeping branch circuits short and using insulation with a dielectric constant less than 3.5 and insulation resistance constant greater than 6100 megohmmeters (20 000 megohm-kilofeet) at 60°F (16°C) reduces leakage from line to ground.

NOTE 3:   Keeping branch circuits short, using insulation with a dielectric constant less than 3.5 and insulation resistance constant greater than 6100 megohmmeters (20 000 megohm-kilofeet) at 60°F (16°C) reduces the monitor hazard current.

NOTE 4:   To correct milliammeter reading to line impedance: Line impedance (in ohms) = V × 1000 divided by I, where V = isolated power system voltage and I = milliammeter reading made during impedance test.

In March 1980, a Formal Interpretation was issued stating that the measurement technique suggested in A-3-5.2.1.3 for grounding systems was acceptable here as well. The Commitee did point out in using this configuration that the test in this section (3-4.3.2.1) was not to be conducted unless the connection between the line isolation monitor and reference ground point was open at the time of the test.

Notes 1 through 4 were added in the 1978 edition of NFPA 56A to help users determine impedance of isolated power wiring [i.e., it is necessary to convert meter reading (in milliamperes) to line impedance (in ohms)].

3-4.3.2.2   An approved capacitance suppressor may be used to improve the impedance of the permanently installed isolated system; however, the resistive impedance to ground of each isolated conductor of the system shall be at least one megohm prior to the connection of the suppression equipment. Capacitance suppressors shall be installed so as to prevent inadvertent disconnecton during normal use.

3-4.3.3 Line Isolation Monitor.

3-4.3.3.1   In addition to the usual control and protective devices, each isolated power system shall be provided with an approved continually operating line isolation monitor that indicates possible leakage or fault currents from either isolated conductor to ground.

NOTE: Protection for the patient is provided primarily by a grounding system. The ungrounded secondary of the isolation transformer reduces the maximum current in the grounding system in case of a single fault between either isolated power conductor and ground. The line isolation monitor provides warning when a single fault occurs, or when excessively low impedance to ground develops, which may expose the patient to an unsafe condition should an additional fault occur. Excessive current in the grounding conductors will not result from a first fault. A hazard exists if a second fault occurs before the first fault is cleared.

The alarm threshold value was raised from 2.0 milliamperes to 5.0 milliamperes in 1978 to account for the larger number of appliances that are now used during operations. It is not uncommon in major procedures to have over 20 electrically powered devices functioning.

Note that 5.0 milliamperes is a maximum threshold value; a facility can choose to retain the previous 2.0 milliampere level or any value in between.

Figure 11(a)   Units with digital readouts of hazard current.

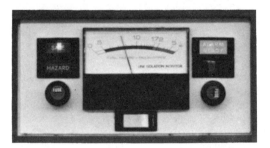

Figure 11(b)   Unit with analog readout of hazard current.

Figure 11 Examples of line isolation monitors (LIMs) used for isolated power systems.

The Committee did not feel that this change increased the risk to patient or staff. While 5.0 milliamperes will produce tingling, it is still well below the 100 to 150 milliamperes required to induce ventricular fibrillation (i.e., external, arm-to-arm contact).

3-4.3.3.2 The monitor shall be designed so that a green signal lamp, conspicuously visible to persons in the anesthetizing location, remains lighted when the system is adequately isolated from ground; and an adjacent red signal lamp and an audible warning signal (remote if desired) shall be energized when the total hazard current (consisting of possible resistive and capacitive leakage currents) from either isolated conductor to ground reaches a threshold value of 5.0 milliamperes under normal line voltage conditions. The line isolation monitor shall not alarm for a fault hazard current of less than 3.7 milliamperes.

NOTE: A 120-volt (nominal) 60-Hz ac system of moderate ampacity is assumed for the description of the specification of the line isolation monitor in 3-4.3.3.1. If other systems are considered, modifications are required, e.g., for other voltages or frequencies, and installed impedance; sensitivity (alarm) levels remain the same, however.

Sentence 2 was reworded to make it clear that it is the hazard current value (5 ma) that is important, and is not to be exceeded, regardless of the voltage, impedance, etc., of the system.

3-4.3.3.3 The line isolation monitor shall have sufficient internal impedance that when properly connected to the isolated system the maximum internal current that can flow through the line isolation monitor, when any point of the isolated system is grounded, shall be one milliampere.

Exception: The line isolation monitor may be of the low-impedance type such that the current through the line isolation monitor, when any point of the isolated system is grounded, will not exceed twice the alarm threshold value for a period not exceeding 5 milliseconds.

The Exception is the result of technology advancement for line isolation monitors. Prior to the 1970s, the usual method of monitoring isolated systems was accomplished by high-impedance monitors. However, a radically different approach using low-impedance technology was developed in the early 1970s and a presentation on it given to the then Technical Committee on Inhalation Anesthetics (now Subcommittee on Anesthesia Services) in 1979. The Committee approved the methodology, and issued a Tentative Interim Amendment on it in July 1980. The TIA was subsequently proposed for inclusion in the text as an Exception in the 1984 edition of NFPA 99.

High-impedance technology uses line isolation monitors that are in parallel with any fault impedance contributing to hazard current. Low-impedance technology uses line isolation monitors that are in series with any fault impedance; however, the time which the low-impedance LIMs are actually in series is very short (one cycle or less; 0.0167 second or less).

NOTE: It is desirable to reduce this monitor hazard current provided this reduction results in an increased "not alarm" threshold value for the fault hazard current.

3-4.3.3.4 An ammeter connected to indicate the total hazard current of the system (contribution of the fault hazard current plus monitor hazard current) shall be mounted in a plainly visible place on the line isolation monitor with the "alarm on" (total hazard current = 5.0 milliamperes) zone at approximately the center of the scale.

NOTE: The line isolation monitor may be a composite unit, with a sensing section cabled to a separate display panel section, on which the alarm and test functions are located, if the two sections are within the same electric enclosure.

It is desirable to locate the ammeter so that it is conspicuously visible to persons in the anesthetizing location.

Until 1970, then NFPA 56A required only a red/green signal system on the wall to indicate when the fault hazard current threshold had been exceeded (an audible signal was and still is required; *see 3-4.3.3.2*). In 1970, the use of an ammeter was added to see more precisely changes in the value of the fault hazard current. This provided more control since devices that significantly increased the current could be spotted, or changes in the baseline current level could be seen.

In 1970, only analog ammeters were generally available. With digital ammeters now available, the phrase "at approximately the center of the scale" should not be construed to exclude digital-type meters. It can be argued that mid-point of the "units" scale of a digital meter (i.e., the 0 to 9 scale) is between 4 and 5. Since the alarm threshold is now up to 5.0 milliamperes, this meets the intent of alarming at approximately the center of the scale.

3-4.3.3.5 Means shall be provided for shutting off the audible alarm while leaving the red warning lamp activated. When the fault is corrected and the green signal lamp is reactivated, the audible alarm silencing circuit shall reset automatically, or an audible or distinctive visual signal shall indicate that the audible alarm is silenced.

3-4.3.3.6 A reliable test switch shall be mounted on the line isolation monitor that will test its capability to operate (i.e., cause the alarms to operate and the meter to indicate in the "alarm on" zone). This switch shall transfer the grounding connection of the line isolation monitor from the reference grounding point to a test impedance arrangement connected across the isolated line. The test impedance(s) shall be of appropriate magnitude to produce a meter reading corresponding to a total hazard current of 5.0 milliamperes at the nominal line voltage. The operation of this switch shall break the grounding connection of the line isolation monitor to the reference grounding point before transferring this grounding connector to the test impedance(s), so that making this test will not add to the hazard of a system in actual use, nor will the test include the effect of the line-to-ground stray impedance of the system. The test switch shall be of a self-restoring type.

3-4.3.3.7 The line isolation monitor shall not generate energy of sufficient amplitude and/or frequency, as measured by a physiological monitor with a gain of at least 10^4 with a source impedance of 1000 ohms connected to the balanced differential input of the monitor, to create interference or artifact on human physiological signals. The output voltage from the amplifier shall not exceed 30 millivolts when the gain is 10^4. The 1000 ohms impedance shall be connected to the ends of typical unshielded electrode leads (which are a normal part of the cable assembly furnished with physiological monitors). A 60-Hz notch filter shall be used to reduce ambient interference (as is typical in physiological monitor design).

Interference on physiological monitors can occur for a variety of reasons: patient electrodes may have dried out or the patient cable may be faulty; sometimes it is the location of the building with respect to transmitting antennas; sometimes it is the line isolation monitor (LIM). This is possible particularly with some models of older LIMs because of the design of switching circuitry. Because of reports of interference from LIMs, the Committee added the above performance test during the processing of the 1984 edition of NFPA 99.

3-4.3.4 Identification of Conductors for Isolated (Ungrounded) Systems. The isolated conductors shall be identified in accordance with 517-104(a)(5) of NFPA 70, *National Electrical Code.*

3-5 Performance Criteria and Testing.

3-5.1 Source (Up to and Including Transfer Switch).

3-5.1.1 Normal. (Reserved)

3-5.1.2 Essential.

3-5.1.2.1 Alternate Power Source Requirements.

(a) *Type I.* The emergency system and the equipment system shall be so arranged that, in the event of failure of the normal power source, an alternate power source shall be automatically connected within 10 seconds to the emergency system loads and to the switching devices (time delay or nonautomatic) supplying the equipment system loads.

> See Commentary on 3-4.2.1.4(d) as to how the time 10 seconds was selected.
> This chapter requires only one level of redundancy for sources of power, but does not require redundancy for transfer switches or distribution wiring. It is left to each facility to make its own determinations concerning possible simultaneous failure of the normal and alternate source of power, and possible failures of transfer switches or distribution wiring. Such determinations are also not required by this chapter.

(b) *Type II.* The emergency system and the critical system shall be so arranged that, in the event of failure of the normal power, an alternate power source shall be automatically connected within 10 seconds to the emergency system loads and to the time delay and/or nonautomatic switching devices supplying the critical system.

> The Commentary under 3-5.1.2.1(a) is applicable here as well.

(c) *Type III.*

(1) The emergency system shall have an alternate source of power separate and independent from the normal source that will be effective for a minimum of 1½ hours after loss of the normal source.[1]

> The 1½-hour requirement is consistent with the minimum requirements of NFPA *101, Life Safety Code.* However, the footnote to 8-5.4.1 is a reminder that 1½ hours may not be sufficient for some medical procedures.

[1]Consideration should be given to medical procedures that may necessitate emergency power being supplied for more than 1½ hours.

(2) The emergency system shall be so arranged that, in the event of failure of normal power source, the alternate source of power shall be automatically connected to the load within 10 seconds.

See Commentary on 3-4.2.1.4(d) as to how the time 10 seconds was selected.

3-5.1.2.2 Transfer Switch Operation Requirements.

(a) *Type I.*

(1) The essential electrical system shall be served by the normal power source except when the normal power source is interrupted or drops below a predetermined voltage level. Settings of the sensors shall be determined by careful study of the voltage requirements of the load.

(2) Failure of the normal source shall automatically start the alternate source generator, either instantaneously or after a short delay [*see 3-4.2.1.4(d)*]. When the alternate power source has attained a voltage and frequency that satisfies minimum operating requirements of the essential electrical system, the load shall be connected automatically to the alternate power source.

Paragraph 3-5.1.2.2(a)(1) states what constitutes a loss of normal power. When this occurs, the generator is to start. However, transfer of loads does not occur until *after* the alternate power source has attained minimum operating requirements for loads. This is assured through requirements of the transfer switch. [*See 3-4.2.1.4(a).*]

(3) Upon connection of the alternate power source, the loads comprising the emergency system shall be automatically reenergized. The load comprising the equipment system shall be connected either automatically after a time delay [*see 3-4.2.1.4(e)*] or nonautomatically and in such a sequential manner as not to overload the generator.

(4) When the normal power source is restored, and after time delay [*see 3-4.2.1.4(f)*], the automatic transfer switches shall disconnect the alternate source of power and connect the loads to the normal power source.

(5) If the emergency power source should fail and the normal power source has been restored, retransfer to the normal source of power shall be immediate, bypassing the retransfer delay timer.

(6) If the emergency power source fails during a test, provisions shall be made to immediately retransfer to the normal source.

This paragraph was added during the processing of the 1984 edition of NFPA 99 because in most testing schemes, a failure (in this instance loss of normal power) must be simulated. However, if the alternate power source fails during the test, nothing would happen to restore the normal power source, since normal power had been simulated to have failed. This new paragraph requires a facility to be able to retransfer to normal power if this situation developed.

(7) Nonautomatic transfer switching devices shall be restored to the normal power source as soon as possible after the return of the normal source or at the discretion of the operator.

(b) *Type II.*

(1) The essential electrical system shall be served by the normal power source except when the normal power source is interrupted or drops below a predetermined voltage level. Settings of the sensors shall be determined by careful study of the voltage requirements of the load.

(2) Failure of the normal source shall automatically start the alternate source generator, either instantaneously or after a short delay [see 3-4.2.1.4(d)]. When the alternate power source has attained a voltage and frequency that satisfies minimum operating requirements of the essential electrical system, the load shall be connected automatically to the alternate power source.

(3) Upon connection of the alternate power source, the loads comprising the emergency system shall be automatically reenergized. The loads comprising the critical system shall be connected either automatically after a time delay [see 3-4.2.1.4(e)] or nonautomatically and in such a sequential manner as not to overload the generator.

(4) When the normal power source is restored, and after time delay [see 3-4.2.1.4(f)], the automatic transfer switches shall disconnect the alternate source of power and connect the loads to the normal power source.

(5) If the emergency power source should fail and the normal power source has been restored, retransfer to the normal source of power shall be immediate, bypassing the retransfer delay timer.

(6) Nonautomatic transfer switching devices shall be restored to the normal power source as soon as possible after the return of the normal source or at the discretion of the operator.

(c) *Type III with Engine Generator Sets.*

The number of transfer switches is not suggested in this section because the number is dependent on the load, etc. (For the number of transfer switches in Type I or Type II facilities with the maximum demand on the essential electrical system, see 3-4.2.2.1 or 3-4.2.3.2, respectively.)

(1) The operation of the equipment shall be so arranged that the load will be served by the normal source except when the normal source is interrupted, or when the voltage drops below the setting of the voltage sensing device. The settings of the voltage sensing relays shall be determined by careful study of the voltage requirements of the load.

(2) When the normal source is restored, and after time delay [see 3-4.2.1.4(f)], the automatic transfer switch shall disconnect the alternate source of power and connect the loads to the normal power source.

(3) If the alternate power source fails and the normal power source has been restored, retransfer to the normal source of power shall be immediate.

(d) *Type III with Battery Systems.*

(1) Failure of the normal source shall automatically transfer the load to the battery system.

(2) Retransfer to the normal source shall be automatic upon restoration of the normal source.

3-5.1.2.3 Maintenance and Testing of Alternate Power Source and Transfer Switches.

(a) *Maintenance of Alternate Power Source.* The generator set or other alternate power source and associated equipment, including all appurtenant parts, shall be so maintained as to be capable of supplying service within the shortest time practicable and within the 10-second interval specified in 3-3.2.1.8, 3-5.1.2.1(a), 3-5.1.2.1(b), and 3-5.1.2.1(c)(2).

This paragraph sets a performance goal for the results of the maintenance program of the alternate power source. The alternate power source is expected to provide power within 10 seconds of interruption of the normal source. The specific test and maintenance activities enumerated for the alternate power source are those of 3-5.1.2.3(b). These are not to be considered as a complete maintenance program. They are only minimum elements. Each facility is expected to prepare a maintenance program that it expects will meet the performance goal of 3-5.1.2.3(b). Appendix C-3-2 contains suggested elements for consideration in preparing such a program. Paragraph 3-6.2.3.2 requires documentation of the implementation of the program.

(b) *Inspection and Testing.*

(1)* Test Interval and Load. Generator sets serving emergency and equipment systems shall be inspected weekly, and shall be exercised under load and operating temperature conditions for at least 30 minutes at intervals of not more than 30 days. The 30-minute exercise period is an absolute minimum, or the individual engine manufacturer's recommendations shall be followed.

NOTE: Records of changes to the essential electrical system should be maintained so that the actual connected load will be within the available capacity.

A-3-5.1.2.3(b)(1) Test Interval.

When indications such as the issuance of storm warnings indicate that power outages may be likely, good practice recommends the warming up of generator sets by a regular exercise period. Operation of generator sets for short intervals should be avoided, particularly with compression ignition engines, since it is harmful to the engines.

The requirements of this section have been reviewed and debated extensively over the past few years. Energy conservation, optimum generator equipment test intervals, actual loading versus simulated loading, and effect on patient safety and equipment have been among the major topics under scrutiny. There is universal agreement that the generator set and the essential electrical system need to be tested periodically to be reasonably certain that they will function in an actual emergency. Differences do exist, however, as to how often and under what conditions this testing should be conducted. The actual running time of the engine must be long enough to ensure that engine parts are properly lubricated; however, this must be balanced by a test load large enough to ensure acids and carbon are purged by the operating temperature of the engine. Thus, the two basic parameters of load and operating temperature are the ones listed for testing purposes.

If, as is the case in many instances, a large generator in relation to the load is installed (e.g., to account for the largest motor connected to the essential electrical system), the operating temperature of the generator may not be reached in thirty minutes. This should be considered when testing the generator.

The Note was added as a reminder that knowledge of what is actually connected to the essential electrical system will prevent a generator overload. A periodic review of the load on the essential electrical system is suggested.

(2) Test Conditions. The scheduled test under load conditions shall include a complete simulated cold start and appropriate automatic and manual transfer of all essential electrical system loads.

Testing procedures might range from manually disconnecting power to the power sensors on transfer switches to manually opening the main incoming feeder breakers. It is very important that each test method be fully understood by all staff through appropriate notification, and that the consequences of each method (if something fails to function) be weighed very carefully. A procedure for returning to the normal power source should also be established, should a failure occur during testing.

(3) Test Personnel. The scheduled tests shall be conducted by competent personnel. The tests are needed to keep the machines ready to function and, in addition, serve to detect causes of malfunction and to train personnel in operating procedures.

3-5.1.2.4 Maintenance and Testing of Circuitry.

(a) *Circuit Breakers.* Main and feeder circuit breakers shall be exercised annually.[1]

A significant percentage of circuit breakers is known to malfunction if not tested and maintained on a periodic basis. The interval of testing circuit breakers was recently reviewed, and annually was considered a reasonable interval for both large and small installations.

The intent is that each circuit breaker of main electrical switchgear, and of each main electrical distribution panel within the facility, be manually opened and closed once per year. Coordination with occupants of the affected areas is suggested. This includes planning for both the expected momentary outages and for the possibility that the circuit breakers cannot be reclosed.

The footnote to 3-5.1.2.4(a) suggests that the functioning of the tripping mechanism be tested with appropriate testing equipment. This type of equipment imposes engineered high values of current on the circuit breaker for a specified time; it also tests the calibration and functioning of the circuit breaker. Although periodic testing is not a requirement, it is strongly recommended by the Committee.

(b) *Insulation Resistance.* The resistance readings of main feeder insulation shall be taken prior to acceptance and whenever damage is suspected.

---

[1]Main and feeder circuit breakers should be periodically tested under simulated overload trip conditions to ensure reliability (*see Appendix C-3.2*).

Taking resistance measurements on a periodic basis has been found to be unnecessary and disruptive of facility activities (it can require shutdown of the entire system). Thus, only those times listed are required for testing.

Knowledge of initial resistance readings, or resistance readings from some past time, when feeders not tested initially were functioning normally, is needed to diagnose certain actual failures or detect certain incipient failures of electrical feeders. The readings are to be recorded and available in the maintenance record. (*See 3-6.2.3.2.*)

3-5.1.2.5 Maintenance of Batteries. Storage batteries used in connection with essential electrical systems shall be inspected at intervals of not more than seven days and shall be maintained in full compliance with manufacturer's specifications. Defective batteries shall be repaired or replaced immediately upon discovery of defects (*see NFPA 70, National Electrical Code, Section 700-4*).

Spare, charged starting batteries for engine generator sets are a prudent investment to provide flexibility to maintenance personnel in taking emergency starting actions when generators do not start. Such spare batteries, however, are not required by this chapter.

Battery-powered lighting systems, not required by this chapter, are often installed in selected areas such as operating rooms and special procedures rooms. When installed, they are intended to provide lighting during the 10-second interval and in the event of simultaneous failure of the alternate source and normal source. When installed, it is suggested that adequate attention be given to the proper maintenance of these optional systems.

3-5.2 Distribution.

3-5.2.1 Grounding System in Patient Care Areas.

3-5.2.1.1* Grounding System Testing. The effectiveness of the grounding system shall be determined by voltage measurements and impedance measurements.

Both voltage and impedance measurements are required because they check two different possible hazards.

Voltage measurement is a check to determine that there is no inadvertent connection or coupling that would raise the potential of the object being tested with respect to other parts of the grounding system. A problem would exist if conductive parts of the building structure became connected to ground but at points remote from the local power system grounds.

Impedance measurement is a check to verify that there is indeed a common grounding path for the power system within a patient vicinity.

(a) *New Construction.* The effectiveness of the grounding system shall be evaluated before acceptance.

(b) *Existing Construction.* The effectiveness of the grounding system of existing construction shall be evaluated and documented. Such evaluation shall be repeated when major sections are modified.

Exception No. 1: Small wall-mounted conductive surfaces, not likely to become energized, such as surface-mounted towel and soap dispensers, mirrors, and so forth, need not be intentionally grounded or tested.

Exception No. 2: Large metal conductive surfaces not likely to become energized, such as windows, door frames, and drains, need not be intentionally grounded or periodically tested.

The distinction between new and existing construction is a practical one: for existing construction, it is not possible to test before acceptance. However, if significant modifications are made on an existing structure, so that the electrical system under construction is essentially new, it is prudent to test that portion as if it were new.

For existing construction, evaluation of the grounding system is to be performed to establish a baseline. This is in addition to determining if the system is within required limits for existing construction. As a result, any subsequent testing should reveal changes or trends.

The fine distinction ("periodically" tested) between Exceptions No. 1 and No. 2 should be noted. The Committee responsible for this chapter was concerned that large metal conductive surfaces be tested at least once to assure that they were not inadvertently carrying excessive potentials. No further testing need be done after this initial check. However, if major changes are made, and there is concern whether conditions have changed, it is a prudent practice to conduct a recheck.

(c) Whenever the electrical system has been altered or replaced, that portion of the system shall be tested.

NOTE: A minimum testing interval of one year is recommended.

The frequency of testing is dependent on many factors: e.g., when the facility was built, usage rate, and staff practices. The annual interval is only a recommendation. It is not intended that testing be performed only if an entire electrical system is replaced. Whatever portion is repaired, replaced, or altered should be tested. In fact, if only one receptacle is replaced, that one receptacle should be checked.

A-3-5.2.1.1 Grounding System Testing. In a conventional *grounded* power distribution system one of the line conductors is deliberately grounded, usually at some distribution panel or the service entrance. This grounded conductor is identified as the *neutral* conductor. The other line conductor (or conductors) is (are) the *high* side of the line. The loads to be served by this distribution system are fed by the high and neutral conductors.

In addition to the high and neutral conductors, a grounding conductor is provided. One end is connected to the neutral at the point where the neutral is grounded, and the other end leads out to the connected loads. For purposes here, the load connection point will be considered to be a convenience receptacle, with the grounding conductor terminating at the grounding terminal of that receptacle.

This grounding conductor may be a separate wire running from the receptacle back to the remote grounding connection (where it joins the neutral conductor). If that separate conductor does not make any intermediate ground contacts between the receptacle and the remote ground, then the impedance of the connection between the receptacle and the remote ground is primarily the resistance of the grounding conductor itself, and is, therefore, predictable.

If, however, the receptacle is also interconnected with the remote ground point by metallic conduit or other metallic building structures, the impedance of the circuit between receptacle and remote ground is not easily predictable, nor is it easy to measure accurately, although one can be sure that the impedance will be less than that of the grounding wire itself because of the additional parallel paths.

Fortunately, as will become apparent in the following paragraphs, the absolute value of the apparent impedance between the grounding contact of an outlet and the remote ground point need not be known or measured with great accuracy.

Ideally, and under no fault conditions, the grounding system described above is supposed to be carrying no current at all. If that were true, then no voltage differences would be found between exposed conductive surfaces of any electrical appliances that were grounded to the grounding contacts of the receptacles from which they were powered. Similarly, there would be no voltage differences between these appliances and any other exposed metal surface that was also interconnected with the grounding system, provided that no currents were flowing in that interconnection.

Ideal conditions, however, do not prevail, and even when there are no "faults" within an appliance, residual "leakage" current does flow in the grounding conductor of each of the appliances, producing a voltage difference between the chassis of that appliance and the grounding contact of the receptacle that feeds it. Furthermore, this current can produce voltage differences among other appliances plugged into various receptacles on the system.

Fortunately, these leakage currents are small, and for reasonably low grounding-circuit impedances, the resulting voltage differences are entirely negligible.

If, however, a breakdown of insulation between the high side of the line and the chassis of an appliance should occur, the leakage current becomes a fault, the magnitude of which is limited by the nature of the breakdown or, in the case of a dead short circuit in the appliance, the magnitude of the fault current is limited only by the residual resistance of the appliance power cord conductors and that of the power distribution system.

In the event of such a short circuit, the impedance of the grounding circuit, as measured between the grounding contact of the receptacle that feeds the defective appliance and the remote ground point where the neutral and grounding conductors are joined, should be so small that a large enough fault current will flow to ensure a rapid breaking of the circuit by the overcurrent protective device that serves that receptacle.

For a 20-ampere branch circuit a fault current of 40 or more amperes would be required to ensure a rapid opening of the branch-circuit overcurrent-protective device. This corresponds to a circuit impedance of 3 ohms or less, of which it is desired that the grounding system contribute 1 ohm or less.

During the time this large fault current flows in the grounding system, the chassis of the defective appliance is raised many volts above other grounded surfaces in the same vicinity. The hazard represented by this condition is minimized by the fact that it exists for only a short time, and unless a patient simultaneously contacts both the defective appliance and some other grounded surface during this short time interval, there is no hazard. Furthermore, the magnitude of an applied voltage required to produce a serious shock hazard increases as its duration decreases, so the rapidity with which the circuit is interrupted helps reduce shock hazard even if such a patient contact should occur.

If, however, the defect in the appliance is not such as to cause an immediate circuit interruption, then the effect of this intermediate level of fault current on the voltages appearing on various exposed conductive surfaces in the patient vicinity must be considered.

Since all of this fault current flows in the grounding conductor of the defective appliance's power cord, then the first effect is to raise the potential of this appliance above that of the receptacle that feeds it by an amount proportional to the power cord grounding conductor resistance. This resistance is required to be less than 0.15 ohm, so fault currents of 20 amperes or less, which will not trip the branch-circuit overcurrent-protective device, will raise the potential of the defective appliance above the grounding contact of its supply receptacle by only 3 volts or less. This value is not hazardous for casual contacts.

The accurate measurement of fractional ohm resistance values is usually beyond the capability of conventional ohmmeters. However, a relatively simple test method will be suggested for making the measurements.

The fault current that enters the grounding system at the grounding contact of any receptacle in the patient vicinity could affect the potential at the grounding contacts of all the other receptacles, and, more importantly, it could produce significant voltage differences between them and other grounded surfaces, such as exposed piping and building structures.

If one grounded point is picked as a reference (a plumbing fixture in or near the patient vicinity, for example), and then the voltage difference is measured between that reference and the grounding contact of a receptacle, produced by driving some known current into that contact, a direct measure of the effectiveness of the grounding system within the patient vicinity is obtained. The "figure of merit" can be stated as so many volts per ampere of fault current. The ratio *volts per ampere* is, of course, impedance; but since the exact path taken by the fault current is not known, and since the way in which the reference point is interconnected with the grounding system is not known, it cannot be stated that this value is the impedance between the receptacle and some specific point, such as the joining of the neutral and grounding conductors. But it can be stated that this measured value of "effective impedance" is indicative of the effectiveness with which the grounding system minimizes voltage differences between supposedly grounded objects in the patient vicinity that are produced by ground faults in appliances used in that vicinity. This impedance, which characterizes the ability of the grounding system to maintain nearly equipotential conditions within the patient vicinity, is of prime importance in assessing shock hazard; but this impedance is not necessarily the same as the impedance between receptacle and remote ground point, which controls the magnitude of the short-circuit current involved in tripping the branch-circuit overcurrent-protective device.

Fault currents on the grounding system can also come from neutral-to-ground faults, which permit some current to flow in the neutral and some in the ground. This type of fault is often the cause of interference on EEG and ECG equipment. It is often not recognized easily because except for 60-Hz interference the equipment works perfectly properly. It is most easily found by causing a substantial change in the line-to-line load and noting changes in the ground-to-reference voltage.

A neutral-to-ground fault, as noted in the last paragraph, is not a common occurrence; but if and when it does occur, it can be difficult to locate (it may not even be in the patient care area) because the only visible manifestation is 60 Hg interference on ECG and EEG equipment. A shock hazard is possible, but very improbable; it is more a diagnostic safety problem.

3-5.2.1.2 Reference Point. The voltage and impedance measurements shall be taken with respect to a reference point. The reference point shall be one of the following:

(a) A reference grounding point (*see Chapter 2, "Definitions"*).

(b) A grounding point, in or near the room under test, that is electrically remote from receptacles. Example: an all-metal cold water pipe.

(c) The grounding contact of a receptacle that is powered from a different branch circuit from the receptacle under test.

This section was added in during the revision for the 1984 edition of NFPA 99 so that more consistent voltage and impedance measurements would be taken.

For subparagraph (b), plastic piping, while electrically remote, would not be acceptable.

3-5.2.1.3* Voltage Measurements. The voltage measurements shall be made under no-fault conditions between a reference point and exposed conductive surfaces (including ground contacts of receptacles) in a patient vicinity. The voltage measurements shall be made with an accuracy of ± 20 percent.

NOTE: The reference point may be the reference grounding point or the grounding contact of a convenient receptacle.

A-3-5.2.1.3 Grounding, and Voltage and Leakage Current Measurement Circuits. Effective grounding to safely handle both fault and leakage currents requires following the requirements of both Chapter 3 and NFPA 70, *National Electrical Code*, having good workmanship, and using some techniques that are not in these documents.

The performance of the grounding system is made effective through the existence of the green grounding wire, the metal raceway, and all of the other building metal. Measurements have shown that it is the metal raceway and building steel that provide most of the effective grounding path of less than 10 milliohms at the receptacle, including plug-to-receptacle impedance. The green grounding wire becomes a backup, not a primary grounding path performer.

Good practice calls for each receptacle to have a good jumper grounding connection to the metal raceway at the receptacle location in addition to having the green grounding wire connecting these points to the grounding bus in the distribution panel. Good workmanship includes seeing that these grounding connections are tight at each receptacle and that all metal raceway joints are secure and tight.

The voltage difference measurements listed in 3-5.2.1.3 in connection with power distribution grounding systems should ideally be made with an oscilloscope or spectrum analyzer in order to observe and measure components of leakage current and voltage differences at all frequencies.

For routine testing, such instruments may be inconvenient. An alternative is to use a metering system that weighs the contribution to the meter reading of the various components of the signal being measured in accordance with their probable physiological effect.

A meter specifically designed for this purpose would have an impedance of approximately 1000 ohms, and a frequency characteristic that was flat to 1 kHz, dropped at the rate of 20 decibels per decade to 100 kHz, and then remained flat to 1 MHz or higher. This frequency response characteristic could be achieved by proper design of the internal circuits of the amplifier that probably precedes the indicating instrument, or by appropriate choice of a feedback network around the amplifier. These details are, of course, left to the instrument designer.

If a meter specifically designed for these measurements is not available, a general-purpose laboratory millivoltmeter can be adapted for the purpose by adding a frequency-response-shaping network ahead of the meter. One such suggested network is shown in Figure A-3-5.2.1.3(a).

The circuit shown in Figure A-3-5.2.1.3(a) is especially applicable to measurements of leakage current, where the current being measured is derived from a circuit whose source impedance is high compared to 1000 ohms. Under these conditions, the voltage developed across the millivoltmeter will be proportional to the impedance of the network. The network impedance will be 1000 ohms at low frequencies, 10 ohms at high frequencies, and the transition between these two values will occur in the frequency range between 1 kHz and 100 kHz.

The basic low-frequency sensitivity will be one millivolt of meter reading for each one microampere of leakage current.

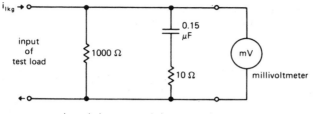

i_{lkg} = leakage current being measured

Figure A-3-5.2.1.3(a)

The millivoltmeter's own input impedance needs to be very large compared to 1000 ohms (100 kilohms), and the meter should have a flat frequency response to well beyond 100 kHz (if the meter impedance is lower than 100 kilohms, then the 1000-ohm resistor can be raised to a higher value, such that the impedance of that resistor in parallel with the meter will still be 1000 ohms).

The circuit of Figure A-3-5.2.1.3(a) can be used for the voltage difference measurements required in Section 3-5, but, because the source impedance will be very low compared to 1000 ohms, the frequency response of the measurement system will remain flat. If any high-frequency components, produced, for example, by pickup from nearby radio frequency transmitters, appear on the circuit being measured, then they will not be attenuated and the meter reading will be higher than it should be.

For meter readings below any prescribed limits this possible error is of no consequence. For borderline cases it could be significant. To avoid this uncertainty when making voltage-difference measurements a slightly more elaborate version of a frequency-response-shaping network is given in Figure A-3-5.2.1.3(b).

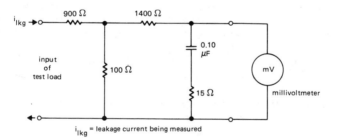

i_{lkg} = leakage current being measured

Figure A-3-5.2.1.3(b)

Here the source being measured is separated from the frequency-response-shaping network by the combination of the 900-ohm and 100-ohm resistors. The frequency response characteristic is now independent of the circuit being tested.

This independence is achieved, however, at a loss in signal delivered to the millivoltmeter. The basic low-frequency sensitivity of this metering circuit is one millivolt of meter reading for ten microamperes of leakage current, or on a voltage basis, one millivolt of meter reading for ten millivolts at the input terminals of the network.

The millivoltmeter should have an input impedance of 150 kilohms, and a frequency response flat to well beyond 100 kHz.

For either of the suggested networks, the resistors and capacitors should be mounted in a metal container close to the millivoltmeter to avoid stray pickup by the leads going to the meter.

Only performance criteria is now listed, as opposed to prior to 1978 when detailed wiring methodology was included in then NFPA 56A, *Standard on the Use of Inhalation Anesthetics*, to achieve the performance desired. How performance is achieved is left to designers, etc. The only requirement is that wiring has to be installed in accordance with NFPA 70, *National Electrical Code*.

The 20 millivolts value in 3-5.2.1.6 reflects correlation between former NFPA 56A and NFPA 76B. Based on reports from various sources, this limit is reasonably attainable and provides a reasonable margin of safety.

Drs. Whaler, Steimer, and MacIntosh, in experiments on human reaction to electrical stimulus, found it was the amount of current that flowed that was critical (i.e., it was the current that induced the ventricular fibrillation). Thus, while the measurement in 3-5.2.1.6 is given in terms of a maximum voltage (20 millivolts) across a specified resistance (1000 ohms), the concern is the amount of current ($I = V/R$) that will flow under this condition. This fact is particularly important when measuring in the microampere range.

3-5.2.1.4 Impedance Measurements. The impedance measurement shall be made with an accuracy of $\pm$ 20 percent.

(a) *New Construction.* The impedance measurement shall be made between the reference point and the grounding contact of each receptacle in the patient vicinity. The impedance measurement shall be the ratio of the 60-Hz voltage developed between a point under test and a reference point to 60-Hz current applied to the point under test.

(b) *Existing Construction.* The impedance (at 60 Hz or at dc) shall be measured between the reference point and the grounding contact of each receptacle in the patient vicinity. The impedance measurement shall be the ratio of the voltage developed between a point under test and a reference point to a current applied to the point under test. If the test is performed when the system is in use on a patient, it must not endanger the patient even if the grounding circuit being tested is faulty.

3-5.2.1.5 Test Equipment. Electrical safety test instruments shall be tested periodically, but not less than annually, for acceptable performance.

(a) Voltage measurements specified in 3-5.2.1 shall be made with an instrument having an input resistance of 1000 ohms $\pm$ 10 percent at frequencies of 1000 Hz or less.

(b) The voltage across the terminals (or between any terminal and ground) of resistance-measuring instruments used in occupied patient care areas shall not exceed 500 mV rms or 1.4 dc or peak to peak.

Concern was expressed during the revision for the 1984 edition of Chapter 9 of NFPA 99 about the safety of patients and staff from use of a test apparatus that had been included for illustration purposes in A-3.4.1 of NFPA 76B-1980. The apparatus was a suggested way of measuring the performance requirements in 3-4.1, etc. of NFPA 76B (3-5.2.1, etc. in this 1987 edition of NFPA 99). In some fault conditions, the test apparatus could harm users as well as self destruct.

Research is still being conducted on the question of how best to measure and verify the integrity of building wiring systems. The high-current test has been found to temporarily "weld" poor connections together; the low-current test will not detect a connection point that is only barely making a connection.

Rather than include any recommendations on tester configuration, a proposal was accepted that specified only instrument input resistance and maximum ohmeter voltage across terminals for resistance-measuring instruments.

Whatever test instrument(s) is used, it is essential for repeatability of measurements that these instruments be checked to verify that they are functioning within their specifications.

3-5.2.1.6 Criteria for Acceptability.

(a) *New Construction*.

(1) Voltage limit shall be 20 mV.

(2) Impedance limit shall be 0.1 ohm.

Exception: For quiet ground systems, the limit shall be 0.2 ohm.

(b) *Existing Construction*.

(1) The voltage limit shall be:

(i) 500 mV for general care areas and wet areas.

NOTE: The 500-mV limit is based on physiological values. Since the actual voltages normally measured in modern construction are usually less than 10 mV with nominal construction, voltages exceeding 20 mV may indicate a deteriorating condition and should be investigated.

(ii) 40 mV for critical care areas.

NOTE: The 40-mV limit is based on physiological values. Since the actual voltages normally measured in modern construction are usually less than 10 mV with nominal construction, voltages exceeding 20 mV may indicate a deteriorating condition and should be investigated.

(2) The impedance limit shall be 0.2 ohm.

3-5.2.2 Receptacles in Patient Care Areas.

3-5.2.2.1 Receptacle Testing.

The continuity of all the grounding circuits may be verified by the impedance test of 3-5.2.1.4. The physical integrity and polarity tests should be performed *before* the continuity test.

(a) The physical integrity of each receptacle shall be confirmed by visual inspection.

(b) The continuity of the grounding circuit in each electrical receptacle shall be verified.

(c) Correct polarity of the hot and neutral connections in each electrical receptacle shall be confirmed.

(d) The retention force of the grounding blade of each electrical receptacle (except locking-type receptacles) shall be not less than 115 grams (4 oz).

Four ounces was considered a reasonable safety factor by the former Technical Committee on Safe Use of Electricity in Patient Care Areas in deciding when it was time to replace a receptacle. A low tension value means the ground pin of the attachment plug (of the appliance) is not making good contact with the grounding blade in the receptacle, thereby defeating the purpose of this configuration (i.e., to provide a low-impedance path to ground for the green ground wire of the appliance).

3-5.2.2.2 Testing Intervals. Testing shall be performed no less frequently than as listed below.

General care areas: 12 months
Critical care areas: 6 months
Wet locations: 12 months

Exception: Where documented performance data are available to justify longer intervals than those shown, such longer intervals shall be permitted.

3-5.2.3 GFCIs in Patient Care Areas.

3-5.2.3.1 Testing. If GFCIs are used, a device or component that causes 6 milliamperes to flow to ground shall be momentarily connected between the energized conductor of the power distribution circuit being protected, and ground, to verify that the GFCI does indeed interrupt the power. If the test is performed when the system is in use on a patient, it must not endanger the patient even if the grounding circuit being tested is faulty.

The test device to be used has deliberately not been specified. Since tests of this type have some level of hazard, they should be performed by competent testing personnel. It is usually best *not* to perform this or other electrical power system tests while a patient is in the room, both for safety and psychological reasons. However, since this is often not practical, testing personnel should be qualified in safety and patient interactions.

3-5.2.3.2 Test Interval. Testing shall be performed no less frequently than every 12 months.

3-5.2.4 Essential Electrical System.

3-5.2.4.1 Type I. The branches of the emergency system shall be installed and connected to the alternate power source specified in 3-3.2.1.2 and 3-3.2.1.3 so that all functions specified herein for the emergency system shall be automatically restored to operation within 10 seconds after interruption of the normal source.

3-5.2.4.2 Type II. The emergency system shall be so installed and connected to the alternate source of power specified in 3-3.2.1.2 and 3-3.2.1.3 that all functions specified herein for the emergency system will be automatically restored to operation within 10 seconds after interruption of the normal source.

3-5.2.4.3 Type III. (Reserved)

3-5.2.5 Isolated Power Systems.

See Commentary under 3-4.3 regarding where isolated power systems are to be installed.

3-5.2.5.1 Patient Care Areas. If installed, the isolated power system shall be tested in accordance with 3-5.2.5.2.

3-5.2.5.2 Line Isolation Monitor Tests. The proper functioning of each line isolation monitor circuit shall be assured by the following:

(a) The LIM circuit shall be tested after installation, and prior to being placed in service, by successively grounding each line of the energized distribution system through a resistor of 200 × V ohms, where V = measured line voltage. The visual and audible alarms (*see 3-4.3.3.2*) shall be activated.

(b) The LIM circuit shall be tested at intervals of not more than one month by actuating the LIM test switch (*see 3-4.3.3.6*). Actuation of the test switch shall activate both visual and audible alarm indicators.

(c) After any repair or renovation to an electrical distribution system and at intervals of not more than six months, the LIM circuit shall be tested in accordance with paragraph (a) above and only when the circuit is not otherwise in use.

3-6 Administration of Electrical System.

3-6.1 Source.

NOTE: Administration is in conjunction with 3-6.2, "Distribution."

3-6.2 Distribution.

3-6.2.1 Responsibilities of Governing Body.

NOTE: See 12-2, 13-2, etc., for responsibilities within specific facilities.

3-6.2.2 Policies. (Reserved)

3-6.2.3 Recordkeeping.

3-6.2.3.1* Normal Electrical Distribution System. A record shall be maintained of the tests required by this chapter and associated repairs or modification. At a minimum, this record shall contain the date, the rooms or areas tested, and an indication of which items have met or have failed to meet the performance requirements of this chapter.

A-3-6.2.3.1 Documentation. While several approaches to documentation exist in hospitals, the minimum acceptable documentation should convey what was tested, when it was tested, and whether it performed successfully. Adopting a system of exception reporting can be the most efficient form of recordkeeping for routine rechecks of equipment or systems and thereby minimize technicians' time in recording the value of each measurement taken. For example, once a test protocol is established, which simply means testing the equipment or system consistent with this chapter, the only item (value) that needs to be recorded is what failure or what deviation from the requirements of the chapter was detected when a corrective action (repair) was undertaken. This approach can serve to eliminate, for example, the need to keep individual room sheets to record measured results on each receptacle or to record measurement values of all types of leakage current tests.

The format of documentation is the responsibility of the facility. However, it is advisable to consult with inspection agencies, insurance companies, etc., for any recommended format.

3-6.2.3.2 Essential Electrical Distribution System. A written record of inspection, performance, exercising period, and repairs shall be regularly maintained and available for inspection by the authority having jurisdiction. (*See Appendix C-3 for general maintenance guide.*)

Use of computers to store recordings of inspections, maintenance, etc., should be acceptable if such information can readily be made available for inspectors.

3-6.2.3.3 Isolated Power System (Where Installed). A permanent record shall be kept of the results of each of the tests.

3-6.2.4 Information and Warning Signs. (Reserved)

4 GAS AND VACUUM SYSTEMS

NOTE 1: The application of requirements contained in this chapter for specific types of health care facilities can be found in Chapters 12 through 18.

NOTE 2: Gases covered include, but are not limited to, oxygen, nitrogen, nitrous oxide, air, carbon dioxide, natural gas, ethylene oxide, hydrogen, helium, acetylene, and vacuum.

NOTE 3: Sections 4-3 through 4-6 cover requirements for pressurized centrally piped gas systems; Sections 4-7 through 4-10 cover requirements for centrally piped vacuum systems.

Note 3 is to clearly emphasize that the requirements of *gas* systems are different from *vacuum* systems. While both systems utilize networks of pipes, alarms, valves, and terminals, the specifics of each are quite different (e.g., location of alarms, direction of flow, type of piping allowed).

Often, these two systems are installed simultaneously. In these instances, care should be taken to assure correct operation (particularly, to prevent cross-connection, and assure correct placement of alarms).

4-1 Scope.

4-1.1 This chapter covers the performance, maintenance, installation, and testing of (1) nonflammable medical gas systems, (2) flammable and nonflammable laboratory gas systems, and (3) vacuum systems used within health care facilities.

4-1.2 Wherever the term *medical gas* occurs in this chapter, the provisions shall apply to all patient gas systems. Wherever the name of a specific gas occurs, the provision applies only to that gas.

4-1.3 This chapter does not apply to portable compressed gas systems.

4-1.4 This chapter applies only to permanently installed, fixed medical-surgical vacuum systems where such systems are intended for patient drainage, aspiration, and suction and, under the conditions set forth in 4-7.2.1, for medical laboratory use. This chapter does not apply to water aspirator systems which dispose of drainage directly into sanitary sewers. This chapter does not cover suction apparatus or appliances attached to the vacuum system terminals (inlets).

4-2 Nature of Hazards.

4-2.1 Gas Systems.

NOTE: See Section 8-2.

The requirements for the installation of medical piped gas systems (as contained in Sections 4-3 to 4-6), are the result of addressing the fire and patient-safety hazards poised by such systems (see below, in addition to 8-2). However, there are other codes that impact on the design and installation of reliable and effective gas systems (e.g. plumbing codes, sizing codes), and they should be consulted as necessary.

In 1932, when the subject of piped gas systems was brought before the then NFPA Committee on Gases some of the initial concerns included the following:

1) a network of pipes was carrying oxidizing gases throughout a building; while these types of gases don't burn, they do support and intensify the burning of combustibles already burning. (Note: There were no restrictions initially on flammable anesthetic gases, but in 1950, their piping was prohibited, thereby eliminating one possible source of explosion and fire);

2) a large quantity of gas in cylinders was being concentrated/stored in one area;

3) there was the possible build up of potentially hazardous gas concentrations should the pipes leak; and

4) a jeopardizing of patient safety should there be a mix-up of gases, (either the supply or from some interruption in the piping system) cross-connection of piping, or an actual loss of gas.

These were of concern in 1932. They are still cogent in 1987.

4-2.2 Vacuum Systems. There are potential fire and explosion hazards associated with medical gas central piping systems and medical-surgical vacuum systems. The various components are usually not independent isolated components, but are parts of a larger system dedicated to total patient care and safety.

Many of these components are covered by existing standards to minimize the fire, explosive, and patient safety hazard. With the increased use of vacuum systems, the potential for mistaken interconnection with oxidizing gases, for ingestion of flammable anesthetic gases, and for undercapacity requiring extended overheated operation all present potential hazards or compound other hazardous conditions which should be properly addressed. While the potential for these problems exists, the Subcommittee on Vacuum Systems and Equipment is unaware of the actual occurrence of any significant fire-related hazards with vacuum systems.

There are also potential hazards to patients in the unplanned shutdown or failure of the systems secondary to a fire and/or the inability of the system to provide adequate levels of performance under normal or emergency situations. There is also the potential for mistaken interconnection with pressurized nonflammable medical gas systems described in Sections 4-3 to 4-6.

The purposes listed in the above paragraph summarize the several diversified but interrelated reasons for NFPA developing requirements on this subject.

For commentary on development of vacuum system requirements, see Prologue just before Section 4-7.

4-3 Gas System Sources.

4-3.1 Patient Gas Supply — Type I.

NOTE: For bulk oxygen systems, see NFPA 50, *Standard for Bulk Oxygen Systems.*

The designation "Type I" is for reference purposes only. In Chapters 12 through 18, the applicability of the type of patient piped gas system is stated. See Sections 12-3.4.1, 13-3.4.1, 14-3.4.1, etc., for applicability in hospitals, ambulatory health care centers, etc.

For historical reference, Type I patient piped gas systems were those covered by Chapters 1 through 5 in NFPA 56F, *Standard for Nonflammable Medical Gas Systems*, which was incorporated into this 1987 edition of NFPA 99.

4-3.1.1 Cylinder and Container Management.

4-3.1.1.1 Cylinders or supply containers shall be constructed, tested, and maintained in accordance with the U.S. Department of Transportation specifications and regulations.[1]

The U.S. Department of Transportation (DOT) regulations for the manufacture and requalification of compressed gas cylinders provide for reasonably safe and economical cylinders. The Committee thus references these regulations to avoid redundancy. Cylinders complying with DOT regulations are also considered safe for the storage of gases in health care facilities.

4-3.1.1.2 Cylinder contents shall be identified by attached labels or stencils naming the components and giving their proportions. Labels and stencils shall be lettered in accordance with ANSI Z48.1 (CGA Pamphlet C-4), *Standard Method of Marking Portable Compressed Gas Containers to Identify the Material Contained.*

4-3.1.1.3 Contents of cylinders and containers shall be identified by reading the labels prior to use. Labels shall not be defaced, altered, or removed.

4-3.1.2 Storage Requirements (Location, Construction, Arrangement).

Prior to the 1984 edition of NFPA 99, each Health Care Facilities Committee and the Committee on Industrial and Medical Gases established storage requirements for its areas of responsibility. The 1984 edition of NFPA 99 brought most of the disciplines together, except nonflammable medical piped gas systems which were still under the auspices of the Technical Committee on Industrial and Medical Gases. With this 1987 edition of NFPA 99 and the restructuring of text, and with the incorporation of NFPA 56F into NFPA 99, all storage requirements for medical gases have been codified, and located in one section (4-3.1.2).

In the restructuring of NFPA 99, requirements have been organized in the following way:

4-3.1.2.1 Nonflammable gases (any quantity; in-storage, connected, or both)

4-3.1.2.2 Additional requirements for nonflammable gases *greater than* 2,000 cu ft

4-3.1.2.3 Additional requirements for nonflammable gases *less than* 2,000 cu ft

4-3.1.2.4 Flammable inhalation agents

---

[1]Regulations of the U.S. Department of Transportation (formerly U.S. Interstate Commerce Commission) outline specifications for transportation of explosives and dangerous articles (*Code of Federal Regulations*, Title 49, Parts 171-190). In Canada, the regulations of the Canadian Transport Commission, Union Station, Ottawa, Ontario, apply.

4-3.1.2.1 Nonflammable Gases (Any Quantity; In-Storage, Connected or Both).

NOTE: This includes oxidizing gases.

(a) Sources of heat in storage locations shall be protected or located so that cylinders or compressed gases shall not be heated to the activation point of integral safety devices. In no case shall the temperature of the cylinders exceed 130°F (54.5°C). Care shall be exercised in handling cylinders that have been exposed to freezing temperature to prevent injury to the skin.

(b) Cylinder storage or manifold enclosures shall be provided for oxidizing agents (nitrous oxide, oxygen mixtures, and compressed air). Such enclosures shall be constructed of an assembly of building materials with a fire-resistive rating of at least one hour and shall not communicate directly with anesthetizing locations. Other nonflammable (inert) medical gases may be stored in the enclosure. Flammable gases shall not be stored with oxidizing agents. Storage of full or empty cylinders is permitted. Such enclosures shall serve no other purpose.

NOTE 1: Conductive flooring is not required in cylinder storage locations that are not a part of a surgical or obstetrical suite.

NOTE 2: Conductive flooring is not required for those cylinder storage locations or manifold enclosures used only for nonflammable medical gases [see 4-3.1.2.4(e)].

> The intent here is for flammable gases to be stored separately from oxidizing gases. It is acceptable for inert gases to be stored with oxidizing or flammable gases. (*See Figure 12.*)

(c) Provisions shall be made for racks or fastenings to protect cylinders from accidental damage or dislocation.

(d) The electric installation in storage locations or manifold enclosures for nonflammable medical gases shall comply with the standards of NFPA 70, *National Electrical Code*, for ordinary locations. Electric wall fixtures, switches, and receptacles shall be installed in fixed locations not less than 152 cm (5 ft) above the floor as a precaution against their physical damage.

(e) Storage locations for oxygen and nitrous oxide shall be kept free of flammable materials [see also 4-3.1.2.1(b)].

(f) The location and ventilation of storage rooms or manifold enclosures for oxygen and nitrous oxide shall comply with 4-3.1.2.1(k) and (l).

(g) Cylinders containing compressed gases and cans containing volatile liquids shall be kept away from radiators, steam pipes, and like sources of heat. Oxygen and nitrous oxide cylinders may be stored in the same room.

(h) Combustible materials, such as paper, cardboard, plastics, and fabrics, shall not be stored or kept near cylinders containing oxygen or nitrous oxide. An exception to the rule may be made in the case of cylinder shipping crates or cartons. Racks for cylinder storage may be of wooden construction. Wrappers shall be removed prior to storage.

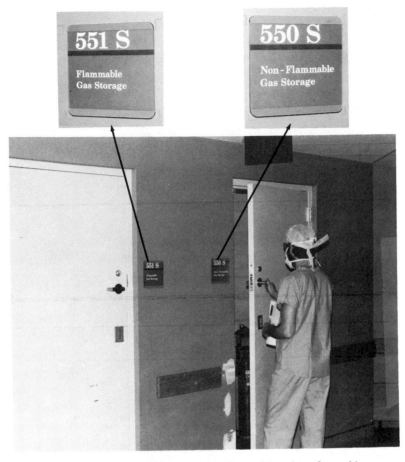

Figure 12   Example of separate enclosures for flammable and nonflammable gases.

An allowance for wooden storage racks was made as a result of a Formal Interpretation by the former Technical Committee on Anesthetizing Agents in July 1976. The Committee incorporated the allowance during the revision for the 1978 edition of NFPA 56A, *Standard on the Use of Inhalation Anesthetics*. The argument of the submitter was that such racks were economical, convenient, and not proven to be a hazard over the test of time. (Note: This is the only exception with respect to combustible materials within gas cylinder storage rooms.)

(i) When cylinder valve protection caps are supplied, they shall be secured tightly in place unless the cylinder is connected for use.

If the cylinder valve protection cap is not present and a cylinder falls, the cylinder valve could snap off. Under same conditions depending on cylinder size, quantity of gas within cylinder, and the orifice size at break, a cylinder could be propelled rapidly and/or violently about.

(a) 95 percent oxygen, 5 percent carbon dioxide.

(b) Nitrous oxide, U.S.P.

(c) Nitrogen.

Figure 13   Typical cylinder supply systems *without* reserve supplies.

(j) Containers shall not be stored in a tightly closed space such as a closet [see 8-2.1.2.3(c)].

Note that this restriction applies only to containers, i.e., low-pressure vessels, since this type of storage vessel continuously vents small amounts of gaseous oxygen vapor to prevent overpressurization of the container.

(k) *Location of Supply Systems.*

(1) Except as permitted by 4-3.1.2.1(k)(2), supply systems for oxygen, nitrous oxide, or mixtures of these gases having total capacities (connected and in storage) not exceeding the quantities specified in 4-3.1.2.2(a) and (b) shall be located outdoors, in a building or enclosure used only for this purpose, or in a room or enclosure used only for this purpose situated within a building used for other purposes.

(2) Locations for supply systems shall not be used for storage purposes other than for containers of nonflammable gases. Storage of full or empty containers is permissible. Other nonflammable medical gas supply systems or storage locations are permitted to be in the same location with oxygen or nitrous oxide or both. However, care shall be taken to provide adequate ventilation to dissipate such other gases in order to prevent the development of oxygen-deficient atmospheres in the event of functioning of cylinder or manifold pressure-relief devices.

(3) Medical air compressors and vacuum pumps shall be located separately from cylinder gas systems or cylinder storage enclosures. Medical air compressors shall be installed in a designated mechanical equipment area, adequately ventilated and with required services.

(l) *Construction and Arrangement of Supply System Locations.*

(1) Walls, floors, ceilings, roofs, doors, interior finish, shelves, racks, and supports of and in the locations cited in 4-3.1.2.1(k)(1) shall be constructed of noncombustible or limited-combustible materials.

(2) Locations for supply systems for oxygen, nitrous oxide, or mixtures of these gases shall not communicate with anesthetizing locations or storage locations for flammable anesthetizing agents.

(3) Enclosures for supply systems shall be provided with doors or gates that may be locked.

There is no requirement that storage rooms for gases be locked. However, in light of reported thefts of nitrous oxide cylinders for substance-abuse purposes, and to prevent unauthorized persons (including small children) from creating a hazard or harming themselves, some means of limiting access to storage rooms would be prudent.

(4) Ordinary electrical wall fixtures in supply rooms shall be installed in fixed locations not less than 5 ft (1.5 m) above the floor to avoid physical damage.

(5) When enclosures (interior or exterior) for supply systems are located near sources of heat, such as furnaces, incinerators, or boiler rooms, they shall be of construction as to protect cylinders from reaching temperatures exceeding 130°F (54°C). Open electrical conductors and transformers

shall not be located in close proximity to enclosures. Such enclosures shall not be located adjacent to oil storage tanks.

(6) Smoking shall be prohibited in supply system enclosures.

(7) Heating shall be by steam, hot water, or other indirect means. Cylinder temperatures shall not exceed 130°F (54°C).

4-3.1.2.2 Additional Storage Requirements for Nonflammable Gases *Greater* than 2000 cu ft (57 m³).

(a) Oxygen supply systems or storage locations having a total capacity of more than 20,000 cu ft (566 m³) (NTP), including unconnected reserves on hand at the site, shall comply with NFPA 50, *Standard for Bulk Oxygen Systems at Consumer Sites.*

(b) Nitrous oxide supply systems or storage locations having a total capacity of 3200 lb (1452 kg) [28,000 cu ft (793 m³) (NTP)] or more, including unconnected reserves on hand at the site, shall comply with Compressed Gas Association, Inc., Pamphlet G-8.1, *Standard for the Installation of Nitrous Oxide Systems at Consumer Sites.*

(c) The walls, floors, and ceilings of locations for systems of more than 2000 cu ft (57 m³) total capacity (connected and in storage) separating the supply system location from other occupancies in a building shall have a fire-resistance rating of at least one hour. This shall also apply to a common wall or walls of a supply system location attached to a building having other occupancy.

(d) Locations for systems of more than 2000 cu ft (57 m³) total capacity (connected and in storage) shall be vented to the outside. If natural venting is used, the vent opening or openings shall be a minimum of 72 sq in. (0.05 m²) in total free area. Mechanical ventilation may be used.

4-3.1.2.3 Additional Storage Requirements for Nonflammable Gases *Less* than 2000 cu ft (57 m³).

(a) Locations for supply systems of 2000 cu ft (57 m³) or less total capacity (connected and in storage) need not be vented to outside. Doors to such locations shall be provided with louvered openings having a minimum of 72 sq in. (0.05 m²) in total free area.

4-3.1.2.4 Flammable Inhalation Anesthetic Agents (Any Quantity; In-Storage, Connected, or Both).

(a) Enclosures in which flammable inhalation anesthetic agents are stored shall be individually and continuously ventilated by gravity or by mechanical means at a rate of not less than eight air changes per hour. The fresh air inlet and the exhaust air outlet within the enclosure shall be located as far apart as feasible consistent with the enclosure layout. The fresh air inlet shall be located at or near the ceiling, and the bottom of the exhaust air outlet shall be located 3 in. (7.6 cm) above the floor. The fresh air supply may be heated. Exhaust air shall be discharged to the exterior of the building at least 12 ft (3.6 m) above grade in a manner to prevent its reentry to the building.

(b) Exhaust fans shall have nonsparking blades. The fan motor shall be connected into the equipment system (either automatic or delayed restoration) (*see Chapter 3, "Electrical Systems"*). All electric installations shall conform to NFPA 70, *National Electrical Code,* and, when inside the storage area or exhaust duct, shall be approved for use in Class I, Group C, Division 2 locations. A visual signal that indicates failure of the exhaust system shall be installed at the entrance to the storage area.

NOTE: Exhaust fans in all new installations, and whenever possible in existing installations, should be located at the discharge end of the exhaust duct.

(c) Approved fire dampers shall be installed in openings through the required fire partition in accordance with the requirements of NFPA 90A, *Standard for the Installation of Air-Conditioning and Ventilating Systems*.

(d) The electric installation in storage locations for flammable inhalation anesthetic agents shall comply with the requirements of 3-4.1.2.1(e)(2).

(e) Enclosures shall not be used for purposes other than storage of flammable inhalation anesthetic agents.

(f) Flooring shall comply with 12-4.1.3.8(b)(1).

(g) Electric wiring and equipment in storage locations for flammable inhalation anesthetic agents shall comply with the requirements of NFPA 70, *National Electrical Code*, Article 500, Class I, Division 2 and equipment used therein shall be approved for use in Class I, Group C, Division 1 hazardous areas (*see 3-5.2.1 for grounding requirements*).

(h) The provisions of 12-4.1.3.2 for ungrounded electric distribution systems do not apply to storage locations for flammable agents.

(i) Storage locations for flammable anesthetics shall meet the construction requirements stated in 4-3.1.2.1(b) and (c), and shall be ventilated as provided in 4-3.1.2.4(a).

(j) Flammable inhalation anesthetizing agents shall be stored only in such locations. Flammable inhalation anesthetizing agents shall not be stored in anesthetizing locations, except for cylinders of flammable anesthetic agents connected to a gas anesthesia apparatus.

(k) Cylinders containing flammable gases (i.e., ethylene and cyclopropane) and containers of flammable liquids (i.e., diethyl ether, divinyl ether, ethyl chloride) shall be kept out of proximity to cylinders containing oxidizing gases (i.e., oxygen or nitrous oxide) through the use of separate rooms.

(l) Storage locations for flammable inhalation agents shall be kept free of cylinders of nitrous oxide, compressed air, oxygen, and mixtures of oxygen.

(m) Sources of illumination and ventilation equipment in storage locations for flammable inhalation anesthetic agents, wherever located, and especially in storage locations that are remote from the operative suite, shall be inspected and tested on a regular schedule. Such procedures shall determine that adequate ventilation is maintained under supervision.

4-3.1.3 Material — Oxygen Compatibility.

4-3.1.3.1 Oxygen system components, including, but not limited to, containers, valves, valve seats, lubricants, fittings, gaskets, and interconnecting equipment including hoses, shall have adequate compatibility with oxygen under the conditions of temperature and pressure to which the components may be exposed in the containment and use of oxygen. Easily ignitible materials shall be avoided unless they are parts of equipments or systems that are approved, listed, or proved suitable by tests or by past experience.[1]

---

[1]Compatibility involves both combustibility and ease of ignition. Materials that burn in air will burn violently in pure oxygen at normal pressure and explosively in pressurized oxygen. Also, many materials that do not burn in air will do so in pure oxygen, particularly under pressure. Metals for containers and piping must be carefully selected, depending on service conditions. The various steels are acceptable for many applications, but some service conditions may call for other materials (usually copper or its alloys) because of their greater resistance to ignition and lower rate of combustion.

Similarly, materials that can be ignited in air have lower ignition energies in oxygen. Many such materials may be ignited by friction at a valve seat or stem packing or by adiabatic compression produced when oxygen at high pressure is rapidly introduced into a system initially at low pressure.

4-3.1.3.2 The provisions of 4-3.1.3.1 apply to nitrous oxide, oxygen-nitrous oxide mixtures, and to other medical gas mixtures containing more than 23.5 percent oxygen.

4-3.1.4 Central Supply Systems. The central supply system shall be a system of cylinders and necessary supply equipment assembled as described in either 4-3.1.5 or 4-3.1.6, or a bulk supply system (4-3.1.7) which may be of the permanently installed type or the trailer type. The medical compressed air source, in addition to the preceding, is permitted to be two or more compressors that deliver medical compressed air and that comply with 4-3.1.2.2(b), 4-3.1.9, and 4-3.1.2.1(k)(2).

4-3.1.5 Cylinder Systems without Reserve Supply. *(See Figure 4-3.1.5 and Appendixes C-4-1 and C-4-2.)*

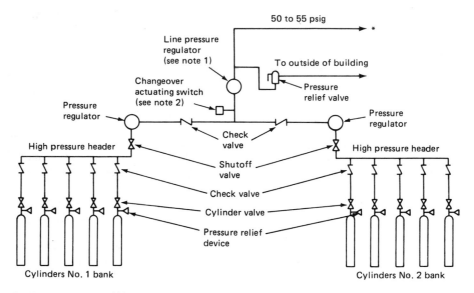

For SI Units: 50 psig = 344 kPa gauge; 55 psig = 377 kPa gauge.
*Piping system continued on Figure 4-3.1.10.1.

    NOTE 1:   See 4-3.1.8.3.
    NOTE 2:   See 4-4.1.1.2(b).

Figure 4-3.1.5 Typical Cylinder Supply System without Reserve Supply (Schematic). Supply systems with different arrangements of valves and regulators are permissible if they provide equivalent safeguards.

4-3.1.5.1 A cylinder manifold shall have two banks (or units) of cylinders that alternately supply the piping system, each bank having a pressure regulator and cylinders connected to a common header. Each bank shall contain a minimum of two cylinders or at least an average day's supply unless normal delivery schedules require a greater supply. When the content of the primary bank is unable to supply the system, the secondary bank shall automatically operate to supply the system. An actuating switch shall be connected to the master signal panels to indicate when, or just before, the changeover to the secondary bank occurs.

4-3.1.5.2 A check valve shall be installed between each cylinder lead and the manifold header to prevent the loss of gas from the manifolded cylinders in the event the pressure relief device on an individual cylinder functions or a cylinder lead (pigtail) fails. The check valve shall be of a material suitable for the gases and pressures involved.

4-3.1.6 Cylinder Supply Systems with Reserve Supply. *(See Figure 4-3.1.6 and Appendixes C-4-1 and C-4-2.)*

4-3.1.6.1 A cylinder supply system with reserve supply shall consist of:

(a) A primary supply, which supplies the piping system.

(b) A secondary supply, which shall operate automatically when the primary supply is unable to supply the system. An actuating switch shall be connected to the master signal panels to indicate when, or just before, the changeover to the secondary bank occurs.

(c) A reserve supply, which shall operate automatically in the event that both the primary and secondary supplies are unable to supply the system. An actuating switch shall be connected to the master signal panels to indicate when, or just before, the reserve begins to supply the piping system.

4-3.1.6.2 The reserve supply shall consist of three or more manifolded high-pressure cylinders connected as required under 4-3.1.8.2, and either shall be equipped with check valves as required in 4-3.1.5.2, or shall be provided with an actuating switch that shall operate the master signals when the reserve supply drops to one day's supply. *(See Appendixes C-4.1 and C-4.2.)*

4-3.1.6.3 A cryogenic liquid cylinder supply system shall be installed either as indicated in Figure 4-3.1.6, or as indicated in Figure 4-3.1.5 with the addition of a reserve supply connected as shown in Figure 4-3.1.6. *(See Appendixes C-4.1 and C-4.2.)*

4-3.1.6.4 When cryogenic liquid cylinder supply systems are designed to prevent the loss of the gas produced by the evaporation of the cryogenic liquid in the secondary supply, they shall be designed so that the gas produced shall pass through the line pressure regulator before entering the piped distribution system.

4-3.1.6.5 Cryogenic liquid cylinder supply systems shall be constructed to withstand high pressure [2200 psig (15.2 MPa gauge)] or shall be provided with suitable pressure relief devices upstream of the control unit.

4-3.1.6.6 Cylinder supply systems designed in accordance with 4-3.1.6 do not require check valves between each cylinder lead and the manifold header on the primary and secondary supplies.

4-3.1.7* Bulk Medical Gas Systems. *(See Figure 4-3.1.7 and Appendixes C-4.1 and C-4.2.)*

A-4-3.1.7 The bulk supply system should be installed on a site that has been prepared to meet the requirements of NFPA 50, *Bulk Oxygen Systems at Consumer Sites*, or Compressed Gas Association Pamphlet G-8.1, *Standard for the Installation of Nitrous Oxide Systems at Consumer Sites*. Storage unit(s), reserve, pressure regulation, and signal actuating switch(es) are components of

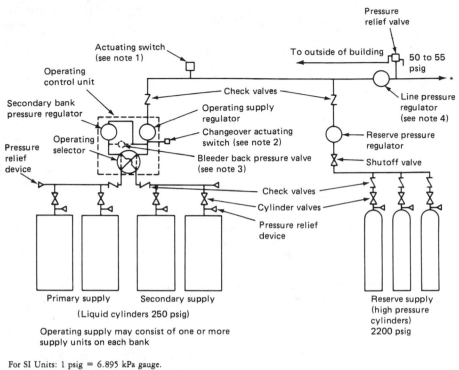

For SI Units: 1 psig = 6.895 kPa gauge.
*Supply piping system continued on Figure 4-3.1.10.1.

NOTE 1:   See 4-4.1.1.2(c).

NOTE 2:   See 4-4.1.1.2(b).

NOTE 3:   See 4-3.1.6.4.

NOTE 4:   See 4-3.1.8.3.

Figure 4-3.1.6 Typical Cylinder Supply System with Reserve Supply (Schematic). Supply systems with different arrangements of valves and regulators are permissible if they provide equivalent safeguards.

the supply system. Shutoff valves, piping from the site, and electric wiring from a signal switch(es) to the master signal panels are components of the piping system.

The bulk supply system is normally installed on the site by the owner of this system. It is the responsibility of the owner or the organization responsible for the operation and maintenance of the bulk supply system to assure that all components of the supply system — main supply, reserve supply, supply system signal actuating switch(es), and delivery pressure regulation equipment — function properly before the system is put in service.

4-3.1.7.1   The bulk system shall consist of two sources of supply, one of which shall be a reserve supply for use only in an emergency. An actuating switch shall be connected to the master signal panels to indicate when, or just before, the reserve begins to supply the system. There are two types of bulk supply systems:

(a) The alternating type with two or more units alternately supplying the piping system. When the primary supply is unable to supply the bulk system, the secondary supply

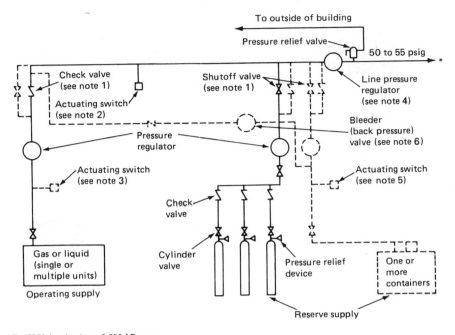

Figure 4-3.1.7 Typical Bulk Supply System (Schematic). Bulk supply systems with different arrangements of valves, regulators, and gas supply units are permissible if they provide equivalent safeguards. The reserve supply shown in dotted lines indicates the arrangements outlined in 4-3.1.7.2(b) or (c).

For SI Units: 1 psig = 6.895 kPa gauge.
*Piping system continued on Figure 4-3.1.10.1.

NOTE 1: See 4-3.1.8.4.

NOTE 2: See 4-4.1.1.2(c).

NOTE 3: See 4-4.1.1.2(b).

NOTE 4: See 4-3.1.8.3.

NOTE 5: See 4-4.1.1.2(d).

NOTE 6: See 4-3.1.7.2(c).

NOTE 7: Dotted lines are alternates.

automatically becomes the primary supply and a new secondary supply, not the reserve supply, is connected when or before this changeover takes place. An actuating switch shall be connected to the master signal panels to indicate when, or just before, the changeover occurs.

(b) The continuous type with one or more units continuously supplying the piping system while another unit remains as the reserve supply and operates only in case of an emergency.

4-3.1.7.2 The secondary supply and the reserve supply referred to in 4-3.1.7.1 shall each contain at least an average day's supply and shall consist of:

(a) three or more manifolded high-pressure cylinders connected as required under 4-3.1.5.1 and 4-3.1.8.2; or

Figure 14   Liquid oxygen sources for bulk-supply piped-oxygen system. "Reserve supply" is the smaller container to the left of the large container.

(b) high-pressure cylinders without check valves provided an actuating switch, which shall operate the master alarm signal when the reserve supply is down to one day's average supply, is installed; or

(c) a cryogenic liquid storage unit used as the reserve for a bulk supply system provided with an actuating switch that shall operate the master alarm signal when the contents of the reserve are reduced to one day's average supply, and another actuating switch that shall operate the master alarm signal if the gas pressure available in the reserve unit is reduced below the pressure required to function properly. It shall also be designed to prevent the loss of gas produced by the evaporation of the cryogenic liquid in the reserve and so that the gas produced shall pass through a line pressure regulator before entering the piped distribution system.

4-3.1.8 General Requirements for Central Supply Systems.

4-3.1.8.1   Cylinders shall be designed, constructed, tested, and maintained in accordance with 4-3.1.1.1. Cylinders in service shall be adequately secured. Cylinders in storage shall be secured and located to prevent them from falling or being knocked over.

4-3.1.8.2   Manifolds shall be of substantial construction and of a design and materials suitable for the gases and pressures involved. Mechanical means shall be provided to assure the connection of cylinders containing the proper gas to the manifold. Cylinder valve outlets and manifold or regulator inlet connections shall comply with the American National-Canadian *Standard for Compressed Gas Cylinder Valve Outlet and Inlet Connections*, ANSI B57.1, CSA B96 (Compressed Gas Association, Inc., Pamphlet V-1). When any nonflammable medical gases or gas mixtures are to be piped, care shall be taken to assure noninterchangeability of cylinders or equipment. Manifolds shall be obtained from and installed under the supervision of a manufacturer or supplier familiar with proper practices for their construction and use.

4-3.1.8.3 Pressure regulating equipment shall be installed in the supply main upstream of the final line-pressure relief valve (*see 4-3.1.8.5*).

4-3.1.8.4 A manually operated shutoff valve shall be installed upstream of each pressure regulator and a shutoff valve or a check valve shall be installed downstream.

4-3.1.8.5 Each central supply system shall have a pressure relief valve set at 50 percent above normal line pressure, installed downstream of the pressure regulator and upstream of any shutoff valve. This pressure relief valve may be set at a higher pressure provided another pressure relief valve set at 50 percent above normal line pressure is installed in the main supply line. All pressure relief valves shall close automatically when excess pressure has been released. Pressure relief valves set at 50 percent above normal line pressure shall be vented to the outside if the total capacity of the supply system is in excess of 2000 cu ft (57 m^3) of gas. Pressure relief valves shall be of brass or bronze and especially designed for the gas service involved.

(a) The pressure relief valve downstream of the line pressure regulator in nitrogen systems, used to provide power for gas-driven medical tools, instruments, or other systems, that vary from the normal 50-55 psig (345-380 kPa gauge) line pressure (for example, systems supplying medical gases to hyperbaric chambers), shall be set at 50 percent above line pressure or 200 psig (1.4 MPa gauge), whichever is lower.

4-3.1.8.6 Supply systems complying with 4-3.1.6 or 4-3.1.7 (*see Figures 4-3.1.6 or 4-3.1.7*) shall have a check valve in the primary supply main, upstream of the point of intersection with the secondary or reserve supply main.

4-3.1.9 Medical Air Compressor Supply Systems. (*See Figure 4-3.1.9.*)

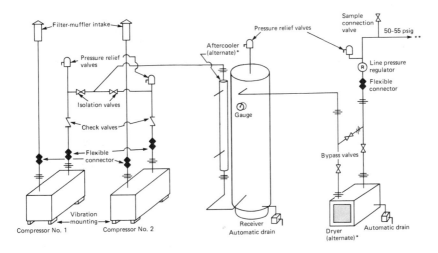

For SI Units: 1 psig = 6.895 kPa gauge.
See paragraph 4-3.1.9.7 for details regarding alternate aftercooler and/or dryer.
**Piping system continued on Figure 4-3.1.10.1.

Figure 4-3.1.9 Typical Duplex Medical Air Compressor System (Schematic).

4-3.1.9.1* The medical air compressor shall be an oil-free air compressor as defined in Chapter 2. The medical air compressor shall take its source from the outside atmosphere and shall not add contaminants in the form of particulate matter, odor, or other gases. It shall be connected only to the medical air piping distribution system and shall not be used for any other purpose.

Maintenance programs in accordance with the manufacturer's recommendations shall be established for the medical air compressor supply system as connected in each individual installation.

A-4-3.1.9.1 The second sentence of 4-3.1.9.1 applies to both the distribution of the air in the piping system and to the use of a compressor as a source.

It is the intent that the medical air piping distribution system support only the intended need for breathable air for such items as IPPB and long-term respiratory assistance needs, anesthesia machines, etc. The system is not intended to be used to provide engineering, maintenance, and equipment needs for general hospital support use. It is the intent that the life safety nature of the medical air be protected by a system dedicated solely for its specific use. The medical air distribution system could also supply air-driven instruments that exhaust into the pharynx. This might be a dental or other surgical device.

As a compressed air supply source, a medical air compressor should not be used to supply air for other purposes because such use could increase service interruptions, reduce service life, and introduce additional opportunities for contamination.

> See Commentary in Chapter 2 under term "Medical Compressed Air" for a discussion on oil-free air compressors.
>
> Connection of the medical air compressors to a laboratory, door opener, or any other nonpatient application can result in adverse consequences with respect to patient care and firesafety.

4-3.1.9.2 Except as provided in 4-3.1.9.2(a), the intake to medical air compressors shall be located outdoors above roof level a minimum distance of 10 ft (3 m) from any door, window, other intake, or opening in the building, and a minimum distance of 20 ft (6 m) above the ground. Intakes shall be turned down and screened. (*See Appendix C-4.2.6.*)

(a) If a source is available that is equal to or better than outside air (air already filtered for use in operating room ventilating systems, for example) it may be used for the medical air compressors.

> It is advisable to conduct periodic tests to verify that the alternative intake is equal to or better than the ambient source, and that it remains that way. Conditions can change, causing the source of air to become unacceptable.

(b) The compressor air intake shall be located where no contamination from engine exhausts, fuel storage vents, vacuum system discharges, particulate matter, or odor of any type is anticipated.

4-3.1.9.3 Two or more air compressors shall be used with provisions for operation alternately or simultaneously dependent on demand. When two compressors are used, each unit shall be capable of maintaining the supply of air to the system at peak calculated demand. When more than two compressors are provided, the peak calculated demand shall be met with the largest compressor out of service. An automatic means shall prevent backflow through off-cycle units.

4-3.1.9.4 Each compressor system shall be provided with disconnect switches, motor starting devices with overload protection, automatic alternation of the units dividing usage evenly, and an automatic means to activate the additional units should the in-service unit be incapable of maintaining adequate pressure.

(a) Manual alternation of larger units is permissible if the system is provided with an automatic means to activate the additional units should the in-service unit be incapable of maintaining adequate pressure.

4-3.1.9.5 The power source for medical air compressors shall be the equipment system of the essential electrical system as described in Chapter 3, "Electrical Systems."

4-3.1.9.6* The receiver shall be equipped with a safety valve, automatic drain, and pressure gauge and shall have the capacity to ensure practical on-off operation. The receiver shall comply with Section VIII ("Unfired Pressure Vessels") of the ASME *Boiler and Pressure Vessel Code*.

A-4-3.1.9.6 A high-water-level alarm sensor connected to the master alarm should be provided to minimize excessive accumulation of water in the receiver tank, which would adversely affect the ability to provide air of the proper quality. Formation of condensed water vapor is the natural result of the air compressor cycle. Failure of certain types of compressors will result in large quantities of water being injected directly and rapidly into the receiver and, if not controlled, ultimately into the air-treatment system and distribution piping system. The high-water-level sensor should disrupt the supply of water being fed to a liquid-ring air compressor and stop the compressor.

• Receiver tanks should be provided with a liquid level switch connected to an alarm to alert responsible persons should a "flooding" of the receiver tank occur. This is particularly important when liquid ring compressors are used.
• Air-treatment systems do what their name implies. They are composed of air compressors, receiver(s), and any additional arrangements of dryers and filtration equipment required to deliver the desired quality of medical air. They also include controls, sensors, and alarms to ensure a continued supply of air of the desired quality. Air-treatment systems are not required and are included in the appendix for guidance only.

4-3.1.9.7* Compressor systems for medical air shall be equipped with intake filter-mufflers of the dry type, aftercooler and/or air dryers, and downstream pressure regulators to ensure the delivery of medical compressed air (*see definition of medical compressed air in Section 2-2*). Appropriate monitoring sensors shall be provided.

To assure optimum operation and protection of the air dryers, they should be located between the receiver tank and the line pressure regulating controls. It is also advisable that items such as dryers, filters, and line pressure controls be redundant to allow maintenance without necessitating shut down of the system.

Medical air compressors should operate within a range of 80-100 psig in order to allow proper operating of the air dryers. Compressors that operate in a range of 45 to 65 psig without the use of line pressure regulators should be considered unacceptable.

A-4-3.1.9.7 The utilization of an air-treatment system is the joint responsibility of the system designer, hospital clinical and engineering staffs, and the authority having jurisdiction. Different types of compressors have characteristics that affect the selection of the type of air-treatment system. Some air-treatment systems impose an additional load upon the compressors which must be accounted for in the sizing of the system (usable capacity). The compressor duty cycle must be chosen in accordance with the manufacturer's recommendation.

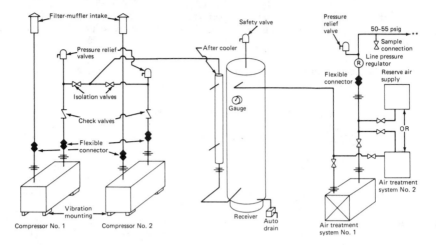

For SI Units: 50 psig = 344 kPa gauge; 55 psig = 377 kPa gauge.
*Note: See paragraph 4-3.1.9.7 for details regarding alternate aftercooler and paragraph A-4-3.1.9.8 for details regarding air treatment system.
**Piping system continued on Figure 4-3.1.10.1.

Figure A-4-3.1.9.7 Typical Duplex Medical Air Compressor System (Schematic).

The presence of high humidity or saturated air from any type of compressor system contributes to degradation of the performance of connected patient equipment and results in additional maintenance.

Nonlubricated reciprocating compressors use Teflon piston rings. Friction can cause localized hot spots where temperatures above 450°F can be encountered. Above these temperatures some of the Teflon can outgas and possibly decompose and produce harmful gases.

Oil- or grease-lubricated reciprocating compressors will add contaminants (liquid and/or vapor) and possibly degradation products, such as carbon monoxide, if temperatures are high enough. Some synthetic oils may have a lower vapor pressure than mineral oils. Upon degradation these synthetic oils may be corrosive in the presence of air and moisture.

4-3.1.9.8* The monitoring of air quality downstream of the dryers and upstream of the piping system, and the monitoring system response when air quality cannot be maintained, shall be in accordance with Table 4-3.1.9.8.

Exception: Existing piping systems, provided such piping systems do not constitute a distinct hazard to life.

Table 4-3.1.9.8 Analytical Tests.

	Dew Point	
Type of Compressor	(1)	(2)
Liquid ring	C	R
Reciprocating:		
Nonlubricated Teflon Ring	C	R
Rotary Vane	C	R

(1) = Frequency
(2) = Alarm
C = Continuous line monitoring
R = Required

While 4-3.1.9.8 calls for monitoring of the dew point of medical compressed air, the subcommittee responsible for this material could not reach a consensus on the minimum temperature of measurement. As a result, only a recommendation is included in the document. (*See Table A-2-2 in Appendix A-2-2 under term "Medical Compressed Air."*)

A-4-3.1.9.8 The facility should have the capability and organization to implement a plan to cope with a complete loss of medical compressed air.

This plan should be part of the overall disaster plan for the facility since a loss of medical air could be disasterous. Loss of any or all portions of centrally piped gas systems, in fact, needs to be considered as a possibility (even with the backup systems required). Emergency measures, until normal system operation is restored, need to be outlined and periodically rehearsed.

Again, it is noted that the use of an air-treatment system in the medical air compressor system is only a recommendation, not a requirement. The subcommittee responsible for medical piped gas systems could not agree on the parameters or their limits for medical compressed air and thus placed material on the subject in the appendix for reader guidance. (*See Table A-2-2 in Appendix A-2-2.*)

4-3.1.9.9 The following tests shall be conducted:

(a) The operation of the system control sensors such as dew point, air temperature, and all other air-quality monitoring sensors and controls shall be checked for proper operation and function before the system is put into service.

(b) The quality of medical compressed air as delivered by the compressor air supply shall be verified upon installation and after 24 hours of operation at a sample point downstream of the pressure regulator and upstream of the piping system as defined in Figure 4-3.1.9.

4-3.1.9.10 The walls, floors, and ceilings of locations for central supply systems of more than 2000 cu ft (57 m³) total capacity (connected and in storage) separating the central supply system location from other occupancy in a building shall have a fire resistance rating of at least one hour. This shall also apply to a common wall or walls of a central supply system location attached to a building having other occupancy.

4-3.1.10 Emergency Oxygen Supply Connection.

4-3.1.10.1 Where the oxygen supply, cryogenic or other, is located outside of the building served, there shall be incorporated in the piping system an inlet for connecting a temporary auxiliary source of supply for emergency or maintenance situations. The inlet shall be located on the exterior of the building served and shall be physically protected to prevent tampering and unauthorized access. It shall be labeled "Emergency Low Pressure Gaseous Oxygen Inlet." This connection shall be installed downstream of the shutoff valve on the main supply line [*see 4-4.1.2.2(b)*] and be suitably controlled with the necessary valves to allow emergency supply of oxygen and isolation of the pipeline to the normal source of supply. It shall have one check valve in the main line between the main line shutoff valve and the tee'd connection and one check valve between the tee'd connection and the emergency supply shutoff valve. (*See Figure 4-3.1.10.1.*)

Table A-4-3.1.9.8 Recommended Analytical Tests.

Type of Compressor	Gaseous Hydrocarbons			Liquid Hydrocarbons			CO			CO_2	Particulate
	(1)	(2)	(3)	(1)	(2)	(3)	(1)	(2)	(3)	(1)	(1)
Liquid ring	Q	NR	NR	A	NR	NR	Q	NR	NR	Q	Q
Reciprocating:											
Nonlubricated											
Teflon Ring	Q	NR	NR	A	NR	NR	C	R	R	Q	Q
Rotary Vane	C	R	R	Q	NR	NR	C	R	R	Q	Q

(1) = Frequency　　　　　　　　C = Continuous Line Monitoring
(2) = Alarm　　　　　　　　　　R = Required
(3) = Reserve Actuated　　　　　Q = Quarterly
　　　　　　　　　　　　　　　NR = Not Required
　　　　　　　　　　　　　　　A = Annually

NOTE 1: Alarm Required: When the air quality is degraded the sensor monitor should activate a master alarm signal.

NOTE 2: Reserve Activated: When the air quality parameters cannot be maintained by any system of primary and secondary components (if any), the alarm should automatically shut down the compressor supply system for medical compressed air, and should activate a reserve supply.

NOTE 3: Reserve supply should be a 24-hour supply from cylinder, bulk containers, reconstituted from oxygen USP and nitrogen NF, or a separate dedicated compressor/air-treatment system that is not part of the normal medical compressed air system.

NOTE 4: The air-treatment system should include a backup which may be a second installed air treatment system or reserve of a one-day supply of medical compressed air.

(a) Monitoring devices to detect degradation of air quality should activate the master alarm signal and the secondary system, which should assure air supply and quality.

(b) The type of air compressor (piston, rotary, liquid ring, etc.) and local atmospheric conditions will govern the design of an air-treatment and monitoring system.

NOTE 5: The reserve supply of medical compressed air may be:

(a) A cylinder system similar to that described in 4-3.1.5 using one bank.

(b) A second medical compressed air system of adequate capacity.

(c) A supply of medical air approved by the authority having jurisdiction.

(a) The emergency-oxygen-supply-connection piping assembly shall be provided with a pressure relief valve of adequate size to protect the downstream piping system and relatedequipment from exposure to pressures in excess of 50 percent higher than normal pipeline pressure.

NOTE 1: See 4-4.1.3.4 and 4-4.1.3.2.

NOTE 2: See 4-4.1.1.2, 4-4.1.1.3, 4-4.1.1.4(b), and 4-4.1.2.2(d).

NOTE 3: See 4-4.1.1.2.

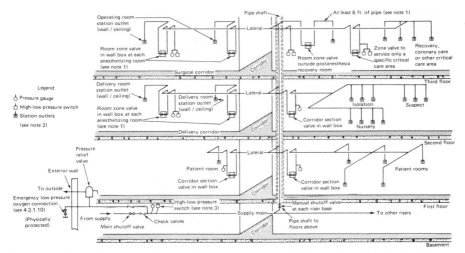

Figure 4-3.1.10.1   Location of Valves, Pressure Switches, and Piping for Medical Gas Systems (Schematic).

4-3.2   Patient Gas Supply — Type II.

• For an explanation of term "Type II," see commentary under Section 4-3.1, "Patient Gas Supply – Type I."

• Type II patient piped gas systems was material from Chapter 6 of NFPA 56F, *Standard for Nonflammable Medical Gas Systems*, that was incorporated into this 1987 edition of NFPA 99. This material was also completely revised during the processing of this edition. The definition of "single treatment facility" was revised in conjunction with clarifications to the scope for Type II systems because of problems reported to the Subcommittee responsible for this material (i.e., when were Type II systems permitted, and when were Type I systems required). (*See Section 4-6.2.4.1 for this scope*.) Application is now based only on storage volume and not the number of use points.

For historical reference, Type II patient piped gas systems were those outlined in Chapter 6 of NFPA 56F, *Standard for Nonflammable Medical Gas Systems*. Where Type II systems are permitted is indicated in Chapters 12 through 18 (Sections 12-3.4.1, 13-3.4.1, 14-3.4.1, etc.)

• One significant change for Type II systems is a new requirement for an automatic alarmed change-over system for both oxygen and nitrous oxide for dual and single treatment facilities with remote cylinder installations. (See Section 4-4.2, particularly 4-4.2.7 and 4-4.2.8). This requirement was added in the interest of clinical (patient) safety.

4-3.2.1   Cylinders shall comply with 4-3.1.1.1.   Cylinders in service shall be adequately secured. Cylinders in storage shall be secured or located to prevent falling or being knocked over.

4-3.2.2   Supply system and storage locations shall comply with 4-3.1.2.1(k); 4-3.1.2.1(l) [except 4-3.1.2.1(l)(3)]; 4-3.1.2.2 [except 4-3.1.2.2(d)]; and 4-3.1.2.3.

4-3.2.2.1*   Enclosures for supply systems shall be provided with doors or gates. If the enclosure is outside and/or remote from the single treatment facility, it shall be kept locked. If the storage area is within the single treatment facility (i.e., is not remote), it may be unlocked.

A-4-3.2.2.1 When the storage/supply enclosure is remote from the single treatment facility, it should be locked for security reasons to prevent tampering. Access should be only via authorized staff or fire department. When the enclosure is within the single treatment facility, it is left to the discretion of the single treatment facility management as to whether greater benefit is achieved by immediate access or by security. An enclosure with direct access from a public hallway should be locked. (*See Figure A-4-3.2.2.1.*)

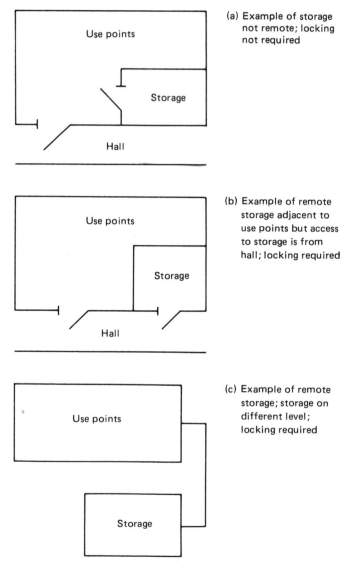

(a) Example of storage not remote; locking not required

(b) Example of remote storage adjacent to use points but access to storage is from hall; locking required

(c) Example of remote storage; storage on different level; locking required

Figure A-4-3.2.2.1

4-3.3 Laboratory Gas Supply.

4-3.3.1 Cylinder and Container Management. Requirements shall be in accordance with 4-3.1.1.

4-3.3.2 Storage Requirements (Location, Construction, Arrangement; Any Quantity; Flammable and Nonflammable Gases).

4-3.3.2.1 Storage shall be in cylinders complying with 4-3.1.1.1.

4-3.3.2.2 The capacities of individual cylinders, in pounds or cubic feet free gas at one atmosphere, shall not exceed:

(a) LP-Gases — 5 lb (2.27 kg)

(b) Acetylene — 350 cu ft (9.9 cu m)

(c) Other flammable gases — 356 cu ft (10 cu m) or water volume of 0.6 cu ft (0.017 cu m).

The capacities listed are the result of considerable discussion by the former Committee on Laboratories and is based on public input.

Rather than designate cylinder size by letter, the capacity of individual cylinders has been set. Capacities are based on safety, current practice and need, and the fact that cylinder sizes and letter designations have varied over the years and between suppliers of gases in cylinders.

4-3.3.2.3 Flammable gas cylinder storage for a laboratory, if inside any health care facility, shall be (except as permitted in 4-4.3.1) in a separate room or enclosure reserved exclusively for that purpose, having a fire-resistance classification of at least two hours, and ventilated in accordance with Section 4-3.1.2.4. Cylinders in storage shall be kept in racks or secured in position.

This section applies to the storage of individual flammable gas cylinders. Requirements for a storage area used to connect cylinders for a manifold system are listed in 4-4.3.1.

The 2-hour rating for this section has been used to be consistent with Federal regulations and NFPA *101*, *Life Safety Code*.

With regard to ventilation, the following recommendations should be observed: there should be eight air changes per hour; air should be ceiling supplied and floor exhausted (with physical separation between each as great as possible); and exhaust should be discharged to the exterior. While a gravity or mechanical ventilation system is allowed, a mechanical one will require additional electrical safety and emergency power requirements. (Refer to Chapter 3 for emergency power requirements.)

Under no condition are flammable and oxidizing gases to be stored or utilized in a common room in any type of (health care) facility.

4-3.3.2.4 Rooms or enclosures for storage of cylinders shall be well ventilated. Electrical equipment in flammable-gas storage areas shall comply with NFPA 70, *National Electrical Code*, for Class I, Division 2 locations.

Figure 15   Labeling on central storage room used for flammable gases and materials.

4-3.3.2.5   Enclosures for storage of nonflammable gases shall have at least one-hour fire-resistive construction, in accordance with 4-3.1.2.1.

This section was reworded in 1984 to address the subject of storage of nonflammable gas cylinders and to be consistent with then NFPA 56F, *Standard for Nonflammable Medical Gas Systems* (now essentially 4-3 to 4-6 in the 1987 edition of NFPA 99). In addition, NFPA 56F prohibited the storage of flammable and nonflammable gases in the same enclosure; a separation of at least 1-hour fire rating is required between flammable and nonflammable gases.

4-3.4 Other Gases.

NOTE: Refer to NFPA 54, *National Fuel Gas Code.*

4-4 Gas System Distribution.

4-4.1 Patient Gas Distribution — Type I (Manifold, Piping, Valving/Controls, Outlets/Terminals, Alarms).

4-4.1.1 Warning Systems.

4-4.1.1.1 General.   *(See Appendix C-4.2.)*

(a) Alarm signals and pressure gauges shall be located to assure continuous responsible surveillance. Each signal device and gauge shall be appropriately labeled.

(b) A master alarm system shall be provided to monitor the operation and condition of the source of supply, the reserve (if any), and the pressure in the main line of the medical gas system. (*See Appendixes C-4.1 and C-4.2.*)

(c) An area alarm system shall be provided in anesthetizing and other critical care locations to monitor the pressure in the local supply line.

(d) The power source for warning systems shall be the life safety branch of the emergency system as described in Chapter 3, "Electrical Sytems."

4-4.1.1.2 Master Alarm Systems.

(a) Two master alarm signal panels shall be located in separate warning locations to assure continuous responsible observation. Audible and noncancellable visual signals shall be installed in the office or principal working area of the individual responsible for the maintenance of the medical gas system and, to assure continuous surveillance, at the telephone switchboard, the security office, or at another suitable location. Separate visual signals, as required, shall be provided for each of the conditions described in 4-4.1.1.2(b) through (f).

> The basic intent of this section is coverage 100 percent of the time with personnel who, upon hearing the alarm, know what to do. It was assumed by the Committee previously responsible for this material that an engineering department would be one of these locations. This was and is a reasonable assumption. If the 100 percent coverage with engineering personnel cannot be met, an alternative location that meets this intent needs to be found.

(b) A signal shall be provided for all medical gas systems when the piping system is supplied by a manifold or an alternating-type bulk system that has as part of its normal operation a changeover from one portion of the operating supply to another portion. An audible and noncancellable visual signal shall indicate when, or just before, this changeover occurs. (*See Appendixes C-4.1 and C-4.2.*)

(c) When a manifold or bulk supply consists of one or more units that continuously supply the piping system while another unit remains as the reserve supply and operates only in case of emergency, audible and noncancellable visual signals shall indicate when, or just before, the reserve supply goes into operation. (*See Appendixes C-4.1 and C-4.2.*)

(d)* When check valves are not provided for each cylinder lead of the reserve supply for a manifold or bulk supply system, an audible and noncancellable visual signal shall indicate when the reserve supply is reduced to one average day's supply. If check valves are provided in each cylinder lead this signal shall not be used. (*See Appendixes C-4.1 and C-4.2.*)

A-4-4.1.1.2(d) This signal will be present only if the reserve supply consists of high-pressure cylinders that do not have check valves in the cylinder leads or is provided by a second bulk liquid storage unit.

(e) All medical gas piping systems shall be provided with audible and noncancellable visual signals to indicate if the pressure in the main line increases or decreases from the normal operating pressure. The actuating switch for these warning signals shall be installed in the main line immediately downstream (on the piping distribution side) of the main-line shutoff valve. (*See Appendix C-4.1.*)

(f) All of the individual alarms as required in 4-3.1.9.8 shall be provided with audible and manually resettable visual signals in accordance with 4-4.1.1.2(a). A manually resettable alarm for each monitored parameter (*see Table 4-3.1.9.8*) shall be provided at the air dryer site.

4-4.1.1.3 Area Alarm Systems.

(a) Warning signals shall be provided for all medical gas piping systems supplying anesthetizing locations and other vital life support and critical care areas such as postanesthesia recovery, intensive care units, coronary care units, etc., to indicate if the pressure in the piping system increases or decreases from the normal operating pressure. (*See Appendix C-4.1.*)

(b) The audible and noncancellable visual signal shall be activated by an actuating switch installed in the individual line supplying each such specific area.

(c)* The actuating switch for anesthetizing locations shall be in the specific line supplying the operating or delivery room suites, with the individual room shutoff valve being the only one between the actuating switch and the room outlets.

A-4-4.1.1.3(c) This signal is intended to provide immediate warning for loss of, or increase in, system pressure for all anesthetizing locations supplied from a single branch line — not for each individual operating or delivery room.

(d)* The area alarm actuating switch for each vital life support and critical care unit shall be in the specific line serving that area. No shutoff valve shall be installed between the actuating switch and the outlets.

A-4-4.1.1.3(d) This signal is intended to provide immediate warning for loss of, or increase in, system pressure for each individual vital life support and critical care area.

(e) The appropriately labeled warning signal panel for area alarms shall be installed at the nurses' station or other suitable location near the point of use that will provide responsible surveillance.

An area alarm panel for a piped medical gas system is not required at all nurses' stations. Only those areas listed in Section 4-4.1.1.3(a) require one since the alarm panel needs to be in a constantly staffed area so alarm is heard. The areas listed in Section 4-4.1.1.3(a) meet this criteria.

When multiple alarms are installed at a common nurse's station and the alarms monitor separate areas controlled by distinct zone valves, the alarms should be labeled for the specific areas they control.

4-4.1.1.4 Pressure Gauges.

(a) A pressure gauge shall be installed in the main line adjacent to the actuating switch required in 4-4.1.1.2(e). It shall be appropriately labeled and be readily visible from a standing position. (*See Appendix C-4.2.*)

(b) An appropriately identified pressure gauge, connected to the line being monitored, shall be installed at each area alarm panel location. (*See Appendix C-4.2.*)

Figure 16 Area piped gas system alarms (in this example, for oxygen and air) along with area piped vacuum alarm. (Note: shutoff valves for area are just below alarms.)

If the alarm panel incorporates gauges for each gas, gauges may not be necessary at zone valves.

4-4.1.2 Piping Systems (General).

4-4.1.2.1 Piping.

(a)* Piping shall be seamless Type K or L (ASTM B88) copper tubing, seamless ACR (ASTM B280) copper tubing, or standard weight (Schedule 40) brass pipe. Piping for all nonflammable medical gas systems shall be cleaned in accordance with 4-4.1.4.1 prior to installation. Pipe sizes shall be in conformity with good engineering practice for proper delivery of maximum volumes specified. Gas piping shall not be supported by other piping but shall be supported with pipe hooks, metal pipe straps, bands, or hangars suitable for the size of pipe, and of proper strength and quality at proper intervals, so that piping cannot be moved accidentally from the installed position as follows:

⅜-in. pipe or tubing	6 ft (2 m)
½-in. pipe or tubing	6 ft (2 m)
¾-in. or 1-in. pipe or tubing	8 ft (2.4 m)
¼-in. or larger (horizontal)	10 ft (3 m)
¼-in. or larger (vertical)	every floor level.

A-4-4.1.2.1(a)   The use of ASTM B280 copper tubing cleaned only for air conditioning and refrigeration use (ACR) may not meet the requirements of 4-4.1.4.1(a) for tubing especially prepared for medical gas use. Such tubing may require additional cleaning in accordance with 4-4.1.4.1.

> The types of piping allowed for nonflammable medical gas systems were expanded during the revision of NFPA 56F-1983 (which has become part of NFPA 99). But, while no structural problems have been reported, more qualifications on cleaning were considered necessary to preclude problems after installation.

(b)   Except as provided in 4-4.1.2.1(c) and (d), fittings used for connecting copper tubing shall be of copper, brass, or bronze suitable for making brazed connections. Brass pipe shall be assembled with screw-type brass fittings or with bronze or copper brazing-type fittings. (*See also 4-4.1.4.2.*)

(c)   Listed or approved metallic gas tubing fittings which, when made up, will provide a permanent joint exhibiting the mechanical, thermal, and sealing integrity of a brazed joint complying with 4-4.1.4.2, may be used anywhere in gas distribution lines.

> The change to allow metallic tube fittings is the same allowance made for vacuum system fittings. See Commentary under 4-8.1.1.2(f) for description of one type of fitting that meets this new criteria.

(d)   Listed or approved gas tubing fittings not complying with 4-4.1.2.1(c), e.g., of the flare or compression type, may be used on gas distribution lines when pipe sizes are ½-in. nominal or less if the fitting is so installed as to be visible in the room. Such fittings may also be used in connecting copper tubing of ¾-in. nominal or less to shutoff valves described in 4-4.1.2.2, providing the fittings are readily accessible.

(e)   Buried piping shall be adequately protected against frost, corrosion, and physical damage. Ducts or casings shall be used wherever buried piping traverses a roadway, driveway, parking lot, or other area subject to surface loads. Medical gas piping may be placed in the same tunnel, trench, or duct with fuel gas piping, electrical lines, or steam lines, if separated, provided that there is good natural or forced ventilation. Medical gas piping shall not be placed in a tunnel, trench, or duct where exposed to contact with oil.

(f)   Medical gas piping installed in combustible partitions shall be protected against physical damage by installation within pipe or conduit. Openings for piping installed in concealed spaces shall be fire-stopped with construction having a fire resistance equal to or greater than the original construction. Medical gas risers may be installed in pipe shafts if suitable protection against physical damage, effects of excessive heat, corrosion, or contact with oil is provided. Medical gas risers shall not be located in elevator shafts.

(g) Where installation of medical gas piping in kitchens, laundries, or other areas of special hazard is unavoidable, the piping shall be protected by an enclosure that will prevent the liberation of medical gas within the room should leaks occur in the piping system installed in the enclosure.

(h) Piping exposed to physical damage, such as might be sustained from the movement of portable equipment such as carts, stretchers, and trucks, in corridors and other locations shall be provided with suitable protection.

(i) Flexible connectors, metallic or nonmetallic, used where required for flexibility, shall have minimized hose lengths. They shall not penetrate walls, floors, ceilings, or partitions.

Prior to this 1987 edition of NFPA 99, former NFPA 56F (now incorporated into NFPA 99) did not cover these "extension cables." However, because they are part of the piping system (i.e., they are *not* removed when *not* in use, and have gas inside them when not in use — just like regular piping), the Subcommittee on Nonflammable Medical Piped Gas Systems considered it time to include minimum performance criteria for these flexible hoses since the same hazards associated with rigid metal pipes exist in these extension cables.
For burst strength criteria, see Section 4-5.1.3.4(d).

4-4.1.2.2 Shutoff Valves. *(See Appendix C-4.2.)*

(a) Shutoff valves accessible to other than authorized personnel shall be installed in valve boxes with frangible or removable windows large enough to permit manual operation of valves.

(b) The main supply line shall be provided with a shutoff valve so located as to be accessible in an emergency.

(c) Each riser supplied from the main line shall be provided with a shutoff valve adjacent to the riser connection.

(d) Station outlets shall not be supplied directly from a riser unless a manual shutoff valve located in the same story is installed between the riser and the outlet with a corridor wall intervening between the valve and the outlets *(see Figure 4-3.1.10.1)*. This valve shall be readily operable from a standing position in the corridor on the same floor it serves. Each lateral branch line serving patient rooms shall be provided with a shutoff valve that controls the flow of medical gas to the patient rooms. Branch line shutoff valves shall be so arranged that shutting off the supply of medical gas to one branch will not affect the supply of medical gas to the rest of the system. A pressure gauge shall be provided downstream of each lateral branch line shutoff valve.

It is a common, but inappropriate practice during both new construction and renovation of medical gas systems to design systems that will allow one of the following conditions to exist:
1. Tie-ins made downstream from an existing zone valve and a second set of zone valves installed. This creates a condition whereby zone valves are installed in series.
2. Zone valves installed in such a manner that the piping for these valves terminate in a common room with outlets on adjacent walls.

Figure 17   Shut-off valves in a corridor outside an operating room.

3. Zone valves and piping installed in such a manner that they traverse specific fire zones.

All of the above conditions compromise both firesafety and patient care since closure of a single set of valves would create undesirable effects.

(e) In-line shutoff valves intended for use to isolate existing systems for piping maintenance or to extend to new piping systems are permitted. These valves shall be located in a secure area or locked open and labeled in accordance with 4-6.4.1.2.

4-4.1.2.3 Surface-Mounted Medical Gas Rail Systems.

This new section was added to reflect new technology — that of a surface-mounted extension of the traditional piped system. It is one way of adding piped gas service in patient care areas at much less cost than the traditional method. It does have limitations and restrictions, as noted below and in the Appendix A material included under the term "Surface-Mounted Medical Gas Rail System" in Chapter 2.

(a) Listed or approved surface-mounted medical gas rail systems may be installed where multiple use of medical gases and vacuum at a single patient location is required or anticipated. The surface-mounted medical gas rail system shall be made of material as identified in Subsection 4-4.1.2.1(a) or a material exhibiting the mechanical, thermal, and sealing integrity of a brazed joint complying with 4-4.1.4.2. Individual gas channel sizes shall be in conformity with good engineering practice for proper delivery of maximum volumes specified. The ends of the surface-mounted medical gas rails shall not be used for station outlets.

It should be noted that there is no reference to a specific type of metal that can be used. Material that is specified in 4-4.1.2.1(a) *or* material that is equivalent in mechanical, thermal, and sealing integrity of a brazed joint can be used. (Note: This equivalency must be determined under actual operating conditions since the melting point of some materials, e.g., aluminum, is below 1000°F when they contain oxygen.) This was deliberate action by the Medical-Gas Application Panel and the Technical Committee on Industrial and Medical Gases which originally proposed this section as a Tentative Interim Amendment to NFPA 56F-1983. The criteria was made as performance oriented as possible to allow suppliers freedom of design. Compliance will thus have to be determined by a testing laboratory acceptable to the authority having jurisdiction.

(b) Station outlet locations for future expansion that are capped shall not be readily removed via screwdriver, pliers, wrench, etc., but shall require a special tool to remove them when expansion is undertaken.

(c) Openings in surface-mounted medical gas rail systems for station outlet assemblies or station outlet plug caps shall be gas specific.

(d) All fittings used for internal and external connection of surface-mounted medical gas rail systems shall be made especially for brazed connection, or shall be assembled with screw thread-type brass fittings with bronze or copper brazing-type fittings.

(e)* Connections of surface-mounted medical gas rail systems to piping systems of dissimilar metals shall require plating of the connecting components to prevent interaction between dissimilar metals.

A-4-4.1.2.3(e) Typical plating would be nickel plating over copper or brass per Federal Specification QQ-N290, Class I Type 7.

(f) The installation of the surface-mounted medical gas rail system shall be tested per 4-4.1.4.

4-4.1.2.4 Station Outlets. (*See Appendix C-4.2.*)

The use of station outlets for other than medical purposes is not condoned, i.e., air station outlets designed for patient use should not be used for equipment blowdown, cleaning, etc. Since these applications are nonmedical, the gas supply should originate from a source other than the medical air source.

(a)* Each station outlet for medical gases, whether threaded or noninterchangeable quick-coupler, shall be gas specific, and shall consist of a primary and a secondary valve (or assembly). The secondary valve (or unit) shall close automatically to stop the flow of medical gas when the primary valve (or unit) is removed. Each outlet shall be legibly identified with the name or chemical symbol of the gas contained. Where chemical symbols are used, they shall be in accordance with Compressed Gas Association Pamphlet P-2, *Characteristics and Safe Handling of Medical Gases*. Where supplementary color identification is used, it shall be in accordance with CGA Pamphlet C-9, *Standard Color-Marking of Compressed Gas Cylinders Intended for Medical Use in the United States*.

A-4-4.1.2.4(a) The purpose of the automatic secondary check valve is to shut off the flow of gas when the primary valve is removed for servicing.

(b) Threaded outlets shall be noninterchangeable connections complying with CGA Pamphlet V-5, *Diameter-Index Safety System — Non-Interchangeable Low Pressure Connections for Medical Gas Applications.*

(c) Each station outlet, including those mounted in columns, hose reels, ceiling tracks, or other special installations, shall be designed so that parts or components that are required to be gas specific for compliance with 4-4.1.2.4(a) cannot be interchanged between station outlets for different gases.

(1) The use of common parts such as springs, O-rings, fasteners, seals, and shutoff poppets is permissible.

(d) Station outlets in patient rooms shall be located at an appropriate height above the floor to prevent physical damage to equipment attached to the outlet. They may be recessed or otherwise protected from damage.

(e) When multiple wall outlets are installed, including those for vacuum, there must be sufficient spacing between outlets to permit the simultaneous use of adjacent outlets with any of the various types of therapy equipment that may be required.

(f) Pressure gauges and manometers for medical gas piping systems shall be cleaned and degreased.

4-4.1.3 Piping Systems — Anesthetizing Locations (Additonal Requirements).

4-4.1.3.1 Anesthetizing locations and other vital life support and critical areas, such as postanesthesia recovery, intensive care units, and coronary care units, shall be supplied directly from the riser without intervening valves except as provided in 4-4.1.3.2 or 4-4.1.3.4.

One way to meet (1) the prohibition of a shutoff valve between the zone valve and riser valve for anesthetizing location (4-4.1.3.1), and (2) the allowance of an "end valve" for extension of a piped gas system {4-4.1.2.2(e)} is by using a "chain-and-lock" feature for the end-valve. After an extension is made, this valve is locked open, with keys restricted to authorized personnel. In essence, the valve is not considered to be there.

4-4.1.3.2 A shutoff valve shall be located immediately outside each vital life support or critical care area in each medical gas line and located so as to be readily accessible in an emergency. Valves shall be protected and marked in accordance with 4-6.4.1.4.

All gas-delivery columns, hose reels, ceiling tracks, control panels, pendants, booms, alarm panels, or other special installations shall be located downstream of this valve.

The change here and in 4-4.1.3.1 to add "other life support and critical care areas" completes an action taken in 1977 for former Figure 5 in NFPA 56F-1977 (now Figure 4-3.1.10.1 in NFPA 99) but not reflected in text. It was the intent of the former Medical Gas Application Panel (now Subcommittee on Nonflammable Medical Piped Gas Systems) to provide these areas with as much protection as anesthetizing locations in terms of no inadvertant shutoff of piped gases. This is achieved by having a valve serve just one area and by having no other valves between this valve and the riser.

New paragraph two is a reminder of where this valve is to be located.

"Birthing centers" or "birthing rooms" present some difficulty in terms of whether they meet the criteria of "vital life support" or "critical" areas. Generally, birthing centers are used when no problems are evident or anticipated. When or if something unusual develops (e.g., the onset of fetal distress), the patient is immediately transferred to a nearby delivery room equipped to handle such complications. Under this arrangement, the group of birthing rooms would not be considered in the same category as critical care areas, etc., and would not have to have individual gas shutoff valves to each room. However, this is not always the case (e.g., a birthing room might be equipped to handle complications and thus be capable of providing life-support measures). Therefore it is necessary to review the level of care that will be provided in each and every birthing room in a facility.

4-4.1.3.3 The main supply line shall be provided with a shutoff valve so located as to be accessible in an emergency. This valve shall be identified.

4-4.1.3.4 A shutoff valve shall be located outside each anesthetizing location in each medical gas line, so located as to be readily accessible at all times for use in an emergency. These valves shall be so arranged that shutting off the supply of gas to any one operating room or anesthetizing location will not affect the others. Valves shall be of an approved type, mounted on a pedestal or otherwise properly safeguarded against physical damage, and marked in accordance with 4-6.4.1.4.

Location of a shutoff valve outside each anesthetizing location is considered by several subcommittees sufficient for emergency and maintenance purposes. Reasons given included:

(1) the outside location provided adequate control;

(2) in an emergency, the Subcommittee wanted people to exit; and

(3) staff outside an operating room, in addition to those inside, would be able to shut off gas supplies.

"Outside" is intended to mean near the main door that leads to a central core, such as where nursing stations are located. It does not mean a rear door through which equipment might be brought, nor a side door where a common scrub room might be located.

If there is more than one operating room in the anesthetizing location, each room should have an independent shutoff valve.

Wording does not preclude a facility from installing a shutoff valve inside an operating room, though additional pressure alarms would be necessary.

4-4.1.3.5* Each yoke insert shall be drilled with two holes of a size and in locations specified in the "Pin-Index Safety System," in ANSI B57.1, *Compressed Gas Cylinder Valve Outlet and Inlet Connections* (CGA Pamphlet V-1) (Canadian Standard CSA-B96) for the gas contained in the pipeline to which it is attached.

A-4-4.1.3.5 Pin-Index Safety System. The Pin-Index Safety System consists of a combination of two pins projecting from the yoke assembly of the apparatus and so positioned as to fit into matching holes drilled into the cylinder valves. It is intended to provide against the possibility of error in attaching the flush-type valves, with which gas cylinders and other sources of gas supply are equipped, to gas apparatus having yoke connections.

Inadvertent mixing of gases can create a gas that is very explosive or injurious to the patient, staff, or both.

Fabrication specifications are contained in CGA Pamphlet V-1 (ANSI B57.1), *Compressed Gas Cylinder Valve Outlet and Inlet Connections.* Connection No. 860, shown in Figure A-4-4.1.3.5, illustrates the system. Connections No. 870 (Oxygen, Medical), 880 (Oxygen–Carbon Dioxide Mixture), 890 (Oxygen-Helium Mixture), 900 (Ethylene), 910 (Nitrous Oxide), 920 (Cyclopropane), 930 (Helium), and 940 (Carbon Dioxide) are for specific medical gases and gas mixtures and utilize the basic dimensions of Connection 860.

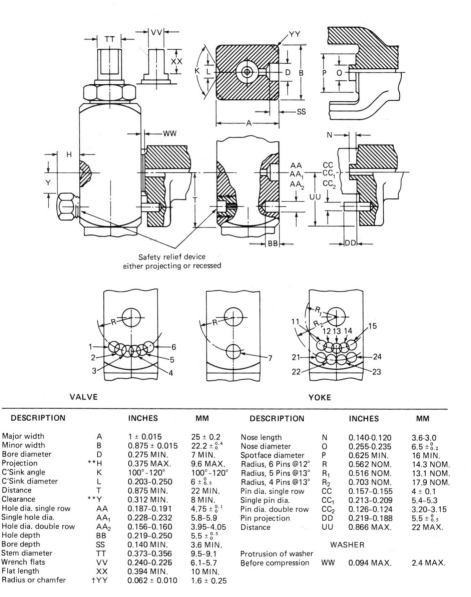

DESCRIPTION		INCHES	MM	DESCRIPTION		INCHES	MM
Major width	A	1 ± 0.015	25 ± 0.2	Nose length	N	0.140-0.120	3.6-3.0
Minor width	B	0.875 ± 0.015	$22.2 \pm_0^{0.4}$	Nose diameter	O	0.255-0.235	$6.5 \pm_{0.2}^{0}$
Bore diameter	D	0.275 MIN.	7 MIN.	Spotface diameter	P	0.625 MIN.	16 MIN.
Projection	**H	0.375 MAX.	9.6 MAX.	Radius, 6 Pins @12°	R	0.562 NOM.	14.3 NOM.
C'Sink angle	K	100°-120°	100°-120°	Radius, 5 Pins @13°	R_1	0.516 NOM.	13.1 NOM.
C'Sink diameter	L	0.203-0.250	$6 \pm_0^{0.5}$	Radius, 4 Pins @13°	R_2	0.703 NOM.	17.9 NOM.
Distance	T	0.875 MIN.	22 MIN.	Pin dia. single row	CC	0.157-0.155	4 ± 0.1
Clearance	**Y	0.312 MIN.	8 MIN.	Single pin dia.	CC_1	0.213-0.209	5.4-5.3
Hole dia. single row	AA	0.187-0.191	$4.75 \pm_0^{0.1}$	Pin dia. double row	CC_2	0.126-0.124	3.20-3.15
Single hole dia.	AA_1	0.228-0.232	5.8-5.9	Pin projection	DD	0.219-0.188	$5.5 \pm_{0.5}^{0}$
Hole dia. double row	AA_2	0.156-0.160	3.95-4.05	Distance	UU	0.866 MAX.	22 MAX.
Hole depth	BB	0.219-0.250	$5.5 \pm_0^{0.5}$				
Bore depth	SS	0.140 MIN.	3.6 MIN.	WASHER			
Stem diameter	TT	0.373-0.356	9.5-9.1	Protrusion of washer			
Wrench flats	VV	0.240-0.225	6.1-5.7	Before compression	WW	0.094 MAX.	2.4 MAX.
Flat length	XX	0.394 MIN.	10 MIN.				
Radius or chamfer	†YY	0.062 ± 0.010	1.6 ± 0.25				

Figure and Notes 1 through 13 reprinted with permission of Compressed Gas Assn., Inc.

Figure A-4-4.1.3.5   Compressed Gas Association Drawing No. 860: Pin-Indexed Yoke Connections for Medical Gases. Basic dimensional drawing for Connection Nos. 870 through 965.*

*Letter symbols [(A, B, C), etc.] and dimensions in millimeters are as shown in ISO Recommendation R407, "Yoke Type Connections for Small Medical Gas Cylinders Used for Anaesthetic and Resuscitation Purposes," December 1964, except for distance T which was increased to accommodate the double row of pins. The American National Standard for Connections 870 through 940 was written in inches and when adopted as ISO R407, the translation of inches to mm was handled by ISO. Little attention was paid to possible discrepancies between the inch and mm dimensions until recently. The metric dimensions are now being reviewed by CGA with a view to recommending changes to make inch and mm dimensions more compatible. It is intended to confer with ISO countries to determine the most suitable manner of presenting dimensions and symbols for international use. In the meantime, it should be understood that the widest possible tolerances shown for each dimension — whether in metric or inches — is considered in compliance with this [CGA] standard.

Notes to Figure A-4-4.1.3.5

1. Each connection (except no. 965) includes two pins in the yoke and two mating holes in the valve, properly indexed for safety.
2. For precise positions of the pins and holes, see the respective connections that follow.
**3. Dimensions H and Y are applicable only if projecting-type safety relief device is used.
4. The rotary movement of the yoke on the valve must be limited to ± 6 degrees prior to pin engagment.
5. Bore D and countersink L must align within 0.020 in. (0.5 mm) T I R of sides and of each other.
6. Pins in yoke must be made of corrosion-resisting material having a minimum tensile strength of 60,000 psi (42 Kg/mm^2).
7. Design must be such that dimension DD cannot be reduced below minimum by force.
8. Face of valve outlet may be grooved and face of yoke washer seating surface may be machined with concentric circles for effective washer seal.
9. A single washer shall be used on the valve outlet or yoke connection to insure a gastight seal. The washer shall be of such thickness that pin engagement of not less than 0.094 in. (³/₃₂ in.) (2.4 mm) is accomplished before washer is compressed.
10. Method of tightening yoke on valve optional except that no pointed object sharper than 100° included angle shall be used as a means to apply tightening pressure at the back of the valve.
11. For non pin-indexed yoke connections, see 2.1.4 of introduction [of CGA document].
†12. Larger chamfer permitted provided face width is ⅝-in. (16 mm) minimum.
13. These dimensions apply to valves manufactured after January 1, 1977. Valves made prior to this date complying with earlier editions of this standard are acceptable for continuing use.

4-4.1.3.6 Each yoke insert or noninterchangeable quick coupler or specifically designed noninterchangeable threaded connection complying with CGA V-5, *Diameter-Index Safety System*, shall be equipped with a backflow check valve designed to prevent flow of gas from the anesthesia apparatus into the pipeline system. Each backflow check valve shall be designed to function properly at pressures up to 190 kg/cm^2 gauge (2700 psig) (18 617 kPa gauge).

4-4.1.3.7 Cylinder valve outlet connections shall conform with ANSI B57.1 (*see 8-3.1.7 and Appendix A-4-4.1.3.5*).

4-4.1.4 Installation and Testing of Piping Systems.

4-4.1.4.1 Before installation, all piping, valves, fittings, and other components for all nonflammable medical gas systems shall be thoroughly cleaned of oil, grease, and other readily oxidizable materials as if for oxygen service. After cleaning, particular care shall be exercised in the storage and handling of such material. Such material shall be temporarily capped or plugged to prevent recontamination before final assembly. Just prior to final assembly, such material shall be examined internally for contamination and shall be recleaned if necessary.

• Before pipes are washed and cleaned, they may be reamed. However, there is no requirement that pipes used for medical gas systems be reamed. Reaming after washing and cleaning would produce copper dust and chips which would, in fact, be very difficult to remove.
• The changes made to the 1983 edition of NFPA 56F (which was also incorporated into the 1987 edition of NFPA 99) still do not restrict manufacturers in the way they may clean pipes. If a manufacturer complies with the requirements of 4-4.1.4.1(a), an inspection of pipes may be all that has to be done. If the manufacturer has not followed requirements, then washing and cleaning according to this section will be necessary at the job site.

(a)* Piping, valves, fittings, and other components may be especially prepared in a facility equipped to clean, rinse, and purge the material in accordance with the requirements of 4-4.1.4.1(a)(1) or may be prepared on the job site in accordance with 4-4.1.4.1(a)(2). *CARBON TETRACHLORIDE SHALL NOT BE EMPLOYED IN ANY CLEANING OPERATION.*

The restriction on carbon tetrachloride is only applicable if cleaning is accomplished at the job site.

(1) Piping, valves, fittings, and other components that have been especially prepared shall have been cleaned in accordance with the provisions of CGA Pamphlet G-4.1, *Cleaning Equipment for Oxygen Service.* Such material shall be delivered capped or plugged and shall be inspected prior to final assembly as required in 4-4.1.4.1. If necessary, recleaning shall be done in accordance with 4-4.1.4.1(a)(2).

• This paragraph was added during the processing of the 1987 edition of NFPA 99 to clarify when *manufacturer-cleaned* piping was acceptable. CGA Pamphlet G-4.1 covers such items as the selection of the type of cleaning process to be used, precleaning, steam or hot water cleaning, caustic cleaning, acid cleaning, solvent washing, vapor degreasing, mechanical cleaning, inspection/quality control procedures, and packaging procedures (to keep cleaned-pipe clean). The CGA document allows the use of cleaning solvents that are prohibited when cleaning is accomplished on the job site because the entire manufacturing process (CGA-4.1) is a very controlled process. In addition, the time lapse from manufacturer-cleaning to use at the job site will allow any residual vapors to evaporate and not cause a problem.
• Piping that has been cleaned and labeled "oxy" or "oxygen" indicates that this piping has been cleaned in such a manner as to be suitable for piping oxygen. It also means that piping is suitable for use with any other nonflammable medical gas. This paragraph [4-4.1.4.1(a)] now requires manufacturer-cleaned piping for *all* nonflammable medical piped gas systems to be suitable for piping oxygen. This restriction precludes the problem of some manufacturer-cleaned piping being suitable for some nonflammable gases but not others, and also eliminates the problem that installers would face in making sure the correct pipe were used.

(2) Piping, valves, fittings, and other components prepared at the job site shall be cleaned by washing in a hot alkaline cleaner-water solution, such as sodium carbonate or trisodium phosphate (proportion of one pound to three gallons of water).Scrubbing shall be employed where necessary to ensure complete cleaning. After washing, the materials shall be thoroughly rinsed in clean, hot water.

• Former NFPA 56F (now essentially Sections 4-3 to 4-6 of NFPA 99) covered the installation of nonflammable medical piped gas systems. Manufacturer pipe-cleaning practices were not covered. Paragraph 4-4.1.4.1(a) was added for 1987 as clarification (see commentary under 4-4.1.4.1(a) for further information).

• Because of paragraph 4-4.1.4.1(a), cleaning by washing at the job site may not be necessary if there is documentation that CGA G-4.1 has been followed, *and* cleaning has not been compromised in shipment or during storage. Thus, washing and cleaning of pipes on site in accordance with above requirements is necessary unless the manufacturer provides written documentation that the requirements of 4-4.1.4.1(a)(1) have been followed, *and* pipes have been capped or plugged.

• This paragraph has been interpreted by many parties to allow systems to be cleaned *after* installation, i.e., installed dirty and then cleaned by injecting the above chemicals into the completed system. This assumption is to be rejected totally since attempts to provide a clean system at that time, in this manner, would create problems of a severe nature. [See also sentence two of paragraph 4-4.1.2.1(a).]

A-4-4.1.4.1(a) The intent of this provision is to not restrict the conducting of the cleaning operation to any particular firm or individual. It may be conducted by the manufacturer, installing contractor, jobber, or other firm or individual in compliance with 4-4.1.4.1(a)(1) or (2).

4-4.1.4.2* All brazed joints in the piping shall be made up using brazing filler alloys that bond with the base metals being brazed and that comply with *Specification for Brazing Filler Metal,* ANSI/AWS A5.8.

A-4-4.1.4.2 All brazed joints should have a brazing alloy exhibiting a melting temperature in excess of 1000°F (538°C) to retain the integrity of the piping system in the event of fire exposure.

• Changes to this section were the result of problems reported to the former Medical Gas Application Panel (now Subcommittee on Nonflammable Medical Piped Gas Systems) when flux was used. These included mechanically weak joints and overheated piping and fittings. Changes thus made were several fold since all were necessary to address the problem. They included:

   (a) reference to a specific American Welding Society (AWS) standard,
   (b) reference to the inclusion of a phosphorous element in the brazing alloy, and
   (c) continuous purging of the pipe with an inert gas (e.g., nitrogen) while brazing.

• The change to referencing ANSI/AWS 5.8 was deliberate to reference a national standard requiring the melting point of the brazing alloy to be a minimum of 1000°F. Reference to a specific type of brazing alloy was deleted to avoid prohibiting new technology.

(a) Copper-to-copper joints shall be made using a copper-phosphorous brazing filler alloy (BCuP series) without flux.

(b) Dissimilar metals such as copper and brass shall be joined using an appropriate flux with either a copper-phosphorous (BCuP series) or a silver (BAg series) brazing filler alloy. Apply flux sparingly and in a manner to avoid leaving any excess inside of completed joints. Use of prefluxed rod is acceptable.

NOTE: Some BAg series filler metals contain cadmium, which, when heated during brazing, can produce toxic fumes.

(c)* While being brazed, joints shall be continuously purged with an inert gas such as dry nitrogen or carbon dioxide to prevent the formation of scale within the tubing.

A-4-4.1.4.2(c) The intent is to provide an oxygen-free atmosphere within the tubing, to prevent the formation of copper atmosphere within the tubing, and to prevent the formation of copper oxide scale during brazing. This is accomplished by filling the piping with a low-volume flow of low-pressure inert gas.

(d) A visual inspection of each brazed joint shall be made to assure that the alloy has flowed completely in and around the joint and, where flux has been used, that hardened flux has not formed a temporary seal that holds test pressure. The outside of all fluxed joints shall be washed with hot water after assembly to remove excess flux for clear visual inspection of brazed connections.

(e) The outside of all tubes, joints, and fittings shall be cleaned by washing with hot water after assembly.

4-4.1.4.3* Threaded joints in piping systems shall be tinned or made up with polytetrafluorethylene (such as Teflon) tape or other thread sealants suitable for oxygen service. Sealants shall be applied to the male threads only.

A-4-4.1.4.3 Where threaded joints are tinned, soft solder should be used. If sealing compound is used, it should be applied sparingly so that excess sealant is not forced inside the system.

4-4.2 Patient Gas Distribution — Type II (Manifold, Piping, Valving/Controls, Outlets/Terminals, Alarms).

4-4.2.1 Mechanical means shall be provided to assure the connection of cylinders containing the proper gas to the piping system. Cylinder valve outlets for nonflammable gases and gas mixtures for medical purposes shall comply with American-Canadian *Standard for Compressed Gas Cylinder Valve Outlet and Inlet Connections* (ANSI B57.1; CSA B96).

4-4.2.2 The provisions of 4-3.1.8.3 shall apply.

4-4.2.3 Threaded connections between the regulators and the piping system shall comply with Compressed Gas Association Standard V-5, *Diameter-Index Safety System*.

4-4.2.4 Flexible connectors of other than all-metal construction used to connect outlets of pressure regulators to fixed piping shall not exceed 5 ft (1.5 m) in length and shall not penetrate walls, floors, ceilings, or partitions. Flexible connectors shall comply with the provisions of 4-4.2.3.

4-4.2.5 A shutoff valve or check valve shall be installed downstream of each pressure regulator.

4-4.2.6 A pressure relief valve set at 50 percent above normal line pressure shall be installed downstream of the shutoff or check valve required in 4-4.2.5. Pressure relief valves shall be of brass or bronze and designed for oxygen service.

4-4.2.7* Supply systems supplying a single treatment facility as outlined in 4-6.2.4.1(c) shall contain as a minimum:

A-4-4.2.7 If the supply system is within the confines of a single treatment facility a simple manual transfer is permissible. Only high/low pressure alarms are required. The gases are to be manifolded so a quick manual transfer is possible without life-threatening consequences.

However, if the supply system is remote, a prompt transfer of gases becomes more difficult. It may require transcending one or more flights of stairs and/or going to a remote location on the same floor. Under these situations an automatic system is required.

4-4.2.7.1 Two cylinders of oxygen and two cylinders of nitrous oxide (if used).

4-4.2.7.2 The cylinders for each gas service shall be manifolded so that the cylinders can alternately supply the piping system. Each bank shall contain at least an average day's supply. When the content of the primary bank is unable to supply the system, the secondary bank shall be capable of being manually switched to supply the system. Automatic switchover is permitted.

4-4.2.7.3 When the supply system is remote the switchover shall be automatic.

4-4.2.8* Supply systems supplying two single treatment facilities as outlined in 4-6.2.4.1(d) shall contain as a minimum:

4-4.2.8.1 Two cylinders of oxygen and two cylinders of nitrous oxide (if used).

4-4.2.8.2 The cylinders for each gas service shall be manifolded so that the cylinders can alternately supply the piping system. Each bank shall contain at least an average day's supply. When the content of the primary bank is unable to supply the piping system, the secondary bank shall automatically operate to supply the piping system.

A-4-4.2.8 The installation of a supply serving more than one single treatment facility creates by its very nature a remote location relative to the other facility. Because more than one practice may be involved, the transfer of oxygen and nitrous oxide gases is to be automatically achieved.

4-4.2.9 Warning Systems.

4-4.2.9.1 An automatic pressure switch, which will actuate a visual and audible alarm when the line pressure drops below or increases above normal line pressure, shall be connected to each main supply line within a single treatment facility. (See *4-5.2.4.1.*) The automatic pressure switch shall be installed downstream of any main supply line shutoff valve that may be required by the provisions of 4-4.2.12.2 or 4-4.2.12.3.

4-4.2.9.2 A warning system as required in 4-4.2.9.1 shall be installed in each single treatment facility served by the supply system. The warning system shall be comprised of an audible and noncancellable visual signal and shall be installed to be heard and seen at a continuously attended location during the time of operation of the facility.

4-4.2.9.3 A warning system as outlined in 4-4.2.9.2 shall be installed to indicate whenever automatic changeover occurs or is about to occur. The signal shall remain uncancellable until the reserve supply bank has been replenished. The sensor alarm shall be independent of the sensor actuator of 4-4.2.9.1. When two treatment facilities are served by a common supply system, the automatic changeover alarm shall indicate in both facilities.

4-4.2.9.4 Warning systems for two single treatment facilities shall conform to 4-4.2.9.1, 4-4.2.9.2, and 4-4.2.9.3, and shall be independent.

4-4.2.10 Pressure Gauges.

4-4.2.10.1 A pressure gauge shall be installed in the main line adjacent to the actuating switch required in 4-4.1.1.2(e). It shall be appropriately labeled and be readily visible from a standing position. (*See C-4.2.14.*)

4-4.2.11 Piping.

4-4.2.11.1* The provisions of Section 4-4.1.2 shall apply.

A-4-4.2.11.1 One of the major concerns is the cross-connection of piping systems of different gases. The problem of cross-connection of oxygen and other gases such as nitrous oxide, air, nitrogen, etc. can readily be recognized/prevented by the use of different sizes of tubing. It is recommended that piping and manifolds for oxygen service be of a different size than the piping intended for other gas services. The piping for other than oxygen may be of a smaller size. Generally, oxygen is installed in ½-in. O.D. tube size and other gases with ⅜-in. O.D. tube size.

4-4.2.12 Shutoff Valves.

4-4.2.12.1* Where the central supply is remote from the medical gas system use points, the main supply line shall be provided with a shutoff valve so located in the single treatment facility as to be accessible from use-point locations in an emergency.

A-4-4.2.12.1 Should a fire occur at night or when the facility is not in use, fire fighters should not be confronted with a potential pressurized gas source which could feed the fire and cause extensive damage and risk of life. Good economics also dictate that when the system is not in use, the leakage of gas through hoses, couplings, etc. can be minimized if the system is shut off and portable equipment disconnected. (*See Figure A-4-4.2.12.1.*)

4-4.2.12.2 When the supply is remote from a single treatment facility, the main supply line shall be provided with a shutoff valve so located in the single treatment facility as to be accessible from use-point locations in an emergency. Such valves shall be labeled to indicate the gas controlled, and shall shut off only the gas to that single treatment facility. A remotely activated shutoff at the supply manifold shall not be used for emergency shutoff. For clinical purposes such a remote actuator shall be of a "fail-open" nature in the event of a loss of electrical power.

4-4.2.12.3 When the central supply system supplies two single treatment facilities, each facility shall be provided with a shutoff valve so located in each treatment facility as to be accessible from the use-point locations in an emergency. Such valves shall be labeled to indicate the gas controlled, and shall shut off only the gas to that single treatment facility. A remotely activated shutoff at the supply manifold shall not be used for emergency shutoff valves for dual treatment facility installations. For clinical purposes such a remote actuator shall be of a "fail-open" nature in the event of a loss of electrical power.

4-4.2.12.4 The provisions of 4-4.1.2.2(c) shall apply to any installation with risers off the main line.

4-4.2.13 Station Outlets.

4-4.2.13.1 The provisions of 4-4.1.2.4 shall apply.

4-4.2.13.2 Station outlets shall be located at an appropriate height above the floor to prevent physical damage to equipment attached to the outlet.

NOTE: They may be recessed or otherwise protected from damage.

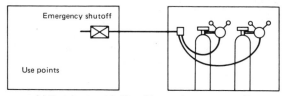

(a) Single treatment facility with manual emergency cutoff

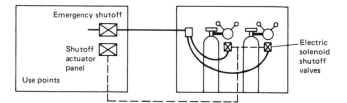

(b) Single treatment facility with remote shutoff at cylinder

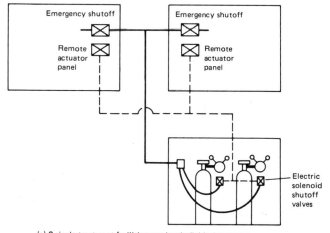

(c) 2 single treatment facilities requires individual emergency
shutoff valves even with remote actuator shutoff at supply

Figure A-4-4.2.12.1   Shutoff Valves.

4-4.2.13.3 Station outlets shall be located to avoid physical damage to the valve and attached equipment.

4-4.3 Laboratory Gas Distribution (Manifold, Piping, Valving/Controls, Outlets/Terminals, Alarms).

4-4.3.1 When a laboratory is intended to be routinely and frequently operated with flammable gases supplied from a manifold compressed system, the containers shall either:

(a) be in a separate room having a fire-resistance classification of at least one hour and ventilated in accordance with 4-3.1.2, or

(b) be located outside of the building and connected to the laboratory equipment by a permanently installed piping system.

Exception: Wherever the volume and nature of the gas, in the judgment of the laboratory safety officer or other authority having jurisdiction, do not offer a hazard, the requirement for the remote locations of the cylinder may be waived.

Previously, the cylinders for a flammable piped gas system had to be located outside the building. However, because 4-3.3.2.3 allows the storage of flammable gas cylinders inside a building, the former Committee on Laboratories modified this section accordingly in 1984.

4-4.3.2 When a laboratory is intended to be routinely and frequently operated with nonflammable gases supplied from a manifold compressed system:

(a) the manifold within the laboratory shall consist of not more than six cylinders;

(b) manifolds larger than six cylinders shall conform to 4-4.3.1; and

(c) cylinders shall be secured in position.

This section was added in 1984 because, although nonflammable piped gas systems are used in laboratories, no guidance on them had been included in then NFPA 56C, *Standard for Laboratories in Health-Related Institutions*. The Committee felt guidance should be included in the interest of safety.

The dividing line of six cylinders was considered a reasonable breakpoint by the Committee. While the gases involved are nonflammable, the Committee felt that the quantity stored inside a laboratory working area should not be open ended.

4-4.3.3 A pressure-reducing valve shall be connected to each gas cylinder and adjusted to a setting to limit pressure in the piping system at the minimum required gas pressure.

4-4.3.4 Pressure regulators shall be compatible with the gas for which they are used.

4-4.3.5* Piping systems for fuel gases, such as manufactured gas, natural gas, and LP-Gas, shall comply with NFPA 54, *National Fuel Gas Code*, and NFPA 58, *Standard for the Storage and Handling of Liquefied Petroleum Gases*.

A-4-4.3.5 Piping Systems. Piping systems supplying medical gases to patients should be reserved exclusively for that purpose so as to protect the patients from administration of gas other than that intended for their use. Therefore laboratory gas piping systems should not be used to pipe gas for use by hospital patients. This warning is also intended to apply to piping systems intended to supply gas to patients within a laboratory facility. Such a system should not be used to supply laboratory equipment other than that directly involved with the patient procedure.

4-4.3.6 Piping systems for gaseous hydrogen shall comply with NFPA 50A, *Standard for Gaseous Hydrogen Systems at Consumer Sites*.

4-4.3.7 Piping systems for nonflammable medical gases shall comply with Type I systems as specified in this chapter.

The Committee responsible for former NFPA 56F (now part of NFPA 99) did not include laboratories within the scope of NFPA 56F. However, because no other standard existed on the subject of nonflammable piped gas systems, the Subcommittee responsible for Laboratories chose to reference it. This has not been a problem because the Subcommittee felt the requirements of former NFPA 56F were adequate for laboratory purposes.

4-4.3.8 Piping systems for acetylene shall comply with NFPA 51, *Standard for the Design and Installation of Oxygen-Fuel Gas Systems for Welding, Cutting, and Allied Processes.*

4-4.3.9 Supply and discharge terminals of piping systems shall be legibly and permanently marked at both ends with the name of the gas to be piped, after testing, to establish their content and continuity.

4-4.3.10 Piping systems shall not be used for gases other than those for which they are designed and identified.

4-4.3.11 If a system is to be connected for use with a gas other than that for which it was originally installed, it shall be inspected for suitability for the proposed gas, purged with an inert gas (such as nitrogen), cleaned if necessary, and pressure tested in accordance with the appropriate piping standard. Each outlet of such a system shall be identified by chemical name and specifically converted for use with the successor gas.

4-4.4 Other Gases. (Refer to NFPA 54, *National Fuel Gas Code.*)

4-5 Gas System Performance Criteria and Testing.

4-5.1 Patient Gas System — Type I.

4-5.1.1 Cross-Connection.

Because of the fatalities that have occurred due to cross-connection of gases, it is absolutely essential to verify that labeling of outlets and delivered gas are the same. The tests listed in this section have been developed for that purpose.

4-5.1.1.1 Before piping systems are intially put into use, the health care facility authority shall be responsible for ascertaining that the gas delivered at the outlet is that shown on the outlet label and that the proper connecting fittings are checked against their labels.

4-5.1.1.2 Gas System Testing and Verification.

(a) To determine that no cross-connection to other piping systems exists, reduce all medical gas systems to atmospheric pressure. Disconnect all sources of test gas from all of the medical gas systems with the exception of the one system to be checked. Pressure this system with oil-free, dry air or nitrogen (see definitions) to a pressure of 50 psig (350 kPa gauge). With appropriate adaptors matching outlet labels, check each individual station outlet of all medical gas systems installed to determine that test gas is being dispensed only from the outlets of the medical gas system being tested.

(1) Disconnect the source of test gas and reduce the system tested to atmospheric pressure. Proceed to test each additional piping system in accordance with 4-5.1.1.2(a).

(2) Where a medical vacuum piping system is installed, the cross-connection testing shall include that piped vacuum system with all medical gas piping systems.

(3) An alternate method of testing to assure that no cross-connections to other piping systems exists is:

Pressures in Table 4-5.1.1.2(a)(3) are *for testing purposes only* and are not reflective of operating pressures.

(i) Reduce the pressure in all medical gas systems to atmospheric.

(ii) Increase the test gas pressure in all medical gas piping systems to the values indicated in Table 4-5.1.1.2(a)(3). Simultaneously maintain these nominal pressures throughout the test.

Table 4-5.1.1.2(a)(3) Alternate Test Pressures.

Medical Gas	Pressure	
	Psig	kPa gauge
Gas Mixtures	20	140
Nitrogen	30	210
Nitrous Oxide	40	280
Oxygen	50	350
Compressed Air	60	420

(iii) Any medical-surgical vacuum systems shall be in operation so that these vacuum systems are tested at the same time the medical gas systems are tested.

(iv) Following the adjustment of pressures in accordance with 4-5.1.1.2(a)(3)(ii) and (iii), each station outlet for each medical gas system shall be tested using the gas-specific connection for each system with a pressure (vacuum) gauge attached. Each pressure gauge used in performing this test shall be calibrated with the line pressure regulator gauge used to provide the source pressure.

(v) Each station outlet shall be identified by label (and color marking, if used), and the pressure indicated on the test gauge shall be that listed in 4-5.1.1.2(a)(3)(ii) for the system being tested.

(b) The presence and correctness of labeling required by this standard for all components (e.g., station outlets, shutoff valves, and signal panels) shall be verified.

4-5.1.2 Cleaning/Purging/Purity.

4-5.1.2.1* After installation of the piping, but before installation of the station outlets and other medical gas system components (e.g., pressure-actuating switches for alarms, manifolds, pressure gauges, or pressure relief valves), the line shall be blown clear by means of oil-free, dry air or nitrogen (*see Chapter 2, "Definitions"*).

A-4-5.1.2.1 Adequate flow rates, based upon system size, should be used to blow out all particulate matter from the piping system prior to installation of station outlets, gauges, and other components.

4-5.1.2.2 Purging. After all medical gas piping systems have been tested in accordance with 4-5.1.1.2 and 4-5.1.3.4, the source of test gas shall be disconnected and the proper gas source of supply connected to each respective system. Following this connection and pressurization, all outlets shall be opened in a progressive order, starting nearest the source and completing the process of purge flushing at the outlet farthest from the source.

(a) Purge gas shall be allowed to pass through a white cloth material at a minimum flow rate of 100 liters per minute until no evidence of discoloration is evident and the test gas used during the previous tests has been removed from the piping systems.

4-5.1.2.3 Analysis.

(a) After completing the purge flushing of the piping system in accordance with 4-5.1.2.2 and 4-5.1.2.2(a), the flow of gas from each station outlet for oxygen, mixed gases containing oxygen, and medical compressed air shall be tested with an oxygen analyzer to confirm the presence of the desired percentage of oxygen.[1]

(1) Where mixtures are piped that involve a low concentration of one component, such as 95 percent oxygen and 5 percent carbon dioxide, an analyzer must be used having sufficient accuracy to properly indicate the mixture. This, in some cases, may require an analyzer specific to each component.

(b) The test specified in 4-5.1.2.3(a) shall be conducted on the downstream portions of the medical gas piping system whenever a system is breached and whenever modifications are made or maintenance performed in anesthetizing locations or vital life support or critical areas.

The only test required when the oxygen (pure or mixed) or medical compressed air portion of an existing piped medical gas system is repaired is an analysis test to assure that no cross-connection of gases has been created. This may seem unnecessary when replacing a broken outlet or zone valve, but is is very important to document that the correct gas is flowing out of a labeled outlet. There can be no compromise in patient safety with respect to gases that will be inhaled by patients.

4-5.1.3 Medical Gas System Test (Pressure, Valves, Etc.).

4-5.1.3.1 A periodic testing procedure for nonflammable medical gas and related alarm systems shall be implemented.

This is usually the function of a maintenance department. However, it should involve the respiratory therapy service.
See Appendix C-4-2 for some recommendations relative to retesting and periodic maintenance.
Caution: Proper performance of some of these tests requires isolation of the system. Thus, tests can be conducted *only* if *no* patients are being served by that portion of system.

4-5.1.3.2 Valves installed in each medical gas piping system shall be tested to verify proper operation and rooms or areas of control. Records shall be made listing the rooms or areas

---

[1]Testing of outlets for other gases to confirm the presence of the designated gas is recommended.

controlled by each valve for each gas. The information shall be utilized to assist and verify the proper labeling of the valves.

4-5.1.3.3 A visual inspection of each brazed joint shall be made to assure that the alloy has flowed completely in and around the joint and, where flux has been used, that hardened flux has not formed a temporary seal that holds test pressure. Remove all excess flux for clear visual inspection of brazed connections.

4-5.1.3.4 Pressure Testing.

(a)* Before attachment of system components (e.g., pressure-actuating switches for alarms, manifolds, pressure gauges, or pressure relief valves), but after installation of the station outlets, with test caps (if supplied) in place (e.g., rough-in assembly), and before closing of the walls, each section of the piping system shall be subjected to a minimum test pressure of 150 psig (1 MPa gauge) [200 psig (1.4 MPa gauge) maximum} with oil-free, dry air or nitrogen (*see Chapter 2, "Definitions"*). This test pressure shall be maintained until each joint has been examined for leakage by means of soapy water or other equally effective means of leak detection safe for use with oxygen. The main-line shutoff valve shall be closed.

(1) Leaks, if any, shall be located, repaired, and retested in accordance with 4-5.1.3.4(a).

A-4.5.1.3.4(a) This is intended to test those stages of construction that may not be accessible at a later time.

(b)* After testing of each individual medical gas system in accordance with 4-5.1.3.4(a), the completely assembled station outlets and all other medical gas system components (e.g., pressure-actuating switches for alarms, manifolds, pressure gauges, or pressure relief valves) shall be installed and all piping systems shall be subjected to a 24-hour standing pressure test at 20 percent above the normal operating line pressure. The test gas shall be oil-free, dry air or nitrogen (*see definitions*). The main-line shutoff valve shall be closed.

(1) After the piping system is filled with test gas, the supply valve and all outlets shall be closed and the source of test gas disconnected. The piping system shall remain leak-free for 24 hours. When making the standing pressure test, the only allowable pressure changes during the 24-hour test period shall be those caused by variations in the ambient temperature around the piping system. Such changes can be checked by means of the pressure-temperature relationship: calculated final absolute pressure (absolute pressure is gauge pressure plus 14.7 psi if gauge is calibrated in "psi") equals the initial absolute pressure times the final absolute temperature (absolute temperature is temperature reading plus 460°F if thermometer is calibrated in Fahrenheit degrees), divided by the initial absolute temperature.

$$\left(P_f = \frac{P_i \times T_f}{T_i}\right)$$

(2) Leaks, if any, shall be located, repaired, and retested in accordance with 4-5.1.3.4(b).

A-4-5.1.3.4(b) This is the final pressure test of the completely installed system and is intended to locate any leaks that would be more likely to occur at lower pressure — e.g., leaks in station outlet valve seals.

The value of 20 percent above normal operating pressure permits testing without damage to other system components and without activation of any installed pressure relief valves.

(c) Prior to the connection of any work or any extension or addition to an existing piping system, the tests in 4-5.1.3.4(a) and (b) and 4-5.1.1.2 shall be successfully performed. Afterconnection to the existing system and before use of the addition for patient care, the tests in 4-5.1.2 shall be completed. Permanent records of these tests shall be maintained in accordance with 4-6.3.1.

(1)* The final connection between the addition and existing system shall be leak tested with the source gas at the normal operating pressure. This pressure shall be maintained until each joint has been examined for leakage by means of soapy water or other equally effective means of leak detection safe for use with oxygen.

A-4-5.1.3.4(c)(1) This leak test uses the source gas and the system pressure for which the system is designed in order to avoid contaminating the existing system.

(d) Flexible connectors, metallic or nonmetallic, shall have a minimum burst pressure of 1000 psig (7 MPa gauge). [See 4-4.1.2.1(i).]

4-5.1.3.5 Shutoff valves shall be tested in accordance with 4-5.1.3.2.

4-5.1.3.6 General Requirements for Central Supply Systems.

(a) Piping systems, with the exception of nitrogen systems, shall be capable of delivering 50 55 psig (345 380 kPa gauge) to all outlets at the maximum flow rate.

(b) A nitrogen system shall be capable of delivering at least 160 psig (1.1 MPa gauge) to all outlets at maximum flow. (See Appendix C-4.2.)

It has been reported that a device has been developed that uses nitrogen and requires a pressure of 200 psig. This is the upper limit for current nitrogen pressure range; the relief valve is required to open at this pressure. This situation cannot be resolved by merely raising the upper pressure limit of medical piped nitrogen systems from 160 to 225 psig (as an example). Supplying nitrogen at this higher pressure could adversely affect current devices designed to operate at a maximum pressure of 200 psig. In addition, the Diameter Index Safety System (DISS) is keyed to 200 psig.

Until the Subcommittee on Nonflammable Medical Piped Gas Systems proposes a solution in terms of changes to or modifications of current requirements, gas-operated devices requiring pressures above present criteria will have to use a high-pressure cylinder with a regulator or a separate *nonmedical* piped nitrogen system operating at 200 psig. This latter system has to be completely independent of the *medical* piped nitrogen system.

4-5.1.4 Alarm Testing.

4-5.1.4.1 General.

(a) All warning systems for each medical gas piping system shall be tested to assure that all components function properly prior to placing the piping system in service. Permanent records of these tests shall be maintained. (See Appendix C-4.2.)

(1) Warning systems that may be included as part of an addition to an existing piping system shall be tested prior to the connection of the new piping to the existing system.

(b) Periodic retesting of audible and visual alarm indicators shall be performed to determine that they are functioning properly and records of the test shall be maintained until the next test. (*See Appendix C-4.2.*)

See Commentary under paragraph 4-5.1.3.1.

4-5.1.4.2 Master Alarm Systems. The audible and noncancellable visual signals of 4-4.1.1.2(e) shall indicate if the pressure in the main line increases or decreases 20 percent from the normal operating pressure.

4-5.1.4.3 Area Alarm Systems. The warning signals for all medical gas piping systems supplying anesthetizing locations and other vital life support and critical care areas such as postanesthesia recovery, intensive care units, coronary care units, etc., shall indicate if the pressure in the piping system increases or decreases 20 percent from the normal operating pressure. [*See 4-4.1.1.3(a) and Appendix C-4.1.*]

4-5.2 Patient Gas System — Type II.

4-5.2.1 (Reserved)

4-5.2.2 (Reserved)

4-5.2.3 Gas System Test (Pressure, Valves, Etc.).

4-5.2.3.1 The medical gas system, including cylinders and pressure regulators, shall deliver gas at a pressure per 4-5.1.3.6.

4-5.2.3.2 Flexible connectors of other than all-metal construction used to connect outlets of pressure regulators to fixed piping shall have a minimum burst pressure of 1000 psig (7 MPa gauge). (*See 4-4.2.4.*)

4-5.2.3.3 The pressure relief valve specified in 4-4.2.6 shall close automatically when excess pressure has been released.

4-5.2.4 Alarm Testing.

4-5.2.4.1 Warning Systems. The automatic pressure switch connected to each main supply line within a single treatment facility shall actuate a visual and audible alarm when the line pressure drops approximately 20 percent below or increases approximately 20 percent above normal line pressure. (*See 4-4.2.9.*)

4-5.2.5* Installation and Testing of Piping Systems. The provisions of 4-5.1.1, 4-5.1.2, and 4-5.1.3 shall apply.

A-4-5.2.5 Testing of all components in accordance with Appendixes C-4.1 and C-4.2 should be conducted as applicable to assure continued proper operation of the system. Testing devices required to conduct tests in 4-5.1.2.3 may be available from local hospitals or medical gas suppliers. This test should be recorded in accordance with 4-6.3.1. Experience indicates that this test is often overlooked.

4-6 Administration (Gas Systems).

4-6.1 Responsibility of Governing Body. (Reserved)

4-6.2 Policies.

4-6.2.1 Gases in Cylinders, and Liquefied Gases in Containers.

4-6.2.1.1* Handling of Gases. Administrative authorities shall provide regulations to assure that standards for safe practice in the specifications for cylinders; marking of cylinders, regulators, and valves; and cylinder connections have been met by vendors of cylinders containing compressed gases supplied to the facility.

A-4-6.2.1.1 Safe Practice for Cylinders Containing Compressed Gases.

Specifications for Cylinders. All cylinders containing compressed gases, such as anesthetic gases, oxygen, or other gases used for medicinal purposes, whether these gases are flammable or not, should comply with the specifications and be maintained in accordance with regulations of the U.S. Department of Transportation.

NFPA has produced a film on this subject entitled, "Safe Handling of Medical Gases" (VC-4). The film illustrates the hazards associated with gases, how cylinders should be handled, how piped systems work, and emergency measures to take in the event of an incident involving medical gases.

4-6.2.1.2 Special Precautions — Oxygen Cylinders and Manifolds. Great care shall be exercised in handling oxygen to prevent contact of oxygen under pressure with oils, greases, organic lubricants, rubber, or other materials of an organic nature. The following regulations, based on those of the Compressed Gas Association Pamphlet G-4, *Oxygen,* shall be observed:

(a) Oil, grease, or readily flammable materials shall never be permitted to come in contact with oxygen cylinders, valves, regulators, gauges, or fittings.

(b) Regulators, fittings, or gauges shall never be lubricated with oil or any other flammable substance.

(c) Oxygen cylinders or apparatus shall never be handled with oily or greasy hands, gloves, or rags.

(d) Particles of dust and dirt shall be cleared from cylinder valve openings by slightly opening and closing the valve before applying any fitting to the cylinder.

(e) The high-pressure valve on the oxygen cylinder shall be opened before bringing the apparatus to the patient or the patient to the apparatus.

The intent of stating both situations is to ensure that the high-pressure valve is opened (thereby indicating if any overheating problem exists) before a patient and an apparatus are brought together.

(f) The cylinder valve shall be opened slowly, with the face of the gauge on the regulator pointed away from all persons.

(g) An oxygen cylinder shall never be draped with any materials such as hospital gowns, masks, or caps.

(h) Oxygen fittings, valves, regulators, or gauges shall never be used for any service other than that of oxygen.

(i) Gases of any type shall never be mixed in an oxygen or any other cylinder.

(j) Oxygen shall always be dispensed from a cylinder through a pressure regulator.

(k) Regulators that are in need of repair or cylinders having valves that do not operate properly shall never be used.

(l) Oxygen equipment that is defective shall not be used until it has been repaired by competent personnel. If competent in-house repairs cannot be made, such equipment shall be repaired by the manufacturer or his authorized agent; or it shall be replaced.

The competence of personnel is a matter of professional judgment by whomever in a facility is responsible for the repair of equipment.

(m) Oxygen cylinders shall be protected from abnormal mechanical shock, which is liable to damage the cylinder, valve, or safety device. Such cylinders shall not be stored near elevators, gangways, or in locations where heavy moving objects may strike them or fall on them.

(n) Cylinder-valve protection caps, when provided, shall be kept in place and be hand tightened, except when cylinders are in use or connected for use.

These caps protect the valve in case the cylinder topples over. (*See Commentary 4-3.1.2.1(i) for hazard if this occurs.*)

(o) Cylinders shall be protected from the tampering of unauthorized individuals.

(p) Valves shall be closed on all empty cylinders in storage.

(q) Oxygen shall be referred to by its proper name, OXYGEN, *not* AIR. Liquid oxygen shall be referred to by its proper name, *not* LIQUID AIR.

(r) Oxygen shall never be used as a substitute for compressed air.

(s) Cylinders or cylinder valves shall not be repaired, painted, or altered.

(t) Safety relief devices in valves or cylinders shall never be tampered with. Sparks and flame shall be kept away from cylinders; a torch flame shall never be permitted under any circumstances to come in contact with cylinder valves or safety devices. Valve outlets clogged with ice shall be thawed with warm — not boiling — water.

(u) The markings stamped on cylinders shall not be tampered with. It is against federal statutes to change these markings without written authority from the Bureau of Explosives.

(v) Markings used for the identification of contents of cylinders shall not be defaced or removed, including decals, tags, stenciled marks, and upper half of shipping tag.

(w) The owner of the cylinder shall be notified if any condition has occurred that might permit any foreign substance to enter a cylinder or valve, giving details and cylinder number.

(x) Even if they are considered to be empty, cylinders shall never be used as rollers, supports, or for any purpose other than that for which they are intended by the supplier.

(y) When small-size (A, B, D, or E) cylinders are in use, they shall be attached to a cylinder stand or to therapy apparatus of sufficient size to render the entire assembly stable.

(z) Cylinders and containers shall not be dropped, dragged, or rolled.

(aa) Freestanding cylinders shall be properly chained or supported in a proper cylinder stand or cart.

There are many commercially available carts that hold a cylinder in such a manner as to make their tipping over very difficult.

(bb) Cylinders shall not be chained to portable or movable apparatus such as beds and oxygen tents.

Even in use, cylinders are to be well secured to a wall, rack, etc., (i.e., something nonmovable) to prevent them from being knocked over.

(cc) Cylinders shall not be supported by, and neither cylinders nor containers shall be placed in proximity of, radiators, steam pipes, or heat ducts.

NOTE: Cylinder and container temperatures greater than 125°F (52°C) may result in excessive pressure increase. Pressure relief devices are sensitive to temperature and pressure. When relief devices actuate, contents are discharged.

(dd) Very cold cylinders or containers shall be handled with care to avoid injury.

(ee) Cylinders and containers shall not be handled with hands, gloves, or other materials contaminated with oil or grease.

4-6.2.1.3 Making Cylinder and Container Connections.

(a) Wrenches used to connect respiratory therapy equipment shall be manufactured of steel or other suitable material of adequate strength.

NOTE: Use of so-called nonsparking wrenches and tools is not necessary.

(b) Cylinder valves shall be opened and connected in accordance with the following procedure:

(1) Make certain that apparatus and cylinder valve connections and cylinder wrenches are free of foreign materials.

(2) Turn the cylinder valve outlet away from personnel. Stand to the side — not in front and not in back. Before connecting the apparatus to cylinder valve, momentarily open cylinder valve to eliminate dust.

(3) Make connection of apparatus to cylinder valve. Tighten connection nut securely with an appropriate wrench [see 4-6.2.1.3(a)].

(4) Release the low-pressure adjustment screw of the regulator completely.

(5) *Slowly* open cylinder valve to full open position.

(6) Slowly turn in the low-pressure adjustment screw on the regulator until the proper working pressure is obtained.

(7) Open the valve to the utilization apparatus.

(c) Connections for containers shall be made in accordance with the container manufacturer's operating instructions.

4-6.2.1.4 Care of Safety Mechanisms.

(a) Personnel using cylinders and containers and other equipment covered in this chapter shall be familiar with the Pin-Index Safety System (see 8-3.1.2) and the Diameter-Index Safety System (see 8-3.1.3), both designed to prevent utilization of the wrong gas.

(b) Safety relief mechanisms, noninterchangeable connectors, and other safety features shall not be removed, altered, or replaced.

4-6.2.1.5 Transfilling Cylinders.

(a) Mixing of compressed gases in cylinders shall be prohibited.

The term "mixing" implies two different gases, not two different cylinders with the same gas (the latter being referred to as transfilling). Mixing of some types of gases can cause an explosion.
This mixing should not be confused with the *administration* of various combinations of gases during surgery or respiratory therapy.

(b) Transfer of gaseous oxygen from one cylinder to another shall be in accordance with CGA Pamphlet P-2.5, *Transfilling of High Pressure Gaseous Oxygen to be Used for Respiration*. Transfer of any gases from one cylinder to another in patient care areas of health care facilities shall be prohibited.

• There has been and continues to be much concern about this subject of transfilling cylinders containing gas under high pressure within health care facilities. While adherence to the CGA document will minimize hazards, there is the question of whether the procedures outlined in the CGA document will be followed. Unfortunately, this places the burden (and associated risks) on the health care facility.

For this 1987 edition of NFPA 99, arguments for and against transfilling within health care facilities were weighed by the Subcommittee on Anesthesia Services, Subcommittee on Gas Equipment, Subcommittee on Laboratories and the Technical Committee on Health Care Facilities. The first two subcommittees favored prohibiting transfilling in health care facilities because of problems noted in paragraph one above. However, the Technical Committee took into consideration that the CGA document, *if followed*, did provide a reasonable level of safety for transfilling. But in the interest of patient, staff, and visitor safety, the Technical Committee restricted transfilling to non-patient care areas. It should be noted that transfilling is allowed only for oxygen since procedures for other gases that take into consideration medical concerns have not yet been developed.

• With the restructuring of NFPA 99 for 1987, the seemingly differing requirements regarding transfilling that appeared in several sections of NFPA 99-1984 have been correlated and placed in this one section [4-6.2.1.5(b)].

• It is further observed that the Compressed Gas Association, which is in the process of revising its P-2.5 pamphlet, will be adding a cautionary note that "the document [P-2.5] is not to be considered an approval of this potentially hazardous activity [transfilling]." The note continues, stating that transfilling is to be accomplished by trained, qualified personnel only, and in areas "where effective controls and safety measures have been established . . ." C.G.A., too, recognizes the inherent risks associated with transfilling and, while it condones the practice, it also places some caveats on it (e.g., how and where it should be done and who should do it). This is in concert with the Technical Committee on Health Care Facilities' actions above.

4-6.2.1.6 Transferring of Liquid Oxygen.

(a) Transferring of liquid oxygen from one container to another, if permitted by the responsible authority of the facility, shall be accomplished in a location remote from patient care areas, utilizing equipment designed to comply with the performance requirements and procedures of CGA Pamphlet P-2.6, *Transfilling of Low-Pressure Liquid Oxygen to Be Used for Respiration*, and adhering to those procedures.

The CGA document outlines specific procedures to be followed in transferring liquid oxygen from one container to another.

4-6.2.1.7 Laboratory Gases.

(a)* *Use of Gases.* Gases shall be handled and used with care and with knowledge of their hazardous properties, both individually and in combination with other materials with which they can come in contact. See NFPA 49, *Hazardous Chemicals Data*, and NFPA 491M, *Manual of Hazardous Chemical Reactions*.

A-4-6.2.1.7(a) Handling of Gas Containers.

The precautions outlined in Compressed Gas Association Pamphlet P-1, Safe Handling of Compressed Gases, and Pamphlet P-2, *Characteristics and Safe Handling of Medical Gases*, should be observed. (*See Appendix B.*) These publications cover such items as moving and storage of cylinders, labeling, withdrawing of cylinder contents, and handling of leaking cylinders. Cryogenic fluids must be used only in containers designed for the purpose, such as a double-walled thermos bottle.

Caps must be replaced promptly after each use to prevent the solidification of atmospheric water vapor in the pouring neck, which otherwise could convert a safe cylinder into a potential bomb.

Protective clothing and eye shields should be used to prevent burns from issuing gases or spilled liquids. Effects of flammable and oxidizing properties are intense and demand special fire protection measures and handling. Inadvertent saturation of clothing by oxygen or spills on asphalt flooring, for example, require prompt and accurate corrective measures. Ample ventilation is needed to prevent hazardous concentrations, for example, of nitrogen, which could cause asphyxiation. For routine cooling operations, liquid air or oxygen should never be used as substitutes for liquid nitrogen.

(b) In a laboratory, gas cylinders being held for prompt use shall not exceed one cylinder of the sizes stated in 4-3.3.2.2 or two days' working needs, except as permitted in 4-4.3.1. Cylinders shall be in racks or secured in position.

The requirement takes into consideration weekday as well as weekend operations.

(c) *Working Supplies.* The aggregate accumulation of cylinders at any one working station shall not exceed one extra cylinder for each cylinder actually connected for use. All cylinders shall be secured in a rack or secured in an upright position.

4-6.2.2 Storage of Cylinders and Containers.

4-6.2.2.1 Facility authorities, in consultation with medical staff and other trained personnel, shall provide and enforce regulations for the storage and handling of containers of oxygen and nitrous oxide in storage rooms of approved construction, and for the safe handling of these agents in anesthetizing locations. Storage locations for flammable inhalation anesthetic agents, established in any operating or delivery suite, shall be limited by space allocation and regulation to not more than a 48-hour normal requirement for any such suite. In storage locations, cylinders shall be properly secured in racks or adequately fastened. No cylinders containing oxygen or nitrous oxide, other than those connected to anesthetic apparatus, shall be kept or stored in anesthetizing locations.

NOTE: Electric wiring and equipment in storage rooms for oxygen and nitrous oxide are not required to be explosionproof.

4-6.2.2.2 Nonflammable Gases.

(a) Storage shall be planned so that cylinders may be used in the order in which they are received from the supplier.

(b) If stored within the same enclosure, empty cylinders shall be segregated from full cylinders. Empty cylinders shall be marked to avoid confusion and delay if a full cylinder is needed hurriedly.

(c) Cylinders stored in the open shall be protected against extremes of weather and from the ground beneath to prevent rusting. During winter, cylinders stored in the open shall be protected against accumulations of ice or snow. In summer, cylinders stored in the open shall be screened against continuous exposure to direct rays of the sun in those localities where extreme temperatures prevail.

4-6.2.2.3 Flammable Agents. Facility administrative authorities, in consultation with the medical staff and others with training and expertise, shall determine the adequacy of storage space for flammable anesthetic and disinfecting agents and medicaments (*see 4-3.1.2.4*), and shall provide and enforce regulations for the storage and handling of containers of such agents. Said regulations also shall provide for the periodic inspection and maintenance of said storage locations.

4-6.2.3 Patient Gas Systems — Type I.

4-6.2.3.1 Piping systems shall not be used for the distribution of flammable anesthetic gases. [1]

4-6.2.3.2 Nonflammable medical gas systems used to supply gases for respiratory therapy shall be installed in accordance with Sections 4-3 and 4-4 of this chapter.

The type of medical piped gas system applicable to a specific type of facility is listed in Chapters 12 to 18.

4-6.2.3.3* Piping System Installation.

(a) The installation shall be made in accordance with the instructions of the manufacturer.

(1) Such instructions shall include directions and information deemed by the manufacturer to be adequate for attaining proper installation, testing, maintenance, and operation of the medical gas systems. These instructions shall be left with the owner.

(2) The installation shall be made by qualified, competent technicians, experienced in making such installations.

A-4-6.2.3.3 The responsible authority of the facility should assure that procedures are established to provide for the testing, maintenance, and operation of nonflammable medical gas piping systems.

4-6.2.3.4* The responsible authority of the facility shall establish procedures to assure that all signal warnings are promptly evaluated and that all necessary measures are taken to reestablish the proper functions of the medical gas system.

A-4-6.2.3.4 Activation of any of the warning signals should immediately be reported to the department of the facility responsible for the medical gas piping system involved. If the medical gas is supplied from a bulk supply system, the owner or the organization responsible for the operation and maintenance of that system, usually the supplier, should also be notified. Provide as much detail as possible.

4-6.2.3.5 Piping systems for gases shall not be used as a grounding electrode.

4-6.2.4 Patient Gas Systems — Type II.

4-6.2.4.1* Type II systems cover nonflammable gas system installations for use primarily in nonhospital-based facilities. These include, but are not limited to, a stand-alone dental office, or practice for dentistry, medicine, surgery, osteopathy, podiatry, veterinary medicine, or

---

[1]These requirements do not restrict the distribution of helium or other inert gases through piping systems.

laboratories or similar office(s) as part of a larger office or retail complex. Type II systems cover cylinder systems installations that:

(a) Have not more than 2000 cu ft (56 m³) total capacity of all gases (excluding nitrogen) connected and in storage at one time, except that the total capacity of all gases may be increased to 5000 cu ft (143 m³) (excluding nitrogen) if oxygen is used in a DOT Specification 4L (liquid) cylinder, and

(b) Have a listed pressure regulator directly connected to each cylinder, and

(c) Supply only a single treatment facility and also as a minimum comply with the specific requirements of 4-4.2.7, or

(d) Supply a maximum of two single treatment facilities and also as a minimum comply with the specific requirements of 4-4.2.8.

A-4-6.2.4.1 It is the intent to provide a simple, safe piping system for small facilities. Although the number of use points could be a consideration, it was felt that actual gas use is a more accurate indicator of complexity. Applications involving a storage in excess of 2000 ft³ (56.6 m³) would have a complexity warranting installation in accordance with the provisions of Type I patient gas distribution systems.

Although the principle intent is to provide simple installations for single treatment facilities, numerous applications exist where a remote use point creates essentially a second treatment facility or where the supply system may be shared by another health care professional such as another dentist, podiatrist, oral surgeon, or general medicine practioner. The addition of an another treatment facility requires incremental safety precautions.

A maximum of two single treatment facilities also approximates the limit with which a 2000 ft³ (57 m³) supply system can provide. [5000 ft³ (143 m³) when liquid oxygen is used.]

It is acknowledged that older user analgesia equipment has offered a nitrous oxide lockout device which requires a minimum of 3 L/min oxygen flow. However, a reasonable percentage of older equipment without this safety feature is in daily use. The storage and piping system is based upon the potential use, either initially or subsequently, of one of the older style analgesia equipment in one of the single treatment facilities.

The quantity of 2000 ft³ (57 m³), or 5000 ft³ (143 m³) if liquid oxygen storage, is to be taken as the total combined storage of gases if there is more than one supply system in the single treatment facility.

4-6.2.4.2 Systems defined in 4-6.2.4.1 may be located within a hospital when they are not served by the hospital's central supply system.

4-6.2.4.3 Single treatment facilities for nonhuman use of medical gas, such as veterinary medicine and laboratories, shall not be subject to the provisions of 4-4.2.7 and 4-4.2.9.2.

4-6.2.4.4 The provisions of 4-3.1.3 and 4-6.2.3.3 apply.

4-6.2.4.5 Type II systems shall be installed in accordance with Type I systems except as provided by 4-6.2.4.

4-6.2.4.6 Medical gas systems not specifically provided for in 4-6.2.4.1 or 4-6.2.4.3, such as systems within a hospital served by a central supply system or systems serving three or more treatment facilities, as may be found in a medical or dental office building, shall comply in all respects with Type I systems.

4-6.2.4.7 Equipment shall be obtained from and be installed under the supervision of a manufacturer or supplier familiar with proper practices for its construction and use.

4-6.3 Recordkeeping.

4-6.3.1 Patient Gas Systems — Type I.

4-6.3.1.1* Prior to the use of any medical gas piping system for patient care, the responsible authority of the facility shall assure that all tests required in Section 4-5.1 have been successfully conducted and permanent records of the test maintained in the facility files.

A-4-6.3.1.1 All testing should be completed before putting a new piping system, or an addition to an existing system, into service. Test procedures and the results of all tests should be made part of the permanent records of the facility of which the piping system forms a part. They should show the room and area designations, dates of the tests, and name(s) of persons conducting the tests.

4-6.4 Information and Warning Signs.

4-6.4.1 Patient Gas Systems — Type I.

4-6.4.1.1 The gas content of medical gas piping systems shall be readily identifiable by appropriate labeling with the name of the gas contained. Such labeling shall be by means of metal tags, stenciling, stamping, or with adhesive markers, in a manner that is not readily removable. Labeling shall appear on the piping at intervals of not more than 20 ft (6 m) and at least once in each room and each story traversed by the piping system. Where supplementary color identification of piping is used, it shall be in accordance with the gases and colors indicated in CGA Pamphlet C-9, *Standard Color-Marking of Compressed Gas Cylinders Intended for Medical Use in the United States.*

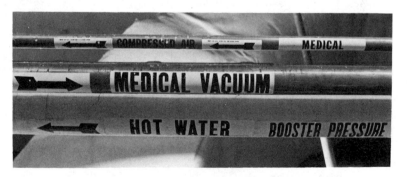

Figure 18   Identifying various pipes. (Note arrows indicating direction of flow of contents of each.)

4-6.4.1.2 Shutoff valves accessible to other than authorized personnel shall be labeled in substance as follows: [*See 4-4.1.2.2(a).*]

> CAUTION — (NAME OF MEDICAL GAS) VALVE
> DO NOT CLOSE EXCEPT IN EMERGENCY
> THIS VALVE CONTROLS SUPPLY TO . . .

4-6.4.1.3 Pressure gauges and manometers for medical gas piping systems shall be identified: (NAME OF GAS) — USE NO OIL!

4-6.4.1.4 The shutoff valve located outside or inside each anesthetizing location or located immediately outside each vital life support or critical care area in each medical gas line shall be marked to prohibit tampering or inadvertent closing, such as: (NAME OF MEDICAL GAS) — DO NOT CLOSE. (*See 4-4.1.3.3 and 4-4.1.3.4.*)

4-6.4.2 Patient Gas Systems — Type II.

4-6.4.2.1 The shutoff valves of 4-4.2.12 shall be labeled to indicate the gas controlled and to indicate that they are to be closed only in an emergency.

4-6.5 Transport and Delivery.

4-6.5.1 Personnel concerned with use and transport of equipment shall be trained in proper handling of cylinders, containers, hand trucks, supports, and valve protection caps.

This training should take place during orientation. Patient, staff, and visitor safety can be compromised if such personnel do not have training first.

4-6.5.2 Large cylinders, exceeding size E and containers larger than 100 lb (45.4 kg) weight, shall be transported on a proper hand truck or cart complying with 8-5.2.

Prologue for Vacuum System Requirements

By the early 1970s, a number of guidelines had been developed by various gas manufacturers, equipment suppliers, industry associations, and engineering publications on the subject of medical-surgical vacuum systems. None were based upon any broad-based documented performance data and each differed significantly from the other on the requirements for such systems. None was accepted by designers, user institutions, and enforcing agency inspectors to the extent that the following were creditable: (1) adequate systems design; (2) appropriate warning systems; and (3) appropriate interface without misinterpretation with other NFPA standards.

Since NFPA had already developed a standard for piped gases (NFPA 56F, *Standard for Nonflammable Medical Gas Systems*, now essentially 4-3 to 4-6 of the 1987 edition of NFPA 99), the development of a document on a system that in some ways paralleled it was considered appropriate. [One of the leading proponents in 1971 for NFPA developing a document on this subject was the Compressed Gas Association (CGA).] Because the mechanics and physics of a vacuum system differ from those of a piped gas system, NFPA established a Committee separate from the Technical Committee on Industrial and Medical Gases that developed NFPA 56F.

At the initial meetings of the Committee in 1971, to which clinical and industry members were invited, it became apparent that there was insufficient data to substantiate any one of the sizing methods in preference to any of the others then available and in use. The consensus of the Committee was that it should not support the development of a new document unless confirming test surveys were carried out. This was achieved by the American Society for Hospital Engineering and the Compressed Gas Association. (The data analysis on the surveys is available from the Secretary of the Technical Committee on Health Care Facilities at NFPA Headquarters in Quincy, Massachusetts.)

Basic testing was done to determine the degree of vacuum, vacuum flow, etc., required to operate the various equipment, such as blood removal, tracheal suction, gastric suction, thoracic suction, etc. The original data was developed with the CGA and various institutional members present. In general, the Committee found that as vacuum increased, the actual displacement curve became flat. A 15-in. Hg factor was ideal; a 12-in. Hg was a minimally acceptable value. At 20-in. Hg vacuum, the displacement curve flattened out.

One question that had been asked was, "Were flow requirements considered when a catheter was left open?" The answer is yes. Air flow is considerably higher with a catheter laying open than when it is inserted in blood. It was found that 0.25 SCFM was required when the catheter was occluded and that 1.5 SCFM was displaced when the suction tip or catheter was left in an open condition. An open catheter running continuously is considered poor suctioning technique and is discouraged (see 4-10.2.1.5) as it reduces the degree of vacuum in the entire system in general, as well as specifically at terminals (inlets) in the same or adjacent rooms.

The Committee, in combination with the American Society for Hospital Engineering and the Compressed Gas Association, collected sizeable data from 1975 through 1980 to make the resulting document (then NFPA 56K) as accurate as possible. It represents a data base significantly beyond that used in other previously promulgated methods. Hospitals were surveyed, and the data from 67 of them was used to confirm and verify the sizing criteria (other data was considered invalid for a variety of reasons). The 67 data points were not used to formulate the sizing criteria; rather they were used to verify and confirm the criteria. The 67 data points had an actual consumption of approximately 34 percent of the NFPA 56K design-rated flow and 17 percent of total source capacity before gas scavenging was considered. When considering gas scavenging and open terminals, actual consumption was 48 percent of the sizing criteria and 24 percent of the total source capacity.

The basic sizing criteria developed by the Committee is based on four major elements:

1. Documented testing on representative pieces of ancillary clinical equipment to determine capabilities and the level of vacuum required to evacuate body fluids and air to simulate outlets accidentally left open.

2. Realistic vacuum levels as established by clinical input.

3. Establishment of a minimum number of vacuum terminals for various locations and use based on empirical input from medical professionals.

4. Empirical development of simultaneous use curves that reflect the fact that as a hospital size (and the number of vacuum terminals) increases, the percentage of utilization of individual terminals decreases.

The surveys also raised the question of whether to design a vacuum system for bed occupancy rather than total bed count. The answer was the latter. For if a hospital had a 34 percent occupancy, the vacuum requirements would not be three times as great if it were at 100 percent occupancy. Looking at the diversity factors, the flow requirement may only be an additional 50 to 100 percent, not 300 percent.

The following Sections (4-7 to 4-10) (essentially former NFPA 56K and former Chapter 6 in NFPA 99-1984) thus provide for reasonable safety factors, although they were developed as a minimum performance standard. They do not, of course, prevent designers, etc., from using greater safety factors if they so desire.

The Committee considered it appropriate to observe testing of various manufacturers' devices since the document would affect such manufacturers, and because such testing provided "worst case" volume displacements and degree of vacuum necessary for various suction-therapy devices. These maximum displacements and levels of vacuum were used as a prime base for the calculations in this chapter, although the displacements are used in less than 50 percent of patient-suction applications, and in less than 10 percent of suctioning time for maximum open aspiration. (Note: the last are always momentary applications.) By using this "worst case" measurement as a prime base, considerable excess safety margin has been incorporated into the requirements that follow.

The testing of five manufacturers' devices was considered a good representation for such purposes and was the basis for these requirements.

In the 1984 revision cycle, when NFPA 56K was incorporated into NFPA 99, the Committee responsible for NFPA 56K voted to change the document from a recommended practice to a standard. This was accomplished for those portions where a consensus on minimum quantitative requirements was reached. (For this 1987 edition of NFPA 99, this material is the requirements contained in Sections 4-7 to 4-10.) Those portions where criteria were still only recommended were retained as recommendations in the form of Notes or Appendix material.

For more history on the development of this chapter, see C-4-6 in Appendix C.

4-7 Vacuum System Sources.

4-7.1 Patient Vacuum Source.

4-7.1.1 Medical-Surgical.

4-7.1.1.1* Pumps.

(a) *Multiple Pumps.* The central vacuum source shall consist of two or more vacuum pumps which, alternately or simultaneously on demand, serve the vacuum system. Each vacuum system shall be served by two or more vacuum pumps which, alternately or simultaneously on demand, supply the vacuum system. In the event that one vacuum pump fails, the remaining pump(s) shall be sized to maintain required vacuum at 100 percent of total system demand. Each pump shall have a shutoff valve to isolate it from the centrally piped system and other pump(s) for maintenance or repair without loss of vacuum in the piping system.

NOTE 1: Depending on anticipated vacuum system demand and utilization, as determined by consultation with the medical hospital staff, two or more centrally piped systems may be considered.

NOTE 2: Where several adjacent buildings are each equipped with vacuum sets, installation of a valved, normally closed, cross-connection line should be considered to provide emergency backup and operating economy under low load conditions. The pipe should be adequately sized. Consideration should also be given to the fact that, when the valve is open, continuous-duty operation of the single vacuum source may pose special design problems.

Previous guidelines recommended that each of the two vacuum pumps provide 75 percent of the calculated system demand. However, 100 percent back-up operation is considered necessary by the Committee since this system is felt to be a critical hospital utility. Failure or shutdown of the pump (causing reduction or loss of vacuum) can be injurious or fatal to patients. Vacuum systems in hospitals are true life-saving, life-support systems.

The requirements of 4-7.1.1.1(b) and (c) in particular ensure against unplanned vacuum loss, which could be life threatening.

The requirements for 100 percent back-up capacity are based on a single fault probability of failure. Thus, in the case of a duplex system, each pump must be designed for 100 percent of the total system design; in a triplex system, each pump should be sized for 50 percent of the demand (the other two pumps will provide

Figure 19   Typical multiple vacuum pump set-up.

the total demand when one is down); and in a quadruplex system, the total demand must be capable of being provided by any three pumps operating.

(b) *Pump Alternation.*   If automatic alternation of pumps in normal service is not provided, a manual alternation shall be achieved through an appropriate schedule determined by the facility.

Alternation of pumps (automatically or manually) is necessary because it provides even wear on both pumps, thereby extending the life of the pumps, reducing the probability of failure at any given time. Most automatic alternators incorporate automatic operation of the second pump in the event of failure or over-demand on the pump in use. Whether pump alternation is automatic or manual, activation of the nonoperating pump would have to be automatic in the event of operating pump failure or overload. Additionally, the pump is to be sized at the stopping point of the operating range so the stop setting can be reached on intermittent operation.

(c) *Backup Operation.*   A device shall be provided to automatically activate the additional pump unit(s) should the pump in operation be incapable of maintaining minimum required vacuum.

(d) *Electrical Power.*   Electrical equipment and wiring shall conform to the requirements of NFPA 70, *National Electrical Code.* Emergency electrical service for the vacuum pumps shall conform to the requirements of Chapter 3 of this document.

(e) *Pump Motors and Controls.*   Each vacuum pump motor shall be provided with a separate motor-starting device and overload protection. A suitable disconnecting device shall be installed in the electrical circuit ahead of each motor-starting device. Electrical control circuits shall be so arranged that shutting off or failure of one vacuum pump will not affect the operation of other pump(s).

(f) *Receivers (Tanks).* Receiver(s) shall be installed where the size of the vacuum system would cause excessive cycling of the pump(s). A suitable method shall be provided for drainage so that substances that might accumulate may be drained from the receiver(s) (tank). The method, if included, shall provide means to drain or service the receiver without interrupting the vacuum system.

NOTE: Characteristics of the vacuum pump and volume of the piping system are considerations for proper receiver sizing.

Figure 20 Typical vacuum receiver (tank). (Note: the two vacuum pumps are just to the right of the receiver.)

(g)* *Noise and Vibration.* Provision shall be made to minimize the transmission of noise and vibration created by the central vacuum source beyond the space in which the equipment is located.

A-4-7.1.1.1(g) Vibration can possibly cause motor deterioration and premature piping failures. Excessive noise can interfere with trouble alarms being heard.

(h) *Exhausts.* The exhaust from vacuum pumps shall be discharged outdoors in a manner that will minimize the hazards of noise and contamination to the hospital and its environment. The exhaust shall be located remote from any door, window, air intake, or other openings in buildings with particular attention given to separate levels for intake and discharge. Care shall also be exercised to avoid discharge locations contraindicated by prevailing winds, adjacent buildings, topography, and other influences. Outdoor exhausts shall be protected against the entry of insects, vermin, debris, and precipitation. Exhaust lines shall be sized to minimize back pressure.

Discharging of exhausts to the *outside* was intended since the discharge from patient drainage is always contaminated. Such discharge can carry infectious organisms, which should never be discharged within the building.

(i) *Typical Vacuum Source.* A schematic of a typical medical-surgical vacuum source is shown in Figure 4-7.1.1.1(i).

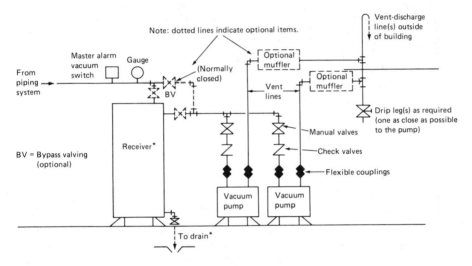

*See 4-7.1.1.1(h).
NOTE: Other arrangements that differ from this schematic in such items as the number of pumps, receivers, piping layout, etc., or other arrangements that meet specific recommendations of the vacuum source equipment manufacturer are permissible.

Figure 4-7.1.1.1(i)   Typical Medical-Surgical Vacuum Source.

A-4-7.1.1.1 Recommended Vacuum Source Sizing.

Unweighted System Demand. Pump sizing is based upon first determining the total number of terminals (inlets) in each of Groups A and B. These totals, each multiplied by 0.25 SCFM, provide the two basic figures necessary to calculate total demand on the system. [*See Table A-4-8.1.1.1(a).*]

Percentage in Use Factor. The two SCFM totals thus determined (one for each group) are multiplied by the appropriate "percent in use" factor as shown on the curves illustrated in Table A-4-8.1.1.1(b), "Simultaneous Use Curves."

Total Weighted System Demand. Adding these two calculated demand totals (for Groups A and B) and, in addition, allowing 1.5 SCFM for each operating room provides the total system demand and the required vacuum pump capacity. The pump should be selected to handle this flow or the maximum flow established for mains, whichever is higher.

Summary. The basic sizing formula is:

Vacuum Pump Size (SCFM) =

$$N_A \times 0.25 \times U.F._A + N_B \times 0.25 \times U.F._B + N_{OR} \times 1.5$$

Where: N_A = number of A-type terminals
N_B = number of B-type terminals
$U.F._A$ = use factor for A-type terminal total
$U.F._B$ = use factor for B-type terminal total
N_{OR} = number of operating rooms.

The issue of recommending a sizing formula has been one of continual debate. If included, should it be in the form of requirements or recommendations? Does sizing go beyond performance, thereby limiting design?

Before NFPA 56K, there were several methods available for calculating pump sizes, but no two methods were in agreement. Thus, designers were left to their own abilities in making the calculations. With no national consensus on the subject, some hospitals had undersized pumps that were burning out, and some had oversized pumps that were excessive in cost and operation, as well as maintenance (i.e., a greater than normal number of breakdowns were occurring due to short cycling). Because of this wide disparity, the Committee felt it appropriate to include at least one way sizing could be accomplished and, to indicate clearly that it was only one way, placed the equation for the calculations in the Appendix of the document. The Committee, in cooperation with the American Society for Hospital Engineering and the Compressed Gas Association, conducted surveys of hospitals to learn how well the formulas fit (*see C-4-6, Derivation of Design Parameters*). Initial testing actually took place in the early 1970s. Full scale surveying was conducted between 1976 and 1980 as noted in C-4-6.

In addition, a 1.5 SCFM factor for each operating room was added to the basic formula. From the 1978-1980 surveys, thirty facilities were analyzed using the existing 1978 formula. All but eight systems fit the then existing formula. Analysis indicated that:
• The number of operating rooms was the single most important parameter effecting all SCFM design.
• The total number of "A" and "B" terminals was the second most important parameter.

When the 1978 formula was adjusted in 1980 to accommodate an additional 1.5 SCFM per operating room, the formula was found to have a virtually 100 percent fit for the entire sixty-seven-hospital data sample.

Finally, a safety factor of 2.5 SCFM per pump was incorporated into the entire sizing methodology; i.e., on the average, the sizing method will give a sizing of total source capacity of five times the observed *peak* demand since two pumps are required (2.5 × 2 = 5). The safety factor was added based on experience and accounting for the heaviest users of vacuum.

4-7.1.2 Waste Anesthetic Gas Disposal.

NOTE: Nonflammable waste anesthetic gases may be disposed of by the medical-surgical vacuum system provided that its inclusion does not affect the performance of other parts of the system as outlined in 4-10.2.1.6 and in 4-7.1.2.1.

In the strictest sense, waste anesthetic gas disposal (WAGD) cannot be considered one of the functions of a medical-surgical vacuum system (MSVS). It does not fall within the scope of this chapter (as listed in 4-1.4). The question then arises: Is WAGD via the MSVS "nonmedical?" Medical-surgical vacuum is the application of suction therapy directly to the patient and in direct support of that therapy; WAGD is an environmental control system and 4-10.2.1.7 states that the MSVS is not to be used for nonmedical or nonsurgical applications.

The Subcommittee responsible for this portion of Chapter 4, recognizing that anesthetizing areas should provide staff protection from pollution by anesthetizing gases, has not prohibited the inclusion of WAGD in the MSVS of new or existing facilities. However, the Subcommittee *strongly discourages* such combined use for reasons listed below. Refer to: (1) Note in Table 4-8.1.1.1; (2) Note to this Section (4-7.1.2); and (3) Note 2 to Section 4-7.1.2.1. On the basis of displacement, a WAGD system would not add measurably to a MSVS. This was found in surveys by the then Committee on Medical-Surgical Vacuum Systems (now Subcommittee on Vacuum Systems and Equipment), and confirmed by an American National Standards Committee in ANSI Z79.11-1982, *Standard for Anesthetic Equipment-Scavenging Systems for Excess Anesthetic Gases.* The absolute maximum volume displaced by a WAGD system is less than 0.54 SCFM which is "worst case" displacement/momentary demand (maximum 5 seconds) of oxygen flush or occluded scavenging equipment (as noted in Table A1 in ANSI/Z79.11). Maximum normal operational displacement is less than 0.35 SCFM (*see Appendix C-4-6, point 3*). Thus, great caution must be exercised in determining the safety anesthesia circuit scavenger interface, if the MSVS is used for WAGD.

The Committee thus advocates separation of MSVS from a WAGD system based on the following factors:

• Nonrecirculating ventilation systems, dedicated blower systems, and passive systems (ambient differential) have all been demonstrated to be effective for WAGD. They meet the intent of ANSI Z79.11-1982 that the pressure of a scavenging system approximate very closely ambient pressure in normal use. These methods are more effective and less costly for WAGD then using the medical-surgical vacuum system.

• Some of the valving and piping material acceptable for use in a MSVS is not acceptable for WAGD. This includes components made of elastomers (many anesthetic agents cause "O" rings made of this material to swell); and aluminum, brass, magnesium, tin, and lead (halothane and other fluorinated agents can attack these metals in the presence of water vapor).

• The alarm systems and monitoring gauges required for a MSVS cannot be used in a WAGD system. The latter requires ultra-sensitive operating indicators. ANSI Z79.11-1982 states that the maximum safe negative pressure for the patient "shall not exceed 0.5 cm H_2O (0.01446847 in. Hg)." This is 0.0012 percent of the minimum degree of vacuum in the MSVS (based on 12 in. of Hg). Another way of stating this is as follows: 12 in. Hg is 829.3 times the maximum safe degree of negative pressure that should be experienced by the anesthetized patient.

• The International Standards Organization and the British Standards Institute both oppose using a MSVS for WAGD, as noted in the following statements made by European representatives at a 1977 ISO meeting on the subject:

(a) There is a great disparity in requirements between the two uses; the vacuum of a MSVS is approximately 1000 times in excess of that required for WAGD.

(b) Mixing the two creates very onerous safety problems. The negative pressure differential is vast [see 3 and 4(a) above], and "pressure swings" can seriously affect patients.

(c) Use of MSVS for WAGD affects pumps, lubricants, and valve seals.

(d) Both organizations concur with 0.5 cm H$_2$O as the maximum safe negative pressure for patients.
- A separate system for WAGD is consistent with the objective of the Subcommittee for a dedicated system for life support/therapy as opposed to a combined system for patient and nonpatient uses (e.g., environmental use such as WAGD). For further information, see:

1. "Waste Anesthetic Gases in Operating Room Air," J. H. Lecky, MD, *Journal of ASA*, 1980.

2. "Gas Scavenging — WAGD," L.D. Bridenbaugh, MD, *Clinical Engineering Series,* Academic Press, 1981.

4-7.1.2.1 Explosion Hazard. Flammable anesthetic or other flammable vapors shall be diluted significantly below the lower flammable limit prior to disposal into the medical-surgical vacuum system.

NOTE 1:   For further information, see Appendix A-5-4.2 on ANSI Z79.11, and Appendix C-12.1.3.1 on flammable anesthetic agents.

NOTE 2:   Flammable and nonflammable gases are known to be incompatible with the seals and piping used in medical-surgical vacuum systems. If waste anesthetic gas disposal is to be included as part of the medical-surgical vacuum system, It should be recognized that this activity will cause certain deterioration of the vacuum system. The terminal performance tests outlined in 4-10.2.1.4 are extremely important in maintaining the integrity of the medical-surgical vacuum system, and they should be made at more frequent intervals if waste anesthetic gas disposal is included in the vacuum system.

Recent information has revealed that none of the nurse anesthetist schools or anesthesiology residency programs have taught flammable anesthetics administration since 1982. It has been further reported to the Subcommittee on Vacuum Systems that the use of flammable anesthetics was encountered in only three locations out of 1,500 in JCAH surveys conducted in 1982.

Nevertheless, the Committee is concerned that the emergency use of flammable anesthetics adds an additional and unnecessary hazard if a medical-surgical vacuum system (MSVS) is used for WAGD. This paragraph was inserted to draw attention to the potential hazard of WAGD for flammable anesthetics. The Subcommittee on Vacuum Systems and Equipment would prefer that no vacuum-operated WAGD be considered when flammable anesthetics are used.

4-7.1.2.2 Pumps.   (Reserved)

4-7.1.2.3 Fans.   (Reserved)

4-7.2 Nonpatient Vacuum Source.

4-7.2.1 Laboratory Vacuum.   Where only one set of vacuum pumps is available for a combined medical-surgical vacuum system and an analysis, research, or teaching laboratory vacuum system, each connection from such a laboratory branch shall be piped through a fluid trap or scrubber with shutoff valves and drain valves, and shall be connected directly to the receiver (tank) and not into the network of piping serving patients.

NOTE: Any laboratory (such as for analysis, research, or teaching) in a hospital that is used for purposes other than direct support of patient therapy should preferably have its own self-supporting vacuum system, independent of the medical-surgical vacuum system. A small (satellite) medical laboratory used in direct support to patient therapy should not be required to be connected directly to the receiver or have fluid traps, scrubbers, etc., separate from the rest of the medical-surgical vacuum system.

A separate vacuum system for nonpatient purposes is recommended for several reasons. Laboratories often require different degrees, operating ranges, and displacements of vacuum from patient care areas. These differences, including usage rates, make planning difficult, particularly if coordination with the system for patients is included. Laboratory systems are also much more likely to aspirate vapors, fumes, and/or liquids of unusual nature, including exotic chemicals which could contaminate the patient portion of a vacuum system and damage pumps and/or other components of the system.

If a separate laboratory vacuum source (receiver tank) is not possible, laboratory piping has to be connected directly into the receiver tank(s), as noted above. This allowance for one source is not permitted for piped medical air systems (*see 4-3.1.9.1*).

4-7.2.2 Other. (Reserved)

4-8 Vacuum System Distribution.

4-8.1 Patient Vacuum Distribution.

4-8.1.1 Medical-Surgical (Piping, Valving/Controls, Inlets/Terminal Units, Alarms).

4-8.1.1.1* Number of Terminals (Inlets). Table 4-8.1.1.1 sets forth the minimum number of vacuum system terminals (inlets) for patient suction therapy, but does not include terminals (inlets) for disposing of waste anesthetic gases.

A-4-8.1.1.1 Number of Terminals (Inlets) and Usage Groups. Table 4-8.1.1.1 sets forth the minimum number of system terminals (inlets) and Table A-4-8-1.1.1(a) establishes usage Groups A and B. Table A-4-8.1.1.1(a) should be used in conjunction with Table A-4-8.1.1.1(b) and Appendix C-4.1 for determining proper pipe and pump sizing. The Group A classification represents a more critical and more frequently used vacuum terminal (inlet) than the Group B classification.

NOTE 1: If the medical-surgical vacuum system is to be used for the disposal of waste anesthetic gases caution must be taken to ensure that the system is designed for the additional volume required. It is recommended that 4-7.1.2, "Waste Anesthetic Gas Disposal," be consulted as well. It is essential that the design team consult with medical and hospital staff when determining the minimum terminal units.

NOTE 2: It should be understood that the percentage in use factors obtained from Table A-4-8.1.1.1(b) represent an average hospital. Hospitals with heavier-than-average use may require higher use factors.

In 1980, the term "waste anesthetic gas evacuation" (WAGE) was agreed upon by the Committee to describe the collecting of anesthetic gases that can be present in the surgical area. For the 1984 edition of NFPA 99, the term "evacuation" was changed to "disposal." This function is sometimes called "scavenging"; however, it is preferable to use the term scavenging in connection with the equipment used between the anesthesia machine and inlet of a disposal system rather than with the function itself. (*See Commentary on waste anesthetic gases under 4-7.1.2.*)

Table 4-8.1.1.1 Minimum Number of Vacuum Terminals
(Without Waste Anesthetic Gas Disposal).

NOTE: If it is intended to use the vacuum system for waste anesthetic gas disposal, provision for an additional terminal (inlet) should be made.

Anesthetizing Locations Operating Room	3/room
Cystoscopy	3/room
Delivery	3/room
Special Procedures	3/room
Other Anesthetizing Locations	3/room
Acute Care Locations (Nonanesthetizing Locations) Recovery Room	3/bed
Intensive Care Units (Except Cardiac)	3/bed
Special Procedures	2/room
Emergency Rooms	1/bed
Emergency Rooms—Major Trauma	3/bed
Cardiac Intensive Care Units	2/bed
Catheterization Lab	2/bed
Surgical Excision Rooms	1/room
Dialysis Unit	(1/2)/bed
Subacute Patient Care Areas (Nonanesthetizing Locations) Nurseries	1/bed
Patient Rooms	1/bed
Exam and Treatment Rooms	1/bed
Respiratory Care	Convenience
Other Autopsy	1/Table
Central Supply	Convenience
Equipment Repair, Calibration and Teaching	Convenience

NOTE: If it is intended to use the vacuum system for waste anesthetic gas disposal, provision for an additional terminal (inlet) should be made.

ANSI Z79.11-1982, *Anesthetic Equipment-Scavenging Systems for Excess Anesthetic Gases*, uses the term "disposal" as opposed to "evacuation." Since that document was developed in coordination with international standards organizations, the Committee responsible for Chapter 6 has dropped its previous use of the term "evacuation."

The simultaneous use curves of A-4.8.1.1.1 are the result of many such curves developed previously by industry; various equipment manufacturers and suppliers, designers, survey inquiries; and from empirical data derived from years of experience by professionals in the field of vacuum technology. The curves reflect the fact that as a hospital increases in size (and increases the number of vacuum inlets), the percentage of utilization of the individual terminals (inlet) decreases. Studies of the past few years have borne out the validity of these curves. (For further information, see C-4-6, "Derivation of Parameters.")

The change to Note 1 under Table A-4-8.1.1.1.(b) reflects the fact that an anesthetic gas disposal system is not considered to be a part of a medical-surgical vacuum system (MSVS).

Table A-4-8.1.1.1(a)   Number of Vacuum Terminals (Inlets) Without Waste Anesthetic Gas Disposal.

	Minimum Terminal Units	Usage Group
Anesthetizing Locations		A
Operating Room	3/rm	A
Cystoscopy	3/rm	A
Delivery	3/rm	A
Special Procedures	3/rm	A
Other Anesthetizing Locations	3/rm	A
Acute Care Locations (Nonanesthetizing Locations)		
Recovery Room	3/bed	A
ICUs (Except Cardiac)	3/bed	A
Special Procedures	2/rm	A
Emergency Rooms	1/bed	A
Emergency Rooms—Major Trauma	3/bed	A
Cardiac ICU (CCU)	2/bed	A
Catheterization Lab	2/rm	B
Surgical Excision Rooms	1/rm	B
Dialysis Unit	(1/2)/bed	B
Subacute Care Areas (Nonanesthetizing Locations)		
Nurseries	1/bed	B
Patient Rooms	1/bed	B
Exam and Treatment Rooms	1/bed	B
Respiratory Care	Convenience	
Other		
Autopsy	1/table	B
Central Supply	Convenience	B
Equipment Repair, Calibration and Teaching	Convenience	B

Table A-4-8.1.1.1(b)   Simultaneous Use Curves.

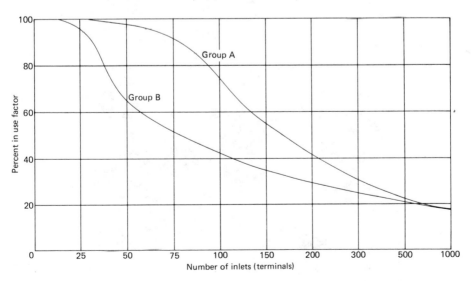

4-8.1.1.2 Vacuum Piping Network.

(a) *Pipe Materials.*   All pipelines shall be constructed of seamless Type K, L, or M copper tubing or other corrosion-resistant metallic tubing such as stainless steel, galvanized steel, etc. If vacuum piping is installed simultaneously with other medical gas piping, either it shall be labeled or otherwise identified prior to installation in order to preclude inadvertent inclusion into a medical gas system, or it shall be cleaned and degreased in accordance with 4-4.1.4. Copper pipelines shall be hard temper for exposed locations and soft temper for underground or concealed locations.

NOTE: The purpose of this requirement is that oxygen, nitrous oxide, and compressed air lines are often installed in hospitals at the same time as vacuum systems, and carelessness and errors in installing the vacuum lines might result in fire, explosion, damage to or contamination of other medical pipelines, or inadvertent switching of pipes. (*Also see Sections 4-3 through 4-6.*)

Corrosion-resistant *metal* piping has always been recommended because of its strength, its resistance to damage and collapse, and its resistance to mechanical and fire damage. These criteria are musts for life-support systems. The Committee studied the issue of piping material very carefully and concluded that there were no valid engineering reasons to exclude noncopper, metal piping in vacuum systems.

In addition, the experience of most Committee members has indicated that (1) copper piping for vacuum systems is sufficiently marked to preclude its installation for medical gas pipelines as required in former NFPA 56F, *Standard for Nonflammable Medical Gas Systems* (now Sections 4-3 to 4-6 in this 1987 edition of NFPA 99), and (2) adhering to recommendations on inspection, in this section and Sections 4-9 and 4-10, can and does reveal any mistakes.

Figure 21 Typical vacuum terminal (inlet) in patient care area.

The use of plastic pipe was considered during the early development phase of NFPA 56K but was not accepted because of the fire hazard imposed by plastics. Concern was for the potential of localized failure of plastic pipe due to heat generated by confined fires. The vacuum system could thus be breached instead of (probably) remaining intact (were metal piping used). There was also concern for toxic and/or noxious fumes from plastic pipe in the event of a fire. Future changes in technology may ultimately allow a revision in this position. However, until then, only corrosion-resistant *metal* piping [as noted in 4-8.1.1.2(a)] is acceptable.

(b)* *Minimum Pipe Sizing.* In both branch and main lines the minimum pipe size shall be not less than ½-in. nominal, except that smaller pipe diameters shall be permitted for drops toindividual terminals (inlets) and static lines to gauges and alarm actuators (vacuum switches).Pipe size for drops to individual terminals (inlets) shall not be less than ¼-in. inner diameter (I.D.).

A-4-8.1.1.2(b) Recommended Minimum Pipe Sizing.

Branch and Riser Sizing. Branch sizing should be on the basis of a flow into the system of 1.5 SCFM per terminal (inlet) served, as described in Table A-4-8.1.1.1(a), commencing with the terminal (inlet) on the branch farthest from the vacuum source(s), until all of the terminals in a room have been accommodated. Branch lines serving more than one room should be sized as mains in accordance with the paragraph below. Operating room suites, ICU suites, and the like, comprising several rooms, should be treated as one room. Risers should be sized in the same manner as branches.

Mains. Sizing should be on the basis of 0.25 SCFM per terminal (inlet) served, as described in Appendix C-4.3, with the further provision that the size of any main line should not be less than the largest pipe in any branch served by that main. The flow rate to be handled at any point in the main should be computed on the number of A and B terminals connected thereto, multiplied by 0.25 SCFM, the simultaneous use percentage plus the allowance of 1.5 SCFM per operating room, or the flow from the largest branch served, whichever is greater.

With regard to pipe sizing, it is the Committee's intent that terminals (inlets) contained in modular walls and consoles be counted individually as opposed to collectively.

(c) *Pipe Supports.* Piping shall not be supported by other piping, but shall be supported by pipe hooks, metal pipe straps, bands, or hangers suitable for the size of the pipe and of proper strength and quality at proper intervals so that the supports are on the joints. [*See Table 4-8.1.1.2(c).*] Pipeline supports shall be insulated from the pipe or be of a compatible material so as to prevent deterioration due to bimetallic electrolyte action.

Table 4-8.1.1.2(c) Intervals of Pipe Support.

½-in. pipe or tubing	6 ft (1.83 m)
¾-in. or 1-in. pipe or tubing	8 ft (2.44 m)
1¼-in. or larger (horizontal)	10 ft (3.05 m)
1¼-in. or larger (vertical)	every floor level

(d) *Permanent Fittings.* All fittings used for connecting copper tubing shall be wrought copper, brass, or bronze made especially for brazed or soldered joining, except as provided in 4-8.1.1.2(e) and (f).

(e) *Nonpermanent Fittings.* Any nonpermanent-type fitting, such as unions, flare connections, etc., when used on vacuum system distribution lines, shall be installed so as to be readily accessible.

(f) *Metallic Shape Memory Fittings.* Listed or approved metallic shape memory fittings that, when made up, will provide a permanent joint equal to the mechanical, thermal, and sealing integrity of a brazed or soldered joint complying with 4-8.1.1.8(a), may be used anywhere in vacuum distribution lines.

This type of fitting is radically different from those requiring the use of a hot flame and solder (brazing) to form a seal at each end of the fitting joining two pipes. It is a new technology that was previously prohibited by prior wording of 4-8.1.1.2(d) and 4-8.1.1.8(a), which allowed only brazing.

Metallic shape memory fittings are made of a special alloy that *contracts upon heating* (e.g., if kept very cold, contraction occurs upon exposure to ambient temperatures). Thus, fittings are kept in liquid nitrogen until ready for use. When removed from the super cold nitrogen, a worker has about 30 seconds to slip half the fitting over the end of one of the pipes to be joined and place the other pipe into the other half of the fitting. The fitting, since it is now exposed to a warmer temperature (in this instance ambient room temperature), will contract, creating a permanent, very tight seal. No flame or solder is required.

(g) *Mechanically Formed Tubing Fittings.* A listed or approved fabricating process, which when completed will provide a permanent joint equal to the mechanical, thermal, and sealing integrity of a brazed or soldered joint complying with 4-8.1.1.8(a), may be used anywhere in vacuum distribution lines.

Like Paragraph 4-8.1.1.2(f), this type of fitting represents technology previously prohibited because prior wording did not envision it.

This paragraph is actually an allowance for any listed fabricating process that creates or produces a permanent fitting equal to those required in Paragraph 4-8.1.1.2(a). (*See Chapter 2 for definition of "listed."*) One method demonstrated to the Subcommittee on Vacuum Systems involved the use of a special drill that first drills a hole in the tubing and then forms out a portion of the tubing, creating a fitting from the tubing itself. This is only *one* method, and thus far it has been considered acceptable only for tubing used for vacuum systems.

(h) *Mechanical and Environmental Protection.* All installations, including buried piping, shall be adequately protected against frost, freezing, corrosion, and physical damage. Ducts or casings shall be used wherever buried piping passes under a roadway, driveway, parking lot, or other area subject to surface loads. Exposed piping shall be suitably protected against physical damage from the movement of portable equipment such as carts, stretchers, and trucks.

4-8.1.1.3 Shutoff Valves.

(a) *General.* Shutoff valves shall be provided to isolate appropriate sections or portions of the piping system for maintenance, repair, or planned future expansion need, and to facilitate periodic testing.

(b) *Valve Types.* Shutoff valves shall be of a type that will create no greater flow restriction than the piping to which they are connected.

(c) *Riser Valves.* Shutoff valves shall be provided at the base of vertical risers servicing more than one floor.

(d) *Section Valves.* A shutoff valve shall be provided on each floor between the riser and the first terminal (inlet) to allow for maintenance and periodic testing without serious disruption of service. In single-story facilities, a shutoff valve shall be installed between the main line and the first terminal of each branch line.

(e) *Valve Boxes.* All shutoff valves in public and anesthetizing areas shall be installed in valve boxes with frangible or removable windows large enough to permit manual operation of the valve.

While Section 4-8.1.1.3(e) is only a declaratory type statement (relative to placing shutoff valves in boxes if they exist in certain areas), Section 4-8.1.1.3(a) clearly requires such valves in certain areas or portions of the system. An anesthetizing location constitutes a portion of the vacuum system. Thus, a shutoff valve would be required for each room in these areas.

This requirement (similar to that for medical piped gas systems), is included so that personnel will learn to quickly identify shutoff valves for all types of piping systems for patient life-support services.

4-8.1.1.4 Terminals (Inlets).

The terms "terminal" and "inlet" are considered the most technically accurate terms from the point of view of use. They were chosen after much Committee discussion because the vacuum system inlets were being confused with positive-pressure medical piped gas system outlets [e.g., those for nonflammable medical gas systems, as specified in former NFPA 56F, *Standard for Nonflammable Medical Gas Systems* (now Sections 4-3 to 4-6 in the 1987 edition of NFPA 99)].

(a) *General.* Each terminal (inlet) for vacuum shall be equipped with a valve mechanism of a type not interchangeable with other systems (such as oxygen, compressed air, etc.) and either a threaded connection or quick coupler.

(b) *Threaded Connections.* Valves with threaded connections shall conform to the Diameter-Index Safety System as described in the Compressed Gas Association pamphlet CGA V-5.

(c) *Secondary Check Valves.* Vacuum terminals (inlets) shall not incorporate a secondary check valve.

NOTE: Area alarms for these systems are just above shutoff valves.

Figure 22   Shutoff valve for piped vacuum system in conjunction with piped gas shutoff valves.

(d) *Physical Protection.*   Terminals (inlets) shall be located so as to avoid physical damage to the valve or attached equipment.

(e) *Physical Spacing.*   Careful consideration shall be given to provide adequate spacing between the terminals (inlets) and adjacent medical gas outlets.

(f) *Removable Assemblies.*   Terminal (inlet) assemblies, as furnished by manufacturers, shall be legibly marked VACUUM or SUCTION so that, in their state of disassembly for hookup to the vacuum system, proper identification is not lost.

Figure 23   Typical vacuum terminal (inlet).

4-8.1.1.5 Master Alarm System.

Suction therapy is truly life supporting since its failure can be injurious and life threatening, and patients receiving suction therapy are generally in serious condition, nonambulatory, and incapable of self-preservation. Thus, the proper functioning of alarms to indicate a failure or shutdown of the medical-surgical vacuum system is most essential.

Warning systems were nonexistent or conflicting in some of the design guidelines prior to the development of NFPA 56K. Requiring such systems was part of the rationale for the development of that document (now essentially Sections 4-7 to 4-10 in the 1987 edition of NFPA 99).

(a) *General.*   The vacuum system master alarm shall provide cancellable audible and noncancellable visual signals at a continuously monitored location so as to indicate when the vacuum in the main line drops below the level required in 4-9.1.5. When one continuously monitored location is not available, a secondary master alarm shall be installed at some location, such as the telephone switchboard or the security office, where it is most likely to be seen or heard.

Twelve-in. Hg vacuum was the minimum value requested by medical personnel on the Committee (i.e., they wanted to know when the vacuum level dropped below 12 in. Hg). Below 12-in. Hg vacuum, the rate and volume of fluid removal (particularly in areas such as surgery and critical care units) is too low for optimum patient care. Less than 12 in. of Hg is considered unsatisfactory for removal of heavy mucus, loose tissue particles, coagulated blood, etc. (*See additional commentary on this subject under 4-9.1.3.1.*)

However, since this 12-in. value is a performance criterion, the value at which the alarm sensor is set is not specified. The designer determines what setting is necessary to meet a minimum of 12-in. Hg vacuum.

Figure 24   Vacuum alarm in conjunction with area gas alarms.

(b) *Actuator Switch.*   The actuator (vacuum switch) for the master alarm shall be connected to the main line immediately upstream (on the terminal or inlet side) of the main-line valve [i.e., the main-line valve is between the receiver (tank) and the master alarm vacuum switch].

(c) *Alarm Panels.*   The master alarm signal panel(s) required in 4-8.1.1.5(a) (each with visual and audible signal) shall be actuated by the vacuum switch described in 4-8.1.1.5(b).

(d) *Panel Labels.*   The master alarm signal panel(s) shall be appropriately labeled.

(e) *Combined Alarm Signals.*   The vacuum alarm signal shall serve only the medical-surgical vacuum system. (*See Sections 4-3 through 4-5 and Chapter 3.*)

NOTE: The master alarm signal panel for the vacuum system may be combined with other alarm signals for other facility systems, such as oxygen, emergency electrical power, fire alarms, etc., provided that the function of this alarm signal is clearly distinguished from the others by labeling as described in 4-8.1.1.5(d).

(f) *Alarm System Power.* The master alarm signal system shall be energized by the essential electrical system described in 4-7.1.1.1(d). (*See Chapter 3.*)

4-8.1.1.6 Area Alarm Systems.

(a) *General.* Vacuum area alarm systems shall be provided in anesthetizing location areas and other life support and critical care areas, such as postanesthesia recovery, intensive care units, coronary care units, etc.

NOTE 1: Two or more adjacent alarm areas may be served by a single signal panel at a location near the points of use, which will provide responsible surveillance.

NOTE 2: For additional information concerning alarms for central medical-gas-piping systems, refer to Sections 4-3 and 4-4.

(b) *Visual and Audible Signals.* The vacuum area alarm system shall incorporate both cancellable audible and noncancellable visual signals that are activated by actuators (vacuum switches) connected to the vacuum line serving each specific area.

(c) *Alarm Panels.* The visual and audible signal panels shall be installed at nurses' stations or other suitable locations in the areas described in 4-8.1.1.6(a) and be appropriately labeled.

(d) *Actuator Switches.* The actuator (vacuum switch) for each area described in 4-8.1.1.6(a) shall connect to the vacuum line for that area and upstream (on the terminal or inlet side) of any shutoff valves, with no shutoff valves intervening between the area alarm actuator (vacuum switch) and the terminals (inlets) in the area.

(e) *Actuator Switch Settings.* Actuators (vacuum switches) for the area alarm signals shall be set to activate their respective warning signals (visual and audible) when the vacuum drops below 12 in. Hg (vacuum).

(f) *Electrical Power.* The area alarm signal system shall be energized by the essential electrical system described in 4-7.1.1.1(d). (*See also Chapter 3.*)

4-8.1.1.7 Vacuum Gauges.

(a) *Main-Line Gauge.* A vacuum gauge shall be provided in the main vacuum line adjacent to the actuator (vacuum switch) for the master alarm, with this gauge located immediately upstream (on the terminal or inlet side) of the main-line valve.

(b) *Area Gauge.* Vacuum gauges shall be located at each area vacuum alarm signal location, with this gauge connected upstream (on the terminal or inlet side) of any valve controlling that area.

Gauges, particularly area gauges, should be checked regularly and calibrated, if necessary, to assure optimum vacuum for patient therapy. (*See also Commentary under 4-10.2.1.2.*)

4-8.1.1.8 Piped Connections.

(a) *Joints.* All joints in copper or stainless steel piping, except those at valves or at equipment requiring pipe thread connections, shall be made with solder, brazing material, or fittings complying with 4-8.1.1.2(f) or (g) having a melting point not less than 450°F (232°C). Joints in galvanized steel piping shall be threaded, flanged, gasketed couplings, or fittings complying with 4-8.1.1.2(f), compatible with the pipe material used.

NOTE: It is recognized that vacuum lines are installed and soldered at the same time as nonflammable medical gas systems. Therefore, silver brazing [at minimum 1000°F (691.4°C) melting point] should be considered in order to avoid inadvertent soft soldering of nonflammable medical gas piping.

The subject of allowing joints to be made of soldering material "having a melting point not less than 450°F" was extensively discussed by the Committee responsible for the development of NFPA 56K (now Sections 4-7 to 4-10 in NFPA 99). Technically, there is no justification for silver brazing vacuum system piping because a vacuum system cannot leak its contents and cause a hazard, even in the event of a fire that causes vacuum lines to leak (i.e., the system is under negative pressure compared to the atmosphere). A melting point not less than 450°F is thus considered adequate for joint integrity, structural consideration, and general safety. Conversely, oxidizing gases (e.g., oxygen, nitrous oxide, compressed air) are gases under 3.5 atmospheres pressure within a piped gas system and can leak into the atmosphere. Therefore, these systems require tubing that cannot ignite in 100 percent oxidizing gases (e.g. copper tubing), as opposed to ferrous metals, which can ignite in such an atmosphere and cause hazards. These piped gas systems also require higher temperature brazing at joints (not less than 1000°F) to reduce the probability of joints leaking and/or breaking in the event of a nearby fire.

Although the Committee considered the requirement portion of this paragraph adequate, it also recognized the possibility of a mixup in soldering joints during new construction when pipe vacuum and gas systems are being installed simultaneously and adjacent to each other. Thus, the requirement portion was worded "not less than" in order not to preclude higher temperatures being used; the Note was added to explain the above to the reader. In addition, for the 1984 edition of NFPA 99, the Committee added recommendations for visual inspection and documentation of pipe and solder material similar to those for nonflammable medical gas piping systems. (See 4-9.)

Given the critical nature of these systems, inspection of joints before walls, ceiling, etc. are closed in is considered essential.

4-8.1.1.9 Threaded Connections. Pipe thread joints shall be installed by tinning the male thread with soft solder, litharge and glycerin, polytetrafluoroethylene (such as Teflon) tape, or a suitable luting compound.

4-8.1.2 Waste Anesthetic Gas Disposal. *(See Note in Table 4-8.1.1.1 and in 4-7.1.2.)*

4-8.2 Nonpatient Vacuum Distribution. (Reserved)

4-9 Vacuum System Performance Criteria and Testing.

4-9.1 Patient Vacuum System.

4-9.1.1 Cross-Connection. Cross-connection testing shall be performed as described in 4-5.1.1.

The Committee felt it essential to ensure that only vacuum use points were connected to the medical-surgical vacuum system. Cross-connection with a nonflammable medical gas system would artificially load the medical-surgical vacuum system during normal operation, and thus inhibit it from achieving design vacuum and flow performance. It would also present a distinct safety problem in the event of a fire (oxygen and nitrous oxide enhance and accelerate combustion). Therefore, the cross-connection test outlined in former NFPA 56F, *Standard for Nonflammable Medical Gas Systems* (now Sections 4-3 to 4-6 in 1987 edition of NFPA 99), was included. Committee documentation reveals that one consultant testing firm that tested 80 facilities over a three-year period encountered cross-connections in ten facilities. Nine specific air/vacuum cross-connections and eight oxygen/vacuum-cross connections were encountered in the ten locations.

4-9.1.2 Purging/Cleaning.

4-9.1.2.1 Flux. Particular care shall be exercised in applying the flux to avoid leaving any excess inside the completed joints.

4-9.1.2.2 Cleaning. The outside of the tube and fittings shall be cleaned by washing with hot water after assembly.

4-9.1.2.3 Purging. After installation of the piping, but before attachment of the vacuum line to the vacuum pumps and receiver(s) (tank), and before installation of the vacuum alarm switches, station terminals (inlets), and gauges, the line shall be blown clear by means of oil-free, dry nitrogen or air.

4-9.1.3 Flow/Standing Pressure.

4-9.1.3.1 Minimum Flow and Pressure Requirements at Vacuum Terminals (Inlets). Piping shall be sized such that 3 SCFM can be evacuated through any one terminal without reducing vacuum pressure below 12 in. Hg at an adjacent terminal.

NOTE: This is not a criterion for pump sizing purposes. See Appendix C-4.3 for pump sizing recommendations.

This paragraph was reworded for the 1987 edition to clarify that the flow and pressure requirements are applicable throughout the vacuum system, and not just at one terminal.

It should not be assumed that a maximum system pressure drop under design flow conditions is 3 in. Hg. The 3 SCFM flow is only a measurement at one terminal when comparing vacuum pressure at an adjacent terminal.

The flow rate of 3 SCFM is representative of a vacuum terminal with none of the normal ancillary equipment attached (i.e., vacuum regulator, suction trap bottle, connecting tubing, and suction tip). This equipment has a restrictive effect on air flow. In fact, tests indicate that the flow of 3 SCFM is about twice the maximum flow through a terminal connected to the normal ancillary equipment. The 3 SCFM flow would probably occur only during a "worse case" test of an unrestricted terminal. Documentation of the Subcommittee responsible for vacuum systems has shown one testing agency finding thousands of terminals, over a five year period, not operating properly.

The 12-in. Hg minimum vacuum level was selected in consultation with the clinical staff, and in coordination with the use of the ancillary vacuum equipment. Normal bronchial or thoracic suction is done under intermittent operation, requiring a low degree of vacuum and a slightly higher volume displacement. In general, the Committee found that as vacuum increased, the actual displacement curve for fluids became flat. A 15-in. Hg vacuum was ideal; 12-in. Hg vacuum, was a minimal accepted value; at 20-in. Hg vacuum, the displacement curve flattened out.

Additionally, the use of artificially high vacuum results in the potential for tissue damage at the catheter tip while in use.

Leaks in the vacuum system result in low-vacuum, high-volume flow. The need to go to higher vacuum levels to achieve a resultant 12-in. Hg vacuum would be a poor use practice (i.e., suction fittings improperly sealing with poor or no maintenance attention; suction left open and running when not in use, artificially increasing the demand load).

Finally, a pump sized for handling a given system designed at 20-in. Hg vacuum would have to be 50 percent higher than a pump sized for the same demand at 15-in. Hg vacuum. This is because the calculated pump capacity for a given hospital demand is inversely proportional to the absolute suction pressure.

For further information on the 12-in. Hg requirement, see Commentary on 4-8.1.1.5.

4-9.1.3.2 Overall System Pressure-Drop Criteria. Pipe sizes shall be in conformity with good engineering practice for delivery of maximum design volumes.

NOTE: It is recommended that vacuum pressure loss, from source to farthest terminal when the calculated demand is drawn on the vacuum system, be limited to 3 in. Hg.

In developing system pressure drop criteria, the Committee responsible for this chapter decided that 3 in. Hg was as restrictive a criterion as was necessary, and so recommended it. However, while only a recommendation, this value is indicative of adequate pipe sizing and of no undue restrictions in mains and risers. (The terminal performance tests of 4-10.2.1.4 will reveal to what degree, if any, the smaller lines to each individual terminal inlet are obstructed.)

A pressure drop (i.e., vacuum pressure loss) greater than 3 in. Hg may indicate that piping or pump capacity is too small. When pressure drop is more than can be tolerated, increased system capacity (parallel piping), larger pumps, and/or a higher setting of operating range may be necessary to stay above the 12-in. Hg vacuum required by 4-9.1.3.3. Such compensation would be more expensive in terms of cost, installation, operation, and maintenance.

4-9.1.3.3 Minimum Vacuum and Operating Range. The vacuum pumps and collection piping shall be capable of maintaining a vacuum of 12 in. of mercury (Hg) at the terminal (inlet) farthest away from the central vacuum source when the calculated demand for the hospital is drawn in the system. The capacity of vacuum pumps shall be based on ACFM calculated at the lead vacuum switch setting. If the pump selected is not capable of continuous duty, the capacity of the pump shall be based on AFCM calculated at the pump's stop setting, or the pump shall be selected so that a stop setting can be reached on intermittent operation. (*See Appendix C-4.3 for examples.*)

NOTE: An operating range of 15 in. to 19 in. Hg is suggested at the receiver.

During the development of NFPA 56K, the Committee pointed out that the operating range criteria of 15 to 19 in. at the receiver was a suggestion based on a medical-user requirement for the most effective and safest suctioning of patients. The recommendation was not related to pump design or size. Any pump that could maintain the minimum vacuum requirement (12 in. Hg) was satisfactory.

The actual operating range for any new system is a factor best left to the system designer. Some vacuum pumps, for example reciprocating types, are often run at higher vacuum levels to ensure equipment protection. The higher compression ratios result in higher operating temperatures and minimize condensation in the pumps. Other types of pumps that are not sensitive to moisture condensation would, by design, want to operate closer to the minimum vacuum requirement of 12 in. Hg.

4-9.1.3.4 Standing Pressure Test. After installing a vacuum system, including terminals (inlets), but before attaching the vacuum lines to the vacuum pumps, receiver(s) (tank), and alarm system(s) switches and gauges, the entire system or sections of the system shall be subjected to a test pressure of not less than 60 psig (413 kPa gauge) by means of oil-free, dry nitrogen or air. After allowance for temperature variation, the pressure at the end of 24 hours shall be within 5 psig (345 kPa gauge) of the initial pressure. Corrective action shall be taken if this performance is not verified. After completion of the test, corrections, and reverification if necessary, the system shall be connected to the vacuum pumps, receiver(s), alarm actuators (vacuum switches), and gauges.

NOTE: For information on how to correct pressure for temperature changes, see Sections 4-3 through 4-5.

The test pressure value was changed in 1984 to "not less than 60 psig" to avoid damage to vacuum terminals (inlets) not designed to withstand the previous recommendation of 150 psig (i.e., vacuum lines normally operate between approximately 12- and 20-in. Hg vacuum).

4-9.1.4 Leakage. The following tests are intended to be performed to certify acceptance of a system after initial installation. Routine tests for maintenance of the system are addressed in 4-10.2. The tests shall be conducted on the upstream portion of the medical-surgical vacuum system whenever it is breached and whenever modifications are made.

The third sentence was added to assure testing of a new system (either a totally new one or the new portion of an existing one), and also to eliminate the need to test an entire system when only a new portion was added or an existing portion changed.

4-9.1.4.1 Inspection. A visual inspection of each joint shall be made to assure that the alloy has flowed completely in and around the joint and that hardened flux has not formed a temporary seal that holds test pressure. All excess flux shall be removed for clear visual inspection of connections.

4-9.1.4.2 Leakage Tests. Before attaching the vacuum lines to the vacuum pumps, receivers(s) (tank), and alarm signaling system(s) switches and gauges, each section of the vacuum piping system shall be subjected to a test pressure not less than 150 psig (1034 kPa gauge) by means of oil-free, dry nitrogen or air. This test pressure shall be maintained until each joint has been examined for leakage by use of soapy water or other suitable means. All leaks shall be repaired and the section retested. (*See Compressed Gas Association Pamphlet G-10.1, Commodity Specification for Nitrogen.*)

4-9.1.4.3 Final Installation Leakage Test. The facility shall perform a final installation leakage test for detecting leaks in the vacuum system.

NOTE: An acceptable method of testing is by means of shutting down portions of the system using the shutoff valves described in 4-8.1.1.3 to determine the capability of the section to maintain a vacuum. An acceptable condition is a vacuum level loss of less than 1.5 in. Hg in one hour with the vacuum system piping initially at a vacuum in excess of 12 in. Hg.

A final installation test is considered essential. However, no specific test can be identified at this time. The example given in the Note (which is a recommendation and not a requirement) must be tempered by the number of installed terminals. For example, a 1.5-in. Hg leak in one hour for a system of 500 installed terminals represents minimal system leakage. The same leakage for a system of 50 installed terminals represents a more serious problem warranting investigation of the leak sources.

4-9.1.4.4 Schedule of Testing. When the piping is intended to be concealed inside of walls or partitions, the tests described in 4-9.1.2.3 and 4-9.1.4.2 shall be completed before the walls or partitions are closed in. Tests described in 4-9.1.3.4 shall be conducted after walls or partitions are closed in.

4-9.1.5 Alarm Testing. The vacuum system master alarm and any secondary master alarm shall signal when the vacuum in the main line drops below the level required to maintain 12 in. Hg (vacuum) at the terminal (inlet) farthest from the source.

4-9.2 Nonpatient Vacuum System. (Reserved)

4-10 Administration (Vacuum System).

4-10.1 Responsibility of Governing Body. (Reserved)

4-10.2 Policies.

4-10.2.1 Vacuum System (Patient).

4-10.2.1.1 General. The locations and number of vacuum system terminals (inlets) in a system shall be determined by consultation with medical and facility staff having knowledge of the requirements for, and the utilization of, vacuum in each space or patient location.

4-10.2.1.2 Maintenance. The facility shall establish routine preventive maintenance programs applicable to both the vacuum piping system and to the secondary equipment attached to vacuum terminals (inlets) to assure the continued good performance of the entire vacuum system.

NOTE: Clogging of regulators, for example, with lint, debris, or dried body fluids reduces vacuum system performance.

During periodic tests of the system, comparative readings of the main line and area gauges will indicate overall system pressure drop and reveal any change from the normal for that system.

While the material in these sections applies only to permanently installed vacuum systems, the Committee noted in the development of maintenance requirements that the operating performance and leakage of secondary apparatus can directly affect the vacuum system and the quality of patient therapy; thus, the reason for the Note. The Committee felt it necessary to advise facilities to adequately maintain these secondary apparatus.

4-10.2.1.3 Leakage Tests. The facility shall perform periodic tests for detecting leaks in the system in accordance with 4-9.1.4.4.

System leaks can degrade performance, compromising the quality of patient care through a reduced degree of vacuum in branches and lines to individual terminal inlets.

The periodicity of such tests has been left to the judgement of the staff of a facility since usage (and thus wear-out) of systems varies markedly between facilities.

4-10.2.1.4 Terminal Performance Tests. Inlet terminal performance, as required in 4-9.1.3.1, shall be tested on a regular preventive maintenance schedule as determined by the hospital maintenance staff. The test shall be based on flow of free air (SCFM) into an inlet terminal while simultaneously checking the vacuum level.

NOTE 1: The test can be conducted using (1) a rotometer or other flow-measuring device, and (2) a vacuum gauge, both devices being fitted with the appropriate inlet terminal connector.

NOTE 2: The test procedure will be to measure the flow with the terminal wide open while simultaneously measuring the vacuum level at an adjacent wall inlet terminal or other inlet terminal on the same branch line.

NOTE 3: It is recognized that this criterion may not be met by some existing systems. It is the responsibility of facility personnel, based on past experience and use, to determine the acceptable alternate performance criterion for their system(s).

4-10.2.1.5 Instruction of Staff. The facility shall instruct its personnel in the proper uses of the vacuum system in order to eliminate practices that reduce the system's effectiveness, such as leaving suction tips and catheters open when not actually aspirating, and using equipment arrangements that are improperly trapped or are untrapped.

NOTE: Suction collection bottles that are used as part of patient treatment equipment should be equipped with an overflow shutoff device to prevent carryover of fluids into equipment of the piping system. It is recommended that a separate vacuum trap with shutoff be used between the suction collection bottle and the vacuum system terminal inlet.

4-10.2.1.6 Contamination. Liquid or debris shall not be introduced into the medical-surgical vacuum system for disposal.

4-10.2.1.7 Nonmedical Use. The medical-surgical vacuum system shall not be used for vacuum steam condensate return or other nonmedical or nonsurgical applications.

4-10.2.2 Vacuum System (Nonpatient). (Reserved)

4-10.3 Recordkeeping. Upon completion of the tests described in 4-9.1, a written record of the performance of these tests shall be maintained in the permanent records of the facility.

4-10.4 Information and Warning Signs.

4-10.4.1 Patient Vacuum Systems.

4-10.4.1.1 Pipe Identification. Vacuum piping shall be readily identified by appropriate labeling, such as MEDICAL-SURGICAL VACUUM. Such labeling shall be by means of metal tags, stenciling, stamping, or adhesive markers, in a manner that is not readily removable. Labeling shall appear on the pipe at intervals of not more than 20 ft (6.1 m) and at least once in or above each room and each story traversed by the pipeline. Arrows (when used) shall point from the terminals (inlets) and toward the receiver or pump.

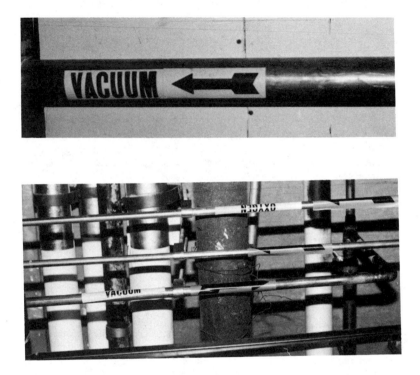

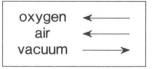

Figure 25   Labeling of piping, including the direction of flow of contents of pipe.

4-10.4.1.2 Valve Boxes. Valve boxes shall be permanently labeled in substance as follows:

CAUTION — MEDICAL-SURGICAL VACUUM VALVE
DO NOT CLOSE EXCEPT IN EMERGENCY
THIS VALVE CONTROLS VACUUM TO. . . .

4-10.4.1.3 Valves Not in Boxes. All shutoff valves that are not in labeled boxes, such as in the main line, risers, above suspended ceilings, etc., shall be identified by means of durable tags, nameplates, or labels in substance as follows:

> CAUTION — MEDICAL-SURGICAL VACUUM VALVE
> DO NOT CLOSE EXCEPT IN EMERGENCY
> THIS VALVE CONTROLS VACUUM TO. . . .

4-10.4.1.4 Terminals (Inlets).   Each terminal (inlet) for vacuum shall be legibly labeled in substance as follows:

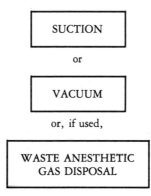

SUCTION

or

VACUUM

or, if used,

WASTE ANESTHETIC
GAS DISPOSAL

4-10.4.1.5 Gauge Identification.   All permanently installed vacuum gauges and manometers for the vacuum system shall be those manufactured expressly for vacuum and labeled: VACUUM.

   NOTE 1:   Vacuum gauges should have an indicated range of 0 in. to 30 in. Hg (vacuum).

   NOTE 2:   Vacuum gauges may be part of shutoff valves in boxes, or incorporated in a unit with gauges for the central medical gas piping systems described in Sections 4-3 through 4-5.

4-10.4.2 Nonpatient Vacuum Systems.   (Reserved)

5
ENVIRONMENTAL SYSTEMS

NOTE: The application of requirements contained in this chapter for specific types of health care facilities can be found in Chapters 12 through 18.

5-1 Scope. This chapter covers the performance, maintenance, and testing of the environmental systems used within health care facilities.

5-2 Nature of Hazards.

(See Sections 3-2 and 8-2 for information on hazards.)

5-3 Source.

5-3.1 Air exhausted from laboratory areas shall not be recirculated to other parts of the facility.

5-4 Distribution.

NOTE: For additional distribution requirements, see NFPA 90A, *Standard for the Installation of Air Conditioning and Ventilating Systems*, and NFPA 90B, *Standard for the Installation of Warm Air Heating and Air Conditioning Systems*.

For air handling as it relates to laminar hoods, readers should consult NFPA 90A, as well as NFPA 101, *Life Safety Code.*
NFPA 90A and 90B cover the safe design and construction criteria for environmental systems (e.g., material, control equipment).

5-4.1* Ventilation — Nonflammable Anesthetizing Locations.

5-4.1.1 The mechanical ventilation system supplying nonflammable anesthetizing locations shall have the capability of controlling the relative humidity within the range of 35 to 50 percent.

A-5-4.1 Ventilation of Anesthetizing Locations.

(See A-5-4.2.)

NOTE: It is recognized that there may be numerous medical hazards associated with the maintenance of relative humidity below 50 percent. These include the danger of producing hypothermia in patients, especially during long operative procedures; the fact that floating particulate matter increases in conditions of low relative humidity; and the fact that the incidence of wound infections is minimized following procedures performed in those operating rooms in which the relative humidity is maintained at the level of 50 to 55 percent.

5-4.1.2 Supply and exhaust systems for windowless anesthetizing locations shall be arranged to automatically vent smoke and products of combustion.

See NFPA 90A, *Standard for the Installation of Air Conditioning and Ventilating Systems* and NFPA 101, *Life Safety Code*, for details on how this venting is to be achieved.

5-4.1.3 Ventilating systems for anesthetizing locations shall be provided that (a) prevent recirculation of smoke originating within the surgical suite, and (b) prevent the circulation of smoke entering the system intake, without in either case interfering with the exhaust function of the system.

Requirements for ventilation are now stated in terms of desired performance rather than particular type of damper or sensing mechanism to be used.

For types of detection for sensing smoke, see NFPA 72E, *Standard on Automatic Fire Detectors.*

5-4.1.4 The electric supply to the ventilating system shall be served by the equipment system of the essential electrical system specified in Chapter 3, "Electrical Systems."

5-4.1.5 Window-type temperature regulating units (air conditioners) may be installed in exterior windows or exterior walls of anesthetizing locations (*see also 5-4.2.4 and 5-4.2.5*). Where such units are employed, the provisions of 5-4.1.1 or 5-4.2.1 shall be met.

5-4.1.6 Scavenging apparatus, if installed, shall exhaust the waste anesthetic gases to the outside of the facility in a manner that will preclude their reentry.

5-4.2* Ventilation — Flammable Anesthetizing Locations.

A-5-4.2 Ventilation of Anesthetizing Locations. Mechanical ventilation is required as a means of diluting flammable gases and maintaining the proper humidity. It is also the most effective and aseptic method of maintaining a uniform humidity within the area.

Care should be taken when recirculating air under current design guidelines so that adequate dilution is maintained, and the requirements of 5-4.1.3 can be satisfied.

General. Anesthetizing locations used solely for the induction of anesthesia need only be ventilated at a rate sufficient to maintain the proper humidity.

Anesthetizing locations in which clinical procedures are performed, such as operating rooms, delivery rooms, and certain treatment rooms, require special ventilation as described below. This special ventilation serves not only to maintain humidity but also to reduce the hazard of infection, which is accomplished by dilution and removal of airborne microbial contamination and dilution of flammable gases. It also contributes to odor control and comfort of personnel.

Dilution of flammable and nonflammable gases is most effectively accomplished by 100 percent fresh air (i.e., 100 percent exhaust) via nonrecirculating air conditioning systems. However, some codes and standards now allow recirculating air conditioning systems in anesthetizing locations, thus reducing the gas-purging effect and increasing the possibility of elevated gas concentrations. Care should be taken to ensure that effective scavenging is available (and used) in these locations.

The Subcommittee on Anesthesia Services recognizes that a hazard may be created by the chronic exposure of anesthesia and other operating room personnel to low concentrations of vapors or commonly employed volatile liquid inhalation anesthetic agents. For further information see:

(a) Cohen, E. N., et al. Anesthesia, pregnancy and miscarriage; A study of operating room nurses and anesthetists. *Anesthesiology* 35:343, 1971.

(b) Whitcher, C. E., et al. Chronic exposure to anesthetic gas in the operating room. *Anesthesiology* 35:348, 1971.

(c) Yanagida, H., et al. Nitrous oxide content in the operating suite. *Anesth. Analg.* 53:347, 1974.

(d) Frey, R., et al. How strong is the influence of chronic exposure to inhalation anesthetics on personnel working in operating theatres? *W.F.S.A. Newsletter* No. 10, June 1974.

The Health Hazard

(a) Cohen, E. N., et al. Occupational disease among operating room personnel — a national study. *Anesthesiology* 41:321-340, 1974.

(b) Spence, A. A., et al. Occupational hazards for operating room-based physicians. *JAMA* 238:955-959, 1977.

(c) Cohen, E. N., et al. A survey of anesthetic health hazards among dentists. *J. Am. Dent. Assoc.* 90:1291-1296, 1975.

(d) Greene, N., Report on American Cancer Society study of causes of death amongst anesthetists. Annual Meeting, American Society of Anesthesiologists, New Orleans, Louisiana, 18 October 1977.

(e) Hazleton Laboratories America, Inc. Final Reports, CDC-99-74-46, National Institute for Occupational Safety and Health, 1014 Broadway, Cincinnati, Ohio. Long-term inhalation reproductive and teratogenic toxicity evaluation of nitrous oxide plus halothane. 14 November 1975. Cytogenic evaluation of spermatogonial cells in the rat following long-term inhalation exposure to nitrous oxide plus halothane. 17 November 1976.

(f) Chang, W. C., et al. Ultrastructural changes in the nervous system after chronic exposure to halothane. *Exp. Neurol.* 45:209-219, 1974.

(g) Quimby, K. L., et al. Behavioral consequences in rats from chronic exposure to 10 ppm halothane during early development. *Anesth. and Analg.* 54:628-633, 1975.

(h) Kripke, B.J., et al. Testicular reaction to prolonged exposure to nitrous oxide. *Anesthesiology* 44:104-113, 1976.

(i) Fink, B. R., ed. *Toxicity of Anesthetics.* Part Four, "Teratogenic Effects." Baltimore, Williams & Wilkins Co., 308-323, 1968.

(j) Bruce, D. L., et al. Trace anesthetic effects on perceptual, cognitive and motor skills. *Anesthesiology* 40:453-458, 1973.

(k) Bruce, D. L., and Bach, M. J. Psychological studies of human performance as affected by traces of enflurane and nitrous oxide. *Anesthesiology* 42:194-196, 1975.

(l) Smith, G., and Shirley, A. W. Failure to demonstrate effects of low concentrations of nitrous oxide and halothane on psychomotor performance. *Br. J. Anaesth.* 48:274, 1976.

(m) Davison, L. A., et al. Psychological effects of halothane and isoflurane anesthesia. *Anesthesiology* 43:313-324, 1975.

(n) Walts, L. F., et al. Critique: Occupational disease among operating room personnel. *Anesthesiology* 42:608-611, 1975.

(o) Cohen, E. W., and Brown, B. W. Comment on the critique. *Anesthesiology* 42:765-766, 1975.

(p) Fink, B. R., and Cullen, B. F. Anesthetic pollution: What is happening to us? *Anesthesiology* 45:79-83, 1976.

(q) Lecky, J. H. Chronic exposure to anesthetic trace levels. *Complications in Anesthesia*, edited by L. H. Cooperman and F. K. Orkin. J. B. Lippincott Co., Phila. In press.

Reduction and Control Methods

(a) Pisiali, R. L., et al. Distribution of waste anesthetic gases in the operating room air. *Anesthesiology* 45:487-494, 1976.

(b) Whitcher, C. E., et al. Control of occupational exposure to nitrous oxide in the dental operatory. *J. Am. Dent. Assoc.* 95:763-766, 1977.

(c) Muravchick, S. Scavenging enflurance from extracorporeal pump oxygenators. *Anesthesiology* 47:468-471, 1977.

(d) Whitcher, C. E., et al. Development and evaluation of methods for the elimination of waste anesthetic gases and vapors in hospitals. HEW Publication No. (NIOSH) 75-137, GPO stock no. 1733-0071. Supt. of Documents, Govt. Print. Off., 1975.

(e) Whitcher, C. E., et al. Control of occupational exposure to N_2O in the dental operatory. HEW Publication No. (NIOSH) 77-171. Cincinnati, U.S. Department of Health, Education and Welfare, Public Health Services Center for Disease Control, National Institute for Occupational Safety and Health.

(f) Lecky, J. H., et al. In-house manual for the control of anesthetic gas contamination in the operating room. University of Pennsylvania Hospital publication.

(g) Lecky, J. H. The mechanical aspects of anesthetic pollution control. *Anesth. and Analg.* 56:769, 1977.

Dealing with Personnel

(a) Lecky, J. H. Notice to employees on the potential health hazards associated with occupational exposure to anesthetics. University of Pennsylvania Hospital publication.

NIOSH — OSHA

(a) Criteria for a recommended standard: Occupation exposure to waste anesthetic gases and vapors. HEW Publication No. (NIOSH) 77-140. Cincinnati, U.S. Department of Health,

Education and Welfare, Public Health Service Center for Disease Control, National Institute for Occupational Safety and Health.

ANSI Z79

(a) American National Standards Institute, Committee Z79, SC-4 *Anesthesia Gas Scavenging Devices and Disposal Systems*, J. H. Lecky, M.D., Chairman, ANSI/Z79.11-1982.

For further information on waste anesthetic gas disposal (scavenging), see Commentary on 4-7.1.2.

A prudent course of action pending further data on this topic lies in the installation of a gas scavenging system for use when inhalation anesthetic techniques are employed with gas flows in excess of metabolic and anesthetic requirements. Care must be taken in the selection and application of any such system to a gas anesthesia apparatus or anesthesia ventilator to avoid exposing the breathing circuit to any pressure less than atmospheric, and also to avoid the dumping of any flammable vapors into a central suction system not designed for such operation.

Operating Rooms, Delivery Rooms, and Special Procedure Rooms. Ventilation air should be supplied from several outlets located on the ceiling or high on the walls of the location. Air should be exhausted by several inlets located near the floor on opposite walls. The air distribution pattern should move air down and through the location with a minimum of draft to the floor for exhaust.

Studies indicate that an air change rate equivalent to 25 room volumes of air per hour dilutes bacteria dispersed into the room by human activity. When properly filtered, 80 percent may be recirculated with no more microbial contamination than 100 percent outdoor air filtered in the same manner. (*See ASHRAE Handbook — 1982 Applications, Chapter 7, "Table on Pressure Relationships and Ventilation of Certain Hospital Areas."*)

A positive air pressure relative to the air pressure of adjoining areas should be maintained in the anesthetizing location. This is accomplished by supplying more air to the location than is exhausted from it. Such pressurization will eliminate the infiltration of contaminated air around perimeter openings of door closures or other wall openings during clinical procedures.

Ventilation systems should incorporate air filters with an efficiency of not less than 90 percent when tested in accordance with ASHRAE Standard 52-76, *Method of Testing Air Cleaning Devices Used in General Ventilation for Removing Particulate Matter. (Summarized in ASHRAE Handbook — 1983 Equipment, Chapter 10).*

Humidity Control. The ventilation system must incorporate humidity equipment and controls to maintain a relative humidity of at least 50 percent or as provided in 5-4.2.1. Although the high level of humidity is not sufficiently reliable for complete dissipation of electrostatic charges, this humidity does reduce the hazard of electrostatic spark discharges under many conditions. The control of airborne bacteria is facilitated in this range of humidity.

The classic reference on bacteria growth and infection versus humidity level is Dunklin and Puck, "Lethal Effect of Relative Humidity on Airborne Bacteria," *Journal of Experimental Medicine*, Vol. 87, pp. 87-101 (1948). Another good reference is McDade and Hall, "Survival of Staphylococci Aures in the Environment," *American Journal of Hygiene*, Vol. 78, pp. 330-7 (1963). A third noteworthy article is Sonneland, "Does Operating Room Modernization Affect Incident of Infection?," *Hospital Topics*, Vol. 44, pp. 149-51 (June 1966).

Temperature. The temperature to be maintained in operating rooms should be chosen on the basis of the well-being of patient and operating teams. It is recommended that the equipment provide for a room temperature in a range of 20°C (68°F) to 24°C (75°F) with controls for selecting any desired temperature within this range.

5-4.2.1   Relative humidity of not less than 50 percent, at a temperature range of 64.4°F (19°C) to 80.6°F (27°C), shall be maintained in flammable inhalation anesthetizing locations.

> See Prologue to 12-4.1 for a discussion of the relative humidity requirements in anesthetizing locations.

5-4.2.2   Other requirements for ventilation and cooling of flammable anesthetizing locations are set forth in 5-4.1.

5-4.2.3 Duct Work for Air Handling.   It is not required that duct work be fabricated of nonsparking material.

> In the past, overzealous interpreters of requirements for flammable anesthetizing locations have thought that the ductwork in such locations, perhaps because of the presence of some flammable vapors, needed to be constructed of nonsparking material (e.g., made out of stainless steel). The Subcommittee on Anesthesia Services has included this paragraph to prevent further misinterpretation of this section.

5-4.2.4   If a window-type temperature regulating unit (air conditioner) is installed so that any part is less than 5 ft (152 cm) from the floor of a flammable anesthetizing location, such unit shall comply with the requirements set forth in 5-4.2.5.

5-4.2.5   Such a window-type temperature regulating unit shall be provided with a vertical divider that effectively prevents airflow from the room side to the outside side, and all electric equipment on the room side of this divider shall meet the requirements of 3-4.1.2.1(e)(2). The installed unit shall tightly fit the opening in the window or wall. Openings in the divider for shafts of fans, other moving parts, or wiring shall be gasketed unless the local air pressure on the room side of the opening when the unit is in operation is less than that on the oudoor side. A fresh-air port may be provided in the divider if it is automatically closed when the unit is not in operation. The rotating parts of fans on the room side of the divider shall not cause percussion sparks if they accidentally contact surrounding objects.

5-4.3 Ventilation — Laboratories.

> General requirements for the design and construction of ventilation systems (ductwork and equipment) are covered in NFPA 90A, *Standard on Air Conditioning and Ventilating Systems.* Requirements in this section are specific for laboratories.
> Previously NFPA 56C (now incorporated into NFPA 99) included a restriction on the type of dampers that could be installed in exhaust ducts serving fume hoods (i.e., preset or barometric only). That restriction was removed by Association action in November 1980. Thus, at present this chapter is silent on this subject, as well as on multiple fume hoods connected to a single exhaust. Proponents of

allowing any damper design cite modern, highly reliable design and energy conservation. Proponents desiring to restrict design to preset dampers only cite the preclusion of inadvertant shutdowns, the environment around dampers, and the inadequate maintenance that is generally given to dampers.

Systems with multiple hoods on a single exhaust and/or with automatic, motorized dampers require monitoring for proper ventilation at any hood immediately prior to its use. Hoods used more or less continuously could have an airflow indicator or a visual/audible alarm installed to warn operators and others in the area if the airflow drops below a safe level. Reliable sensing equipment that is not located in the exhaust steam, provides an alarm, and can be easily maintained is now available.

The use, inspection, and maintenance of ventilation systems in the laboratory should be coordinated between all areas involved. Whenever any cycling of fans or ventilation systems is instituted, or energy management programs are employed, the impact of the positive/negative pressure differentials of laboratories and other sensitive areas must be considered. Where pressure differentials are required, those systems should be provided with priority overrides or imbalance alarms connected to a constantly attended location.

5-4.3.1* Laboratories provided with mechanical ventilation throughout or employing fume hoods as a fixed part of the exhaust system shall have the air supply and exhaust balanced to provide a negative pressure with respect to surrounding hospital occupancies.

Exception: Laboratories for procedures requiring maximum protection against contamination and not involving infectious or noxious materials may be arranged for slight positive pressure when the safety of the arrangement is affirmed by a responsible laboratory official.

A-5-4.3.1 Ventilation Design. Prevalent practice when laboratories are provided with supply and exhaust ventilation is to design the fume hood exhaust as an integral part of the balanced ventilating system, so that the fume hood exhaust is in constant operation.

However, for energy conservation, and if variable-volume fume hood exhaust controls are employed, using fume hoods as a fixed part of the ventilation system should be avoided. Variable volume control of the primary laboratory ventilating system (to offset variable hood exhaust quantities while simultaneously maintaining the required relative pressure between the laboratory and its adjacent areas) can introduce complexities of these controls that are difficult to reliably set and maintain. This is particularly true if pneumatic controls are used. Other means (controls) are available to maintain fume hood exhaust flows at variable, but desired, levels when hood sashes are moved. Electronic and direct digital control equipment is becoming available to solve this problem; but for the present, it is best to keep energy conservation controls simple.

5-4.3.2 Exit corridors shall not be used as plenums to supply or exhaust air from laboratory areas.

This refers to "access to exit" corridors. It does not apply to circulation corridors within the laboratory.

5-4.3.3 Exhaust systems for laboratory ventilation shall be arranged with motors and fans located at the discharge end of the systems, and with the exhaust air discharged above the roof in such a manner that it will not be drawn into any air intake or blown into windows.

NOTE: The discharge side of fume hood exhaust fans is under positive pressure and often leaks toxic fumes into the surrounding environment; therefore, all fume hood exhaust fans should be installed out-of-doors, and not inside penthouses or other mechanical equipment enclosures that have to be frequented by maintenance and service personnel.

A Formal Interpretation was issued in March 1980 after the then Committee on Laboratories received a question regarding the meaning of the term "roof." Since the term was not then defined in the Glossary of NFPA 56C, the Interpretation Committee considered it the intent of the Technical Committee that the term had the following meaning (as defined in Webster's 3rd International Dictionary): "The outside cover of a building or structure including the roofing and all the materials and construction necessary to maintain the cover upon its walls or other support."

The requirement for discharge "above the roof" was extensively discussed again by the then Committee on Laboratories during the revision of the 1980 edition of NFPA 56C. Public comments noting some difficulty in meeting this requirement had been received. The Committee responded that the requirement applied to new construction only, that it reflected good engineering design practice, and, in essence, that any other location for discharge included too many variables to reasonably ensure the safety of laboratory or other personnel (e.g., wind pressure on side of building could defeat side wall fans; erection of a new building adjacent to laboratory could eliminate clear area around side of building).

The Committee noted that even with above-the-roof discharge, cases have been reported of exhaust fumes drawn in through air intake ducts of nearby higher buildings.

The Note (new for 1987) is to call attention to the problem of an accumulation of fume hood exhausts in areas where maintenance personnel, who may not be aware of the hazard, may light a cigarette or flip an electrical switch, thus creating a spark of sufficient magnitude to ignite the accumulated gases.

5-4.3.4 Air exhausted from areas in which highly infectious or radioactive materials are processed or used shall pass through high-efficiency (99.7 percent) filters before discharging to the atmosphere.

The need for this paragraph has been questioned, particularly in view of the lack of details on types of filters acceptable, removal procedures, etc. The Subcommittee on Laboratories noted that there are detailed Federal regulations prohibiting the release of infectious or radioactive waste directly into the atmosphere. Thus, the implementation of this requirement should not pose a problem. It is included to call attention to a problem that would be hazardous if not addressed. Users should therefore follow directions (if any) of filter manufacturers, or of regulatory bodies (e.g., Nuclear Regulatory Commission) on disposal procedures.

5-4.4* Fume Hoods — Laboratories.

A-5-4.4 The American Industrial Hygiene Association, the American Conference of Governmental and Industrial Hygienists, and the American Society of Heating, Refrigeration, and Air Conditioning Engineers have published guidelines on the design, installation, face velocities, location, and test procedures for laboratory hoods.   The Scientific Apparatus Makers Association also has published a standard on laboratory hoods. (*See Appendix B.*)

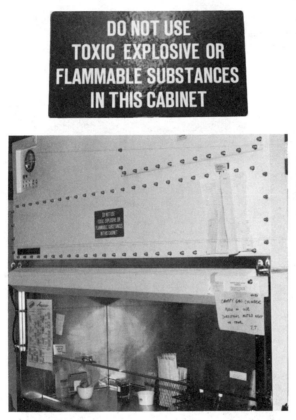

Figure 26(a) Typical fume hood (not in use). This unit is not suitable for toxic explosive or flammable substances (via large sign).

• Another source for fume hood details can be found in Appendix A-6-3 through A-6-14 in NFPA 49, *Standard for Laboratories using Chemicals.*

• Fume hoods are most susceptible to ventilation fluctuations and can cause varying levels of hazards depending on the process or activity taking place within the hood. Locations of hoods for minimum traffic or air turbulence, construction specifications for the hood and associated utilities and shut-offs, warning signs and emergency directions and procedures, and periodic tests and inspections for performance must all be accommodated within the facility safety and/or hazard surveillance program.

• Where hood operation involves hazardous or flammable materials, an audible and visual alarm should signal lack of proper hood operation.

5-4.4.1 Fume hoods shall be located in areas of minimum air turbulence and away from doors and windows, and in a manner that will not impede access to egress.

Figure 26(b) Typical fume hood. This unit cautions user about acid within fume hood (via label on left).

5-4.4.2 Glazing at the face of the hood shall be of a material that will provide protection to the operator or environment against the hazards normally associated with the use of the hood.

> Prior text (in NFPA 56C) included specification of a particular type of glazing. This has been replaced with performance criteria.

5-4.4.3 Fume hoods, and their associated equipment in the air stream, intended for use with perchloric acid and other strong oxidants, shall be constructed of stainless steel or other material consistent with special exposures, and be provided with a water wash and drain system to permit periodic flushing of the duct and hood. Electrical equipment intended for installation within such ducts shall be designed and constructed to resist penetration by water. Lubricants and seals shall not contain organic materials.

Exception: When perchloric acid or other strong oxidants are transferred from one container to another.

> Other strong oxidants besides perchloric acid pose the same hazard of causing an explosion if vapors (from heating) are allowed to settle on the walls of the duct and form crystals. These crystals are very corrosive and can explode with only a little friction. However, just transferring these types of chemicals within a fume hood does not create the same hazardous situation; thus, the reason for the Exception.
>   For further information on this subject, see Section 6-12 in NFPA 45, *Standard for Laboratories Using Chemicals.*

5-4.4.4 Fume hoods intended for use with radioactive isotopes shall be constructed of stainless steel or other material suitable for the particular exposure and shall comply with NFPA 801, *Recommended Fire Protection Practice for Facilities Handling Radioactive Materials.*

5-4.4.5 Fume hood ventilating controls shall be so arranged that shutting off the ventilation of one fume hood will not reduce the exhaust capacity or create an imbalance between exhaust and supply for any other hood connected to the same system.

The operation of the these controls shall be tested annually by a qualified person who shall certify the result of the test. The qualified person may be a staff member of the facility.

- Fume hood users worry (and justifiably so) when they shut off their hood and airflow reserves, allowing air from the hood to enter the room. For an individual hood with a fan serving just that hood, this flow reversal often occurs, but is not as serious a concern as the flow reversal when a fume hood is ganged with other fume hoods onto one fan. In this latter situation, when the fan is shut off, the contents of the exhaust from one hood may accidentally arrive in the laboratory space of another area via the fume hood in that area.

Reliable sensors can detect this condition when the fume hood fan is turned on, but none is available when the fan is shut off. Thus, serious thought should be given to the consequence of ganging fume hood exhausts together.

- The second paragraph was added for several reasons: 1) fume hood ventilating controls today are complex and require an understanding of air movement to balance properly; 2) improper balance and operation of these controls can create hazardous conditions in terms of fire (e.g., an inadequate exhaust can trap flammable gases and cause them to ignite should an ignition source such as a bunsen burner, be present), and can endanger personnel (e.g., back draft of toxic fumes); and 3) an annual check was considered a reasonable interval of time to assure adequate operation and reveal any signficant drifts in settings.

The stipulation that the person be "qualified" was considered necessary to assure that only competent persons worked on these systems. Many health care facilities do have persons on their staff who are quite competent in inspecting and testing fume hood controls. This paragraph is intended to allow the utilization of these persons in lieu of contracting for such services from an outside source.

5-4.4.6* Fume hoods shall be so designed that the face velocity ventilation is adequate to prevent the backflow of contaminants into the room, especially in the presence of cross drafts or the rapid movements of an operator working at the face of the hood.

A-5-4.4.6 The minimal face velocity of a fume hood is generally considered to be 100 ft (30.5 m) per minute; unusual conditions may require velocities greatly in excess of this flow. Engineers require complete data on the function of a fume hood for the adequate design of its exhaust facilities.

5-4.4.7 Shutoff valves for services, including gas, air, vacuum, and electricity, shall be outside of the hood enclosure in a location where they will be readily accessible in the event of fire in the hood. The location of such shutoffs shall be legibly lettered in a related location on the exterior of the hood.

5-5 Performance Criteria and Testing. (Reserved)

5-6 Administration.

5-6.1 Anesthetizing Locations.

5-6.1.1 Ventilating and humidifying equipment for anesthetizing locations shall be kept in operable condition and be continually operating during surgical procedures (*see Appendix A-5-4.1*).

5-6.1.2 All gas storage locations or manifold enclosures shall be routinely inspected to assure that the ventilation requirements stated in 4-3.1.2.1(a) are not obstructed.

5-6.2 Laboratories. Warning signs describing the nature of any hazardous effluent content shall be posted at fume hoods' discharge points.

6 MATERIALS

NOTE: The application of requirements contained in this chapter for specific types of health care facilities can be found in Chapters 12 through 18.

6-1 Scope. This chapter covers the hazards associated with the use of flammable and combustible materials used within health care facilities.

6-2 Nature of Hazards.

6-2.1 Flammability. (Reserved)

6-2.2 Combustible Loading. (Reserved)

6-2.3 Toxicity of Products of Combustion. Many substances, when subjected to a fire, may undergo a chemical change resulting in a new toxic product. This is especially true of many plastic substances. Many highly toxic combustion products may cause sudden unconsciousness, cardiovascular collapse, and severe injury or death, even though the person injured is relatively remote from the fire. These combustion products have been found to cause injury after passing through halls, ventilating systems, and even through electrical conduit.

6-2.4 Chemical Burns. (Reserved)

6-2.5 Safety. (Reserved)

6-2.6 Radioactivity. (Reserved)

6-3 Source. (Reserved)

6-4 Distribution. (Reserved)

6-5 Performance Criteria and Testing. (Reserved)

6-6 Administration. (Reserved)

7 ELECTRICAL EQUIPMENT, HEALTH CARE FACILITIES

NOTE 1: The application of requirements contained in this chapter for specific types of health care facilities can be found in Chapters 12 through 18.

NOTE 2: For requirements of manufacturers of equipment, see Chapter 9.

Prologue

In the late 1960s, many health care personnel became concerned with the problem of electric currents in the microampere range causing ventricular fibrillation. This occurs when a conductive pathway carrying these small currents flows within or adjacent to the chambers of the heart. Such pathways include cardiac pacemakers or catheters containing ionizable fluids. The problems associated with the use of these devices, plus the continuous increase in the instrumentation of patients (both direct contact and ancillary to) led to the concepts of "electrically susceptible patient location" and "electrically susceptible patient." An NFPA Committee was established in the late 1960s to address the subject. The result of its efforts, a document designated NFPA 76B, was adopted as a manual in 1971, as a tentative standard in 1973, and, after several rejections and major revisions, as a full standard in 1980. In 1984 it was one of eleven health care documents combined to form NFPA 99.

Since the initial years of discussion on the subject of electric currents and ventricular fibrillation, there have been significant improvements in equipment design and in practices involving equipment. In addition, it was realized that the terms "electrically susceptible patient location" and "electrically susceptible patient" were misleading in the sense that all living organisms are affected by electricity imposed on them. As a result, these two terms are no longer used in this document.

Originally, NFPA 76B covered the performance criteria for the electrical wiring system, and the design, maintenance, and safe use of portable and fixed line-powered electrical appliances as they relate to electrical safety in hospitals. In 1984, as part of NFPA 99, it became Chapter 9 of that edition. In this edition, the former (wiring) has been incorporated into requirements for electric systems (Chapter 3) and the latter (appliances) into this chapter (7) and Chapter 9 (facility and manufacturer requirements), respectively.

Concern about electrical safety in the health care community increased as physicians and surgeons started to probe below the surface of that protective barrier, the skin. In particular, probing on the surface and inside the heart revealed that this organ was very sensitive to any electrical current impressed upon it. Although experimentation on human response to external electrical stimuli had been conducted in the 1700's by Benjamin Franklin and even earlier by others, electrical contacts in the cardiac region, through catheterization procedures, did not become common until the early 1960s. By the mid 1960s, after reports of cardiac catheterizations in which patients went into ventricular fibrillation for no apparent reason, resultant research showed that small electrical current (at levels well below the perceptible threshold) could cause fibrillation. Insurance mortality statistics for noncatheterized electrical accidents seemed to support the same conclusion. Efforts began on various fronts — medical, engineering, manufacturing, maintenance — to reduce the likelihood that extra electrical current could find its way through patients (and also health care personnel) and cause cardiac among other problems.

The initial health care community reaction and media coverage had the benefit of focusing attention on the problem. Over the years, however, with improvements in equipment design, and more and *better* understanding of the problem, more tempered views have prevailed. Thus, NFPA 76B (finally adopted as a standard in 1980) reflected a general consensus of reasonable measures to take in the area of electrical safety in patient care areas of hospitals.

Much discussion has taken place as to whether there was a need for an individual NFPA document on the subject of safe use of electricity. There appears to be little question that most of this subject is well outside the responsibilities of electrical inspecting authorities: the subject extended beyond the installation of the wiring system, and included manufacturing criteria and operational practices. While other organizations may have addressed portions of this subject, the need for a document that tied all facets of the problem together was, and still is, vital to all involved: builders, inspectors, operators, engineers, and practitioners. Thus, this chapter and Chapter 3 are linked together because electric equipment interfaces with the electrical system in a facility. The developers of NFPA 76B were very much aware of this interrelationship, which is not diminished even though the material from that document is now to be found in 3 chapters. Thus, electrical safety is addressed as a system *phenomena*, allowing flexibility in achieving a reasonable level of safety in health care facilities.

7-1* Scope.

A-7-1 This chapter originated from a concern about electrical safety in the hospital. It resulted in NFPA 76B-1980, *Safe Use of Electricity in Patient Care Areas of Hospitals* (incorporated into NFPA 99 in 1984).

This chapter states the basic electrical safety performance criteria for patient care areas to be followed by personnel. Chapter 9 provides performance criteria for manufacturers of appliances. Chapter 3 provides performance criteria for the installation implementation requirements contained in Article 517, NFPA 70, *National Electrical Code*. The purpose of these chapters is the practical safeguarding of patients and staff from the hazards arising from the use of electricity in medical diagnosis and therapy.

The material in this appendix, as it relates to electrical safety (Sections A-3 and A-7), interprets some of the basic criteria by presenting different methodologies and alternative procedures to achieve the level of safety defined by the criteria.

The scope of this chapter (which is substantially the patient-care-related electrical appliances as contained in former NFPA 76B) has been questioned many times regarding its similarity to that of other NFPA and non-NFPA documents. NFPA 70, *National Electrical Code*, has been frequently mentioned in this regard. The scope of the then Committee responsible for this chapter was reviewed in 1979 by the Standards Council, particularly in relation to a new scope for Panel 17 of the National Electrical Code Committees. While no changes in the scope of the Committee were made, the relation of the two documents was clarified. The former Health Care Facilities Technical Committees (replaced by standing subcommittees) were (and still are), responsible for the criteria for performance, maintenance and testing of, among other things, electrical systems and electrical appliances; Panel 17, responsible for Article 517 of NFPA 70, was and is responsible for electrical construction and installation requirements based on such performance criteria.

While it could be argued that it might be simpler to place all factors relating to health care firesafety in one document, the Standards Council chose to divide up responsibilities in the aforementioned way for several reasons. First, the division is a very practical one: electrical installation requirements are largely the same in all occupancies. Electrical inspectors, contractors, and others concerned with installation are familiar with the *National Electrical Code*. Although Article 517 contains special requirements peculiar to health care facilities, these requirements are similar to general provisions as well. Designers, while they need some knowledge of installation requirements for wiring, are primarily concerned with equipment interacting with users to achieve safe design and use. A second compelling reason for this division of responsibilities is the problem in coordination and correlation that would exist if separate installation documents were developed for different occupancies. It has thus been a long-established policy that electrical installation requirements for all occupancies would be contained in the *National Electrical Code*.

As noted above, the scope of this chapter is not limited to just electrical appliances. Rather, the multifaceted aspects of electricity and its associated hazards are covered. (With restructuring of NFPA 99 for 1987, hazards associated with the electrical wiring systems have been moved to Chapter 3.)

The scope of this chapter is not at odds with the Medical Devices Amendment Act of 1976 (PL 94-295), which now governs medical devices. This chapter sets up minimum performance criteria for appliances; the Food and Drug Administration can use this voluntary document for its purposes if it wishes, just as other agencies or organizations use NFPA documents.

While this chapter does not require formal approval or listing of appliances, it does indicate that authorities having jurisdiction might do so. Users should consult appropriate authorities on this matter.

7-1.1 This chapter covers the performance, maintenance, and testing of electrical equipment used within health care facilities.

7-1.2 Although an appliance that yields erroneous data or functions poorly may be dangerous, quality and assurance of full appliance performance is not covered except as it may relate to direct electrical or fire injury to patients or personnel.

7-1.3 This chapter does not require formal approval or listing of experimental or research apparatus built to order, or under development, provided such apparatus is used under qualified supervision and provided the apparatus is demonstrated to have a degree of safety equivalent to that described herein or whose degree of safety has been deemed acceptable by the facility.

7-1.4 This chapter does not require formal approval or listing of any appliance.

7-2 Nature of Hazards.

NOTE: See also Section 3-2 in Chapter 3 for related electrical hazards.

7-2.1 Fire and Explosion. (Reserved)

7-2.2 Electrical Shock.

7-2.2.1 Elimination of Shock Hazards.

7-2.2.1.1 Personnel are cautioned to be aware of the hazards presented by defective or improperly employed electrical equipment (*see 7-2.2.2*) and shall avoid the use of defective electrical equipment (*see 7-6.2.3.5*).

To keep personnel from becoming lax in checking electrical equipment for defects, an orientation and annual in-service review program should be provided. A record of these programs should be kept.

7-2.2.1.2 All electrical equipment shall be grounded according to applicable provisions of 9-2.1.3.

7-2.2.2 Electrical equipment, such as those items detailed in 7-6.2.3, is often employed on patients who are receiving respiratory therapy. Aside from the fire ignition hazard [*see 8-2.1.2.4(c)*], there may be a serious shock hazard if such equipment is defective and generates leakage currents, or if it is employed without careful thought, and particularly if more than one item of electrical equipment is being used simultaneously.

NOTE: Therapy gases containing nebulized mists and vapors render the therapy equipment conductive. If the equipment is connected to a nonflammable medical gas system, the patient may be grounded through the therapy apparatus, and leakage currents may pass through the patient to the gounded therapy equipment.

7-2.3 Burns.   (Reserved)

7-2.4 Interruption of Power.   (Reserved)

7-2.5 R.F. Interference.

(*See Annex 2, "The Safe Use of High-Frequency Electricity in Health Care Facilities."*)

7-2.6 Mechanical Injury.   (Reserved)

7-3 Source.

7-3.1 Electrical System.

NOTE: See Chapter 3.

7-3.2 Battery.   (Reserved)

7-4 Distribution.   (Reserved)

7-5 Performance Criteria and Testing.

7-5.1 Patient-Care-Related Electrical Appliances and Equipment.

7-5.1.1 Fixed.

7-5.1.1.1 Grounding of Appliances. Patient-connected electric appliances shall be grounded to the equipment grounding bus in the distribution panel by an insulated grounding conductor run with the power conductors.

7-5.1.1.2 All exposed metal of permanently installed equipment shall be grounded in accordance with the requirements of 7-5.1.1.1.

For discussion of this requirement, see Commentary under 12-4.1.2.6(c).

7-5.1.1.3 Wiring for fixed equipment installed outside the hazardous area of a flammable inhalation anesthetizing location shall comply with 3-4.1.2.1(e)(1).

7-5.1.1.4 All service equipment, switchboards, or panelboards shall be installed outside hazardous areas.

7-5.1.1.5 Control Devices. Devices or apparatus such as motor controllers, thermal cutouts, switches, relays, the switches and contactors of autotransformer starters, resistance and impedance devices, which tend to create arcs, sparks, or high temperatures, shall not be installed in hazardous areas unless devices or apparatus are of a type approved for use in Class I, Group C atmospheres in accordance with Sections 501-6(a), 501-7(a), or Sections 501-6(b) and 501-7(b) of NFPA 70, *National Electrical Code.*

NOTE: It is recommended that control devices for such purposes be installed in a nonhazardous area and actuated by some suitable mechanical, hydraulic, or other nonelectric remote-control device which may be operated from any desired location. This recommendation applies particularly to foot and other switches that must be operated from a location at or near the floor.

7-5.1.1.6 Equipment in storage locations for flammable anesthetic locations shall comply with 4-3.1.2.4(g).

7-5.1.1.7 For anesthetizing locations, devices, appliances, fixtures, or equipment, if of a type incorporating sliding contacts or arcing or sparking parts, including switches and overcurrent devices, shall be of the totally enclosed type or shall have all openings guarded or screened so as to prevent the dispersion of hot particles.

7-5.1.1.8 Ceiling-Suspended Fixtures. In anesthetizing locations, ceiling-suspended fixtures for illumination of the operative field, if installed, shall comply with the following requirements:

(a) *Fixture.* The light source of the fixture shall be suitably protected against physical damage.

(b) *Supports.* Boxes, box assemblies, or fittings used for these fixtures shall be approved for the purpose, and so supported that the supporting means does not become disengaged from its fastening during or as a result of movement of the fixture. The fixture shall be suspended by suitable rigid stems or other approved means. For stems longer than 12 in. (30.5 cm), flexibility in the form of a fitting or flexible connector approved for the purpose shall be provided not more than 12 in. (30.5 cm) from the point of attachment to the supporting box or fitting.

7-5.1.2 Portable.

7-5.1.2.1 Grounding of Appliances.
All cord-connected electrically powered appliances used in the patient vicinity shall be provided with a three-wire power cord and a three-pin grounding-type plug.

Exception: Double-insulated appliances shall be permitted to have two conductor cords.

Household or office appliances not commonly equipped with grounding conductors in their power cords shall be permitted provided they are not located within the patient vicinity. For example, electric typewriters, pencil sharpeners, and clocks at nurses' stations, or electric clocks or TVs that are normally outside the patient vicinity but may be in a patient's room, shall not be required to have grounding conductors in their power cords.

> During revision for the 1984 edition of NFPA 99, the Committee responsible for this chapter received several proposals recommending allowance in patient vicinities of appliances enclosed in plastic cases but not technically double insulated. The Committee did not accept these recommendations, stating that the present minimum level of safety (i.e., grounded or double insulated) was necessary within the patient vicinity. Appliances not meeting either of these requirements are acceptable outside the patient vicinity, as noted in the second paragraph of text.
>
> Double-insulated appliances are not just appliances with some nonconductive coating around a metal chassis. Double insulation involves deliberate efforts to prevent noncurrent-carrying conductive components from becoming energized and accessible to contact by persons using the appliance.
>
> One type of double-insulated appliance has a normal insulation plus a second layer of insulation in case the normal one fails or is broached. Another type uses a single insulation that is much heavier than normal, plus other protective measures. Whatever method is used, appliances qualifying as double insulated require special testing or examination by qualified personnel (*see also Commentary in Chapter 2 on the definition of Double-Insulated Appliances*).
>
> The problem of electromagnetic interference (EMI) should be considered for sensitive monitoring equipment that may be double-insulated. Operation of equipment in various locations at various times may be necessary to learn of any problems.
>
> Another recent concern has been raised over appliances that operate from low-voltage power supplies: if these power supplies are three-wire, grounded configuration type, but have only a two-wire "isolated" output, did the case of the appliance necessarily have to be grounded? Answer: if the output of the power supply is truly "isolated" (i.e., meets the electrical safety requirements for isolated leads), then the case does not have to be grounded.
>
> It should be noted that if the appliance is, can be or has to be operated in physical contact with the case of the power supply (e.g., can be clamped together, or the ground shield of the output cable of the power supply has to contact the chassis of the appliance), then the electrical safety requirements for a three-wire appliance apply to the appliance, in addition to the power supply.

7-5.1.2.2 Line Voltage Equipment — All Anesthetizing Locations.

(a) Photographic lighting equipment for use in anesthetizing locations shall be of the totally enclosed type or so constructed as to prevent the escape of sparks or hot metal particles. The exposed metal parts of photographic lighting equipment shall be grounded as specified in 7-5.1.2.2(b).

(b) Exposed metal parts of electric equipment such as the frames or metal exteriors of motors, portable lamps and appliances, fixtures, cabinets, and cases, intended for use in anesthetizing locations, shall be grounded as provided in Article 250 and in Section 501-16 of NFPA 70, *National Electrical Code (see 3-5.2.1).*

(c) Portable equipment shall be provided with a storage device for its flexible cord, designed to minimize damage to the cord during storage.

Storage mechanisms can be of variable types. The intent is that some method of storage be provided.

(d) Flexible cord for portable lamps or portable electric appliances operating at more than ten volts between conductors, intended for use in all anesthetizing locations, shall be continuous and without switches from the appliance to the attachment plug and of a type designated for extra-hard usage in accordance with Section 501-11 of NFPA 70, *National Electrical Code.* Such flexible cord shall contain one extra insulated conductor to form a grounding connection between the ground terminal of the polarized plug and metal lamp guards, motor frames, and all other exposed metal portions of portable lamps and appliances. Cords shall be protected at the entrance to equipment by a suitable insulating grommet. The flexible cord shall be of sufficient length to reach any position in which the portable device is to be used and the attachment plug shall be inserted only in a fixed, approved receptacle. For correct use and maintenance of adapters, the provisions of 7-6.2 shall apply.

The change to ten volts in the first sentence above was for consistency with prior changes to 7-5.1.2.3(a) and 7-5.1.2.4(f).

Also in the first sentence, the phrase "shall be continuous and without switches from the appliance to the attachment plug" has been interpreted by the former Committee on Anesthetizing Agents (now Subcommittee on Anesthesia Services) to mean that extension cords are not permitted in any type of anesthetizing location (flammable and nonflammable). (The Formal Interpretation issued in 1974 is still applicable since the text is still the same.) Comments by the Interpretation Committee noted that the original requirement prohibiting the use of extension cords related to the vicinity around flammable gases where arcs or sparks could cause explosions (for example, where an applicance mated with a receptacle). Reasons noted for continuing the prohibition in nonflammable anesthetizing locations included the following:
• mechanical damage to the cord connector while lying on the floor;
• short circuits resulting from spilled fluids and liquids typically found in operating rooms;
• short circuits resulting from the lack of controlability over inventory (typical for extension cords);
• the unreliability inherent in the introduction of additional connectors into a circuit;
• the probability of using a cord or connectors of inadequate ampacity;
• the probability of incorrect polarization;
• the compromise of overcurrent protection caused by the introduction of increased grounding wire resistance; and
• the probability that a prohibited extension cord might subsequently be used in the presence of flammable anesthetics.

Exceptions 5 and 6 below were developed in 1980 as a way of meeting the current needs in anesthetizing locations without resorting to extension cords.

The last sentence on adapters was added during the 1984 revision of NFPA 99 when it was pointed out to the Committee that such adapters may be necessary in emergency situations. Regular use of such adapters is not the intent of the Committee, as seen by Exceptions 5 and 6.

Exception No. 1: Foot-treadle-operated controllers are permitted in any anesthetizing location if appended to portable electric appliances in an approved manner or if integral with the supply cord and equipped with a connector containing a flammable anesthetizing location receptacle approved for use in Class I, Group C, Division 1 hazardous locations into which the equipment plug {see 7-5.1.1.5 and 3-4.1.2.4(g) and (h)} may be inserted.

Exception No. 2: Foot-treadle-operated controllers and their connector shall be splashproof but need not be explosionproof if used in a nonflammable anesthetizing location.

Exception No. 3: Listed double-insulated appliances with two-wire cords shall be permitted.

Exception No. 4: Small metal parts not likely to become energized (e.g., nameplates, screws) shall not be required to be grounded.

Exception No. 5: Two or more power receptacles supplied by a flexible cord may be used to supply power to plug-connected components of a movable equipment assembly that is rack-, table-, or pedestal-mounted in a nonflammable anesthetizing location provided:

(a) the receptacles are an integral part of the equipment assembly, permanently attached; and

(b) the sum of the ampacity of all appliances connected to the receptacles shall not exceed 75 percent of the ampacity of the flexible cord supplying the receptacles; and

NOTE: Whole-body hyperthermia/hypothermia units should be powered from a separate branch circuit.

(c) the ampacity of the flexible cord is suitable and in accordance with the current edition of NFPA 70; and

(d) the electrical and mechanical integrity of the assembly is regularly verified and documented through an ongoing maintenance program.

NOTE: See 3-4.1.2.4(d) for criteria of receptacles.

This Exception reflects the Committee's concern about extension cords and the proliferation of devices now being used at one time in an operating room. The Committee noted when first proposing this Exception (TIA 56A-78-8) that the receptacles involved were intended to serve a common function only. This was subsequently clarified when subparagraph (b) of Exception No. 5 was changed to consider the ampacity of the load, as well as to indicate that high-power devices, such as hyperthermia/hypothermia units, were not to be powered from these extended receptacles.

Exception No. 6: Overhead power receptacles, not in a hazardous location, may be supplied by a flexible cord (ceiling drop) that is connected at a ceiling-mounted junction box either:

(a) permanently; or

(b) utilizing a locking-type plug cap and receptacle combination, or other method of retention. In either connection mode, suitable strain relief shall be provided.

NOTE 1: The disconnection means is permitted only to facilitate replacement; as such, ceiling drop cords may not be disconnected for alternative usage.

NOTE 2: See 3-4.1.2.4(d) for criteria of receptacles.

This configuration (overhead receptacles) is one method of alleviating the number of electrical cords on the floor, where they are subject to more abuse, than if they are plugged into an overhead receptacle.

7-5.1.2.3 Low-Voltage Equipment and Instruments — All Anesthetizing Locations.

See NFPA 70, *National Electrical Code,* Article 517-105 for installation requirements associated with low-voltage equipment.

(a) Low-voltage equipment that is frequently in contact with the bodies of persons or has exposed current-carrying elements shall:

(1) operate on an electrical potential of 10 volts or less, or

A previous 8-volt level was raised to 10 volts because many devices now operate on six 1½-volt batteries or one 9-volt battery. The former Committee on Safe Use of Electricity in Patient Care Areas (now Subcommittee on Electrical Equipment) did not feel that the voltage increase compromised patient safety.

(2) be approved as intrinsically safe or double-insulated equipment, and

(3) be moisture resistant.

(b) Power shall be supplied to low-voltage equipment from:

(1) an individual isolating transformer (autotransformers shall not be used) connected to an outlet receptacle by means of a listed cord and plug [*see 3-4.1.2.4(d) through (f)*], or

(2) a common isolating transformer installed in a nonhazardous location, or

(3) individual dry-cell batteries, or

(4) common batteries made up of storage cells located in a nonhazardous location.

(c) Battery-powered appliances shall not be capable of being charged while in operation unless their charging circuitry incorporates an integral isolating-type transformer.

7-5.1.2.4 Line Voltage Equipment — Flammable Anesthetizing Locations.

(a) All equipment intended for use in anesthetizing locations shall be labeled by the manufacturer to indicate whether it may be used in a flammable anesthetizing location. Electric equipment presently in use shall be so labeled by the user. Labeling shall be permanent, conspicuous, and legible when the equipment is in the normal operating position [see 7-5.1.2.4(f)].

(b) Suction, pressure, or insufflation equipment, involving electric elements and located within the hazardous area, shall be of a type approved for use in Class I, Group C, Division 1 hazardous areas. Means shall be provided for liberating the exhaust gases from such apparatus in such a manner that gases will be effectively dispersed without making contact with any possible source of ignition.

NOTE: Suction of pressure apparatus serving flammable anesthetizing locations but located outside such flammable anesthetizing locations need not be approved for Class I, Group C, Division 1 hazardous areas, providing the discharge from suction machines is kept away from sources of ignition.

(c) Portable X-ray equipment intended for use in flammable anesthetizing locations shall be approved for use in Class I, Group C, Division 1 hazardous areas and may be provided with an approved positive-pressure system for the tube head and cables within the hazardous area [see 7-5.1.2.4(f)(2)]. All devices and switches for X-ray equipment within the hazardous area shall conform to requirements of 7-5.1.1.4 and 12-4.1.3.5(f) and (h). X-ray equipment shall be provided with an approved method of eliminating electrostatic accumulation [see 12-4.1.2.6(c) and 12-4.1.3.5(f))].

(d) High-frequency equipment intended for use in flammable anesthetizing locations shall be approved for use in Class I, Group C, Division 1 hazardous areas.

NOTE 1: Remote-control switches are recommended [see 7-5.1.1.5 and 12-4.1.3.9(c)].

NOTE 2: For recommendations in connection with the use of cautery and high-frequency equipment in flammable anesthetizing locations, see 12-4.1.3.8(j); Appendix C-12.3, Regulation Set (1), 4(d) and Set (3), 4(e); and Annex 2, "Safe Use of High-Frequency Electricity in Health Care Facilities."

(e) Portable electric equipment, such as incubators, lamps, heaters, motors, and generators, used in flammable anesthetizing locations in which anesthesia equipment is present or in operating condition, shall comply with the requirements of Articles 500, 501, and 517 of NFPA 70, National Electrical Code, for Class I, Division 1 locations and shall be approved for Class I, Group C, Division 1 hazardous areas except as permitted in 7-5.1.2.4(f).

NOTE: The resistance and capacitive reactance between the conductors and the noncurrent-carrying metallic parts must be high enough to permit the use of the equipment on an ungrounded distribution system having a line isolation monitor specified in 3-4.3.3.

(f) The following shall be considered exceptions to 7-5.1.2.4(a) and (e).

(1) Equipment designed to operate on circuits of ten volts or less shall comply with 7-5.1.2.3.

See Commentary on 7-5.1.2.3(a)(1) for the reason for changing to ten volts.

(2) Portable electric or electronic equipment mounted within an enclosure and protected by an approved positive-pressure ventilating system that conforms with the following requirements shall otherwise comply with the standards of NFPA 70, National Electrical Code, for ordinary locations. The enclosure of such a system shall be supplied with air taken from a nonhazardous area and circulated to maintain within the enclosure a pressure of at least 1 in. (2.5 cm) of water above that of the hazardous area, and shall be provided with means to deenergize the equipment

if the air temperature exceeds 140°F (60°C), or if the pressure differential drops below 1 in. (2.5 cm) of water. The positive pressure shall be continuously maintained whether or not the equipment is in use, or means shall be provided to ensure that there are at least ten changes of air within the enclosure before any electric equipment within the enclosure that does not comply with the requirements of 7-5.1.1.6 is energized. The enclosure with its equipment shall be approved for use in Class I, Group C, Division 1 hazardous areas.

(3) Portable electric or electronic equipment, if it is mounted on a floor-borne movable assembly that will not overturn either when it is tilted through an angle of 20 degrees or when in a normal operating position a horizontal force of 25 lb (11.3 kg) is applied at a height of 5 ft (152 cm) above the floor; and if the equipment, together with its enclosure, cannot be lowered within 5 ft (152 cm) of the floor without tilting the assembly, need not be approved for use in Class I, Group C, Division 1 hazardous areas, but shall comply with the requirements of 7-5.1.2.4(e). The entire assembly shall be approved for use in anesthetizing locations as defined in Section 2-2.

(4) Intrinsically safe electric or electronic equipment, which is incapable of releasing sufficient electric energy under normal or abnormal conditions to cause ignition of flammable anesthetic mixtures, may be approved for use in Class I, Group C, Division 1 hazardous areas as provided in Section 500-1 of NFPA 70, *National Electrical Code.*

(g) Photographic lighting equipment used in flammable anesthetizing locations shall comply with provisions of 7-5.1.2.4 to prevent ignition of flammable gases [*see 7-5.1.2.2(a)*]. Lamps used above the hazardous area shall be suitably enclosed to prevent sparks and hot particles falling into the hazardous area. Photoflash and photoflood lamps that are not suitably enclosed shall not be used within an anesthetizing location. Neither flash tubes nor their auxiliary equipment shall be used within the hazardous area. Flash-tube operation may be accompanied by sparking at switches, relays, and socket contacts, and by corona discharge of flashovers from high-voltage circuits.

(h) The exposed metal parts of photographic lighting equipment shall be grounded as specified in 7-5.1.2.2(b).

7-5.1.2.5 Low-Voltage Equipment — Flammable Anesthetizing Locations. Specifications for portable equipment operating on low-voltage power supplies that are not stated in 7-5.1.2.4(f)(1) and 12-4.1.3 are stated in 7-5.1.2.3.

7-5.1.3 Testing Requirements (Fixed and Portable).

7-5.1.3.1 The physical integrity of the power cord and attachment plug and cord-strain relief shall be confirmed by visual inspection or other appropriate tests.

Verification of the integrity of the power cord and its conductors and insulation, and of the power plug with particular attention to the condition of the grounding means, can prevent the possible introduction to, or the utilization of, unsafe appliance in the clinical area.
Physical deteriorations can be identified by simple inspection.

7-5.1.3.2* The resistance between the appliance chassis, or any exposed conductive surface of the appliance, and the ground pin of the attachment plug shall be measured. The resistance shall be less than 0.50 ohm. The cord shall be flexed at its connection to the attachment plug or

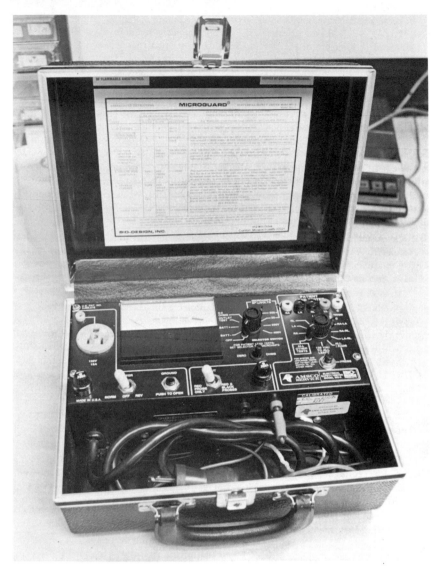

Figure 27   A testing device that can be used to perform a variety of tasks (e.g., chassis and patient-lead leakage current, resistance between chassis and plug, isolated lead test, reversed polarity check).

connector and at its connection to the strain relief on the chassis during the resistance measurement. This measurement shall only apply to appliances that are used in the patient vicinity. (*See Appendix A-7-5.1.3.2 for suggested test methods.*)

Exception: The requirement does not apply to escutcheon or nameplates, small screws, etc., that are unlikely to become energized.

While a value lower than 0.50 ohm is better, and can be measured, the Subcommittee responsible for this material left unchanged for 1987 the 0.50 ohm requirement for health care facilities. A review of this criteria is planned for the next edition of NFPA 99. (*See also Commentary below on A-7-5.1.3.2.*)

A-7-5.1.3.2 There are several methods for measuring ground-wire resistance accurately. Three examples are described below:

(a) *Two-Wire Resistance Technique.*

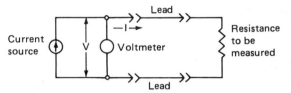

A known current is fed through the unknown resistance. A high-input-impedance voltmeter measures the voltage drop across the resistance and R is calculated as V/I. This technique measures the lead resistance in series with the unknown resistance. When the unknown resistance is a ground wire (less than 0.15 ohm), the lead resistance is appreciable. This is accounted for by shorting the lead wires together and "zeroing" the voltmeter. The actual resistance in effect subtracts out the lead wire resistance. In order for this technique to be reasonably accurate for measuring ground wires, an active high-impedance millivoltmeter must be used.

(b) *Four-Wire Resistance Technique.*

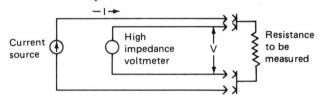

This technique is very similar to the two-wire resistance technique. The difference is that the known current is fed to the resistance to be measured through a pair of leads separate from the pair of leads to the voltmeter. The voltmeter is measuring the true voltage across the resistance to be measured regardless of the resistance of the measuring leads. This method eliminates the need for zeroing out the measuring lead resistance.

(c) *AC Current Method.*

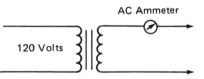

This technique utilizes a step-down transformer of known voltage output to feed current through the ground wire and measure the current that flows. The impedance of the ground wire is then calculated by Ohm's Law.

NOTE: The internal impedance of the measuring circuit must be established with the test leads shorted. This value needs to be subtracted from the test measurement.

The maximum resistance allowed for an appliance used within a patient care area of a facility has lately been a subject of much debate. The value required of manufacturers has long been accepted as 0.15 ohm, and is based on the total resistance of 15 ft of No. 18 wire, the contact resistance at connectors, and a safety factor. Thus, 9-5.3.2.1 lists this value of 0.15 ohm.

In 1980, when manufacturer requirements were moved into a separate chapter of NFPA 76B, the Committee recognized that there could be some differences between hospital and manufacturer requirements (e.g., allowance for deterioration, less sophisticated instrumentation, tighter time constraints, etc.). One of these differences was the value of the resistance of the ground wire. In the 1980 edition of NFPA 76B, the value was the same for hospitals and manufacturers: 0.15 ohm. However, for the 1984 edition of NFPA 99 (into which NFPA 76B was incorporated), public proposals were submitted to raise the measured value for hospitals to 0.20 and 0.50 ohm. The major reasons given for these proposed increases included the inaccuracy of measuring devices and the lack of data showing a safety hazard for values greater than 0.15 ohm.

These proposals prompted extensive Committee debate. Issues included an assurance factor, double standard, reasonableness, and changes being based on technology rather than safety. The Committee accepted a recommendation of 0.20 ohm on the basis that reasonably priced instrumentation was available to make repeatable measurements in the 0.1-ohm range, that some degradation of connections can be expected, and that a 10-year record of cord-resistance measurements by a clinical engineering department in a Connecticut hospital showed that most problems were readily correctable when the initial value of 0.15 ohm began to rise over the 0.20-ohm level (much more effort was required when the value was between 0.15 and 0.18 ohm).

At the NFPA 1983 Fall Meeting, members present accepted the public proposal that increased the acceptable level of the total grounding resistance value (between chassis and ground pin of plug) to 0.50 ohm. The major reason given was the lack of data to show that this higher value would create an electrical safety hazard. The then Committee on Safe Use of Electricity in Patient Care Areas of Health Care Facilities in turn accepted the proposal.

7-5.1.3.3* Leakage Current Tests — General. The following requirements shall apply to all tests.

(a) The resistance tests of 7-3.1.3.2 shall be conducted before undertaking any leakage current measurements.

It is important to first verify power cord integrity, and then the condition of the wall receptacle and the test equipment, with the latter two connected to a proper grounding point. Operator safety and test results can be impacted.

(b) *Techniques of Measurement.* Each test shall be performed with the appropriate connection to a properly grounded ac power system.

(c) *Frequency of Leakage Current.* The leakage current limits stated in 7-5.1.3.3 shall be rms values for dc and sinusoidal waveforms up to 1 kHz. For frequencies above 1 kHz the leakage current limits shall be the values given in 7-5.1.3.3 multiplied by the frequency, in kHz, up to a maximum multiplier of 100.

NOTE 1: The limits for nonsinusoidal periodic, modulated, and transient waveforms remain to be determined.

NOTE 2: For complex leakage-current waveforms, a single reading from an appropriate metering system can represent the physiologically effective value of the composite waveform, provided that the contribution of each component to the total reading is weighted in accordance with 7-5.1.3.3(c). This weighting can be achieved by a frequency-response-shaping network that precedes a flat-response meter, or by a meter whose own frequency-response characteristic matches 7-5.1.3.3(c).

(d) *Leakage Current in Relation to Polarity.* Leakage current measurements shall be made with the polarity of the power line normal, the power switch of the appliance "on" and "off," and with all operating controls in the positions to cause maximum leakage-current readings. The leakage current limits in 7-5.1.3 and 7-5.2.2.1 shall not be exceeded in any of these conditions.

A-7-5.1.3.3 Leakage Current Measurements.

For complex leakage current waveforms, a single reading from an appropriate metering system can represent the physiologically effective value of the composite waveform, provided that the contribution of each component to the total reading is weighted in accordance with 7-5.1.3.3 or 9-2.1.13.3(a).

This "weighting" can be achieved by a frequency-response-shaping network that precedes a flat-response meter, or by a meter whose own frequency response characteristic matches 7-5.1.3.3 or 9-2.1.13.3(a).

If the required performance is obtained by a meter with integral response shaping properties, then that meter should have a constant input resistance of 1000 ohms. (A high-input-impedance meter may be used by shunting a 1000-ohm resistor across the meter's input terminals.)

If, however, the required frequency response is obtained by a network that precedes an otherwise flat-response meter, then the input impedance of the network should be 1000 ohms ± 10 percent, over the frequency range from 0 to 1 MHz, and the frequency response of the network-meter combination must be substantially independent of the impedance of the signal source.

A suggested input network is shown below.

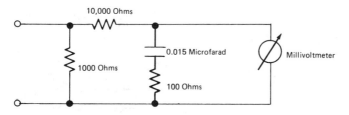

Figure A-7-5.1.3.3/A-9-2.1.13.3(a) Leakage Current Measurements. (1.0 millivolt meter reading corresponds to input current of 1.0 microamperes.)

When manufacturer requirements were placed in a separate chapter of NFPA 76B-1980, some tests for manufacturers were inadvertently left out or incorrectly combined; one test for hospitals was also inadvertently excluded. The tests described below are now in the same sequence as those for manufacturers in Section 9-2.1:

Chassis:
- permanently wired
- cord-connected

Patient leads:
- lead-to-ground (nonisolated input)
- lead-to-ground (isolated input)
- isolated test (isolated input)
- between leads (nonisolated input)
- between leads (isolated input)

The values for leakage currents reflect exhaustive discussion of studies on humans and dogs, actual measurements during cardiac surgery, and manufacturing capabilities. For further information, see A-9-2.1.13.4(c), Chassis Leakage Current Limits.

See A-9.2.1.13.3(a) for Commentary on test equipment changes.

7-5.1.3.4 Chassis Leakage Current, Fixed Equipment. Permanently wired appliances in the patient vicinity shall be tested prior to installation while the equipment is temporarily insulated from ground. The leakage current from frame to ground of permanently wired appliances installed in general or critical patient care areas shall not exceed 5.0 milliamperes with all grounds lifted. After installation, such appliances shall be tested periodically in accordance with 3-5.2.1.3 ("Voltage Measurements") and 3-5.2.1.6(b) ("Existing Construction").

After installation, it may not be easy to disconnect ground(s) or temporarily insulate an appliance from ground. However, it is also very unlikely that the grounding will be disturbed after being permanently wired. Thus, permanently wired appliances can be considered a part of the building wiring system after installation. This is the reason the tests conducted after installation are the same as those as given in Section 3-5.2.1.

7-5.1.3.5 Chassis Leakage Current, Portable Equipment.

(a) The leakage current for cord-connected appliances shall be measured. The limit shall be 100 microamperes. Figure 7-5.1.3.5 shows one method of performing this test.

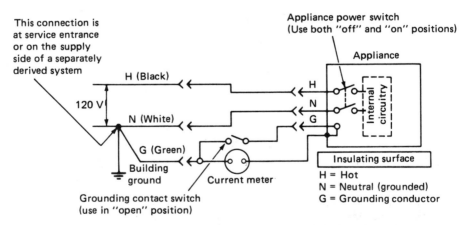

Figure 7-5.1.3.5   Test Circuit for Measuring Chassis Leakage Current.

If multiple appliances are mounted together by the hospital in a single cart or rack, and one power cord supplies power, the leakage current shall be measured as an assembly.

The second paragraph (referring to multiple appliances) was added during revision for the 1984 edition of NFPA 99. For rack-mounted or cart-mounted appliances with one power cord, the leakage current is the sum from each appliance. It is this sum that will pass through a person should the ground of the power cord be broken and the person touch the chassis of the cart/rack and some ground. (*See also Commentary under 9-2.1.3.8.*)

Exception No. 1: Existing appliances with leakage currents up to 250 microamps shall be permitted to be used provided an appropriate inspection and maintenance program is established for these items to ensure that the integrity of the grounding connection is reliably maintained.

Exception No. 2: Where existing or special equipment (such as mobile X-ray machines) exhibit chassis leakage current between 250 and 500 microamperes, this condition does not represent a hazard to the patient as long as the grounding connection is intact. Such equipment shall be permitted to be kept in service provided a documented maintenance schedule is established to assure the integrity of the grounding connection. A three-month interval is a nominal period. Depending on the intensity of the use of the appliance and prior test data, the hospital shall be permitted to establish a protocol with shortened or lengthened time intervals.

NOTE: Where existing equipment exceeds 500 microamps, such as some types of ultrasound therapy devices or portable hypothermia units, etc., methods to reduce leakage current, such as the addition of a small isolation transformer to that device, or methods to provide equivalent safety by adding redundant equipment ground are permissible.

(b) Measurements shall be made with the appliance ground broken in two modes of appliance operation: power plug connected normally and with the appliance on and with the appliance off (if equipped with an on/off switch). When the appliance has fixed redundant grounding (e.g., permanently fastened to the grounding system), the chassis leakage current test shall be conducted with the redundant grounding intact.

•   It may seem unproductive to measure the leakage current with the redundant ground intact since redundant grounding presents a dead short across the meter input, causing the measured leakage current to read zero. The Subcommittee on Electrical Equipment believes that the leakage current measurement should still be made, however, as a check that the redundant grounding is indeed in place. Since redundant grounding is used only in potentially hazardous circumstances, it is worthwhile to check its presence.
•   The polarity-reversal test was eliminated from users (facilities) when former NFPA 76B was adopted in 1980. (Manufacturers were, and still are, required to test appliances in both the normal and reversed polarity modes.) Since manufacturers did conduct both tests, there was seen only a low probability of a problem occurring when received by the end user; thus, the relaxation of testing by the end-user.
   However, when an appliance is repaired, or "grows old," normal/reverse polarity testing should be considered, particularly since most medical test equipment have a built in polarity-reversal switch.

7-5.1.3.6 Lead Leakage Current Tests and Limits, Portable Equipment.

(a) *Lead to Ground (Nonisolated Input).*   The leakage current between all patient leads connected together and ground shall be measured with the power plug connected normally and the device on. Figure 7-5.1.3.6(a) is an example of an acceptable test configuration. The leakage current shall be less than 100 microamperes.

(b) *Lead to Ground (Isolated Input).*   The leakage current between each patient lead and ground for an appliance with isolated leads shall be measured with the power plug connected normally

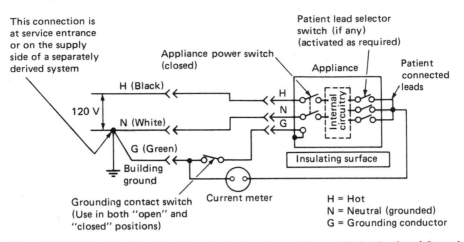

Figure 7-5.1.3.6(a)   Test Circuit for Measuring Leakage Current Between Patient Leads and Ground (Nonisolated).

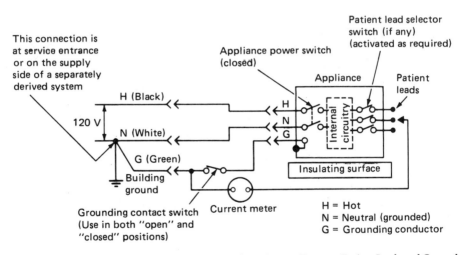

Figure 7-5.1.3.6(b)   Test Circuit for Measuring Leakage Current Between Patient Leads and Ground (Isolated).

and the device on. Figure 7-5.1.3.6(b) is an example of an acceptable test configuration. The leakage current shall be less than 10 microamperes.

(c) *Isolation Test (Isolated Input)*.   The current driven into the leads of an appliance that has isolated leads, when an external power source at line voltage and frequency is applied between each lead and ground, shall be measured in accordance with Figure 7-5.1.3.6(c). The leakage current shall be less than 20 microamperes in each case. The test is made with the appliance's normal patient cables.

Suitable safety precautions (such as including a resistance in series to limit the current, insulation of the meter, and a momentary switch) shall be taken to protect the operator. In appliances without a power cord or with ungrounded, exposed conductive surfaces, measurements

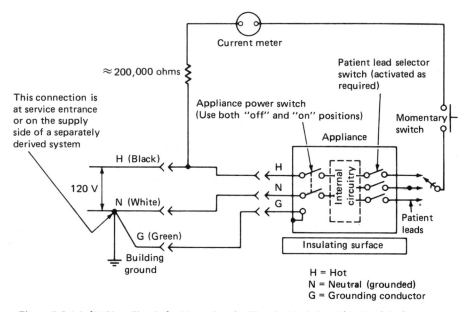

Figure 7-5.1.3.6(c) Test Circuit for Measuring the Electrical Isolation of Isolated Patient Leads.

shall be made with the exposed conductive surfaces temporarily grounded. If there is no exposed conductive surface, measurement shall be made with a simulated surface, as described in 9-2.1.13.4(b), "Appliances with No Exposed Conductive Surfaces," that is also temporarily grounded.

Only isolated patient leads shall be connected to intracardiac catheters or electrodes.

The cautionary language of the second paragraph was added for the 1984 edition of NFPA 99 since the hazard associated with this test is present wherever it is accomplished. (The cautionary note had previously been included only in manufacturer requirements.)

(d) *Between Leads (Nonisolated Input).* The leakage current between any one lead (not ground) and each other lead shall be measured. Figure 7-5.1.3.6(d)/(e) is an example of an acceptable test configuration. The leakage current shall be less than 50 microamperes for the ground wire open and closed.

(e) *Between Leads (Isolated Input).* The leakage current between any one lead (not ground) and each other lead shall be measured. Figure 7-5.1.3.6(d)/(e) is an example of an acceptable test configuration. The leakage current shall be less than 10 microamperes for the ground wire open and closed.

7-5.1.3.7 Testing Intervals.

(a) The facility shall establish policies and protocols for the type of test and intervals of testing for each appliance.

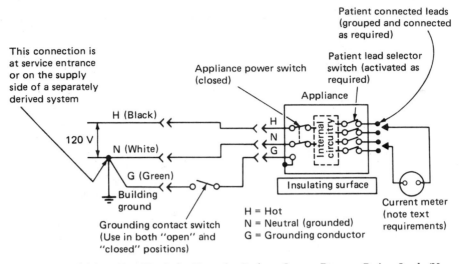

Figure 7-5.1.3.6(d)/(e) Test Circuit for Measuring Leakage Current Between Patient Leads (Non-isolated and Isolated).

(b) All appliances that may be used in patient care areas shall be tested in accordance with 7-5.1.3 before being put into service for the first time and after repair or modification. Patient-care-related electrical appliances shall be retested at intervals determined by their normal location or area of normal use, but not exceeding the intervals listed below.

General Care Areas (Class G): 12 months
Critical Care Areas (Class H): 6 months
Wet Locations (Class W): 6 months.

Exception No. 1: The testing intervals listed are intended to be nominal values and hospitals shall be permitted to adopt a protocol using either longer or shorter intervals provided that there is a documented justification based on previous safety testing records for the equipment in question, unusually light or heavy utilization, or similar considerations.

Exception No. 2: Facility-owned household or other appliances that may be in the patient vicinity, but that are not intended to contact the patient, shall be tested at intervals deemed appropriate by the facility. Some equipment in this category may require only an infrequent visual inspection. The facility shall be permitted to structure a testing protocol and frequency for some equipment that may be more limited than that prescribed in 7-5.1.3.

Exception No. 3: The tests specified in 7-5.1.3.6, "Lead Leakage Current Tests and Limits, Portable Equipment," shall be required for incoming inspections and following repairs and modifications that may have compromised the patient lead leakage current.

• Exception No. 3 was included since this isolation test should not be a routine test. It can be hazardous if not performed by knowledgeable persons, and it may damage nonisolated patient equipment.
• Determination of testing intervals is intended to eliminate the possibility of utilizing unsafe devices in patient care areas. Justification for interval periods may be based on the device's design, manufacturing guidelines, application or life supportability, age, performance history and institutional experiences with similar devices, and finally its risk level (i.e., the type of possible hazard to be prevented).

7-5.2 Nonpatient Electrical Appliances and Equipment.

7-5.2.1 Fixed. (Reserved)

7-5.2.2 Portable.

7-5.2.2.1 Patient Care Area.

(a) *Facility-Owned Household Appliances.* The leakage current for facility-owned household appliances (e.g., housekeeping or maintenance appliances) that may be used in a patient vicinity and are likely to contact the patient shall be measured. The leakage current shall be less than 500 microamperes.

Requirements, as well as commentary, relative to *non*facility-owned appliances are covered in 7-6.2.1.10.

7-5.2.2.2 Laboratory.

(a) Portable equipment intended for laboratory use shall be grounded or otherwise arranged with an approved method to protect personnel against shock, in accordance with NFPA 70, *National Electrical Code.*

(b) All electrical heating equipment to be used for laboratory procedures shall be equipped with overtemperature-limit controls so arranged that thermostatic failure will not result in hazardous temperatures. When such equipment is intended for use with flammable or combustible liquids, its electrical components shall be explosionproof, intrinsically safe, or ventilated in a manner that will prevent accumulation of flammable atmospheres under normal conditions of operation.

(c) Heating equipment equipped with fans shall be arranged with an interlock arranged to disconnect the heating elements when the fan is inoperative, unless the fan is not essential to safe operation.

7-6 Administration.

7-6.1 Responsibilities of Governing Body. (Reserved)

7-6.2 Policies.

7-6.2.1 General.

7-6.2.1.1 Medical and surgical electrical instrumentation and monitoring devices, as well as all electric appliances used for the care and entertainment of the patient, purchased or otherwise acquired for use by the facility (e.g., leased, donated, constructed on-site, loaned, etc.), shall meet the safety performance criteria of 9-2.1, "Patient-Care-Related Electrical Equipment," in Chapter 9, "Manufacturer Requirements."

7-6.2.1.2 General. The facility shall perform the testing procedures at intervals as specified in 7-5.1.3.7.

7-6.2.1.3 Protection of Patients with Direct Electrical Pathways to the Heart. Only equipment that is specifically designed for the purpose, i.e., provided with suitable isolated patient leads or connections (*see 9-2.1.12, "Direct Electrical Pathways to the Heart"*), shall be connected directly to electrically conductive pathways to a patient's heart. Such electrically conductive pathways include intracardiac electrodes such as implanted pacemaker leads and guide wires. The facility shall have a policy that prohibits the use of external cardiac pacemakers and pacing leads with external terminals that are not properly protected from potentially hazardous contact with conductive surfaces.

> The leakage current limits of 7-5.1.3 are based in part on the premise that the most stringent leakage current requirements are necessary only for those patient leads that can be expected to be connected to electrical conductive pathways going directly to the heart. Other patient leads, as well as chassis leakage current levels, do not require such stringent levels.

7-6.2.1.4 Electrical appliance controls, (such as bed controls, pillow speakers, television controls, and nurse-call controls) that do not meet the minimum requirements of 9-2.1, "Patient-Care-Related Electrical Equipment," shall be mounted so that they cannot be taken into the bed.

Exception: Existing low-voltage controls may be used in general patient-care areas.

7-6.2.1.5 Adapters. With the exception of three-to-two-prong adapters, adapters shall be permitted to be used to permit appliances fitted with distinctive plugs (such as those that may still be in use in anesthetizing locations) to be used with conventional power receptacles. The wiring of the adapter shall be tested for physical integrity, polarity, and continuity of grounding at the time of assembly and periodically thereafter. Construction of adapters and cords shall be adequate for the application to avoid overload (i.e., 16 AWG or greater) and shall meet the requirements of 9-2.1.2.1, "Attachment Plugs," and 9-2.1.2.2, "Power Cords."

> Conducting periodical performance verification of adaptors as part of the equipment control program will enhance hazard avoidance only if *all* adaptors are properly identified. Thus, each adaptor introduced into patient care areas needs to be so labeled as to facilitate its identification and subjection to periodic testings.

7-6.2.1.6 Appliances Intended to Deliver Electrical Energy. Electrical-energy-delivering appliances shall conform to the leakage, grounding, and other requirements of this chapter when powered, but not delivering energy.

NOTE 1: When delivering energy, such appliances may deviate from these requirements only to the extent essential for their intended clinical function.

NOTE 2: Appliances that intentionally or that may inadvertently apply electrical energy to the patient or to components in contact with the patient require special safety considerations.

NOTE 3: Since there is a wide range of power levels, output frequencies, and purposes of appliances that apply electricity directly to patients or to patient-connected devices, it is not feasible to cite them in detail.

This requirement was previously included only in the manufacturer portion of NFPA 99, but it is also applicable to health care facility personnel conducting leakage current tests.

Although it is primarily the responsibility of the manufacturer to design safe power-delivering equipment, facility personnel are responsible for ensuring that the equipment is functioning properly and being used correctly. This responsibility becomes particularly pertinent if repairs are made by facility personnel.

7-6.2.1.7 Specification of Conditions of Purchase. The procurement authority shall include in its purchasing documents any appropriate requirements or conditions specifically related to the hospital's use of the appliance, which may include, but are not restricted to, the following:

NOTE: The facility may wish to reference compliance with this chapter and Chapter 9 on its purchasing document.

(a) the type of appliance listing or certification required, if any,

(b) the delivery of manufacturer's test data, where pertinent,

(c) special conditions of use (such as in anesthetizing or other locations with special hazards),

(d) unusual environmental conditions (such as high humidity, moisture, salt spray, etc.), and

(e) the type of electric power system (i.e., grounded or isolated) intended to energize the appliance, the nature of the overcurrent devices, the use of auxiliary emergency power, etc., when pertinent.

It has been reported to the editor of this Handbook that a specific preprinted document addressing, among other issues, items (a) through (e) above has been incorporated by some hospitals for several years. The document is attached to all purchase requisitions issued for electrically powered patient care appliances. Over the years, it has helped curb the introduction of items with compliance deficiencies as well as assuring the owners' future access to replacement parts and product safety enhancements.

7-6.2.1.8* Manuals for Appliances. Purchase specifications shall require the vendor to supply suitable manuals for operators or users upon delivery of the appliance. The manuals shall include installation and operating instructions, inspection and testing procedures, and maintenance details. [See 9-2.1.8.1(m).]

A-7-6.2.1.8 Manuals For Appliances. Consideration should be given to requiring the vendor to sell parts to the individual or group designated by the hospital to service the equipment following the warranty period.

These requirements and recommendations can be incorporated into a condition-of-purchase document. (See 7-6.2.1.7.) In addition, a vendor can be requested to provide to the user with all safety-related enhancements for the duration of the life of the device.

7-6.2.1.9 System Demonstration. Any system consisting of several electric appliances shall be demonstrated as a complete system, after installation, by the vendor designated to assume system responsibility, and prior to acceptance of the system by the facility. The vendor shall demonstrate the operation of the system and provide appropriate initial instruction to operators and maintenance personnel.

NOTE: This section is not intended to prevent facilities from assembling their own systems.

7-6.2.1.10 Appliances Not Provided by the Facility. Policies shall be established for the control of appliances not supplied by the facility.

Specific policies will depend on the facility's resources and staff, but some type of control over appliances is essential — both for patient and staff safety and legal liability purposes.

Some of the factors that need to be considered include: Is the appliance a "medical device" or does the manufacturer make no claims as to its design or use as a medical device? Is device to be used by the staff of the facility on the patient? Is the appliance owned by the patient and to be used only by the patient?

To one hospital clinical engineer, from the results of a six-month, two-hospital incoming inspection review of appliances *not* provided by the facilities, it was obvious that the noncompliance level was high. On the average, one third of the devices did not pass the incoming inspection and were thus not permitted to be used in the facilities.

7-6.2.2 Anesthetizing Locations.

7-6.2.2.1 Physical safeguards built into the anesthetizing locations or storage areas will not provide protection unless safe practices are followed and good maintenance is provided.

7-6.2.2.2 Scheduled inspections shall be maintained.

7-6.2.2.3 Defective electrical equipment shall be replaced promptly or repaired by competent personnel.

7-6.2.2.4 If patients with externalized cardiac pacemakers are treated in ambulatory care facilities, care shall be taken to prevent contact of the exposed leads with conductive surfaces.

7-6.2.2.5 Administrative vigilance is required to prohibit the use of portable electric equipment and appliances — such as electric drills — of a type unsuitable for use in hazardous areas in flammable anesthetizing locations during their occupancy by patients or near anesthesia equipment in operating condition and in storage locations containing flammable inhalation anesthetic agents.

7-6.2.3 During Administration of Respiratory Therapy.

7-6.2.3.1 Electrical equipment used within the site of intentional expulsion shall have no hot surfaces.

When only the remote control or signal leads of a device are to be used in the site of intentional expulsion, only the control or signal leads shall be required to comply with this section.

Exception: Small (less than 2-watt) hermetically sealed heating elements such as light bulbs.

For 1987, the term and concept of "site of administration" were replaced by the term and concept of "site of intentional expulsion." The former was established when NFPA 56B, *Standard for Respiratory Therapy*, was being developed in the 1960s. It was a way of creating an easily indentifiable and enforceable boundary (i.e., one foot around oxygen-delivery equipment) into which no electrical equipment was to be brought unless it was listed for use in an oxygen-enriched atmosphere. This one foot boundary was a conservative value (i.e., it was known, and has since been measured in a controlled study, that any escaping oxygen is quickly diluted into the atmosphere, and oxygen concentrations return to normal levels at approximately 2 to 5 in.).

Because of (1) a recent study by a hospital, (2) the number *and type* of incidents reported over the years, and (3) the practices taking place in hospitals today, a proposal was accepted during the revision for this 1987 edition of NFPA 99 that redefined the hazardous area to just that area where oxygen or an oxygen-enriched atmosphere was deliberately vented to the atmosphere. (For examples of this concept, refer to the definition of site of international expulsion in Chapter 2.) However, while the hazardous area is now smaller and more reflective of where higher-than-normal oxygen levels will occur, it does not negate all the other precautions that need to be observed when oxygen is being administered (e.g., no smoking in the room, etc.).

7-6.2.3.2 Electrical equipment used within oxygen-delivery equipment shall be listed for use in oxygen-enriched atmospheres, or sold with the intent to be used in oxygen-enriched atmospheres.

NOTE: For further information concerning the criteria for equipment used in oxygen delivery equipment, see Chapter 9, Section 9-2.1.

Sections 7-6.2.3.1 and 7-6.2.3.2 reflect a major change in the extent of area considered hazardous when oxygen is administered for respiratory therapy purposes. (*See Commentary under Section 7-6.2.3.1 and under the definition of new term "Site of Intentional Expulsion" in Chapter 2 for a description of this change.*)

For changes in manufacturer criteria associated with this change, see Paragraph 9-2.1.9.3.

7-6.2.3.3 When high-energy-delivering probes (such as defibrillator paddles) or other electrical devices that do not comply with 7-6.2.3.1 are deemed essential to the care of an individual patient and must be used within a site of administration or within oxygen-delivery equipment, they shall be used with extreme caution.

NOTE: Where possible, combustible materials such as hair, fabric, and paper should be removed from the vicinity of where the energy is delivered. Water-soluble surgical jelly has been shown to dramatically reduce the combustibility of these materials.

Some of these types of devices have to be used in instances such as cardiac arrest. As noted, extreme caution is to be exercised if oxygen is being used.

7-6.2.3.4 Electrical equipment, apparatus, and wiring for respiratory therapy equipment used in anesthetizing locations shall be in accordance with Chapter 3 and 12-4.1.

7-6.2.3.5 Defective electrical apparatus shall be tagged and repaired or discarded.

7-6.2.3.6 Servicing and Maintenance of Equipment.

(a) Defective equipment shall be immediately removed from service.

(b) Defective electrical apparatus shall not be used.

(c) Areas designated for the servicing of oxygen equipment shall be clean, free of oil and grease, and not used for the repair of other equipment.

(d) Only repair parts recommended by the manufacturer shall be employed.

(e) Service manuals, instructions, and procedures provided by the manufacturer shall be used in the maintenance of equipment.

(f) A scheduled preventive maintenance program shall be followed.

7-6.2.4 Laboratory.

The use, inspection, and maintenance of electrical equipment and appliances in laboratories needs to be coordinated between all areas responsible for the equipment and appliances. Typically, the electrical safety, preventive maintenance, and hazard surveillance programs are all involved in laboratory electrical safety.

It is a good practice to include all aspects of electrical safety within the laboratory (equipment, wiring, maintenance, and testing), and to review them in conjunction with the facility-wide safety program to determine if they conform to the requirements of the authority having jurisdiction.

7-6.2.4.1* Electrical equipment for laboratory use shall be tested for electrical safety against standards acceptable to the authority having jurisdiction.

A-7-6.2.4.1 One reason for requiring testing of all electrical equipment used in the laboratory is to provide minimum assurance against electrical macroshock hazards.

Since an electrical safety document for laboratory equipment does not currently exist, the Subcommittee responsible for laboratory requirements considered it reasonable that electrical safety criteria for equipment intended for use in laboratories be tested for electrical safety by a testing laboratory acceptable to authority having jurisdiction. (In the restructuring process for the 1987 edition of NFPA 99, electrical safety requirements for all electrical equipment were placed in Chapter 7.)

7-6.2.4.2* Electrical equipment intended for use in hazardous areas in laboratories shall be approved by the authority having jurisdiction. (*See definition of hazardous area in laboratories in Section 2-2 of Chapter 2.*)

A-7-6.2.4.2 Electrical equipment has been a frequent source of ignition of flammable concentrations of gases and vapors when combustible and flammable liquids and gases have been used in or near equipment not designed or safe for such use. While general and special ventilation will usually prevent the accumulation of flammable concentrations of gases and vapors in health care laboratories, the hazards should be recognized. Recommended practice is to evaluate at least annually what combustible and flammable liquids and gases are being used in the laboratory, what electrical equipment is exposed to flammable vapors and gases routinely or under reasonably foreseeable circumstances, whether special listed and labeled electrical equipment is available and justified, or whether equivalent safety can be provided more economically and practically by ventilation or quantity limitations.

As an educational measure in laboratories that have many personnel and electrical devices and that handle combustible or flammable liquids in containers larger than 1.69 oz (50 ml), electrical equipment not listed or labeled for use in hazardous atmospheres should be marked with precautionary signs or labels with a legend such as:

> May ignite flammable vapors or gases. Not safe for use with exposed organic liquids with flash point temperatures below 100°F (37.8°C) (or the temperature of the high-limit cutoff if the equipment is designed for heating, e.g., oil bath or hot plate).

Several proposals were previously submitted to the Subcommittee on Laboratories (responsible for this material) regarding the deletion of this paragraph. However, the Committee believes sufficient hazard exists when electrical equipment is used in hazardous areas in laboratories to warrant equipment approval in such areas by an authority having jurisdiction. Note that this paragraph does not apply to all laboratory equipment—only to electrical equipment used in hazardous areas.

A definition of the term "hazardous areas in laboratories" was created since the Committee responsible for laboratories is also responsible for defining the boundaries of such areas.

7-6.3 Recordkeeping.

7-6.3.1 Patient Care Appliances.

7-6.3.1.1 Instruction Manuals. A permanent file of instruction and maintenance manuals as described in 9-2.1.8.1 shall be maintained and be accessible. It shall preferably be in the custody of the engineering group responsible for the maintenance of the appliance. Duplicate instruction manuals shall be available to the user. Any safety labels and condensed operating instructions on an appliance shall be maintained in readable condition.

7-6.3.1.2* Documentation. A record shall be maintained of the tests required by this chapter and associated repairs or modifications. At a minimum, this record shall contain the date, unique identification of the equipment tested, and an indication of which items have met or have failed to meet the performance requirements of this section.

A-7-6.3.1.2 Documentation. (*See A-3-6.2.3.1.*)

7-6.3.1.3 Test Logs. A log of test results and repairs shall be maintained and kept for an appropriate time.

7-6.4 Use. (Reserved)

7-6.5 Qualification and Training of Personnel.

7-6.5.1 Personnel concerned with the application and maintenance of electric appliances, including physicians, nurses, nurse aids, engineers, technicians, and orderlies, shall be cognizant of the risks associated with their use. To achieve this end the hospital shall provide appropriate programs of continuing education for its personnel.

Continuing education programs are extremely important in hazard prevention. While all professional personnel are involved in ongoing training, this activity is especially important for engineers and technicians as they install, repair, and maintain medical appliances and systems, and determine their performance.

7-6.5.2 Equipment shall be serviced by qualified personnel only.

Compliance with this standard will eliminate hazardous conditions mainly through the servicing and testing of medical appliances. The Subcommittee responsible for the material in this chapter felt, therefore, that only qualified professionals can determine compliance with these standards. Due to the complexity of the hospital environment and the interdisciplinary training and background required to perform such tasks appropriately, safety technology for patient care appliances should thus be provided only by trained professionals.

8 GAS EQUIPMENT (POSITIVE AND NEGATIVE PRESSURE), HEALTH CARE FACILITIES

NOTE: The application of requirements contained in this chapter for specific types of health care facilities can be found in Chapters 12 through 18.

Prologue

In the past, fires occasionally occurred in and around oxygen tents and other respiratory therapy apparatus. While the frequency of these incidents was not great, fatalities to patients (especially those in oxygen tents) usually accompanied these blazes. Recognizing that respiratory therapy equipment and treatment, especially in the presence of oxygen-enriched atmospheres, posed a significant hazard, Dr. Carl Walter, then Chairman of the Hospitals Committee, appointed a Subcommittee in 1964 to develop a safety standard for respiratory therapy. That standard, designated NFPA 56B, was adopted as a tentative standard in 1966 and officially adopted two years later. The standard recognized the many sources of respiratory therapy and the hazards associated with use of this equipment, especially when oxygen-enriched atmospheres were utilized.

Since the oxygen-enriched atmosphere is usually an essential component of respiratory therapy, the prevention of fires revolves around the elimination of sources of ignition and the presence of flammable substances within this atmosphere. A study of fires in oxygen tents revealed that the most likely causes of these fires had been attempts by patients to smoke and parents supplying children on the pediatric ward with sparking toys. Precautions relating to these hazards were incorporated into the standard.

That standard (Chapter 5 in the 1984 edition of NFPA 99; mostly Chapters 4 and 8 of the 1987 edition of NFPA 99) is now recognized by respiratory therapists and other hospital and firesafety personnel. Its enforcement has essentially resulted in the elimination of fires in and around respiratory therapy equipment.

8-1 Scope.

8-1.1 This chapter covers the performance, maintenance, and testing of gas equipment used within health care facilities.

8-1.2* This chapter applies to the use of nonflammable medical gases, vapors, and aerosols, and the equipment required for their administration, at normal atmospheric pressure.

The phrase "at normal atmospheric pressure" may cause confusion. Some equipment, such as IPPB machines, ventilators, and resuscitation equipment, function internally at pressures above normal (room) atmospheric pressure. The

241

phrase "above normal atmospheric pressure" refers to unusual atmospheres in a room to which this chapter does *not* apply. (*See 8-1.4.*)

A-8-1.2 Respiratory therapy is an allied health specialty employed with medical direction in the treatment, management, control, diagnostic evaluation, and care of patients with deficiencies and abnormalities of the cardiopulmonary system.[1]

In 1983, it was estimated that there were over 80,000 respiratory therapy practitioners in the United States. These professionals are key personnel in health care facilities in applying the requirements established in this chapter.

Respiratory therapy includes the therapeutic use of the following: medical gases and administration apparatus, environmental control systems, humidification, aerosols, medications, ventilatory support, broncho-pulmonary drainage, pulmonary rehabilitation, cardiopulmonary resuscitation, and airway management.[2]

With medical knowledge increasing and changes in the state of the art of science and technology, this list of uses is subject to additions and/or changes.

There is a continual need for human diligence in the establishment and maintenance of safe practices for respiratory therapy.

It is essential for personnel having responsibility for respiratory therapy to establish and enforce appropriate programs to fulfill provisions of this chapter.

It is the responsibility of the administrative and professional staff of a hospital, or safety director if one is appointed, to adopt and enforce appropriate regulations for a hospital. In other health care facilities, responsibility may be assigned to a safety director or other responsible person, who is, in turn, responsible to the administration.

In institutions having a respiratory therapy service, it is recommended that this service be directly responsible for the administration of this chapter.

Hazards can be mitigated only when there is continual recognition and understanding.

8-1.3 When used in this chapter, the term *oxygen* is intended to mean 100 percent oxygen as well as mixtures of oxygen and air.

This should not be confused with air, which contains 21 percent oxygen under normal conditions.

8-1.4 This chapter does not apply to special atmospheres, such as those encountered in hyperbaric chambers. (*See Chapter 19, "Hyperbaric Facilities."*)

8-2 Nature of Hazards.

NOTE: See Chapter 7, Paragraph 7-2.2.2, for electrical hazards associated with gas equipment.

---

[1]Courtesy of the American Association for Respiratory Therapy, 1720 Regal Row, Dallas, TX 75235.
[2]Ibid.

8-2.1 Fire and Explosions.

8-2.1.1 Inhalation Anesthetizing Locations.

8-2.1.1.1 Oxygen and nitrous oxide, the gases normally used for relative analgesia and as a component of general anesthesia, are strong oxidizing gases, and individually or as a mixture support combustion quite readily.

Nitrous oxide will, in fact, support combustion in the absence of oxygen.

8-2.1.1.2 Inhalation gases or vapors introduce fire, chemical, mechanical, and electrical hazards which are all interrelated. Any mixture of inhalation gases will support combustion. In an oxygen-enriched atmosphere, materials that are flammable and combustible in air ignite more easily and burn more vigorously. The materials that may be found on or near patients include hair oils, oil-based lubricants, skin lotions, clothing, linens, paper, rubber, alcohols, acetone, and some plastics.

8-2.1.1.3 A hazard exists if any of the components of an oxygen or nitrous oxide supply system become contaminated with oil or grease.

8-2.1.1.4 Sources of ignition may include open flames, burning tobacco, electric heating coils, defective electrical equipment, and adiabatic heating of gases.[1]

NOTE: The use of carpeting is a matter of concern. It is recognized that some carpeting contributes to the possible generation of high-energy static charges. Until more experience is obtained, it is advisable that carpeting not be used.

8-2.1.1.5 A hazard exists if either oxygen or nitrous oxide leaks into a closed space, creating an oxygen-enriched atmosphere.

8-2.1.1.6 A hazard exists if improper components are employed to connect equipment containing pressurized oxygen or nitrous oxide.

8-2.1.2 During Respiratory Therapy Administration.

8-2.1.2.1 The occurrence of a fire requires the presence of combustible or flammable materials, an atmosphere of oxygen or other oxidizing agents, and a source of ignition. Combustible materials may be unavoidably present when oxygen is being administered, but flammable liquids and gases and ignition sources are avoidable.

(a) Any mixture of breathing gases used in respiratory therapy will support combustion. In an oxygen-enriched atmosphere, materials that are combustible and flammable in air ignite more easily and burn more vigorously.

(b) Materials not normally considered to be combustible may be so in an oxygen-enriched atmosphere.

8-2.1.2.2 Combustible materials that may be found near patients who are to receive respiratory therapy include hair oils, oil-based lubricants, skin lotions, facial tissues, clothing, bed linen,

---

[1]Sudden compression or recompression of a gas to high pressure can generate large increase in temperature [up to 2000°F (1093°C)] that can ignite any organic material present, including grease. See also NFPA 53M, *Fire Hazards in Oxygen-Enriched Atmospheres*.

tent canopies, rubber and plastic articles, gas-supply and suction tubing, cyclopropane, ether, alcohols, and acetone.

8-2.1.2.3 A particular hazard exists when high-pressure oxygen equipment becomes contaminated with oil, grease, or other combustible materials. Such contaminants will ignite readily and burn more rapidly in the presence of high oxygen concentrations and make it easier to ignite less-combustible materials with which they come in contact.

(a) An oxygen-enriched atmosphere normally exists in an oxygen tent, croup tent, incubator, and similar devices when supplemental oxygen is being employed in them. These devices are designed to maintain a concentration of oxygen higher than that found in the atmosphere.

(b) Oxygen-enriched atmospheres may exist in the immediate vicinity of all oxygen administration equipment. (*See definition of site of intentional expulsion in Section 2-2 of Chapter 2.*)

The transfer of liquid oxygen from one container to another container may create an oxygen-enriched atmosphere within the vicinity of the containers.

(c) If oxygen is supplied by a container that stores the oxygen as a liquid, there will be a small amount of oxygen vented into the vicinity of the container after a period of nonuse of the equipment. Larger amounts of oxygen will be vented if the container is accidentally tipped over or placed on its side. This venting may create an oxygen-enriched atmosphere if the container is stored in a confined space [*see 4-3.1.2.1(i)*].

8-2.1.2.4 Sources of ignition include not only the usual ones in ordinary atmospheres, but others that become significant hazards in oxygen-enriched atmospheres [*see 8-2.1.2.1(a)*].

(a) Open flames, burning tobacco, and electric radiant heaters are sources of ignition.

Lit cigarettes, cigars, and pipes are the most common sources of ignition when respiratory therapy is administered. Smoking regulations should be developed to eliminate the introduction of this ignition source into the area of administration. (See Chapter 2 for the definition of "Area of Administration" and 8-6.2.1 for requirements on elimination of sources of ignition.)

(b) The discharge of a cardiac defibrillator may serve as a source of ignition.

(c) Arcing and excessive temperatures in electrical equipment are sources of ignition. Electrically powered oxygen apparatus and electrical equipment intended for use in an oxygen-enriched atmosphere are sources of ignition if electrical defects are present.

Electrically powered cautery devices and knives with energy levels of 10-100 watts are common open-spark sources in or near oxygen-enriched atmospheres.
An electrical safety inspection program should be instituted to detect problems before equipment deteriorates to the point where it can cause ignition.

(d) Electrical equipment not conforming to the requirements of 7-6.2.3.1, which may include but is not limited to electric razors, electric bed controls, hair dryers, remote television controls, and telephone handsets, may create a source of ignition if introduced into an oxygen-enriched atmosphere (*see 7-6.2.3.1*).

(e) A static discharge having an energy content that can be generated under normal conditions in respiratory therapy will not constitute an ignition source as long as easily ignited substances (such as ether, cyclopropane, alcohols, acetone, oils, greases, or lotions) are not present (*see* *8-6.2.2.4*).

NOTE: Experience and research indicate that static-accumulating materials such as plastics, synthetic fibers, and wool may be used under these conditions. The use of carpeting in patient care areas of hospitals is a relatively new innovation. It is recognized that some carpeting contributes to the generation of significant static charges on personnel. Until more experience is obtained with this potential problem, it is advisable that carpeting of wool and acrylic, nylon, and other synthetic fibers not be used in the area of administration unless treated to render them permanently antistatic.

A study by R. J. Plano (*Modern Hospital*, Vol. 95, No. 3, Sept. 1960) confirmed that blankets and sheets are not a fire hazard from static sparks inside an oxygen tent. Therefore, there is even a lower hazard when oxygen is administered by cannula.

This condition (static discharge) is not the same as that of spark-generating toys. The latter are a definite hazard inside oxygen tents.

(f) Rapid opening of cylinder valves can cause sudden increase in downstream gas pressure and temperature caused by the adiabatic heat of recompression with consequent ignition of combustible materials in contact with the hot gas downstream, including the valve seat.

Extreme caution should be used when opening cylinder valves. They should be opened slowly because of the phenomenon of adiabatic heating.

There should also be a policy to ensure that valves and regulators are maintained free of contaminants.

8-2.2 Toxicity.

8-2.2.1 Inhalation Anesthetizing Locations.
The use of some modern nonflammable inhalation anesthetic agents with high-flow techniques and in the absence of venting of the exhaled gases to the atmosphere may create low-grade toxicity in personnel who work regularly in the facility.

8-2.2.2 During Respiratory Therapy Administration.

8-2.2.2.1 Chemical hazards may be associated with the presence of residual sterilant in high-pressure equipment.

8-2.2.2.2 Some breathing mixtures may decompose in contact with hot surfaces and produce toxic or flammable substances (*see* 8-6.2).

8-2.2.2.3 Smoldering combustion of flammable substances may occur with the production of significant amounts of toxic gases and fumes.

8-2.3 Safety (Mechanical Injury; Cross-Connection, etc.).

8-2.3.1 Inhalation Anesthetizing Locations.

8-2.3.1.1 A large amount of energy is stored in a cylinder of compressed gas. If the valve of a cylinder is struck (or strikes something else) hard enough to break off the valve, the contents of the cylinder may be discharged with sufficient force to impart dangerous reactive movement to the cylinder.

8-2.3.2 During Respiratory Therapy Administration.

8-2.3.2.1 Mechanical Hazards.

(a) Cylinders and containers may be heavy and bulky and can cause personal injury or property damage (including to the cylinder or container) if improperly handled.

Cylinders and containers should never be left standing without some type of physical support (i.e., a stand, a cart, straps to wall, etc.). (See 4-6.5.)

(b) In cold climates, cylinders or containers stored outdoors or in unheated ventilated rooms may become extremely cold [see 4-6.2.1.2(dd) and 4-6.2.1.2(ee)]. A hazardous situation could develop if these cylinders or containers are heated [see 4-6.2.1.2(cc)].

If such cold cylinders or containers are suddenly brought into a warm room, pressure will suddenly increase in the cylinder or container, causing the "pop-off" mechanism to be activated. If this occurs, an oxygen-enriched atmosphere will develop around the "pop-off."

8-2.3.2.2 Improper maintenance, handling, or assembly of equipment may result in personal injury, property damage, or fire.

8-2.3.2.3 A hazardous condition exists if cylinders or containers are improperly located so that they may become overheated or tipped over. If a container is tipped over or placed on its side, liquid oxygen may be spilled. The liquid can cause frostbite on contact with skin.

See Commentary on 8-2.3.2.1(b).

8-2.3.2.4 A hazardous condition exists if there is improper labeling of cylinders or containers or inattention to the manufacturer's label or instructions.

All cylinders and containers should be checked for color coding, labeling, attached labeling, and proper Pin-Index Safety System or Diameter-Index Safety System fitting before being placed in service. If there is any doubt about the contents of a cylinder or container, a sample of the content should be analyzed. (See 8-6.4.1.6 for requirements on labeling.)

8-2.3.2.5 A hazardous condition exists if care is not exercised in making slip-on and other interchangeable connections when setting up equipment.

8-2.3.2.6 Safety features, including relief devices, valves, and connections, are provided in equipment and gas supply systems. Altering or circumventing these safety features by means of adapters creates a hazardous condition.

8-2.3.2.7 **Extreme danger to life and property can result when compressed gases are mixed or transferred from one cylinder to another.**

The boldface type emphasizes the Committee's concern about transfilling gases between cylinders or mixing gases. The uncertainty of results underscores this concern.

See 4-6.2.1.5 regarding conditions under which transfilling is allowed. Mixing is never allowed.

8-2.3.2.8 A hazardous condition exists if devices, such as fixed or adjustable orifices and metering valves, are directly connected to cylinders or systems without a pressure-reducing regulator.

8-2.3.2.9 Hazardous conditions are created when pressure-reducing regulators or gauges are defective.

8-2.4 Electric Shock. (Reserved)

NOTE: See 7-2.2 for additional information.

8-3 Source.

8-3.1 Cylinders and Containers.

8-3.1.1 Cylinders and containers shall comply with 4-3.1.1.1.

8-3.1.2 Cylinder valve outlet connections shall conform to ANSI B57.1, *Standard for Compressed Gas Cylinder Valve Outlet and Inlet Connections* (includes Pin-Index Safety System for medical gases). (*See 4-3.1.1.1.*)

8-3.1.3 When low-pressure threaded connections are employed, they shall be in accordance with the Compressed Gas Association standard for noninterchangeable, low-pressure connections for medical gases, air and suction, Pamphlet V-5, *Diameter-Index Safety System*.

8-3.1.4 Low-pressure quick-coupler connections shall be noninterchangeable between gas services.

8-3.1.5 Regulators and gages intended for use in high-pressure service shall be listed for such service.

8-3.1.6 Pressure-reducing regulators shall be used on high-pressure cylinders to reduce the pressure to working pressures.

8-3.1.7 Approved regulators or other gas-flow control devices shall be used to reduce the cylinder pressure of every cylinder used for medical purposes. All such devices shall have connections so designed that they can be attached only to cylinders of gas for which they are designated.

8-3.1.8 Equipment that will permit the intermixing of different gases, either through defects in the mechanism or through error in manipulation in any portion of the high-pressure side of any system in which these gases may flow, shall not be used for coupling cylinders containing compressed gases. It is particularly important that the intermixing of oxidizing and flammable gases under pressure be scrupulously avoided, as such mixing may result in violent explosion.

See text and Commentary for 8-3.2.7 concerning this hazard.
See 4-6.2.1.5 regarding the subject of transfilling.

8-3.1.9 Cylinder valve outlet connections for oxygen shall be Connection No. 540 as described in ANSI B57.1, *Standard for Compressed Gas Cylinder Valve Outlet and Inlet Connections.*

8-3.1.10 Cylinder valve outlet connections for nitrous oxide shall be Connection No. 326 as described in ANSI B57.1, *Standard for Compressed Gas Cylinder Valve Outlet and Inlet Connections.*

8-3.2 Generators. (Reserved)

8-3.3 Gas Systems. *(See Chapter 4.)*

8-4 Distribution. (Reserved)

8-5 Performance Criteria and Testing.

8-5.1 Patient-Care-Related Gas Equipment.

8-5.1.1 Fixed. (Reserved)

8-5.1.2 Portable.

8-5.1.2.1 Anesthetic Apparatus.

NOTE: Portable Supply Systems. If the sole source of supply of nonflammable medical gases, such as nitrous oxide and oxygen, is a system of cylinders attached directly to and supported by the device (such as a gas anesthesia apparatus) used to administer these gases, it is recommended that two cylinders of each gas be attached to the administering device.

(a) Anesthetic apparatus shall be subject to approval by the authority having jurisdiction.

(b)* Each yoke on anesthetic apparatus constructed to permit attachment of small cylinders equipped with flush-type valves shall have two pins installed as specified in ANSI B57.1 (Pin-Index Safety System) *(see 4-4.1.3.7 and Appendix A-4-4.1.3.5).*

A-8-5.1.2.1(b) Pin-Index Safety System. The Pin-Index Safety System consists of a combination of two pins projecting from the yoke assembly of the apparatus and so positioned as to fit into matching holes drilled into the cylinder valves. It is intended to provide against the possibility of error in attaching the flush-type valves, with which gas cylinders and other sources of gas supply are equipped, to gas apparatus having yoke connections.

(c) After any adjustment or repair involving use of tools, or any modification of the gas piping supply connections or the pneumatic power supply connections for the anesthesia ventilator, or other pneumatically powered device if one is present, and before use on patients, the gas anesthesia apparatus shall be tested at the final common path to the patient to determine that oxygen and only oxygen is delivered from the oxygen flow meters, and the oxygen flush valve if any. Interventions requiring such testing shall include, but not be limited to:

(1) alteration of pipeline hoses or fittings;

(2) alteration of internal piping;

(3) adjustment of selector switches or flush valves;

(4) replacement or repair of flowmeters of bobbins.

Before the gas anesthesia apparatus is returned to service, each fitting and connection shall be checked to verify its proper indexing to the respective gas service involved.

A paramagnetic or polarographic oxygen analyzer, or a similar device, known to be accurate at 0 percent, 21 percent, and 100 percent oxygen, is a suitable test instrument (*see Appendix C-12.2*).

(d)* Yoke-type connections between anesthesia apparatus and flush-type cylinder valves (commonly used with anesthetic gas cylinders) shall be Connection No. 860 as described in ANSI B57.1, *Compressed Gas Cylinder Valve Outlet and Inlet Connections* (*see Appendix A-4-4.1.3.5*).

A-8-5.1.2.1(d) Fabrication specifications are contained in CGA Pamphlet V-1 (ANSI B57.1), *Compressed Gas Cylinder Valve Outlet and Inlet Connections*. Connection No. 860 shown in that document illustrates the system. Connection Nos. 870 (Oxygen, Medical), 880 (Oxygen-Carbon Dioxide Mixture), 890 (Oxygen-Helium Mixture), 900 (Ethylene), 910 (Nitrous Oxide), 920 (Cyclopropane), 930 (Helium), and 940 (Carbon Dioxide) are for specific medical gases and gas mixtures and utilize the basic dimensions of Connection 860.

8-5.1.2.2 Apparatus for Administering Respiratory Therapy.

(a) Oxygen tent circulation/conditioning apparatus, pressure breathing apparatus, and other equipment intended to rest on the floor shall be equipped with a base designed to render the entire assembly stable during storage, transport, and use. If casters are used, they shall conform to Class C of Commercial Standard 223-59, *Casters, Wheels and Glides for Hospital Equipment*. (*See 20-1.2.4.1*.)

(b) Oxygen tent canopies having flexible components shall be fabricated of materials having a maximum burning rate classification of "slow burning." (*See definition of slow burning in Section 2-2 of Chapter 2*.)

(1) Oxygen enclosures of rigid materials shall be fabricated of noncombustible materials.

(c) Equipment supplied from cylinders or containers shall be designed and constructed for service at full cylinder or container pressure, or constructed for use or equipped with pressure-reducing regulators.

(d) Humidification or reservoir jars containing liquid to be dispersed into a gas stream shall be made of clear, transparent material, impervious to contained solutions and medications, and shall permit observation of the liquid level and consistency.

In today's hospitals, use of devices prefilled with sterile water is common. They meet the requirements of this section as they are clear and allow observation of the liquid level.

(e) Humidifiers and nebulizers shall be equipped with provisions for overpressure relief or alarm if the flow becomes obstructed.

Alarms can be easily tested by occluding the outlet port briefly to see if "pop off" occurs.

(f) Humidifiers and nebulizers shall be incapable of tipping or shall be mounted so that any tipping or alteration from the vertical shall not interfere with function or accuracy.

8-5.2 Nonpatient Gas Equipment.

8-5.2.1 Carts and Hand Trucks.

8-5.2.1.1 Carts and hand trucks for cylinders and containers shall be constructed for the intended purpose and shall be self-supporting. They shall be provided with appropriate chains or stays to retain cylinders or containers in place.

8-5.2.1.2 Carts and hand trucks that are intended to be used in anesthetizing locations or cylinder and container storage rooms communicating with anesthetizing locations shall comply with the appropriate provisions of 12-4.1.

8-5.2.1.3 Gas Equipment — Laboratory. Gas appliances shall be of an approved design and installed in accordance with NFPA 54, *National Fuel Gas Code*. Shutoff valves shall be legibly marked to identify the material they control.

8-6 Administration.

8-6.1 Responsibility of Governing Body. (Reserved)

8-6.2 Policies.

The hazard does not exist when oxygen is only being *supplied* to a room via piping. It is when oxygen is actually being *used* that the precautions (policies) in this section (8-6.2) have to be taken.

8-6.2.1 Elimination of Sources of Ignition.

8-6.2.1.1 Smoking materials (matches, cigarettes, lighters, lighter fluid, tobacco in any form) shall be removed from patients receiving respiratory therapy and from the area of administration.

A facility-wide policy on smoking should be developed to avoid confusion and to generally reduce the hazard from smoking.

8-6.2.1.2 No sources of open flame, including candles, shall be permitted in the area of administration.

8-6.2.1.3 Patients and hospital personnel in the area of administration shall be advised of respiratory therapy hazards and regulations.

(a) Visitors shall be cautioned of these hazards through the prominent posting of signs (*see* 8-6.4.2).

It is very important that visitors be informed of a facility's policies in order not to jeopardize the safety of the patient they are visiting, other patients, visitors, and staff.

(b) Prudent practice dictates that in pediatric hospitals, or in pediatric wards of general hospitals, parents and other visitors to the nursing units be placed on actual notice of the hazards created by potential sources of ignition such as sparking toys.

Young children cannot be expected to know the hazards present when respiratory therapy is being administered. Thus, it is necessary for respiratory therapy personnel and others to personally explain the situation to parents and visitors.

(c) It may be desirable to preclude the introduction of all such toys into any pediatrics nursing unit in which oxygen tents or oxygen hoods are used.

8-6.2.2 Misuse of Flammable Substances.

8-6.2.2.1 Flammable or combustible aerosols or vapors, such as alcohol, shall not be administered in oxygen-enriched atmospheres as outlined in 8-2.1.2.3(a).

Alcohol/oxygen mixture vapor may be necessary in the treatment of pulmonary disorders. Reference to 8-2.1.2.3(a) is included to indicate that such vapors are prohibited in tents, etc., but not in masks, nasal catheters, etc.

8-6.2.2.2 Oil, grease, or other flammable contaminants shall not be used with oxygen equipment.

8-6.2.2.3 Flammable and combustible liquids, and flammable gases, such as ether, shall not be permitted within the site of intentional expulsion. When flammable anesthetics, such as ether, are administered, the area shall be considered a flammable anesthetizing location. (*See 12-4.1 for requirements for flammable anesthetizing locations.*)

Only water-based lubricants are to be used around the face when oxygen is being administered by cannula or mask, or for diaper rashes on babies in croup tents. This is an important point since oxygen can be very drying to the skin.
Reference to flammable anesthetics is only an alert to those few facilities that still use flammable anesthetics.

8-6.2.2.4 High-pressure oxygen equipment shall not be sterilized with a flammable sterilizing agent such as ethylene oxide or alcohol. Sterilizing agents shall be oil-free and shall not damage materials.

(a) High-pressure oxygen equipment shall not be sterilized in polyethylene bags.

NOTE: Sloughed particles of polyethylene produced by abrasion and flexure of such bags are pure hydrocarbons and therefore constitute a severe flammability hazard in high-pressure oxygen atmospheres. Nylon films produce practically no sloughing.

(b) Equipment operated at oxygen pressures under 60 psig (0.414 kPa gauge) may be sterilized with nonflammable mixtures containing ethylene oxide and carbon dioxide or ethylene oxide and fluorocarbon diluents.

(c) Cylinders and containers shall not be sterilized.

Since cylinders and containers are not normally designed for sterilizing, this prohibition is included to exclude them from the requirements of 8-6.2.2.4(b). However, in the future, this restriction may have to be changed in view of decontaminating procedures associated with immunosuppressed patients (e.g., cancer chemotherapy, AIDS, burns, etc.).

8-6.2.3 Prevention of Chemical Breakdown.

8-6.2.3.1 Equipment capable of producing surface temperatures sufficient to cause chemical breakdown of the atmosphere within a patient enclosure shall not be permitted therein.

(a) Where diethyl ether vapor is involved, surface temperatures shall not exceed 248°F (120°C).

NOTE 1: Such a potentially hazardous atmosphere can be created by the placement in an incubator of a recently anesthetized infant or one whose mother received an inhalation anesthetic during delivery.

NOTE 2: Diethyl ether vapor can produce formaldehyde upon contact with a heating element.

This requirement originated when flammable anesthetics were used for expectant mothers during delivery; the flammable gases got into the fetus' lungs through the mother's blood. This requirement also dates from the time when flammable anesthetics were used in surgery on infants.

While not associated with a medical problem, a study on the thermal decomposition of ether was conducted by M. K. Menderhall in the late 1950s. A paper on it appeared in the *Journal of the American Medical Association* (173:123, 1960).

8-6.2.4 Servicing and Maintenance of Equipment.

8-6.2.4.1 Defective equipment shall be immediately removed from service.

8-6.2.4.2 Defective electrical apparatus shall not be used.

8-6.2.4.3 Areas designated for the servicing of oxygen equipment shall be clean, free of oil and grease, and not used for the repair of other equipment.

8-6.2.4.4 Only repair parts recommended by the manufacturer shall be employed.

8-6.2.4.5 Service manuals, instructions, and procedures provided by the manufacturer shall be used in the maintenance of equipment.

8-6.2.4.6 A scheduled preventive maintenance program shall be followed.

8-6.2.5 Ambulatory Patients.
Ambulatory patients on oxygen therapy, whether in or out of a health care facility, shall be permitted free access to all areas that prohibit smoking and that have no open flames.

The use of portable oxygen systems is growing dramatically in the United States. As such, the Subcommittee on Gas Equipment felt it appropriate to address the subject since administration of oxygen is usually initiated in medical facilities.

It is acknowledged that the scope of the Health Care Facility Project limits it to the confines of health care facilities. However, since the Subcommittee felt it reasonable for patients in health care facilities to be allowed to enter areas under the restrictions listed, the same allowance should be afforded these patients outside the health care facility.

This new provision places some responsibilities on both users and owners of establishments. The user has to be aware of the environment he/she is entering and whether or not a "no-open-flame" policy exists. Owners have to enforce whatever policy is established for designated areas. Thus, the posting of appropriate warning signs about oxygen in use or where oxygen users can sit, etc., must accompany this extended use of oxygen.

The situation is further compounded if a language barrier exists.

However, there are still many persons who think oxygen is a flammable or explosive gas (which it is not). This new provision is intended to show that the use of oxygen is safe when reasonable precautions are taken.

8-6.3 Recordkeeping. (Reserved)

8-6.4 Use (Including Information and Warning Signs).

8-6.4.1 Labeling.

8-6.4.1.1 Equipment listed for use in oxygen-enriched atmospheres shall be so labeled.

8-6.4.1.2 Oxygen metering equipment and pressure-reducing regulators shall be conspicuously labeled: OXYGEN — USE NO OIL.

8-6.4.1.3 Flowmeters, pressure-reducing regulators, and oxygen-dispensing apparatus shall be clearly and permanently labeled, designating the gas or mixture of gases for which they are intended. Apparatus whose calibration or function is dependent on gas density shall be labeled as to the proper supply gas pressure (psig/kPa) for which it is intended.

8-6.4.1.4 Canopies or enclosures intended to contain patients shall be labeled advising that oxygen is in use and that precautions related to the hazard shall be observed. The labels shall be located on the enclosure interior in a position to be read by the patient and on two or more opposing sides of the enclosure exterior.

(a) A suggested minimum text for labels is:

```
CAUTION

OXYGEN IN USE
KEEP FLAMES AWAY
NO SMOKING
NO ELECTRICAL APPLIANCES
```

8-6.4.1.5 Oxygen-metering equipment, pressure-reducing regulators, humidifiers, and nebulizers shall be labeled with the name of the manufacturer or supplier.

8-6.4.1.6 Cylinders and containers shall be labeled in accordance with ANSI Z48.1, *Standard Method of Marking Portable Compressed Gas Containers to Identify the Material Contained.* Color coding shall not be utilized as a primary method of determining cylinder or container content.

See commentary on 8-2.3.2.4 for further information.

8-6.4.1.7 All labeling shall be durable and withstand cleansing or disinfection.

8-6.4.2 Signs. Precautionary signs, readable from a distance of 5 ft (1.4 m), shall be conspicuously displayed at the site of administration and in aisles and walkways leading to the area. They shall be attached to adjacent doorways or to building walls, or supported by other appropriate means. Precautionary signs should be approximately 8 in. by 11 in. (21 cm by 28 cm) in size.

NOTE: Special signs and additional precautionary measures should be employed whenever foreign languages present a communication problem.

It is incumbent upon staff to learn if a language barrier does exist, and to provide material in the appropriate language. This can normally be determined at the time of admission.

Signs with bright, clear letters, such as red letters on a white background, should be used.

8-6.4.2.1 A suggested minimum text for precautionary signs is:

CAUTION
OXYGEN IN USE
NO SMOKING
NO OPEN FLAMES

Any material that can burn in air will burn more rapidly in the presence of oxygen. No electrical equipment is allowed within an oxygen enclosure or within 5 ft (1.5 m) of it.

NOTE: This sign is intended to caution those not familiar with this chapter.

8-6.4.2.2 A suggested text for precautionary signs for oxygen tent canopies and oxygen hoods (*see 8-6.4.2.1*) used in pediatric nursing units is:

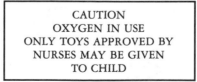

CAUTION
OXYGEN IN USE
ONLY TOYS APPROVED BY
NURSES MAY BE GIVEN
TO CHILD

8-6.4.3 Transportation, Storage, and Use of Equipment.

8-6.4.3.1 Flow-control valves on administering equipment shall be closed prior to connection and when not in use.

Release of pressure on the gauge for the flow control valve while the cylinder is not in use will extend the life of the gauge itself.

8-6.4.3.2 Apparatus shall not be stored or transported with liquid agents in reservoirs.

8-6.4.3.3 Care shall be observed in attaching connections from gas services to equipment and from equipment to patients.

Accepted procedures should always be followed when making attachments.

8-6.4.3.4 Fixed or adjustable orifice mechanisms, metering valves, regulators, and gauges shall not be connected directly to high-pressure cylinders unless specifically listed for such use and provided with appropriate safety devices.

8-6.4.3.5 Nasal respiratory therapy catheters shall be color coded green. Verification of proper connection to oxygen therapy equipment is necessary to prevent accidental attachment to gastric or intestinal catheters.

The use of nasal catheters is extremely rare today; however, since they are still employed, especially in centers that treat persons with chronic lung disease, this requirement is to be observed.

8-6.4.3.6 Equipment for respiratory therapy need not be electrically conductive unless intended for use in a hazardous location.

8-6.5 Qualification and Training of Personnel.

8-6.5.1 Equipment shall be serviced by qualified personnel only.

9 MANUFACTURER REQUIREMENTS

NOTE 1: The application of requirements contained in this chapter for specific types of health care facilities can be found in Chapters 12 through 18.

NOTE 2: Sections of Chapter 9 identified by a dagger (†) include figures extracted from NFPA 493-1978, *Standard for Intrinsically Safe Apparatus and Associated Apparatus for Use in Class I, II and III, Division 1 Hazardous Locations.* Requests for interpretations or revisions of the extracted figures will be referred to the Technical Committee on Electrical Equipment in Chemical Atmospheres.

9-1 Scope. This chapter covers the performance, maintenance, and testing, with regard to safety, required of manufacturers of equipment used within health care facilities.

9-2 Electrical Equipment.

9-2.1 Patient-Care-Related Electrical Equipment.

The requirements in this section were originally developed for inclusion in NFPA 76B-1980, *Standard for Safe Use of Electricity in Patient Care Areas of Hospitals.* As in Chapters 3 to 8, this chapter is not facility applicable unless referenced in Chapters 12 to 18, unless prior chapters reference this chapter (as is the case in Chapter 7), or unless a facility or some authority chooses to enforce the requirements contained herein.

NOTE 1: It is the intent that 9-2.1 should not be used by authorities having jurisdiction over health care facilities to limit health care facilities' purchases to patient-care-related electrical appliances meeting these requirements; rather it is the intent to encourage equipment manufacturers to conduct the specified tests in order to ensure state-of-the-art electrical safety in their patient-care-related electrical appliances. Similarly, it is not the intent of the Technical Committee to require health care facilities to conduct tests using these manufacturer requirements to verify that their patient-care-related electrical appliances are in conformance with the requirements of this chapter. In this respect, it is the intent of the Committee that health care facilities perform only those tests specified in 7-5.1.

NOTE 2: See Chapter 2, "Definitions," for the definition of patient-care-related electrical appliance.

9-2.1.1 Mechanical Construction.

9-2.1.1.1 Separation of Patient Circuits. Patient-connected circuits within an appliance shall be sufficiently separated or insulated from all other circuits within the appliance to prevent accidental contact with hazardous voltages or currents.

9-2.1.1.2 Mechanical Stability. The appliance shall be mechanically stable in the position of normal use. If the appliance is intended for use in an anesthetizing location, 12-4.1 applies.

9-2.1.2 Electrical Requirements — Appliances Equipped with Power Cords.

9-2.1.2.1 Attachment Plugs.

(a) *General.*   Attachment plugs listed for the purpose shall be used on all cord-connected appliances.

NOTE: Hospital grade listing is acceptable, but not required.

In the past, health care facility appliances were frequently provided with molded or other light-duty plugs appropriate for household use but not for hospital use where severe conditions can be experienced. The recognition of this problem led to the development of heavy-duty plugs that could stand "hospital abuse." These plugs were labeled "hospital grade" and appropriately marked. (The term "hospital grade" was used since the heaviest use of appliances occurred in hospitals).

Recently, other users have been attracted to these plugs, and manufacturers now provide heavy-duty plugs that are equivalent to, but not labeled as, "hospital grade." They are sometimes less expensive. It is the intent of this section to allow the use of such plugs. Household or other light-duty plugs, however, are not acceptable. In particular, molded rubber plugs, which secure the grounding pin only by rubber, are not acceptable.

(b) *Construction and Use.*   The plug (cap) shall be a two-pole, three-wire grounding type. (*See ANSI C73.11, C73.12, C73.45, C73.46; and 410-56, 410-57, 410-58 of NFPA 70, National Electrical Code.*)

Exception No. 1: Appliances used in special locations or purposes may be equipped with plugs approved for the location (e.g., 3-4.1.2.4).

Exception No. 2: If the power cord of an appliance does not require and does not contain a grounding conductor it shall not be fitted with a grounding-type plug {see 9-2.1.2.2(e), "Cords Without Grounding Conductors"].

Exception No. 3: Appliances supplied by other than 120-V single-phase systems shall use the grounding-type plug (cap) appropriate for the particular power system (e.g., ANSI C73.16, C73.17, C73.18, C73.28, C73.83, C73.84, C73.86, C73.87, C73.88, C73.89, C73.90, C73.91, C73.92, C73.94, and C73.95).

The grounding prong shall be constructed so that it cannot be easily broken. The grounding prong of the plug shall be the first to be connected to and last to be disconnected from the receptacle. If screw terminals are used, the stranded conductor shall be twisted to prevent stray strands, but the bundle shall not be tinned after twisting; if the conductor is not twisted, it shall be attached by an approved terminal lug. The power cord conductors shall be arranged so that the conductors are not under tension in the plug. The grounding conductor shall be the last one to disconnect when a failure of the plug's strain relief allows the energized conductors to be disrupted.

Having phase conductors disengage first is normally achieved by making the green ground wire longer than the phase conductors, and/or making the grounding prong on the plug longer than the phase prongs.

On the issue of tinning, it has been the intent of the Subcommittee on Electrical Equipment (formerly the Technical Committee on Safe Use of Electricity in Patient Care Areas of Health Care Facilities) that twisted wires not be tinned. This position is based on experience, as well as reports, such as in *Health Devices* (4:75, 1975), which indicated more occurrences of loosening of connections with tinned, twisted wires than with untinned, twisted wires. No controlled studies of late have been conducted, however.

(c) *Strain Relief.* Strain relief shall be provided. The strain relief shall not cause thinning of the conductor insulation. The strain relief of replaceable plugs shall be capable of being disassembled. Plugs may be integrally molded onto the cord jacket if the design is listed for the purpose.

(d) *Testing.* The wiring of each cord assembly shall be tested for continuity and polarity at the time of manufacture, when assembled into an appliance, and when repaired.

9-2.1.2.2 Power Cords.

(a) *Material and Gauge.* The flexible cord, including the grounding conductor, shall be of a type suitable for the particular application, listed for use at a voltage equal to or greater than the rated power line voltage of the appliance, and have an ampacity, as given in Table 400-5 of NFPA 70, *National Electrical Code*, equal to or greater than the current rating of the device.

"Hard Service" (SO, ST, or STO) or "Junior Hard Service" (SJO, SJT, or SJTO) or equivalent listed flexible cord shall be used (*see Table 400-4 of NFPA 70, National Electrical Code*) except where an appliance with a cord of another designation has been listed for the purpose.

NOTE: "Hard Service" cord is preferable where the cord may be subject to mechanical abuse. A cord length of 10 ft (3.1 m) is recommended for general locations, and 18 ft (5.5 m) for operating rooms, but may be of a different length if designed for a specific location.

(b) *Grounding Conductor.* Each electric appliance shall be provided with a grounding conductor in its power cord. The grounding conductor shall be no smaller than No. 18 AWG. The grounding conductor of cords longer than 15 ft (4.6 m) shall be no smaller than No. 16 AWG. Grounding conductors shall meet the resistance requirements of 9-2.1.13.2, "Grounding Circuit Continuity."

Exception: A grounding conductor in the power cord need not be provided for listed double-insulated appliances, but such a grounding conductor shall be permitted to be used to ground exposed conductive surfaces (see 9-2.1.3.2, "Grounding of Exposed Conductive Surfaces").

(c) *Separable Cord Sets.* A separable power cord set shall be permitted to be used if it can be shown that an accidental disconnection is unlikely or not hazardous. Separable power cord sets shall be designed so that the grounding conductor is the first to be connected and the last to be disconnected. Cord-set plugs and receptacles at the appliance shall be polarized in accordance with ANSI C73.13 and C73.17.

Appliances with separable cord sets shall meet the grounding-wire-resistance requirements of 9-2.1.13.2, "Grounding Circuit Continuity," when the cord set is connected to the appliance. Both the cord set and the means of connection to the appliance shall be listed for the purpose.

(d) *Connection to Circuit and Color Codes.* Power cords, regardless of whether intended for use on grounded or isolated power systems, shall be connected in accordance with the conventions of a grounded system. (*See 200-2 to 200-10 of NFPA 70, National Electrical Code.*)

The circuit conductors in the cord shall be connected to the plug and the wiring in the appliance so that any of the following devices, when used in the primary circuit, are connected to the ungrounded conductor: the center contact of an Edison base lampholder; a solitary fuseholder; a single-pole, overcurrent-protective device; and any other single-pole, current-interrupting device. (*See Exception No. 2 to 210-5(b) of NFPA 70, National Electrical Code.*)

Exception: If a second fuseholder or other overcurrent-protective device is provided in the appliance, it may be placed in the grounded side of the line.

The Exception was added in 1984 to correlate with other United States and international documents.

(e) *Cords Without Grounding Conductors.* If the power cord of an appliance does not require and does not contain a grounding conductor, it shall not be fitted with a grounding-type plug.

(f) *Testing.* The wiring of each cord assembly shall be tested for continuity and polarity at the time of manufacture, when assembled into an appliance, and when repaired.

(g) *Cord Strain Relief.* Cord strain relief shall be provided at the attachment of the power cord to the appliance so that mechanical stress, either pull, twist, or bend, is not transmitted to internal connections. If the strain relief is molded onto the cord, it shall be bonded to the jacket and shall be of compatible material.

9-2.1.3 Wiring Within Appliances Equipped with Power Cords.

9-2.1.3.1 Protection of Wiring in Appliances.
Within the appliance, the power conductors of the cord and the associated primary wiring (other than the grounding conductor) shall be mounted and dressed to minimize the likelihood of accidental electrical contact with the frame or exposed conductive parts of the appliance.

9-2.1.3.2 Grounding of Exposed Conductive Surfaces.
All exposed conductive surfaces of an electric appliance likely to become energized from internal sources shall be bonded together to provide electric continuity with the connection to the grounding conductor.

NOTE 1: Size and location are the main criteria used in determining what is not likely to become energized and thus may be exempted from the bonding and grounding requirements. Items such as screws, nameplates, hinges, metal trim, handles, and other hardware are unlikely to become energized because of their size. If they are sufficiently isolated from internal sources they need not be grounded.

NOTE 2: Also, it is unnecessary for exposed conductive surfaces to be grounded separately with individual or looped grounding wires if, by reliable contact or connection with other grounded metal portions (frame), these surfaces can maintain ground.

9-2.1.3.3 Connection to Permit Replacement.
The connection of the power cord to the appliance shall permit ready replacement of the cord except where the power cord is not intended to be replaced by the user.

9-2.1.3.4 Connection of the Grounding Conductor.
The grounding conductor shall be connected to the exposed metal or frame of the appliance by a terminal or bolt so that a reliable electrical connection is always maintained. The connection shall be arranged so that it will not be broken during electrical or mechanical repair of the appliance, except replacement of the power cord.

The power cord shall be arranged so that the grounding conductor is the last to disconnect when a failure of the strain relief at the appliance allows the cord to be pulled free. When a grounding conductor is not required and is not provided, the appliance shall be visibly labeled to indicate that fact.

9-2.1.3.5 Connections with Grounding Conductor. Any component, such as a filter or test circuit, within an appliance that intentionally reduces the impedance between the energized conductors and the grounding conductor shall be in operation when the leakage current tests specified in 9-2.1.13.4, "Leakage Current from Appliance to Ground," are performed.

9-2.1.3.6 Overcurrent Protection. An overcurrent protective device shall be permitted to be placed in the attachment plug, the power cord, or in the main body of the appliance.

NOTE: It is recommended that a listed overcurrent protective device be used in the power input circuit of all appliances.

The then Committee on Safe Use of Electricity in Patient Care Areas of Health Care Facilities intended that overcurrent devices not be mandatory (i.e., permitted, but not required). If overcurrent protection is included, the requirements of this section are to be followed.

Overcurrent protection within an appliance is a way of protecting an appliance itself, as well as other appliances on the same branch circuit. A fault within an appliance, which causes current to flow in excess of the rating of the overcurrent protector, will cause the overcurrent protector to open. Since an appliance's overcurrent protection rating should be less than the rating of the branch circuit breaker feeding current to appliances on that branch circuit, the branch circuit breaker will not open as a result of a fault within any one appliance on that circuit. Thus, while only appliances are protected directly, the loss of only one appliance instead of a branch circuit can be very significant to patients relying on the continuous functioning of medical electrical appliances on that circuit.

The overcurrent protective device shall precede any other components within the appliance, including the primary power-control switch.

Exception: Listed insulated terminal blocks or strips, listed connecting devices, and RFI filters for use on power systems shall be permitted to precede the overcurrent device (see 9-2.1.3.5).

This requirement shall not preclude the use of overcurrent protective devices within the appliance. The power control switch and overcurrent protective device shall be permitted to be combined into one component provided it is identified to indicate the combined function.

9-2.1.3.7 Primary Power-Control Switch. When a primary power-control switch is provided on an appliance it shall interrupt all primary power conductors, including the neutral conductor. The grounding conductor shall not be interrupted by the switch.

Exception: When the primary power wiring of an appliance is polarized so as to ensure the proper connection of its neutral conductor to the electric distribution system of the building, that neutral conductor need not be interrupted by a primary power-control switch.

An in-line switch shall be permitted in a primary power cord only if the switch is listed with the appliance with which it is intended to be used.

The former Committee on Safe Use of Electricity in Patient Care Areas of Health Care Facilities recognized the hazards associated with in-line switches, but noted that there were circumstances where they were the preferred way to control power. As a result, the Committee allowed their use, but only under the conditions specified above.

9-2.1.3.8 Rack- or Cart-Mounted Equipment. Each appliance mounted in an equipment rack or cart, when rated by the manufacturer as a stand-alone appliance, shall independently meet the requirements of 9-2.1.13.

When multiple appliances, as designated by the manufacturer, are mounted together in a cart or rack, and one power cord supplies power, the cart or rack shall meet the requirements of 9-2.1.13.

The requirements of the first paragraph were revised in 1984 to make provisions for stand-alone appliances that could be included in a rack or cart. The addition of a new paragraph requiring a rack or cart with one power cord to meet the requirements of this chapter takes into consideration that all the leakage current passes through the one main power cord; if the ground in this main power cord is broken, all the leakage current could pass through a person touching any one of the appliances mounted on the cart or rack. The Committee therefore felt that, because of this cumulative effect, the entire system should be treated as one appliance, and thus meet the requirements of this chapter as one appliance.

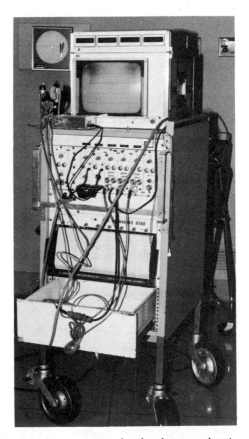

Figure 28   Combination cart-mounted and rack-mounted patient equipment.

9-2.1.4 Connectors and Connections to Devices.

9-2.1.4.1 Indexing of Receptacles for Patient Leads. Receptacles on appliances shall be designed and constructed so that those contacts that deliver electric current in a way and of a magnitude greater than 500 microamperes, when measured in accordance with 9-2.1.13.5(a), (b), (d), and (e), are female and indexed. Receptacles and plugs shall be polarized if improper orientation can create a hazard.

Dictating appliance design is not intended; however, it is recommended that careful study be given to connector selection. Inputs of multimodality monitoring equipment should be distinctive; otherwise, for example, an ECG signal could be confused with a pressure signal, possibly resulting in improper signals and unexpected patient injury.

9-2.1.4.2 Distinctive Receptacles for Patient Leads. Where reversal or misconnection of patient leads to an appliance might constitute a hazard (for example: reversal of active and dispersive electrodes of electrosurgical machines), distinctive, noninterchangeable connections shall be employed.

NOTE: The purpose of these requirements is to prevent interchanging connectors in any manner that permits the inadvertent delivery of a hazardous current to a patient.

9-2.1.5 Line Voltage Variations and Transients — General.

All appliances shall be capable of operating within line voltage variations that conform with ANSI C84.1-1977 (and 1980 supplement), *Voltage Ratings for Electrical Power Systems and Equipment*.

NOTE: The design of an appliance intended for life support should minimize the effects on performance of transient, line voltage variations, or other electrical interference. The design of all appliances should minimize the production of line variations and transients.

9-2.1.6 General Design and Manufacturing Requirements.

9-2.1.6.1 Thermal Standards. Electric appliances not designed to supply heat to the patient, and operated within reach of a nonambulatory patient, shall not have exposed surface temperatures in excess of 122°F (50°C). Surfaces maintained in contact with the skin of patients and not intended to supply heat shall not be hotter than 104°F (40°C).

9-2.1.6.2 Toxic Materials. Surfaces that contact patients shall be free of materials that commonly cause toxic reactions. Coatings used on these surfaces shall conform to ANSI Z66.1-1964 (R 1972), *Specifications for Paints and Coatings Accessible to Children to Minimize Dry Film Toxicity*.

9-2.1.6.3 Chemical Agents. Electric appliances containing hazardous chemicals shall be designed to facilitate the replenishment of these chemicals without spillage to protect the patient, the operating personnel, and the safety features of the appliance from such chemicals.

NOTE: Preference should be given to the use of replaceable sealed canisters of chemicals.

9-2.1.7 Fire and Explosion Hazards.

9-2.1.7.1 Materials and Supplies. Materials used in the construction of, and supplies for, electric appliances shall be noncombustible or flame retardant and impermeable to liquids and gases to the extent practicable; or the materials used in the construction of, and supplies for, electric appliances shall not ignite from internal heating or arcing resulting from any and all possible fault conditions. This includes spillage of liquids such as water and intravenous solutions onto the appliance.

Exception: Materials used in the construction and operation of electric appliances shall be permitted to be combustible when it is essential to their intended function.

9-2.1.7.2 Oxygen-Enriched Atmospheres. Electric appliances employing oxygen, or that are intended to be used in oxygen-enriched atmospheres, shall comply with the appropriate provisions of Chapter 8, "Gas Equipment (Positive and Negative Pressure), Health Care Facilities"; Chapter 19, "Hyperbaric Facilities"; and NFPA 99B, *Standard for Hypobaric Facilities*, in addition to all applicable provisions of this chapter.

NOTE: See also NFPA 53M, *Manual on Fire Hazards in Oxygen-Enriched Atmospheres.*

9-2.1.7.3 Inhalation Anesthetizing Locations. Electric appliances used in inhalation anesthetizing locations shall comply with the provisions of Chapter 7, "Electrical Equipment, Health Care Facilities" and 12-4.1, in addition to all applicable provisions of this chapter.

9-2.1.8 Instruction Manuals and Labels.

9-2.1.8.1 Manuals. The manufacturer of the appliance shall furnish operator's, maintenance, and repair manuals with all units. These manuals shall include operating instructions, maintenance details, and testing procedures.

The manuals shall include the following where applicable:

(a) illustrations that show location of controls,

(b) explanation of the function of each control,

(c) illustrations of proper connection to the patient and other equipment,

(d) step-by-step procedures for proper use of the appliance,

(e) safety considerations in application and in servicing,

(f) difficulties that might be encountered, and care to be taken if the appliance is used on a patient simultaneously with other electric appliances,

(g) schematics, wiring diagrams, mechanical layouts, parts lists, and other pertinent data for the appliance as shipped,

(h) functional description of the circuit,

(i) electrical supply requirements (volts, frequency, amperes, and watts), heat dissipation, weight, dimensions, output current, output voltage, and other pertinent data,

(j) the limits of electrical supply variations — performance specifications of the appliance shall be given for the applicable limits of electrical supply variations,

(k) technical performance specifications including design levels of leakage current,

(l) instructions for unpacking (readily available upon opening), inspecting, installing, adjusting, and aligning,

(m) comprehensive preventive and corrective maintenance and repair procedures.

Where appropriate, the information itemized shall be permitted to be supplied in the form of a separate operating manual and a separate maintenance manual, except that the separate maintenance manual shall also include essentially all the information included in the operating manual.

The Committee responsible for this chapter has noted that its requirements would be satisfied if a manufacturer provides at least one complete set of manuals. Additional sets (either complete or operators' manuals or service manuals) are a matter between the purchaser and the manufacturer.

9-2.1.8.2 Operating Instructions on Appliances. Condensed operating instructions shall be visibly and permanently attached to, or displayed on, any appliance that is intended to be used in emergency situations, and that could result in injury or death to the operator or patient if improperly used.

9-2.1.8.3 Labeling. The manufacturer shall furnish, for all appliances, labels that are readily visible and legible, and that remain so after being in service for the expected life of the appliance under hospital service and cleaning conditions. Controls and indicators shall be labeled to indicate their function. When appropriate, appliances shall be labeled with precautionary statements. All appliances shall be labeled with model numbers, date of manufacture, manufacturer's name, and the electrical ratings including voltage, frequency, current and/or wattage of the device. Date of manufacture shall be permitted to be a code, if its interpretation is provided to the user. Appliances shall be labeled to indicate if they (1) are listed for use as medical equipment, and (2) have isolated patient leads. Appliances intended for use in anesthetizing locations shall be labeled in an approved manner. *(See 12-4.1.)*

Adequate and appropriate labeling is considered necessary to reduce chances of misuse. Thus, Section 9-2.1 (formerly part of NFPA 76B-1980) does not require appliances to be listed, but if they are, they should be so labeled.

9-2.1.9 Additional Requirements for Special Appliances.

9-2.1.9.1 Signal Transmission Between Appliances.

(a)* *General.* Signal transmission lines from an appliance in a patient location to remote appliances shall employ a signal transmission system designed to prevent hazardous current flowing in the grounding interconnection of the appliances.

A-9-2.1.9.1(a) Signal Transmission. This may be accomplished by using a signal transmission system that is isolated from ground or presents a high impedance to ground; that employs a common signal grounding wire between appliances served from the same reference grounding point; that employs an additional grounding path between the common signal grounding wire and reference grounding point in the patient vicinity; or by other means intended to reduce potential differences in the patient vicinity due to grounding currents to a safe level.

The Appendix material indicates that there are several possible methods to prevent hazardous current levels.

(b) *Outdoor Signal Transmission.* Outdoor signal transmission lines from appliances attached to patients shall be equipped with surge protection appropriate to the type of transmission line used. Such appliances or signal transmission lines shall be designed to prevent a hazard to the patient from exposure of the lines to lightning, power contact, power induction, rise in ground potential, radio interference, etc.

9-2.1.9.2 Appliances Intended to Deliver Electrical Energy.

(a) *Conditions for Meeting Safety Requirements.* Electrical-energy-delivering appliances shall conform to the leakage, grounding, and other requirements of this chapter when powered but not delivering energy.

NOTE 1: When delivering energy, such appliances may deviate from these requirements only to the extent essential for their intended clinical function.

NOTE 2: Appliances that intentionally or that may inadvertently apply electrical energy to the patient or to components in contact with the patient require special safety considerations.

NOTE 3: Since there is a wide range of power levels, output frequencies, and purposes of appliances that apply electricity directly to patients or to patient-connected devices, it is not feasible to cite them in detail.

(b) *Specific Requirements by Type of Device.*

(1) Electrically Powered Transducers. Exposed metal parts of these devices shall be considered electrodes and meet the applicable requirements of 9-2.1.13, "Manufacturers' Tests for Safety of Patient-Care-Related Electrical Appliances." Connectors shall be designed to prevent inadvertent interchange of leads if interchange could constitute a hazard to the patient or operator.

NOTE: Electrically powered transducers include pressure transducers, flowmeters, endoscopes, etc. The electrical energy is not intended to be applied to the patient but to a device that contacts the patient.

The intent here is the prohibition of interconnections that could cause a shock hazard, not necessarily the prohibition of all interconnections. It is good design practice to prevent interconnections to prevent signal interference, but that subject is outside the scope of the Committee responsible for this chapter. (*See Figure 29.*)

(2) Patient Impedance Measuring Devices. For a particular application, the combination of frequency and current levels shall limit the applied current to the minimum necessary to achieve the medical purposes, but not to exceed the limits given in 9-2.1.13.5, "Lead Leakage Current Tests and Limits," whichever is appropriate.

NOTE: Assessment of physiologic functions by electric impedance measurements usually requires direct contact with the patient and injection of electric current.

(3) Electrotherapeutic Devices. Appliances that require specific pulse forms or high power levels shall be designed to protect the operator and attendant personnel from accidental electric shock.

NOTE: Electrotherapeutic devices include devices for electrosleep, electroanesthesia, and electroshock.

(4)* Electrosurgery. Electrosurgical devices shall meet the requirements of 9-2.1.9.2(a), "Conditions for Meeting Safety Requirements."

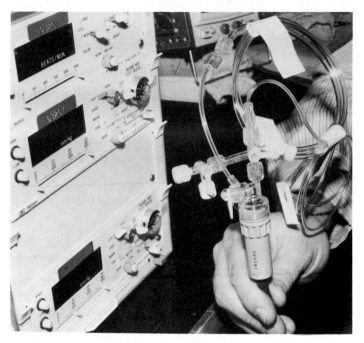

Figure 29   Transducer for monitoring blood pressure continuously.

A-9-2.1.9.2(b)(4) Electrosurgery. Electrosurgical unit output circuits are commonly designated as isolated or ground-referenced on the basis of their isolation at their operating (RF) frequency. No assumption about isolation at 60 Hz should be made unless the device is specifically labeled as having an "isolated patient circuit (60 Hz)" in which case the device is to conform to the requirements of 9-2.1.13.5(c), "Isolation Test."

The Appendix material calls attention to the possibility of an electrosurgical unit not being isolated at 60 Hz current. For more guidance on this subject, see Annex 2.

NOTE 1:   See Annex 2, "Use of High-Frequency Electricity in Health Care Facilities," for information on electrosurgical devices.

NOTE 2:   Electrosurgery uses high levels of continuous or pulsed radio frequency power. It presents some unique hazards. It generates sparks with the attendant ignition hazard. It generates radio frequency interference that may obstruct monitoring. It may cause burns at inadvertent ground return paths if its return circuit is inadequate. Demodulation products may contain components that cause fibrillation or stimulation. DC monitoring currents may cause chemical burns. Capacitive or inductive coupling may occur.

(5) Cardiac Defibrillation. Since the operator holds the high-voltage patient electrode paddles and defibrillation may be a hurried emergency procedure, the appliance shall be designed to protect the operator and attendant personnel from accidental electric shock.

NOTE: Cardiac defibrillation applies high-voltage, short-duration pulses to the patient.

9-2.1.9.3 Oxygen Delivery Equipment. Electrically powered oxygen delivery equipment shall comply with either (a) or (b) or (c) or (d) or (e) as listed below. When only a remote control or signal leads of a device are to be used in the site of intentional expulsion, only the control or signal leads shall be required to comply with this section.

(a) Listed for use in oxygen-enriched atmospheres.

(b) Comply with the requirements of NFPA 493, *Standard for Intrinsically Safe Apparatus*.

(c) Sealed so as to prevent an oxygen-enriched atmosphere from reaching electrical components. The sealing material shall be of the type that will still seal even after repeated exposure to water, oxygen, mechanical vibration, and heating from the external circuitry.

(d) Ventilated so as to limit the oxygen concentration surrounding electrical components to below 23.5 percent by volume.

(e) Both of following:

(1) No hot surfaces over 300°C (573°F).

Exception: Small (less than 2-watt) hermetically sealed heating elements such as light bulbs.

(2) No exposed switching or sparking points of electrical energy that fall to the right of the curve for the appropriate type of circuit contained in Figures 9-2.1.9.3 (a) through (f). The dc (or peak ac) open-circuit voltage and short-circuit current shall be used.

> Previously, only equipment complying with Subparagraph (a) (i.e., equipment listed for use in oxygen-enriched atmospheres) was considered acceptable for use within the "site of administration" (i.e., one foot around oxygen-delivery equipment). For this 1987 edition of NFPA 99, site of administration has been replaced by the concept of the "site of intentional expulsion" *(see commentary in Chapter 2 under this term, and in Chapter 7 under Section 7-6.2.3.1).* This reduced the area considered hazardous to that where an oxygen-enriched atmosphere was intentionally vented to the atmosphere. In addition, the Subcommittee on Gas Equipment approved the allowance of four other safety measures for electrically powered oxygen-delivery equipment [(b) through (e) above]. *(See Section 7-6.2.3 for further criteria for users of electrical equipment within the site of intentional expulsion, and of electrical equipment used within oxygen delivery equipment.)*

9-2.1.10 Low-Voltage Appliances and Appliances Not Connected to the Electric Power Distribution System.

9-2.1.10.1 General. Appliances and instruments operating from batteries or their equivalent, an external source of low voltage, or that are not connected to the electric power distribution system shall conform to all applicable requirements of 9-2.1, "Patient-Care-Related Electrical Equipment." This shall include communication, signaling, entertainment, remote-control, and low-energy power systems.

Exception: Telephones.

9-2.1.10.2 Rechargeable Appliances. Battery-operated appliances that are rechargeable while in use shall meet all the requirements of 9-2.1.13.3, "Leakage Current Tests," for line-operated appliances.

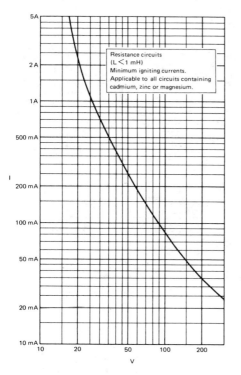

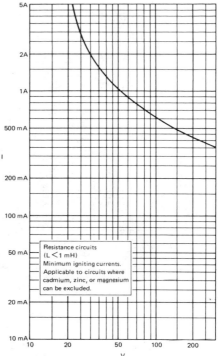

Figure 9-2.1.9.3(a)†

NOTE: Extracted from NFPA 493, *Standard for Intrinsically Safe Apparatus and Associated Apparatus for Use in Class I, II, and III, Division 1 Hazardous Locations.*

Figure 9-2.1.9.3(b)†

NOTE: Extracted from NFPA 493, *Standard for Intrinsically Safe Apparatus and Associated Apparatus for Use in Class I, II, and III, Division 1 Hazardous Locations.*

9-2.1.10.3 Low-Voltage Connectors. Attachment plugs used on low-voltage circuits shall have distinctive configurations that do not permit interchangeable connection with circuits of other voltages.

9-2.1.10.4 Isolation of Low-Voltage Circuits. Low-voltage circuits shall be electrically isolated from the electric power distribution system.

9-2.1.11 Cardiac Monitors and Electrocardiographs. Monitoring of cardiac activity is crucial to effective defibrillation. Design of electrocardiographs, cardiac monitors, or blood-pressure monitors intended for use on patients in Class H areas shall include protection against equipment damage during defibrillation of the patient.

9-2.1.12 Direct Electrical Pathways to the Heart. The requirements of this section shall apply only to manufacturers except where specifically noted.

NOTE: This section is concerned with the patient who may have either of two types of direct electrical connections to the heart. The obvious and most hazardous conductor comprises a wire in contact with the heart muscle. This may be a pacemaker electrode, a guide wire, or a transthoracic or implanted electrode. The second type of conductor is a liquid column contained within a nonconductive catheter with the internal end in the heart.

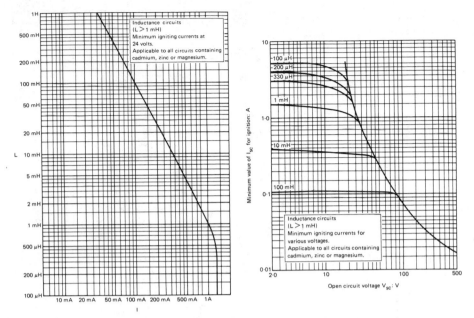

Figure 9-2.1.9.3(c)†

NOTE: Extracted from NFPA 493, *Standard for Intrinsically Safe Apparatus and Associated Apparatus for Use in Class I, II, and III, Division 1 Hazardous Locations.*

Figure 9-2.1.9.3(d)†

NOTE: Extracted from NFPA 493, *Standard for Intrinsically Safe Apparatus and Associated Apparatus for Use in Class I, II, and III, Division 1 Hazardous Locations.*

In the Note, "transthoracic" refers to electrodes that enter the heart through the chest wall.

Also, a simple invasive procedure to a peripheral vessel does not establish a direct electrical pathway to the heart. The end of the electrical probe or liquid-filled conductor inside the body must come in contact with the heart to establish a direct electrical pathway to the heart.

Although this section is intended primarily to guide manufacturers in the design of safe equipment, hospital personnel must be aware of these design requirements so that they are not compromised. Some of the requirements listed apply specifically to facility operating personnel, but were placed in this section because of their relationship to manufacturer's requirements, and so that facility personnel would appreciate the totality of the problem. Thus, close liaison must be maintained between manufacturers and users in meeting the requirements of this critical area of electrical safety.

9-2.1.12.1 Cardiac Electrodes.

(a) *General.* Appliances that have isolated patient leads shall be labeled as having isolated patient leads in accordance with 9-2.1.13.5, "Lead Leakage Current Tests and Limits."

(b) *Insulation of Cardiac Leads.* Pacemaker leads and other wires intended for insertion into the heart, together with their adapters and connections to appliances, shall be insulated except for their sensing or stimulation areas.

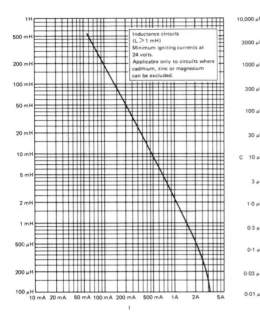

Figure 9-2.1.9.3(e)†

NOTE: Extracted from NFPA 493, *Standard for Intrinsically Safe Apparatus and Associated Apparatus for Use in Class I, II, and III, Division 1 Hazardous Locations.*

Figure 9-2.1.9.3(f)†

NOTE: Extracted from NFPA 493, *Standard for Intrinsically Safe Apparatus and Associated Apparatus for Use in Class I, II, and III, Division 1 Hazardous Locations.*

NOTE: The user is required to have a policy to protect pacing leads with external terminals from potentially hazardous contact with conductive surfaces (*see 7-6.2.1.3, "Protection of Patients with Direct Electrical Pathways to the Heart"*).

Exception No. 1: Metal stylets or guide wires temporarily introduced into a vein or artery for purposes of positioning a catheter need not be insulated. When such guide wires are inside the heart the operator shall exercise extreme care to ensure safe use. When used in conjunction with electrical devices (e.g., positioning catheters by use of ECG recordings), the guide wire shall be insulated as required above.

Exception No. 2: Insulated wires designed to be introduced through a surgical needle, or other special wires where it is not practicable to maintain insulation, shall not be required to maintain insulation during introduction or manipulation. At such times the operator shall take appropriate safeguards.

(c) *Safety Requirements for Cardiac Electrodes.* The electrode catheter, fitting, and associated appliance, when assembled, shall meet the applicable requirements of 9-2.1.13.5, "Lead Leakage Current Tests and Limits," for isolated patient leads.

(d) *Insulation of Pacemaker Connections.* Uninsulated or open-type connectors shall not be used for external cardiac pacemaker terminals.

9-2.1.12.2 Liquid-Filled Catheters.

(a) *Cardiac Catheter System.* Any conductive element of a liquid catheter system that can come in contact with the liquid column shall be insulated from ground or electric energy sources.

NOTE: A liquid catheter system may consist of the catheter itself, pressure transducers, electronic appliances, and associated accessories.

(b) *Nonconductive Cardiac Catheters.* A nonconductive catheter containing a conductive liquid, when connected to its appropriate system, shall meet the applicable requirements of 9-2.1.13.5, "Lead Leakage Current Tests and Limits," for isolated patient leads, with the patient end of the liquid-filled catheter considered to be an electrode.

(c) *Conductive Cardiac Catheters.* If the liquid column is contained in a catheter made of conductive material having an electrical conductivity approximating that of blood, the system shall not require connection to an isolated patient lead. Conductive catheters shall be appropriately identified.

9-2.1.12.3 Angiographic Catheters. Appliances used to inject contrast media into the heart or major vessels shall meet the same safety requirements as other liquid-filled catheter systems.

NOTE: Although contrast injectors are not intended to apply electrical energy to the patient, they may deliver current from the power source and also may generate transient voltages large enough to be hazardous.

The Committee has noted that the contrast media is the major hazard, not the injector. The injector, however, should be designed to reduce the hazard.

9-2.1.13 Manufacturers' Tests for Safety of Patient-Care-Related Electrical Appliances.

9-2.1.13.1 General. This section describes tests by manufacturers for the safe operation of an appliance. The tests in this subsection are in addition to the design requirements of the entire Section 9-2.1, "Patient-Care-Related Electrical Equipment." The appliance manufacturer shall perform the testing adequate to ensure that each finished appliance will meet the specified test limits of this section.

Exception: Tests that are potentially destructive need only be performed by the manufacturer to assure design compliance for new appliances.

It is not necessary for manufacturers to perform all the tests in this section, only those necessary to ensure that appliances meet the requirements of this section.

9-2.1.13.2 Grounding Circuit Continuity.

(a) *Measurement of Resistance.* The resistance between the appliance chassis, or any exposed conductive surface of the appliance, and the ground pin of the attachment plug shall be measured. The resistance shall be less than 0.15 ohm. The cord shall be flexed at its connection to the attachment plug or connector, and at its connection to the strain relief on the chassis during the resistance measurement.

If there is no grounding conductor (as is the case in most listed double-insulated appliances), this test cannot be performed. However, if there is a grounding conductor, even if unnecessary, it should be tested. This will avoid a possible misunderstanding on the part of the user concerning the significance of the grounding.

9-2.1.13.3* Leakage Current Tests.

Material on manufacturer leakage current testing was reorganized and made congruent with facility testing procedures. *(See also commentary on 7-5.1.3.3.)*

(a)* *General.*

A-9-2.1.13.3(a) General. *(See A-7-5.1.3.3.)*

The test equipment requirements outlined in this section were revised in 1984 to better account for frequency weighting to low-impedance sources. Appendix A-7-5.1.3.3 was added during the revision for the 1984 edition of NFPA 99 to explain how frequency weighting was achieved. The network shown is in concert with international documents on the subject.

During that revision, the frequency range for testing was modified from "essentially dc" to "dc" since the Committee's intent was to make measurements from dc to 1 kHz.

(1) Techniques of Measurement. Each test shall be performed with the appropriate connection to a properly grounded ac power system.

(2) Frequency of Leakage Current. The leakage current limits stated in 9-1.1.13.4, "Leakage Current From Appliance to Ground," and 9-2.1.13.5, "Lead Leakage Current Tests and Limits," shall be rms values for dc and sinusoidal waveforms up to 1 kHz. For frequencies above 1 kHz, the leakage current limits shall be the values given in 9-2.1.13.4 and 9-2.1.13.5 multiplied by the frequency, in kHz, up to a maximum multiplier of 100.

NOTE 1: The limits for nonsinusoidal periodic, modulated, and transient waveforms remain to be determined.

NOTE 2: For complex leakage current waveforms, a single reading from an appropriate metering system can represent the physiologically effective value of the composite waveform, provided that the contribution of each component to the total reading is weighted in accordance with 9-2.1.13.3(a)(2).

This "weighting" can be achieved by a frequency-response-shaping network that precedes a flat response meter, or by a meter whose own frequency response characteristic matches 9-2.1.13.3(a)(2).

(3) Leakage Current in Relation to Polarity. Leakage current measurements shall be made with the polarity of the power line normal and reversed, the power switch of the appliance "on" and "off," and with all operating controls in the positions to cause maximum leakage current readings. The leakage current limits in 9-2.1.13.4 and 9-2.1.13.5 shall not be exceeded under any of these conditions.

A-9-2.1.13.3 Leakage Current Tests.

These currents usually derive from the line power by resistive paths, or capacitive or inductive coupling. However, they also include currents from other sources generated within the appliance and are measured by the tests described in this chapter.

These leakage current limits are based on acute events, i.e., sensation, duration tetany, or ventricular fibrillation. Appliance design should aim to reduce such current as much as possible. In properly grounded appliances, maximum chassis leakage current is in the grounding conductor and not through the patient.

These tests are not known to be adequate where currents (such as dc or high frequency) are introduced into the patient for long periods and where low-level effects must be considered.

9-2.1.13.4 Leakage Current from Appliance to Ground.

(a) *Test Methods.* The current shall be measured from the exposed conductive surfaces of the appliance to ground with all grounding conductors open at the end nearest the power receptacle. The appliance shall not be grounded by any other means. The current meter shall be inserted between the exposed conductive surfaces and ground. This test shall be made under the conditions of 9-2.1.13.3(a)(1) and (2). This test is illustrated in Figure 9-2.1.13.4(a).

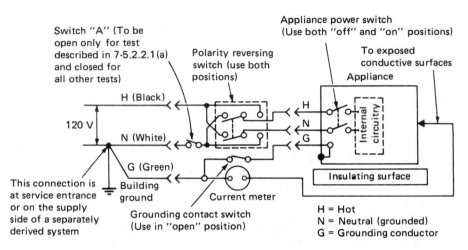

Figure 9-2.1.13.4(a) Test Circuit for Measuring Leakage Current from Exposed Conductive Surfaces.

A change to Figure 9-2.13.4(a) better reflected the way leakage current is measured (i.e., by connecting a probe to exposed conductive surfaces).

The phrasing of text in 7-5.2.2.1(a) may seem at odds with the requirements in paragraph two of this section [9-2.1.13.4(a)]. However, they have the same meaning — that of addressing nonpatient appliances that have found their way into (and will be used in) the patient vicinity. These types of appliances are not intended to contact the patient, but they may do so.

Appliances required to meet the limits of 7-5.2.2.1(a), "Facility-Owned Household Appliances," (i.e., appliances not intended to contact a patient) shall be tested with switch "A" open (open neutral). All other appliances meeting the limits of 9-2.1.13.4(c)(1) and (2), "Chassis Leakage Current Limits," shall be tested with switch "A" closed (connected neutral).

(b) *Appliances with No Exposed Conductive Surfaces.* When the appliance has no exposed conductive surface, one shall be simulated by placing a 3.9 by 7.8 in. (10 by 20 cm) bare metal foil in intimate contact with the exposed surface. This shall be considered the "exposed metal surface" of the appliance and all appropriate tests shall be performed to the foil.

The dimensions of the metal foil are considered to approximate the surface area of a hand touching an appliance. Hence, the leakage current measured here is a capacity-coupled area measurement instead of a point measurement. The Committee felt this was a reasonable test for manufacturers to conduct for such appliances. It is a particularly pertinent test when appliances are covered with an insulating film, but are not listed as "double insulated."

(c)* *Chassis Leakage Current Limits.*

(1) Cord-Connected Appliances. Cord-connected appliances that are intended for use in the patient vicinity shall not exceed 100 microamperes of chassis leakage current as measured in 9-2.1.13.4(a), "Test Methods."

(2) Permanently Wired Equipment. Permanently wired equipment installed in the patient vicinity shall not have leakage current from the frame to ground in excess of 5.0 milliamperes. The leakage current shall be measured prior to installation by the installer and verified and accepted by the facility. This measurement shall be made in accordance with 9-2.1.13.4(a) while the equipment is temporarily insulated from ground.

A-9-2.1.13.4(c) Chassis Leakage Current Limits. The chassis leakage current limits given in 9-2.1.13.4(c) and in other sections, combined with the grounding wire requirements, are based on a concept of two layers of protection. Either the limited leakage current or an intact grounding system will provide protection. However, it is becoming generally agreed that, not only with medical equipment but also with conventional appliances, there should be two levels of protection. This means that both safeguards must fail before the subject is at hazard.

For general application (household appliances) the leakage current limit is generally set at 500 microamperes at 60 Hz. The limit of 500 microamperes is based on the work of Dalziel and others which indicates that different individuals in the general population will exhibit responses to electrical shock at differing levels. A small percentage, perhaps 5 percent, will react to a current level of 500 microamperes with an involuntary movement that could trigger a secondary accident. Some individuals are sensitive to an electric shock sensation as low as 100 microamperes. A reasonable compromise seems to be to set the limit at 500 for the general public. It should be noted that in 7-5.2.2.1(a), "Facility-Owned Household Appliances," this is the limit for household-type appliances.

References:

Dalziel, C. F., and Lee, W. R., Reevaluation of lethal, electric currents effects of electricity on man. *Transactions on Industry and General Applications.* Vol. IGA-4, No. 5, September/October 1968.

Roy, O. A., Park, G. R., and Scott, J. R., Intracardiac catheter fibrillation thresholds as a function of duration of 60 Hz current and electrode area. *IEEE Trans. Biomed. Eng.* BME 24:430-435, 1977.

Roy, O. A., and Scott, J. R., 60 Hz ventricular fibrillation and pump failure thresholds versus electrode area. *IEEE Trans. Biomed. Eng.* BME 23:45-48, 1976.

Weinberg, D. I., et al., Electric shock hazards in cardiac catheterization. *Elec. Eng.* 82:30-35, 1963.

Watson, A. B., Wright, J. S., and Loughman, J., Electrical thresholds for ventricular fibrillation in man. *Med. J. Australia* 1:1179-1181, 1973.

For equipment in the patient vicinity it seems reasonable to reduce this limit by a safety factor of 5 to 100 microamperes, because of the special circumstances involved in hospitals. Some of these factors are:

(a) Some patients may be wet or have some other low-impedance connection to the ground. For this reason the assumption usually made for the general public that they are moderately insulated from ground is not valid.

(b) Patients are sick, tend to be unresponsive, tend to be obtunded, and may not be able to perform the evasive maneuvers that an alert adult would perform when experiencing an electrical shock.

(c) The nature of the patient's illness may exacerbate the response to electric shock.

(d) Hospital patients are increasingly in close proximity to more and more electrical equipment.

(e) Hospital equipment is subject to industrial-type abuse. It is handled roughly, is sometimes wet, and sometimes not properly maintained. All of this increases the probability of deterioration and consequent increase in leakage.

(f) The economics of the problem has been considered. The medical appliance industry has responded to the requirement for 100 microamperes maximum leakage by designing equipment within that limit. It has been shown to be feasible and not unduly uneconomical. In the few cases where, for technical reasons, it is impractical to reach these limtis, other solutions are available.

For the above reasons it has not been considered unreasonable to utilize a safety factor of 5 below conventional equipment. It should be emphasized that this number is not based on clear technical evidence but represents considered opinion. Therefore, if a particular appliance has a leakage current somewhat above 100 microamperes, it is not implied that it is dangerously unsafe. It does indicate that such an appliance should be examined to determine whether there is a reason for the higher leakage. If the leakage cannot be reduced it can be compensated for by more-intensive preventive maintenance to ensure that the grounding conductor is intact.

It should be further noted that the shock hazards produced by these current levels apply to external contacts, e.g., body surface ECG lead or a skin contact with the chassis of an appliance. These current values do not apply to intracardiac leads. For such leads the hazard is not startle, involuntary muscular motion, or "let-go." It is frank fibrillation of the heart, and is caused at levels a factor of 1000 below those necessary to cause fibrillation by external contacts. It is impractical to provide protection to the patient who has an intracardiac lead by means of the control of chassis leakage current, isolated power systems, ground fault interrupter circuits, or other similar external devices. Protection for such patients can be achieved only by the protection of the intracardiac lead. This is discussed in 9-2.1.12, "Direct Electrical Pathways to the Heart." For such patients the limit of such leads has been placed at 10 microamperes. Again there is a safety factor involved. The lower limit of hazardous currents seems to be about 100 microamperes at 60 Hz. A safety factor of 10 has been established because of most of the reasons above, and because of the following:

(a) Patients with intracardiac leads are usually ones whose hearts are already in jeopardy.

(b) Such patients usually have even more electrical equipment near them than does the average patient.

(c) It has been shown to be economically quite feasible to maintain such leads at a limit of 10 microamperes.

Section 9-2.1, it should be recalled, is applicable only to manufacturers of patient-care-related electrical appliances.

The former Committee on Safe Use of Electricity in Patient Care Areas of Health Care Facilities rejected the concept of subdividing these types of appliances into two categories: appliances likely to contact the patient, and appliances not likely to contact the patient. The Committee also noted that it was *not* its intent to have two categories of patient-care-related electrical appliances. All cord-connected patient-care-related electrical appliances in a patient vicinity are likely to contact patients. The Committee thus modified the previous title of subsection 9-2.1.13.4(c)(1), intending to apply the 100 microampere requirements to all cord-connected patient-care-related electrical appliances. Exception No. 2 to 7-5.1.3.5(a) should also be noted in this regard.

Reference to "facility" in subsection 9-2.1.13.4(c)(2) of text (not Appendix) is made since that paragraph requires both manufacturer and facility to participate in the test.

9-2.1.13.5 Lead Leakage Current Tests and Limits.

(a) *Lead to Ground (Nonisolated Input).* The lead leakage current to ground shall be measured under the conditions of 9-2.1.13.3(a), "Leakage Current Tests — General." The test shall be made between each patient lead and ground, and between the combined patient leads and ground. The test shall be made with the patient leads active (e.g., in the case of a multilead instrument, the lead selector switch shall be advanced through all operating positions). Each measurement shall be performed with the grounding conductors both opened and closed. For this purpose the grounding conductor shall be interrupted at the plug end of the appliance cord. Figure 9-2.1.13.5(a) is an example of an acceptable test configuration. The leakage current shall be less than 50 microamperes.

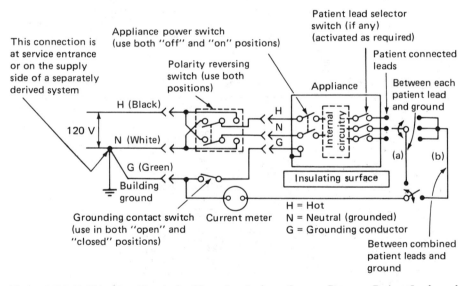

Figure 9-2.1.13.5(a)   Test Circuit for Measuring Leakage Current Between Patient Leads and Ground (Nonisolated).

While the organization of leakage current tests for manufacturers and hospitals has been made congruent (see commentary on 7-5.1.3.3), the test and value for one lead leakage current test has been made more exacting for manufacturers: the lead-to-ground test for nonisolated inputs.

For health care facilities, this lead test is to be conducted with the patient leads combined (connected together). For manufacturers, this test is, as noted in the above text, to be conducted between each patient lead and ground, and between combined patient leads and ground. In addition, the maximum leakage current criteria for manufacturers has been lowered to 50 microamperes.

These changes were made for several reasons. First, although the change in leakage current value has the effect of lowering the chassis leakage current limit to 50 microamperes for those devices with nonisolated input leads, the major concern is the value of those items that will be in constant contact with the patient (e.g., the patient leads); this 50-microampere value was required in prior editions and drafts of former NFPA 76B. Second, making both measurements (individual and combined) is technically more accurate in the instance of active driven leads (i.e., the current would be only in the driven leads, and their contribution of leakage current could be shunted off through another lead when measured in the combined configuration, thus not giving an accurate meter reading). Third, requiring both tests brings this requirement into conformity with another United States document on the subject by the Association for Advancement of Medical Instrumentation.

The former Committee on Safe Use of Electricity on Patient Care Areas of Health Care Facilities did not feel that health care facilities, in making the lead-to-ground test for nonisolated inputs, needed to be this exacting in their measurements.

(b) *Lead to Ground (Isolated Input).* The leakage current to ground between each patient lead and ground shall be measured under the conditions of 9-2.1.13.3(a), "Leakage Current Tests — General." The test shall be made with the patient leads active (e.g., in the case of a multilead instrument, the lead selector switch shall be advanced through all operating positions). Each measurement shall be performed with the grounding conductors both opened and closed. For this purpose the grounding conductor shall be interrupted at the plug end of the appliance cord. Figure 9-2.1.13.5(b) is an example of an acceptable test configuration. The leakage current shall be less than 10 microamperes.

(c) *Isolation Test (Isolated Input).* The isolation between each patient lead and ground for an appliance that has been labeled as having isolated patient leads shall be measured by observing

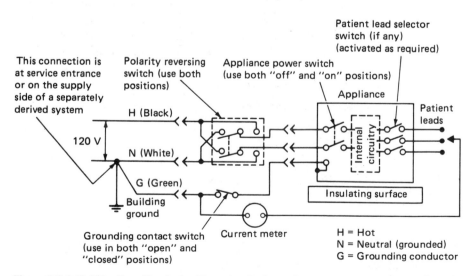

Figure 9-2.1.13.5(b)   Test Circuit for Measuring Leakage Current Between Patient Leads and Ground (Isolated).

the current produced by applying an external source of power-line frequency and voltage between the lead and ground while the leads are approximately 8 in. (20 cm) from a grounded conductive surface. Similarly, the isolation at the apparatus terminals to the patient cables shall be measured. Figure 9-2.1.13.5(c) is an example of an acceptable test configuration. At the patient end of the leads the leakage current shall be less than 20 microamperes and at the apparatus terminals less than 10 microamperes. Only appliances meeting this requirement shall be permitted to be identified as having isolated patient leads.

Suitable safety precautions (such as including a resistance in series to limit the current, insulation of the meter, and a momentary switch) shall be taken to protect the operator. In appliances without a power cord or with ungrounded, exposed conductive surfaces, measurements shall be made with the exposed conductive surfaces temporarily grounded. If there is no exposed conductive surface, measurement shall be made with a simulated surface, as described in 9-2.1.13.4(b), "Appliances with No Exposed Conductive Surfaces," which is also temporarily grounded.

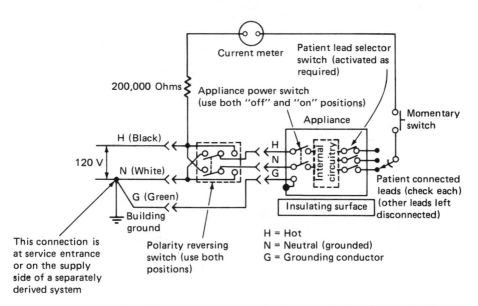

Figure 9-2.1.13.5(c)   Test Circuit for Measuring the Electrical Isolation of Isolated Patient Leads.

(d) *Between Leads (Nonisolated Input)*.   The current between any pair of leads or any single lead and all others shall be measured under the conditions of 9-2.1.13.3(a), "Leakage Current Tests — General." Each measurement shall be performed with the grounding conductors both opened and closed. For this purpose the grounding conductor shall be interrupted at the plug end of the appliance cord. Figure 9-2.1.13.5(d)/(e) is an example of an acceptable test configuration. The leakage current shall be less than 50 microamperes.

Exception: Measuring leakage current between any single lead and all other leads need only be performed to assure the approval agency of design compliance.

(e) *Between Leads (Isolated Input)*.   The current between any pair of leads or any single lead and all others shall be measured under the conditions of 9-2.1.13.3(a), "Leakage Current Tests — General." Each measurement shall be performed with the grounding conductors both opened and closed. For this purpose the grounding conductor shall be interrupted at the plug end of the appliance cord. Figure 9-2.1.13.5(d)/(e) is an example of an acceptable test configuration. The leakage current shall be less than 10 microamperes.

Exception: Measuring leakage current between any single lead and all other leads need only be performed to assure the approval agency of design compliance.[7]

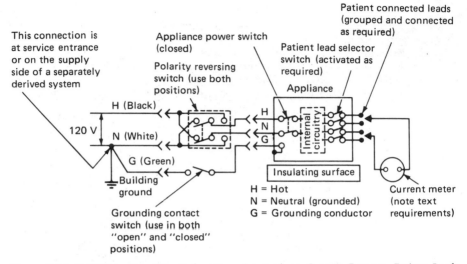

Figure 9-2.1.13.5(d)/(e) Test Circuit for Measuring Leakage Current Between Patient Leads (Nonisolated and Isolated).

As with the two testing configurations in 9-2.1.13.5(a), the change requiring manufacturers to measure leakage current both with and without patient leads is both for accuracy and to ensure that the maximum value at apparatus terminals is safe as well as consistent between manufacturers. This requirement makes this test conform with other United States documents. Again, health care facilities need make the measurement only with the patient cable connected.

9-2.1.14 Flammable Gases.   Additional design and construction requirements for appliances used in flammable anesthetizing locations are contained in 7-5.1.2.4 and 7-5.1.2.5.

9-2.2 Nonpatient Electrical Equipment.   (Reserved)

9-3 Gas Equipment.   (Reserved)

9-4 Material.   (Reserved)

10 LABORATORIES

NOTE: The application of requirements contained in this chapter for specific types of health care facilities can be found in Chapters 12 through 18.

Prologue

In 1966, a Subcommittee on Hospital Laboratories of the Committee on Hospitals was created. This Subcommittee was charged with developing a standard intended to recognize and mitigate the hazards associated with the operation of laboratories within health care facilities. It was recognized, for example, that clinical laboratories require the immediate presence of flammable and combustible gases, solvents, and solids; but there were no general requirements for their safe use in laboratories with respect to fire or explosion hazards.

The proximity of many laboratories to patient care areas for convenience and efficiency was also noted. (Patients may have to be taken to the laboratory for certain testing; laboratory specimens and results have to be transmitted between the laboratory and the nursing units.) As a result, the Subcommittee was concerned about construction criteria for laboratories since they posed a serious fire exposure hazard to patients.

In 1968, the Subcommittee on Hospital Laboratories presented for adoption a manual, NFPA 56CM, on the subject. In 1969, the document was proposed and adopted as a full standard. Among other things, it set forth safety precautions when storing and handling flammable and combustible substances. It also required the posting of hazard symbols as detailed in NFPA 704, *Standard on Identification of the Fire Hazards of Materials.*

Recognition of hazards leads to the development and implementation of safety standards and of safe practices. This in turn may lead to the development of better equipment. One such development took place in the early 1970s. Many hospitals stored diethyl ether in conventional laboratory refrigerators to retard vaporization. The volatility of diethyl ether is such that when it is refrigerated to the range of 4° to 6°C, mixtures of ether vapor and air tend to form a stoichiometric mixture. In a number of situations, personnel entering the laboratory following a long weekend discovered that an explosion had taken place in a refrigerator, and the refrigerator door was found buried in an opposite wall. These problems led to the development (via requirements included in the NFPA 56C) of "laboratory-safe" refrigerators that eliminated means by which vapors could be ignited (e.g., sealing, or externally mounting, contact points of thermostats).

An issue of overlap and/or conflict with NFPA 45, *Standard on Fire Protection for Laboratories Using Chemicals*, was resolved with changes in the scope of NFPA 56C in 1980. This precluded NFPA 45 and NFPA 56C from being applied simultaneously to health care laboratories.

Over the years, NFPA 56C (now Chapter 10 of the 1987 edition of NFPA 99) has undergone continual refinement. The adoption and enforcement of the provisions contained herein have virtually eliminated hospital and other health care facility laboratories as a source of danger to patients and laboratory personnel.

10-1 Introduction and Scope.

10-1.1 Hazards and Responsibilities. Laboratory facilities present fire hazards of a nature not encountered elsewhere in health-related institutions.

10-1.2* Scope.

For the 1980 edition of NFPA 56C, all references to nonflammable gases were deleted. In addition, requirements for liquefied gases were also deleted as they are generally not used in clinical laboratories. However, for 1984 (when NFPA 56C was incorporated into NFPA 99), guidance on nonflammable piped gas systems was added in the interest of safety for laboratory personnel.

A-10-1.2 Chapter 10 includes many special operational requirements that should be used in all laboratories affiliated with health care facilities, even those located in separate buildings where there may be no patients incapable of self-preservation.

NFPA 45, *Standard on Fire Protection for Laboratories Using Chemicals*, contains comprehensive general requirements for laboratories that can be used for additional reference.

- Because of the nature of activities in laboratories, operational and safety requirements have been developed for use by all laboratories. While construction and equipment requirements are applicable to new laboratories (per Section 1-2), safety with respect to activities is *always* applicable.
- The requirements of NFPA 45 go beyond those of this chapter, but note also that A-10-1.2 is a recommendation and not a requirement.

10-1.2.1 This section is not intended to cover hazards resulting from the misuse of chemicals, radioactive materials, or biological materials that will not result in fires or explosions. Although it deals primarily with hazards related to fires and explosions, many of the requirements to protect against fire or explosion, such as those for hood exhaust systems, also serve to protect persons from exposure to nonfire health hazards of these materials.

Requirements and recommendations of other organizations and agencies should be reviewed and integrated with requirements in this chapter to ensure firesafety and environmental/chemical/biological safety requirements do not interfere with one another.

10-1.3 Interface with Existing Codes and Standards.

10-1.3.1 Where interface with existing NFPA or other consensus codes and standards occurs, reference is made to the appropriate source in the text.

10-1.3.2 Where necessary, due to the special nature of laboratories, codes and standards are supplemented in this text, so as to apply more specifically to buildings or portions of buildings devoted to laboratory usage.

10-2 Nature of Hazards.

This portion of Chapter 10 was extensively revised in 1980. Fire loss-prevention procedures were updated and expanded.

Laboratories using large quantities of materials that could cause explosions should be particularly observant of the safety procedures below, in addition to any other practices required by enforcing authorities.

The development of a manual may be helpful to facilitate the listing and incorporation of safety procedures for laboratory emergencies. A manual is also useful for documentation and review of procedures and as an orientation tool for new employees.

10-2.1* General. Laboratory work may involve the use of flammable, combustible, and explosive materials that can be safely handled only if they are treated with a respect for and a knowledge of their hazardous properties.

A-10-2.1 Before a hazardous chemical is ordered, controls should be established to assure that adequate facilities and procedures are available for receiving, storing, using, and disposing of the material. Information sources include:

NFPA 49, *Hazardous Chemicals Data*;

NFPA 491M, *Manual of Hazardous Chemical Reactions*;

NFPA 325M, *Fire Hazard Properties of Flammable Liquids, Gases and Volatile Solids*;

Flash Point Index of Trade Name Liquids.

Class IA and IB flammable liquids in glass containers larger than the 1-quart (0.91-L) size should be transported in suitable containers of sufficient size to hold the contents of the glass containers.

10-2.2 Fire Loss Prevention.

10-2.2.1 Hazard Assessment.

10-2.2.1.1 An evaluation shall be made of hazards that may be encountered during laboratory operations before such operations are begun. The evaluation shall include hazards associated with the properties of the chemicals used, hazards associated with the operation of the equipment, and hazards associated with the nature of the proposed reactions (e.g., evolution of acid vapors or flammable gases).

The utilization of NFPA 49, *Hazardous Chemicals Data*, and NFPA 704, *Identification of the Fire Hazards of Materials*, can greatly assist in evaluating the hazard potential of flammables in a laboratory.

10-2.2.1.2 Periodic reviews of laboratory operations and procedures shall be conducted with special attention given to any change in materials, operations, or personnel.

Most authorities, as well as recommended good practice, indicate that reviewing and updating of laboratory operations and procedures be conducted and documented annually.

10-2.2.1.3 Unattended operations and automatic laboratory equipment shall be provided with periodic surveillance or with automatic monitoring devices to detect and report abnormal operation.

Periodic observation of unattended operations and automatic laboratory equipment can be provided by security personnel on their normal rounds, support service personnel (i.e., housekeeping, transport, etc.), or supervisors or other laboratory personnel in adjacent or nearby laboratories. The person(s) responsible for the equipment should inform these personnel what constitutes abnormal operation, how often equipment needs checking, and what actions should be taken should something abnormal be observed (e.g., an emergency shutdown switch/sequence; an emergency phone number).

10-2.2.1.4 When chemicals and reagents are ordered, steps shall be taken to determine the hazards and to transmit that information to those who will receive, store, use, or dispose of the chemicals.

NFPA 49, *Hazardous Chemicals Data*, and NFPA 704, *Identification of the Fire Hazards of Materials*, can provide identification of hazards to personnel who receive, store, use, or dispose of hazardous chemicals.

10-2.2.2 Fire Prevention Procedures.   Fire prevention procedures shall be established. (*See Section 10-8.*)

10-2.2.3 Emergency Procedures.

10-2.2.3.1 Procedures for laboratory emergencies shall be developed. Such procedures shall include alarm actuation, evacuation, and equipment shutdown procedures, and provisions for control of emergencies that may occur in the laboratory, including specific detailed plans for control operations by an emergency control group within the organization or a public fire department.

The emergency procedures for a laboratory are usually specific to that laboratory, and must therefore be custom designed to address those hazards significant to that location. Common to most, however, is the need to consider alternative plans for evening, weekend, or holiday operation when fewer staff are present; and for emergency conditions (severe weather, civil disorder, etc.) when staff resources might be altered. Persons who will be responding to emergencies should review procedures for clarity and specific understanding of all plans. Emergency procedures should be written and reviewed at regular intervals with all employees.

10-2.2.3.2 Emergency procedures shall be established for controlling chemical spills.

A chemical spill procedure and spill kit should be readily available to receiving, storage, use, and disposal personnel for their handling of hazardous chemicals. Kits containing neutralizers, absorbants, clean-up tools (scoops, brushes, boxes, or bags) and personal protective items (goggles, aprons, gloves) may be purchased or assembled by knowledgeable laboratory personnel. Written procedures and training of potential users are required for the use of any spill kit.

The type of spill kit selected should be appropriate for the chemical hazards present in an area. For example, spillage of some chemicals, such as hydrofluoric acid and mercury, requires a special spill kit. Other spills, however, may be handled by a standard chemical spill kit.

10-2.2.3.3* Emergency procedures shall be established for extinguishing clothing fires.

A-10-2.2.3.3 Laboratory personnel should be thoroughly indoctrinated in procedures to follow in cases of clothing fires. The single most important instruction, one that should be stressed until it becomes second nature to all personnel, is to immediately drop to the floor and roll. All personnel should recognize that, in case of ignition of another person's clothing, they should immediately knock that person to the floor and roll that person around to smother the flames. Too often a person will panic if his clothing ignites and will run, resulting in more severe, often fatal burn injuries.

It should be emphasized that safety showers or fire blankets are of secondary importance. They should be used only when immediately at hand. It should also be recognized that rolling on the floor not only smothers the fire, but also helps to keep flames out of the victim's face and reduce inhalation of smoke. Improper use of fire blankets can increase the severity of smoke and fire injuries if the blanket funnels smoke towards the face or if the blanket is not removed after the flames have been extinguished.

One method for extinguishing clothing fires is the "Stop, Drop, and Roll" procedure recommended by NFPA. As noted in the Appendix material, it should be an automatic reflex reaction.

Instructions for clothing fires in a laboratory should emphasize the following:

1. If your clothes catch fire, lie down (keeping flame and toxic gases away from face). Roll and beat flames out. Call for help. Above all, do not run (running can fan flames and increase size and intensity of fire).

2. If you are using a "fire blanket" on a person whose clothing is on fire, take the blanket to the victim. Bring the blanket across the victim *from head toward feet* (pushing flames and toxic gases away from face) to smother out flames. After flames are out, use blanket to treat for shock. Remove all smoldering clothing immediately (do not allow blanket to trap heat from remaining smoldering clothing). Fire blankets can be particularly harmful when synthetics are involved. They can increase the amount and severity of burns. Thus, once fire is extinguished, blankets should be immediately removed, as noted above.

10-2.2.4 Orientation and Training.

Orientation and training of laboratory personnel is particularly important for new personnel so that they may become familiar with specific procedures and features of a laboratory. Frequent safety in-service training programs can reinforce safety information to new staff and provide a valuable review to existing staff.

Figure 30   A fire blanket, clearly labeled, for use in a laboratory.

In addition, laboratory safety policies, procedures, and emergency plans should be coordinated with institution-wide emergency plans to avoid conflict and contradiction in an emergency.

10-2.2.4.1   New laboratory personnel shall be taught general safety practices for the laboratory and specific safety practices for the equipment and procedures they will use.

10-2.2.4.2   Continuing safety education and supervision shall be provided, incidents shall be reviewed monthly, and procedures shall be reviewed annually.

10-3 Structure.

This section (10-3) and Section 10-5 were extensively revised in 1980 to reflect current practices and to correlate more closely with requirements of NFPA *101*, *Life Safety Code* (e.g., exit access travel distance, openings in corridor barriers, fire protection features).

10-3.1* **Construction and Arrangement.**

A-10-3.1   The types of construction are defined in NFPA 220, *Standard on Types of Building Construction*. Also, for a discussion of fire-resistive construction and fire resistance of building

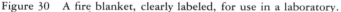

materials and construction assemblies, see the NFPA *Fire Protection Handbook*. For information on the fire resistance, installation, and maintenance of fire doors, see NFPA 80, *Standard for Fire Doors and Windows*.

10-3.1.1 Health care laboratories shall be separated from surrounding health care areas and from exit corridors by fire-resistive construction with a minimum rating of one hour, and all openings protected by ¾-hour-rated assemblies.

Exception No. 1: Laboratories that are protected by automatic extinguishing systems and that are not classified as a severe hazard are not required to be separated.

Exception No. 2: Any opening in a laboratory corridor barrier may be held open only by an automatic release device complying with the applicable requirements in NFPA 101, Life Safety Code.

The level of fire separation for laboratories is based on the working supplies of flammable or combustible liquids. The total amount of flammable or combustible liquids and the type of storage will determine whether a laboratory is classified as an ordinary or severe hazard. Quantities in excess of those identified in 10-7.2.2 would be considered severe hazards.

For ordinary hazard laboratories, the following is required: either a 1-hour fire separation with at least "C"-labeled 45-minute rated doors, or a smoketight room (equal to 30-minute walls and 20-minute doors for existing construction; 1-hour walls in new construction) protected by an automatic fire extinguishing system.

For severe hazard laboratories, the following is required: either a 2-hour fire separation with at least "B"-labeled 1½-hour rated doors, or a 1-hour fire separation with at least a "C"-labeled 45-minute rated door and an automatic fire extinguishing system.

Separation Requirements

Ordinary Hazard	Severe Hazard
<10 gal flammable liquids or <60 gal flammable liquids stored in a flammable liquids cabinet	>10 gals flammable liquids or >60 gals flammable liquids stored in a flammable liquid cabinet
requires: 1-hour separation with "C"-labeled 45-minute doors	*requires:* 2-hour separation with "B"-labeled 1½-hour doors
or: smoketight room with automatic fire extinguishing system	*or:* 1-hour separation with "C"-labeled 45-minute doors and an automatic fire extinguishing system

Refer to NFPA *101, Life Safety Code*, Sections 12-2.11.6 and 13-2.11.5 for applicable requirements. Any automatic release device can hold open a door to a hazardous area if the device is activated by the manual fire alarm system, a local smoke detector, or a complete fire detection or extinguishing system.

10-3.1.2 Interior finish in laboratories and means of egress shall comply with the applicable sections of NFPA *101, Life Safety Code*.

10-3.2 Exit Details.

Requirements in this section were revised in 1980 to bring them into line with NFPA *101, Life Safety Code*.

10-3.2.1* Any room arranged for laboratory work that has an area in excess of 1000 sq ft (92.9 sq m) shall have at least two exit access doors remote from each other, one of which shall open directly onto a means of egress.

A-10-3.2.1 A door to an adjoining laboratory work area or laboratory unit is considered to be a second access to an exit.

Exit access door requirements were revised in 1980 to make them less restrictive, but still provide an equivalent degree of safety (i.e., one door could open to another room, assuming 1-hour fire-resistive construction, etc., separated the two areas). Note that at least one door is required to open onto a means of egress.

10-3.2.2 Travel distance between any point in a laboratory unit and an exit access door shall not exceed 75 ft (22.9 m).

This requirement was added in 1984 to emphasize the importance of not creating tenuous situations in laboratories. It is in compliance with NFPA *101, Life Safety Code*.

10-3.2.3 Exit access doors from laboratories shall meet the requirements of NFPA *101, Life Safety Code*.

10-3.2.4 Laboratory corridors constituting access to an exit shall meet the requirements of NFPA *101, Life Safety Code*. Corridors shall be maintained clear and unobstructed at all times.

Prior editions of laboratory requirements contained corridor width requirements in excess of those contained in NFPA *101, Life Safety Code*. This was not a conflict; it just meant former NFPA 56C (and then NFPA 99) requirements were more restrictive. With this new (1987) edition of NFPA 99, the Subcommittee on Laboratories (responsible for Chapter 10) is deferring all corridor requirements to NFPA *101* (sentence one). It should be noted that the width of corridors that constitute access to an exit will vary depending on the occupancy classification of a laboratory (e.g., *business/industrial* if properly separated from the rest of a health care facility; *health care* if not separated). If the laboratory will be used by patients on litters or beds, then the requirement of 10-3.2.5 takes precedence.

Sentence two is a result of experience that, while a corridor can be built to NFPA *101* criteria, the maintainance of the width of corridors may be narrowed by the placement of objects in the corridors (e.g., water coolers, boxes, chairs, "temporary" equipment).

10-3.2.5 Laboratory corridors, used for the transporting of patients in beds or litters, and constituting access to an exit, shall be not less than 96 in. (243.8 cm) in clear and unobstructed width.

This section was added in 1980 to take into consideration those laboratory corridors (or portions therein) through which patients in beds or litters might be wheeled *and* which constitute an access to an exit. This section applies only to laboratories performing in vivo procedures requiring patients to be transported into the laboratory for the test or procedure. This requirement, it should be noted, is applicable only to new construction.

The 96-in. value takes into consideration the need to be able to turn a bed around in the corridor, and for beds to be able to pass each other. This is the same value as in NFPA *101, Life Safety Code*, for patient areas in new health care occupancies.

10-3.3 Exhaust Air.   Exhaust air shall conform to 5-3.1.

10-3.4 Ventilation.   Ventilation shall conform to 5-4.4.

10-3.5 Fume Hoods.   Fume hoods shall conform to 5-4.4 and 5-6.2.

10-4 Equipment.

For general safety requirements for electrical appliances used in laboratories, see Chapter 7.

10-4.1 Equipment Employing Liquids.

10-4.1.1 Tissue processors and similar automatic equipment employing flammable or combustible reagents shall be operated at least 5 ft (1.52 m) from the storage of combustible materials, unless separated by one-hour fire-resistive construction.

Appendix C-10-1 describes a tissue processor fire, fueled by combustible reagents in glass containers stored below the processor. The intent of this section (10-4.1.1) is to isolate equipment capable of igniting such reagents during unattended periods of operation. Although a safety cabinet less than 5 ft away could satisfy the 1-hour construction requirement, great care should be exercised in the location of combustible reagent storage near equipment intended to be operated in an unattended mode.

10-4.1.2* Unattended laboratory operations employing flammable or combustible reagents shall be conducted in an area equipped with an automatic fire extinguishing system.

A-10-4.1.2 One method of safeguarding unattended processes is to place the equipment in a pan large enough to contain any spilled materials, preferably within a fume hood protected by some form of automatic fire extinguishment or detection.

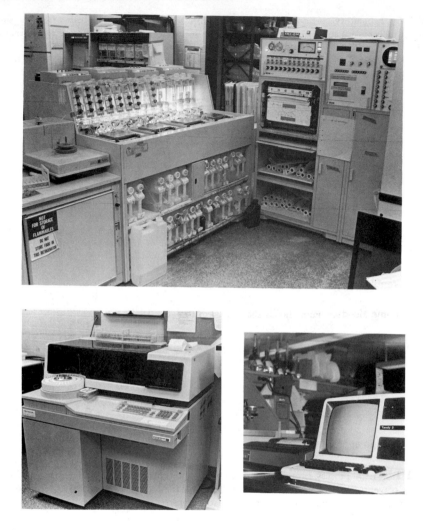

Figure 31   Equipment of all kinds, including computers, is now found in many laboratories.

Paragraph 10-2.2.1.3 is the general requirement for unattended operation and automatic laboratory equipment. This paragraph (10-4.1.2) is specifically for those unattended operations or equipment that employ flammable or combustible reagents. It was revised based on Committee knowledge of actual fires involving unattended experiments where no automatic fire protection was present.

Routine operations performed by tissue processors, solvent recovery stills, and other automated equipment, increase the possibility of fire due to the repetitive nature of the process and the casual attitude some personnel may adopt after setting up routine operations. The Committee believes special attention must be directed toward the design and installation of the automatic fire detection and extinguishing equipment specifically intended for such unattended operation.

When a sprinkler system is used for automatic fire extinguishment, one such design consideration is the elimination of the possibility of an accidental discharge. (Laboratory occupancies in health care facilities often contain very expensive equipment that could be destroyed and/or become extremely hazardous if exposed to an accidental discharge from a sprinkler system.) This is accomplished by a system called a "pre-action" system and is defined in NFPA 13, *Standard for the Installation of Sprinkler Systems*, as "a system employing automatic sprinklers attached to a piping system containing 'air' that may or may not be under pressure, with a supplemental fire detection system installed in the same areas as the sprinklers; actuation of the fire detection system, as from a fire, opens a valve, permitting water to flow into the sprinkler piping system and to be discharged from any sprinklers that may be open." Thus, no water need be within the sprinkler stationed over special equipment. It is only when the fire detection system senses a fire, heat, etc., that water is released into the sprinkler piping system.

10-5* Fire Protection.

A-10-5 Fire Protection. Examination of laboratory fire records demonstrates the extra vulnerability of premises with substantial amounts of combustible contents. The use of noncombustible shelving, benches, and furniture will reduce production of smoke and damage to facilities and with substantial savings where expensive laboratory equipment is present, even in sprinklered areas.

Self-contained breathing apparatus should be considered for equipping personnel for rescue operations in areas with special fire hazards. Training is required for effective use of such equipment. It is desirable to coordinate equipment and training with local fire department personnel.

10-5.1* Automatic fire extinguishing protection shall be provided in all laboratories, including associated storage rooms, when:

10-5.1.1 Laboratories are not separated from surrounding areas by at least one-hour fire-resistive construction with door openings protected by Class C self-closing fire doors, and employ quantities of flammable, combustible, or hazardous materials less than that which would be considered severe.

10-5.1.2 Laboratories are not separated from surrounding areas by at least two-hour fire-resistive construction with door openings protected by Class B self-closing doors, and employ quantities of flammable, combustible, or hazardous materials considered severe.

NOTE: Where there is a critical need to protect data in process, reduce equipment damage, and facilitate return to service, considerations should be given to the use of Halon 1301 total flooding systems in sprinklered or unsprinklered computer rooms. Chapter 5 of NFPA 75, *Standard for the Protection of Electronic Computer/Data Processing Equipment*, provides general information on the protection of computer room equipment.

A-10-5.1 The hazard level of a laboratory is considered severe if quantities of flammable, combustible, or hazardous materials are present that are capable of sustaining a fire condition of sufficient magnitude to breach a one-hour fire separation.

To determine the combustible content or heat potential of flammable or combustible materials capable of breaching or penetrating a one-hour-rated fire separation, one method is included in the 14th edition of the NFPA *Fire Protection Handbook*, where formulas and tables for calculating the equivalence of time versus fire severity are given. Specific reference is made to Section 6, Chapter 8, "Confinement of Fire and Smoke in Buildings" and Table 6-8A. Heat of combustion

(Btu/lb) for materials common to laboratories can be found in Section 3, Chapter 11, "Fire Hazard of Materials — Tables and Charts" of the *Handbook*. Specific reference is made to Table 3-11B, Table 3-11G, Table 3-11H, and Table 3-11L.[1]

NOTE: The weights of combustible contents in Table 6-8A are those of ordinary combustible materials taken at 8000 Btu/lb. For converting other than ordinary combustibles to pounds per square foot (psf), divide the total Btu value by 8000/Btu/lb.

The above, it should be noted, is only one of several methods for calculating the hazard level of a laboratory with regard to combustibles breaching a one-hour fire separation.

The following chart can be used as a guide in making the above determination:

| Wall Rating | Hazard | |
	Not Severe	Severe
Less than 1-Hour	Automatic fire extinguishing system required.	Not allowed.
1-Hour	No automatic fire extinguishing system required.	Automatic fire extinguishing system required.
2-Hour	No automatic fire extinguishing system required.	No automatic fire extinguishing system required.

Requirements for automatic fire extinguishing protection were substantially revised for the 1980 edition of NFPA 56C. Instead of requiring their installation in all laboratories, several criteria were listed as to when such systems were required. Here, separation and quantity/severity of materials is concerned. However, the subject of automatic fire extinguishing protection strictly with respect to *separation requirements* can be found in 10-3.1.1 (see commentary on 10-3.1.1 for further information).

In 1980, while the above requirements were being proposed, arguments were submitted suggesting that an appropriate number of portable extinguishers were adequate for fire protection instead of an automatic extinguishing system. The Committee pointed out that laboratories are not always staffed, and that an automatic system was required only when the fuel load was anticipated to exceed the fire rating of the enclosure.

To help determine how severity can be calculated, the Committee (in 1980) included in the Appendix one method, as shown above, that could be used for making the calculation.

The chart in A-10-5.1 was added in 1984 as a result of some confusion about the requirements of 10-5.1. It was the intent of the Committee that laboratories employing hazardous material less than severe, and not separated by a 1-hour rated wall, have an automatic fire extinguishing system.

The Note below 10-5.1.2 was also added in 1984 to call attention to the fact that there are types of extinguishment systems other than water, and that they should be reviewed for use in such areas as computer rooms (which may or may not be sprinklered) where equipment sensitive to water is used.

---

[1] In 16th edition of the *NFPA Fire Protection Handbook*, see Section 7, Chapter 9, Table 7-9A; and Section 5, Chapter 11, respectively.

10-5.2 Automatic fire extinguishment and fire detection systems, when required, shall be connected to the facility fire alarm system and shall be arranged to immediately sound an alarm.

This paragraph would be applicable only if an automatic fire detection or extinguishing system were installed.

If a laboratory met one of the criteria in 10-5.1 above, no connection to a facility fire alarm system would be necessary, since there would be no extinguishing system.

10-5.3 Fire extinguishers suitable for the particular hazards shall be located so that they will be readily available to personnel in accordance with NFPA 10, *Standard for Portable Fire Extinguishers*.

Beyond the selection, distribution, inspection, maintenance, and recharging of portable fire extinguishers as specified in NFPA 10, *Standard for Portable Fire Extinguishers*, Section 31-4 of NFPA *101*, *Life Safety Code*, sets forth operational plans and staff responsibilities in a fire emergency. It includes provisions within the fire plan for fire extinguishment. This familiarity with extinguishing characteristics, and the location, operation, and use of fire extinguishers, should be incorporated into new employee orientation, periodic retraining, and drills or rehearsals.

Considerations such as minimizing damage to equipment and/or specimens, records, etc., contained therein may warrant the installation of halon or other alternatives to water extinguishing systems.

10-6* Emergency Shower. Where the eyes or body of any person may be exposed to injurious corrosive materials, suitable fixed facilities for quick drenching or flushing of the eyes and body shall be provided within the work area for immediate emergency use. Fixed eye baths shall be designed and installed to avoid injurious water pressure.

If shutoff valves or stops are installed in the branch line leading to safety drenching equipment, the valves shall be OS and Y (outside stem and yoke), labeled for identification, and sealed in the open position. The installation of wall-mounted portable eye-wash stations shall not preclude the adherence to the provisions of this section.

A-10-6 Protective Devices. Showers should be controlled by a nonautomatic shutoff device. Although a self-closing shower valve (favored by most designers) would minimize flooding of the building if, for example, maliciously activated, it does not afford maximum help to the injured user. Since a person would have to use one hand to keep the valve open, efforts to remove clothing or wipe away offending materials would be greatly hampered.

Although emergency showers are rarely used, their use when necessary can mean the difference between superficial burns and serious disfigurement, or loss of life. In some cases where such showers have not been activated for long periods, they have been found inoperative. It is essential that emergency showers be provided and tested from time to time to determine that their valves are in good operating condition. Advance planning must be made to handle the water that will flow in a test.

Floor drains are not recommended for hospital areas because traps tend to dry out and permit passage of gases, vermin, and odors.

Another consideration is to be sure that all holes in floor slabs that have not been sealed around pipes to prevent the passage of smoke, be so sealed, and in a manner that will prevent water from flowing to lower floors from the discharge of an emergency shower or sprinkler head.

Wall-mounted portable eye wash stations do not contain an adequate supply of water for the 15-minute flushing recommended by chemical manufacturers.

Shower heads on flexible water lines at sink locations may be useful for eye flush and skin or clothing spills. (*See 10-8.1.4 for maintenance procedures.*)

Shutoff valves for showers allow repair, replacement, testing, etc., without necessitating the shutdown of an entire sprinkler system.

10-7 Flammable and Combustible Liquids.

The material in this section was revised in coordination with NFPA 30, *Flammable and Combustible Liquids Code*, which contains general requirements for such liquids. Unless otherwise noted, the term "liquids" in Section 10-7 refers to flammable or combustible liquids.

10-7.1 General.

10-7.1.1 Flammable and combustible liquids shall be handled and used with care and with knowledge of their hazardous properties, both individually and in combination with other materials with which they can come in contact. (*See references in Chapter 20 and Appendix B.*)

10-7.2* Storage and Use.

A-10-7.2 Flammable Liquids. Plastic containers are sometimes used to avoid breakage problems posed by glass containers or contamination problems with metal containers. Plastic containers must be chosen with particular attention to their compatibility with the liquid to be contained. For example, polyethylene containers are generally unsuitable for aldehydes, ketones, esters, higher molecular-weight alcohols, benzene, toluene, various oils, silicone fluids, and halogenated hydrocarbons. In addition to labeling containers for identification of contents, it is important to label plastic containers for identification of their constituent materials to avoid misuse.

In some cases, listed or labeled stainless steel or tin-lined safety containers offer a solution to contamination problems.

10-7.2.1* Flammable or combustible liquids shall be used from and stored in approved containers, in accordance with NFPA 30, *Flammable and Combustible Liquids Code*.

A-10-7.2.1† Table A-10-7.2.1 is a portion of Table 4-2.3 in NFPA 30, *Flammable and Combustible Liquids Code*.

Table A-10-7.2.1 Maximum Allowable Size of Containers and Portable Tanks.

Container Type	Flammable Liquids			Combustible Liquids	
	Class IA	Class IB	Class IC	Class II	Class III
Glass	1 pt	1 qt	1 gal	1 gal	5 gal
Metal (other than DOT drums) or approved plastic	1 gal	5 gal	5 gal	5 gal	5 gal
Safety Cans	2 gal	5 gal	5 gal	5 gal	5 gal

For SI Units: 1 pt = 0.49 L; 1 qt = 0.95 L; 1 gal = 3.8 L.

To determine the maximum size container for a flammable or combustible liquid, the liquid's hazard classification needs to be known. This can be done by first reviewing NFPA 325M, *Fire Hazard Properties of Flammable Liquids, Gases and*

Figure 32(a) metal type.   Figure 32(b) nonmetallic type.

Figure 32   Typical laboratory safety cans. Cutaway views show flame arrestors.
(Courtesy Justrite Corp., Chicago, IL)

Volatile Solids. Then, Table 4-2.3 in NFPA 30, *Flammable and Combustible Liquids Code*, can be checked for maximum allowed size.´

10-7.2.2*   Established laboratory practices shall limit working supplies of flammable or combustible liquids. The total capacity of flammable or combustible liquids outside of approved storage cabinets shall not exceed 10 gal (37.85 L) per 5000 sq ft (464.4 sq m). The total capacity of all approved storage cabinets in a laboratory shall not exceed 60 gal (227.1 L) per 5000 sq ft (464.4 sq m). No flammable or combustible liquids shall be stored or transferred from one vessel to another in any exit corridor or passageway leading to an exit. At least one approved flammable or combustible liquid storage room shall be available within any health care facility regularly maintaining a reserve storage capacity in excess of 300 gal (1135.5 L). Quantities of flammable and combustible liquids for disposal shall be included in the total inventory.

A-10-7.2.2   Constant effort must be exerted to prevent the overstocking of hazardous chemicals. The laboratory chief can help keep stocks at a safe level by encouraging small and more frequent requisitions, by developing a reliable stock inventory system, by assuring convenient and prompt deliveries from the central stock room, by selecting brands that are the most popular and not necessarily the cheapest, and by discouraging (except perhaps for large-scale research-type projects) the practice of purchasing the largest containers, including bulk supplies in 55 gal (208.2 L) drums.

This section (10-7.2.2) was extensively revised in 1980 to clarify how much flammable or combustible liquid was permitted outside of storage cabinets per 5000 sq ft of laboratory area, and how much could be stored in a laboratory per

5000 sq. ft. Also, the last sentence (on flammable or combustible liquids still within the laboratory but destined for disposal since they still present the same level of hazard as liquids that will be used) was added.

Depending on the quantity and type, chemicals within a laboratory — and particularly flammable liquids — can constitute a serious fire hazard. Serious consideration should be given to the quantities and reactive qualities of chemicals stored in a laboratory. A systematic review of chemical inventory by qualified laboratory personnel can aid in providing the most appropriate (safe) level of flammable storage within the laboratory.

Approved storage cabinets are described in NFPA 30, *Flammable and Combustible Liquids Code*. Approved cabinets can be of either metal or wood, as long as the materials and construction techniques appropriate for each are followed. One advantage of wooden cabinets is that they often can be constructed locally or in-house, and custom designed to fit into the space available, as opposed to trying to locate a manufactured cabinet to fit the desired space.

A Formal Interpretation (99-84-1) was issued in 1984 on the subject of the 10-gallon value (outside of storage) and the size of the laboratory. (Did a laboratory smaller than 5000 sq ft have a proportionately lower gallon limit?)

The former Technical Committee on Laboratories in Health Care Facilities (now Subcommittee on Laboratories) reviewed the matter and noted that it was their intent that the 10-gallon limit be applied to *any* laboratory up to 5000 sq ft (i.e., there was *no* proportioning just because a laboratory was smaller). Some procedures required considerable flammable liquids to be on hand. Thus, the amount (10 gal) was not directly related to the size of the laboratory.

It should be kept in mind, however, that this 10-gal/5000-sq-ft limit outside of approved storage cabinets is a maximum, and that laboratories should have only the minimum amount necessary for efficient laboratory operation.

10-7.2.3 Venting of storage cabinets shall be permitted. Storage cabinets with approved flame arresters shall be permitted to be exhausted through a fume hood exhaust system. Construction of the venting duct within the laboratory shall be equal to the rating of the cabinet.

The venting criteria were added so that those laboratories that chose to vent would have safety guidelines. It should be noted, however, that venting is optional.

The reasons for venting include preventing the building of positive pressure within cabinets and reducing the accumulation of fumes that pose a fire hazard.

10-7.2.4 Flammable or combustible liquids shall not be positioned near Bunsen burners, ovens, hot pipes and valves or other sources of heat, in corridors, or within exhaust canopies.

10-7.2.5* Class I flammable or combustible liquids shall not be stored in refrigerators. Storage of other combustible liquids in well-sealed containers is permissible in listed flammable I, Division 1, Groups C and D. The outside of doors to refrigerators shall be labeled to denote whether or not they are acceptable for storage of flammable or combustible liquids. If the refrigerator is not listed for the purpose, the warning shall be worded to prohibit all storage of flammable or combustible liquids.

The subject of the storage of flammable and combustible liquids in refrigerators has been debated considerably in recent years. The current position of the

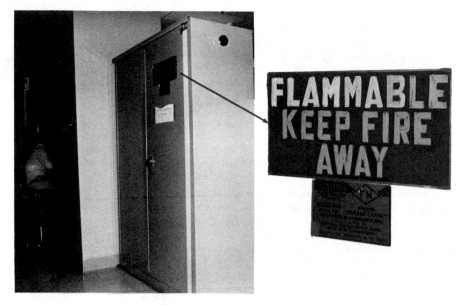

Figure 33   Storage cabinet with cap on side for venting.

Committee responsible for this chapter is that there are hazards associated with the storage of Class I flammable and combustible liquids in any type of refrigerator. Other adequate means for storage of such liquids exist, as noted in 10-7.2.1 and 10-7.2.3.

Previously, modification of clinical lab refrigerators by health care personnel was tacitly condoned; this is no longer the situation. For refrigerators storing flammable material, the Committee changed "approved" to "listed" to indicate its intent that such refrigerators are to be tested and listed by an organization acceptable to the authority having jurisdiction.

A-10-7.2.5 Walk-In Thermal-Controlled Boxes.   Procedures likely to result in toxic or flammable atmospheres should be discouraged within "walk-in" refrigerators or other types of temperature-controlled boxes. A warning sign such as the one indicated here should be posted on every box.

DANGER
NOT EXPLOSIONPROOF
NOT VENTILATED

GROUND ALL ELECTRICAL
EQUIPMENT

DO NOT STORE DRY ICE
DO NOT SMOKE

New boxes should include at least the following features: a latch that can be released by a person inside the box when the door is locked from the outside; latch and door frames designed to allow actuation under all conditions of freezing; a floor with a nonconductive surface; neoprene matting to insulate up to 10,000 volts; a view-window in the door; an independently circuited high-temperature thermostat and alarm (for warm boxes); vaporproof duplex electrical receptacles; an alarm that can be heard throughout the occupied work area and an alarm button at the inside door frame that will keep operating after actuation; conduits sealed (in cold boxes) in a manner to prevent accumulation of water vapor such as in the globe protectors of the light fixtures; and adjustable exhaust vent and air intake of at least 15 CFM for general ventilation, with provisions for installing a flexible hose and miniature canopy in a manner to provide local ventilation at a specific work site. As explosionproof laboratory apparatus becomes available, it should be substituted for less safe equipment used in enclosed thermal-control boxes.

Non-Walk-in Refrigerators. The use of domestic refrigerators for the storage of typical laboratory solvents presents a significant hazard to the laboratory work area. Refrigerator temperatures are almost universally higher than the flash points of the flammable liquids most often stored in them. In addition to vapor accumulation, a domestic refrigerator contains readily available ignition sources, such as thermostats, light switches, and heater strips, all within or exposing the refrigerated storage compartment. Furthermore, the compressor and its circuits are typically located at the bottom of the unit, where vapors from flammable liquid spills or leaks may easily accumulate.

Explosionproof refrigeration equipment is designed to protect against ignition of flammable vapors both inside and outside the refrigerated storage compartment. This type is intended and recommended for environments such as pilot plants or laboratory work areas where all electrical equipment is required to be explosionproof.

The design concepts of the flammable material storage refrigerators are based on the typical laboratory environment. The primary intent is to eliminate ignition of vapors inside the storage compartment from sources also within the compartment. In addition, flammable material storage refrigerators incorporate such design features as thresholds, self-closing latch doors, friction latches or magnetic door gaskets, and special methods for the inner shell. All of these features are intended to control or limit the loss potential should an exothermic reaction occur within the storage compartment. Finally, the compressor and its circuits and controls are often located at the top of the unit to further reduce the potential for ignition of floor-level vapors. In general, the design features of a commercially available flammable material storage refrigerator are such that they provide several safeguards not available through modification of domestic models.

Every laboratory refrigerator should be clearly labeled to indicate whether or not it is acceptable for storage of flammable materials. Internal laboratory procedures should ensure that laboratory refrigerators are being properly used. The following are examples of labels that can be used on laboratory refrigerators:

DO NOT STORE FLAMMABLE SOLVENTS
in this refrigerator

NOTICE

This is not an "explosionproof" refrigerator, but it has been designed to permit storage of materials producing flammable vapors. Containers should be well-stoppered or tightly closed.

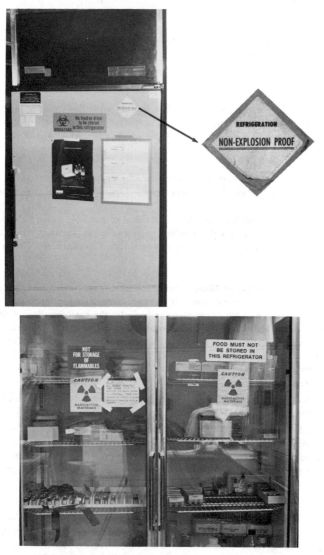

Figure 34   Labels on refrigerators used in laboratories.

10-7.3 Transfer of Flammable or Combustible Liquids.   Transfer from bulk stock containers to smaller containers shall be made in storage rooms as described in NFPA 30, *Flammableand-Combustible Liquids Code,* or within a fume hood having a face velocity of at least 100 ft (30.5 m) per minute.

10-7.4 Handling of Flammable and Combustible Liquids.

Procedures and policies for handling flammable and combustible liquids must be incorporated into laboratory procedures. They must also be monitored to assure that they are being carried out. General requirements for policies, procedures, and training are contained in 10-2.2.4.

Paragraph 10-7.4.1 is a refinement of previous guidelines on heating flammable and combustible liquids, using the flash point as the hazard criterion. This means that laboratories have to know the flash point of the type of liquid they are using. Paragraph 10-7.4.2 is a reaffirmation of the prohibition of open flames when heating any flammable or combustible liquid.

10-7.4.1 Flammable liquids and combustible liquids with flash points lower than 200°F (93.3°C) (Class I, II, and IIIA liquids) shall be heated in hoods or with special local exhaust ventilation if the quantities exceed 10 ml, or if the liquid is heated to within 30° (16.6°) of the flash point of the liquid.

10-7.4.2 Flammable or combustible liquids shall be heated with hot water, steam, or an electric mantle, depending upon their boiling points. Open flames shall not be employed.

10-7.5* Disposal of Hazardous Materials. Disposal of hazardous materials shall be accomplished off the premises by a disposal specialist, or at a safe location away from the health care facility by competent personnel using procedures established in concurrence with the authority having jurisdiction.

A-10-7.5 Disposal of Hazardous Materials. Because disposal techniques for various hazardous materials produced in hospital research involve complicated problems, they cannot be adequately discussed herein. Such materials may include: the toxic product of mixing sodium cyanide and acids in the drain system; nuisance or alarming odors such as produced by mercaptans or lutidine; violently water-reactive solids or liquids like phosphoric anhydride and thionyl chloride; potential explosives like picric acid; strong oxidizers like perchloric acid; and radioactive, pathogenic, corrosive, or potentially harmful wastes, such as television picture tubes, syringes, and aerosol cans.

Many chemicals can be disposed of at the bench through the ingenuity of the chemist, such as the reacting of small quantities of potassium with tertiary butyl alcohol.

Flammable and combustible liquids that are miscible with water in all proportions may be flushed down a drain within a laboratory room in quantities not exceeding one pint (0.45 L), thoroughly mixed with at least 3 gal (11.4 L) of cold water. This precaution for minimizing flammable vapor concentrations in building drains may not be acceptable to pollution-control authorities.

Vaporization should not be used for routine disposal of liquids.

Drain lines and traps from laboratory benches, safety showers, hood floors, mechanical equipment rooms, storage rooms, etc. should have water added at regular intervals to assure that traps will not be the source of flammable or toxic vapor release. Where self-priming traps are provided, an annual inspection for proper operation should be made. Addition of mineral oil or similar liquids is sometimes used to reduce evaporation of water from traps.

Previous changes made by the then Committee on Laboratories were for the purpose of clarification: disposal is possible by any disposal specialist or by whatever procedures are acceptable to the authority having jurisdiction.

10-8* Maintenance and Inspection.

A-10-8 Maintenance and Inspection. Detailed specifications for the contents of manuals intended to describe the installation, operation, and maintenance of medical equipment are established in a standard developed by the National Committee for Clinical Laboratory Standards

(ASI-1, *Preparation of Manuals for Installation, Operation and Repair of Laboratory Instruments*). *(See Appendix B.)* Whenever such manuals accompany new equipment, they should be carefully preserved and consulted for guidance in all phases of the setting up and safe operation of the equipment.

10-8.1 Procedures.

The laboratory safety program should be part of, and coordinated with, the facility-wide safety program. Preventive maintenance programs and electrical safety tests and inspections should also encompass appropriate laboratory items.

10-8.1.1 For adequate laboratory safety, careful maintenance and watchfulness are imperative.

10-8.1.2 A safety officer shall be appointed to supervise safe practices in the laboratory. Responsibilities shall include ensuring that the equipment and preparation for fire fighting are appropriate for the special fire hazards present. These responsibilities shall be in addition to surveillance of hazards attendant to caustics, corrosives, compressed gases, electrical installations, and other hazards indigenous to laboratories in health care facilities. This individual shall also supervise the periodic education of laboratory personnel, including new employee orientation, in the nature of combustible and flammable liquids and gases, first-aid fire fighting, and the use of protective equipment, and shall review unsafe conditions observed or reported.

NOTE: This individual may be the safety officer for the health care facility or may be a specifically designated laboratory safety officer.

The Committee broadened the responsibilities for the laboratory safety officer because it believes all hazards associated with clinical laboratories and their functioning should be under the purview of the laboratory safety officer. The Note is to ensure that the best qualified individual is appointed.

10-8.1.3 Regular rounds of the health care facility laboratory shall be made by a member of the security force or another designated individual whenever the laboratory is unattended, but particularly and especially in the hours immediately following the departure of the laboratory staff for the night. The laboratory safety officer shall inform the security force of those areas and items of equipment of a hazardous nature requiring special surveillance.

These requirements are to help ensure that the persons who make inspection and rounds of laboratories, particularly when unattended operations are involved, are made aware of particular hazards so that they can identify problems early.

10-8.1.4* Operations and equipment related to safe operations and practices, including such items as ventilating provisions; fire protection apparatus; periodical flushing of sinks; emergency showers and eye-wash units; shelf stocks and storage of flammable and combustible materials; and caustic and corrosive liquids shall be reviewed at appropriate, regular intervals. A system of prompt reporting of defective equipment and its prompt repair shall be instituted, and periodic inspections shall be made of all electrical and gas equipment. The laboratory safety officer shall prepare and supervise the proper completion of a safety checklist that can be preserved for record.

A-10-8.1.4 Regulations should be adopted for routine housekeeping and laboratory cleanup practices.

The laboratory safety officer should make periodic inspections of the laboratory premises to determine that electric cords in use are of adequate conductor size with safe insulation and that circuits are not overloaded through the use of multiple taps.

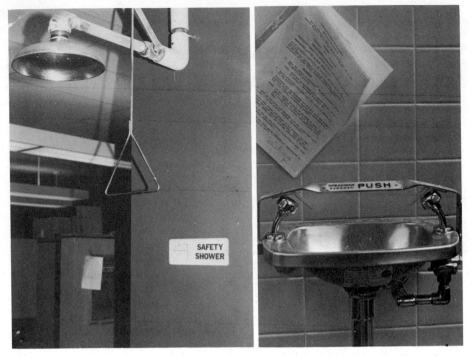

Figure 35(a) A safety shower in a laboratory.   Figure 35(b). Eyewashes in a laboratory. (Note labeling.)

Several good laboratory safety checklists are available, such as the one developed by the College of American Pathologists Inspection and Accreditation Program (*see Appendix B*). The laboratory safety officer may wish to augment or modify one of these for his own facility.

The list should not be considered exhaustive. Sources that may know of other checklists include the National Committee for Clinical Laboratory Standards and the Joint Commission on Accreditation of Hospitals.

Hazards peculiar to each laboratory should be evaluated to determine frequency of inspection.

10-8.1.5 Periodic safety inspection shall include the testing of all emergency showers, eye baths, and other emergency equipment.

Periodic safety inspections can be conducted by the laboratory safety officer or incorporated into other safety programs.

10-8.1.6* A system for disposing of hazardous chemicals and combustible trash shall be established and regularly maintained. Disposal of chemical wastes shall be in accordance with good safety practices and environmental standards.

A-10-8.1.6 Information sources for safe handling and disposal of hazardous chemicals include NFPA 49, *Hazardous Chemicals Data*. The guidance of a technically qualified person is recommended for the disposal of hazardous chemicals.

The reference to environmental standards reflects the Committee's concern for safety and environmental protection when disposing of hazardous chemicals.

10-8.2 Identification of Hazards.

10-8.2.1 All doors leading to laboratories in health-related facilities shall be marked with the emblem described in NFPA 704, *Standard System for the Identification of Fire Hazards of Materials*, to indicate the fire hazards of materials intended to be used within this area.

Figure 36 Sign posted outside a laboratory warning of the various types of gases in cylinders found in the laboratory.

Figure 37 The "704" Diamond.

1. Numbers range from 0 to 4, with 4 being the *most* hazardous (e.g., a "4" in flammability box means extremely flammable; a "0" in flammability box means "will not burn."

2. Several color arrangements are allowed:
   a) Background of each square is the colored listed, and numbers are some contrasting color (e.g., black, white)
   b) Backround is white, and color of numbers correspond to color assigned for hazard

3. Any "special hazards" are indicated by the use of a symbol, e.g.,

 means "avoid the use of water" because of an unusual reactivity to water.

 means materials possess oxidizing properties.

 means materials possess radioactivity hazards.

4. Review of laboratory contents needs to be conducted on periodic basis or when changes in functions in laboratory result in changes in contents stored in laboratory.

5. The "704" diamond is used and recognized by many fire service personnel.
   The Subcommittee on Laboratories has retained the reference to NFPA 704, *Standard on Identification of the Fire Hazards of Materials*, because of this widespread recognition of the standard by fire service personnel.
   Any major changes in the types or quantity of flammable or biohazard level of material should be brought to the attention of the laboratory safety officer so that the 704 diamond can be updated.

10-8.2.2 It shall be the responsibility of the laboratory safety officer to assure periodically that the emblem properly indicates the nature of the materials being used within the identified space.

Other laboratory staff are urged to become familiar with this ID system as well.

10-8.2.3 It shall be the duty of the senior person responsible for activities in respective laboratory areas to inform the laboratory safety officer of changes in protocol and procedures that involve variations in the fire hazards of materials used in individual spaces.

Close coordination must occur between laboratory personnel and facility-wide disaster planners to assure that hazards related to laboratories are identified and properly addressed in the facility's disaster plans. (*See also Annex 1, Health Care Emergency Preparedness.*)

10-9 Transfer of Gases.

10-9.1 Transfer of gaseous oxygen shall be in accordance with 4-6.2.1.5(b).

For background on this allowance, see commentary on 4-6.2.1.5(b).

10-9.2 Transfer of all other gases from one cylinder to another within the laboratory shall be prohibited.

10-9.3 Transfer of liquid oxygen shall be in accordance with 4-6.2.1.6(a).

11 (Reserved)

12

HOSPITAL REQUIREMENTS

Prologue

As noted in Chapter 1, this Chapter (12) lists requirements from Chapters 1 to 11 that are applicable for *hospitals*. [Similarly, Chapters 13 to 18 list requirements for their respective facilities]. The definition of "hospital," and thus the types of hospitals for which this chapter is applicable, is given in Chapter 2.

The subcommittee of the Technical Committee on Health Care Facilities that devised the new structure for NFPA 99 considered this listing of requirements for each type of health care facility to be the best method, given the many different users of NFPA 99. [Several other matrixes (or methods) were considered, but rejected, by the subcommittee]. Users generally know the type of facility for which they are interested in finding requirements. Thus, with this new structure, a reader can first turn to the "facility" chapter (12 to 18) to learn the requirements from Chapters 1 to 11 that are applicable to the facility under review. The reader can then review the specific paragraph(s) cited and study the requirements listed.

12-1 Scope.   This chapter addresses safety requirements of hospitals.

12-2 General Responsibilities.

12-2.1   As used in this chapter, the term *hospital* (except where it obviously refers to the physical structure) shall mean the entity and that portion of its internal governing structure that has the responsibility for the elements of hospital operation covered by this chapter, including building design, purchasing specifications, inspection procedures, maintenance schedules, and training programs affecting such use.

12-2.2   It is understood that the individuals who are responsible will vary from one hospital to another, although in most cases the hospital's administration exercises the concomitant authority. It is further recognized that fulfillment of this responsibility frequently occurs by means of delegating appropriate authority to staff, consultants, architects, engineers, and others.

12-2.3   To achieve the performance criteria of Chapters 1 through 11 the governing body of the hospital shall be permitted to assign responsibility to appropriate hospital personnel, consultants, architects, engineers, or others.

12-2.4   The hospital shall ensure that policies are established and maintained that permit the attending physician to satisfy the emergency needs of any patient that may supersede the requirements of this chapter. Each such special use shall be clearly documented and reviewed to attempt to have future similar needs met within the requirements of this chapter.

12-2.5 Electricity. It shall be the responsibility of the hospital to provide an environment that is reasonably safe from the shock and burn hazards attendant with the use of electricity in patient care areas.

The hospital shall establish policies and procedures related to the safe use of electric appliances.

Each hospital shall be permitted to select a specific electrical safety program that is appropriate to its particular needs.

The physical protection afforded by the installation of an electrical distribution system that meets the requirements of this chapter and the purchase of properly constructed and tested appliances shall be augmented by having designated departments of the facility assume responsibility for the continued functioning of the electrical distribution system (Chapter 3) and the inspection, testing, and maintenance of electrical appliances (Chapter 7).

The hospital shall adopt regulations and practices concerning the use of electric appliances, and shall establish programs for the training of physicians, nurses, and other personnel who may be involved in the procurement, application, use, inspection, testing, and maintenance of electrical appliances for the care of patients.

12-2.6 Patient Care Areas. Areas of a hospital in which patient care is administered are classified as general care areas, critical care areas, and wet locations. The governing body of the facility shall designate these areas in accordance with the type of patient care anticipated, and with the following definitions of the three types of areas. (*See definition of patient care area in Chapter 2.*)

Patient care areas have been grouped into three types because it would be inappropriate to have one set of electrical safety requirements for all areas. Patients in the different areas may be at different levels of electrical risk. Thus, differing requirements have been developed.

It is important to note that the governing body of the facility is responsible for the designation of these areas. This can and should be done in consultation with medical staff, engineering staff, etc., taking into consideration the conditions and practices taking place in the facility. While this imposes a responsibility on the facility, it also provides a safeguard because it is considered better to have facilities themselves make the designations than it is to have external agencies impose the designations.

Variations in assignments within facilities can be expected since a surgical recovery rooms will be far different from dental-operating recovery rooms.

These three terms (general care area, critical care area, and wet location) appear in Chapter 12 because they were developed for NFPA 76B which applied only to hospitals. In this 1987 edition of NFPA 99, the term "patient care area" was seen as needing a definition since the text above only stated the categories into which patient care areas should be classified; the "area" itself was not defined. Thus, the term "patient care area" is now found in Chapter 2, "Definitions." Also for this edition, the definition of "wet location" was considered sufficiently generic to warrant applicability throughout the document (i.e. in all types of health care facilities). Thus, this last term is also now included in Chapter 2.

(a) General care areas are patient bedrooms, examining rooms, treatment rooms, clinics, and similar areas in which it is intended that the patient shall come in contact with ordinary appliances such as a nurse-call system, electric beds, examining lamps, telephones, and entertainment devices. In such areas, it may also be intended that patients be connected to electromedical devices (such as heating pads, electrocardiographs, drainage pumps, monitors, otoscopes, ophthalmoscopes, intravenous lines, etc.). (Class G)

(b) Critical care areas are those special care units, intensive care units, coronary care units, angiography laboratories, cardiac catheterization laboratories, delivery rooms, operating rooms, and similar areas in which patients are intended to be subjected to invasive procedures and connected to line-operated, electromedical devices. (Class H)

NOTE: Inhalation anesthetizing locations shall be classified in accordance with Section 12-4.1, "Anesthetizing Locations."

(c) Wet locations are those patient care areas that are normally subject to wet conditions, including standing water on the floor, or routine dousing or drenching of the work area. Routine housekeeping procedures and incidental spillage of liquids do not define a wet location. (Class W)

See commentary in Chapter 2, "Definitions," under "wet location" for explanation of term.

Electrical requirements for wet locations are listed in 3-4.1.2.6. Further commentary on wet locations and anesthetizing locations is included under 12-4.1.2.6(a).

12-2.7 Anesthesia. It shall be the responsibility of the governing body of the hospital to designate anesthetizing locations.

12-2.8 Laboratories. The governing boards of hospitals shall have the responsibility of protecting the facilities (for patient care and clinical investigation) and the personnel employed therein.

12-3 General Requirements.

12-3.1 (Reserved)

12-3.2 (Reserved)

12-3.3 Electrical System Requirements.

12-3.3.1 The normal electrical distribution system for patient care areas shall conform to the requirements in Chapter 3, "Electrical Systems."

These requirements apply to new construction. Existing installations need not be modified, provided that they meet the operational safety requirements in 3-5.2.1 through 3-5.2.3.

12-3.3.2 The essential electrical distribution system shall conform to a Type I system, as described in Chapter 3, "Electrical Systems."

12-3.4 Gas and Vacuum System Requirements.

12-3.4.1 Patient piped gas systems shall conform to Type I systems in Sections 4-3 through 4-6 of Chapter 4, "Gas and Vacuum Systems."

12-3.4.2 Laboratory piped gas systems shall conform to 4-3.3, 4-4.3, and 4-6.

12-3.4.3 Patient piped vacuum systems shall conform to 4-7 through 4-10.

12-3.4.4 Laboratory piped vacuum systems shall conform to 4-7 through 4-10.

12-3.4.5 For nonmedical piped gas systems, 4-3.4 shall apply.

12-3.5 Environmental System Requirements. (Reserved)

(See 12-4.1 and 12-4.2 for requirements for anesthetizing locations and laboratories, respectively.)

12-3.6 Material Requirements. (Reserved)

12-3.7 Electrical Equipment Requirements.

12-3.7.1 Patient Care Areas. Electrical appliances shall conform to Chapter 7, "Electrical Equipment, Health Care Facilities" as applicable to patient care areas. *(See 7-5.1 and 7-5.2.2.1.)*

NOTE: The requirements of Chapter 7 apply to all electrical appliances. Chapter 7 requirements and procedures are intended to be implemented by the hospital to evaluate existing equipment or to evaluate new equipment as part of routine incoming inspection procedures for all appliances in patient care areas.

12-3.7.2 Laboratories. Equipment shall conform to the nonpatient electrical equipment requirements in Chapter 7. *(See 7-5.2.2.2.)*

12-3.8 Gas Equipment Requirements.

12-3.8.1 Patient. Equipment shall conform to the patient equipment requirements in Chapter 8, "Gas Equipment (Positive and Negative Pressure), Health Care Facilities."

12-3.8.2 Nonpatient. Equipment shall conform to the nonpatient equipment requirements in Chapter 8, "Gas Equipment (Positive and Negative Pressure), Health Care Facilities."

12-4 Specific Area Requirements.

NOTE: This is in addition to any applicable requirements in Section 12-3.

This Note is a very important reminder, stressing the new structure of NFPA 99 and how requirements are to be applied for each type of facility called out in Chapters 12 to 18. As an example, Section 12-3 lists requirements that are applicable to all hospitals. Section 12-4 lists requirements for specific areas within hospitals (e.g., 12-4.1 covers anesthetizing locations; 12-4.2 covers laboratories). However, it should be clearly understood that the requirements of Section 12-4 *cannot* be considered *alone*, but must be applied in conjunction with the requirements of Section 12-3. Section 12-4 requirements can be considered supplemental to any of the general requirements listed in Section 12-3.

12-4.1 Anesthetizing Locations.

Prologue

The first health-care-related document produced by the NFPA, "Anesthetic Gases and Oxygen in Hosptials," was published in 1934 and was originally the responsibility of the Committee on Gases. This document covered piping and storage of medical gases and "oxygen chambers" (the latter resembling a room within a room, with oxygen being pumped into the inner room).

A separate Committee on Hospitals was established in the late 1930s to address only the use of flammable anesthetics in operating rooms. It published a guideline in 1941 and a recommended practice in 1944, designated NFPA 56. Over the years, the name of this publication has changed a number of times. (*See Cross-Reference to Previous Individual Documents at the end of this Handbook.*) In 1962, it became the *Standard on the Use of Flammable Anesthetics* and in 1970, the *Standard on the Use of Inhalation Anesthetics.*

During the initial development of fire and explosion precautions for hospital operating suites, it became apparent that one of the principle sources of ignition of flammable anesthetic gases was static electricity. Through efforts of the Bureau of Mines, and especially Dr. George Thomas, an anesthesiologist and one of the earliest advocates of firesafety in the hospital operating suite, studies were conducted to determine the cause of static electricity in operating suites and methods for mitigating this hazard. As a result of these studies, a number of precautions were incorporated into the very first editions of NFPA 56, beginning in 1944. These precautions applied not only to permanently installed equipment and fixtures, but also to supplies and personnel attire used in the operating rooms, and to personal safety practices as well. These precautions included the following:

1. Installation of conductive flooring;
2. Maintenance of a 50 to 55 percent relative humidity;
3. Elimination of garments and drapes of synthetic fibers;
4. Use of conductive and antistatic materials;
5. Use of conductive shoes or conductive shoe covers, and the testing of their efficacy before personnel entered flammable anesthetizing locations; and
6. Use of isolation transformers to supply ungrounded electric power, and line isolation monitors to detect if ungrounded power were being compromised.

As a result of the promulgation, adoption, and enforcement of these provisions, the incidence of fires and explosions in operating rooms fell drastically. While there has never been a retrospective study to evaluate the effects of the original requirements on operating room fires, adherence to these principles has made operating room personnel more cognizant of dangers.

In 1956, a totally nonflammable inhalation anesthetic agent, halothane, was introduced into anesthesia practice. In subsequent years, a number of other nonflammable, polyhalogenated anesthetic agents were introduced. Because many anesthesiologists and anesthetists recognized the dangers of fires and explosions, and because the use of electrosurgery burgeoned, the use of these nonflammable agents became widespread, while the administration of cyclopropane and diethyl ether declined.

At the recommendation of the then Chairman of the Sectional Committee on Flammable Anesthetics, provisions for the use of nonflammable anesthetics were incorporated into NFPA 56, and the concepts of the nonflammable anesthetizing location and the mixed facility were included in the 1970 edition. That edition (designated NFPA 56A) recognized for the first time those operating suites in which flammable agents were no longer employed. If none were employed in the hospital, each of the operating rooms became a nonflammable anesthetizing location. In those hospitals where some anesthetizing locations were designated for flammable anesthetics use and others for the use of nonflammable anesthetics only, the term "mixed facility" was applied.

Because the provisions for flammable and nonflammable anesthetizing locations were intermixed, in 1972 the Chairman of the Sectional Committee on Flammable Anesthetics completely edited and revised NFPA 56A, placing provisions for all facilities (flammable and nonflammable anesthetizing locations and mixed facilities) into separate chapters. No substantive changes were made in the standard during that particular revision. The structure of NFPA 56A remained in that form through the 1984 edition of NFPA 99 (when it became, essentially, Chapter 3). For this 1987 edition of NFPA 99, much of that material is now Section 12-4.1. Anesthetizing location requirements appear in NFPA 99, but only where they differ from requirements for patient care areas.

By the mid 1970s, training programs in the United States were no longer teaching the use of flammable anesthetics, resulting in a continually decreasing number of operating room personnel familiar with the use of flammable agents. Some practitioners, however, feel that flammable agents (cycloprane and ether) still have a great deal to offer and should not be abandoned. Furthermore, flammable anesthetic agents, owing to economy, physiologic safety, and simplicity of administration, may be used in other parts of the world wherein authorities having jurisdiction may choose to look to NFPA guidance in regard to firesafety. For these reasons, the Committee has retained those portions that apply to flammable agents and has not relaxed requirements.

The requirements for isolated power were developed to eliminate from the hospital operating suite one source of ignition of flammable anesthetic gases, namely electrical sparks from line-powered equipment. With the firm acceptance of the concept of the nonflammable anesthetizing location and the abandonment of the use of flammable anesthetics in a significant number of American hospitals, efforts were made by various members of the former Technical Committee on Anesthetizing Agents to modify the requirements for isolated power. Other members of the Committee, however, pointed to the frequent spillage of biological and other fluids, the increasing use of electrical equipment in operating rooms, and the ready access to opportunities for grounding of personnel; these, in combination, could present a serious hazard of electrical shock to personnel. In 1984, changes were made allowing relaxation of some of these requirements, and provisions now allow for the elimination of isolated power under certain circumstances. (*See 12-4.1.2.6.*)

Before the concept of nonflammable anesthetizing locations, the maintenance of a relative humidity of 50 to 55 percent was mandatory because of the significant role humidity plays in reducing static electricity. With the advent of nonflammable anesthetizing locations, the maintenance of relative humidity in this range was no longer necessary strictly from an explosion prevention standpoint. Hospital engineers have pointed out that it is very costly to maintain relative humidity in this range during winter, when the outside temperature may be very low and the amount of water vapor contained in the ambient air is minimal. As a result, requirements for humidity control in nonflammable anesthetizing locations were dropped for the 1978 edition of NFPA 56A. There was extensive discussion on this subject for the 1984 edition of NFPA 99 (into which NFPA 56A was incorporated), and a range of humidity control was established.

Although the use of flammable anesthetic agents has diminished almost into obscurity, this does not mean that flammable agents (e.g., alcohol, flammable prepping agents, bone cement) do not exist in anesthetizing locations. These flammable agents, combined with a large combustible load in the operating room and the use of oxidizing agents (oxygen and nitrous oxide), have not as yet been addressed by the Committee. In addition, the almost universal use of electrosurgical units, which results in a combination of sparks and small flames, is still of concern.

12-4.1.1 General.

12-4.1.1.1 Foreword. When this material was first published in 1941 as a separate document, the majority of inhalation anesthetics were administered with flammable agents, and fires and explosions in operating rooms occurred with disturbing frequency. Promulgation of this material by NFPA and the use of this material by hospitals has lowered the incidence of such tragedies significantly.

Since 1950, nonflammable inhalation anesthetics possessing relatively safe properties have been developed. The increasing use of these agents has curtailed, and in most institutions completely eliminated, the use of flammable agents. This change in anesthetic practice has made it desirable to delineate standards of construction and operation of rooms in locations where flammable agents will never be used. It must be emphasized that many safety recommendations pertain to hazards other than those related to fires and explosions, e.g., electric shock. It must also be recognized that these agents may possess toxicologic hazards to patients and personnel.

This material has been formulated in the belief that, although materials and mechanical equipment must be relied upon to the fullest possible extent for the mitigation of fire, explosion, and electric shock hazards, such physical safeguards are most effective only when augmented by safety precautions conscientiously applied by operating room and supporting personnel. This section emphatically calls attention to the need for constant human diligence in the maintenance of safe practices because of the peculiar intermixing of flammable anesthetic hazards and electric shock hazards, together with the mental strain in the environment of surgical operations.

Studies of these operating room hazards by many investigators over more than 30 years have pointed to the conclusion that the greatest degree of safety possible within the limitations of our present knowledge is secured only through a completely coordinated program rather than by the application of individual and unrelated safeguards. Compliance with certain requirements of this section will be effective, or even permissible, only when accompanied by compliance with the full program of precautionary measures.

It is necessary that all personnel having any responsibility for safety in anesthesia collaborate in the precautionary program. In the case of hospitals, this will apply to members of the governing body, physicians, administrative personnel, nursing staff, and maintenance staff. Not only must such personnel achieve an understanding of the hazards involved, but, in addition, they must be reminded periodically of the dangers posed by electric shock, compressed gases and their cylinders, the explosive nature of all flammable agents, and the hazards created by oxygen-enriched atmospheres. (*See NFPA 53M, Fire Hazards in Oxygen-Enriched Atmospheres.*)

For further discussion on the nature of the hazards, see Appendix C-12.1.

12-4.1.1.2 Scope. The purpose of this section is to establish performance and maintenance criteria for anesthetizing locations and for equipment and facilities ancillary thereto in order to safeguard patients and health care personnel from fire, explosion, electrical, and related hazards associated with the administration of both flammable and nonflammable inhalation anesthetics.

This section covers all anesthetizing locations and related storage areas within hospitals in which inhalation anesthetics are administered.

This section covers ambulatory care facilities that are part of a hospital as well as ambulatory care facilities in which flammable inhalation anesthetics are administered. This section does not apply to anesthetizing locations situated in freestanding ambulatory care facilities in which only nonflammable anesthetics are administered (*see Section 13-4.1*).

This section is intended to provide requirements to protect against explosions or fires, electric shock, mechanical injury from compressed gases or compressed gas cylinders, or anoxia from erroneous gas connections and similar hazards, without unduly limiting the activities of the surgeon or anesthesiologist. This principle, without minimizing any of the aforementioned dangers, recognizes that the physicians shall be guided by all the hazards to life that are inherent to surgical procedures carried out in anesthetizing locations.

This section does not cover animal operative facilities unless the animal operative facility is integral to a hospital and uses flammable anesthetics.

The provisions of this section do not apply to the manufacture, storage, transportation, or handling of inhalation anesthetics prior to delivery to the consuming health care facility. They do not apply to any use other than in an anesthetizing location and related storage areas.

12-4.1.1.3 Purpose. This section contains the requirements for administration and maintenance that shall be followed as an adjunct to physical precautions specified in 12-4.1.2.

12-4.1.1.4* Recognition of Hazards and Responsibility.

(a) The hazards involved in the use of inhalation anesthetic agents can be successfully mitigated only when all of the areas of hazard are fully recognized by all personnel, and when the physical protection provided is complete and is augmented by attention to detail by all personnel of administration and maintenance having any responsibility for the functioning of anesthetizing locations. Since 12-4.1.1 and 12-4.1.2 are expected to be used as a text by those responsible for the mitigation of associated hazards, the requirements set forth herein are frequently accompanied by explanatory text.

(b) Responsibility for the maintenance of safe conditions and practices in anesthetizing locations falls mutually upon the governing body of the hospital, all physicians using the anesthetizing locations, the administration of the hospital, and those responsible for hospital licensing, accrediting or other approval programs.

(c) Inasmuch as the ultimate responsibility for the care and safety of patients in a hospital is that of the governing board of the hospital, that body in its responsibility for enforcement of requirements contained in this chapter shall determine that adequate regulations with respect to anesthesia practices and conduct in anesthetizing locations have been adopted by the medical staff of the hospital and that adequate regulations for inspection and maintenance are in use by the administrative, nursing, and ancillary personnel of the hospital.

(d) By virtue of its responsibility for the professional conduct of members of the medical staff of the hospital, the organized medical staff shall adopt adequate regulations with respect to the use of inhalation anesthetic agents and to the prevention of electric shock and burns (*see Appendix C-12.3*) and through its formal organization shall ascertain that these regulations are regularly adhered to.

(e) In meeting its responsibilities for safe practices in anesthetizing locations, the hospital administration shall adopt or correlate regulations and standard operating procedures to assure that both the physical qualities and the operating maintenance methods pertaining to anesthetizing locations meet the standards set in this chapter. The controls adopted shall cover the conduct of professional personnel in anesthetizing locations, periodic inspection to ensure the proper grounding of dead metal (*see 3-5.2.1*), and inspection of all electrical equipment, including testing of line isolation monitors.

A-12-4.1.1.4 In determining whether existing construction or equipment does or does not constitute a hazard to life, due consideration should be given to the record of incidents or accidents of the facility in question and whether equipment used in the facility is subject to documented preventive maintenance. Absence of incidents and accidents, and the existence of a well-documented preventive maintenance program covering all electrical equipment used in anesthetizing locations in the facility, indicates that minimal hazard to life exists.

For example, isolated power systems would not be required in existing anesthetizing locations in health care facilities meeting the above criteria.

It is the intent of the Subcommittee on Anesthesia Services that changes to future editions of this (now) Section be applied judiciously to existing facilities (similar to NFPA 101, *Life Safety Code*, which specifically differentiates between new and existing occupancies).

The Appendix material is a further clarification with respect to the specific issue of existing anesthetizing locations that do not have isolated power systems. It was originially drafted as a Tentative Interim Amendment in 1980.

12-4.1.1.5 Rules and Regulations.

(a) Hospital authorities and professional staff shall jointly consider and agree upon necessary rules and regulations for the control of personnel concerned with anesthetizing locations. Upon adoption, rules and regulations shall be prominently posted in the operating room suite. Positive measures are necessary to acquaint all personnel with the rules and regulations established and to assure enforcement.

(b) This section recognizes that some hospitals contain operating and delivery rooms designed and maintained for the use of flammable anesthetic agents. It also recognizes that there may be some operating rooms and even entire operating suites designed for the exclusive use of nonflammable agents. A particular hazard exists where personnel elect to employ a flammable agent in a room not designed for it, or where a flammable agent is employed in a nonflammable anesthetizing location without taking the proper administrative steps.

The first sentence of Subparagraph (b) reflects the diminished use of flammable anesthetics in the last few years.

(c) Appendix C-12.3 contains three sets of proposed regulations applying to the specific types of inhalation anesthetizing locations as defined in Section 2-2.

Set (1) contains regulations for flammable anesthetizing locations that may be adopted by hospitals for all anesthetizing locations designed for the safe administration of flammable inhalation anesthetic agents.

Set (2) contains regulations for nonflammable anesthetizing locations that may be adopted by hospitals for all anesthetizing locations designed for the exclusive administration of nonflammable inhalation anesthetic agents.

Set (3) contains regulations for mixed facilities that may be adopted by hospitals in which flammable anesthetizing locations and nonflammable anesthetizing locations coexist within the same building, allowing interchange of personnel and equipment between flammable and nonflammable anesthetizing locations.

(d) Anesthetizing locations shall be identified as noted in 12-4.1.5.5(a).

(e) The hazard symbols contained in NFPA 704, *Identification of the Fire Hazards of Materials*, shall be employed throughout the hospital, as appropriate. Such use is particularly important in the operating suite and in gas and volatile liquid storage facilities.

NFPA 704 provides a very simple method for identifying the level of hazard of an area. Fire departments use NFPA 704, and can thus quickly translate the coding used in the document into the vernacular, and take appropriate measures when extinguishing a fire in that area. Once identified, areas should be checked periodically to learn if the assigned coding is still applicable.

For a picture of the 704 "diamond," see Commentary on Section 10-8.2.1.

(f) All pieces of equipment used in anesthetizing locations shall be labeled to indicate that they comply with applicable safety regulations.

NOTE: A generally recognized mark or symbol will meet the intent of this requirement.

(g)* Transportation of patients while an inhalation anesthetic is being administered by means of a mobile anesthesia machine shall be prohibited, unless deemed essential for the benefit of the patient in the combined judgment of the surgeon and anesthetist.

A-12-4.1.1.5(g) Hazards During Transport of Anesthetized Patients. Transporation of patients while an inhalation anesthetic is being administered from a machine separate from the table supporting the patient has resulted in injury or death of patients. Two hazards have been recognized: significant accumulation of electrostatic charge and mechanical disruption of the anesthesia circuit. Respiratory tract damage has resulted due to tugging of indwelling tubes when the anesthesia machine was not moved with the operating table. Asphyxiation resulted when the rebreathing tubes became detached and were reconnected to the wrong nipples.

12-4.1.2 Requirements for ALL Anesthetizing Locations.

12-4.1.2.1 Ventilation. Ventilation of anesthetizing locations shall conform to 5-6.1; and to 5-4.1 for nonflammable anesthetizing locations and 5-4.2 for flammable anesthetizing locations.

12-4.1.2.2 Germicides.

(a) Medicaments, including those dispersed as aerosols, may be used in anesthetizing locations for germicidal purposes, for affixing plastic surgical drape materials, for preparation of wound dressing, or for other purposes.

(b) Liquid germicides used in anesthetizing locations, whenever the use of cautery or electrosurgery is contemplated, shall be nonflammable.

(c) Whenever flammable aerosols are employed, sufficient time shall be allowed to elapse between deposition and application of drapes to permit complete evaporation and dissipation of any flammable vehicle remaining.

NOTE: Inhibited 1,1,1 trichloroethane and 1,1,1 trifluoro 2,2,2 trichloroethane are suitable defatting agents. Ether and tinctures of disinfecting agents are flammable and often are improperly used during surgical procedures. Tipping containers, accidental spillage, and the pouring of excessive amounts of such flammable agents on patients expose them to injury in the event of accidental ignition of the flammable solvent.

12-4.1.2.3 Smoking and open flames shall be prohibited in all anesthetizing locations.

12-4.1.2.4 Electrical Safeguards.

(a) Physical safeguards built into the anesthetizing locations or storage areas will not provide protection unless safe practices are followed and good maintenance is provided.

(b) Scheduled inspections and written reports shall be maintained.

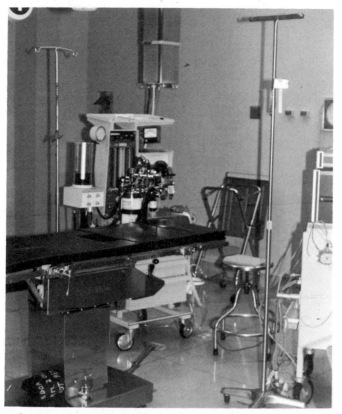

(a) Anesthesia machine is in background; monitoring equipment is on right.

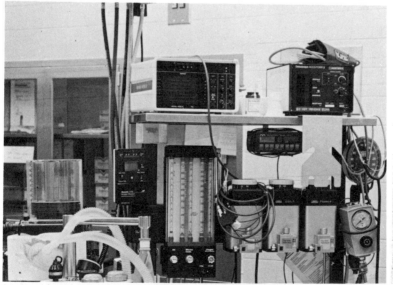

(b) Anesthesia machine is in middle, with a small patient monitor on shelf. Overhead stanchion provides electricity, gases, vacuum.

Figure 38   Typical set-ups in operating rooms.

(c) Rules to require prompt replacement of defective electrical equipment shall be adopted and rigidly enforced.

(d) Maintenance employees shall be properly acquainted with the importance of the work they are expected to do in storage locations for flammable anesthetic agents and anesthetizing locations, in order that their informed cooperation may be assured.

(e) All electrical equipment used in inhalation anesthetizing locations and areas ancillary thereto, or in other areas using conductive floors constructed in accordance with this section, shall be periodically tested for electrical safety. (*See Appendix C-12.1.2.1.2.*)

(f) Members of the professional staff shall be required to submit for inspection and approval any special equipment they wish to introduce into anesthetizing locations. Such equipment shall meet the requirements for the protection against electric shock as given in Chapter 7 (*see 7-5.1.1.1 and 7-5.1.1.2*).

> From a safety perspective, it is very important that electrical and mechanical appliances be tested before they are used on patients.

(g) Line-powered equipment that introduces current to the patient's body shall have the output circuit isolated from ground to ensure against an unintentional return circuit through the patient.

Exception: Equipment whose output circuit is grounded or ground-referenced shall be permitted, provided that the design provides equivalent safety to an isolated output.

> This Exception was added to the 1978 edition of NFPA 56A because new designs of electrosurgical units "ground-referenced" patients, but limited current that could flow through a patient via the designated return electrode to a nonhazardous level.

12-4.1.2.5 Electric Connections and Testing.

(a) Administrative authorities shall ascertain that electric maintenance personnel are completely familiar with the function and proper operation of ungrounded electric circuits required by 12-4.1.3.2. The significance of the signal lamps and audible alarms installed to indicate accidental grounds shall be explained to all personnel affected. A permanent sign shall be installed close to the position of the signal lamps to indicate their significance. Circuits in the panel boxes shall be clearly labeled, distinguishing between grounded and ungrounded, emergency and normal circuits, so that immediate recognition is possible.

(b) Extension cords shall not be connected to lighting fixtures in anesthetizing locations under any circumstances.

12-4.1.2.6 Electrical Systems.

(a) A grounded electrical distribution system shall be permitted to be installed in facilities that have a written policy prohibiting the use of flammable inhalation anesthetizing agents.

NOTE: If a nonflammable anesthetizing location is a wet location, the provisions of 3-4.1.2.6 apply.

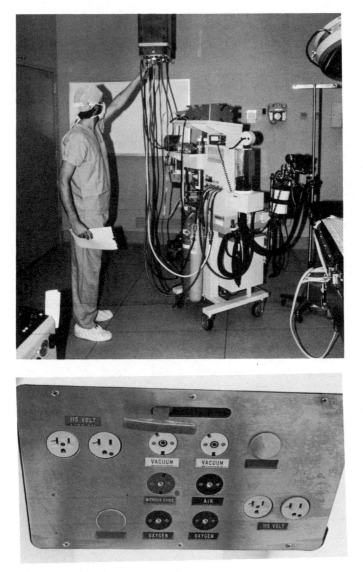

Figure 39   Example of an overhead stanchion in an operating room, containing electrical and gas outlets and vacuum inlets.

The Note on wet location was added to call attention to a fact that became necessary to consider when allowance of grounded electrical systems in nonflammable anesthetizing locations was approved for the 1984 edition of NFPA 99. While a grounded electrical system was permitted, the degree of wetness (and the additional electrical safety measures required in "wet locations") was another matter that required consideration.

Much discussion was again held during the revision for the 1987 edition of NFPA 99 on the subject of isolated power systems. (*See commentary under the definition of "isolated power systems" in Chapter 2, as well as the commentary under*

3-2.4.2 *for details of this discussion*). On this particular paragraph [12-4.1.2.6(a)] there was extensive debate because the 1984 change allowing grounded electrical systems in nonflammable anesthetizing locations unknowingly raised an issue that hitherto had not been an issue: that of another requirement in NFPA 99 dealing with wet locations in patient care areas.

Former NFPA 76B (Chapter 9 in NFPA 99-1984) required an additional level of electrical safety in patient care areas designated "wet locations." A definition of "wet location" was provided [*see 12-2.2(c)*]. The level of safety essentially called for GFCIs or isolated power systems, depending on whether power interruption was tolerable. [*See 3-4.1.2.6(a)*.] This requirement was moot for nonflammable anesthetizing locations as long as IPSs were required in these locations (through former NFPA 56A). With the change in 1984 and the allowance of grounded electrical systems in nonflammable anesthetizing locations, the requirement for an additional level of safety became a matter of consideration since nonflammable anesthetizing locations *are* patient care areas.

For this 1987 edition of NFPA 99, three subcommittees (Anesthetizing Services, Electrical Equipment, and Electrical Systems) and the Technical Committee on Health Care Facilities reviewed the situation. In addition, there were about a dozen proposals and comments recommending reverting to the previous criteria of requiring isolated power systems in all anesthetizing locations (some based on patient/staff electrical safety; others on the power-continuation issue). The only change that the Technical Committee on Health Care Facilities could agree on was the addition of the Note referring to wet location provisions (now located in Chapter 3).

Because of the history of this issue (i.e., IPSs), and the current reference to wet locations, the Chairman of the Technical Committee on Health Care Facilities plans to appoint an Ad Hoc Subcommittee in 1987 to review the entire situation and present recommendations to the Technical Committee. Open meetings will be held to solicit as much input as possible.

For a discussion on the need to maintain power, see commentary under 3-2.4.2.

(b) High-voltage wiring for X-ray equipment shall be effectively insulated from ground and adequately guarded against accidental contact.

(c) Approved permanently installed equipment may be supplied through a grounded single-phase or three-phase distribution system if installed in accordance with 12-4.1.3.3.

This paragraph and 7-5.1.1.2 reflect previously made changes in 12-4.1.3.3 and 12-4.1.3.4 allowing three-phase *grounded* power in anesthetizing locations for certain permanently installed equipment. These revisions were originally prepared as a Tentative Interim Amendment to NFPA 56A-1978 (TIA 56A-78-2) when the problem of three-phase power was brought before the Committee in early 1980. With the allowance of a grounded electrical system in nonflammable anesthetizing locations, this paragraph is moot for those locations (though it does have applicability for those facilities that do install isolated power systems in nonflammable anesthetizing locations).

The former NFPA 56A allowed only X-ray equipment in anesthetizing locations to be supplied by a grounded electrical system. The change extended the allowance to all fixed equipment.

The reasoning behind this change is that fixed equipment will be bolted to structural metal, and thus permanently grounded. It will be grounded also through rigid or flexible metallic conduit. In the event of an electrical fault within the equipment, the case of the equipment cannot be raised to a potentially hazardous to personnel who may be grounded.

Consistent with this reasoning, and recognizing the vulnerability of flexible cords, *cord*-connected attachments and accessories to fixed equipment are required (by 12-4.1.3.3) to operate at 24 volts or less supplied by an isolating transformer, or to be supplied by isolated power at line voltage.

Nonmetallic conduit is not (at present) permitted in hospitals. (Exception Number 3 in 517-11 of NFPA 70-1987, *National Electrical Code*, does not apply to hospitals.) Should this exclusion be revised, 12-4.1.2.6(c) might merit reconsideration inasmuch as it is observed that some equipment (e.g., the electrically powered operating table) may be fixed only to studs set in concrete.

(d) An isolation transformer shall not serve more than one operating room except as provided in 12-4.1.2.6(c). For purposes of this section, anesthetic induction rooms are considered part of the operating room or rooms served by the induction rooms. If an induction room serves more than one operating room, the isolated circuits of the induction room may be supplied from the isolation transformer or any one of the operating rooms served by that induction room.

Exception: In existing hospitals where one isolation transformer is serving more than one inhalation anesthetizing location, provided the system has been installed in accordance with previous editions of this section (formerly NFPA 56A) where such systems were permitted.

While one transformer cannot serve more than one operating room in new facilities, there is no restriction on using more than one transformer in one operating room. This is to reduce cumulative leakage current from tripping line isolation monitor alarms.

The Exception is an example of the differentiation in requirements between new and existing anesthetizing locations. The Exception reflects that the requirement of 12-4.1.2.6(d) was only a recommendation until 1971. A Formal Interpretation in December 1977 clarified the issue of nonretroactive application. This clarification, however, was incorporated as an Exception in the 1978 edition of NFPA 56A (which was incorporated into NFPA 99), and thus addressed the needs of existing facilities.

(e) Isolation transformers may serve single receptacles in several patient areas when the receptacles are reserved for supplying power to equipment requiring 150 volts or higher, such items as portable X-ray units, and when the receptacles and mating plugs are not interchangeable with the receptacles on the local isolated power system.

12-4.1.2.7 Gases.

(a) *Storage Locations or Manifold Enclosures for Oxygen and Nitrous Oxide.* The location and ventilation of storage roooms or manifold enclosures for oxygen and nitrous oxide shall comply with Chapter 4 and Chapter 5.

(b) *Nonflammable Medical Gas Piping Systems.* Oxygen and nitrous oxide manifolds and piping systems that supply anesthetizing locations shall comply with Chapter 4.

12-4.1.2.8 Anesthetic Apparatus. Anesthetic apparatus shall conform to the requirements in 8-5.1.2.1.

12-4.1.2.9 Electrical Equipment. *(See 12-3.7.1.)*

12-4.1.3 Requirements for Flammable Anesthetizing Locations.

This section applies only to anesthetizing locations where flammable anesthetics are still used. Facilities that no longer use flammable anesthetics will find requirements in Section 12-4.1.4 for any conductive floors they still have in nonflammable anesthetizing locations. But, otherwise, the requirements in this section need not be followed for institutions that prohibit the use of flammable anesthetics in anesthetizing locations.

As discussed in the Prologue to 12-4.1, the use of flammable anesthetics for general anesthesia has fallen off dramatically in the past ten years. Articles have, in fact, been written on the subject. *(See: "The Case for Abandonment of Explosive Anesthetic Agents," H. V. Fineberg, et al, New England Journal of Medicine, September 11, 1980; and "Flammable Anesthetics are Nearing Extinction," Deryck Duncalf, MD, Anesthesiology, Vol. 56, No. 3, March 1982.)*

There are several reasons for the growing use of nonflammable anesthetics, the most obvious one being the elimination of the explosion hazard. This switchover became possible when nonflammable anesthetizing agents became acceptable alternatives to the various flammable agents previously in use. The switch has sparked debate in the medical community about whether to ban the use of flammable anesthetics. This issue, however, is outside the scope of the Committee responsible for Section 12-4.1 since, over the years, the Committee has developed a set of procedures for the use of flammable anesthetics. In fact, the very infrequent use of flammable anesthetics has been cited as a strong reason for more closely adhering to the requirements in Section 12-4.1.3. The lack of familiarity with their use, in and of itself, can be hazardous. As long as flammable anesthetics are available and are not prohibited, it will be incumbent upon the Subcommittee on Anesthesia Services to provide requirements for their safe use.

12-4.1.3.1 Areas Adjoining Flammable Inhalation Anesthetizing Locations and Flammable Anesthetizing Storage Locations.

(a) An adjoining area connected by a closable doorway, such as a corridor, sterilizing room, scrub room, X-ray control room, or monitoring room, where it is not intended to store or administer flammable inhalation anesthetics, is not considered a hazardous area.

(b) Areas described in 12-4.1.3.1(a) may be ventilated in accordance with the applicable sections of NFPA 70, *National Electrical Code*, for ordinary locations.

(c) Conductive flooring is required in these adjoining areas to remove static charges from personnel or objects before they enter the flammable inhalation anesthetizing location or agent storage location [*see 12-4.1.3.8(b)*].

(d) Postanesthesia recovery rooms are not considered to be hazardous areas unless specifically intended for the induction of inhalation anesthesia with flammable anesthetic agents [*see 12-4.1.3.9(b)*].

(e) All doorways leading to flammable inhalation anesthetic agent storage locations shall be identified with NFPA 704, *Identification of Fire Hazards of Materials*, symbols as appropriate.

12-4.1.3.2* Isolated Power Systems. A local ungrounded electric system shall be provided.

NOTE 1: The isolated system reduces the ignition hazard from arcs and sparks between a live conductor and grounded metal and mitigates the hazard of shock or burn from electric current flowing through the body to ground. The latter hazard usually follows inadvertent contact with one live conductor or results from unrecognized failure of insulation.

NOTE 2: Such a system provides protection from spark and electric shock hazards due to the most common types of insulation failure. It does not, however, prevent all electric sparks or completely eliminate the possibility of electric shock from insulation failure. Electric shock hazards are particularly aggravated in operating rooms because of the physiological predisposition to injury of persons in such locations and because of the generally low electric resistance resulting from moisture on the floors or the use of conductive shoes and the installation of conductive floors necessary for dissipation of static electricity. Patients and personnnel often are wet with prepping solutions, blood, urine, and other conductive fluids that greatly reduce resistance to the passage of unintended electrical current. More than ordinary care is crucially necessary in the use and maintenance of all electric systems and equipment.

The installation of isolated power systems in anesthetizing locations was one of several measures instituted in 1941 to reduce the spark hazard in operating rooms. At that time, flammable inhalation anesthetics were still generally used and electrical equipment was being used more frequently. Because these protective measures reduced the number of incidents, they have been retained in flammable anesthetizing locations.

For further discussion on isolated power systems, see Commentary under isolated power systems in Chapter 2.

For performance criteria for isolated power systems, see 3-4.3 in Chapter 3.

(a) Hospitals complying with NFPA 56A, *Standard for the Use of Inhalation Anesthetics*, prior to 1970 shall not be required to change ground fault detectors to a line isolation monitor.

The Committee has taken into consideration existing conditions by precluding the retroactive application of new editions of the standard on this subject.

(b) The isolated electric system shall only be required to be explosionproof if installed in the hazardous areas of a flammable inhalation anesthetizing location.

It is not required or necessary that the isolated power system be installed in the hazardous area of the flammable anesthetizing location.

A-12-4.1.3.2 Isolated Power Systems. The ungrounded electrical distribution system specified in 12-4.1.3.2 is intended to reduce the possibility of electric shocks and recurring arcs and sparks in the event of insulation failure of the electrical wiring system in anesthetizing locations. Because of the difficulty in achieving a sufficiently high level of insulation to permit operation of a line isolation monitor, and in recognition of evolving capabilities in medical care, an exception has been made so that permanently installed equipment as well as nonadjustable lighting fixtures in specified locations need not be supplied by the ungrounded system. (*See 12-4.1.3.3 and 12-4.1.3.4.*)

The Appendix material refers to the new material in 12-4.1.3.3 and 12-4.1.3.4 on fixed equipment and lighting. Prior to the 1984 edition of NFPA 99 (i.e., when there were individual health care documents), only permanently installed X-ray equipment could be supplied by grounded power.

12-4.1.3.3 Power for Fixed Equipment. Approved, fixed, therapeutic and diagnostic equipment, permanently installed in nonflammable anesthetizing locations or outside the hazardous area of a flammable anesthetizing location, may be supplied by a grounded single- or three-phase system of less than 600 volts provided (a) the equipment complies with 7-5.1.1.2; (b) cord-connected accessories (such as positioning controls, aiming lights and fiberoptic light sources, slaved monitors, motorized cameras and video cameras, dosimeters, and exposure triggers) likely to come in contact with patients or personnel are supplied by isolated power at line voltage, or operate at 24 volts or less, supplied by an isolating transformer; and (c) wiring is installed in accordance with NFPA 70, *National Electrical Code*, Section 517-104.

NOTE: It is intended that this section apply to positioning motors for patient tables associated with radiographic and other imaging equipment, and to sometimes massive equipment for radiotherapy or for the delivery of other forms of energy.

Previously, only fixed lighting fixtures and permanently installed X-ray equipment had been exempted from the requirement that electrical equipment in anesthetizing locations be supplied by an isolated power source. Certain fixed-type equipment was added to the exemption (originally TIA 56A-78-2) because of the difficulty of achieving a sufficiently high level of insulation to permit operation of line isolation monitors, and because of the massive size of the line isolation transformers that would be required. In addition, allowance for three-phase power was made (only single-phase power had previously been allowed in anesthetizing locations), with the Committee noting (in TIA 56A-78-2) that conditions and state of the art no longer warranted this exclusion.

12-4.1.3.4 Fixed Lighting. Branch circuits supplying only fixed lighting may be supplied by a conventional grounded system provided (a) such fixtures are located at least 2.4 m (8 ft) above the floor; (b) switches for the grounded circuits are wall-mounted and installed in accordance with NFPA 70, *National Electrical Code*, Section 517-104; and (c) wiring for grounded and ungrounded circuits is installed in accordance with NFPA 70, *National Electrical Code*, Section 517-104.

NOTE: Wall-mounted remote-control stations for lighting control switches operating at 24 volts or less may be installed in any anesthetizing location.

12-4.1.3.5 Ceiling-Suspended Fixtures.

(a) Ceiling-suspended surgical lighting fixtures shall be supplied from an ungrounded electric distribution system (*see 12-4.1.3.2*), which shall be monitored by a line isolation monitor as required by 3-4.3.3.1. Switching or dimmer devices shall control secondary circuit conductors only.

Exception No. 1: Where interruption of illumination is acceptable, as with single-filament lights, ceiling-suspended surgical lighting fixtures may be connected to a grounded source of supply, protected by approved individual ground fault circuit interrupters.

Exception No. 2: The secondary circuit of the ceiling-mounted surgical lighting fixture supplied by a step-down isolation transformer need not be equipped with a line isolation monitor provided that the step-down transformer is located in the same enclosure as the lamp fixture, or that the conductors carrying the current from the transformer to the lamp fixture are contained in metallic conduit that forms an integral electrical (ground) pathway between the transformer enclosure and the lamp fixture, and provided that the voltage in the secondary (lamp) circuit is not greater than 30 volts.

This Exception was added because it was brought to the Committee's attention that some new ceiling-mounted surgical fixtures include a step-down transformer mounted externally to the lighting fixture itself. As such, it was questioned whether this constituted an isolated power system and thus required a line isolation monitor. The Committee deemed it reasonable to address this configuration as similar to low-voltage signal and control circuits, and as isolation transformers that are an integral part of an assembly of components. Though technically "isolated," such secondary circuits are not required to be monitored.

(b) The light source of ceiling-suspended surgical lighting fixtures installed above hazardous areas shall not enter the hazardous area, and, if in an enclosure, the enclosure shall not enter the hazardous area in its lowest position, unless it is approved for hazardous areas.

(c) If installed above a hazardous area, fixtures with sliding contacts or arcing or sparking parts shall be installed so that in any position of use, no sliding contacts or arcing or sparking parts shall extend within the hazardous area.

(d) Integral or appended switches, if installed on ceiling-suspended surgical lighting fixtures, shall be approved for use in Class I, Group C, Division 1 hazardous areas if a switch is installed in, or can be lowered into, the hazardous area.

(e) Lamps installed in fixed position in hazardous areas shall be enclosed in a manner approved for use in Class I, Group C, Division 1 hazardous areas and shall be properly protected by substantial metal guards or other means where exposed to breakage. Lamps shall not be of the pendant type unless supported by and supplied through hangers of rigid conduit or flexible connectors approved for use in Class I, Group C, Division 1 hazardous areas in accordance with Section 501-9(a) or Section 501-9(b) of NFPA 70, *National Electrical Code.*

(f) Tube heads and cable of permanently installed X-ray equipment in flammable anesthetizing locations shall be approved for use in Class I, Group C atmospheres.

(g) *Viewing Box Lighting.* Film viewing boxes in hazardous areas shall either comply with the requirements of Section 501-9(a) of NFPA 70, *National Electrical Code*, or they shall be of a type that excludes the atmosphere of the room. If located above the 5-ft (152-cm) level in a flammable anesthetizing location or mixed facility, or in a nonflammable anesthetizing location, the film viewing box may be of the totally enclosed type or so constructed as to prevent the escape of sparks or hot metal. Such viewing boxes may be connected to a conventional grounded supply circuit if the device is protected by an approved system of double insulation. Where such an approved system is employed, the equipment shall be distinctly marked.

(h) Control units and other electric apparatus installed or intended for use in a flammable anesthetizing location shall comply with the requirements of 7-5.1.1 [*see also 12-4.1.3.5(d) and 12-4.1.5.6(d)*].

12-4.1.3.6 Signaling and Communications Systems. All equipment of signaling and communications systems in hazardous areas, irrespective of voltage, shall be of a type approved for use in Class I, Group C, Division 1 hazardous areas in accordance with Section 501-14(a) or Section 501-14(b) of NFPA 70, *National Electrical Code.*

12-4.1.3.7 This section (12-4.1) prohibits the piping of flammable anesthetic gases (*see 4-6.2.3.1*).

12-4.1.3.8 Reduction in Electrostatic Hazard.

(a) *Purpose.*

(1) The requirements of this section have been promulgated to reduce the possibility of electrostatic spark discharges, with consequent ignition of flammable gases (*see C-12.1.3.1*).

(2) The prevention of the accumulation of static charges revolves about a number of safeguards which shall be complied with in flammable anesthetizing locations; in corridors and passageways adjacent thereto; in rooms connecting directly to anesthetizing locations, such as scrub rooms and sterilizing rooms; and in storage locations for flammable anesthetics located in an operating suite.

(3) The methods employed to prevent such accumulation include the installation of conductive flooring [*see 12-4.1.3.8(b)*], the maintenance of the relative humidity at 50 percent at least, and the use of certain items of conductive equipment, accessories, and wearing apparel.

(b)* *Conductive Flooring.*

As mentioned at the beginning of 12-4.1, safety is composed of many links — conductive flooring is one link in that chain when flammable anesthetics are used.

(1) Conductive flooring shall be installed in those areas specified in 12-4.1.3.8(a)(2). Conductive flooring installed in corridors or passageways in compliance with 12-4.1.3.8(a)(2) shall extend the width of the corridor and along the corridor a minimum of 9.84 ft (3 m) on each side of door frames.

(2) A conductive floor shall meet the resistance provisions through its inherent conductive properties. The surface of the floor in the locations specified by 12-4.1.3.8(a)(2) and 12-4.1.3.8(b)(1) shall provide a patch of moderate electric conductivity between all persons and equipment making contact with the floor to prevent the accumulation of dangerous electrostatic charges. No point on a nonconductive element in the surface of the floor shall be more than ¼ in. (6.4 mm) from a conductive element of the surface, except for insulated floor drains.

(3) The resistance of the conductive floor shall be less than an average of 1,000,000 ohms as measured in accordance with 12-4.1.3.8(b)(7).

This upper value (1,000,000 ohms) for conductive floors in flammable anesthetizing locations was selected for several interrelated reasons. Part of the reasoning included balancing the need to dissipate static electricity (lowering floor resistance) with the protection against grounding personnel (raising floor resistance). Values of 20,000,000 ohms or more are technically acceptable to discharge static electricity [*see A-12-4.1.3.8(b) for further information*]. However, other factors influenced the Committee to reduce that value. These included the long-term characteristics of conductive floors; the need for some safety factor; and the maintenance necessary to reduce dirt build-up and, thus, resistance build-up.

(4) The resistance of the floor shall be more than an average of 25,000 ohms, as measured in accordance with 12-4.1.3.8(b)(7).

A lower limit of 25,000 ohms is necessary to limit the current flow that could occur under fault conditions.

(5) A deliberate connection of the conductive floor to the room ground shall not be required.

The purpose of the conductive floor is to interconnect equipment and personnel to equalize static potentials. This is achieved whether or not the conductive floor is connected to the room ground.

(6) The resistance of conductive floors shall be initially tested prior to use. Thereafter measurements shall be taken at intervals of not more than one month. A permanent record of the readings shall be kept.

(7) The following test method shall be used (see 12-4.1.3.12).

(i) The floor shall be clean and dry and the room shall be free of flammable gas mixtures.

(ii) Each electrode shall weigh 5 lb (2.268 kg) and shall have a dry, flat, circular contact area 2½-in. (6.35 cm) in diameter, which shall comprise a surface of aluminum or tin foil 0.0005 in. (0.013 mm) to 0.001 in. (0.025 mm) thick, backed by a layer of rubber ¼ in. (6.4 mm) thick and measuring between 40 and 60 durometer hardness as determined with a Shore Type A durometer (ASTM D2240-68).

(iii) Resistance shall be measured by a suitably calibrated ohmmeter that shall have a nominal open circuit output voltage of 500 volts dc and a nominal internal resistance of not less than 100,000 ohms, with tolerance defined as follows:

Revision for the 1978 edition of NFPA 56A took into account those existing test instruments that had output resistance of approximately 200,000 ohms and a short circuit current of 2.5 milliamperes.

1. Short-circuit current of from 2.5 mA to 5 mA.

2. At any value of connected resistance, Rx, the terminal voltage, V, shall be

$$\left[\frac{Rx}{Rx + \text{internal resistance}} \right] \times 500V \pm 15\%$$

(iv) Measurements shall be made between five or more pairs of points in each room and the results averaged. For compliance with 12-4.1.3.8(b)(3) the average shall be within the limits specified and no individual measurement value shall be greater than five megohms, as measured between two electrodes placed 3 ft (91 cm) apart at any points on the floor. For compliance with 12-4.1.3.8(b)(4) the average value shall be no less than 25,000 ohms with no individual measurement's value less than 10,000 ohms as measured between a ground connection and an electrode placed at any point on the floor, and also as measured between two electrodes placed 3 ft (91 cm) apart at any points on the floor. There is no upper limit of resistance for a measurement between a ground connection and an electrode placed on the conductive floor.

NOTE: If the resistance changes appreciably with time during a measurement, the value observed after the voltage has been applied for about five seconds shall be considered to be the measured value.

While 12-4.1.3.8(b)(5) does not prohibit a deliberate connection between the conductive floor and room ground, if such a connection is made, the resistance value between the two electrodes on the floor still has to meet both parts of sentence three, i.e., 25,000 ohms (average) with no value less than 10,000 ohms.

A-12-4.1.3.8(b) Conductive Flooring. A conductive floor serves as a convenient means of electrically connecting persons and objects together to prevent the accumulation of electrostatic charges.

A resistance not exceeding 50 megohms between objects or persons is generally sufficient to prevent accumulation of dangerous voltages. The upper limit of 1,000,000 ohms for the resistance of the floor has been chosen as meeting this requirement with a reasonable factor of safety and with reasonable provision for other resistances in the conductive path.

The resistance of some flooring materials changes with age. Floors of such materials should have an initial resistance that permits changes in resistance with age without exceeding the limits prescribed in 12-4.1.3.8(b)(3) and (4).

(c) *Accessories.*

(1) Coverings of operating tables, stretcher pads, pillows and cushions, etc., shall be fabricated from conductive materials throughout. Conductive sheeting shall be tested on a nonconductive surface. The resistance between two electrodes placed 3 ft (91 cm) apart, or as close to this distance as the size of the material will permit, on the same surface, and between two electrodes placed in the middle of opposite surfaces, shall not exceed one megohm. Individual items covered with conductive sheeting shall be tested on a metal surface. The resistance between an electrode placed on the upper surface of the covered item and another electrode placed on the metal surface shall not exceed one megohm. The electrodes and ohmmeter used for these tests shall be of the type specified in 12-4.1.3.8(b)(7)(ii) and (iii) respectively.

(d) *Interconnecting Conductive Accessories.*

(1) All accessories that are required to be resilient or flexible on the anesthesia machine, and that form part of an interconnecting electrically conductive pathway, such as tubing, inhalers, rebreathing bags, headstraps, retainers, face masks, handbulbs, and similar items, shall be of conductive material throughout. Electric resistance of such accessories shall be not greater than one megohm when tested as specified in 12-4.1.3.8(e)(1).

High-pressure flexible tubing used to interconnect the gas anesthesia apparatus with the central piping station outlets shall be antistatic and shall be conductive throughout with a maximum resistance of 100,000 ohms per linear foot during the specified life of the material.

NOTE: When a nonconductive endotracheal catheter is in use, the conductive path from the patient to the anesthesia machine should be maintained by the use of a conductive headstrap.

(2) Tubing and connectors used for suctioning shall provide a continuous electrically conductive pathway to the vacuum bottle and to the vacuum outlet. The materials used shall be conductive throughout or, where it is necessary for visual monitoring, may be of antistatic material with antistatic properties good for the specified life of the material provided the tubing or connector embodies a continuous integral conductive pathway designed so that in normal use the conductive pathway shall make and maintain conductive contact with conducting materials.[1]

---

[1]*Specified life* refers to the permanence of the antistatic property with respect to the stated life of the material, including storage, and is of particular importance if the material is expected to be used and cleaned (e.g., washed) several times.

Electric resistance of such tubing and connectors shall be not greater than one megohm when tested as specified in 12-4.1.3.8(e).

The following configuration (Figure 40) for suctioning was interpreted in July 1976 by the Committee responsible for NFPA 56A as meeting the intent of "conductive throughout." The Committee indicated, however, that the configuration below was not acceptable for use elsewhere (e.g., on anesthesia machines).

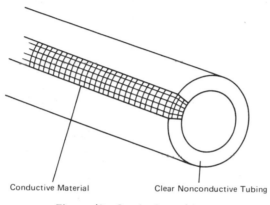

Conductive Material   Clear Nonconductive Tubing

Figure 40   Suctioning tubing.

(3) All belting used in connection with rotating machinery shall have incorporated in it sufficient material to prevent the development of electrostatic charges. A conductive pulley shall be used.

NOTE: The conductivity of the path from the pulley to the ground should be considered. If ball bearings are used, the contact between the balls and the races will probably be sufficient when bearings are lubricated with graphitized oil or grease. If sleeve bearings are used, some means of conducting the charge from the pulley should be provided.

(4) Wherever possible, items that are not parts of a machine shall be of conductive materials throughout, particularly where the item is depended on to provide a conductive pathway between other conductive items and/or the patient [*see Note after 12-4.1.3.8(d)(1)*].

NOTE: For essential elements in surgery, such as prosthetic and therapeutic devices, bacterial barriers, instruments, gloves (thermoplastic: for example, PVC), or biomechanical equipment, antistatic materials should be used if conductive materials are not available or are impractical. Regular materials may be used in approved devices shown by test to be nonhazardous.

(5) Nonconductive nonantistatic parts shall be used where necessary as electric insulators or heat-insulating handles on approved devices. Where exposed metal parts of machines of necessity are insulated from each other by other nonconductive parts, they shall be electrically interconnected. The resistance of the grounding path between these metal parts shall not exceed 0.1 ohm.

(6) Antistatic materials are not acceptable where they are relied upon to provide an interconnecting electrically conductive pathway.

(e) *Testing for Conductivity.*

(1) An ohmmeter of the type specified in 12-4.1.3.8(b)(7)(iii) shall be used for testing. Where possible, electrodes shall be of the type to make contact with metal positions across which it is desired to ensure a conductive pathway provided by the accessory, but care must be taken to ensure that the placing of the electrodes has not inadvertently provided an alternate conductive path to that under test; or, electrodes shall be of the type specified in 12-4.1.3.8(b)(7)(ii), where applicable; or, equivalent electrode contact shall be employed as practical. All items that are parts of a machine such as tubing, bags, face masks, etc., shall be tested either in place or detached from the machine in accordance with one of the methods listed under 12-4.1.3.8(e)(2) through (8).

(2) When tested in place on the machine, it is first necessary to purge the entire system of flammable or explosive gases. The anesthesia jar and cylinders of flammable gases shall be removed from the machine and all the remaining parts purged by flowing air through them in sufficient quantity to assure that all residual anesthetic gases have been removed. All parts shall be tested and each part shall be tested separately.

(3) For interconnecting parts that are to be classed as conductive throughout, one electrode shall be attached in a satisfactory manner to the metal frame of the machine, and the conductivity shall be determined by measuring the resistance between this first electrode and a second electrode consisting of a metal band snugly fitted around the midpart of the item being tested, or, for face masks and similar objects, between the first electrode and a second electrode [*see 12-4.1.3.8(b)(7)(ii)*] resting on the item.

(4) For interconnecting parts that are to be classed as antistatic with a continuous integral conductive pathway, the conductivity test shall be performed as given in 12-4.1.3.8(e)(1) above except that, in place of the metal band electrode or the standard electrode of 12-4.1.3.8(b)(7)(ii), there shall be a suitable second electrode making contact with the part in a manner that simulates the actual second contact area made when the part is connected for use.

(5) Metal parts of machines that are of necessity apparently insulated from each other by other nonconductive parts shall be suitably tested for electric interconnection; this may be an ohmmeter test. The resistance of the grounding path between these metal parts shall not exceed 0.1 ohm.

(6) When tubing and other accessories are tested for conductivity while detached from a machine, each part shall be fitted with a clean brass nipple of the same outside diameter as the connector by which the part is normally connected to the machine. A nipple shall be inserted into each such opening of the part. When two or more nipples are involved, satisfactory conductivity shall be determined by measuring the resistance between nipples. If only one nipple is involved, as in the case of a face mask or breathing bag, the resistance shall be measured between the nipple and another electrode suitably connected elsewhere (e.g., a standard electrode resting on the part).

(7) While the above are given as standard test methods, where these methods cannot be applied, an equivalent test method may be used. Interconnecting conductivity is acceptable if the measured resistance is not greater than one megohm.

(8) Conductive items containing antistatic material shall have the antistatic properties tested as described in 12-4.1.3.8(f)(3) and (4).

(f) *Antistatic Accessories and Testing.*

(1) For conductive accessories containing antistatic material see 12-4.1.3.8(d)(1) and (2); the antistatic material of these accessories shall be tested as given in 12-4.1.3.8(f)(3) and (4). For other individual items that may be of antistatic material see 12-4.1.3.8(d)(4).

(2) Plastic sheeting, film, and other nontextile, nonmetal materials, if not required to form a conductive interconnecting pathway between machines, objects, and persons, need not be conductive but shall be of antistatic material except as given in 12-4.1.3.8(d)(4). They shall be of antistatic material throughout their specified life when tested as described in 12-4.1.3.8(f)(3) and (4).

(3) Antistatic sheeting, film, and textiles shall meet the specified requirements of at least one of the following test methods when preconditioned at 50 percent ± 2 percent RH at 23° ± 1°C for 25 hours or until equilibrium is reached, and tested at 50 percent ± 2 percent RH at 23° ± 1°C.

(i) Method 4046 of Federal Test Method Standard 101B. After the specimen has received its maximum charge from the application of 5000 volts, the time for the indicated specimen potential to drop to 10 percent of its maximum value shall not exceed ½ second.

NOTE: The static detector head should be of a type that is adequately shielded to minimize responses to potentials on the electrodes, and other stray pickup. The sample is held between electrically interconnected electrodes. The 5000 volts are applied to the electrodes for 10 seconds after the indicated potential of the sample reaches equilibrium before the charge decay rate is measured.

(ii) Method 76-1972 of the AATCC (ANSI L14.112). Applied voltage should be 102 volts per in. (40 volts per cm) of interelectrode spacing. The measured resistivity shall be less than 1×10^{11} ohms per unit square of material.

A Formal Interpretation to NFPA 56A issued in July 1976 reaffirmed the requirement that sheeting, etc., needs to meet *one* of the test methods listed, not necessarily both.

Another Formal Interpretation was issued in January 1978 regarding a test specimen that could not be charged to the 5,000 volts, as prescribed by the Federal Test Method (FTM) Standard. After charging as high as possible, if the specimen otherwise decayed as prescribed in the FTM Standard, the specimen could be considered to meet the intent of the FTM Standard.

A third Formal Interpretation was issued in January 1978 regarding the test method of the AATCC. This method requires that the resistivity of the material be less than 10^{11} ohms/unit square of material, and that for textiles the measurement be made in several different directions parallel to the textile's yarn or thread. The Interpretation Committee affirmed that the less than 10^{11}-ohm value be met regardless of direction or side.

This testing is applicable only to manufacturers, as noted in 12-4.1.3.8(f)(5).

(4) Antistatic items other than sheeting, film, and textiles shall be tested in a manner as closely as possible equivalent to that given in 12-4.1.3.8(f)(3).

(5) The supplier of conductive and antistatic accessories shall certify that the item or items supplied meet the requirements of one of the tests specified in 12-4.1.3.8(f)(3). The supplier shall certify the conditions of storage, shelf life, and, in the case of reusable items, the methods of

repreparation necessary to allow the product or device to return to its antistatic or conductive properties.

(g) *Conductive Footwear.*

(1) The resistance of any static conductive footwear or any equivalent static conductive device used in conjunction with nonconductive footwear shall have a value before the item is first put in use not exceeding 500,000 ohms when tested in the following manner. The static conductive shoe or any equivalent static conductive device attached to a nonconductive shoe shall have clean contact surfaces. It shall be placed on a nonoxidizing metal plate wetted with water. A brass electrode having a contact area of 1 sq in. (6.5 sq cm) shall be placed on the inside of the sole or heel of the shoe after the surface under the electrode has been wetted by water. The resistance shall be measured between the plate and the electrode using a dc ohmmeter supplying a potential in excess of 100 volts [*e.g., see 12-4.1.3.8(b)(7)(iii)*].

(2) In the case of static conductive booties, the test shall be made as follows: The bootie shall be laid flat on an insulating surface. Two brass electrodes, each 1.5 in. (3.8 cm) long, having a contact area of 1 sq in. (6.5 sq cm), shall be used. One electrode shall be placed on the bootie near the toe and on the part of the bootie that normally comes in contact with the floor. The other electrodes shall be placed on the ankle section. The booties shall be wetted under the electrodes only.

(3) If the tests as here described are not technically feasible for the device under consideration, an alternative equivalent means of testing shall be used. The static conductive footwear and any static conductive device used with nonconductive footwear shall also meet, during use, the requirements of 12-4.1.3.10(a), (b), and (c) and 12-4.1.3.13(c).

(4) For protection of personnel against electric shock and high-frequency burns, static conductive footwear and equivalent static conductive devices shall not have any metal parts (nails, etc.) that normally come in contact with the floor.

(h) *Textiles.* [*See also 12-4.1.3.10(d), (e), and (f).*]

(1) Silk, wool, synthetic textile materials, blends of synthetic textile materials with unmodified cotton or rayon, or nonwoven materials shall not be permitted in hazardous locations as outer garments or for nonapparel purposes, unless such materials have been tested and found to be antistatic by meeting the requirements of 12-4.1.3.8(f)(3).

In the case of reusable materials the manufacturer shall certify that the antistatic properties shall be maintained through 50 wash-autoclave cycles or throughout the useful life of the material, whichever is greater.

In the case of nonreusable material the manufacturer shall certify that the antistatic properties shall be maintained throughout the useful life of the material.

NOTE: It is preferable to use only one textile material because static electricity is more readily generated by contact between articles of different materials than by contact between articles of the same material.

(i)* *Furniture.*

(1) If the furniture is conductive but not made of metal, then it shall have casters, tires, or legs of metal, conductive rubber, or equivalent conductive material with a floor contact surface having one dimension of at least ⅝ in. (1.58 cm). Approved equivalent means of making conductive contact between the piece of furniture and the floor is acceptable, provided the contact device is securely bonded to the piece of furniture and is of material that will not oxidize under

conditions of normal use (so as to decrease the conductivity of the circuit), and that uninterrupted contact with the floor is at least ⅝ in. (1.6 cm) in one dimension [*see also 12-4.1.3.13(d)*].

(2) Surfaces on which movable objects may be placed shall be without insulating paint, lacquer, or other nonconductive finish.[1]

(3) The resistance between the conductive frame of the furniture referred to in 12-4.1.3.8(i)(2) and a metal plate placed under one supporting member but insulated from the floor shall not exceed 250,000 ohms, measured with an ohmmeter of the type described in 12-4.1.3.8(b)(7)(iii).

A-12-4.1.3.8(i)   In its requirement for furniture in a flammable anesthetizing location to be constructed of conductive materials, the Subcommittee on Anesthesia Services specifically intends that any shelves within such furniture as well as the top also be conductive. Furniture is intended to include movable and permanently installed objects in the room, such as stools, tables, and cabinets. Wooden racks, however, are permitted for storage of cylinders of flammable as well as nonflammable gases.

A two-part Formal Interpretation was issued on NFPA 56A in July 1976 relative to furniture used in flammable anesthetizing locations. The first part ruled affirmatively on the question of using insulating or nonconductive materials in furniture in such locations, provided the furniture has a conductive frame that meets the requirements of 12-4.1.3.8(i). The second part ruled negatively on the question of a vertical surface bulletin board constituting a "surface" on which movable objects may be placed such that 12-4.1.3.8(i)(2) would apply. In either case, the Interpretation Committee emphasized that these interpretations were not to be construed as allowing the use of nonconductive seats or cushions on stools and chairs in flammable anesthetizing locations.

(j) *High-Frequency Equipment.*   Potential sources of ignition, such as electrosurgical units, shall be prohibited during the administration of flammable anesthetizing agents.

The prior allowance of electrosurgical units (ESUs) in flammable locations under certain circumstances became a controversial issue in recent years. As a result of public comments in 1983, the former Committee on Anesthetizing Agents (now Subcommittee on Anesthesia Services) removed even limited use of ESUs because of the very low use of flammable anesthetics and the concurrent lack of knowledge in the safe use of the anesthetic agents by operating room personnel.

12-4.1.3.9 General Requirements for Flammable Anesthetizing Locations.

(a) Hospital authorities in consultation with others as noted in 4-6.2.2.3 shall adopt regulations to control apparel and footwear allowed, the periodic inspection of conductive materials, the control of purchase of static-conductive and antistatic materials, and the testing of conductive floors.

---

[1]An economical way to make painted furniture conform to this requirement is to attach unpainted sheet metal to the furniture's shelf or top with screws, rivets, or similar fasteners that provide electrical continuity to the frame and casters of the furniture.

(b)* All required precautions shall apply to all anesthetizing locations in which flammable inhalation anesthetics are used.

A-12-4.1.3.9(b)   The use of flammable anesthetic agents is not uncommon in such areas as cystoscopy rooms and emergency units. Such areas must be properly equipped for safe administration of flammable agents, and administrative regulations must apply unless the use of flammable anesthetics in the area is specifically prohibited by an official and specific resolution of the governing board of the hospital, and a conspicuous sign detailing the prohibition is posted in the area.

(c) Hospital regulations shall be established and enforced to control the use of electronic equipment such as television equipment, diathermy equipment, public address systems, monitoring equipment, and similar electronic and high-frequency apparatus in the presence of flammable inhalation anesthetic agents.

(d) Hospital regulations shall prohibit the use of X-ray equipment in flammable anesthetizing locations if such equipment is not approved for operation in hazardous locations [*see 12-4.1.3.5(f) and (g) and 7-5.1.2.4(c)*].

(e) Covers of fabric or of any form of sheeting shall not be used on anesthesia equipment capable of utilizing flammable anesthetizing agents because a cover will confine gas that may leak from a cylinder. When the cover is removed from the anesthesia machine under such conditions a static charge may be created that could ignite the gas confined beneath the cover.

(f) The use of rebreathing techniques in administering flammable anesthetic agents at all times is highly desirable. Through the use of these techniques the escape of flammable mixtures is substantially limited.

(g) Residual ether remaining in ether vaporizers at the end of each day shall be returned to its original containers for disposal or laboratory use only. The ether vaporizer, container, and such shall be thoroughly washed and dried before being returned to use (*see Appendix C-12.4.1*).

(h) Waste liquid ether and other flammable volatile liquid inhalation anesthetic agents shall be disposed of outside of the hospital building according to the recommendations of the authority having jurisdiction. One method is to allow the agent to evaporate in a shallow pan, well removed from possible sources of ignition under supervision.

While the evaporative technique is acceptable, it is very important that supervision be *constant* when allowing the ether to evaporate in a shallow pan.

(i) Members of the professional staff shall be required to submit for inspection and approval any special equipment they wish to introduce into flammable anesthetizing locations [*see 12-4.1.2.4(f)*]. Such equipment shall be approved for use in Class I, Group C, Division 1 hazardous areas or comply with 7-5.1.2.4(e). It shall be equipped with approved cords and attachment plugs [*see 7-5.1.2.2(c) and (d) and 3-4.1.2.4(g) and (h)*].

(j) High-frequency electric and electronic equipment, such as electrosurgery amplifiers, monitors, recorders, television cameras, portable electrical tools, maintenance equipment, and certain sterilizing equipment that does not comply with the provisions of 7-5.1.2.4(e), shall not be used when flammable inhalation anesthetic agents are being administered.

Cautery and electric surgical equipment shall not be used during procedures involving flammable inhalation anesthetic agents unless the equipment complies with the requirements of 7-5.1.2.4(d).

NOTE: See Annex 2, "Safe Use of High-Frequency Electricity in Health Care Facilities."

12-4.1.3.10 Electrostatic Safeguards.

NOTE: Section 12-4.1.3.8 of this chapter deals with the elements required to be incorporated into the structure and equipment to reduce the possibility of electrostatic spark discharges, which are a frequent source of the ignition of flammable anesthetic agents. The elimination of static charges is dependent on the vigilance of administrative activities in material selection, maintenance supervision, and periodic inspection and testing. It cannot be too strongly emphasized that an incomplete chain of precautions will generally increase the electrostatic hazard. For example, conductive flooring [see 12-4.1.3.8(b)] may contribute to the hazard unless all personnel wear conductive shoes and unless all objects in the room are electrically continuous with the floor.

(a)* All personnel entering flammable anesthetizing locations, mixed facilities, or storage locations for flammable anesthetics located in the surgical suite shall be in electrical contact with the conductive floor through the wearing of conductive footwear or an alternative method of providing a path of conductivity. The provision of conductive floors in corridors and rooms directly communicating with flammable anesthetizing locations [see 12-4.1.3.8(b)] will minimize the possibility of static discharge from patients or personnel entering such anesthetizing locations.

A-12-4.1.3.10(a) Personnel. One method for electrically connecting all persons to conductive floors is through the wearing of shoes conforming to the following specifications:

Each shoe having a sole and heel of conductive rubber, conductive leather, or equivalent material, should be so fabricated that the resistance between a metal electrode placed inside the shoe and making contact with the inner sole equivalent in pressure and area to normal contact with the foot, and a metal plate making contact with the bottom of the shoe, equivalent in pressure and area to normal contact with the floor, be not more than 250,000 ohms.

(b) Electric connection of the patient to the operating table shall be assured by the provision of a high-impedance strap in contact with the patient's skin, with one end of the strap fastened to the metal frame of an operating table.

The term "high-impedance strap" is somewhat a misnomer in the sense that the strap has a high impedance compared to electric wire, but it actually has some conductive properties impregnated into it. It could be termed a "conductive strap."

(c) Because of the possibility of percussion sparks, shoes having ferrous nails that may make contact with the floor shall not be permitted in flammable anesthetizing locations or mixed facilities nor in storage locations for flammable anesthetic agents in the surgical suite.

(d) Silk, wool, or synthetic textile materials, except rayon, shall not be permitted in flammable anesthetizing locations or mixed facilities as outer garments or for nonapparel purposes, unless these materials have been approved as antistatic in accordance with the requirements of 12-4.1.3.8(f)(3) and (4).

NOTE: Rayon refers to regenerated cellulose, not cellulose acetate. Cotton and rayon must be unmodified; i.e., must not be glazed, permanently starched, acetylated, or otherwise treated to reduce their natural hygroscopic quality. Fabrics of intimate blends of unmodified cotton or rayon with other textile materials are not acceptable unless tested and found to be antistatic.

(e) Hosiery and underclothing in which the entire garment is in close contact with the skin may be of silk, wool, or synthetic material.

(f) Undergarments with free-hanging skirts, such as slips or petticoats, shall be of cotton, rayon, or other materials demonstrated to be antistatic by the requirements of 12-4.1.3.8(f)(3) and (4).

(g) Antistatic materials for use in flammable anesthetizing locations shall be handled and used in the following manner:

(1) Antistatic materials shall be stored at the temperature and humidity required for flammable anesthetizing locations or they shall be allowed to equilibrate to the humidity and temperature of the flammable anesthetizing location prior to use.

(2) Antistatic materials shall be stored in such a manner that will ensure that the oldest stocks will be used first.

(3) Controls shall be established to ensure that manufacturers' recommendations as to use are followed in the case of antistatic materials.

(h) All antistatic accessories intended for replacement, including belting, rubber accessories, plastics, sheeting, and the like, shall meet pertinent requirements for conductivity as specified in 12-4.1.3.8(f).

12-4.1.3.11 Discretionary Use of Nonconforming Materials.

(a) Suture material, alloplastic or therapeutic devices, bacterial barriers, instruments, gloves (thermoplastic), surgical dressings, and biologic interfaces of these otherwise prohibited materials may be used at the discretion of the surgeon.

(b) Disposable supplies that contribute to the electrostatic hazard shall be so labeled on the unit package.

12-4.1.3.12 Maintenance of Conductive Floors.

A Formal Interpretation was issued on NFPA 56A in August 1977, ruling that sealers or dressings intended to adjust the resistivity of a floor are acceptable. The only criteria of such items is that they do not adversely affect the conductivity of the floor. A second question in the Formal Interpretation, on the permanence of sealers or dressings, subsequently resulted in an Exception being formally adopted for the 1978 edition of NFPA 56A; this is the Exception to 12-4.1.3.12(b).

(a) The surface of conductive floors shall not be insulated by a film of oil or wax. Any waxes, polishes, or dressings used for maintenance of conductive floors shall not adversely affect the conductivity of the floor.

(b) Floors that depend upon applications of water, salt solutions, or other treatment of a nonpermanent nature for their conductivity are not acceptable.

Exception: Treatment of the floor to modify conductivity shall be considered permanent provided the floor meets the requirements of this section (12-4.1) for a period of not less than two years, during which no change or modification beyond normal washing is performed.

(c) Cleaning procedures for conductive floors shall be established, then carefully followed to assure that conductivity characteristics of the floor are not adversely affected by such treatment.

(d) Conductive floors shall be tested as specified in 12-4.1.3.8(b).

12-4.1.3.13 Other Conductive Equipment.

(a) The resistance of conductive accessories shall be tested prior to use as described in 12-4.1.3.8(c) or (d). Thereafter, measurements shall be taken at intervals of not more than one month. A permanent record of the readings shall be kept.

(b) Antistatic plastics shall meet the requirements of 12-4.1.3.8(f)(2). It shall be the responsibility of the hospital to ensure that antistatic sheeting, etc., is used in accordance with the manufacturer's instructions. Failure to do so could in some cases lead to loss of antistatic properties. Antistatic materials that are reused [e.g., antistatic tubing incorporating a continuous conductive pathway as described in 12-4.1.3.8(d)(1)] shall be tested [see 12-4.1.3.8(f)(1)] periodically to ensure retention of conductive properties.

(c) Conductive footwear and other personnel-to-floor connective devices shall be tested on the wearer each time they are worn. An approved resistance-measuring device having a short-circuit current not exceeding 0.5 milliamperes shall be used.

NOTE: The reading may be taken between two insulated, nonoxidizing, metal plates so located that the wearer can stand in a normal manner with a foot on each, in which case the indicated resistance shall not exceed 1,000,000 ohms (1 megohm). [See also Appendix A-12-4.1.3.10(a).]

(d) The resistance of furniture [see 12-4.1.3.8(i) and Appendix A-12-4.1.3.8(i)] and equipment shall be tested prior to use as described in 12-4.1.3.8(i)(3). Thereafter, measurements shall be taken at intervals of not more than one month. A permanent record of the readings shall be kept. The monthly tests can conveniently consist of measurements of the resistance between an electrode placed on the floor and an electrode placed successively on each article of furniture in the room. Additional tests of any individual item shall be made if the measured resistance exceeds five megohms.

(e) Periodic inspection shall be made of leg tips, tires, casters, or other conductive devices on furniture and equipment to ensure that they are maintained free of wax, lint, or other extraneous material that may insulate them and defeat the purpose for which they are used, and also to avoid transporting to conductive floors such materials from other areas.

(f) Excess lubrication of casters shall be avoided to prevent accumulation of oil on conductive caster wheels and sides. Dry graphite or graphitized oil are preferable lubricants.

12-4.1.4 Requirements for Nonflammable Anesthetizing Locations.

This section was developed in response to those facilities no longer using flammable inhalation anesthetics anywhere in their institutions.

While there are no restrictions in nonflammable anesthetizing locations on the types of fabric that can be worn by personnel or used for draping patients, institutions should be sure that such materials are *not* highly combustible. The increased use of flammable liquids, the presence of oxygen, and the use of electrocuting devices pose a problem should a fire involving these materials occur.

12-4.1.4.1 Requirements contained in this part are in addition to those contained in 12-4.1.2.

12-4.1.4.2 All nonflammable anesthetizing locations shall be identified by prominently posted permanent signs at all entrances to the location and within the location indicating that only nonflammable anesthetic agents may be employed.

NOTE: Suggested explanatory text of such a sign is as follows:

> RESTRICTED TO NONFLAMMABLE
> INHALATION ANESTHETIC AGENTS

12-4.1.4.3 Each operating suite containing only nonflammable anesthetizing locations shall contain prominently posted regulations similar to those contained in Appendix C-12.3, Set (2).

12-4.1.4.4* Flooring in nonflammable anesthetizing locations shall not be required to be conductive. If conductive flooring exists, the monthly testing of floors shall not be required provided that at least one test of the floors, as detailed in 12-4.1.3.8(b)(7), is carried out, and in no case shows a single reading of less than 10,000 ohms. At least five readings shall be taken in each room. In the event that the check shows any reading of less than 10,000 ohms, the facility shall revert to the monthly check of the flooring specified in 12-4.1.3.8(b)(6) until the flooring again exceeds 10,000 ohms resistance. There is no need to average the readings. Conductive floors are permitted to be rendered nonconductive by means that will modify their conductive properties. [*See 12-4.1.3.12(b)*.]

NOTE: No requirements on upper limit.

A-12-4.1.4.4 The provision for testing the conductivity of floors once in nonflammable anesthetizing locations is intended to circumvent the need for monthly tests of the approximately 90 percent of such floors that increase in resistivity (decrease in conductivity) as they age.

The resistance value of conductive flooring in nonflammable anesthetizing locations can be allowed to rise in value since it would then resemble that of regular flooring. (The concern here is with conductive floors becoming too conductive and thus posing an electric shock hazard; the static discharge problem is not an issue in nonflammable anesthetizing locations, so rise in resistance of the floor is not of concern.)

There are various options with regard to conductive flooring in nonflammable anesthetizing locations, from checking to make sure the resistance of the floor is rising (or at least not falling below required values), to physically removing conductive flooring, to covering the conductive floor in some manner.

Testing of conductive floors in nonflammable anesthetizing locations may be conducted only once, as a result of recent data from the American Hospital Association indicating that conductive flooring generally only rises in value.

In the event a floor reading drops below 10,000 ohms, remedial action needs to be taken. When readings again exceed 10,000 ohms, testing need be conducted only as indicated. (From a use perspective, the 10,000-ohm lower limit is a moot point because it is almost routine in major surgical procedures for floors to become covered with fluids, and thus be rendered highly conductive. Testing, however, is to be conducted when flooring is dry and clean.)

12-4.1.4.5 In nonflammable facilities the requirements of 12-4.1.3.10, "Electrostatic Safeguards," do not apply. Antistatic clothing and conductive footwear shall not be required. Furniture in nonflammable anesthetizing locations shall not be required to be tested.

12-4.1.5* Requirements for Mixed Facilities.

Items acceptable for use in flammable anesthetizing locations can safely be used in nonflammable anesthetizing locations, but the opposite is not always true. Thus, while a facility could elect to make all movable items suitable for both locations, Section 12-4.1.5 allows the two types of locations to exist independently in the same facility, as long as requirements peculiar to each location are observed.

The term "mixed facilities" was introduced by the Committee for two reasons: (1) while the use of flammable anesthetics has diminished, many institutions wanted to retain some locations suitable for the use of such anesthetics; and (2) even if only a few locations were being maintained for flammable anesthetics, many enforcing authorities were requiring all anesthetizing locations in a facility to meet flammable requirements.

A mixed facility places another burden on anesthesiologists and nurse anesthetists, since these staff are usually the ones assigned the responsibility of ensuring adherence to requirements for mixed facilities. For fixed equipment, this presents no problem; however, movable items (portable equipment, furniture, supplies) present the situation of nonflammable items being able to be moved into flammable locations. Although procedures can be established and followed under normal conditions, in an intense, life-threatening situation, it is unlikely that these procedures will be followed no matter how disasterous the outcome could be.

A-12-4.1.5 A serious behavioral hazard exists in a "mixed facility," i.e., where there are some rooms where flammable agents are prohibited. In the latter situation, inadvertent use of a flammable agent in the "nonflammable" room could be disastrous. It is important to understand the regulations recommended in Appendix C-12.3.

12-4.1.5.1 General. The mixed facility is defined in Chapter 2.

12-4.1.5.2 Construction of Anesthetizing Locations and Storage Locations.

(a) Flammable anesthetizing locations shall be designed, constructed, and equipped as stated in 12-4.1.2 and 12-4.1.3.

(b) The requirements for nonflammable anesthetizing locations are stated in 12-4.1.2 and 12-4.1.4.

(c) Storage locations for flammable anesthetics shall be constructed as provided in 4-3.1.2.4. Storage locations for nonflammable medical gas cylinders shall be constructed as provided in 4-3.1.2.1.

12-4.1.5.3 Conductive Flooring. The provisions of 12-4.1.4.4 shall apply to permanently designated and posted nonflammable anesthetizing locations that exist within a mixed facility.

12-4.1.5.4 Provision for Connection of Patient to Operating Table. Electric connection of the patient to the operating table shall be assured by the provision of a high-resistance (conductive) strap in contact with the patient's skin, with one end of the strap fastened to the metal frame of an operating table.

Conductive straps are an example of an item that can be moved from one anesthetizing location to another since they are suitable for flammable and nonflammable anesthetizing locations. Thus, only one type of straps, suitable in both locations, need be maintained.

An item suitable only for nonflammable anesthetizing locations, however, would not be acceptable in flammable anesthetizing locations.

12-4.1.5.5 Precautionary Signs.

(a) The entrances to all anesthetizing locations shall be identified by prominently posted signs denoting individually whether the anesthetizing location is designed for flammable inhalation anesthetic agents or for nonflammable anesthetic agents.

NOTE: Suggested explanatory texts of such signs are as follows:

```
SUITABLE FOR USE WITH FLAMMABLE
INHALATION ANESTHETIC AGENTS
```

or

```
RESTRICTED TO NONFLAMMABLE INHALATION ANESTHETIC AGENTS
```

(b) In addition, a removable sign shall be posted to all entrances to the anesthetizing location indicating whether a flammable inhalation anesthetic agent is being employed.

NOTE: Suggested explanatory text of such a sign is as follows:

```
CAUTION
FLAMMABLE INHALATION ANESTHETIC IN USE
OBSERVE AND OBEY ALL SAFETY REGULATIONS
```

It shall be the responsibility of the anesthesiologist or nurse anesthetist to ensure that the room is suitably designated for use of the particular agent, whether flammable or nonflammable.

(c) Regulations for the conduct of personnel, administration, and maintenance in mixed facilities shall be posted in at least one prominent location within the operating and, if applicable, delivery suite [see 12-4.1.1.5(c)]. Suggested text of such regulations is contained in Appendix C-12.3, Set (3).

12-4.1.5.6 Movable Equipment and Furniture.

(a) All equipment intended for use in both flammable and nonflammable anesthetizing locations shall meet the antistatic requirements of 12-4.1.3.8.

(b) Equipment intended for use only in nonflammable anesthetizing locations shall be labeled in accordance with 7-5.1.2.4(a), and shall not be introduced into flammable anesthetizing locations. This equipment is not required to meet the antistatic requirements of 12-4.1.3.8.

(c) No portable equipment, including X-ray equipment, shall be introduced into mixed facilities unless it complies with requirements of 7-5.1.2.4(c) and is approved for use in Class I, Group C, Division 1 hazardous areas, or unless it is prominently labeled for use only in the presence of nonflammable anesthetic agents and then restricted to such use.

(d) Portable electric equipment, such as incubators, lamps, heaters, motors, and generators used in mixed facilities in which flammable anesthetics are being employed shall comply with the requirements of Articles 500, 501, and 517 of NFPA 70, *National Electrical Code*, for Class I, Division 1 locations and shall be approved for Class I, Group C, Division 1 hazardous areas, except as permitted in 7-5.1.2.4(f).

NOTE: The resistance and capacitive reactance between the conductors and the noncurrent-carrying metallic parts must be high enough to permit the use of the equipment on an ungrounded distribution system having a line isolation monitor specified in 3-4.3.3.

(e) Furniture intended for use in both flammable and nonflammable anesthetizing locations of mixed facilities shall meet the antistatic requirements of 12-4.1.3.8(i).

(f) Furniture intended for use only in nonflammable anesthetizing locations of mixed facilities shall comply with 12-4.1.3.8(i) or shall be conspicuously labeled and not be introduced into flammable anesthetizing locations.

12-4.2 Laboratories. Laboratories in hospitals shall comply with the requirements of Chapter 10 as applicable.

13

AMBULATORY HEALTH CARE CENTER REQUIREMENTS

Prologue

This chapter lists requirements from Chapters 1 to 11 that are applicable for *ambulatory health care centers*. [Readers should review the Commentary (Prologue) at the beginning of Chapter 12 to understand how this structuring of requirements is intended to be used for each type of health care facility (Chapters 12 to 18)]. The definition of "ambulatory health care center" is given in Chapter 2.

13-1 Scope. This chapter addresses safety requirements for ambulatory health care centers.

13-2 General Responsibilities.

13-2.1 Laboratories. The governing boards of ambulatory health care centers shall have the responsibility of protecting the facilities (for patient care and clinical investigation) and the personnel employed therein.

13-3 General Requirements.

See Commentary under Section 12-3 for explanation of how Section "-3" is to be used.

13-3.1 (Reserved)

13-3.2 (Reserved)

13-3.3 Electrical System Requirements.

13-3.3.1 Normal Electrical Distribution System. (Reserved)

13-3.3.2 The essential electrical distribution system shall conform to the Type III system as described in Chapter 3 if inhalation anesthetics are not administered in any concentration, or if patients do not require electrical life-support equipment. Otherwise, the essential electrical system shall conform to the Type I system as described in Chapter 3.

- See commentary under 16-3.3.2, Exception (a) regarding term "electrical life-support equipment."
- The difference between Sections 13-3.3.2 and 13-3.3.2.1 is slight but necessary. Section 13-3.3.2 specifies conditions when a Type I (as opposed to a Type III) essential electrical system can be used. Section 13-3.3.2.1 specifies conditions

under which a battery system can be used as the alternate source. Thus, while an ambulatory care center meets Type III criteria under Section 13-3.3.2, Section 13-3.3.2.1 allows the facility the option, if it meets the same criteria, to use a battery system in lieu of a generator set for the alternate source of power.

13-3.3.2.1 Ambulatory health care centers that do not administer inhalation anesthetics in any concentration, or have no patients requiring electrical life-support equipment, shall be permitted to use a battery system or self-contained battery integral with equipment in lieu of the alternate power source required in 3-4.2.4.3.

13-3.4 Gas and Vacuum System Requirements.

13-3.4.1 Patient piped gas systems shall conform to Type II systems in Sections 4-3 through 4-6 of Chapter 4 if they are nonhospital-based and meet the criteria of 4-6.2.4.1. Otherwise, conformance to Type I systems, as listed in Sections 4-3 through 4-6 of Chapter 4, is required.

13-3.4.2 Laboratory piped gas systems shall conform to 4-3.3, 4-4.3, and 4-6.

13-3.4.3 Patient Vacuum Systems. (Reserved)

If ambulatory health care centers perform invasive (as opposed to superficial) emergency surgery, and provide continuous suctioning, such facilities should consider complying with the requirements of Sections 4-7 to 4-10 (which were originally developed just for hospitals). Such facilities, however, may have a limited number of vacuum terminals. As such, the Subcommittee on Vacuum Systems and Equipment may develop alternate diversification (use) curves specifically for ambulatory care facilities. (The use curves in Appendix A-4-8.1.1.1 were developed with the intent that they be used by hospitals, which have both surgical/treatment rooms and inpatient care rooms. Ambulatory health care centers would have only the former.)

13-3.4.4 Laboratory Vacuum Systems. (Reserved)

13-3.4.5 For nonmedical piped gas systems, 4-3.4 shall apply.

13-3.5 Environmental Systems. (Reserved)

13-3.6 Material Requirements. (Reserved)

13-3.7 Electrical Equipment Requirements.

13-3.7.1 Patient Care Areas. Electrical appliances shall conform to Chapter 7, "Electrical Equipment, Health Care Facilities," as applicable to patient care areas.

This one new sentence represents several things. First, it shows how the new structure for NFPA 99 can clearly and easily handle changes to facility requirements.

Second, the change itself extends requirements for electric appliances in patient care areas to ambulatory health care centers (AHCC). The requirements in Chapter 7 for electric appliances in patient care areas were originally developed only for patient care areas in hospitals. Arguments were presented during the revision for the 1987 edition of NFPA 99 that the level of electrical hazards for patients in AHCCs has become comparable to those for patients in hospitals. Thus, the Subcommittee on electrical Equipment proposed the extension. The NFPA membership concurred.

13-3.7.2 Laboratories. Equipment shall conform to 7-5.2.2 and 7-6.

13-3.8 Gas Equipment Requirements.

13-3.8.1 Patient. Equipment shall conform to the patient equipment requirements in Chapter 8.

13-4 Specific Area Requirements.

NOTE: This is in addition to any applicable requirements in Section 13-3.

See Commentary under Section 12-4 for explanation of how Section "-4" is to be used.

13-4.1 Anesthetizing Locations.

Prologue

Inhalation anesthetic agents have been employed in dental offices for decades. In the 1960s, Dr. Wallace Reed of Phoenix, Arizona, developed the concept of the Surgicenter®. This facility was the first freestanding operation of its type in the United States to offer general anesthesia for minor surgical procedures performed on wholly ambulatory patients. At about the same time, dental practitioners began popularizing the concept of relative analgesia, a term denoting the administration of nitrous oxide in carefully controlled concentrations sufficient to produce analgesia without loss of consciousness. Relative analgesia is employed for many dental procedures other than extractions and oral surgical work.

An impetus for the development of NFPA 56G (Chapter 4 in the 1984 edition of NFPA 99; now mostly this section of NFPA 99) came as a result of several serious fires in dental offices caused by the improper installation of piping systems. (*See Chapter 4 on medical piped gas systems.*)

The Committee thus decided that a safety standard should be published for the anesthetizing locations of these freestanding facilities. Rather than modify then NFPA 56A, which contained too many requirements and restrictions for such facilities, the Committee decided to draft a separate standard on the subject.

The resultant standard, NFPA 56G, was developed by a specially appointed subcommittee of the then Technical Committee on Inhalation Anesthetics. It was adopted as a tentative standard in 1973 and as a full standard in 1975. This standard was not intended to apply to anesthetizing locations located within hospitals.

The following concepts were included in the original development of NFPA 56G. However, patient and gas limitations were not formally incorporated into the document.

- The requirements of hospital-based flammable anesthetic locations would apply to ambulatory care facilities (ACFs) because, no matter how small or limited in scope, there was no way to lessen requirements when flammable anesthetics were used.
- The standard would apply only to small facilities (six or fewer patients total in either the anesthetic or postanesthetic phase). Large facilities were thought to have the same gas and electrical systems as hospital-based facilities.
- Central gas systems would be limited to 2000 cu ft or less, and the requirements for such systems would continue to be written by the Committee on Industrial and Medical Gases via NFPA 56F, *Standard on Nonflammable Medical Gas Systems*. (Note: NFPA 56F has been incorporated into this 1987 edition of NFPA 99; it has essentially become Sections 4-3 to 4-6, with associated appendix material.)
- With regard to emergency electrical power, if each life support device, as well as lighting, had its own power source (usually batteries), a central generator would not be needed. The Committee on Essential Electrical Systems wrote these requirements. (*See Chapter 3, Type III essential electrical systems.*)
- The only area of severe controversy centered on whether to produce two separate standards: one for anesthetic locations and one for analgesic locations. It was the opinion of the practitioners on the Committee that this was a subjective judgment and could not be equated to number(s), i.e., concentrations, gas flows, anesthetic blood levels, etc. Since the plumbing apparatus was the same, no distinction was made between the two locations.

With many ambulatory care facilities becoming part of multibuilding health care facilities, concern was expressed over whether then NFPA 56A or NFPA 56G would be applicable. This concern primarily related to ungrounded electric power and centrally piped gas systems. In 1980, the Committee emphasized again that NFPA 56G applied to ambulatory care facilities that were not part of health care facilities with inpatients. At the same time, the Committee redefined the criteria for ungrounded (isolated) electric power in NFPA 56A to avoid a conflict between the two documents.

13-4.1.1 General.

13-4.1.1.1 Foreword.

(a) This section has been formulated in the belief that, although material and mechanical equipment must be relied upon to the fullest possible extent for the mitigation of fire and electric shock hazards, such physical safeguards are most effective only when augmented by safety precautions conscientiously applied by personnel staffing ambulatory care facilities. This chapter emphatically calls attention to the need for constant human diligence in the maintenance of safe practices because of the hazards cited together with the mental strain in the environment of surgical, dental, and similar procedures.

(b) Studies of hazards associated with hospital operating rooms by many investigators for more than 30 years have pointed to the conclusion that the greatest degree of safety possible, within the limitations of our present knowledge, is secured only through a completely coordinated program, rather than by the application of individual and unrelated safeguards. Compliance with certain requirements of this chapter will be effective, or even permissible, only when accompanied by compliance with the full program of precautionary measures.

(c) It is necessary for all ambulatory care personnel having any responsibility for safety in anesthesia to collaborate in the precautionary program. Not only must such personnel achieve an understanding of the hazards involved, but in addition, they must be reminded periodically of the dangers posed by electrical shock, compressed gases and their cylinders, and the fire hazards created by oxygen-enriched atomspheres.

13-4.1.1.2 History. A significant number of general anesthetic agents, especially nitrous oxide, are employed in ambulatory care facilities, both as an adjunct for the production of general anesthesia and for the production of relative analgesia. This section was prepared because of the variety of hazards attendant upon the use of some of these agents in the outpatient setting.

13-4.1.1.3 Scope.

(a) This section states the composite methods by which hazards of fire and the handling of compressed gases, when these agents are employed in anesthetizing locations in the ambulatory care facility, can be mitigated.

(b) This section is intended to provide requirements to protect against fires, electric shock, mechanical injury from compressed gases or compressed gas cylinders, and anoxia from erroneous gas connections, without unduly limiting the activities of the practitioner, be he/she a surgeon, oral surgeon, dentist, anesthetist, or anesthesiologist.

(c) Provisions of this section do not apply to the manufacture, storage, transportation, or handling prior to the delivery to the consuming facility of any of these gases. This section does not apply to any use other than in an anesthetizing location.

(d) Although neither nitrous oxide nor oxygen will burn, both support combustion quite readily and pose a potential fire hazard even when flammable agents are not employed concurrently. Additionally, cylinders containing these gases pose a threat to life because of the large amount of pneumatic energy contained therein and the danger of accidental cross-connection between supplies of nitrous oxide and oxygen.

13-4.1.1.4 This section is concerned with certain features in the construction of ambulatory care facilities. This section, with equal emphasis, deals with the installation, maintenance, performance, and use of equipment within these facilities.

13-4.1.1.5 The material of this section and Appendix C-13 are interdependent. For the informed development of an effective ambulatory-care safety program, it is necessary that thorough reference be made to all parts of these requirements.

13-4.1.1.6 Recognition of Hazards and Responsibility. The hazards involved in the use of anesthetic agents, whether used for general anesthesia or relative analgesia, can be successfully mitigated only when all of the areas of hazard are fully recognized by all personnel, and when the physical protection provided is complete and is augmented by attention to detail by all personnel of administration and maintenance having any responsibility for the functioning of anesthetizing locations.

13-4.1.1.7 Applicability.

(a) This section applies to nonhospital-based facilities wherein general anesthesia or relative analgesia are administered to ambulatory patients.

(b) This section does not apply to hospital-based ambulatory care facilities. In such facilities, appropriate provisions of 12-4.1, "Anesthetizing Locations [in Hospitals]," Chapter 8, "Gas Equipment, Health Care Facilities," and Chapter 4, "Gas and Vacuum Systems," shall apply.

Because NFPA 56G was not being applied as intended, the Committee responsible for that document reviewed the issue of hospital-based versus nonhospital-based ambulatory care facilities. In ambulatory care facilities physically connected to hospitals, anesthetizing locations could and would be used for inpatients if the need arose. In that situation, where there was the probability of common piping of gases and of common staffing, the Committee deemed it appropriate to have these anesthetizing locations meet the requirements of NFPA 56A. The Committee thus defined the term "hospital-based" (*see Section 2-2*), noting that it was the physical connection of a facility, whether patient flow or gas or electrical connection, that determined which document should be applied to anesthetizing locations in an ambulatory care facility.

The Committee also took note of NFPA 56A being applied to hospital-based ambulatory care facilities and of the changes in that document that exempted these facilities from certain portions of its requirements (e.g., the change in criteria for installing an isolated power system).

13-4.1.2 Requirements for All Anesthetizing Locations.

The numerous use of "(Reserved)" in this section reflects the desire to have requirements in this chapter listed in the same order as those in Chapter 12 (*see 12-4.1.2*). The "(Reserved)" only means that no requirements have been generated on the subject for anesthetizing locations in ambulatory health care centers. If requirements are proposed, they will have to be processed in accordance with NFPA procedures.

13-4.1.2.1   (Reserved)

13-4.1.2.2   (Reserved)

13-4.1.2.3   Smoking shall be prohibited in all anesthetizing locations.

13-4.1.2.4   (Reserved)

13-4.1.2.5   (Reserved)

13-4.1.2.6   (Reserved)

13-4.1.2.7   (Reserved)

13-4.1.2.8 Anesthetic Apparatus.   Anesthetic apparatus shall conform to the requirements in 8-5.1.2.1.

13-4.1.2.9 Electrical Equipment.   (*See 13-3.7.1.*)

13-4.1.3 Requirements for Flammable Anesthetizing Locations.   This section does not apply to the administration of flammable agents. In ambulatory care facilities wherein flammable agents are employed, the provisions of 12-4.1.3, "Requirements for Flammable Anesthetizing Locations [in Hospitals]," shall apply.

13-4.1.4 Requirements for Nonflammable Anesthetizing Locations.

13-4.1.4.1 Equipment.

(a) *Central Supply Systems.* Central supply systems shall be installed and tested in accordance with 13-3.4.1.

Type II gas systems in Chapter 4 would apply to the installation of piped gas systems for nonhospital-based facilities.

(b) *Special Precautions — Oxygen Cylinders, Manifolds and Cylinder Storage Facilities.* The requirements of 4-6.2.1.2 shall apply.

13-4.1.4.2 Posted Regulations.

(a) Rules and regulations necessary for the implementation of this chapter (*see Appendix C-13.2 for suggested text*), where appropriate, shall be posted in the ambulatory care facility.

13-4.2 Laboratories. Laboratories in ambulatory health care centers shall comply with the requirements of Chapter 10, as applicable.

14 CLINIC REQUIREMENTS

Prologue

This chapter lists requirements from Chapters 1 to 11 that are applicable for *clinics*. [Readers should review the Commentary (Prologue) at the beginning of Chapter 12 to understand how this structuring of requirements is intended to be used for each type of health care facility (Chapters 12 to 18)]. The definition of "clinic" is given in Chapter 2.

14-1 Scope. This chapter addresses safety requirements of clinics.

14-2 General Responsibilities.

14-2.1 Laboratories. The governing boards of clinics shall have the responsibility of protecting the facilities (for patient care and clinical investigation) and the personnel employed therein.

14-3 General Requirements.

See Commentary under Section 12-3 for explanation of how Section "-3" is to be used.

14-3.1 (Reserved)

14-3.2 (Reserved)

14-3.3 Electrical System Requirements.

14-3.3.1 Normal Electrical Distribution System. (Reserved)

14-3.3.2 The essential electrical distribution system shall conform to the Type III system as described in Chapter 3 if inhalation anesthetics are not administered in any concentrations, or if patients do not require electrical life-support equipment. Otherwise, the essential electrical system shall conform to the Type I system as described in Chapter 3.

See Commentary under 16-3.3.2, Exception (a) regarding term "electrical life support equipment."
See Commentary under 13-3.3.2 to understand the difference between 14-3.3.2 and 14-3.3.2.1.

14-3.3.2.1 Clinics that do not administer inhalation anesthetics in any concentration or have no patients requiring electrical life-support equipment shall be permitted to use a battery system or self-contained battery integral with equipment in lieu of the alternate power source required in 3-4.2.4.3.

14-3.4 Gas and Vacuum System Requirements.

14-3.4.1 Patient piped gas systems shall conform to Chapter 4, Sections 4-3 through 4-6, Type II systems if they are nonhospital-based and meet the requirements of 4-6.2.4.1. Otherwise, conformance to Type I systems, as listed in Sections 4-3 through 4-6 of Chapter 4, is required.

14-3.4.2 Laboratory piped gas systems shall conform to 4-3.3, 4-4.3, and 4-6.

14-3.4.3 Patient Vacuum Systems. (Reserved)

14-3.5 Environmental Systems. (Reserved)

14-3.6 Material Requirements. (Reserved)

14-3.7 Electrical Equipment Requirements.

14-3.7.1 Patient Care Areas. (Reserved)

14-3.7.2 Laboratories. Equipment shall conform to 7-5.2.2 and 7-6.

14-3.8 Gas Equipment Requirements.

14-3.8.1 Patient. Equipment shall conform to patient equipment requirements in Chapter 8.

14-4 Specific Area Requirements.

NOTE: This is in addition to other clinic requirements listed in Section 14-3.

See Commentary under Section 12-4 for explanation of how Section "-4" is to be used.

14-4.1 Laboratories. Laboratories in clinics shall comply with the requirements of Chapter 10, as applicable.

15 MEDICAL AND DENTAL OFFICE REQUIREMENTS

Prologue

This chapter lists requirements from Chapters 1 to 11 that are applicable for *medical and dental offices*. [Readers should review the Commentary (Prologue) at the beginning of Chapter 12 to understand how this structuring of requirements is intended to be used for each type of health care facility (Chapters 12 to 18)].

15-1 Scope. This chapter addresses safety requirements of medical and dental offices.

15-2 General Responsibilities.

15-2.1 Laboratories. The governing boards of medical and dental offices shall have the responsibility of protecting the facilities (for patient care and clinical investigation) and the personnel employed therein.

15-3 General Requirements.

See Commentary under Section 12-3 for explanation of how Section "-3" is to be used.

15-3.1 (Reserved)

15-3.2 (Reserved)

15-3.3 Electrical System Requirements.

15-3.3.1 Normal Electrical Distribution System. (Reserved)

15-3.3.2 The essential electrical distribution system shall conform to the Type III system as described in Chapter 3 if inhalation anesthetics are not administered in any concentrations, or if patients do not require electrical life-support equipment. Otherwise, the essential electrical system shall conform to the Type I system as described in Chapter 3.

See Commentary under 16-3.3.2, Exception (a) regarding term "electrical life support equipment."
See Commentary under 13-3.3.2 to understand the difference between 15-3.3.2 and 15-3.3.2.1.

15-3.3.2.1 Medical and dental offices that do not administer inhalation anesthetics in any concentration or have no patients requiring electrical life-support equipment shall be permitted to use a battery system or self-contained battery integral with equipment in lieu of the alternate power source required in 3-4.2.4.3.

15-3.4 Gas and Vacuum System Requirements.

15-3.4.1 Patient piped gas systems shall conform to Chapter 4, Sections 4-3 through 4-6, Type II systems if they are nonhospital-based and meet the requirements of 4-6.2.4.1. Otherwise, conformance to Type I systems, as listed in Sections 4-3 through 4-6 of Chapter 4, is required.

15-3.4.2 Laboratory piped gas systems shall conform to 4-3.3, 4-4.3, and 4-6.

15-3.4.3 Patient Vacuum Systems. (Reserved)

15-3.5 Environmental Systems. (Reserved)

15-3.6 Material Requirements. (Reserved)

15-3.7 Electrical Equipment Requirements.

15-3.7.1 Patient Care Areas. (Reserved)

15-3.7.2 Laboratories. Equipment shall conform to 7-5.2.2 and 7-6.

15-3.8 Gas Equipment Requirements. (Reserved)

15-3.8.1 Patient. Gas equipment shall conform to the patient equipment requirements in Chapter 8.

15-4 Specific Area Requirements.

See Commentary under Section 12-4 for explanation of how Section "-4" is to be used.

NOTE: This in addition to other medical and dental office requirements listed in Section 15-3.

15-4.1 Laboratories. Laboratories in medical and dental offices shall comply with the requirements of Chapter 10, as applicable.

16 NURSING HOME REQUIREMENTS

Prologue

This chapter lists requirements from Chapters 1 to 11 that are applicable for *nursing homes*. [Readers should review the Commentary (Prologue) at the beginning of Chapter 12 to understand how this structuring of requirements is intended to be used for each type of health care facility (Chapters 12 to 18)]. The definition of "nursing home" is given in Chapter 2.

16-1 Scope. This chapter addresses safety requirements of nursing homes.

16-2 General Responsibilities.

16-2.1 Laboratories. The governing boards of nursing homes shall have the responsibility of protecting the facilities (for patient care and clinical investigation) and the personnel employed therein.

16-3 General Requirements.

See Commentary under Section 12-3 for explanation of how Section "-3" is to be used.

16-3.1 (Reserved)

16-3.2 (Reserved)

16-3.3 Electrical System Requirements.

16-3.3.1 Normal Electrical Distribution System. (Reserved)

16-3.3.2 Essential electrical distribution systems shall conform to the Type II systems as described in Chapter 3.

Exception: Any freestanding nursing home that:

(a) maintains admitting and discharge policies that preclude the provision of care for any patient or resident who may need to be sustained by electrical life-support equipment, and

The term "electrical life support equipment" was adopted in 1984 to more accurately reflect the type of equipment that would require a generator set

357

supplying ac power. Only if a device supports life and requires electricity (ac) to function is an essential electrical system required. (*See definition of "electrical life support equipment" in Chapter 2.*)

(b) offers no surgical treatment requiring general anesthesia, and

(c) provides an automatic battery-powered system or unit equipment that will be effective for at least 1½ hours and is otherwise in accordance with NFPA 101, Life Safety Code, and NFPA 70, National Electrical Code, and that will be capable of supplying lighting of at least one footcandle to exit lights, exit corridors, stairways, nursing stations, medication preparation areas, boiler rooms, and communication areas. This system must also supply battery power to operate all alarm systems.

The length of time and light level are in agreement with Chapter 5 of NFPA *101, Life Safety Code.*

While reference is made to a battery-powered system for supplying emergency power {subparagraph (c) of Exception}, any suitable method of supplying electric power would be acceptable, provided the criteria of 1½ hours of electric power is met. It was not the intent of the former Technical Committee on Essential Electrical Systems that a battery-powered system *had* to be provided or was the only way emergency power could be provided. The Exception just *allows* a battery-powered system to be used under certain conditions. A regular emergency generator-set system is acceptable.

16-3.3.2.1 Nursing homes that meet the requirement in the Exception to 16-3.3.2 shall be permitted to use a battery system or self-contained battery integral with equipment in lieu of the alternate power source required in 3-3.2.1.3.

16-3.4 Gas and Vacuum System Requirements.

16-3.4.1 Patient piped gas systems shall conform to Chapter 4, Sections 4-3 through 4-6, Type II systems if they meet the requirements of 4-6.2.4.1. Otherwise, conformance to the Type I systems, as listed in Sections 4-3 through 4-6 of Chapter 4, is required.

16-3.4.2 Laboratory piped gas systems shall conform to 4-3.3, 4-4.3, and 4-6.

16-3.4.3 Patient Vacuum Systems. (Reserved)

16-3.5 Environmental Systems. (Reserved)

16-3.6 Material Requirements. (Reserved)

16-3.7 Electrical Equipment Requirements.

16-3.7.1 Patient Care Areas. (Reserved)

16-3.7.2 Laboratories. Equipment shall conform to 7-5.2.2 and 7-6.

16-3.8 Gas Equipment Requirements.

16-3.8.1 Patient equipment shall conform to requirements for patient equipment in Chapter 8.

16-4 Specific Area Requirements.

NOTE: This is in addition to other nursing home requirements listed in Section 16-3.

See Commentary under Section 12-4 for explanation of how Section "-4" is to be used.

16-4.1 Laboratories. Laboratories in nursing homes shall comply with the requirements of Chapter 10, as applicable.

17 CUSTODIAL CARE FACILITY REQUIREMENTS

Prologue

This chapter lists requirements from Chapters 1 to 11 that are applicable for *custodial care facilities*. [Readers should review the Commentary (Prologue) at the beginning of Chapter 12 to understand how this structuring of requirements is intended to be used for each type of health care facility (Chapters 12 to 18)]. The definition of "custodial care facility" is given in Chapter 2.

17-1 Scope. This chapter covers safety requirements of custodial care facilities.

17-2 General Responsibilities.

17-2.1 Laboratories. The governing boards of custodial care facilities shall have the responsibility of protecting the facilities (for patient care and clinical investigation) and the personnel employed therein.

17-3 General Requirements.

See Commentary under Section 12-3 for explanation of how Section "-3" is to be used.

17-3.1 (Reserved)

17-3.2 (Reserved)

17-3.3 Electrical System Requirements.

17-3.3.1 Normal Electrical Distribution System. (Reserved)

17-3.3.2 Essential electrical distribution systems shall conform to the Type II systems as described in Chapter 3.

Exception: Any freestanding custodial care facility that:

(a) maintains admitting and discharge policies that preclude the provision of care for any patient or resident who may need to be sustained by electrical life-support equipment, and

See Commentary under 16-3.3.2, Exception (a) regarding term "electrical life support equipment."

(b) offers no surgical treatment requiring general anesthesia, and

(c) provides an automatic battery-powered system or unit equipment that will be effective for at least 1½ hours and is otherwise in accordance with NFPA 101, Life Safety Code, and NFPA 70, National Electrical Code, and that will be capable of supplying lighting of at least one footcandle to exit lights, exit corridors, stairways, nursing stations, medication preparation areas, boiler rooms, and communication areas. This system must also supply battery power to operate all alarm systems.

> See Commentary under 16-3.3.2, Exception (c) regarding time requirements, light level, and use of a regular generator set instead of a battery-powered system.

17-3.3.2.1   Custodial care facilities that meet the requirements in the Exception to 17-3.3.2

shall be permitted to use a battery system or self-contained battery integral with equipment in lieu of the alternate power source required in 3-3.2.1.3.

17-3.4 Gas and Vacuum System Requirements.   (Reserved)

17-3.5 Environmental Systems.   (Reserved)

17-3.6 Material Requirements.   (Reserved)

17-3.7 Electrical Equipment Requirements.

17-3.7.1 Patient Care Areas.   (Reserved)

17-3.7.2 Laboratories.   Equipment shall conform to 7-5.2.2 and 7-6.

17-3.8 Gas Equipment Requirements.   (Reserved)

17-4 Special Area Requirements.

> NOTE: This is in addition to other custodial care facility requirements listed in Section 17-3.

> See Commentary under Section 12-4 for explanation of how Section "-4" is to be used.

17-4.1 Laboratories.   Laboratories in custodial care facilities shall comply with the requirements of Chapter 10, as applicable.

18 SUPERVISORY CARE FACILITY REQUIREMENTS

Prologue

This chapter lists requirements from Chapters 1 to 11 that are applicable for *supervisory care facilities*. [Readers should review the Commentary (Prologue) at the beginning of Chapter 12 to understand how this structuring of requirements was intended to be used for each type of health care facility (Chapters 12 to 18)]. The definition of "supervisory care facility" is given in Chapter 2.

18-1 Scope. This chapter covers safety requirements of supervisory care facilities.

18-2 General Responsibilities. (Reserved)

18-3 General Requirements.

See Commentary under Section 12-3 for explanation of how Section "-3" is to be used.

18-3.1 (Reserved)

18-3.2 (Reserved)

18-3.3 Electrical System Requirements.

18-3.3.1 Normal Electrical Distribution System. (Reserved)

18-3.3.2 Essential electrical distribution systems shall conform to the Type III systems as described in Chapter 3 if inhalation anesthetics are not administered in any concentrations, or if patients do not require electrical life-support equipment. Otherwise, the essential electrical system shall conform to Type I systems as described in Chapter 3.

See Commentary under 16-3.3.2, Exception (a) regarding term "electrical life support equipment."
See Commentary under 13-3.3.2 to understand the difference between 18-3.3.2 and 18-3.3.2.1.

18-3.3.2.1 Supervisory care facilities that do not administer inhalation anesthetics in any concentration or have no patients requiring electrical life-support equipment shall be permitted to use a battery system or self-contained battery integral with equipment in lieu of the alternate power source required in 3-4.2.4.3.

18-3.4 Gas and Vacuum System Requirements. (Reserved)

18-3.5 Environmental Systems. (Reserved)

18-3.6 Material Requirements. (Reserved)

18-3.7 Electrical Equipment Requirements. (Reserved)

18-3.8 Gas Equipment Requirements.

18-3.8.1 Patient. Equipment shall conform to patient equipment requirements in Chapter 8.

19 HYPERBARIC FACILITIES

Prologue

Hyperbaric medicine is not new; the US Navy has been employing hyperbaric chambers for deep sea diving, research, and treatment of physiologic and pathologic problems experienced by divers since long before the Second World War. During the late 1950s and early 1960s, many health care institutions in the United States began using hyperbaric facilities, both single-patient and multi-occupancy chambers. The former were developed to allow ready hyperoxygenation of patients for treating gas gangrene, carbon monoxide poisoning, and similar problems. The latter were constructed for those procedures that required medical personnel to be in attendance. Additionally, operating facilities were installed in some larger chambers to allow operative procedures, notably open-heart operations, on patients who, because of their severe illness, would not receive enough oxygen if operated on at ambient atmosphere.

Because of the extensive development and widespread application of these techniques in the modern health care facility, a Subcommittee on Hyperbaric Facilities was appointed in 1964. The Subcommittee membership included representatives from manufacturers of chambers and chamber components, users of chambers, fire service personnel, and others interested in hyperbaric chamber safety. Progress in drafting a standard was slow, however, since there had never been a similar publication.

A significant but unfortunate impetus for the development of a standard came on January 23, 1967, when a fatal fire erupted in the Apollo I Command Module on its pad at Cape Canaveral, Florida, killing all three astronauts inside. Lessons learned from this fire, as well as from a fatal fire occurring a few days later in a US Air Force hypobaric chamber in San Antonio, Texas, spurred development and adoption of NFPA 56D (Chapter 10 in NFPA 99-1984; Chapter 19 in this 1987 edition of NFPA 99). In 1968, it was adopted as a tentative standard, and in 1970, it became a full standard.

In the past few years, the safety precautions contained in that document have been relaxed somewhat as a result of safe experiences in the operation of chambers in both the uniformed services and the private sector. Another factor affecting relaxation was a review of the concept of an oxygen-enriched atmosphere, based on test data for hyperbaric conditions. The compression of air (because of the increased pressure of nitrogen as well as oxygen) does not necessarily create, in and of itself, an oxygen-enriched atmosphere.

19-1 Introduction and Scope.

19-1.1 General.

19-1.1.1 During the past twenty years there has been a widespread interest in the use of oxygen therapy at elevated environmental pressures to drench the tissues of a patient's body with oxygen, to treat certain medical conditions, or to prepare a patient for surgical or radiographic therapy. These techniques are also employed widely for the treatment of decompression sickness (e.g., bends, caisson worker's disease) and carbon monoxide poisoning.

19-1.1.2 Such treatment involves placement of the patient, with or without attendants, in a hyperbaric chamber or pressure vessel, the pressure of which is raised above ambient pressure. In the course of the treatment the patient breathes up to 100 percent oxygen.

The use of closed chambers to treat patients places a special burden on the operators and administrators of these facilities to provide a safe environment. Unlike military and industrial applications, in health care facilities a patient can be expected to be nonambulatory and, in addition, unfamiliar with the equipment and its safety features. This added dimension of concern is evidenced by the requirements that have been included for health care hyperbaric facilities.

19-1.1.2.1 In addition to being used for patient care, these chambers also are being employed for research purposes, using experimental animals, and in some instances humans.

19-1.1.2.2 The partial pressure of oxygen present in a gaseous mixture is the determinant factor of the amount of available oxygen. This pressure will rise if the volume percentage of oxygen present increases or if the total pressure of a given gas mixture containing oxygen increases or if both factors increase. Since the sole purpose of the hyperbaric technique of treatment is to raise the total pressure within the treatment chamber, an increased partial pressure of oxygen always is available during treatment unless positive means are taken to limit the oxygen content. In addition, the patient is often given an oxygen-enriched atmosphere to breathe.

Recently there has been some debate about the increase in flammability of materials in regular air mixtures at higher pressures. The argument is given that regular air mixtures at higher pressures are not particularly hazardous and only increased concentrations of oxygen lead to greater hazards. In Figure A-2-2(a), included in the definition of "oxygen-enriched atmosphere" *(see Chapter 2)*, the graph of burning rate for filter paper versus pressure seems to indicate that this is not true; that is, as pressure increases, holding oxygen percent constant (21 percent line), the burning rate increases from about 0.85 cm/second to about 2.9 cm/second at 10.1 atmospheres. On this basis, either increased partial pressure of oxygen or increased percent oxygen will cause an increased risk and requires special care.

19-1.1.3 There is continual need for human diligence in the establishment, operation, and maintenance of hyperbaric facilities.

19-1.1.3.1 It is the responsibility of the chief administrator of the facility possessing the hyperbaric chamber to adopt and enforce appropriate regulations for hyperbaric facilities. In formulating and administering the program, full use should be made of technical personnel highly qualified in hyperbaric chamber operations and safety.

19-1.1.3.2 It is essential that personnel having responsibility for the hyperbaric facility establish and enforce appropriate programs to fulfill the provisions of this chapter.

19-1.1.4 Potential hazards can be controlled only when continually recognized and understood by all pertinent personnel.

As indicated in 19-1.1.2.1, hyperbaric chambers are used in many different locations for a wide variety of reasons. Each installation and use will present unique concerns which must be recognized and addressed by the operators. This is the reason for 19-1.1.3 and 19-1.1.4.

19-1.2 Purpose.

19-1.2.1 The purpose of this chapter is to set forth minimum safeguards for the protection of patients or other subjects of, and personnel administering, hyperbaric therapy and experimental procedures. Its purpose is also to offer some guidance for rescue personnel who might not ordinarily be involved in hyperbaric chamber operation, but who might become so involved in an emergency.

NOTE: In view of the experimental nature of hyperbaric medicine, many of the hazards and attendant safeguards have not yet been investigated adequately. The Subcommittee on Hyperbaric and Hypobaric Facilities believes that, despite the lack of knowledge needed to prescribe fully for safe practices in hyperbaric medicine, the publication of this chapter is needed for general guidance. Comments based on continuing experience are solicited so that this chapter may be revised from time to time.

The Subcommittee has frequently invited users to make presentations at Committee meetings so that users, designers, and manufacturers will benefit from their experience.

19-1.3 Scope.

19-1.3.1 This chapter applies to hyperbaric chambers and associated facilities that are used, or intended to be used, for medical applications and experimental procedures at pressures from 0 psig to 100 psig (14.7 psia to 114.7 psia) (0 to 690 kPa gauge).

NOTE: This chapter does not apply to respiratory therapy employing oxygen-enriched atmospheres at ambient pressures. [See Chapter 8, "Gas Equipment (Positive and Negative Pressure), Health Care Facilities".]

- The critical concern here is the use of an enclosed space in which the occupants must rely on the outside staff for life safety.
- Even if training chambers are used only occasionally for medical purposes, the requirements set forth in this chapter would be applicable:
- fire protection and building construction requirements are intended to protect building occupants and the building itself; and
- mistakes are more likely to occur in nonmedical (e.g. training) chambers when suddenly used for medical-related purposes.

19-1.3.1.1 This chapter covers the recognition of and protection against hazards of an electrical, explosion, or implosion nature, as well as fire hazards.

The very nature of hyperbaric operations lends itself to all of the above hazards, any of which can produce fire.

19-1.3.1.2   Medical complications of hyperbaric procedures are discussed primarily to acquaint rescue personnel with these problems.

19-1.3.2   This chapter applies to both single- and multiple-patient-occupancy hyperbaric chambers, to animal chambers the size of which precludes human occupancy, and to those in which the chamber atmosphere contains an oxygen partial pressure greater than 0.21 atmosphere absolute (3.09 psia).

NOTE: Hazards differ significantly depending on the occupancy and chamber atmosphere. For this reason, chambers are classified (*see 19-1.5*) for the purpose of defining the hazards and setting forth the safeguards within the chapter.

19-1.4 Application of this Chapter.   This chapter shall be applied only to new construction and new equipment. It shall not require the alteration or replacement of existing construction or equipment. Existing construction or equipment shall be permitted to be continued in use when such use does not constitute a distinct hazard to life.

This paragraph, like that in Chapter 1, is included to emphasize that this edition of Chapter 19 should be applied only to new facilities. Where the Committee felt it warranted, requirements for existing facilities are included for minimum safety. New facility requirements would be overly burdensome to existing facilities and should not be applied to them.

19-1.5 Classification of Chambers.

19-1.5.1 General.   Chambers shall be classified according to occupancy in order to establish appropriate minimum essentials in construction and operation.

19-1.5.2 Occupancy.

(a) Class A — Human, multiple occupancy

(b) Class B — Human, single occupancy

(c) Class C — Animal, no human occupancy.

NOTE: Chambers designed for animal experimentation but equipped for access of personnel to care for the animals are classified as Class A for the purpose of this chapter.

The concern is for the safety of any individual who may be required to enter the chamber (i.e., the enclosed space).

19-1.6 Nature of Hazards.

19-1.6.1   This chapter for the use of hyperbaric facilities is intended to provide protection against fire, explosion, and other hazards without unduly limiting the activities of professional personnel involved in patient (in the case of hospitals) or other care. This principle, without minimizing the hazards, recognizes that professional personnel shall be guided by all of the hazards to life that are inherent in and around hyperbaric treatment procedures.

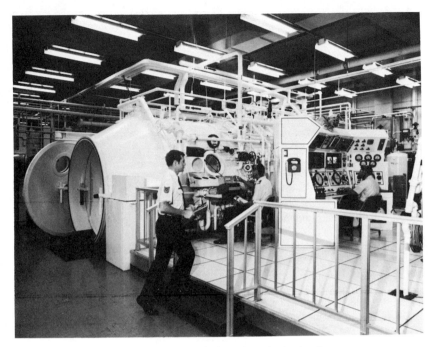

Figure 41(a)   Typical Class A hyperbaric chamber.
(Courtesy of US Air Force School of Aerospace Medicine)

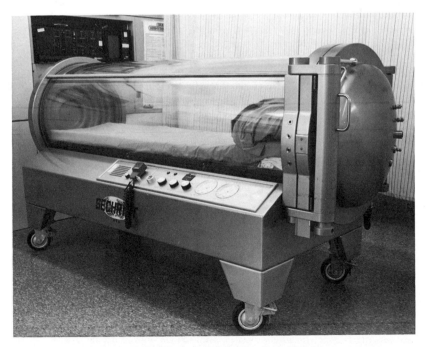

Figure 41(b)   Typical Class B hyperbaric chamber.

19-1.6.2 Potential hazards involved in the design, construction, operation, and maintenance of hyperbaric facilities are formidable. For a discussion of these hazards, see the information in Appendix C-19.

NOTE: The navies of the world have established an enviable safety record in their use of hyperbaric facilities for deep-sea diving research, training, and operations. A knowledge of this safety record must not lull hyperbaric personnel into a false sense of security, however. The potential hazards remain. Where civilian personnel — patients, experimental subjects, and chamber attendants — are involved, an appreciation of these hazards and their mitigation becomes even more important.

With regard to the last sentence in the Note, hospital chambers are of special concern, since they can be expected to house nonambulatory patients who are completely unfamiliar with the chambers and their operational features.

19-2 Construction and Equipment.

19-2.1 Housing for Hyperbaric Facilities.

19-2.1.1 Class A chambers and all ancillary service equipment shall be housed in fire-resistant construction of not less than two-hour classification, which shall be a building either isolated from other buildings or separated from contiguous construction by two-hour noncombustible (under standard atmospheric conditions) wall construction.

This section applies to the noncombustibility of materials used outside the chamber and is the reason that the term "under standard atmospheric conditions" was added in 1980. The environment surrounding the chamber is as important to the safety of the occupants as the interior. The life support systems, controls, safety equipment and, most importantly, the outside support staff must be protected so they can fulfill their function of protecting the occupants of the chamber.

19-2.1.1.1 If there are connecting doors through such common walls of contiguity, they shall be at least B-label, 1½-hour fire doors. All construction and finish materials shall be noncombustible under standard atmospheric conditions.

NOTE: Characteristics of building construction housing hyperbaric chambers and ancillary facilities are no less important to safety from fire hazards than are the characteristics of the hyperbaric chambers themselves. It is conceivable that a fire emergency occurring immediately outside a chamber, given sufficient fuel, could seriously endanger the life or lives of those inside the chamber. Since the service facilities such as compressors, cooling equipment, reserve air supply, oxygen, etc., will in all probability be within the same building, these will also need protection while in themselves supplying life-maintaining service to those inside.

19-2.1.1.2 The room or rooms housing the Class A chambers and service equipment, such as described in 19-2.1.1, shall be for the exclusive use of the hyperbaric operation.

A wet-pipe sprinkler system for the room(s) having a Class A chamber and service equipment is considered necessary because the time required for the fusible link of a sprinkler head to melt in response to a fire would make the area uninhabitable for chamber operators and occupants. The fire would also destroy equipment. Sprinklers are for saving the structure and preventing a fire from spreading beyond an area.

With respect to sprinkler head reliability, inadvertant activation is extremely rare.

Regarding the differences between fire protection outside Class A and Class B chambers, the Committee has noted that for Class A chambers, a sprinkler system is intended to protect persons within a chamber from the effects of a fire outside the chamber; for Class B chambers (19-2.1.2), the intent is to protect the building and its occupants from a fire within the Class B chamber. (It is not usually feasible or, unfortunately, very helpful to install a sprinkler system inside a Class B chamber. *See 19-2.6, Fire Protection in Class B and C Chambers.*)

19-2.1.1.3 The supporting foundation for any chamber should be sufficiently strong to support the chamber. Consideration shall be given to any added floor stresses that will be created during any on-site hydrostatic testing.

The floor has to be capable of supporting the entire chamber filled with water.

19-2.1.2 During use, Class B chambers fabricated of nonmetallic pressure-containing component(s) shall be housed and sprinkler protected as specified in 19-2.1.1, 19-2.1.1.1, and 19-2.1.3.

Exception: Class B chambers constructed according to ANSI/ASME PVHO-1, Safety Standard for Pressure Vessels for Human Occupancy, supplied by an oxygen piping system installed according to Chapter 4, "Gas and Vacuum Systems," and equipped to discharge the effluent gas from the chamber to the exterior of the building, need not be housed and sprinkler protected as specified in 19-2.1.1, 19-2.1.1.1, and 19-2.1.3.

The Subcommittee responsible for requirements for hyperbaric facilities is aware of the differences in building sprinkler requirements between Class A chambers and those Class B chambers that meet the Exception. The Subcommittee intends to conduct a thorough review of this matter for the next edition of NFPA 99.

19-2.1.3 A hydraulically calculated automatic wet pipe sprinkler system shall be installed in the room housing the Class A chamber and in any ancillary equipment rooms. The room shall have automatic wet pipe sprinkler system heads equipped with fusible links installed in accordance with NFPA 13, *Standard for the Installation of Sprinkler Systems.*

This requirement is to protect operators and support equipment in the event of a fire external to the chamber and to ensure sufficient time to bring the chamber to normal atmosphere and evacuate the chamber occupants.

19-2.2 Fabrication of the Hyperbaric Chamber.

19-2.2.1 Class A, B, and C chambers shall be designed and fabricated to meet ANSI/ASME PVHO-1, *Safety Standard for Pressure Vessels for Human Occupancy*, by personnel qualified to fabricate vessels under such codes.

Since this chapter applies only to new construction and equipment, the Committee believes all new chambers should be designed and fabricated to the ANSI/ASME Standard.

Even though the limits of operating pressure in ANSI/ASME PVHO-1 are different (i.e. higher) from those in Chapter 19 of NFPA 99, the Subcommittee on Hyperbaric and Hypobaric Facilities still requires Class A, B, and C chambers to be designed and built to that document. Chambers intended for low pressurization present many of the same hazards as those designed for higher operating pressures (e.g., elevated oxygen levels or concentrations).

19-2.2.2 Class A chambers shall be equipped with a floor that is structurally capable of supporting equipment and personnel necessary for the operation of the chamber according to its expected purpose.

19-2.2.2.1 The floor of Class A chambers shall be noncombustible.

This prohibits the use of wooden or other combustible duckboards.

19-2.2.2.2 If the procedures to be carried out in the Class A hyperbaric chamber require antistatic flooring, the flooring shall be installed in accordance with the provisions of 12-4.1, "Anesthetizing Locations."

Some patients are electrically unstable and may be adversely affected by small electrical currents. A conductive floor will eliminate the buildup of any static charge on occupants as they move about the chamber (e.g., if flammable anesthetics are to be used).

19-2.2.2.3 If a bilge is installed, access to the bilge shall be provided for cleaning purposes. The floor overlying the bilge shall be removable or, as an alternative, there shall be other suitable access for cleaning the bilge.

NOTE 1: Where feasible, it is recommended that Class A chambers be constructed without a bilge or other enclosures that will collect dirt, dust, or liquids.

NOTE 2: It may not be feasible or practical to construct certain chambers without a bilge.

The buildup of dirt, dust, or liquids in a bilge cannot be tolerated in hyperbaric operation since it could pose a fire hazard. In addition, for sanitary reasons, the bilge (and entire chamber) should be readily accessible for cleaning.

19-2.2.3 The interior of Class A chambers shall be unfinished or treated with a finish that is inorganic-zinc-based or high-quality epoxy or equivalent, or that is flame resistant.

Finishes such as inorganic zinc-based, etc., were included in the 1984 revision of NFPA 99 because previously, the referenced test methods listed under the definition of flame resistant were not applicable to the types of interior finishes generally used for the inside walls of hyperbaric chambers. Some finish is required for steel chambers to prevent rusting. The Committee did retain the option of finishes being flame resistant since, in the future, there may be finishes that meet the criteria in the definition of flame resistant.

Because of the need for periodic cleaning of the interiors of chambers, steel surfaces cannot normally be left uncoated. However, any coatings used should provide maximum protection for the occupants in the event of fire.

19-2.2.3.1 If sound-deadening materials are employed within a hyperbaric chamber, they shall be flame resistant as defined in Chapter 2, "Definitions."

19-2.2.4 A sufficient number of viewing ports and access ports for piping and monitoring and related leads shall be installed during initial fabrication of the chamber. Prudent design considerations dictate that at least 150 percent excess pass-through capacity be provided, for future use.

Since chambers are designed and tested, when first constructed, to meet code requirements, any subsequent construction to add ports or other openings in the chamber will require retesting of the pressure vessel, an expensive and disruptive process. Installing extra ports during the original construction will save both time and effort later.

19-2.2.4.1 Access ports in Class A chambers for monitoring and other electrical circuits shall be housed in enclosures that are weatherproof both inside and outside the chamber for protection in the event of sprinkler activation.

Weatherproofing enclosures also makes cleaning possible without shorting electrical components in addition to making the cleaning of the chamber considerably easier and safer.

19-2.2.4.2 Viewports shall be designed and fabricated according to ANSI/ASME PVHO-1, *Safety Standard for Pressure Vessels for Human Occupancy*.

19-2.3 Illumination.

19-2.3.1 Wherever possible, all sources of illumination shall be mounted outside the pressure chamber and arranged to shine through chamber ports.

Mounting lighting outside the chamber, if possible, substantially reduces the hazards that could occur should a lamp break. In addition, it is generally easier to change and maintain externally mounted lamps.

19-2.3.1.1 Lighting fixtures used in conjunction with viewports shall be designed as specified in ANSI/ASME PVHO-1.

19-2.3.1.2 Gasket material shall be of a type that permits the movement of thermal expansion and shall be suitable for the temperatures, pressures, and composition of gases involved. Where practical, noncombustible gasket material shall be employed. Gaskets of O-rings shall be confined to grooves or enclosures, which will prevent their being blown out or squeezed from the enclosures or compression flanges.

19-2.3.2 Fluorescent lamps may be employed for general illumination within Class A chambers provided the ballasts are positioned outside the chamber and the fixtures are housed in self-contained, vented containers.

A concern inside hyperbaric chambers is the presence of sources of explosion and ignition. Lighting is one such source. However, by arranging the ballast of fluorescent lights outside chamber and venting fixtures, the hazard can be mitigated.

19-2.3.3 If it is necessary to employ portable surgical spot-illumination units in the chamber, these units shall be installed in a self-contained, vented, shatterproof fixture.

19-2.3.4 Permanent lighting fixtures installed within the hyperbaric chamber, and any portable lighting fixtures brought into the chamber, shall comply with the requirements of NFPA 70, *National Electrical Code*, Article 500, Class I, Division 1, and approved for use in Class I, Group C atmospheres at the maximum proposed pressure and oxygen concentration.

19-2.3.4.1 All lighting fixtures shall be type-tested and approved in an external pressure of 1 ½ times maximum allowable working pressure. All lighting units to be placed inside a chamber (fluorescent or portable surgical spot lamps) shall be individually pressure tested to withstand the maximum proposed pressure of the chamber.

Increased stringency of testing of lighting fixtures reflects the concern of the Subcommittee for the safety of chamber occupants.

19-2.4 Ventilation of Class A Chambers.

19-2.4.1 Whenever the Class A chamber is used as an operating room, it shall be adequately ventilated and the air supply thereto conditioned according to the minimum requirements for temperature for hospital operating rooms as specified in 12-4.1, "Anesthetizing Locations."

Exception: Class A chambers that are not used in the capacity of an operating room should maintain a temperature that is comfortable for the occupants {usually 75° ± 5°F (22° ± 2°C)}. The thermal control system should be designed to maintain the temperature below 85°F (29°C) during pressurization if possible, and above 65°F (19°C) during depressurization if possible.

NOTE: Section 12-4.1, "Anesthetizing Locations," specifies a desirable temperature of 68°F (20°C). It is impractical to maintain such a temperature during pressurization, but efforts should be made in the design and operation of thermal control systems to maintain the temperature as close to 75°F (22°C) as possible. The air-handling system of all Class A chambers should be capable of maintaining relative humidity in the range of 50 to 70 percent during stable depth operations.

The Exception is included because the temperature levels of 19-2.4.1 for non-operating room conditions would be too cold for patients.

In addition, controlling humidity between 50 and 70 percent is recommended for static electricity control, patient comfort, and avoidance of prolonged exposure to high humidity, which can cause medical problems.

19-2.4.1.1 The minimum ventilation of a Class A chamber shall be 3 cu ft (0.085 cu m) (of pressurized air) per occupant per minute with no less than 3 cu ft per minute (0.085 cu m per minute).

Exception: When a mask oxygen overboard dump system is used to exhaust exhaled gases, the ventilation schedule shall be based on the number of occupants who are not using the overboard dump system, except that the ventilation schedule shall be not less than 3 cu ft per minute (0.085 cu m per minute).

Regular users of hyperbaric chambers indicate that the environment can become "foul" very quickly if proper ventilation is not maintained. Also, carbon dioxide exhaled by chamber occupants must be removed. A rate of 3 cu ft per occupant per minute was determined as a minimum in this situation.

19-2.4.1.2 If volatile agents are being utilized (e.g., nitrous oxide, methoxyflurane, halothane) the minimum continuous ventilation for Class A chambers shall be eight compartment changes per hour.

NOTE: Experience and practice may dictate the need for a threshold sanitary ventilation in excess of the minimum rates specified.

19-2.4.1.3 Provision shall be made for ventilation during nonpressurization of Class A chambers as well as during pressurization.

Since a hyperbaric chamber is gastight, little infiltration can be expected; thus, some form of powered ventilation should be provided during periods of disuse to prevent stale conditions.

19-2.4.1.4 Individual breathing apparatus shall be supplied for each occupant of a Class A chamber for use in case air in the chamber is fouled by combustion or otherwise. Each breathing apparatus shall be available for immediate use and the breathing mixture shall be independent of chamber atmosphere. The air supply shall be sufficient for simultaneous use of all breathing apparatus. Such apparatus shall function at all pressures that may be encountered in the chamber.

Availability to the occupants of a source of air for breathing will allow for an orderly decompression in the event of an accident outside (or inside) the chamber that fouls the chamber air.

19-2.4.1.5 Portable self-contained breathing apparatus shall be available outside a Class A chamber for use by personnel in the event that the air in the vicinity of the chamber is fouled by smoke or other combustion products of fire.

Immediate evacuation of patients and staff in the event of fire or smoke conditions is not possible when operating a chamber. Self-contained breathing apparatus for chamber operators should be designed to provide adequate time for the operators to bring the chamber down to normal atmosphere to allow for evacuation.

19-2.4.2 Sources of air for Class A chamber atmosphere shall be such that toxic or flammable gases are not introduced. Intakes shall be located so as to avoid air contaminated by exhaust from vehicles, stationary engines, or building exhaust outlets.

19-2.4.2.1 Positive efforts shall be undertaken to assure that air for a Class A chamber atmosphere is not fouled by handling (i.e., by oil bath compressors and the like).

Air-handling equipment (i.e., compressors) that use oil must be monitored carefully to ensure that oil seals and oil removal devices are intact and working properly to provide an oil-free atmosphere in the chamber.

19-2.4.3 Warming or cooling of the atmosphere within a Class A chamber may be accomplished by circulating the ambient air within the chamber over or past coils through which a constant flow of warm or cool water is circulated. Dehumidification may be accomplished through the use of cold coils; humidification, by the use of an air-powered water nebulizer. Suitable noncombustible packing and nonflammable lubricant shall be employed on the fan shaft.

19-2.5 Fire Protection in Class A Chambers.

The Committee on Hyperbaric and Hypobaric Facilities reaffirmed its position in 1984 that an automatic fire extinguishment system for Class A chambers is optional. With a change in 19-2.5.2.3 (i.e., that extinguishing system controls be located both inside and outside the chamber), and with Class A chambers always supervised by personnel outside the chamber, a manual extinguishing system is considered sufficient for fire suppression purposes.

19-2.5.1 The system design shall be such that prior to activation of the water deluge system, whether operated in the automatic or manual mode, interior chamber power shall be automatically deactivated first and the emergency lighting and communication system shall be activated.

This sequence of operation is to avoid electrical shocks to chamber occupants when the fire extinguishing system is activated. This design feature is critical to minimize possible electrical hazard to patients and staff.

19-2.5.2 A fixed extinguishing system shall be installed within all Class A chambers. It shall be capable of manual activation. When operated in the automatic mode, activation shall occur within one second of perception of sensible flame development. When operated in the manual mode, system activation shall occur within one second of the manual activation signal.

NOTE: Since inadvertent discharge of the extinguishing agent can disrupt operation of the facility, proper precautions to prevent such an occurrence should be observed. See 19-3.2.1.2.

An automatic extinguishing system is not mandated as it is recognized that discharge of the system in the midst of surgery could cause serious complications to the patient. However, a fixed extinguishing system, activated either manually or automatically, must be installed and available.

19-2.5.2.1 The duration of application of extinguishers in Class A chambers shall be governed by the type of system. The quantity of agent discharged shall provide the necessary concentration or saturation throughout the chamber for complete extinguishment.

This places the burden of engineering the capacity of the extinguishing system to suit the needs of the chamber on chamber designers.

19-2.5.2.2 For water systems in Class A chambers, sufficient spray nozzles shall be installed to provide reasonably uniform spatial coverage with horizontal and vertical jets and an average density at floor level of 2 to 3 gpm per sq ft (27.8 L/min/m^2).

NOTE: Experience has shown that when water is discharged through conventional sprinkler heads into a hyperbaric atmosphere, the spray angle is reduced because of the increased density of the atmosphere, even though the water pressure differential is maintained above atmospheric pressure. Therefore, it is necessary to compensate by increasing the number of sprinkler heads.

19-2.5.2.3 The limit on duration of application of water-based extinguishers in Class A chambers shall be governed by the capacity of the chamber and its drainage system. There shall be sufficient water available to maintain the flow specified in 19-2.5.2.2 for approximately one-minute duration. Extinguisher controls shall be located both inside and outside the chamber.

Recommendations on durations are included because excessive extinguisher application could be disasterous. There must be consideration for balancing a quick, thorough extinguishment (deluge) with a mechanism to prevent flooding.

19-2.5.3 Automatically activated extingushment systems for Class A chambers are optional. If installed, they shall meet the requirements of 19-2.5.3.1 through 19-2.5.3.7.

This reinforces the requirements of 19-2.5.2: automatic activation of the fixed extinguishing system is optional, but a fixed system must be installed.

19-2.5.3.1 Surveillance fire detectors responsive to the radiation from flame shall be employed for automatic activation in Class A chambers. Type and arrangement of detectors shall be such as to activate within one second of fire origination.

19-2.5.3.2 The number of such detectors employed in Class A chambers and their location will be dependent upon the sensitivity of each detector and the configuration of the space or spaces to be protected.

NOTE: Additional detectors are required to avoid "blind" areas if the chamber contains compartmentation.

19-2.5.3.3 There shall be a manual activator located at the operator's console outside the Class A chamber, and at at least two locations inside the chamber. As an alternative method of in-chamber activation, a chain running the length of the chamber adjacent to the ceiling may be provided.

19-2.5.3.4 The fire detection system in Class A chambers shall have automatic or "floating" battery standby. The extinguishing system shall have stored pressure to operate at least 15 seconds without electrical supply.

The critical fire detection and suppression systems should be capable of operation despite power failures, as might occur in fire situations.

19-2.5.3.5 The power supply for booster pumps when used with deluge water sprinkler systems in Class A chambers, and for other emergency facilities, shall be separate from that supplying all other electrical equipment. Activation control circuitry shall have emergency standby provisions. (*See 19-2.7.1.4.*)

See Commentary on 19-2.5.3.4.

19-2.5.3.6 A visual and aural indication of the activation of the extinguishing system in Class A chambers shall be provided at the chamber operator's control console and at the switchboard of the telephone operator or a suitable authority to activate the emergency fire/rescue network of the institution containing the hyperbaric facility.

NOTE: The requirements in 19-2.5.3.6 do not preclude the use of an alarm system affording direct fire department contact.

The activation of an alarm alerting person or group who can provide quick and appropriate help is essential. Fire in or around the chamber is most serious. It is important, therefore, to mobilize the staff of the hospital quickly to assist in fire suppression and rescue efforts.

19-2.5.3.7 The alarm system for Class A chambers shall include continuous electrical supervision to indicate occurrence of a break or ground fault condition in the circuit. A distinctive trouble signal, which shall be activated by this occurrence, shall be provided.

19-2.5.4 A manual extinguishing system also shall be provided inside Class A chambers.

Persons experienced in the use of hyperbaric chambers indicate that the small hand lines, as required by this section, are most effective in quickly suppressing fires within chambers since personnel inside the chamber can pinpoint the line directly on the fire for maximum effect.

19-2.5.4.1 This system for Class A chambers shall consist of two ½-in. water handlines, located strategically within the chamber, preferably adjacent to opposite ends of the chamber. Fire blankets and portable carbon dioxide extinguishers shall not be installed or carried into the chamber.

NOTE: Experience has shown that fire blankets and portable carbon dioxide extinguishers are not effective in controlling fires in oxygen-enriched atmospheres. Valuable time can be lost in attempting to use such devices.

19-2.5.4.2 In the case of Class A chambers having personnel locks, at least one such line shall also be located in each lock.

While "locking in or out" of the chamber, users are isolated from both the chamber and the exterior. Should a fire occur at this point in time, only the hand lines in the lock would be available to them.

19-2.5.4.3 Each handline in a Class A chamber shall be activated by a manual quick-opening quarter-turn valve located within the chamber or the personnel lock.

19-2.5.4.4 The handlines in a Class A chamber shall be supplied from water mains, augmented where necessary with a "surge tank," which will assure 50 psi (345 kPa) minimum water pressure above the maximum hyperbaric chamber pressure.

19-2.5.4.5 Power and control circuits for this booster pump for Class A chambers shall be supplied as noted in 19-2.5.3.5.

19-2.5.4.6 Both the handlines and (where applicable) the deluge sprinkler system of a Class A chamber shall be equipped with manual override valves located at the chamber operator's console and appropriately identified.

This will ensure that the lines can be turned off from the outside if the chamber occupants become incapacitated.

19-2.5.5 Activation of any of the fire extinguishing systems of a Class A chamber shall cause the electrical circuits within the chamber, except the sound-powered telephone circuits and intrinsically safe circuits provided with ground fault circuit interrupters where required by NFPA 70, *National Electrical Code*, to be inactivated automatically and rendered electrically dead.

The exception for telephone circuits was added to maintain as much contact as possible with personnel inside a chamber if a fire occurs in the chamber and the fire extinguishing system activates. The deactivation of other electrical circuits is to prevent the possibility of electrical hazard to occupants in the chamber during the activation of water spray systems.

19-2.5.6 Visibility within the chamber shall be maintained through the continued operation of externally mounted fixtures. (*See 19-2.3.1 through 19-2.3.1.2.*)

This is another reason to have externally mounted, inwardly directed light sources: they will not be affected by activation of the fire suppression system and will still provide much needed illumination during a fire or other emergency.

19-2.6 Fire Protection in Class B and C Chambers. Since Class B and C chambers may be portable, sprinkler systems similar to those described above shall be installed in all areas in which such chambers will be used. (*See 19-2.1.3 except as modified by 19-2.1.2.*)

As noted above, it is critical to protect the areas in which chambers are used to allow operators to decompress the chamber in an orderly fashion to evacuate occupants.

19-2.6.1 The provisions of NFPA 13, *Standard for the Installation of Sprinkler Systems*, shall be referred to when applicable to any class of chamber.

19-2.7 Electrical Systems.

Because uncontrolled decompression can be life threatening, the systems supporting hyperbaric chambers are critical. Electrical service, which is needed to supply power and light for the critical portions of the chamber's control and life support features, should be powered by a secondary emergency power system.

19-2.7.1 Source of Power to Hyperbaric Chambers.

19-2.7.1.1 All essential electric equipment and circuits associated with a hyperbaric chamber, whether within or outside of the chamber, shall have a minimum of two independent sources of electric power, one to be fed from a prime mover-driven generator set located on the premises of the facility.

This is the general requirement for essential electricity for hyperbaric chamber operation. It is critical that power to essential equipment not be interrupted.

19-2.7.1.2 The electrical circuits contained within the chamber and all permanent lighting, whether within or outside of the chamber, and all circuits used for communication and alarm systems shall be connected to the emergency system. (*See Chapter 3, "Electrical Systems."*)

19-2.7.1.3 Electric motor-driven compressors and auxiliary electrical equipment used for atmospheric control within the chamber and normally located outside the chamber shall be connected to the equipment system. (*See Chapter 3, "Electrical Systems."*)

Exception: When reserve air tanks of sufficient capacity to maintain pressure and airflow within the hyperbaric enclosure and to supply high-pressure air for the rapid pressurization of the decompression chamber are provided, the compressor and auxiliary equipment need not have an alternate source of power. It is the intent of this paragraph that the chamber occupants be protected from rapid decompression due to failure of the normal source of power.

19-2.7.1.4 The circuits and equipment listed in 19-2.5.3.1, 19-2.5.3.4, 19-2.5.3.5, 19-2.7.1.2, and 19-2.7.1.3 shall be so installed and connected to an alternate source of power that they will be automatically restored to operation within 10 seconds after interruption of the normal source.

19-2.7.2 Electrical Wiring and Equipment.

19-2.7.2.1 No electrical equipment, with the exception of intrinsically safe equipment and equipment listed for use in 100 percent oxygen at 3 ATA pressure, shall be used in any chamber in which the percent by volume of oxygen exceeds 23.5 percent. Equipment that is used in chambers with concentrations of oxygen of 23.5 percent by volume or less shall be continuously purged with nitrogen or shall be intrinsically safe for that atmosphere.

The requirements on electrical equipment used in hyperbaric chambers were extensively reviewed during the revision for the 1984 edition of NFPA 99 in light of: (1) the need for electrical equipment in Class B chambers; (2) the limited value of a deluge-water system for a fire in Class B chambers with 100 percent oxygen; and (3) the experience of a physician who has been operating in a chamber that uses only compressed air.

Previously, for (1) and (2) above, electrical equipment was not permitted in Class B chambers. However, given the need to place some equipment inside the chamber, and advances in Class B chamber design, the Committee on Hyperbaric and Hypobaric Facilities eliminated the restriction.

For (3), the Committee received a presentation in August 1982 by a physician who, for twenty years, had been operating in a Class A chamber with only compressed air even though he utilized a cautery unit. No incidents had occurred. Because of this record, the Committee modified requirements to distinguish between chambers that used only compressed air (nominal 21 percent oxygen) and those chambers that used oxygen-enriched atmospheres (above 23.5 percent oxygen). (The value 23.5 percent is specified to allow for minor deviations in measurement.)

If the atmosphere in the chamber is oxygen enriched (above 23.5 percent oxygen), the chamber and all internal electrical equipment must still meet the standards for 100 percent oxygen at two atmospheres.

If, however, the atmosphere is only compressed air (nominal 21 percent oxygen), electrical equipment used in the chamber may be intrinsically safe or purged with nitrogen to render the atmosphere in and around the equipment inert. The latter requirement is, of course, much less stringent.

19-2.7.2.2 All electrical circuits serving equipment located adjacent to, or in the vicinity of, the Class A hyperbaric chamber shall be installed in rigid metal conduit so equipped as to prevent water from entering the conduit system, including boxes and fittings used therewith. Conduit shall be equipped with approved drains. All switches, connectors, terminals, and junction boxes shall be completely waterproof.

NOTE: In the event of a fire in the vicinity of the chamber while it is in operation, it is necessary that these circuits be protected from exposure to water from the sprinkler system protecting the chamber housing.

19-2.7.2.3 All electrical circuits contained within the chamber shall be supplied from an ungrounded electrical system, fed from isolating transformers located outside the chamber, and equipped with a line isolation monitor with appropriate signal lamps as specified in Chapter 3, "Electrical Systems." It is desirable that this indicator be capable of sensing single or balanced capacitive-resistive faults, as well as leakage of current to ground.

Use of an ungrounded system minimizes both the possibility of direct faults to ground and the electrical hazard to chamber occupants.

19-2.7.2.4 All electrical wiring installed in the hyperbaric chamber shall comply with the requirements of NFPA 70, *National Electrical Code*, Article 500, Class I, Division 1. Equipment installed therein shall be approved for use in Class I, Group C atmospheres at the maximum proposed pressure and oxygen concentration. Either threaded rigid metal conduit or Type MI cable with termination fittings approved for the location shall be the wiring method employed. All boxes, fittings, and joints shall be explosionproof. (*See Article 501, NFPA 70, National Electrical Code.*)

Enclosure of electrical wiring accomplishes the following:

1. It protects the wiring during normal cleaning operations (in steel tanks, wire runs may well be exposed).
2. It protects wiring in the event of activation of the fire suppression system.
3. It protects wiring from the tank atmosphere.
4. It encloses the wiring in the event of a breakdown to prevent release of noxious fumes into the chamber.

19-2.7.2.5 Fixed electrical equipment within the hyperbaric enclosure shall comply with the requirements of NFPA 70, *National Electrical Code*, Article 500, Class I, Division 1. Equipment installed therein shall be approved for use in Class I, Group C atmospheres at the maximum proposed pressure and oxygen concentration.

NOTE: It is the intention of this chapter that no electrical equipment be installed or used within the chamber that is not intrinsically safe or designed and tested for use under hyperbaric conditions. Any electrical component within the chamber may constitute an intolerable hazard, and should not be permitted without exhaustive study. Control devices, wherever possible, should be installed outside of the hyperbaric chamber and actuated by some suitable mechanical, hydraulic, or other nonelectrical control device, which may be operated from any desired location within the chamber.

19-2.7.2.6 Overcurrent protective devices shall comply with the requirements of NFPA 70, *National Electrical Code*, Article 240, and shall be installed outside of, and adjacent to, the hyperbaric enclosure. Equipment used inside the hyperbaric enclosure may have its own individual overcurrent devices incorporated within the equipment, provided this device is approved for Class I, Division 1, Group C atmospheres at the maximum proposed pressure and oxygen concentration. Each circuit shall have its own individual overcurrent protection in accordance with Section 240-11 of NFPA 70, *National Electrical Code*.

Many overcurrent devices consist of a fusible link (fuse) that heats up, melts, and in many cases, burns to interrupt the circuit. Although adequate in ordinary atmosphere, it may provide a source of ignition in a hyperbaric situation. All such devices must be suitable for service under the conditions expected in the chamber.

19-2.7.2.7 Each ungrounded circuit within or partially within the hyperbaric enclosure shall be controlled by a switch outside the enclosure having a disconnecting pole for each conductor. These poles shall be ganged.

The reason for location of the switch outside the chamber is the sparking that usually occurs when such switches are thrown. Both poles are disconnected because voltage is impressed on both sides of the secondary of an isolation transformer.

19-2.7.2.8 Switches, receptacles, and attachment plugs designed for electrical systems used in ordinary locations are prohibited from use in hyperbaric chambers because of the frequent sparks or arcs that result from their normal use. All receptacles and attachment plugs shall conform to 3-4.1.2.4(g), which addresses receptacles and attachment plugs in hazardous areas.

Ordinary switches draw an arc when activated and thus become a source of ignition. Similarly, regular receptacles and plugs (attachment caps) can draw an arc if the plug is pulled out while power is flowing. Suitable switches, receptacles, and plugs are to be used in the chamber.

19-2.7.3 Hyperbaric Chamber Service Equipment. All hyperbaric chamber service equipment, switchboards, or panelboards shall be installed outside of, and adjacent to, the hyperbaric enclosure, and so arranged as to readily permit manual supervisory control by operators in visual contact with the chamber interior.

19-2.8 Intercommunications and Monitoring Equipment.

Ordinary communication equipment may not be suitable for use under the rigorous conditions of hyperbaric service. Switches may spark, and microphones can produce arcing. Any devices used in the chamber for communications should be carefully checked, as indicated in the subsequent paragraphs, to ensure that they are safe for use in hyperbaric chambers.

19-2.8.1 Intercommunications equipment is mandatory to the safe operation of a hyperbaric facility.

19-2.8.1.1 All intercommunications equipment shall be approved as intrinsically safe. (*See Chapter 2, "Definitions."*) All fixed conductors inside the chamber shall be insulated with insulation that is flame resistant in accordance with the definitions given in Chapter 2, for example Type MI cable or Teflon-insulated cable.

19-2.8.1.2 Microphones, loudspeakers, and hand phones located in the chamber and personnel locks shall be approved as intrinsically safe at the maximum proposed pressure and oxygen concentration and shall operate on less than five volts. All other components of the intercommunications equipment, including the audio output transformers, shall be located outside of the hyperbaric facility.

Exception: Oxygen mask microphones with external relays designed to operate on equal to or less than 28 volts and not to exceed a current of 0.25 amperes may be used provided they qualify as intrinsically safe at the maximum proposed pressure and oxygen concentration. If push-to-talk switches are used, they shall be of the hermetically sealed, pressure-tested type and arc-suppressed circuits shall be incorporated in the switch.

This Exception was added in 1984 since it was reported to the Committee that the National Aeronautics and Space Administration in Houston, Texas, had conducted fire tests on these systems in hyperbaric chambers with satisfactory results. These microphone systems are the standard AIC-10 aviator mask microphone systems.

The term "intrinsically safe" is defined in Chapter 2.

19-2.8.1.3 Voice sensors when part of an oxygen mask shall be approved as intrinsically safe for 95 ± 5 percent oxygen at the maximum proposed pressure.

19-2.8.1.4 All electrical conductors inside the chamber and personnel locks shall be insulated with insulation that is flame resistant in accordance with the definitions given in Chapter 2.

Exception: Grounds through the piping system need not be insulated.

The Exception was added to the 1982 edition of NFPA 56D for clarification — grounding wires do not have to be insulated since they are at the same potential as the surrounding chamber (ground).

19-2.8.1.5 The intercommunications system also shall connect all personnel locks with both the main chamber and the chamber operator's control panel.

NOTE: It is recommended that each Class A chamber be equipped with a system with dual channels, and a sound-powered telephone or surveillance microphone system be furnished in addition.

19-2.8.2 All patient-monitoring equipment shall be located on the outside of the chamber and the monitoring leads conveyed through appropriate pass-throughs. Information about the status of an anesthetized patient should be transmitted to members of the operating team via the intercommunications equipment. As an alternative, the oscilloscopic screen or other monitoring device indicator may be placed adjacent to one of the viewing ports. As another alternative, monitors continuously purged with inert gas and designed so as not to exceed maximum safe operating temperature and pressure changes may be employed.

Although many modern electronic devices may function in high-pressure locations, the oscilloscope is a large, evacuated glass tube that can implode if placed under pressure.

19-2.8.2.1 The conductors or patient leads extending into the hyperbaric chamber shall be intrinsically safe, up to seven atmospheres pressure, as defined in NFPA 70, *National Electrical Code*, and shall be listed for use in Class I, Group C, Division 1 hazardous locations under pressures up to 100 psig (114.7 psia) (690 kPa gauge) pressure.

NOTE: The minimum electrical energy required to ignite explosive atmospheres decreases as the pressure of the explosive atmosphere increases. Therefore, intrinsically safe circuits that have been tested and found suitable for explosive atmospheres at ambient pressures (atmospheric) may not be intrinsically safe when used in the presence of flammable anesthetic gas (or vapor) air mixtures above atmospheric pressure.

19-2.8.3 Any other electrically operated equipment brought into the hyperbaric chamber, or installed in the chamber, including monitoring and intercommunications equipment, shall be explosionproof or be intrinsically safe as defined by NFPA 70, *National Electrical Code*, in 95 ± 5 percent oxygen and up to 100 psig (114.7 psia) (690 kPa gauge) pressure.

19-2.8.4 Automatic fire detection equipment is covered in 19-2.5.3 through 19-2.5.3.7.

19-2.8.5 Sensors shall be installed to detect levels of carbon dioxide (above 0.2 percent), carbon monoxide (above 15 ppm), and volatilized hydrocarbons (above 500 ppm). As an alternative, periodic sampling of chamber air in Class A chambers without oxygen-enriched environments shall be accomplished at least once each month of operation. (*See ventilation requirements in 19-2.4.1 and 19-2.4.1.2.*)

Exception: Sensors are not required in the case of the Class B chamber continuously purged with 95 ± 5 percent oxygen.

The use of sensors or periodic sampling to monitor for the presence of hydrocarbon pollutants is designed to alert operators to the possible fouling of air inside the chamber. This condition is caused by drawing in fouled air or by breakdown of seals or other systems in the air-compressing mechanisms.

The second sentence was added in 1981 for the benefit of clinical hyperbaric chambers since continuous venting is required for this type (*see 19-2.4.1*). In addition, it was reported to the Committee that monthly monitoring of CO_2 and hydrocarbons in USAF hyperbaric chambers over the past thirteen years had been found to be adequate (i.e., no accidents had occurred).

19-2.8.6 All detectors or sensors mounted inside the hyperbaric chamber shall be intrinsically safe and implosionproof at the maximum proposed operating pressure and oxygen concentration. Control equipment shall be installed outside the chamber.

The Committee on Hyperbaric and Hypobaric Facilities felt that such devices needed to meet both requirements in view of the severe environmental conditions to which these devices are subjected.

19-2.9 Other Equipment and Fixtures.

19-2.9.1 All furniture used in the hyperbaric chamber shall be grounded as recommended for installation and use in hazardous locations in 12-4.1, "Anesthetizing Locations."

While the space inside a Class B hyperbaric chamber is considered a hazardous location, the *room* in which the chamber is located is *not* a hazardous location, particularly with exhausts vented to the exterior of the building. (*See 19-2.1.2.*) Thus, there is no requirement for a conductive floor, etc., in the room where this type of chamber is located. Prudency would suggest grounding the chamber if it is nonelectric (i.e., a three-wire power cord would provide a ground through the green "ground" wire).

19-2.9.2 Exhaust from all classes of chambers shall be piped outside of the building, the point of exit being clear of all neighboring hazards and clear of possible reentry of exhaust gases into the building, and protected by a grille or fence of at least 2-ft (0.6-m) radius from the exhaust port. A protective grille or fence is not required when the exhaust is above the building height.

External exhaust requirements were extended to Class C chambers (thereby affecting all chambers) because health hazards exist as a result of the exhausts from all classes of chambers.

19-2.9.3 Requirements cited in this section are minimum ones. Discretion on the part of chamber operators and others may dictate the establishment of more stringent regulations.

19-3 Administration and Maintenance.

19-3.1 General.

19-3.1.1 Purpose. Section 19-3 contains requirements for administration and maintenance which shall be followed as an adjunct to physical precautions specified in Section 19-2.

It cannot be to strongly stressed: the best systems in the world can be rendered unsafe if they are not checked regularly and maintained. This includes careful monitoring of written controls, such as written safety procedures, to ensure that they remain current. This is in addition to adherence to the controls themselves and inspection of the physical facility.

19-3.1.2 Recognition of Hazards. The hazards involved in the use of hyperbaric facilities can be mitigated successfully only when all of the areas of hazard are fully recognized by all personnel and when the physical protection provided is complete and is augmented by attention to detail by all personnel of administration and maintenance having any responsibility for the functioning of the hyperbaric facility. The nature and degree of these hazards are outlined in Appendix C-19 of this document and should be reviewed by all personnel. Since Section 19-3 is expected to be used as a test by those responsible for the mitigation of hazards of hyperbaric facilities, the requirements set forth herein are frequently accompanied by explanatory text.

19-3.1.3 Responsibility.

19-3.1.3.1 Responsibility for the maintenance of safe conditions and practices both in and around hyperbaric facilities falls mutually upon the governing body of the institution, all personnel using or operating the hyperbaric facility, the administration of the institution, and those responsible for licensing, accrediting, or approving institutions or other facilities in which hyperbaric installations are employed.

This paragraph sets up a four-point safety check over the hyperbaric chamber. The governing body of the institution in which the chamber is housed must set a firm policy to ensure safe operation of the chamber. The management of the institution, in concert with the technical staff of the chamber, must develop procedures for the safe operation of the chamber. The technical operating staff is then responsible for the correct execution of the procedures. Finally, licensing and accrediting agencies must periodically review all three (policy, procedures, and compliance) to ensure the safety of patients and staff who use hyperbaric chambers.

19-3.1.3.2 A safety director shall be in charge of all hyperbaric equipment. The safety director shall have the authority to restrict potentially hazardous supplies and equipment from the chamber [*see 19-3.1.3.3 and 19-3.1.5.5(c)*].

19-3.1.3.3 The complexity of Class A chambers is such that one person should be designated chamber operator, such as one in a position of responsible authority. Before starting a hyperbaric run, this person should acknowledge, in writing, in an appropriate log, the purpose of the run or test, duties of all personnel involved, and a statement that he or she is satisfied with the condition of all equipment. Exceptions should be itemized in the statement.

19-3.1.3.4 The ultimate responsibility for the care and safety of patients (in the case of a hospital) and personnel (in any institution) is that of the governing board. Hence it is incumbent upon that body to insist that adequate rules and regulations with respect to practices and conduct in hyperbaric facilities be adopted by the medical or administrative staff of the institution, and that adequate regulations for inspection and maintenance are in use by the administrative, maintenance, and ancillary (and in the case of a hospital, nursing and other professional) personnel.

It is important to remember that, while the governing board does not write safety procedures, it must ensure that they are written and adhered to.

19-3.1.3.5 By virtue of its responsibility for the professional conduct of members of the medical staff of the health care facility, the organized medical staff shall adopt adequate regulations with respect to the use of hyperbaric facilities located in health care facilities (*see Appendix C-19-2 and C-19-3*) and through its formal organization shall ascertain that these regulations are regularly adhered to. The safety director shall be included in the planning phase of these regulations.

Good medical staff regulations are important. Although the needs of the medical staff may be different from those of the institution's management, the ultimate goal of safety must be addressed by both.

19-3.1.3.6 In meeting its responsibilities for safe practices in hyperbaric facilities, the administration of the facility shall adopt or correlate regulations and standard operating procedures to assure that both the physical qualities and the operating maintenance methods pertaining to hyperbaric facilities meet the standards set in this chapter. The controls adopted shall cover the conduct of personnel in and around hyperbaric facilities, and the apparel and footwear allowed. They shall cover periodic inspection of static-dissipating materials and of all electrical equipment, including testing of ground contact indicators. Electrical, monitoring, life-support, protection, and ventilating arrangements in the hyperbaric chamber shall be inspected and tested regularly.

NOTE: In the case of a hyperbaric facility located in a hospital, hospital licensing and other approval bodies, in meeting their responsibilities to the public, should include in their inspections not only compliance with requirements for physical installations in hyperbaric facilities, but also compliance with the requirements set forth in Section 19-3 of this chapter.

Hospital hyperbaric chambers have to simultaneously meet the needs of both regular hospital operating rooms and of high-pressure chambers.

19-3.1.4 Rules and Regulations.

19-3.1.4.1 General. It is recommended that administrative, technical, and professional staffs jointly consider and agree upon neccessary rules and regulations for the control of personnel concerned with the use of hyperbaric facilities. Upon adoption, rules and regulations shall be prominently posted in and around the hyperbaric chamber. Positive measures are necessary to acquaint all personnel with the rules and regulations established and to assume enforcement. Training and discipline are mandatory.

19-3.1.4.2 It is recommended that all personnel, including trainees and those involved in the operation and maintenance of hyperbaric facilities, and including professional personnel and (in the case of hospitals) others involved in the direct care of patients undergoing hyperbaric therapy, be familiar with this chapter. Personnel concerned should maintain proficiency in the matters of life and fire safety by periodic review of this chapter, as well as any other pertinent material.

19-3.1.4.3 All personnel, including those involved in maintenance and repair of the facility, shall become familiar with emergency equipment — its purposes, applications, operation, and limitations.

It must be stressed that merely writing emergency procedures is not enough. Procedures must be practiced regularly to ensure that, if they are needed, chamber personnel will react quickly and correctly when called upon. In addition, it is important to train all personnel involved, as it is impossible to know in advance which persons will be available in an emergency, or what special conditions the emergency itself will impose on the facility and staff.

19-3.1.4.4 Emergency procedures best suited to the needs of the individual facility shall be established. All personnel shall become thoroughly familiar with these procedures and the methods of implementing them. Individual circumstances dictate whether such familiarization can best be afforded through the medium of a procedure manual. Personnel shall be trained to safely decompress occupants when all powered equipment has been rendered inoperative.

The Subcommittee on Hyperbaric and Hypobaric Facilities changed previous guidance on establishing emergency procedures from "recommendations" to "requirements" because such procedures are considered critical in the event of a fire.

19-3.1.4.5 A suggested outline for emergency action in the case of fire is contained in Appendix C-19.2.

19-3.1.4.6 Fire training drills shall be carried out at regular intervals.

NOTE: A calm reaction (without panic) to an emergency situation can be expected only if the above recommendations are familiar to and rehearsed by all concerned.

19-3.1.5 General Requirements.

19-3.1.5.1 Open Flames and Hot Objects. Smoking, open flames, hot objects, and ultraviolet sources, which would cause premature operation of flame detectors, when installed, shall be prohibited from hyperbaric facilities, both inside and outside, but in the vicinity of the chamber. The immediate vicinity of the chamber is defined as the general surrounding area from which activation of the flame detector can occur.

The second sentence was added to the 1982 edition of NFPA 56D to clarify the term "vicinity."

19-3.1.5.2 Flammable Gases and Liquids. The use of flammable agents inside a hyperbaric facility or in proximity to the compressor intake shall be forbidden. Burners employing natural or bottled gas for laboratory purposes, and cigarette lighters fall into this category.

Exception: When potentially flammable agents must be used for patient treatment (e.g., alcohol swabs, parenteral alcohol-based pharmaceuticals, topical creams), such agents shall be approved by a board of competent authorities.

NOTE: Many "inert" halogenated compounds have been found to act explosively in the presence of metals, even under normal atmospheric conditions, despite the fact that the halogen compound itself does not ignite in oxygen, or, in the case of solids such as polytetrafluoroethylene, is self-extinguishing. Apparently these materials are strong oxidizers whether as gases, liquids (solvents, greases), or solids (electrical insulation, fabric, or coatings). Some halogenated hydrocarbons that will not burn in the presence of low-pressure oxygen will ignite and continue to burn in high-pressure oxygen. Customarily, Class A chambers maintain internal oxygen concentration that does not exceed 23.5 percent.

The Exception was added by the Committee on Hyperbaric and Hypobaric Facilities, but caution should be exercised with regard to allowing the use of such potentially flammable agents in a chamber.

19-3.1.5.3 Parts of this chapter deal with the elements required to be incorporated into the structure of the chamber to reduce the possibility of electrostatic spark discharges, which are a possible cause of ignition in hyperbaric atmospheres. The elimination of static charges is dependent on the vigilance of administrative activities in materials, purchase, maintenance supervision, and periodic inspection and testing. It cannot be emphasized too strongly that an incomplete chain of precautions generally will increase the electrostatic hazard. For example, conductive flooring may contribute to the hazard unless all personnel wear conductive shoes, all objects in the room are electrically continuous with the floor, and humidity is maintained. Maximum precautions within reason shall be taken.

The last sentence was added to the 1982 edition of NFPA 56D to allow for judgment by the user.

19-3.1.5.4 Personnel.

(a) The number of occupants of the chamber shall be kept to the minimum number necessary to carry out the procedure.

(b) All personnel entering a Class A chamber equipped with a conductive floor shall be in electrical contact with the conductive floor through the wearing of conductive footwear or an alternative method of providing a path of conductivity. In Class A chambers that are not equipped with conductive floors, antistatic procedures as directed by the safety director shall be employed whenever oxygen-enriched atmospheres are used.

(c) In Class A chambers with oxygen-enriched atmospheres, and in all Class B chambers, electrical grounding of the patient shall be assured by the provision of a conductive strap in contact with the patient's skin, with one end of the strap fastened to the metal frame of an operating table (or other equipment) meeting the requirements of 12-4.1, "Anesthetizing Locations."

• The intent of subparagraphs (b) and (c) is to minimize the buildup of static electricity in chambers, while at the same time allowing medical procedures to be carried out.
• There are various methods of grounding the patient to the frame of the chamber. Conductive material that meets the conductivity requirements in Section 12-4.1.3 (requirements for flammable anesthetizing locations) are acceptable.

(d) Because of the possibility of percussion sparks, shoes having ferrous nails that may make contact with the floor shall not be permitted to be worn in Class A chambers.

(e) Equipment of cerium, magnesium, magnesium alloys, and similar manufacture shall be prohibited. (*See also Note under 19-3.2.2.*)

Many light metals are capable of burning in air. (Magnesium is particularly known for this and is used for incendiary bombs.) Placement in a hyperbaric chamber where the atmospheric pressure (normal or oxygen enriched) is elevated would only make it easier for such metals to burn.

19-3.1.5.5 Textiles.

(a) Cotton, silk, wool, or synthetic textile materials shall not be permitted in Class A hyperbaric chambers, unless the fabric meets the requirements of 19-3.1.5.5(d).

These materials, unless treated, are strong producers of static electricity.

(b) Only garments of cotton or antistatic synthetic materials (*see 12-4.1.3*) shall be permitted in Class B hyperbaric chambers.

(c) Suture material, alloplastic devices, bacterial barriers, surgical dressings, and biologic interfaces of otherwise prohibited materials may be used at the discretion of the physician or surgeon in charge with the concurrence of the safety director. This permission shall be stated in writing for all prohibited materials employed (*see 19-3.1.3.3*).

(d) Where flame resistance is specified, the fabric shall meet the requirements set forth for the small-scale test in NFPA 701, *Standard Methods of Fire Tests for Flame-Resistant Textiles and Films*, except that the test shall be performed in an atmosphere equivalent to the maximum oxygen concentration and pressure proposed for the chamber.

NFPA 701 does not consider the hyperbaric situation. Thus, the Exception clause was added to assure that textiles remain flame resistant at the oxygen concentration and pressure to be experienced.

19-3.1.5.6 All chamber personnel shall wear garments of the overall or jumpsuit type, completely covering all skin areas possible, and as tight-fitting as possible.

19-3.1.5.7 Whenever possible patients shall be stripped of all clothing, particularly if it is contaminated by dirt, grease, or solvents, and then reclothed as specified in 19-3.1.5.6. All cosmetics, lotions, and oils shall be removed from the patient's body and hair.

NOTE: It may be impractical to clothe some patients (depending upon their disease or the site of any operation) in such garments. Hospital gowns of flame-resistant textile should be employed in such a case.

19-3.1.5.8 All other fabrics used in the chamber such as sheets, drapes, and blankets shall be of inherently flame-resistant materials. Free-hanging drapes should be minimized.

19-3.1.5.9 The use of flammable hair sprays, hair oils, and skin oils shall be forbidden for all chamber occupants — patients as well as personnel.

19-3.2 Equipment.

19-3.2.1 All equipment used in the hyperbaric facility shall comply with Section 19-2. This includes all electrical and mechanical equipment necessary for the operation and maintenance of the hyperbaric facility, as well as any medical devices and instruments used in the facility. Use of unapproved equipment shall be prohibited. [See 19-3.1.5.5(c).]

With the last sentence, the Committee emphasized the need to have equipment meet the requirements set forth in this chapter.

19-3.2.1.1 Portable X-ray devices, electrocautery equipment, and other similar high-energy devices shall not be operated in the hyperbaric chamber unless approved for such use. Photographic equipment employing photoflash, flood lamps, or similar equipment shall not remain in the hyperbaric chamber when the chamber is pressurized. Lasers shall not be used under any condition.

19-3.2.1.2 Equipment known to be, or suspected of being, defective shall not be introduced into any hyperbaric chamber or used in conjunction with the operation of such chamber until repaired, tested, and accepted by qualified personnel and approved by the safety director (see 19-2.5.2).

19-3.2.1.3 The use of paper shall be kept to an absolute minimum in hyperbaric chambers, and any paper brought into the chamber shall be stored in a closed metal container. Containers shall be emptied after each chamber operation.

The use of paper products in hyperbaric chambers is discouraged by the Committee because of the fire hazard they present. This includes paper cups, towels, or tissues. If they must be used, a minimal number should be brought inside the chamber, and then they are to be stored in a closed metal container.

19-3.2.2 Oxygen containers, valves, fittings, and interconnecting equipment shall be all metal to the extent possible. Valve seats, gaskets, hoses, and lubricants shall be selected carefully for oxygen compatibility under service conditions.

NOTE: Users should be aware that many items if ignited in pressurized oxygen-enriched atmospheres are not self-extinguishing. Iron alloys, aluminum, and stainless steel are, to various degrees, in that category as well as human skin, muscle, and fat, and plastic tubing such as polyvinyl chloride (Tygon). Testing for oxygen compatibility is very complicated. Very little data exists and many standards still have to be determined. Suppliers do not normally have facilities for testing their products in controlled atmospheres, especially high-pressure oxygen. Both static conditions and impact conditions are applicable. Self-ignition temperatures normally are unknown in special atmospheres.

19-3.2.3 Equipment requiring lubrication shall be lubricated with oxygen-compatible flame-resistant material.

19-3.3 Handling of Gases.

19-3.3.1 General.

19-3.3.1.1 Flammable gases shall not be used or stored within, or in the immediate vicinity of, a hyperbaric facility. Nonflammable gases may be piped into the hyperbaric facility. Pressurized containers of gas may be introduced into the hyperbaric chamber, provided the container and contents are approved for such use. The institution's administrative personnel shall ensure that rules and regulations are provided to ensure the safe handling of gases in the hyperbaric facility (*see 19-3.1.5.2 and Appendix C-19.1.1.3.2*).

Pressurized containers are those used for specific purposes such as blood gas analyzers and emergency air supplies.

19-3.3.2 Quantities of oxygen stored in the chamber shall be kept to a minimum. Oxygen and other gases shall not be introduced into the chamber in the liquid state.

Gases in a liquid state are prohibited because liquid gases could "boil off," and quickly change the composition of the atmosphere in the chamber, creating a hazardous condition.

19-3.4 Maintenance.

19-3.4.1 General.

19-3.4.1.1 The hyperbaric safety director shall be ultimately responsible for ensuring that all valves, regulators, meters, and similar equipment used in the hyperbaric chamber are properly compensated for safe use under hyperbaric conditions, and tested periodically. Pressure relief valves shall be tested and calibrated periodically.

Most gas regulators depend on atmospheric pressure as a reference point to operate properly. No device of this type should ever be used in a chamber unless it has been properly checked by the hyperbaric safety director to ensure that the use is appropriate.

19-3.4.1.2 The hyperbaric-safety director shall also be ultimately responsible for ensuring that all gas outlets in the chambers are properly labeled or stenciled in accordance with ANSI Z48.1, *Standard Method of Marking Portable Compressed Gas Containers to Identify the Material Contained.*

19-3.4.1.3 Before piping systems are initially put into use, it shall be ascertained that the gas delivered at the outlet is shown on the outlet label and that proper connecting fittings are checked against their labels, in accordance with 4-3 through 4-6 in Chapter 4, "Gas and Vacuum Systems."

Although this requirement is rudimentary, accidents that have occurred repeatedly could have been avoided if this simple procedure had been conducted.

19-3.4.1.4 The guidelines set forth in Sections 4-3 through 4-6 of Chapter 4, "Gas and Vacuum Systems," concerning the storage, location, and special precautions required for compressed gases shall be followed.

19-3.4.1.5 All storage areas shall be located remote from the hyperbaric environment and flammable gases shall not be used or stored in the facility.

The Committee believes flammable gases should not be used or stored in hyperbaric facilities under any circumstances. It does recognize the need for items such as alcohol swabs, etc., and has allowed their use *(see 19-3.1.5.2)*, but only if approved by authorities knowledgeable of the hazards involved in hyperbaric operations.

19-3.4.2 Radiation equipment, whether infrared or roentgen ray, can make hyperbaric chambers even more hazardous. In the event that such equipment is introduced into a hyperbaric chamber, hydrocarbon detectors shall be installed. In the event that flammable gases are detected in excess of 1000 parts per million, such radiation equipment shall not be operated until the chamber atmosphere is cleared.

19-3.4.3 Maintenance Logs.

Careful attention to details, such as maintenance logs, is of immeasurable aid toward achieving a safe environment.

19-3.4.3.1 Installation, repairs, modifications of equipment, etc. related to a chamber should be evaluated by engineering personnel, tested under pressure, and approved by the safety director. Logs of the various tests shall be maintained.

19-3.4.3.2 Operating equipment logs shall be maintained by engineering personnel. They shall be signed before chamber operation by the person in charge *(see 19-3.1.3.3)*.

19-3.4.3.3 Operating equipment logs shall not be taken inside the chamber.

19-3.5 Electrical Safeguards.

19-3.5.1 Electrical equipment shall be installed and operated in accordance with 19-2.7.

19-3.5.1.1 All electrical circuits shall be tested before chamber pressurization. This test shall include a continuity check to verify that no conductors are grounded to the chamber, as well as a test of normal functioning *(see 19-2.7.2.3)*.

19-3.5.1.2 In the event of fire, all nonessential electrical equipment within the chamber shall be deenergized insofar as possible before extinguishing the fire. Smouldering, burning electrical equipment shall be deenergized before extinguishing a localized fire involving only the equipment *(see 19-2.5.5)*.

Once electrical equipment is de-energized, a fire in a hyperbaric chamber becomes a simple "Class A" fire, readily extinguishable with water.

19-3.6 Electrostatic Safeguards.

19-3.6.1 Administration.

19-3.6.1.1 General. The elimination of static charges is dependent on the vigilance of administrative supervision of materials purchased, maintenance, and periodic inspection and testing.

19-3.6.1.2 Textiles. Textiles used or worn in the hyperbaric chamber shall conform to 19-3.1.5.5 through 19-3.1.5.8.

19-3.6.2 Maintenance.

19-3.6.2.1 Conductive Floors. *(See 12-4.1, "Anesthetizing Locations.")*

19-3.6.2.2 Furniture.

(a) Periodic inspection shall be made of leg tips, tires, casters, or other conductive devices on furniture and equipment to ensure that they are maintained free of wax, lint, or other extraneous material that may insulate them and defeat the purpose for which they are used; also to avoid transporting to conductive floors such materials from other areas. Metals capable of impact sparking shall not be allowed for casters or furniture leg tips.

NOTE: Ferrous metals may cause such sparking. So may magnesium or magnesium alloys if contact is made with rusted steel.

(b) Casters shall not be lubricated with oils or other flammable materials. Such lubricants shall be oxygen compatible and flame resistant.

For firesafety in hyperbaric chambers, lubricants need to be both oxygen compatible and flame resistant. *(See 19-3.2.3, which also states this requirement.)*

19-3.6.2.3 Conductive Accessories. Replacement belting, rubber accessories, plastics, covers, sheeting, and other conductive accessories shall be of conductive material, and shall meet the requirements of 12-4.1, "Anesthetizing Locations."

19-3.6.3 Testing. Conductive testing, if required, shall be in accordance with requirements in 12-4.1.3, "Requirements for Flammable Anesthetizing Locations."

Inspection is considered vital since deterioration of material occurs in oxygen-enriched atmospheres.

19-3.6.3.1 Materials containing rubber shall be inspected regularly, especially at points of kinking.

NOTE: Materials containing rubber deteriorate rapidly in oxygen-enriched atmospheres.

Conductive rubber materials contain large amounts of carbon which can lessen their mechanical strength (particularly in oxygen-enriched atmospheres). They should be checked more frequently than ordinary rubber products to ensure their safe condition.

19-3.6.4 Fire Protection Equipment. Electrical switches, valves, and electrical monitoring equipment associated with fire detection and extinguishment shall be visually inspected before each chamber pressurization. Fire detection equipment shall be tested each week and full testing, including discharge of extinguishing media, conducted annually. Testing shall include activation of trouble circuits and signals. Discharge of extinguishant may be limited to 10 percent of the system capacity.

19-3.6.5 Housekeeping. It is absolutely essential that all areas of, and components associated with, the hyperbaric chamber be kept meticulously free of grease, lint, dirt, and dust. A regular housekeeping program shall be implemented whether or not the facility is in regular use. The persons assigned to this task shall be thoroughly indoctrinated in the hazards to occupants under normal operation.

Such accumulations are, of course, very undesirable from a sanitation viewpoint. In a hyperbaric chamber, however, there is the added concern that materials, objects, equipment laden with grease, etc., could introduce additional fire hazards by being more-than-ordinarily flammable.

20 REFERENCED PUBLICATIONS

20-1 The following documents or portions thereof are referenced within this standard and shall be considered part of the requirements of this document. The edition indicated for each reference shall be the current edition as of the date of the NFPA issuance of this document. These references shall be listed separately to facilitate updating to the latest edition by the user.

20-1.1 NFPA Publications. National Fire Protection Association, Batterymarch Park, Quincy, MA 02269.

NFPA 10-1984, *Standard for Portable Fire Extinguishers*

NFPA 13-1987, *Standard for the Installation of Sprinkler Systems*

NFPA 30-1984, *Flammable and Combustible Liquids Code*

NFPA 45-1986, *Standard on Fire Protection for Laboratories Using Chemicals*

NFPA 49-1975, *Hazardous Chemicals Data*

NFPA 50-1985, *Standard for Bulk Oxygen Systems at Consumer Sites*

NFPA 50A-1984, *Standard for Gaseous Hydrogen Systems at Consumer Sites*

NFPA 51-1987, *Standard for the Design and Installation of Oxygen-Fuel Gas Systems for Welding, Cutting, and Allied Processes*

NFPA 54-1984, *National Fuel Gas Code*

NFPA 58-1986, *Standard for the Storage and Handling of Liquefied Petroleum Gases*

NFPA 70-1987, *National Electrical Code*

NFPA 78-1986, *Lightning Protection Code*

NFPA 80-1986, *Standard for Fire Doors and Windows*

NFPA 90A-1985, *Standard for the Installation of Air-Conditioning and Ventilating Systems*

NFPA 101-1985, *Life Safety Code*

NFPA 110-1985, *Standard for Emergency and Standby Power Systems*

NFPA 220-1985, *Standard on Types of Building Construction*

NFPA 259-1987, *Standard Test Method for Potential Heat of Building Materials*

NFPA 493-1978, *Standard for Intrinsically Safe Apparatus and Associated Apparatus for Use in Class I, II, and III, Division 1 Hazardous Locations*

NFPA 701-1977, *Standard Methods of Fire Tests for Flame-Resistant Textiles and Films*

NFPA 704-1985, *Standard System for the Identification of Fire Hazards of Materials*

NFPA 801-1986, *Recommended Fire Protection Practice for Facilities Handling Radioactive Materials.*

20-1.2 Other Publications.

20-1.2.1 CGA Publications.
Compressed Gas Association, Inc., 1235 Jefferson Davis Highway, Arlington, VA 22202.

Pamphlet C-4-1978, *Standard Method of Marking Portable Compressed Gas Containers to Identify the Material Contained* (ANSI Z48.1)

Pamphlet C-9-1980, *Standard Color-Marking of Compressed Gas Cylinders Intended for Medical Use in the United States*

Pamphlet G-4-1980, *Oxygen*

Pamphlet G-4.1-1985, *Cleaning Equipment for Oxygen Service*

Pamphlet G-7.1-1973, *Commodity Specification for Air* (ANSI Z86.1)

Pamphlet G-8.1-1979, *Standard for the Installation of Nitrous Oxide Systems at Consumer Sites*

Pamphlet G-10.1-1976, *Commodity Specification for Nitrogen*

Pamphlet P-1-1974, *Safe Handling of Compressed Gases*

Pamphlet P-2-1978, *Characteristics and Safe Handling of Medical Gases*

Pamphlet P-2.5-1981, *Transfilling of High Pressure Gaseous Oxygen to be Used for Respiration*

Pamphlet P-2.6-1983, *Transfilling of Low-Pressure Liquid Oxygen to be Used for Respiration*

Pamphlet V-1-1977, *Standard for Compressed Gas Cylinder Valve Outlet and Inlet Connections* (ANSI B57.1)

Pamphlet V-5-1978, *Diameter-Index Safety System — Non-Interchangeable Low Pressure Connections for Medical Gas Applications.*

20-1.2.2 ASME Publications.
American Society of Mechanical Engineers, 345 East 47th Street, New York, NY 10017.

ANSI/ASME PVHO-1-1978, *Safety Standard for Pressure Vessels for Human Occupancy*

ASME Boiler and Pressure Vessel Code (1980).

20-1.2.3 ASTM Publications.
American Society for Testing and Materials, 1916 Race Street, Philadelphia, PA 19103.

ASTM B88-1981, *Specification for Seamless Copper Water Tube*

ASTM B280-1983, *Specification for Seamless Copper Tubing for Air Conditioning and Refrigeration Field Service*

ASTM D2240-1981, *Test Method for Rubber Property — Durometer Hardness*

ASTM D5-1971, *Test for Penetration of Bituminous Materials*

ASTM D2863-1977, *Method for Measuring the Minimum Oxygen Concentration to Support Candle-like Combustion of Plastics (Oxygen Index)*

ASTM E136-1979, *Standard Method of Test for Behavior of Materials in a Vertical Tube Furnace at 750°C.*

20-1.2.4 U.S. Government Publications.

20-1.2.4.1
U.S. Government Printing Office, Superintendent of Documents, Washington, DC 20402.

Federal Test Method Standard No. 101B, Method 4046

Code of Federal Regulations, Title 49, Parts 171 through 190 (U.S. Dept. of Transportation, *Specifications for Transportation of Explosives & Dangerous Articles*). (In Canada, the regulations of the Board of Transport Commissioners, Union Station, Ottawa, Canada, apply.)

Commercial Standard 223-59, *Casters, Wheels, and Glides for Hospital Equipment.*

20-1.2.4.2 U.S. Dept. of Defense, Naval Publications & Form Center (NPFC 103), 5801 Tabor Avenue, Philadelphia, PA 19120.

MIL-Standard 104B, *Limit for Electrical Insulation Color.*

20-1.2.5 AATCC Publication. American Association of Textile Chemists and Colorists, P.O. Box 886, Durham, NC 27701.

AATCC Test Method 76-1972 (ANSI L14.112-1973), *Determination of the Electrical Resistivity of Fabrics,* included in 1962 Technical Manual.

20-1.2.6 UL Publication. Underwriters Laboratories Inc., 333 Pfingsten Rd., Northbrook, IL 60062.

UL Subject 94, *Burning Tests for Plastics.*

20-1.2.7 NCCLS Publications. National Committee for Clinical Laboratory Standards, 771 East Lancaster Avenue, Villanova, PA 19085.

NCCLS ASI-5, *Power Requirements for Clinical Laboratory Instruments and for Laboratory Power Sources*

NCCLS ASI-1, *Preparation of Manuals for Installation, Operation and Repair of Laboratory Instruments.*

20-1.2.8 ASHRAE Publications. American Society of Heating, Refrigerating and Air Conditioning Engineers, Inc., 1791 Tullie Circle, N.E., Atlanta, GA 30329.

ASHRAE *Guide and Data Book — Applications Table on Pressure Relationships and Ventilation of Certain Hospital Areas,* published annually.

ASHRAE Handbook of Fundamentals-1985, Chapter 24.

20-1.2.9 ANSI Publications. American National Standards Institute, Inc., 1430 Broadway, New York, NY 10018.

ANSI B57.1 See CGA V-1

ANSI C73-1973, *Plugs and Receptacles*

ANSI C84.1-1977 (1980 Supplement), *Voltage Ratings for Electrical Power Systems and Equipment*

ANSI Z48.1 See CGA C-4

ANSI Z66.1-1964 (R 1972), *Specifications for Paints and Coatings Accessible to Children to Minimize Dry Film Toxicity.*

20-1.2.10 AWS Publication. American Welding Society, 2501 NW 7th St., Miami, FL 33125.

ANSI/AWS A5.8-1977, *Specification for Brazing Filler Metal.*

APPENDIX A

The material contained in Appendix A is included in the text within this *Handbook* and therefore is not repeated here.

APPENDIX B INFORMATORY REFERENCED PUBLICATIONS

B-1 The following documents or portions thereof are referenced within this standard for informational purposes only and thus are *not* considered part of the requirements of this document. The edition indicated for each reference should be the current edition as of the date of the NFPA issuance of this document. These references should be listed separately to facilitate updating to the latest edition by the user.

B-1.1 NFPA Publications. National Fire Protection Association, Batterymarch Park, Quincy, MA 02269.

NFPA 10-1984, *Standard for Portable Fire Extinguishers*

NFPA 30-1984, *Flammable and Combustible Liquids Code*

NFPA 37-1984, *Standard for the Installation and Use of Stationary Combustion Engines and Gas Turbines*

NFPA 45-1986, *Standard on Fire Protection for Laboratories Using Chemicals*

NFPA 49-1975, *Hazardous Chemicals Data*

NFPA 50-1985, *Standard for Bulk Oxygen Systems at Consumer Sites*

NFPA 53M-1985, *Manual on Fire Hazards in Oxygen-Enriched Atmospheres*

NFPA 75-1987, *Standard for the Protection of Electronic Computer/Data Processing Equipment*

NFPA 80-1986, *Standard for Fire Doors and Windows*

NFPA 90A-1985, *Standard for the Installation of Air Conditioning and Ventilating Systems*

NFPA 90B-1984, *Standard for the Installation of Warm Air Heating and Air Conditioning Systems*

NFPA 99B-1987, *Standard for Hypobaric Facilities*

NFPA 220-1985, *Standard on Types of Building Construction*

NFPA 325M-1984, *Fire Hazard Properties of Flammable Liquids, Gases, and Volatile Solids*

NFPA 491M-1986, *Manual of Hazardous Chemical Reactions*

NFPA 704-1985, *Standard System for the Identification of Fire Hazards of Materials*

Flash Point Index of Trade Name Liquids

NFPA *Fire Protection Handbook*, 16th edition, 1986

NFPA FR 61-1, "Occupancy Fire Record — Hospitals"

B-1.2 Other Publications. The following publications are available from the addresses listed.

B-1.2.1 ASHRAE Publications. American Society of Heating, Refrigeration and Air Conditioning Engineers, Inc., 1791 Tullie Circle, NE, Atlanta, GA 30329.

ASHRAE Guide and Data Book—Equipment, Chapter 10, 1969

ASHRAE Guide and Data Book—Applications, Chapter 14, 1969

ASHRAE Handbook on Equipment, Chapter 10, 1983

ASHRAE Handbook on Applications, Chapter 7, 1982

B-1.2.2 CGA Publications. Compressed Gas Association, Inc., 1235 Jefferson Davis Highway, Arlington, VA 22202.

CGA Pamphlet G-8.1-1979, *Nitrous Oxide Systems at Consumer Sites*

CGA Pamphlet P-1, *Safe Handling of Compressed Gases*

CGA Pamphlet P-2, *Characteristics of Safe Handling of Medical Gases*

B-1.2.3 JCAH Publication. Joint Commission on the Accreditation of Hospitals, 875 N. Michigan Avenue, Chicago, IL 60611.

Accreditation Manual for Hospitals

B-1.2.4 NCCLS Publication. National Committee for Clinical Laboratory Standards, 771 East Lancaster Avenue, Villanova, PA 19085.

NCCLS ASI-1, *Preparation of Manuals for Installation, Operation and Repair of Laboratory Instruments*

B-1.2.5 Ocean Systems Publication. Ocean Systems, Inc. Research and Development Laboratory, Tarrytown, NY 10591. Work carried out under U.S. Office of Naval Research, Washington, DC, Contract No. N00014-67-A-0214-0013.

Technical Memorandum UCR1-721, *Chamber Fire Safety*

B-1.2.6 ASTM Publications. American Society for Testing and Materials, 1916 Race St., Philadelphia, PA 19103.

ASTM D56-1982, *Test Method for Flash Point by Tag Closed Tester*

ASTM D93-1985, *Test Methods for Flash Point by Pensky-Martens Closed Tester*

B-1.2.7 U.S. Government Publication. U.S. Government Printing Office, Superintendent of Documents, Washington, DC 20025.

NRC Publication 1132, *Diesel Engines for Use with Generators to Supply Emergency and Short Term Electric Power* (Also available as Order No. O.P.52870 from University Microfilms, P.O. Box 1366, Ann Arbor, MI 48106.)

B-2 Published Articles on Fire Involving Respiratory Therapy Equipment, and Related Incidents.

Benson, D. M., and Wecht, C. H. Conflagraton in an ambulance oxygen system. *Journal of Trauma*, vol. 15, no. 6:536-649, 1975

Dillon, J. J. Cry fire! *Respiratory Care*, vol. 21, no. 11: 1139-1140, 1976

Gjerde, G. E., and Kraemer, R. An oxygen therapy fire. *Respiratory Care*, vol. 25, no. 3:362-363, 1980

Walter, C. W. Fire in an oxygen-powered respirator. *JAMA* 197:44-46, 1960

Webre, D. E., Leon, R., and Larson, N.W. Case History; Fire in a nebulizer. *Anes. and Analg.* 52:843-848, 1973

B-3 Addresses of Some Other Organizations Publishing Standards or Guidelines.

American Industial Hygiene Assoc., 475 Wolf Ledges Parkway, Akron, OH 44311

American Conference of Governmental and Industrial Hygienists, P.O. Box 1937, Cincinnati, OH 45201

College of American Pathologists, 7400 Skokie Blvd., Skokie, IL 60077

Scientific Apparatus Makers Assoc., 1101 16th Street, NW, Washington, DC 20036

APPENDIX C ADDITIONAL EXPLANATORY NOTES TO CHAPTERS 1–19

This Appendix is not a part of the requirements of this NFPA document but is included for information purposes only.

NOTE: Sections of Appendix C identified by a dagger (†) include text extracted from NFPA 30-1984, *Flammable and Combustible Liquids Code*, and NFPA 704-1985, *Standard System for the Identification of the Fire Hazards of Materials*. Requests for interpretations or revisions of the extracted text will be referred to the Technical Committee on General Storage of Flammable Liquids and the Technical Committee on Fire Hazards of Materials, respectively.

Appendix C-3 Additional Explanatory Information on Chapter 3, "Electrical Systems"

Appendix C-3 consists of the following:

C-3.1 Typical Hospital Wiring Arrangement;

C-3.2 Maintenance Guide for an Essential Electrical System;

C-3.3 Suggested Format for Listing Functions to be served by the Essential Electrical System in a Hospital.

C-3.1 Typical Hospital Wiring Arrangement.

(See Figure C-3.1 on next page.)

C-3.2 Maintenance Guide for an Essential Electrical System.

This generalized maintenance guide is provided to assist administrative, supervisory, and operating personnel in establishing and evaluating maintenance programs for emergency electric generating systems.

Monthly:

(1) Testing of generator sets and transfer switches under load and operating temperature conditions at least every 30 days. A 30-minute exercise period is an absolute minimum, or the engine manufacturer's recommendations should be followed.

(2) Permanently record all available instrument readings during the monthly test.

(3) During the monthly test, check the following system or systems applicable to your installation:

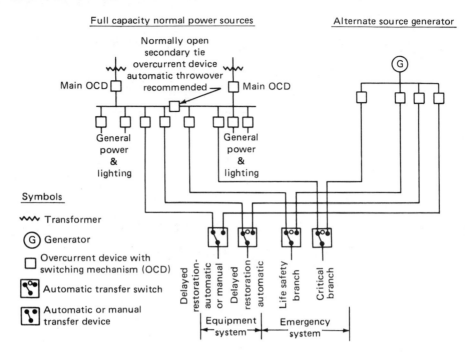

Separate transfer switches for each branch, as shown, are required only if dictated by load considerations. Smaller facilities may be served by a single transfer switch.

Figure C-3.1   Typical Hospital Wiring Arrangement.

Natural Gas or Liquid Petroleum Gas System:

    Operation of solenoids and regulators
    Condition of all hoses and pipes
    Fuel quantity

Gasoline Fuel System:

    Main tank fuel level
    Operation of system

Diesel Fuel System:

    Main tank fuel level
    Day tank fuel level
    Operation of fuel supply pump and controls

Turbine Prime Movers:

    Follow manufacturer's recommended maintenance procedure

Engine Cooling System:

    Coolant level
    Rust inhibitor in coolant
    Antifreeze in coolant (if applicable)
    Adequate cooling water to heat exchangers
    Adequate fresh air to engine and radiators

Condition of fan and alternator belts
Squeeze and check condition of hoses and connections
Functioning of coolant heater (if installed)

Engine Lubricating System:

Lubricating oil level
Crankcase breather not restricted
Appearance of lubricating oil
Correct lubricating oil available to replenish or change
Operation of lubricating oil heater (if installed)
Oil pressure correct

Engine Electrical Starting System:

Battery terminals clean and tight
Add distilled water to mainten proper electrolyte level
Battery charging rate
Battery trickle charging circuit operating properly
Spare batteries charged if provided

Engine Compressed Air Starting System:

Air compressor operating properly
Air compressor lubricating oil level
Spare compressed air tanks full
Main compressed air tanks full
Drain water from compressed air tanks

Engine Exhaust System:

Condensate trap drained
No exhaust leaks
Exhaust not restricted
All connections tight

Transfer Switch:

Inside clean and free of foreign matter
No unusual sounds
Terminals and connectors normal color
Condition of all wiring insulation
All covers tight
Doors securely closed

General:

Any unusual condition of vibration, deterioration, leakage, or high surface temperatures or noise
Maintenance manuals, service log, basic service tools, jumpers, and supplies readily available
Check and record the time intervals of the various increments of the automatic start-up and shutdown sequences
Overall cleanliness of room
No unnecessary items in room

(4) After the monthly test:

Take prompt action to correct all improper conditions indicated during test
Check that the standby system is set for automatic start and load transfer

Quarterly:

(1) On generator sets:

Engine Electrical Starting System:

Check battery electrolyte specific gravity
Check battery cap vents

Engine Lubricating System:

Check lubricating oil (or have analyzed if part of an engineered lube oil program)

(2) Fuel System:

Drain water from fuel filters (if applicable)
Drain water from day tank (if applicable)
Check fuel gauges and drain water from main fuel tanks
Inspect all main fuel tank vents

Semiannually:

(1) On generator sets:

Engine Lubricating System:

Change oil filter (if sufficient hours)
Clean crankcase breather

Fuel System:

General inspection of all components
Change fuel filter
Change or clean air filter

Governor:

Check all linkages and ball joints
Check oil level (if applicable)
Observe for unusual oil leakage

Generator:

Check brush length and pressure
Check appearance of slip rings and clean if necessary
Blow out with clean, dry compressed air

Engine Safety Controls:

Check operation of all engine operating alarms and safety shutdown devices (generator not under load during this check)

Annually:

(1) On generator sets:

Fuel System:

Diesel:
Analyze fuel for condition (replace if required)

Gasoline:
Replace fuel

Natural Gas or Liquefied Petroleum Gas:
Examine all supply tanks, fittings, and lines

Lubricating Systems:

Change oil
Change oil filter
Replace carburetor air filter

Cooling System:

Check condition and rod-out heat exchangers if necessary
Change coolant on closed systems
Clean exterior of all radiators
Check all engine water pumps and circulating pumps
Examine all duct work for looseness
Clean and check motor-operated louvers

Exhaust System:

Check condition of mufflers, exhaust lines, supports, and connections

Ignition System:

Spark ignition engines
Replace points and plugs
Check ignition timing
Check condition of all ignition leads

Generator:

Clean generator windings
Check generator bearings
Measure and record resistance readings of generator windings using insulation tester
(megger)

Engine Control:

General cleaning
Check appearance of all components
Check meters

(2) Transfer Switch:

Inspect transfer switch and make repairs or replacements if indicated

(3) On main switchgear and generator switchgear:

Operate every circuit breaker manually
Visually check bus bars, bracing, and feeder connections for cleanliness and signs of
    overheating

Every Three Years:

(1) System Controls:

Reevaluate the settings of the voltage sensing and time delay relays

(2) Main Switchgear and Generator Switchgear:

Determine whether changes to the electrical supply system have been made that require a
revision of the main circuit breaker, fuse, or current-limiting bus duct coordination.

Calibrate and load test main circuit breakers. Spot-check bus bar bolts and supports for
tightness. Obtain and record insulation tester readings on bus bars and circuit breakers. Obtain
and record insulation tester readings on internal distribution feeders.

Periodically:

(1) Prime Mover Overhaul:

Each prime mover should have a periodic overhaul in compliance with the manufacturer's
recommendation or as conditions warrant.

(2) Connected Load:

Update the record of demand and connected load and check for potential overload.

C-3.3 Suggested Format for Listing Functions to be Served by the Essential Electrical System in a Hospital.

Explanation. It may be advantageous, in listing the specific functions for a given construction
project or building review, to list them, at the outset, by geographical location within the
project, in order to assure comprehensive coverage. Every room or space should be reviewed for
possible inclusion of:

(a) lighting (partial or all),

(b) receptacles (some or all),

(c) permanently wired electrical apparatus.

The format suggested herein is offered as a convenient tool, not only for identifying all
functions to be served and their respective time intervals for being reenergized by the alternate
electric source, but also for documenting other functions that were considered, discussed, and
excluded as nonessential. This last column is considered worthy of attention. It may be that the
hospital engineer or the reviewing authority will wish to keep on file a final copy of the list, which
would be the basis for the electrical engineer's detailed engineering design.

Although this suggested format is intended for use by a hospital it may, with suitable changes,
be useful for other health care facilities.

ESSENTIAL ELECTRICAL SYSTEMS

Hospital _____ Date _____

Room No.	Room Name	Function Served*	EMERGENCY SYSTEM		EQUIPMENT SYSTEM		NON-ESSEN-TIAL
			Life Safety Branch	Critical Branch	Delayed Auto.**	Delayed Manual	

* Indicate precise lighting, receptacles and/or equipment. Use a separate line for each function.
** Indicate time interval.

Appendix C-4 Additional Explanatory Information on Chapter 4, "Gas and Vacuum Systems"

Appendix C-4 consists of the following:

C-4.1 Initial Testing of Nonflammable Medical Piped Gas Systems (formerly Appendix B in NFPA 56F-1983);

C-4.2 Retesting and Maintenance of Nonflammable Medical Piped Gas Systems (formerly Appendix C in NFPA 56F-1983);

C-4.3 Examples, Medical-Surgical Vacuum System Sizing;

C-4.4 Vacuum Flow Chart and Formulas;

C-4.5 Metric Conversion Factors;

C-4.6 Comments on Derivation of Design Parameters for Medical-Surgical Vacuum Systems.

C-4.1 Initial Testing of Nonflammable Medical Piped Gas Systems (formerly Appendix B in NFPA 56F-1983).

NOTE: Numbers in brackets refer to paragraphs in Chapter 4 of text.

C-4.1.1 [4-3.1.5] The contractor installing the system apparatus should test the system for proper function, including the changeover from one cylinder bank to the other and the actuation of the changeover signal before the system is put into service.

C-4.1.2 [4-3.1.6] The contractor installing the system apparatus should test the system for proper function, including the changeover from primary to secondary supply (with its changeover signal) and the operation of the reserve (with its reserve in use signal), before the system is put into service.

C-4.1.3 [4-3.1.6.2] If the system has an actuating switch and signal to monitor the contents of the reserve, its function should be tested before the system is put into service.

C-4.1.4 [4-3.1.7] The contractor installing the bulk supply signals and the master signal panels should arrange with the owner or the organization responsible for the operation and maintenance of the supply system for the testing of the bulk supply signals to assure proper identification and activation of the master signal panels to be sure the facility can monitor the status of that supply system. These tests should also be conducted when changing storage units.

C-4.1.5 [4-3.1.8.5] The pressure relief valve, set at 50 percent above normal line pressure, should be tested to assure proper function prior to use of the system for patient care.

C-4.1.6 [4-3.1.9.4] The installing contractor should test for the proper functioning of the system before it is put into service. This should include a purity test for air quality. It should also include a test of the alarm sensors after calibration and setup per the manufacturer's instructions and automatic switchover as outlined in 4-3.1.9.8.

C-4.1.7 [4-3.1.9.6] The proper functioning of the safety valve, automatic drain, pressure gauge, and high-water-level sensor should be verified before the system is put into service.

C-4.1.8 [4-4.1.1.1] Tests of warning systems for new installations (initial tests) should be performed after the pressure testing (Section 4-5.1.3.4) and the cross-connecting testing (Section 4-5.1.1), but before the purging (Section 4-5.1.2) and analyzing (Section 4-5.1.2.3). Initial tests of warning systems that may be included in an addition or extension to an existing piping system should be completed before connection of the addition to the existing system. Test gases for the initial tests should be those in Chapter 2, "Definitions."

C-4.1.9 [4-4.1.1.1(b)] Tests should be performed for each of the nonflammable medical gas piping systems. Permanent records of these tests should be maintained with those required under Section 4-6.3.1.

C-4.1.10 [4-4.1.1.2(a)] Follow the manufacturer's operating instructions or request the assistance of the owner or the organization responsible for the operation and maintenance of the bulk supply system.

(1) Pressurize the piping system and connect the electric power to the signal panels.

(2) Check the main-line pressure gauge [4-4.1.1.4(a)] to ascertain that it indicates the desired pressure (4-5.1.3.6) and is properly labeled. Check the alarm signal panels to assure that they indicate normal operation and that none of the warning signals are activated.

C-4.1.11 [4-4.1.1.2(b)] Changeover Warning Signal — Manifold or Alternating Bulk Supply — 4-3.1.5.1, 4-3.1.6.1(b), and 4-3.1.7.1(b).

(1) Start a flow of gas from an outlet of the piping system.

(2) Close the shutoff valve or cylinder valves on the number 1 bank (Figure 4-3.1.5), the primary supply of the manifold (Figure 4-3.1.6), or the primary unit of the alternating bulk supply to simulate its depletion. Changeover should be made to the number 2 bank, secondary supply, or the alternate bulk unit.

(3) Check main-line pressure gauge to assure maintenance of the desired pressure.

(4) Check signal panels for activation of the proper changeover signal.

(5) Silence the audible signal; visual signal should remain.

(6) Open the valves closed in step 2. Close the valve on the number 2 bank, secondary supply, or alternate bulk unit. When changeover back to original primary supply has occured, reopen the valve. This will reinstate system to its original status.

(7) Check signal panels for deactivation of warning signals.

(8) Stop flow of gas from the piping system.

C-4.1.12 [4-4.1.1.2(c)] Reserve-In-Use Warning Signal — 4-3.1.6.1(c), 4-3.1.6.3, and 4-3.1.7.1.

(1) Start a flow of gas from the piping system.

(2) Close the proper shutoff valves to simulate depletion of the operating supply. Reserve should begin to supply the piping system.

(3) Check the main-line pressure gauge. Pressure should remain at the desired level.

(4) Check the master signal panels to determine that the reserve-in-use signals have been activated.

(5) Silence the audible signal. Visual signal should remain.

(6) Open the shutoff valves closed in step 2.

(7) Check master signal panels for deactivation of the warning signals.

(8) Stop the flow of gas from the piping system.

C-4.1.13 [4-4.1.1.2(d)] Reserve Supply Low (Down to an average one-day supply) — 4-3.1.6.2 and 4-3.1.7.2(b) and (c).

High-Pressure Cylinder Reserve.

(1) Start a flow of gas from the piping system.

(2) Close all operating supply shutoff valves. (To use pressure from the reserve.)

(3) Close the reserve supply shutoff valve or, if necessary, the reserve cylinder valves, depending on the exact location of the actuating switch (to reduce pressure on the actuating switch, simulating loss of reserve).

(4) Open the operating supply valves closed in step 2 (so that only the "reserve low" signal should be activated).

(5) Check the master signal panels for activation of the proper signal.

(6) Silence the audible signal. Visual signal should remain.

(7) Open reserve supply valve or cylinder valves closed in step 3.

(8) Check master signal panels for deactivation of the warning signals.

(9) Stop flow of gas from the piping system.

Liquid Bulk Unit Reserve.

This type of reserve requires an actuating switch on the contents gauge and another actuating switch for the gas pressure being maintained in the reserve unit. Reduced contents or gas pressure in the reserve unit would indicate less than a day's supply in reserve.

Simulation of these conditions requires the assistance of the owner or the organization responsible for the operation and maintenance of the supply system as it will vary for different styles of storage units.

C-4.1.14 [4-4.1.1.2(e)] High or Low Pressure in Piping System.

Initial test of the area alarms covered in 4-4.1.1.3(a) can be done at the same time.

(1) Increase the pressure in the piping system to the high-pressure signal point (20 percent above normal pressure).

(2) Check all master signal panels (and area signals) to assure that the properly labeled warning signal is activated; also check main-line pressure gauge and area gauges to assure their function.

(3) Silence the audible signal. Visual signal should remain.

(4) Reduce piping system pressure to the normal. A flow from the system is required to lower the pressure and permit readjustment of the line regulator.

(5) Check all signal panels for deactivation of the signals.

(6) Close main-line shutoff valve.

(7) Continue the flow from the system until pressure is reduced to the low-pressure signal point (20 percent below normal).

(8) Check all signal panels for activation of the properly labeled warning signal; also check main-line gauge and area pressure gauges to assure their function.

(9) Silence the audible signal. Visual signal should remain.

(10) Open main-line shutoff valve.

(11) Check main-line gauge for proper line pressure.

(12) Check all signal panels for deactivation of warning signals.

C-4.1.15 [4-4.1.1.3(a)]   This signal should be initially tested at the time the tests of C-4-1.12 are performed.

C-4.2 Retesting and Maintenance of Nonflammable Medical Piped Gas Systems (formerly Appendix C in NFPA 56F-1983)

NOTE: Numbers in brackets refer to paragraphs in Chapter 4 of text.

C-4.2.1 [4-3.1.5]   These systems should be checked daily to assure that proper pressure is maintained and that the changeover signal has not malfunctioned. Periodic retesting of the routine changeover signal is not necessary as it will normally be activated on a regular basis.

C-4.2.2 [4-3.1.6]   These systems should be checked daily to assure that proper pressure is maintained and that the changeover signal has not malfunctioned. Periodic retesting of the routine changeover signal is not required. Annual retesting of the operation of the reserve and activation of the reserve-in-use signal should be performed.

C-4.2.3 [4-3.1.6.2]   If the system has an actuating switch and signal to monitor the contents of the reserve, it should be retested annually.

C-4.2.4 [4-3.1.7]   Maintenance and periodic testing of the bulk system is the responsibility of the owner or the organization responsible for the operation and maintenance of that system. The staff of the facility should check the supply system daily to assure that medical gas is ordered when the contents gauge drops to the reorder level designated by the supplier. Piping system pressure gauges and other gauges designated by the supplier should be checked regularly and gradual variation, either increases or decreases, from the normal range should be reported to the supplier. These variations may indicate the need for corrective action.

Periodic testing of the master signal panel system, other than the routine changeover signal, should be performed. Request assistance from the supplier or detailed instruction if readjustment of bulk supply controls is necessary to complete these tests.

C-4.2.5 [4-3.1.8.3]   The main-line pressure gauge should be a checked daily to assure the continued presence of the desired pressure. Variation, either increases or decreases, should be investigated and corrected.

C-4.2.6 [4-3.1.9.2]   Quarterly rechecking of the location of the air intake should be made to assure that it continues to be a satisfactory source for medical compressed air.

C-4.2.7 [4-3.1.9.6] Proper functioning of the pressure gauge and high-water-level sensor should be checked at least annually. Check the receiver drain daily to determine if an excessive quantity of condensed water has accumulated in the receiver.

C-4.2.8 [4-3.1.9.7] An important item required for operation of any medical compressed air supply system is a comprehensive preventive maintenance program. Worn parts on reciprocating compressors can cause high discharge temperatures resulting in an increase of contaminants in the discharge gas. Adsorber beds, if not changed at specified time intervals, can become saturated and lose their effectiveness. It is important that all components of the system be maintained in accordance with the manufacturer's recommendations. It is important that any instrumentation, including analytical equipment, be calibrated routinely and maintained in operating order. Proper functioning of the dew point sensor should be checked at least annually.

C-4.2.9 [4-4.1.1.1(b)] When test buttons are provided with signal panels, activation of the audible and visual signals should be performed on a regular basis (monthly).

C-4.2.10 [4-4.1.1.2(b)] Changeover Warning Signal — Manifold or Alternating Supply — 4-3.1.5.1, 4-3.1.6.1(b), and 4-3.1.7.1(b).

As this is a routine signal that is activated and deactivated at frequent intervals, there is no need for retesting UNLESS it fails. If the reserve-in-use signal is activated because both units of the operating supply are depleted without the prior activation of the changeover signal, it should be repaired and retested.

C-4.2.11 [4-4.1.1.2(c)] Reserve-In-Use Warning Signal — 4-3.1.6.1(c), 4-3.1.6.3, and 4-3.1.7.1.

All components of this warning signal system should be retested annually in accordance with steps 2 through 7 of the procedure given in Appendix C-4.1.12. Audible and visual signals should be tested periodically during the year (monthly).

C-4.2.12 [4-4.1.1.2(d)] Reserve Supply Low (Down to an average one-day supply) — 4-3.1.6.2 and 4-3.1.7.2(b) and (c).

High-Pressure Cylinder or Liquid Reserve.

All components of these signal warning systems should be retested annually in accordance with Steps 2 through 8 of the procedure given in Appendix C-4-1.13. If test buttons are provided, audible and visual signals should be periodically tested throughout the year (monthly).

C-4.2.13 [4-4.1.1.2(f)] The medical compressed air system alarms in A-4-3.1.9.6 and A-4-3.1.9.7 should be checked at least annually.

C-4.2.14 [4-4.1.1.4(a)] This pressure gauge should be checked on a daily basis to assure proper piping system pressure. A change, increase or decrease, if noted, may give evidence that maintenance may be required on the line pressure regulator, and could thus avoid a problem.

C-4.2.15 [4-4.1.1.4(b)] This pressure gauge should be checked on a daily basis to assure proper system pressure. A gradual change, increase or decrease, if noted, will give an indication of a developing problem that could be avoided by preventive maintenance.

C-4.2.16 [4-5.1.4.1(a)] Annual retesting of all components of warning systems, if it can be done without changing piping system line pressure, should be performed.

C-4.2.17 [4-5.1.4.1(b)] If test buttons are provided, the retesting of audible and visual alarm indicators should be performed monthly.

C-4.2.18 [4-4.1.2.2] Shutoff valves should be periodically checked for external leakage by means of a test solution or other equally effective means of leak detection safe for use with oxygen.

C-4.2.19 [4-4.1.2.4] Station outlets should be periodically checked for leakage and flow. Instructions of the manufacturer should be followed in making this examination.

Flow rates for a given pressure can vary between systems (i.e., they vary between manufacturers and between models of a manufacturer). Thus, the Subcommittee responsible for this material has not included a recommended value. What is important is the consistency of readings over a time after a facility has determined its minimum acceptable flow rates for the devices it will be connecting to the system.

C-4.3 Examples, Medical-Surgical Vacuum System Sizing.

These are *only* examples to illustrate how sizing of medical-surgical vacuum system should be approached.

C-4.3.1 Example 1. Vacuum Source Sizing Example. Calculate the required vacuum pump capacity to meet the demands of a hypothetical hospital with rooms and terminal quantities described below:

Table C-4.3.1(a) Hospital Parameters.

Room Designation	Number of Rooms or Beds	Number of Terminals	Type/ Usage Group [See Table A-4-8.1.1.1(a)]
Operating Rooms	6	18	A
Cystoscopy Rooms	2	6	A
Delivery Rooms	4	12	A
Recovery Beds	13	39	A
ICUs	24	72	A
Emergency Rooms	10	10	A
Emergency Rooms—Major Trauma	2	6	A
Patient Rooms	385	385	B
Nurseries	30	30	B
Treatment and Examination Rooms	20	20	B
Autopsy	1	1	B
Respiratory Care	1	1	B
Dialysis Unit	4	2	B

Table C-4.3.1(b) Calculations.

Type of Room	No. of Terminals	SCFM	Use Factor*	Adjusted SCFM
Type A	163	163 × 0.25 = 41	0.52	21
Type B	439	439 × 0.25 = 110	0.22	24
Operating Rooms	6	6 × 1.5 = 9	1.0	9
				54**

*Per Table A-4-8.1.1.1(a).
**Does not include waste anesthetic gas evacuation.

Pump Sizing for 3 in. Hg
Piping Pressure Drop:

Minimum allowable system vacuum	12 in. Hg Vac.
Design pressure drop (Appendix C-4.2)	3 in. Hg Vac.
Minimum operating vacuum at receiver	15 in. Hg Vac.

To maintain the minimum operating vacuum at the receiver, typical control settings for a duplex vacuum pump installation might be as follows (assuming pumps are located at the receiver):

	Start	Stop
Lead Switch	16 in. Hg Vac.	19 in. Hg Vac.
Lag Swtich	15 in. Hg Vac.	18 in. Hg Vac.

NOTE: Three-inch vacuum pressure loss used in the illustration can be varied to suit system design.

The pumps are rated for the ACFM load at the lead switch setting of the vacuum pump; in this example, 16 in. Hg vacuum.

Required single pump capacity (ACFM):

$$\text{ACFM} = (\text{Adjusted SCFM}) \times \left(\frac{29.92}{29.92\text{-Vac}} \right) \times \left(\frac{T + 460}{528} \right)$$

$$= 54 \times \left(\frac{29.92}{29.92\text{-}16} \right) \times \left(\frac{68 + 460}{528} \right)$$

$$= 116.$$

Therefore, the hospital requires two vacuum pumps, each with a minimum capacity of 116 ACFM at 16 in. Hg vacuum.

NOTE: For final vacuum source sizing, see "Total Weighted System Demand" in Appendix A-4-7.1.1.1. The pump size selected should handle this flow (116) or the maximum flow established for mains, whichever is higher.

C-4.3.2 Example 2. Pipe Sizing Example (Not Related to Examples 1 and 3). See Figure C-4.3(a).

C-4.3.3 Example 3. Pipe Sizing Example (Not Related to Examples 1 and 2). See Figure C-4.3(b).

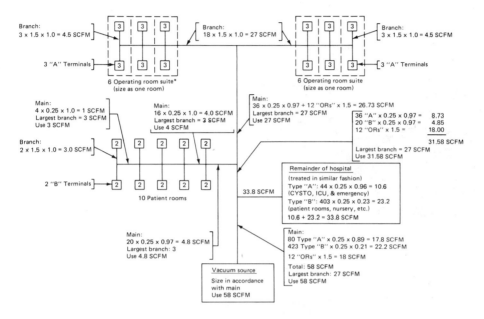

*In the event of a branch line serving more than six (6) operating rooms, or the like, only the first six should be considered as one room. The branch sizing for the remaining rooms should use the same procedure as for other branch lines. See Figure C-4.3(b).

Figure C-4.3(a)   Typical Branch and Main Sizing.

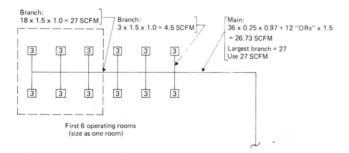

Figure C-4.3(b)   Sizing Branch Lines Serving Large Operating Suites.

C-4.4 Vacuum Flow Chart and Formulas.

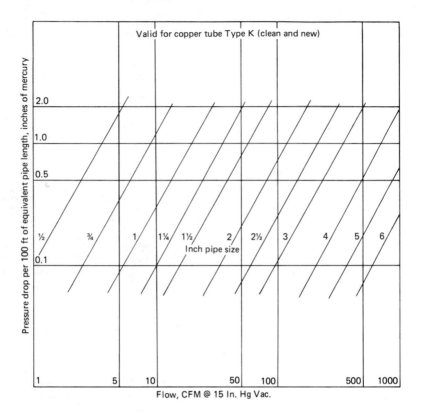

Flow, CFM @ 15 In. Hg Vac.

NOTE: Pressure drops at other vacuum levels may be closely approximated by multiplying the pressure drop found from the chart (for a given CFM and pipe size) times the ratio:

$$\left[\frac{30 - \text{new vacuum level}}{15} \right]$$

Formulas for Calculating Pressure Drop for Other Types and Sizes of Pipe

(Eq. 1)   Darcy's Formula:

$$P = 0.00341 \; f\left(\frac{L}{D}\right) \times \frac{\rho V^2}{2g}$$

where:

P = pressure drop in. Hg abs.

f = friction factor determined from Moody Diagram

L = length of pipe, ft

D = internal diameter of pipe, ft

ρ = density of air at upstream pressure, lb/ft³

V = velocity of air at upstream pressure, ft/sec

g = gravitation constant, 32.2 ft/sec².

For clean new copper tube K, L, or M, the friction factor may be closely approximated by the following relation:

(Eq. 2) $$f = \frac{0.184}{(Re_N)^{0.2}}$$

where:

Re_N = Reynolds's Number, $\dfrac{\rho VD}{\mu}$

μ = absolute (dynamic) viscosity, $\dfrac{lb}{sec\ ft}$.

Friction factors of commercial steel pipe are higher.

C-4.5 Metric Conversion Factors.

1 in. = 2.540 cm
1 ft = 30.48 cm
1 atm = 29.92 in. Hg = 760 mmHg
1 lb per sq in. = 4.882 kg per sq m
1 cu ft per min = 28.32 L per min

C-4.6 Comments on Derivation of Design Parameters for Medical-Surgical Vacuum Systems.

This material was prepared by the Committee on Medical-Surgical Vacuum for reader education as well as for historical purposes.

While most vacuum system design parameters, such as pressure drop, are derived from the laws of physics, two very important items are almost entirely empirical. These two are: first, the number of vacuum terminals (or inlets) needed for various types of rooms or functional areas of a health care facility [Table A-4-8.1.1.1(a)] and second, the number of terminals (or inlets) that are in simultaneous operation at any given time [Table A-4-8.1.1.1(b)].

The reasons for this empiricism are obvious. The number of terminals needed for any particular room depends not only on the medical needs of the patients being treated, but also upon the location of those terminals within each room and the individual characteristics of each vacuum device attached to the terminals. The number of terminals in simultaneous use (the diversity factor) depends not only on the type of medical facility involved but also, to some extent, on the geographical area that the facility serves.

The number of vacuum terminals needed and the diversity factor determine the "load" on the vacuum system. This load is then used to determine the required vacuum pump capacity as well as the sizing of the piping between terminals and pumps. One design approach would be to assume a "worst-case" situation (such as all installed terminals are in simultaneous use). Another would be to assume a fixed diversity factor regardless of facility size.

All such arbitrary approaches can be criticized as being either unnecessarily expensive or resulting in inadequate systems. Clearly, design recommendations must be based upon the actual vacuum needs in "real-life" facilities. Given the obvious limitations of time and money, these recommendations can be based only on a survey of a fraction of the total number of health care facilities in existence at any one time.

In 1974, the then NFPA Sectional Committee on Medical-Surgical Vacuum Systems[1] examined representative samples of suction apparatus to determine the design requirements (i.e., flow rates and vacuum) for the associated terminals. "As-delivered" samples of the apparatus of five leading manufacturers, covering an estimated 90 percent of all equipment then in common use in the United States, were measured in the presence of Sectional Committee members at the engineering laboratories of one of the manufacturers. Field conditions were simulated by the use of saline solutions and whole-blood samples provided for this purpose by a member of the Sectional Committee. The flow rate given in 4-9.1.3.1 and minimum vacuum given in 4-9.1.1.3 are based on these measurements. Periodic review of these 1974 measurements indicated that they were still valid as of 1980.

In 1976, the Sectional Committee on Medical-Surgical Vacuum Systems examined the vacuum systems of nine hospitals to determine the types and locations of their vacuum terminals (inlets), the number of terminals in use throughout the day, and total demand on the vacuum source(s) as the various terminals were used. These hospitals ranged in size from 100 beds to 1200 beds, and, in terms of the types of medical procedures performed and demands placed on their vacuum systems, were considered a fair representation of hospitals in the United States. Flow-rate and pressure-recording instruments were provided by one of the manufacturers. The original data for Table A-4-8.1.1.1(a) and Table A-4-8.1.1.1(b) were based on these measurements.

Between 1976 and 1977, the vacuum systems of approximately 20 additional hospitals were examined by one or more members of the Sectional Committee. Several of these systems were being examined because of malfunctions or inadequate performance. The others were new systems being designed and installed, or new extensions to existing systems. The information obtained from these hospitals was used to make minor corrections to Table A-4-8.1.1.1(a) and Table A-4-8.1.1.1(b).

The sampling of hospital vacuum systems was expanded in 1978. Whereas previous data were based upon short, 90-minute data observations, newer data were based upon one-week data acquisition. Although 13 hospital systems were studied, only 9 contained usable data. This information was later expanded in 1980 by data from 21 additional hospital systems. In total, data from 67 vacuum systems have been gathered by the CGA, industry members of the Technical Committee on Medical-Surgical Vacuum Systems, and by the American Society for Hospital Engineering. Hospital sizes varied from 40 to 1200 beds and constituted a broader representation than before.

The data from the 1978-1980 surveys (30) were analyzed using the existing 1978 formulae. All but eight systems fit the existing formulae. The important conclusions from an analysis indicated that:

(1) The number of operating rooms was found to be the single most important parameter affecting SCFM demand.

(2) The total number of A-type and B-type terminals was the second most important parameter.

(3) Whether the hospital used the central vacuum system for waste anesthetic gas disposal was not found to be statistically significant in this group of data.

---

[1]In 1974, the Sectional Committee was actually an ad hoc Subcommittee (formed in 1971) of the Committee on Hospitals. In 1975, it became a full Sectional Committee under the jurisdiction of the Correlating Committee on Health Care Facilities. In 1976, Sectional Committees were raised to Technical Committee level. In 1985, the Health Care Facilities Project was reorganized, with the Technical Committee on Medical-Surgical Vacuum Systems becoming the standing Subcommittee on Vacuum Systems and Equipment.

The basic 1978 formulae were subsequently adjusted in 1980 to accommodate an additional 1.5 SCFM requirement for each operating room. The formulae were now found to have virtually 100 percent unanimity with all 67 data samples. Additionally, the formulae provide for a sizing that gives 2½ times the observed peak demand, a margin that should be enough for even the most conservative users.

Over the years several members of the Technical Committee on Medical-Surgical Vacuum Systems have planned, designed, and supervised the installation of a number of these systems using the procedures outlined in Chapter 4 and its associated Appendixes A-4 and C-4. These systems have continued to perform as intended.

Appendix C-8 Additional Explanatory Information on Chapter 8, "Gas Equipment (Positive and Negative Pressure) Health Care Facilities"

Appendix C-8 consists of the following:

C-8.1 Medical Safeguards, Respiratory Therapy;

C-8.2 Glossary of Respiratory Therapy Terminology;

C-8.3 Suggested Fire Reponse, Respiratory Therapy;

C-8.4 Typical Gas Cylinders.

C-8.1 Medical Safeguards, Respiratory Therapy.

C-8.1.1 General.

C-8.1.1.1 Personnel setting up, operating, and maintaining respiratory therapy equipment, including suction apparatus, should familiarize themselves with the problems of the use of each individual unit.

C-8.1.1.2 Respiratory therapy equipment should be stored and serviced in an area apart from that used for other functions. Preferably the respiratory therapy service should be supplied with its own workroom/storeroom. Such a room or area may be divided into three sections — clean-up and sterilization, repair, and storage and reissue.

C-8.1.1.3 Storage of respiratory therapy equipment should be systematic and segregated from areas of storage of other items of medical equipment. If drawers or cabinets are employed, proper labeling should be utilized to assure ready availability of equipment.

C-8.1.1.4 Personnel must be aware of the exact location of equipment in storage to facilitate emergency use.

C-8.1.2 Handling of Equipment.
Proper procedures must be established for mechanical cleansing and sterilization of equipment coming in contact with patients or through which patients breathe. There must be no residual chemical deposits that might be toxic to the patient and no residual bacteria that might cause cross-infection.

C-8.1.2.1 Mechanical cleansing and sterilization should be carried out after each patient application.

C-8.1.2.2 Mechanical cleansing should be sufficiently thorough to remove blood, saliva, mucus, residual adhesive tape, and other debris.

C-8.1.2.3 Use of improper combinations of medication in therapy equipment should be avoided.

C-8.1.3 Tracheotomy and Endotracheal Tube Connection.

C-8.1.3.1 Pressure breathing apparatus may be connected directly to a tracheotomy or endotracheal tube. Connectors designed to afford a tight fit between breathing tubes of a pressure breathing apparatus and the tracheal tube should have an internal diameter at least as large as that of the tube.

C-8.1.3.2 A tracheotomy collar should not obstruct movement of gas through the tracheotomy tube.

C-8.1.3.3 To avoid reducing the effective lumen of tracheotomy tubes and interfering with movement of gas in and out of the lungs, suction tubes or other devices must not remain in the tracheotomy tubes.

Suction catheters should be no larger than one-half the diameter of the lumen. The suction procedure should not last more than 15 seconds, and re-oxygenation of the patient should occur before suctioning is carried out again.

C-8.1.4 Suction Equipment for Respiratory Care.

C-8.1.4.1 Equipment employed for patient suction includes the source of suction, the interconnecting tubing, and collection and trap bottles. The bottle used for collection may contain the trap. A trap is a mechanism preventing spillage of liquid contents into the source of suction if the bottle overfills.

C-8.1.4.2 Suction equipment should be set up and applied only by qualified individuals.

C-8.1.4.3 Sources of suction without pressure regulation should not be connected directly to a tube to be inserted into a body cavity for continuous suction. Regulation of suction pressure is not required for clearing of the oral cavity or removal of blood or other bodily fluids from open wounds.

Sentence two was added since the kinds of body fluids present in oral cavities and open wounds affect vacuum regulators after short periods of time. In addition, rapid evacuation is often critical for these situations; vacuum regulators, by design, restrict suction.

C-8.1.4.4 Suction regulators should be serviced by qualified individuals. Defective regulators should not be employed.

C-8.1.4.5 Trap bottles should be fixed to the wall or other appropriate stationary object to prevent tipping and subsequent spillage of liquid contents into the source of suction.

C-8.1.4.5.1 Trap bottles should be utilized between collection bottles and the source of suction to prevent spillage (*see C-8.1.4.1 and C-8.1.4.5*).

C-8.1.4.5.2 Collection bottles should be placed below the site of suction drainage from the patient, thus allowing gravitational pull to aid rather than impede flow into the collection bottle.

C-8.1.4.5.3 Collection bottles should be placed as close as practical to the patient to reduce the length of tubing required and to increase the efficiency of suction.

C-8.1.4.5.4 The overflow-preventive mechanism of the trap bottle should be cleaned each time the bottle is emptied and should be tested periodically to assure proper functioning.

C-8.1.4.6 Suction tips or tubes with the largest practical internal diameter should be employed.

The Commentary on C-8.1.3.3 applies here as well.

C-8.1.4.7 Tubing employed for connection of the various components of the suction system should possess an internal diameter of at least 0.25 in. (6.4 mm). The wall thickness of the tubing should be sufficient to prevent collapse during all conditions of use.

C-8.1.4.8 Suction tubing employed in a hazardous location is to be electrically conductive.

C-8.2 Glossary of Respiratory Therapy Terminology.

Arrhythmia. Irregularity of heartbeats.

Asphyxia. Suffocation from lack of oxygen and an accumulation of carbon dioxide.

Aspiration. Removal of accumulated mucus by suction.

Bronchi. The two primary divisions of the trachea.

C.P.A.P. Continuous positive airway pressure.

C.P.R. Cardiopulmonary resuscitation.

Croup Tent. Equipment utilized to provide environmental control inside a canopy in relation to oxygen concentration, temperature, humidity, and filtered gas.

Cyanosis. A bluish discoloration of skin and mucus membranes due to excessive concentration of reduced hemoglobin in the blood.

Defibrillate. Use of electrical shock to synchronize heart activity.

Diffusion. Transfer of gases across the alveolar capillary membrane.

EKG, ECG. Electrocardiogram.

Hemoglobin. The chemical compound in red blood cells that carries oxygen.

Hypoxia. An abnormally decreased supply or concentration of oxygen.

I.M.V. Intermittent mandatory ventilation.

I.P.P.B. Intermittent positive pressure breathing.

P.E.E.P. Positive end expiratory pressure.

Respiration. The exchange by diffusion of gases between the alveoli, the blood, and the tissue.

R.L.F. A disease entity of the premature infant causing blindness.

Reference to oxygen has been deleted since there are questions in the medical community concerning the role of oxygen in the production of R.L.F.

Thorax. The chest; the upper part of the trunk between the neck and the abdomen.

Trachea. The windpipe leading from the larynx to the bronchi.

Ultrasonic Nebulizer. A device that produces sound waves that are utilized to break up water into aerosol particles.

Ventilation. Movement of air into and out of the lungs.

Ventilator. Machine used to support or assist nonbreathing or inadequately breathing patient.

C-8.3 Suggested Fire Response, Respiratory Therapy.

Suggested procedure in the event of fire involving respiratory therapy apparatus.

C-8.3.1 General. Fires in oxygen-enriched atmospheres spread rapidly, generate intense heat, and produce large volumes of heated and potentially toxic gases. Because of the immediate threat to patients and personnel, as well as the damage to equipment and possible spread to the structure of the building, it is important that all personnel be aware of the steps necessary to save life, preserve limb, and, within reason, to extinguish or contain the fire.

C-8.3.2 Steps to Take in Event of Fire.

C-8.3.2.1 The following steps are recommended in the event of a fire, in the approximate order of importance:

(a) Remove the patient or patients immediately exposed from the site of the fire if their hair and clothing are not burning; if they are burning, extinguish the flames. (*See C-8.3.4 and C-8.3.5.*)

(b) Sound the fire alarm by whatever mode the hospital fire plan provides.

(c) Close off the supply of oxygen to the therapy apparatus involved if this step can be accomplished without injury to personnel. (*See C-8.3.3.*)

(d) Carry out any other steps specified in the fire plan of the hospital. For example:

    (1) remove patients threatened by the fire,

    (2) close doors leading to the site of the fire,

    (3) attempt to extinguish or contain the fire (*See C-8.3.4*),

    (4) direct fire fighters to the site of the fire,

    (5) take whatever steps necessary to protect or evacuate patients in adjacent areas.

C-8.3.3 Closing Off of Oxygen Supply.

C-8.3.3.1 In the event of a fire involving respiratory therapy equipment connected to an oxygen station outlet, the zone valve supplying that station is to be closed.

C-8.3.3.1.1 All personnel are cautioned to be aware of the hazard of such a step to other patients receiving oxygen supplied through the same zone valve. Steps should be taken to minimize such hazards, realizing that closing the valve is of foremost importance.

C-8.3.3.2 In the case of oxygen therapy apparatus supplied by a cylinder or container of oxygen, it is desirable to close the valve of the cylinder or container, provided that such closure can be accomplished without injury to personnel.

    NOTE: Metallic components of regulators and valves can become exceedingly hot if exposed to flame. Personnel are cautioned not to use their bare hands to effect closure.

C-8.3.4 Extinguishment or Containment of Fire.

C-8.3.4.1 Fire originating in or involving respiratory therapy apparatus generally involves combustibles such as rubber, plastic, linen, blankets, and the like. Water or water-based extinguishing agents are most effective in such fires.

C-8.3.4.1.1 Precautions should be observed if electrical equipment is adjacent to or involved in the fire, because of the danger of electrocution of personnel if streams of water contact live 115-volt circuits.

C-8.3.4.1.2 Before attempting to fight such a fire with water or a water-based extinguishing agent, such electrical apparatus should be disconnected from the supply outlet, or the supply circuit deenergized at the circuit panel.

C-8.3.4.1.3 If such deenergization cannot be accomplished, water should not be employed. (*See C-8.3.4.2.*)

C-8.3.4.2 Fires involving or adjacent to electrical equipment with live circuits may be fought with extinguishers suitable for Class C fires, in accordance with NFPA 10, *Standard on Portable Fire Extinguishers.*

    NOTE: Chemical extinguishers are not effective against fires in oxygen-enriched atmospheres unless the source of oxygen is shut off. See C-8.3.3 for closing off oxygen supply.

C-8.3.5 Protection of Patients and Personnel.

C-8.3.5.1 Because of the intense heat generated, serious and even fatal burns of the skin or of the lungs from inhaling heated gases are possible sequelae to the oxygen-enriched-atmosphere fire. Thus, it is essential that patients be removed from the site of the fire whenever practical.

NOTE: Where a nonambulatory patient is connected to a burning piece of therapy equipment, it may be more practical as the initial step to remove the equipment and/or extinguish the fire than to remove the patient.

C-8.3.5.2 The large quantities of noxious gases produced constitute a threat to life from asphyxia, beyond the thermal burn problem.

C-8.3.5.2.1 Personnel are cautioned not to remain in the fire area after patients are evacuated if quantities of gaseous combustion products are present.

C-8.3.6 Indoctrination of Personnel.

C-8.3.6.1 It is highly desirable that personnel involved in the care of patients, including nurses, aides, ward secretaries, and physicians, irrespective of whether or not they are involved in respiratory therapy practices, be thoroughly indoctrinated in all aspects of firesafety, including:

(a) The location of zone valves of nonflammable medical gas systems where employed, and the station outlets controlled by each valve.

(b) The location of electrical service boxes, and the areas served thereby.

(c) The location of fire extinguishers, indications for their use, and techniques for their application.

(d) The recommended methods of evacuating patients, and routes by which such evacuation is accomplished most expeditiously. Reference should be made to the facility's fire plan.

(e) The steps involved in carrying out the fire plan of the hospital.

(f) The location of fire alarm boxes, or knowledge of other methods, for summoning the local fire department.

C-8.4 Typical Gas Cylinders. See Table C-12.5, "Typical Gas Cylinders."

Appendix C-10 Additional Explanatory Information on Chapter 10, "Laboratories"

Appendix C-10 consists of the following:

C-10.1 Fire Incidents in Laboratories;

C-10.2 Related Definitions, Laboratories.

C-10.1 Fire Incidents in Laboratories.

Descriptions of a few laboratory fires are included in NFPA FR 61-1, "Occupancy Fire Record — Hospitals." Some laboratory fires and explosions are described below:

Tissue Processor Fire.   Operated 24 hours per day, but unattended from 11 p.m. to 7 a.m., a tissue processor was suspected of causing $200,000 damage because the incident occurred after 11 p.m. and there were no detectors or automatic extinguishing equipment in the laboratory. Flammable liquids in glass containers stored in an open shelf below the equipment contributed to the intensity of the fire.

Aside from damage to the laboratory, electrical cables in the corridor near the incident shorted and caused power to be interrupted in the hospital. Fire doors closed, but the fire alarm was not sounded.

"Walking" Motor Fire.   A motor, which had been connected to inadequately secured apparatus, "walked" off a bench and caught fire.

Incinerator Explosion.   The operators received minor burns as they dumped contents of GI cans into a top-feed incinerator; detonations were caused by "empty" ether cans.

Perchloric Acid Explosion.   A maintenance worker was killed by an explosion resulting from the prodding of the cover plate of a fan that had been routinely exhausting perchloric acid fumes.

Cellulose Nitrate Centrifuge Tubes.   A technician suffered severe injuries when an explosion blew the door from a steam autoclave that had been sterilizing blood samples contained in cellulose nitrate tubes. In a different instance, cellulose nitrate culture tubes were destroyed by fire while within the closed compartment.

A technician noticed nitrogen oxide fumes seeping from the oven that was drying cellulose nitrate tubes. Upon opening the door to inspect, a mild explosion occurred followed by the tubes bursting into flames. A new employee had assumed that the oven control dial read in centigrade when actually it was marked with an arbitrary graduation. The damage was slight but the potential was reminiscent of the 1929 Cleveland Clinic X-ray film fire, which killed 125 people.

Explosion Hazard of Scintillation Counters.   In a refrigerated scintillation counter, enough solvent vapor may penetrate through plastic bottles or leak from plastic snap-type caps to form an explosive concentration in the box. Many organics penetrate at varying rates through some plastics.

Hot Plate Fires.   Acetone, being poured at the sink in a patient treatment lab, was ignited by a nearby hot plate that had just been turned off. The technican dropped the container, which was metal and which, fortunately, fell in an upright position. The patient was safely evacuated but the fire was intense enough to melt the sweated water pipe fittings of the window ventilator.

Petroleum ether caught fire while a chemist was pouring it in a fume hood from its large glass container — presumably ignited by a nearby hot plate that had recently been turned off. He dropped the glass container on the floor and ran from the room. The bottle broke; ignition caused enough pressure to blow open the lab escape hatch and slam the entrance door shut.

Refrigerator Explosion.   Eighty ml of diazomethane dissolved in ether detonated in a domestic-type refrigerator. The door blew open, the frame bowed out, and the plastic lining ignited, causing a heavy blanket of soot to be deposited far down the adjoining corridor. (See 10-7.2.5.)

Pressure Filter Fire.   At an eastern hospital pharmacy, a fire-conscious technician prepared for pressure filtering of 50 gal of isoprophyl alcohol by placing a towel on a table adjacent to the pump; in the event of fire he planned to smother flames of alcohol inadvertently spilled on his person. As he attempted to turn on the pump, the defective switch ignited alcohol on his hands. Instinctively, he reached for the towel as he had previously rehearsed in his mind but, in doing so, he tripped over the hose that was conducting alcohol by gravity from a large open kettle to the suction side of the pump. The hose slipped from its fittings thereby dumping 50 gal of the flaming solvent onto the floor. He escaped with minor injuries but the pharmacy was destroyed.

(Many fires are intensified by an unfortunate sequence of minor unsafe practices that in themselves seem almost too insignificant to worry about.)

Ampuls Explode. An ampul of tissue exploded like a firecracker moments after being removed from a liquid nitrogen refrigerator. The legs of the assistant were peppered with powdered glass. Such an explosion occurs as a result of liquid nitrogen being drawn into an imperfectly sealed ampul through pinhole imperfections. As the ampul is removed from the bath, room temperature expands the entrapped nitrogen rapidly, causing it to burst with much violence.

Chromatography Fire Hazard. Chromatography apparatus operating through the night had collected 2500 ml of cyclohexane with 200 ml remaining in the solvent reservoir when two explosions occurred. Ignition was attributed to sparks from electrical controls on the sampling device. (Based on *DuPont Safety News* of May 24, 1965.)

Water Bath Fire. When the thermostat on a water bath malfunctioned, the bath overheated, causing the acrylic lid to sag and contact the heater elements. A fire resulted. Heater equipment should always be protected by overtemperature shutoffs. (Based on *DuPont Safety News*, June 14, 1965.)

Cyclopropane Explosion. Upon opening the valve of a cylinder supposedly containing only cyclopropane, the cylinder exploded with extensive fragmentation, killing six and mutilating three others. This occurred in a Chilean hospital operating room in 1964.

The cylinder had been partially filled, in error, with oxygen and subsequently charged with cyclopropane. The valve, regulator, and fittings were unsuitable for oxygen, thus providing the conditions for a classic organic-oxidizer explosion. (From *NFPA Quarterly*, January, 1964, page 222.) (*See 4-4.3.5.*)

Centrifuge Fire. A small centrifuge, being used under a lab hood to separate a flammable hydrocarbon slurry, flashed in the operator's face. The motor was nonexplosionproof: the exhaust fan had been turned off. (*See 7-6.2.4.1.*)

Peroxide Explosion. A distillation apparatus exploded within a lab fume hood. It was caused by the detonation of the residual peroxide. The drawn sash prevented injury, although the electric mantle was torn to shreds. The investigator was using "some isopropyl ether" which had been kept in a clear glass bottle. He allowed the distillation to continue to dryness.

Investigators should become more aware of the nature of ether peroxide formations. Dioxane and ethyl and isopropyl ethers are the most common offenders. Age, sunlight, air space above liquid, and clear glass containers help to create these explosive peroxides. Test frequently for peroxide; filter out peroxides through a column of 80 mesh Alorco activated alumina, as suggested by Dasler and Bauer, *Ind. Eng. Chem. Anal.*, Ed. 18, 52 (1964). Never leave distillations unattended.

Spinning Gas Cylinder. While a large uncapped gas cylinder was being loaded on a freight elevator prior to laboratory delivery, it fell over. The valve opened slightly on the floor. A quick-thinking attendant shut off the valve before damaging momentum could be attained. Moving an uncapped cylinder within a limited area is permissible provided it is strapped to a carrying cart. [*See 4-6.2.1.7(c).*]

Steam Bath Flash. Flammable vapors from a batch of solvent that had been poured into a drain upstairs floated into the chamber of a steam bath fixture. As the investigator lit a Bunsen burner adjacent to the steam bath, the flammable vapors ignited, causing a quick hot flash. The rubber tubing was burned beyond recognition. The hood sash protected the investigator's face so he escaped with no injury other than singed eyebrows. ROOM OCCUPANTS SHOULD RUN WATER INTO UNUSED STEAM BATH TRAPS AND ALL OTHER UNUSED TRAPS ABOUT TWICE A MONTH.

Fume Hood Operation. About an hour after the electrical system failed because of a substation fire, toxic gases began to permeate through portions of the hospital.

Closing down the electrical system, either accidentally or announced, cuts off all hood and room ventilation and lack of ventilation may lead to sudden contamination of large areas. Upon announcement that the electrical system has failed, or is about to be shut down, experimental processes that produce hazardous exhaust should be slowed down or stopped.

C-10.2 Related Definitions, Laboratories. The following definitions are taken from other NFPA documents and are critical to the understanding of Chapter 10.

C-10.2.1† The following definitions are taken from NFPA 30, *Flammable and Combustible Liquids Code*:

(a) Flammable liquid shall mean a liquid having a flash point below 100°F (37.8°C) and having a vapor pressure not exceeding 40 lb per sq in. (2.76 bar) (absolute) at 100°F (37.8°C) and shall be known as Class I liquid.

Class I liquids shall be subdivided as follows:

(1) Class IA shall include those having flash points below 73°F (22.8°C) and having a boiling point below 100°F (37.8°C).

(2) Class IB shall include those having flash points below 73°F (22.8°C) and having a boiling point at or above 100°F (37.8°C).

(3) Class IC shall include those having flash points at or above 73°F (22.8°C) and below 100°F (37.8°C).

(b) Combustible liquid shall mean a liquid having a flash point at or above 100°F (37.8°C).

Combustible liquids shall be subdivided as follows:

(1) Class II liquids shall include those having flash points at or above 100°F (37.8°C) and below 140°F (60°C).

(2) Class III liquids shall include those with flash points at or above 140°F (60°C). Class III liquids shall be subdivided in two subclasses:

a. Class IIIA liquids shall include those with flash points at or above 140°F (60°C) and below 200°F (93.4°C).

b. Class IIIB liquids shall include those with flash points at or above 200°F (93.4°C).

C-10.2.2† The following definition is also taken from NFPA 30, *Flammable and Combustible Liquids Code*:

(a) The flash point of a liquid having a viscosity less than 45 SUS at 100°F (37.8°C) and a flash point below 200°F (93.4°C) shall be determined in accordance with ASTM D56-1975, *Standard Method of Test for Flash Point by the Tag Closed Tester.*

(b) The flash point of a liquid having a viscosity of 45 SUS or more at 100°F (37.8°C) or a flash point of 200°F (93.4°C) or higher shall be determined in accordance with ASTM D93-1973, *Standard Method of Test for Flash Point by the Pensky-Martens Closed Tester.*

C-10.2.3† The following definitions are based on NFPA 704, *Standard System for the Identification of the Fire Hazards of Materials.*

C-10.2.3.1 Health Hazard. A health hazard is any property of a material which, either directly or indirectly, can cause injury or incapacitation, either temporary or permanent, from exposure by contact, inhalation, or ingestion.

C-10.2.3.1.1 Degrees of Health Hazard.

4 — Materials which on very short exposure could cause death or major residual injury even though prompt medical treatment were given, including those which are too dangerous to be approached without specialized protective equipment. This degree should include:

(a) Materials which can penetrate ordinary rubber protective clothing;

(b) Materials which under normal conditions or under fire conditions give off gases which are extremely hazardous (i.e., toxic or corrosive) through inhalation or through contact with or absorption through the skin.

3 — Materials which on short exposure could cause serious temporary or residual injury even though prompt medical treatment were given, including those requiring protection from all bodily contact. This degree should include:

(a) Materials giving off highly toxic combustion products;

(b) Materials corrosive to living tissue or toxic by skin absorption.

2 — Materials which on intense or continued exposure could cause temporary incapacitation or possible residual injury unless prompt medical treatment were given, including those requiring use of respiratory protective equipment with independent air supply. This degree should include:

(a) Materials giving off toxic combustion products;

(b) Materials giving off highly irritating combustion products;

(c) Materials which either under normal conditions or under fire conditions give off toxic vapors lacking warning properties.

1 — Materials which on exposure would cause irritation but only minor residual injury even if no treatment is given, including those which require use of an approved canister-type gas mask. This degree should include:

(a) Materials which under fire conditions would give off irritating combustion products;

(b) Materials which on the skin could cause irritation without destruction of tissue.

0 — Materials which on exposure under fire conditions would offer no hazard beyond that of ordinary combustible material.

C-10.2.3.2 Flammability Hazard. Flammability describes the degree of susceptibility of materials to burning. The form or condition of the material, as well as its inherent properties, affects its flammability.

C-10.2.3.2.1 Degree of Flammability Hazard.

4 — Materials which will rapidly or completely vaporize at atmospheric pressure and normal ambient temperature or which are readily dispersed in air, and which will burn readily. This degree should include:

(a) Gases;

(b) Cryogenic materials;

(c) Any liquid or gaseous material which is a liquid while under pressure and having a flash point below 73°F (22.8°C) and having a boiling point below 100°F (37.8°C) (Class IA flammable liquids).

(d) Materials which on account of their physical form or environmental conditions can form explosive mixtures with air and which are readily dispersed in air, such as dusts of combustible solids and mists of flammable or combustible liquid droplets.

3 — Liquids and solids that can be ignited under almost all ambient temperature conditions. Materials in this degree produce hazardous atmospheres with air under almost all ambient temperatures, or, though unaffected by ambient temperatures, are readily ignited under almost all conditions. This degree should include:

(a) Liquids having a flash point below 73°F (22.8°C) and having a boiling point at or above 100°F (37.8°C) and those liquids having a flash point at or above 73°F (22.8°C) and below 100°F (37.8°C) (Class IB and Class IC flammable liquids);

(b) Solid materials in the form of coarse dusts which may burn rapidly but which generally do not form explosive atmospheres with air;

(c) Solid materials in a fibrous or shredded form which may burn rapidly and create flash fire hazards, such as cotton, sisal, and hemp;

(d) Materials which burn with extreme rapidity, usually by reason of self-contained oxygen (e.g., dry nitrocellulose and many organic peroxides);

(e) Materials which ignite spontaneously when exposed to air.

2 — Materials that must be moderately heated or exposed to relatively high ambient temperatures before ignition can occur. Materials in this degree would not under normal conditions form hazardous atmospheres with air, but under high ambient temperatures or under moderate heating may release vapor in sufficient quantities to produce hazardous atmospheres with air. This degree should include:

(a) Liquids having a flash point above 100°F (37.8°C), but not exceeding 200°F (93.3°C);

(b) Solids and semisolids which readily give off flammable vapors.

1 — Materials that must be preheated before ignition can occur. Materials in this degree require considerable preheating, under all ambient temperature conditions, before ignition and combustion can occur. This degree should include:

(a) Materials which will burn in air when exposed to a temperature of 1500°F (816°C) for a period of five minutes or less;

(b) Liquids, solids, and semisolids having a flash point above 200°F (93.3°C). This degree includes most ordinary combustible materials.

0 — Materials that will not burn. This degree should include any material which will not burn in air when exposed to a temperature of 1500°F (816°C) for a period of five minutes.

C-10.2.3.3 Reactivity (Instability) Hazards.
Reactivity describes the ability of a material to chemically react with other stable or unstable materials. For purposes of this hazard identification system, the other material is water, if reaction with water releases energy. Reactions with common materials other than water may release energy violently, but are beyond the scope of this identification system.

Unstable materials are those which, in the pure state or as commercially produced, will vigorously polymerize, decompose, or condense; become self-reactive, or undergo other violent chemical changes.

Stable materials are those that normally have the capacity to resist changes in their chemical composition, despite exposure to air, water, and heat encountered in fire emergencies.

C-10.2.3.3.1 Degree of Reactivity (Instability) Hazard.

4 — Materials which in themselves are readily capable of detonation or of explosive decomposition or explosive reaction at normal temperatures and pressures. This degree should include materials which are sensitive to mechanical or localized thermal shock at normal temperatures and pressures.

3 — Materials which in themselves are capable of detonation or of explosive decomposition or explosive reaction but which require a strong initiating source or which must be heated under confinement before initiation. This degree should include materials which are sensitive to thermal or mechanical shock at elevated temperatures and pressures or which react explosively with water without requiring heat or confinement.

2 — Materials which in themselves are normally unstable and readily undergo violent chemical change but do not detonate. This degree should include materials which can undergo chemical change with rapid release of energy at normal temperatures and pressures or which can undergo violent chemical change at elevated temperatures and pressures. It should also include those materials which may react violently with water or which may form potentially explosive mixtures with water.

1 — Materials which in themselves are normally stable, but which can become unstable at elevated temperatures and pressures or which may react with water with some release of energy, but not violently.

0 — Materials which in themselves are normally stable, even under fire exposure conditions, and which are not reactive with water.

Appendix C-12 Additional Explanatory Information on Chapter 12, "Hospital Requirements"

Appendix C-12 consists of the following:

C-12.1 Nature of Hazards, Anesthetizing Locations;

C-12.2 Related Hazards and Safeguards, Anesthetizing Locations;

C-12.3 Text of Suggested Signs and Posters for Inhalation Anesthetizing Locations;

C-12.4 Suggested Procedures in Event of a Fire or Explosion, Anesthetizing Locations;

C-12.5 Cylinder Table.

C-12.1 Nature of Hazards, Anesthetizing Locations.

C-12.1.1 General.   The environment of the modern operating room poses numerous hazards, even in those rooms in which flammable agents are prohibited.

C-12.1.2 Hazards Present in all Anesthetizing Locations.

C-12.1.2.1 Electric Shock and Spark Hazards — High-Frequency Burn.

C-12.1.2.1.1   When a human body becomes the connecting link between two points of an electric system that are at different electric potentials, the person is likely to suffer an electric shock or high-frequency burns. When there is a highly conductive pathway from outside the body to the heart or great vessels, small electric currents may cause ventricular fibrillation or cardiac arrest. If a conductive material bridges two points of an electric system that are different electric potentials, the contact is likely to create a spark or an arc and intense heating of one or more of the conductors involved.

C-12.1.2.1.2   Electric equipment that is defective or faultily grounded produces a definite shock hazard if connected to conventional grounded electric circuits and employed in the presence of purposely conductive flooring, as installed in corridors adjacent to operating rooms, or wet flooring as may be encountered in sterilizing or scrub rooms during use.

C-12.1.2.1.3   Improper use of the high-frequency electrosurgical unit, alone or in combination with certain items of medical monitoring equipment, may cause serious high-frequency burns to the patient or to personnel. (*See Annex 2, "Safe Use of High-Frequency Electricity in Health Care Facilities."*)

C-12.1.2.2 Toxicologic Hazards.

C-12.1.2.2.1   The use of some modern nonflammable inhalation anesthetic agents with high-flow techniques and in the absence of venting of the exhaled gases to the atmosphere may create low-grade toxicity in personnel who work regularly in the operating room (*see Appendix A-5.1/A-5-4.2*).

C-12.1.2.3 Mechanical Hazards.

C-12.1.2.3.1 A large amount of energy is stored in a cylinder of compressed gas. If the valve of a cylinder is struck (or strikes something else) hard enough to break off the valve, the contents of the cylinder may be discharged with sufficient force to impart dangerous reactive movement to the cylinder.

C-12.1.2.3.2 A hazard exists when hospital personnel attempt to transfer the contents of one compressed gas cylinder into another.

C-12.1.3 Hazards Related to the Use of Flammable Substances.

C-12.1.3.1 Flammable Anesthetic Agents.

C-12.1.3.1.1 The use of flammable anesthetic agents is attended by considerable fire and explosion risk because these agents form flammmable mixtures with air, oxygen, or nitrous oxide. In many cases, these mixtures are violently explosive. Fatal accidents have resulted from explosions of such mixtures during anesthesia.

C-12.1.3.1.2 The following inhalation agents are considered flammable during conditions of clinical use in anesthesia: cyclopropane, diethyl ether, ethyl chloride, and ethylene.

The flammability of a compound may be reduced by substitution of a halogen (fluorine, chlorine, or bromine) for hydrogen at one or more positions in the molecular structure. Several inhalational anesthetics are thus halogenated. Halogenated agents are not necessarily nonflammable under all conditions.

Conflicting reports in the literature as to flammability limits probably represent differences in experimental techniques. Both the nature of the source of ignition and the configuration of the test chamber are critical. Some agents can be ignited only under optimal conditions never duplicated in clinical anesthesia. In one study, ignition of chloroform in oxygen could be obtained only in a closed steel bomb with a fuse producing an ignition temperature of 2000°C to 3000°C (1093°F to 1649°F) and with a chloroform concentration of 20 percent to 25 percent.[1]

Trichloroethylene, used in concentrations higher than recommended, is flammable in oxygen and nitrous oxide. Methoxyflurane is nonflammable in concentrations obtainable at room temperature; however, a heated vaporizer can produce flammable mixtures.

Halothane, enflurane, and isoflurane are nonflammable under almost all conditions encountered in clinical anesthesia. High concentrations of nitrous oxide increase the range of flammability. Given laboratory conditions employing a closed tube, zero humidity, and sufficient ignition energy (far greater than that obtainable from incidental static electricity) it is possible to ignite a mixture of 4.75 percent halothane in 30 percent oxygen provided the balance of the atmosphere is nitrous oxide. If the oxygen concentration in a mixture with nitrous oxide is allowed to fall to 20 percent, 3.25 percent halothane is flammable. In these same nitrous oxide–oxygen atmospheres, the corresponding minimal flammable concentrations of enflurane are 5.75 percent and 4.25 percent respectively, and of isofluorane, 7.0 percent and 5.25 percent.[2]

---

[1]Brown, T. A. and Morris, G. The ignition risk with mixtures of oxygen and nitrous oxide with halothane. *Brit. J. Anaesth.* 38:164-173, 1966.

[2]Cruice, M. S. Lower explosion limits of three anesthetics in mixtures of oxygen and nitrous oxide. Hazards Research Corp. Report 3296 to Ohio Medical Products, Madision, Wisconsin, 5 March 1974.

The fact that halothane has for years been widely employed without significant problems relating to flammability suggests that the data in the preceding paragraph are of more theoretical than practical concern.

C-12.1.3.1.3 The use of closed rebreathing systems for the administration of flammable anesthetic agents normally tends to restrict the region likely to be hazardous. To secure a reasonable measure of protection, however, it has been found necessary to apply certain basic safeguards in any room in which these agents may be used.

C-12.1.3.2 Flammable Medicaments, Including Aerosol Products.

C-12.1.3.2.1 Medicaments, including those dispersed as aerosols, frequently are used in anesthetizing locations for germicidal purposes, for affixing plastic surgical drape materials, for preparation of wound dressings, or for other purposes.

C-12.1.3.2.2 A particular hazard is created if cautery or high-frequency electrosurgical equipment is employed following use of a flammable medicament for preparation of the skin (*see Appendix C-12.1.3.2.1*), since the liquid remaining on the skin or vapors pocketed within the surgical drapes may be ignited.

C-12.1.3.3 Sources of Ignition.

C-12.1.3.3.1 Potential sources of ignition of flammable anesthetics in anesthetizing locations include the following: (a) fixed electric equipment, (b) portable electric equipment, (c) accumulation of static electricity, (d) electrosurgical equipment, and (e) open flames and heated objects above the ignition temperature of the flammable gases in use. Other potential sources of ignition may be percussion sparks, ignition of oxidizing and flammable gases from accidental mixing under pressure (8-3.1.8), and ignition from improper handling of oxygen cylinders (4-6.2.1.2).

The Technical Committee on Anesthetizing Agents is cognizant of suggestions that the detonation of ether peroxides formed by the oxidation of ether over a period of time may be a cause of explosions in anesthesia machines. Frequent emptying of the ether bottle and cleaning of the ether evaporator inside anesthetizing locations is a simple and desirable precaution.

Many types of hospital construction afford reasonable protection against lightning hazards. However, because of the storage and use of combustible anesthetic agents, the increased protection offered by the installation of lightning rods may be desirable for some types of buildings, particularly those of wood (frame) construction in outlying areas. Lightning protection, if installed, should conform to the requirements of NFPA 78, *Lightning Protection Code*.

C-12.1.3.3.2 Experience indicates that the ignition of flammable mixtures by electrostatic spark is a great hazard. Electrostatic charges may accumulate on personnel and metallic equipment. Electrostatic charges can set up dangerous potential differences only when separated by materials that are electrically nonconducting. Such insulators act as barriers to the free movement of such charges, preventing the equalization of potential differences. A spark discharge can take place only when there is no other available path of greater conductivity by which this equalization may be affected. Such a spark may ignite a flammable mixture of gases.

C-12.1.3.3.3 In many cases, the hazards of electric shock and electrostatic discharge coexist. Measures to mitigate one hazard may enhance the other, however. It is necessary, therefore, to weigh both hazards in recommending precautionary measures for either.

C-12.1.3.3.4 An obvious and, hence, less frequent cause of the ignition of flammable anesthetic agents is by open flame or hot materials at or above the ignition temperature of the agents. The lowest ignition temperature in air of any of the anesthetic agents mentioned in Appendix C-12.1.3.1.2 is that of diethyl ether: 180°C (365°F). The most effective safeguard against this source of ignition is a constant vigilance on the part of the operating room personnel to prevent the introduction of sources of flames and hot objects into the anesthetizing locations (*see 12-4.1.2.3*).

An example of this inverse relationship is a damp or high-humidity environment where the electric shock hazard is increased, but electrostatic discharge is decreased.

C-12.1.4 Hazards that May Be Present in Nonflammable Anesthetizing Locations.

C-12.1.4.1 Electrostatic Hazard.

C-12.1.4.1.1 Conductive flooring is not a requirement for nonflammable anesthetizing locations. The uncontrolled use of static-producing materials in such locations, however, may lead to:

(a) electrostatic discharge through sensitive components of electronic equipment, causing equipment failure;

(b) inadvertent use of these materials in flammable anesthetizing locations where mixed facilities exist (*see definition of mixed facility in Chapter 2*);

(c) impaired efficiency because of electrostatic clinging; or

(d) the involuntary movement of personnel subject to electrostatic discharges.

C-12.1.4.2 Hazard of Flammable Substances.

C-12.1.4.2.1 Nonflammable anesthetizing locations are neither designed nor equipped for the use of any flammable substances, be they inhalation anesthetic agents or medicaments containing benzene, acetone, or the like. A hazardous situation is created any time any such flammable substance is inadvertently or intentionally introduced into a nonflammable anesthetizing location (*see also Appendix C-12.1.3.2*).

C-12.1.5 Hazards that May Be Present in Mixed Facilities.

C-12.1.5.1 Mixed facilities contain both flammable and nonflammable anesthetizing locations. Movable furniture, portable equipment, and conductive accessories intended for sole use in nonflammable anesthetizing locations may be introduced inadvertently into a flammable anesthetizing location, with the attendant dangers of ignition of flammable gas mixtures from electrical or electrostatic sparks.

C-12.1.5.2 Personnel working in mixed facilities may not take the proper precautions in reference to wearing apparel and the use of conductive grounding devices when entering flammable anesthetizing locations.

C-12.1.5.3 A particular hazard exists if regulations [*see Appendix C-12.3, Set (3)*] are not adopted, posted, and complied with or if the anesthetizing locations are not identified as noted in 12-4.1.4.2, 12-4.1.4.3, and 12-4.1.5.5(a) and (b).

C-12.2 Related Hazards and Safeguards, Anesthetizing Locations.

C-12.2.1 General.

C-12.2.1.1 The gas anesthesia apparatus and anesthetic ventilators constitute essential items (in most cases) for the administration of inhalation anesthesia. The safe use of these devices is predicated upon their cleanliness and proper function, as well as an understanding of their proper operation, maintenance, and repair.

C-12.2.2 Selection of a Gas Anesthesia Apparatus.

C-12.2.2.1 The individual selecting a gas anesthesia apparatus, either for initial purchase or for application in a given case, should be certain that the apparatus is the proper one for the given application or applications and that it is in good repair. See C-12.2.3, "Suggested Method for Assuring Proper Delivery of Oxygen and Nitrous Oxide"; C-12.2.4, "Disposable Masks, Bags, Tubing, and Bellows"; and C-12.2.5, "Decontamination and Routine Cleaning of Reusable Items."

C-12.2.3 Suggested Method for Assuring Proper Delivery of Oxygen and Nitrous Oxide.

C-12.2.3.1 This method is recommended to prevent delivery of a gas different from that indicated by the flowmeters, and to detect mixing of gases inside the machine that may result in delivery of dangerous gas mixtures to the patient. The following materials are needed:

(a) 91.5 cm (3 ft) of anesthesia delivery hose, and

(b) an accurate oxygen meter, analyzer, or detector [*see 8-5.1.2.1(c)*]; this device may be of the paramagnetic, platinum electrode, gas chromatographic, or mass spectrometer type.

C-12.2.3.2 Detailed steps of a method of testing anesthesia machines to assure the absence of hazard due to crossed connections between oxygen and nitrous oxide follow.

C-12.2.3.2.1 Premises.

(a) It is reasonable to conclude that no hazardous cross-connections or cross-leakages are present if gas from the only source available is delivered by only those valves intended for that gas, and that no gas is delivered by those valves when their intended source is unavailable, but other sources are available.

(b) It is not necessary to know the composition of a gas in order to determine the extent of the circuit it supplies.

(c) The operation of the oxygen circuit is independent, but the operation of some or all of the other circuits may be at least partially dependent on the operability of the oxygen circuit, e.g., fail-safe valves.

C-12.2.3.2.2 Method.

All anesthesia machines have at least one source of oxygen. This may be a large cylinder, one or two small cylinders, or a pipeline supply. Some machines have two such sources, and a very few have all three. Each should be tested separately. Proceed as follows:

(a) Disconnect all gas sources and open all needle valves and flush valves until all gas has stopped flowing from the machine outlet. Then close all needle valves and flush valves. Be certain that all cylinder pressure gauges read zero. Connect an oxygen cylinder to an oxygen hanger yoke and open the cylinder valve. Pressure must rise in the corresponding oxygen pressure gauge only. Close the cylinder valve.

(b) Repeat step (a) exactly for each oxygen hanger yoke, including any fed by high-pressure lines from large cylinders. Leave the cylinder in the last hanger yoke tested, with the cylinder valve open.

(c) Open in succession and leave open all the needle valves for gases other than oxygen. Briefly open any flush valve for a gas other than oxygen. No flow should occur at the machine outlet. An easy way to test for gas flow is to simply place the machine outlet tube in a glass of water and observe bubbling. Stand clear when flush valves are operated.

(d) Open and close in succession each of the oxygen needle valves, including any that provide an independent source of oxygen for vaporizers, and the oxygen flush valve. Flow should occur at the associated flowmeter or the machine outlet each time a valve is opened.

(e) If the machine is equipped for a pipeline oxygen supply, close the oxygen clydinder valve and open the oxygen flush valve. When gas stops flowing at the machine outlet, close the flush valve and all needle valves and connect the oxygen pipeline inlet to an oxygen pipeline outlet with the oxygen supply hose. Then repeat steps (c) and (d).

(f) Since it is now established that oxygen is delivered to the oxygen needle and flush valves, and is not delivered to any other needle or flush valve, it remains to be determined that oxygen and oxygen alone is also available to perform any other function for which it is essential. A valve that shuts off the supply of any other gas to the appropriate needle valve in the event of oxygen supply pressure failure, commonly called a "fail-safe" valve, performs such a function. It should be tested as follows:

(g) Disconnect the pipeline supply and open the oxygen flush valve until flow stops at the machine outlet, then close the flush valve. Install a cylinder of nitrous oxide in one hanger yoke, open the cylinder valve, and note the pressure on all cylinder pressure gauges. Only the nitrous oxide gauge should show any pressure.

(h) Open in succession and leave open all the needle valves for gas other than nitrous oxide. Briefly open any flush valve for a gas other than nitrous oxide. No flow should occur at the machine outlet, nor at any flowmeter.

NOTE: An easy way to test for gas flow is to simply place the machine outlet tube in a glass of water and observe bubbling. Stand clear when flush valves are operated.

(i) Open and close in succession each of the nitrous oxide needle valves and nitrous oxide flush valves. If any delivers flow, all should do so.

(j) If neither the nitrous oxide needle valves nor the nitrous oxide flush valve deliver flow, open the oxygen cylinder valve and repeat steps (h) and (i). Each nitrous oxide needle valve and flush valve should deliver flow to the machine outlet.

(k) Close the nitrous oxide cylinder valve and open a nitrous oxide needle valve until all gas stops flowing, then remove the nitrous oxide cylinder and close the needle valve. Repeat steps (g) through (j) using any other nitrous oxide yoke.

(l) If the machine is equipped for a pipeline nitrous oxide supply, close the nitrous oxide cylinder valve and open a nitrous oxide needle valve until all gas stops flowing, then close all needle valves and flush valves. Connect the nitrous oxide pipeline inlet to a nitrous oxide pipeline outlet with the nitrous oxide supply hose. Then repeat steps (h) through (j).

C-12.2.4 Disposable Masks, Bags, Tubing, and Bellows.

C-12.2.4.1 It is well recognized that newer technologies often lead to the introduction of new equipment and techniques, 'which in turn may lead to new hazards, or the potentiation of old ones. For example, the use of disposable and nondistensible conductive accessories potentiate the hazards of excessive airway pressures. These components should be employed only when it is assured that system pressure cannot become excessive.

C-12.2.4.1.1 Many plastic items are combustible. Most of these materials will emit toxic compounds when subjected to thermal decomposition. Special care must be exercised during storage, use, and disposal of these items in order to preclude accidental ignition. Due consideration must be given to on-site storage of trash prior to removal from the operating suite. The presence of these items on the hospital premises contributes significantly to the solid waste disposal problem facing the modern hospital.

C-12.2.4.1.2 The Subcommittee on Anesthesia Services recommends that purchasing policies of an institution, as well as the practices of individual physicians and nurses, take into consideration the multiple problems posed by plastic items, and limit purchases and use of them to those items deemed essential for the proper function of the institution.

C-12.2.5 Decontamination and Routine Cleaning of Reusable Items.

C-12.2.5.1 Under certain circumstances, infectious organisms can be cultured from the breathing passages of ventilators, anesthesia valves, absorbers, tubing, bags, masks, and connectors. Some of these organisms can remain viable for many days. Although evidence that cross-infection from such sources can and does occur is very scanty, it is suggested that the user of such equipment consider implementation of one of the following methods. Mechanical cleansing with soap and water should precede sterilization. Alternative approaches to routine cleansing include:

(a) mechanical cleansing with soap and water, followed with air drying in a stream of compressed air;

(b) mechanical cleansing with soap and water, followed by exposure to a preparation such as dialdehyde solution;

(c) mechanical cleansing with soap and water, followed by ethylene oxide, steam, or dry heat sterilization.

C-12.2.5.2 Following gross contamination, the step outlined in C-12.2.5.1(b) or C-12.2.5.1(c) should be employed.

NOTE 1: Whenever ethylene oxide or dialdehyde is used, care must be taken to assure complete removal of residuals.

NOTE 2: Recommendations for cleansing and sterilization supplied by the manufacturer of the item of equipment should be followed.

C-12.2.5.2.1 External contamination of the gas anesthesia apparatus, ventilator, and other equipment employed on and around the patient at least at weekly intervals, as well as immediately after use in an infectious case, is likewise recommended.

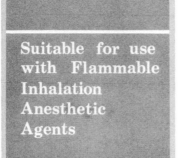

(a) Room suitable for flammable inhalation anesthetics (flammable *and* nonflammable anesthetics permitted.)

(b) Room restricted to nonflammable inhalation anesthetics only.

Figure 42   Signs posted outside operating rooms indicating type of anesthetics allowed.

C-12.3 Text of Suggested Signs and Posters for Inhalation Anesthetizing Locations.

SET (1)
REGULATIONS FOR SAFE PRACTICE IN
FLAMMABLE ANESTHETIZING LOCATIONS

The following rules and regulations have been adopted by the Medical Staff and by the Administration. Paragraph 12-4.1, "Anesthetizing Locations," of NFPA 99-1987 shall apply in all inhalation anesthetizing locations.

_____   _____
(Insert Date)   (Insert Name of Hospital Authority)

By reason of their chemical compositions, the following flammable anesthetic agents present a hazard of explosion in anesthetizing locations:

cyclopropane   ethyl chloride
ethyl ether   ethylene

REGULATIONS

1. Flammable Anesthetizing Location.

(a) *Definition.* The term flammable anesthetizing location shall mean any area of the hospital designated for the use of flammable anesthetizing agents.

2. Equipment.

(a) No electrical equipment except that judged by the Engineering Department of Hospital as being in compliance with Section 12-4.1, "Anesthetizing Locations," of NFPA 99-1987 shall be used in any flammable anesthetizing location.

(b) When a physician wishes to use his or her personal electrical equipment, it shall first be inspected by the Engineering Department and, if judged to comply with 12-4.1, "Anesthetizing Locations," of NFPA 99-1987, it shall be so labeled.

(c) Portable X-ray equipment used in flammable anesthetizing locations shall be approved for use in hazardous areas.

(d) Only approved photographic lighting equipment shall be used in flammable anesthetizing locations. Because of occasional bursting of bulbs, suitable enclosures shall be used to prevent sparks and hot particles from falling into the hazardous area.

(e) Covers shall not be used on anesthesia machines designed for flammable anesthetic agents.

3. Personnel.

(a) Outer garments worn by the operating room personnel and visitors shall not include fabrics of silk, wool, or synthetic textile materials such as nylon, polyester, acrylic, or acetate, unless such fabrics have been tested and found to be antistatic in accordance with the requirements of Section 12-4.1, "Anesthetizing Locations," NFPA 99-1987.

(b) Silk, wool, or synthetic textile materials, except untreated rayon, shall not be permitted in anesthetizing locations as outer garments, or for nonapparel purposes, unless such fabrics have been tested and found to be antistatic in accordance with the requirements of Section 12-4.1, "Anesthetizing Locations," NFPA 99-1987. Hosiery and underclothing in which the entire garment is in close contact with the skin may be of silk, wool, or synthetic material.

(c) All personnel and visitors entering flammable anesthetizing locations shall wear conductive footwear or other floor-contacting devices, which shall have been tested on the wearer and found to be satisfactorily conductive.

(d) It shall be the responsibility of each individual entering a flammable anesthetizing location to determine at least once daily that he is in electrical contact with the conductive floor. Apparatus for testing shall be available.

(e) Moving of patients from one area to another while a flammable anesthetic is being administered shall be prohibited.

(f) Smoking shall be limited to dressing rooms and lounges with the doors leading to the corridor closed.

4. Practice.

(a) Flammable anesthetic agents shall be employed only in flammable anesthetizing locations.

(b) Woolen and synthetic blankets shall not be permitted in flammable anesthetizing locations.

(c) Electrical connection of the patient to the conductive floor shall be assured by a high-impedance (conductive) strap in contact with the patient's skin with one end of the strapfastened to the metal frame of an operating table or shall be electrically interconnected by other means.

(d) If cautery, electrosurgery, or electrical equipment employing an open spark is to be used during an operation, flammable anesthetics shall not be used. Flammable germicides or flammable fat solvents shall not be applied for the preoperative preparation of the field.

(e) A visual (lighted red lamp) or audible warning signal from the line isolation monitor serving an anesthetizing location indicates that the total hazard current has exceeded allowable limits. This suggests that one or more electrical devices is contributing an excessively low impedance to ground, which might constitute a fault, which would expose the patient or hospital personnel to an unsafe condition should an additional fault occur. Briefly and sequentially unplugging the power cord of each electrical device in the location will usually cause the green signal lamp to light, showing that the system has been adequately isolated from ground, when the potentially defective device has been unplugged. The continuing use of such a device, so identified, should be questioned, but not necessarily abandoned. At the earliest opportunity the device should be inspected by the hospital engineer or other qualified personnel and, if necessary, repaired or replaced.

5. Enforcement.

It shall be the responsibility of _____

(name)

[an anesthesiologist or other qualified person appointed by the hospital authority to act in that capacity] to enforce the above regulations.

SET (2)
**REGULATIONS FOR SAFE PRACTICE IN
NONFLAMMABLE ANESTHETIZING LOCATIONS**

The following rules and regulations have been adopted by the Medical Staff and Administration. NFPA 99-1987, Section 12-4.1, "Anesthetizing Locations," shall apply in all inhalation anesthetizing locations.

_____   _____
(Insert Date)   (Insert Name of Hospital Authority)

The use or storage of any of the following flammable agents or germicides shall be prohibited from all operating rooms, delivery rooms, and other anesthetizing locations in this hospital.

By reason of their chemical composition, these agents present a hazard of fire or explosion:

cyclopropane	ethyl chloride
diethyl ether	ethylene

1. Nonflammable Anesthetizing Location.

(a) *Definition.* The term nonflammable anesthetizing location shall mean any anesthetizing location designated for the exclusive use of nonflammable anesthetizing agents.

2. Equipment.

(a) No electrical equipment except that judged by the Engineering Department of Hospital as being in compliance with NFPA 99-1987, Section 12-4.1, "Anesthetizing Locations," shall be used in any anesthetizing location.

(b) When a physician wishes to use his or her personal electrical equipment, it shall first be inspected by the Engineering Department and, if judged to comply with NFPA 99-1987, Section 12-4.1, "Anesthetizing Locations," it shall be so labeled.

(c) Photographic lighting equipment shall be of the totally enclosed type or so constructed as to prevent the escape of sparks or hot metal particles.

3. Personnel.

Smoking shall be limited to dressing rooms and lounges with doors leading to the corridor closed.

4. Practice.

(a) The use or storage of flammable anesthetic agents shall be expressly prohibited in a nonflammable anesthetizing location.

(b) If cautery, electrosurgery, or a hot or arcing device is to be used during an operation, flammable germicides or flammable fat solvents shall not be applied for preoperative preparation of the skin.

(c) A visual (lighted red lamp) or audible warning signal from the line isolation monitor serving an anesthetizing location indicates that the total hazard current has exceeded allowable limits. This suggests that one or more electrical devices is contributing an excessively low impedance to ground, which might constitute a fault, that would expose the patient or hospital personnel to an unsafe condition should an additional fault occur. Briefly and sequentially unplugging the power cord of each electrical device in the location will usually cause the green lamp to light, showing that the system has been adequately isolated from ground, when the potentially defective device has been unplugged. The continuing use of such a device, so identified, should be questioned, but not necessarily abandoned. At the earliest opportunity the device should be inspected by the hospital engineer or other qualified personnel and, if necessary, repaired or replaced.

(d) Transportation of patients while an inhalation anesthetic is being administered by means of a mobile anesthesia machine shall be prohibited, unless deemed essential for the benefit of the patient in the combined judgment of the surgeon and anesthesiologist.

(e) If, in the combined judgment of the anesthesiologist responsible for the administering of the anesthetic and the surgeon performing the operation, the life of the patient would be jeopardized by not administering a flammable anesthetic agent, the following steps shall be taken:

(1) Both surgeon and anesthesiologist involved in the case shall attest to the reason for administering a flammable anesthetic in a nonflammable anesthetizing location on the patient's record and in the operating room register.

(2) The hazard of static sparks shall be reduced by electrically interconnecting the patient, operating room table, anesthesia gas machine, and anesthesiologist by wet sheets or other conductive materials. Conductive accessories shall be used for the electrically conductive pathways from the anesthesia gas machine to the patient.

(3) If cautery, electrosurgery, or electrical equipment employing an open spark is to be used during an operation, flammable anesthetics shall not be used. Flammable germicides or flammable fat solvents shall not be applied for the preoperative preparation of the field.

5. Enforcement.

It shall be the responsibility of _____
(name)

[an anesthesiologist or other qualified person appointed by the hospital authority to act in that capacity] to enforce the above regulations.

SET (3)

REGULATIONS FOR SAFE PRACTICE IN MIXED FACILITIES

The following rules and regulations have been adopted by the Medical Staff and by the Administration. NFPA 99-1987, Section 12-4.1, "Anesthetizing Locations," shall apply in all inhalation anesthetizing locations. This hospital is a mixed facility. Personnel are cautioned as to the existence of both flammable and nonflammable inhalation anesthetizing locations within the hospital building and the different practices that apply to each location.

(Insert Date)	(Insert Name of Hospital Authority)

By reason of their chemical composition, these flammable anesthetic agents present a hazard of explosion in anesthetizing locations:

cyclopropane   ethyl chloride
ethyl ether   ethylene

REGULATIONS

1. Mixed Facility.

(a) *Definition.* The term mixed facility shall mean a hospital wherein flammable anesthetizing locations and nonflammable anesthetizing locations coexist within the same building, allowing interchange of personnel and equipment between flammable and nonflammable anesthetizing locations.

(b) *Definition.* Flammable anesthetizing location shall mean any area of the hospital designated for the administration of flammable anesthetic agents.

(c) *Definition.* Nonflammable anesthetizing location shall mean any anesthetizing location permanently designated for the exclusive use of nonflammable anesthetizing agents.

2. Equipment.

(a) No electrical equipment except that judged by the Engineering Department of Hospital as being in compliance with NFPA 99-1987, Section 12-4.1, "Anesthetizing Locations," shall be used in any flammable anesthetizing location.

(b) When a physician wishes to use his or her personal electrical equipment, it shall first be inspected by the Engineering Department and, if judged to comply with NFPA 99-1987, Section 12-4.1, "Anesthetizing Locations," it shall be so labeled.

(c) Portable X-ray equipment used in flammable anesthetizing locations shall be approved for use in hazardous areas.

(d) Only approved photographic lighting equipment shall be used in flammable anesthetizing locations. Because of occasional bursting of bulbs, suitable enclosures shall be used to prevent sparks and hot particles from falling into the hazardous area.

(e) Covers shall not be used on anesthesia machines designed for flammable anesthetic agents.

(f) All portable electrical equipment shall meet the requirements for flammable anesthetizing locations.

3. Personnel.

(a) Outer garments worn by the operating room personnel and visitors in mixed facilities shall not include fabrics of silk, wool, or synthetic textile materials such as nylon, polyester, acrylic, or acetate, unless such fabrics have been tested and found to be antistatic in accordance with the requirements of NFPA 99-1987, Section 12-4.1, "Anesthetizing Locations."

(b) Silk, wool, or synthetic textile materials, except untreated rayon, shall not be permitted in mixed facilities as outer garments, or for nonapparel purposes, unless such fabrics have been tested and found to be antistatic in accordance with the requirements of NFPA 99-1987, Section 12-4.1, "Anesthetizing Locations." Hosiery and underclothing in which the entire garment is in close contact with the skin may be made of silk, wool, or synthetic material.

(c) All personnel and visitors entering all anesthetizing locations in mixed facilities shall wear conductive footwear or other floor-contacting devices that shall have been tested on the wearer and found to be satisfactorily conductive.

(d) It will be the responsibility of each individual entering an anesthetizing location of a mixed facility to determine at least once daily that he is in electrical contact with the conductive floor. Apparatus for testing shall be available.

(e) Moving of patients from one area to another while a flammable anesthetic is being administered shall be prohibited.

(f) Smoking shall be limited to dressing rooms and lounges with the doors leading to the corridor closed.

4. Practice.

(a) Flammable anesthetic agents shall be employed only in flammable anesthetizing locations.

(b) The administration or the intended administration of a flammable anesthetic agent shall be brought to the attention of all personnel within the flammable anesthetizing location by verbal communication by the anesthesiologist and by posting prominent signs in the operating room and at all entrances to the operating room stating that a flammable anesthetic agent is in use.

(c) Woolen and synthetic blankets shall not be permitted in anesthetizing locations.

(d) Electrical connection of the patient to the conductive floor in a flammable anesthetizing location shall be assured by a high-impedance conductive strap in contact with the patient's skin with one end of the strap fastened to the metal frame of an operating table or shall be electrically interconnected by other means.

(e) If cautery, electrosurgery, or electrical equipment employing an open spark is to be used during an operation, flammable anesthetics shall not be used. Flammable germicides and flammable fat solvents shall not be applied for the preoperative preparation of the field.

(f) If, in the combined judgment of the anesthesiologist responsible for the administration of the anesthetic and the surgeon performing the operation, the life of the patient would be jeopardized by not administering a flammable anesthetic agent in a nonflammable anesthetizing location, the following steps shall be taken:

(1) Both surgeon and anesthesiologist involved in the case shall attest to the reason for administering a flammable anesthetic in a nonflammable anesthetizing location on the patient's record and in the operating room register.

(2) The hazard of static sparks shall be reduced by electrically connecting the patient, operating room table, anesthesia gas machine, and anesthesiologist by wet sheets or other conductive materials. Conductive accessories shall be used for the electrically conductive pathways from the anesthesia gas machine to the patient.

(g) A visual (lighted red lamp) or audible warning signal from the line isolation monitor serving an anesthetizing location indicates that the total hazard current has exceeded allowable limits. This suggests that one or more electrical devices is contributing an excessively low impedance to ground, which might constitute a fault, which would expose the patient or hospital personnel to an unsafe condition should an additional fault occur. Briefly and sequentially unplugging the power cord of each electrical device in the location will usually cause the green signal lamp to light, showing that the system has been adequately isolated from ground, when the potentially defective device has been unplugged. The continuing use of such a device, so identified, should be questioned, but not necessarily abandoned. At the earliest opportunity the device should be inspected by the hospital engineer or other qualified personnel and, if necessary, repaired or replaced.

(h) Interchange of personnel and portable equipment between flammable and nonflammable anesthetizing locations shall be strictly controlled.

(i) Transportation of patients while an inhalation anesthetic is being administered by means of a mobile anesthesia machine shall be prohibited, unless deemed essential for the benefit of the patient in the combined judgment of the surgeon and anesthetist.

5. Enforcement.

It shall be the responsibility of _____

(name)

[an anesthesiologist or other qualified person appointed by the hospital authority to act in that capacity] to enforce the above regulations.

C-12.4 Suggested Procedures in the Event of a Fire or Explosion, Anesthetizing Locations.

C-12.4.1 General.

C-12.4.1.1 Fires in hospitals pose unique problems for hospital personnel, patients, and fire service personnel. Hospitals store and use relatively large quantities of flammable and combustible substances. Oxygen-enriched atmospheres are often employed in medical therapy, and are utilized routinely during administration of anesthesia. The presence of flammable and combustible substances and oxygen-enriched atmospheres under the same roof with nonambulatory patients presents an extra-hazardous situation. All hospital personnel should understand the steps to take to save life, preserve limb, and contain smoke and/or limit fire until the fire department arrives. It is recommended that the procedures delineated herein, or similar ones, become a part of the firesafety regulations of every hospital.

C-12.4.2 Steps to Take in the Event of a Fire or Explosion.

C-12.4.2.1 The following steps, listed in the approximate order of their importance, should be taken by all personnel, should fire occur. If an explosion occurs, and it is not followed by fire, follow the procedure outlined under C-12.4.2.2. If a fire follows an explosion, proceed as follows:

(a) Remove the immediately exposed patient or patients from the site of the fire, if their hair or clothing are not burning. If they are burning, extinguish the flames (*see C-12.4.4 and C-12.4.5*).

(b) Sound the fire alarm by whatever mode the hospital fire plan provides.

NOTE: It is assumed that each hospital has a fire plan, prepared in consultation with representatives of the local fire department. In such a plan, immediate notification of the local fire department is essential.

(c) Close off the supply of oxygen, nitrous oxide, and air to any equipment involved, if this step can be accomplished without injury to personnel (*see C-12.4.3*).

(d) Close doors to contain smoke and isolate fire.

(e) Remove patients threatened by the fire.

(f) Attempt to extinguish or contain the fire (*see C-12.4.4*).

(g) Direct the fire fighters to the site of the fire.

(h) Take whatever steps are necessary to protect or evacuate patients in adjacent areas.

NOTE 1: In the event of a fire in an operating room while an operative procedure on an anesthetized patient is in progress, it may be necessary to extinguish the fire prior to removing the patient from the room.

NOTE 2: During an operation, it may be more hazardous to move patients than to attempt to extinguish or contain the fire. The attending physician must determine which step would present the lesser hazard —

hurriedly terminating an operative procedure or continuing the procedure and exposing the members of the operating team and the patient to the hazards stemming from the fire.

C-12.4.2.2 The following steps are recommended in the event of an explosion involving inhalation anesthesia apparatus:

(a) Disconnect the patient from the apparatus;

(b) Procure a new gas anesthesia apparatus and make every effort to save the life of the patient and prevent injury to the patient.

C-12.4.2.3 It is essential that all equipment involved in a fire or explosion by preserved for examination by an authority attempting to determine the cause. Additionally, pertinent administrative data, including photographs, should be recorded. The report should state:

(a) Whether wearing apparel of all persons in the room at the time of the fire or explosion met the requirements of 12-4.1.3.8(g) and (h) of Chapter 12;

(b) Whether portable equipment, low-voltage instruments, accessories, and furniture met the requirements of 7-5.1.2.4, 7-5.1.2.5, and 12-4.1.3.8(c), (d), and (i), of Chapters 7 and 12, respectively.

(c) Whether the ventilating system was being operated in accordance with 5-4.3 of Chapter 5.

C-12.4.2.3.1 The area involved, with all involved items in place, should be closed off and secured for later examination by a responsible authority.

C-12.4.3 Closing Off Oxygen, Nitrous Oxide, and Air Supply.

C-12.4.3.1 In the event of a fire involving equipment connected to an oxygen, nitrous oxide, and air station outlet, the zone valve supplying that station is to be closed [*see C-12.4.6.1(a)*].

C-12.4.3.1.1 Immediately, all patients receiving oxygen through the same zone valve must be supplied with individual oxygen cylinders.

NOTE: Each gas line to an operating room should have an individual zone valve (*see Sections 4-3 through 4-6 in Chapter 4, "Gas and Vacuum Systems"*). Thus, closing of all valves to one room would not endanger patients in other rooms.

C-12.4.3.2 If fire involves apparatus supplied by a cylinder of oxygen, it is desirable to close the cylinder valve, if this can be done without injuring personnel.

NOTE: Metal components of regulators and valves can become excessively hot if exposed to flame. Personnel are cautioned not to use their bare hands to effect closure.

C-12.4.4 Extinguishment or Containment of Fire.

The issue of fire extinguishers being used inside operating rooms is very complicated because of the unusual environment during surgery (i.e., one person, the patient, either unconscious or immobile; and the exposure of the internal body cavity, and the resultant need for the maintenance of sterility). While staff is always present during surgery, their ability to respond to a fire may not always be immediately possible. The effects of extinguishers, including water-based extinguishers, can be disasterous to the patient.

NFPA *101, Life Safety Code,* and NFPA 10, *Standard for Portable Fire Extinguishers,* offer some general criteria vis-a-vis fire extinguisher placement. One of the best solutions, of course, is taking steps to prevent fire from occurring in operating rooms. This involves reviewing procedures that can create hazards (e.g., the use of flammable liquids), as well as educating staff on the need to prevent incidents.

Periodic training involving all persons who work in operating rooms is essential.

C-12.4.4.1 Fire originating in or involving inhalation anesthesia apparatus generally involves combustibles such as rubber. Water or water-based extinguishing agents are most effective in such fires.

(a) Precautions should be taken if line-powered electrical equipment is adjacent to or involved in fire, because of the danger of electrocution of personnel if streams of water contact live circuits.

(b) Before attempting to fight fire with water or a water-based extinguishing agent, electrical apparatus should be disconnected from the supply outlet, or the supply circuit deenergized at the circuit panel.

(c) If such deenergization cannot be accomplished, water should not be employed (*see C-12.4.4.3*).

C-12.4.4.2 Fires involving, or adjacent to, electrical equipment with live circuits must be fought with extinguishers suitable for "Class C" fires in accordance with NFPA 10, *Standard for Portable Fire Extinguishers.*

C-12.4.4.3 Fire extinguishers are classified according to the type of fire for which each is suited.

(a) Fires involving ordinary combustibles such as rubber, plastic, linen, wool, paper, and the like are called "Class A" fires. These may be fought with water or water-based extinguishing agents. Hose lines are suitable for this purpose. Portable extinguishers suitable for "Class A" fires are identified with the letter *A* contained in a (if colored) green triangle.

(b) "Class B" fires involve flammable liquids and should be fought only with an extinguisher identified by the letter *B* contained in a (if colored) red square.

(c) "Class C" fires involve electrical equipment and should be fought only with an extinguisher identified by the letter *C* contained in a (if colored) blue circle.

(d) Carbon dioxide and some dry chemical extinguishers are labeled for "Class B" and "Class C" fires. Some dry chemical units may be used for all three types (*see NFPA 10, Standard for Portable Fire Extinguishers, Appendix B*).

C-12.4.5 Protection of Patients and Personnel.

C-12.4.5.1 Serious and even fatal burns of the skin or lungs, from inhaling heated gases, are possible. Thus, it is essential that patients be removed from the scene of the fire whenever practical. Where an anesthetized patient is connected to a burning piece of equipment, it may be more practical as the initial step to remove the equipment and/or extinguish the fire than to remove the patient.

C-12.4.5.2 Noxious gases produced by fire constitute a threat to life from asphyxia, beyond the thermal burn problem.

(a) Personnel are cautioned not to remain in the fire area after patients are evacuated, unless they are wearing proper emergency apparatus.

C-12.4.6 Indoctrination of Personnel.

C-12.4.6.1 It is highly desirable that personnel involved in the care of patients, including nurses, aides, ward secretaries, and physicians, irrespective of whether they are involved in anesthesia practices, be thoroughly indoctrinated in all aspects of firesafety, including:

(a) the location of zone valves of nonflammable medical gas systems and the station outlets controlled by each valve;

(b) the location of electrical service boxes and the areas served thereby;

(c) the location and proper use of fire extinguishers (*see C-12.4.4*);

(d) the recommended methods and routes for evacuating patients (*see Annex 1, "Health Care Emergency Preparedness"*);

(e) the steps involved in carrying out the fire plan of the hospital;

(f) the location of fire alarm boxes, or knowledge of other methods for summoning the fire department.

C-12.4.6.2 To ensure that personnel are familiar with the procedures outlined above, regular instructive sessions and fire drills should be held.

C-12.5 Cylinder Table. See Table C-12.5.

Appendix C-13 Additional Explanatory Information on Chapter 13, "Ambulatory Health Care Center Requirements"

Appendix C-13 consists of the following:

C-13.1 Typical Gas Cylinders, Anesthetizing Locations;

C-13.2 Text of Suggested Regulations, Anesthetizing Locations.

C-13.1 Typical Gas Cylinder Table, Anesthetizing Locations. (*See Table C-12.5.*)

C-13.2 Text of Suggested Regulations for Nonflammable Inhalation Anesthetizing Locations and Gas Storage Areas in Nonhospital-based Ambulatory Care Facilities.

The following rules and regulations have been adopted. The requirements of Section 13-4.1, "Anesthetizing Locations," of NFPA 99-1987 shall apply to all anesthetizing locations and gas storage areas in this facility.

Table C-12.5   Typical Medical Gas Cylinders Volume and Weight of Available Contents.* All Volumes at 70°F (21.1°C).

Cylinder Style & Dimensions	Nominal Volume Cu In./ Liter	Contents	Name of Gas							Mixture of Oxygen	
			Air	Carbon Dioxide	Cyclo-Propane	Helium	Nitrogen	Nitrous Oxide	Oxygen	Helium	CO²
B 3½″ od × 13″ 8.89 × 33 cm	87/ 1.43	psiq Liters Lbs.-Oz. Kilograms		838 370 1–8 .68	75 375 1–7¼ .66				1900 200 — —		
D 4½″ od × 17″ 10.8 × 43 cm	176/ 2.88	psig Liters Lbs.-Oz. Kilograms	1900 375 — —	838 940 3–13 1.73	75 870 3–5½ 1.51	1600 300 — —	1900 370 — —	745 940 3–13 1.73	1900 400 — —	** 300 ** **	** 400 ** **
E 4¼″ od × 26″ 10.8 × 66 cm	293/ 4.80	psiq Liters Lbs.-Oz. Kilograms	1900 625 — —	838 1590 6–7 2.92		1600 500 — —	1900 610 — —	745 1590 6–7 2.92	1900 660 — —	** 500 ** **	** 660 ** **
M 7″ od × 43″ 17.8 × 109 cm	1337/21.9	psiq Liters Lbs.-Oz. Kilograms	1900 2850 — —	838 7570 30–10 13.9		1600 2260 — —	2200 3200 — —	7.45 7570 30–10 13.9	2200 3450 122 cu ft —	** 2260 ** **	** 3000 ** **
G 8½″ od × 51″ 21.6 × 130 cm	2370/38.8	psiq Liters Lbs.-Oz. Kilograms	1900 5050 — —	838 12,300 50–0 22.7		1600 4000 — —		745 13,800 56–0 25.4		** 4000 ** **	** 5330 ** **
H or K 9¼″ od × 51″ 23.5 × 130 cm	2660/43.6	psiq Liters Lbs.-Oz. Kilograms	2200 6550 — —			2200 6000 — —	2200 6400 — —	745 15,800 64 29.1	2200† 6900 244 cu ft —		

NOTES: (*) These are computed contents based on nominal cylinder volumes and rounded to no greater variance than ±1%.
(**) The pressure and weight of mixed gases will vary according to the composition of the mixture.
(†) 275 cu ft/7800 liter cylinders at 2490 psig are available upon request.

This table reprinted with permission from the Compressed Gas Association, Inc.

The use of any of the following flammable agents shall be prohibited from the premises. By reason of their chemical composition, these agents present a hazard of fire or explosion:

cyclopropane
divinyl ether
ethyl ether

fluroxene
ethyl chloride
ethylene

Smoking shall be limited to those areas of the premises not directly connected with the anesthetizing location or the location for storage of compressed gas cylinders.

Compressed gas cylinders shall be connected to the manifold, and otherwise handled and stored, as provided in Chapter 13 of NFPA 99-1987.

Defective electrical equipment shall not be used on the premises.

Gas pipeline alarm systems shall be monitored, and responsible personnel notified of any fall in pressure or alarm condition.

Appendix C-19 Additional Explanatory Information on Chapter 19, "Hyperbaric Facilities"

Appendix C-19 consists of the following:

C-19.1 Nature of Hazards;

C-19.2 Suggested Procedures to Follow in Event of Fire in Class A Chambers;

C-19.3 Suggested Procedures to Follow in Event of Fire in Class B Chambers;

C-19.4 Pressure Table.

C-19.1 Nature of Hazards.

C-19.1.1 Fire and Explosion.

C-19.1.1.1 The occurrence of a fire requires the presence of combustible or flammable materials, an atmosphere containing oxygen or other oxidizing agent(s), and heat or energy source of ignition.

NOTE: Certain substances such as acetylenic hydrocarbons can propagate flame in the absence of oxygen.

C-19.1.1.2 Under hyperbaric conditions utilizing compressed air, the partial pressure of oxygen is increased. Leakage of oxygen into the atmosphere of the chamber (for example from improper application of respiratory therapy apparatus) may further increase markedly the oxygen partial pressure.

C-19.1.1.2.1 The flammability or combustibility of materials generally increases as the partial pressure of oxygen increases, even when the percentage of oxygen in the gas mixture remains constant. Materials that are nonflammable or noncombustible under normal atmospheric conditions may become flammable or combustible under such circumstances.

C-19.1.1.3 Sources of Fuel.

C-19.1.1.3.1 Materials that may not ignite in air at atmospheric pressure or require relatively high temperatures for their ignition but that burn vigorously in 100 percent oxygen include, but are not necessarily limited to: tricresyl phosphate (lubricant); certain types of flame-resistant fabrics; silicone rubber; polyvinyl chloride; asbestos-containing paint; glass fiber-sheathed silicone rubber-insulated wire; polyvinyl chloride-insulated asbestos-covered wire and sheet; polyamides; epoxy compounds; and certain asbestos blankets.

NOTE: Flammable lubricants are used widely in equipment designed for conventional use, including shafts, gear boxes, pulleys and casters, and threaded joints, which are coupled and uncoupled.

This list is for information purposes only, and does not necessarily reflect what may be practiced today in the United States (i.e., some materials are no longer allowed, but may be in use in existing chambers).

C-19.1.1.3.2 The flammability of certain volatile liquids and gases containing carbon and hydrogen is well known. Hazards and safeguards for their use in oxygen-enriched atmospheres at ambient pressure are well documented in Section 12-4.1, "Anesthetizing Locations." See also NFPA 325M, *Fire Hazard Properties of Flammable Liquids, Gases, and Volatile Solids.*

NOTE: Repeated reference to 12-4.1 is made throughout Chapter 19. These references do not imply, and should not be construed to mean, that flammable anesthetics can or should be employed in or around hyperbaric facilities.

C-19.1.1.3.3 Human tissues will burn in an atmosphere of 100 percent oxygen. Body oils and fats, as well as hair, will burn readily under such circumstances.

C-19.1.1.3.4 When a conventional loose cotton outergarment, such as scrub suits, dresses, and gowns employed in hospital operating suites, is ignited in an atmosphere of pure oxygen, the garment will become engulfed in flame rapidly, and will be totally destroyed within 20 seconds or less.

C-19.1.1.3.4.1 If such a garment is ignited in a compressed air atmosphere, the flame spread is increased. When oxygen concentration exceeds 23.5 percent at elevated total pressure, flame spread is much more rapid, and at 6 ATA, is comparable to 95 ± 5 percent at 1 ATA. Flame spread in air (21 percent oxygen) is somewhat increased at 6 ATA, but not to the level of 95 ± 5 percent at 1 ATA.

C-19.1.1.3.4.2 Combustible fabrics have tiny air spaces which become filled with oxygen when exposed to oxygen-enriched environments. Once removed to atmospheric air (e.g., room air outside the chamber), the fabric will burn, if ignited, almost as rapidly as if it were still in the oxygen environment. This hazard will remain until the oxygen trapped in the air spaces in the fabric has had time to diffuse out and be replaced by air.

This phenomenon should be remembered if clothing, etc., catches fire. Burning clothes should be removed from the body as quickly as possible.

C-19.1.1.3.5 Oil-based or volatile cosmetics (facial creams, body oils, hair sprays, and the like) constitute a source of fuel that is highly flammable in an oxygen-enriched atmosphere.

C-19.1.1.4 Sources of Ignition.

C-19.1.1.4.1 Sources of ignition that might be encountered in a hyperbaric chamber include, but are not necessarily limited to: defective electrical equipment, including failure of high-voltage components of radiological or monitoring equipment; heated surfaces in broken vacuum tubes or broken lamps used for general illumination, spot illumination, or illumination of diagnostic instruments; the hot-wire cautery or high-frequency electrocautery; open or arcing switches, including motor switches; bare defibrillator paddles; overheated motors; and electrical thermostats.

C-19.1.1.4.2 Sources of ignition that should not be encountered in a hyperbaric facility, but that might be introduced by inept practice, include: lighted matches or tobacco; static sparks from improper use of personal attire; electrical wiring not complying with 19-2.7 of Chapter 19; cigarette lighters; and any oil-contaminated materials that present a spontaneous heating hazard.

C-19.1.1.4.3 In oxygen-enriched atmospheres, the minimum energy necessary to ignite flammable or combustible materials is reduced in most instances below the energy required in atmospheres of ambient air.

C-19.1.2 Mechanical Hazards.

C-19.1.2.1 General.

C-19.1.2.1.1 A large amount of potential energy is stored in even a small volume of compres sed gas. In hyperbaric chambers of moderate or large size, the potential energy of the chamber's compressed atmosphere, if released suddenly, can produce devastating destruction to adjacent structures and personnel, as well as to structures and personnel remote from the site of the chamber. Such sudden release could result from failure of the vessel structure, its parts, or its piping.

C-19.1.2.1.2 A particular hazard can be created if individuals attempt to drill, cut, or weld the vessel in a manner contrary to ASME *Pressure Vessel Codes*.

C-19.1.2.2 The restriction on escape and the impedance to rescue and fire-fighting efforts posed by the chamber create a significant hazard to life in case of fire or other emergency.

C-19.1.2.2.1 A particular hazard exists to chamber personnel in the event of a fire within the structure housing the chamber. Inability to escape from the chamber and loss of services of the chamber operator would pose serious threats to the lives of all occupants of the chamber.

C-19.1.2.2.2 All personnel involved in hyperbaric chamber operation and therapy, including patients and family, must be made aware of the risks and hazards involved. Fire prevention is essential. Extinguishment of a fire within a Class B chamber is impossible. Extinguishment of a fire within a Class A chamber is only possible utilizing equipment already installed in such a chamber, and then often only by the efforts of the occupants of such a chamber or the chamber operator.

Because the oxygen level is elevated and the patient is the sole occupant of the chamber, a fire in a Class B chamber is to be prevented by all means possible.

C-19.1.2.3 The necessity for restricting viewing ports to small size limits the vision of chamber operators and other observers, reducing their effectiveness as safety monitors.

C-19.1.2.4 Containers and enclosures may be subjected to collapse or rupture as a consequence of the changing pressures of the hyperbaric chamber. Items containing entrained gas include, but are not necessarily limited to: ampuls; partially filled syringes; stoppered or capped bottles; cuffed endotrachael tubes; and pneumatic cushions employed for breathing masks or aids in positioning patients. The rupture of such containers having combustible or flammable liquids would also constitute a severe fire or explosion hazard.

C-19.1.2.4.1 The sudden collapse of containers from high external pressures will result in adiabatic heating of the contents. Therefore the collapse of a container of flammable liquid would consitute a severe fire or explosion hazard both from heating and from a spill of the liquid. (*See 19-3.1.5.2 and C-19.1.1.3.2.*)

C-19.1.2.5 Other mechanical hazards relate to the malfunction, disruption, or inoperativeness of many standard items when placed in service under pressurized atmospheres. Hazards that might be encountered in this regard are: implosion of illuminating lamps and vacuum tubes; overloading of fans driving gas at higher density; and inaccurate operation of standard flowmeters, pressure gauges, and pressure-reducing regulators.

C-19.1.2.5.1 Illuminating lamps or vacuum tubes, which implode, or overloaded fans, are sources of ignition.

C-19.1.3 Physiological and Medical Hazards.

C-19.1.3.1 Medical hazards that may be encountered routinely include compression problems, nitrogen narcosis, oxygen toxicity, and the direct effects of sudden pressure changes.

C-19.1.3.1.1 Inability to equalize pressure differentials between nasopharynx (nose) and nasal sinuses or the middle ear can result in excruciating pain and may cause rupture of the eardrum or hemorrhage into the ear cavity or nasal sinus.

C-19.1.3.1.2 The breathing of air (78 percent nitrogen) under significant pressures (as by chamber personnel breathing chamber atmosphere) can result in nitrogen narcosis, which resembles alcoholic inebriation. The degree of narcosis is directly related to the amount of pressurization and, up to a certain point, the duration of pressurization. Nitrogen narcosis results in impairment of mental functions, loss of manual dexterity, and interference with alertness and ability to think clearly and act quickly and intelligently in an emergency.

C-19.1.3.1.3 Oxygen toxicity may develop from breathing of oxygen at partial pressures above 0.21 atmosphere absolute for a significant length of time. Oxygen toxicity can affect the lungs (pain in the chest, rapid shallow breathing, coughing), nervous system (impaired consciousness and convulsions), and/or other tissues and organs, or combinations thereof.

C-19.1.3.1.4 Direct effects of reduction in pressure may include inability to equalize pressures between the nasopharynx and sinuses or middle ear; expansion of gas pockets in the gastrointestinal tract; and expansion of trapped gas in the lungs.

C-19.1.3.1.5 The presence of personnel within the cramped confines of the hyperbaric chamber in close proximity to grounded metallic structures on all sides creates a definite shock hazard if accidental contact is made with a live electrical conductor or a defective piece of electrical equipment. Such accidental contact also could be a source of ignition of flammable or combustible materials. (See C-19.1.1.4.)

C-19.1.3.2 Medical hazards that are not ordinarily encountered during hyperbaric oxygen therapy, but that may arise during malfunction, fire, or other emergency conditions, include electric shock and fouling of the atmosphere of the chamber with oxygen, nitrous oxide, carbon dioxide, carbon monoxide, pyrolysis products from overheated materials, or the toxic products of combustion from any fire.

C-19.1.3.2.1 Increased concentrations of carbon dioxide within the chamber, as might result from malfunction of the systems responsible for monitoring or removal thereof, can be toxic under increased pressures.

C-19.1.3.2.2 The development of combustion products or gases evolved from heated nommetallics within the closed space of the hyperbaric chamber can be extremely toxic to life because of the confining nature of the chamber and the increased hazards of breathing such products under elevated pressure.

NOTE: Extreme pressure rises have accompanied catastrophic fires in confined atmospheres. These pressures have driven hot, toxic gases into the lungs of victims as well as exceeding the structural limits of the vessel in at least one case.

C-19.1.3.3 Physiological hazards include exposure to high noise levels and decompression sickness. Rapid release of pressurized gases may produce shock waves and loss of visibility.

C-19.1.3.3.1 During hyperbaric therapy, and especially during compression, the noise level within the chamber becomes quite high. Such a level can be hazardous because it is distractive, interferes with communication, and may produce headaches or other problems in susceptible individuals.

C-19.1.3.3.2 Decompression sickness (bends, caisson worker's disease) results from the elution into the blood stream or extravascular tissues of bubbles of inert gas (mainly nitrogen) which becomes dissolved in the blood and tissue fluids while breathing air at elevated pressures for a significant period of time.

NOTE: Rapid decompression of the chamber may occur if the pressure relief valve is damaged from exposure to a fire external to the chamber or from the venting of hot products of combustion from within the chamber.

C-19.1.3.3.3 The use of decompression procedures will prevent immediate escape from the Class A chamber by occupants during emergency situations.

NOTE: These procedures are not followed if chamber occupants are exposed to a "no-decompression exposure" [compression to less than 2 atmospheres absolute (ATA) air]; or when compressed to 2 ATA or higher pressures and breathing 100 percent oxygen.

C-19.1.3.3.4 The sudden release of gas, whether by rupture of a container or operation of a device such as used in fire fighting, will produce noise, possible shock waves, reduced or obscured visibility, and temperature changes. The initial effect may be to cool the air, but resulting pressure rises will cause adiabatic heating.

C-19.1.3.4 In summary, the hazards of fire and related problems in hyperbaric systems are real. By the very nature of the hyperbaric atmosphere, increased partial pressures of oxygen are present routinely. Flammability and combustibility of materials are increased. Ignition energy is lowered. Both immediate escape and ready entry for rescue are impeded. Finally, attendants within the chamber, through effects of the elevated noise level and nitrogen pressure, may be unable to respond to emergencies quickly and accurately.

C-19.2 Suggested Procedures to Follow in Event of Fire in Class A Chambers.

NOTE: The procedures contained in Appendix C-19.2 are adopted from those employed by the United States Air Force. These procedures are published herein only as a guide for those who are preparing procedures for their own hyperbaric facilities. Their publication herein is not to be construed as implying that they become a literal part of the standard procedure in any hyperbaric facility.

The procedures listed below reflect the latest emergency practices of the U.S. Air Force. The Subcommittee on Hyperbaric and Hypobaric Facilities considers it appropriate to include such an example for user benefit.

C-19.2.1 Fire Inside Chamber.

Inside Observer.

(a) Advise outside.

(b) Don breathing air mask.

(c) Activate fire suppression system and/or hand-held hoses.

Console Operator.

(a) Maintain chamber depth.

(b) Activate the fire suppression system, if needed.

(c) Ensure breathing gas is compressed air.

(d) Notify the fire department by activating fire alarm station or telephone.

(e) Note time of fire and record progress of events.

Hyperbaric Chamber (System) Technician (Outside).

(a) Stand by with a fire extinguisher.

(b) Assist in unloading chamber occupants.

Physician/Safety Monitor (Outside).

(a) Direct operations and assist crew members wherever necessary.

(b) Terminate procedure as soon as possible.

Other Personnel.

(a) Stand by to evacuate chamber personnel.

C-19.2.2 Fire Outside Chamber.

Console Operator.

(a) Notify the inside observer to stand by for emergency return to normal atmospheric pressure.

(b) Notify fire department by activating fire alarm station or telephone.

(c) Change chamber breathing gas to compressed air.

(d) Don fire mask.

(e) Note time of fire and record progress of events.

Hyperbaric Chamber (System) Technician (Outside).

(a) Assure that compressor intake is drawing outside air.

(b) Man fire extinguisher.

(c) Help chamber operator to don fire mask.

Physician/Safety Monitor (Outside).

(a) Direct operations.

(b) Determine whether procedure should be terminated.

Other Personnel.

(a) Stand by to evacuate chamber personnel.

C-19.3 Suggested Procedures to Follow in Event of Fire in Class B Chambers.

C-19.3.1 For fires within facility not involving the chamber:

(a) Turn off oxygen source.

(b) Decompress chamber.

(c) Remove patient and evacuate to safe area.

C-19.3.2   For fire within chamber:

(a) Turn off oxygen source.

(b) Decompress chamber.

(c) Remove patient.

(d) Sound fire alarm of facility.

(e) Evacuate area.

(f) Attempt to suppress fire, or close door and await arrival of fire service personnel.

NOTE 1:   The oxygen percentage in the chamber environment, not the oxygen partial pressure, is of principal concern, as concentrations above 23.5 percent oxygen increase the rate of flame spread. Thirty percent oxygen in nitrogen at 1 ATA (228 mmHg pO_2), increases burning rate. However, 6 percent oxygen in nitrogen will not support combustion, regardless of oxygen partial pressure (at 5 ATA, 6 percent oxygen gives 228 mmHg pO_2).

Note 1 was added in the 1982 edition of NFPA 56D to clarify that it is the percent of oxygen in the atmosphere that is of fire concern, not the partial pressure of oxygen.

NOTE 2:   The Subcommittee on Hyperbaric and Hypobaric Facilities recommends that one unit of pressure measurement be employed. Since a variety of different units are now in use, and since chamber operators have not settled upon one single unit, the above table includes the five units most commonly employed in chamber practice.

C-19.4   Pressure Table:

Absolute	mmHg	psia	psig	Equivalent Depth in Ft Seawater	Equivalent Depth in Meters Seawater	mmHg Oxygen Pressure of Compressed Air	mmHg Oxygen Pressure of Oxygen-Enriched Air (23.5%)
1	760	14.7	0	0	0	160	179
1.5	1140	22	7.35	16.5	2.24	240	268
2.0	1520	29.4	14.7	33	4.48	320	357
2.5	1900	36.7	22.0	49.7	6.71	400	447
3.0	2280	44.1	29.4	66.2	8.96	480	536
3.5	2660	51.4	36.7	82.9	11.19	560	625
4.0	3040	58.8	44.1	99.2	13.44	640	714
5.0	3800	73.5	58.8	132.4	17.92	800	893

ANNEX 1 HEALTH CARE EMERGENCY PREPAREDNESS

A Plan for Emergency Expansion of Facilities and Disaster Preparedness for Health Care Facilities

This annex is not a part of the requirements of this NFPA document but is included for information purposes only.

NOTE: Cross-references (of numbered paragraphs) refer to paragraphs within this annex unless otherwise noted.

Prologue

NFPA 3M, now Annex 1 of NFPA 99, grew out of a need to provide guidance in meeting requirements for fire drills as contained in NFPA *101, Life Safety Code*. Because of the inability to readily evacuate patients in a hospital, a detailed plan of action was needed for the various emergencies that could befall a hospital and require exiting. These included both internal emergencies (such as fires), as well as external ones (such as train wrecks, that could cause many injured to be brought to the hospital or necessitate evacuation of the hospital because of toxic fumes).

Initially, only hospital emergency preparedness was addressed. However, in 1975, other health care facilities were included because these facilities faced the same emergencies. In addition, the plans of these other occupancies could involve coordination with other health care facilities, such as hospitals (e.g., a small nursing home coordinating plans with a nearby hospital).

1-1 Introduction.

1-1.1 Purpose. The purpose of this annex is to provide the information necessary for the preparation of a disaster plan for a health care facility.

The responsibility of a health care facility to its community during a disaster is not simply one of moral commitment or mission; it is also a part of regulatory standards and insurance considerations to preserve the resources of the facility.

One of the greatest threats to good emergency functioning of a health care facility is the prevalence of the "it can't happen here" syndrome. This real possibility underscores the need for heightened awareness of possible hazards, even those so remote physically (e.g, a brush fire) as to escape initial appraisal by planners. Either the events themselves, or their side effects, should be considered for the problems they could cause the facility.

1-1.2 Scope. This annex covers types of disasters that need to be anticipated, factors to be considered in responding to a disaster, a sample of a typical disaster plan, guidance on implementing a disaster plan, and the obligations of the governing body and staff of the health care facility. While this annex primarily addresses hospitals, many parts are readily usable in upgrading emergency preparedness of nursing and custodial-care facilities.

Every health care facility should have a plan of action for the various emergencies that can affect the facility.

1-1.3 Applicability.

1-1.3.1 External Disasters. This annex is applicable to any health care facility that is intended to provide first aid or long-term medical treatment to the victims of a disaster in the community at large. Such facilities include, but are not limited to: hospitals, clinics, convalescent or nursing homes, and first aid stations. Such facilities may be formally designated by a government authority as a disaster treatment center, or may reasonably be assumed by the layman as being a disaster treatment center because of appearance, tradition, or location.

External disasters include those events that impact a community. Also included are those that can adversely affect the health care facility and create a volume of victims that would require such a facility to institute special procedures and resources. During such disasters, staffing patterns and health care services will be altered to address increased demands; additional information and communications systems will be instituted; and the overall activities of the facility will be adjusted to the different demands made necessary to provide services to injured victims.

1-1.3.2 Internal Disasters. This annex is applicable to any facility used for medical or other treatment or care of persons suffering from physical or mental illness, disease, or infirmity. Such facilities include hospitals, clinics, and convalescent or nursing homes. Such facilities would not normally include doctors' or dentists' offices, medical laboratories, or school nurseries, unless such facilities are used for treatment of external disaster victims (*see 1-1.3.1*).

Internal disasters include those events that impact the functions of a health care facility due to an internal or external cause. Many external disasters can create damage to, or cause utility failures in, health care facilities.

1-1.4 Life Safety Code. This annex is intended to assist the governing body and staff of a health care facility in meeting the requirements of NFPA *101®, Life Safety Code®*. The *Life Safety Code* establishes the basic mechanical or architectural requirements (such as exits, fire alarms, and smoke partitions) for fire safety in all occupancies, including health care facilities. It also requires that adequate plans for drills, evacuation, etc., be made (*see* NFPA *101, Life Safety Code*). This annex will assist in making such plans but is not limited solely to the requirements of the *Life Safety Code*.

1-1.5 Organization of this Annex. Since no single model of a disaster plan is feasible for every health care facility, this annex is intended to provide guidance in the preparation and implementation of an individual plan. Because of the diversity of health care facilities it cannot state mandatory requirements that would be appropriate in every case. Accordingly, it is presented as an annex to this standard.

1-1.6 Responsibility of the Governing Body. It is the responsibility of the governing body of the health care facility to provide its staff, patients, and visitors with plans necessary to respond to a disaster. Further, a government authority may impose upon the governing body the responsibility for participating in a community disaster plan. In order to discharge those obligations, the governing body may elect to delegate to its medical staff, consultants, architects, engineers, and others the authority for writing and implementing a disaster plan.

The governing body should review and evaluate the disaster plan not only for its functional ability but also to assure that the plan is not in conflict with other rules, regulations, and practices. If a conflict does occur, there should be an authorized transitional plan so that the disaster plan can be activated.

1-1.7 Authority Having Jurisdiction. In time of disaster all persons are subject to certain constraints not present during normal circumstances. During peacetime such restrictions are exercised by civil authority, such as a fire department, police department, public health department, or emergency medical service councils. During wartime, or declaration of martial rule, it would be exercised by a civil defense or military authority. It is imperative that all disaster plans written by a health care facility be reviewed and coordinated with such authorities so as to prevent confusion or unnecessary hardship.

1-1.8 Interpretations. The National Fire Protection Association does not approve, inspect, or certify any installation, procedure, equipment, or material. With respect to this annex, and to disaster planning, its role is limited solely to an advisory capacity. The acceptability of a particular disaster plan is solely a matter between the health care facility and the authority having jurisdiction. However, to assist in the determination of such acceptability, the National Fire Protection Association has established interpretation procedures. These procedures are outlined in the NFPA *Regulations Governing Committee Projects.*

1-2 Types of Disasters.

1-2.1 Definition of Disaster. Within the context of this annex, a disaster is defined as any situation that seriously overtaxes or threatens to seriously overtax the routine capabilities of a health care facility. Such a situation creates the need for emergency expansion of facilities, as well as operation of this expanded facility in an unfamiliar environment. Under this definition, the recognition of a disaster situation will vary greatly from one facility to another and from time to time in any given facility. Such recognition and concomitant activation of the Health Care Disaster Plan is dependent upon facility type, geographic location, bed capacity, bed occupancy at a given time, staff size, staff experience with disaster situations, and other factors. For example, the routine workload of the emergency department of a large metropolitan general hospital would constitute a disaster, requiring activation of the Health Care Disaster Plan, were this same workload to be suddenly applied to a small community hospital.

1-2.2 Causes of Disaster. Disasters have a variety of causes, all of which must be considered in effective emergency preparedness planning. Among the most common are natural disasters such as earthquakes, hurricanes, tornadoes, and floods; mass food poisoning; industrial accidents involving explosion or environmental release of toxic chemicals; transportation accidents involving crashes of trains, planes, or automobiles with resulting mass casualties; civil disturbances; building fires; extensive or prolonged utility failure; collapse of buildings or other occupied structures; and toxic smogs in urban areas. The ultimate disaster, nuclear warfare, must be given extensive consideration in disaster planning. Conventional bombing in warfare is another possibility that cannot be overlooked. Arson attempts and bomb threats have been made on health care facilities and must therefore be considered, as must the potential admission to the facility of VIPs. While the last does not involve mass casualties or the potential of mass casualties, the degree of disruption of normal routine will be sufficient to qualify it as a disaster-like situation.

NOTE: Disaster plans should reflect a facility's location from internal and external disasters. As an example, areas subject to frequent wildland fires should invoke countermeasures for smoke management and air quality maintenance.

The prospect of nuclear warfare and the potential for survival afterward make planning necessary in the event that the facility remains functional.

Some disasters do not physically affect a facility (e.g., a nearby plane crash; a bomb threat). However, any serious disruption to the function of patient care can and should be viewed as a disaster and should be planned for accordingly.

The Note was added to reinforce the Subcommittee on Disaster Planning concern that facilities consider their location and how it could affect the types of disasters that could affect the facility.

1-2.3 Location of the Disaster vs. Impact on a Health Care Facility. The location of the disaster will create different degrees of impact upon a health care facility's ability to respond effectively. For the purposes of this annex, disasters may be categorized as either internal or external.

An internal disaster is an event that causes or threatens to cause physical damage and injury to the hospital personnel or patients within the facility. Examples of internal disasters are fire (including arson), explosion, radiation accident, or telephoned bomb threat.

An external disaster is an event that requires expansion of facilities to receive and care for a large number of casualties resulting from a disaster that produces no damage or injury to the health care facility and staff. This is the most common type of disaster and, in a relative sense, the easiest for a health care facility to handle since facility and staff remain intact. Examples of external disasters are transportation accidents with mass casualties, mass food poisoning in the community, nuclear accidents/incidents, and natural disasters such as a tornado occurring at a distance from the facility itself. Obviously, the most serious disaster a health care facility might face is the combined internal-external disaster, such as an earthquake or nuclear warfare, in which the facility's physical plant and its staff have been degraded at the same time that it faces a mass influx of casualties resulting from the same disaster.

1-3 Basic Considerations in Health Care Disaster Planning.

1-3.1 Differences Between Standard Operating Procedure and Disaster Operating Procedure. Under routine procedures, the individual patient receives the highest quality of medical care the health care facility is capable of providing. In a disaster situation the philosophy changes to that of providing the best available medical care for the greatest number of patients. Austerity of treatment and triage play progressively greater roles as the magnitude of the disaster increases. In a general sense, triage occurs routinely in any hospital emergency department, in that the seriously injured or ill patient is usually treated before the patient with less serious injury or illness. However, in the extreme disaster situation the most seriously ill or injured patient is not necessarily treated first and perhaps is not treated at all. If the injury or illness is of such magnitude as to prove fatal despite treatment, the available treatment will be given preferentially to the serious injury or illness of lesser severity in which such treatment will prove life saving.

A "difference" that is conjured up by inexperienced planners is the false contrasting of daily versus disaster modes of functioning. On the contrary, proper plans have people use the same skills (and preferably in or near the same places) under all circumstances. Planners must be alert to avoid the pitfalls offered by the temptation to cast personnel in dissonant roles, thus wasting valuable skills and tending toward conditions of chaos.

1-3.2 Flexibility. The key to effective emergency preparedness planning is flexibility, which is attained by contingency planning (i.e., consideration of all likely possibilities and development of options for action that are maximally effective under each such possibility). Thus, the first step in disaster planning is to review the various types of disasters that can occur, emphasizing the types of disasters most likely to affect a given facility. For example, a California hospital might give special emphasis to earthquakes, whereas a Gulf Coast hospital might give special emphasis to hurricanes. The second step in disaster planning is the assessment of resources (facilities, material, and personnel), including resources on hand, resources required to effectively cope with disaster, and potential remaining resources following degradation due to internal disaster. The final step is then the meshing of disaster type and magnitude (number of casualties) with the potentially available medical resources in each given case into options for action.

The key element of a disaster plan is that it be functional for any time of day or night, any day of the year. The plan should not rely on any special individual or group to be put into effect; rather, the people on duty at the time of the disaster should be capable of implementing it. The overall coordination, which must be developed and rehearsed regularly, is the critical issue. A cohesive community resource working along with the medical/nursing/administrative services of a health care facility can provide all the components required for victims of a disaster.

1-3.3 Coordination. Having developed a flexible plan, it is essential that this plan be coordinated both internally and externally.

1-3.3.1 Internal Coordination. Internal coordination is necessary to assure that each professional staff member and employee of the health care facility is aware of his individual role under the Health Care Disaster Plan and to assure that all available resources are most efficiently and effectively utilized. Each supervisor at each level of organization within the health care facility must assure that his or her staff and employees are aware of their individual roles and responsibilities during a disaster, stressing the flexibility of such roles and responsibilities.

All roles and responsibilities must be delineated in written form so they can be studied, incorporated into training programs, and then rehearsed, drilled, and evaluated for effectiveness. (*See Figure 43.*)

1-3.3.2 External Coordination. Since no health care facility is completely self-sufficient, external coordination is essential if a hospital is to effectively function under disaster conditions. Such external coordination is best accomplished through a community emergency medical service council composed of representatives of the local fire department, law enforcement agencies, civil defense office, military units, search and rescue groups, ambulance services, volunteer agencies (Red Cross, Salvation Army, etc.), local professional medical associations, local hospital and nursing home associations, and local hospitals and nursing homes. Ideally, regional disaster councils composed of representatives from constituent local councils should also be established.

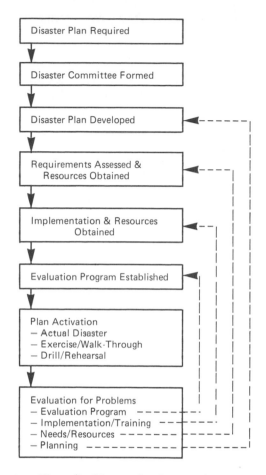

Figure 43   Disaster planning procedure.

Often, through the work of such local and regional councils in planning patient distribution in the event of disaster, the necessity for health care facilities to activate their individual disaster plans can be averted. For example, through the informed and cooperative action of on-scene ambulances equipped with two-way radio and in communication with local or regional emergency operations centers (civil defense, sheriffs' offices, C-meds or E-M-S communication control centers, etc.), 40 victims of a train wreck might be distributed among a number of available health care facilities, rather than bringing all 40 casualties to the single nearest facility. In some large urban areas, the council can often designate certain large health care facilities, with well-equipped and well-staffed emergency rooms providing around-the-clock service, as primary receiving facilities for disaster victims, thus giving smaller facilities with lesser resources the additional time to prepare to accept an influx of patients hours or days later, i.e., at such time as the primary receiving facilities require additional beds or treatment capability.

In some rural areas, a small nursing home might well be the only health care facility; it would thus become an assembly area until transfer to hospitals could be accomplished.

As mentioned in 1-1-2, every health care facility should anticipate what could befall it and what its role might be in an emergency. A plan for as many eventualities as is reasonably probable should be developed (e.g., an aircraft crash plan if a major airport is close by). Plans should be based on the strengths of the resources available. Only by matching disaster potentials with resources can the emergency plan provide maximum benefit to the community.

Figure 44   A helicopter used to transport patients from accident scenes or other facilities to this facility. (Battery charger in front of helicopter ensures starting.) Regional coordination is necessary.

1-3.4 Communications Systems.   The better the internal and external communications systems available to a health care facility in the disaster situation, the more effectively it can respond to the disaster. Functional communication systems, effectively utilized, can provide the facility with advance warning of external disaster, thus permitting time to better prepare response; can be used to mobilize mutual aid and other disaster assistance; and can be used to coordinate all aspects of facility functioning to assure maximum efficiency in using available resources to provide the best available patient care.

The simplest communication system is face-to-face verbal communication, using runners; this system can be used to contact those areas of the facility without other means of communication. Telephone communications are invaluable in the disaster situation — providing such systems remain intact. However, it must be emphasized that even with intact telephone systems, switchboards are invariably swamped with incoming calls in the disaster situation, thus effectively cancelling out the use of routine telephone systems. For this reason, it is highly desirable that the health care facility have one or more unlisted telephone numbers for use in making outgoing calls during emergencies. Existing phone systems can be expanded simply if arrangements are made with the telephone company.

An increase in telephone communication can almost always be expected in a disaster. Thus, a means of expanding telephone service quickly should be included in any plan.

Extra lines can be added, and lines used infrequently can be bridged in, to augment principal numbers. Pay telephones, usually found in most facility wards or in lobbies, can also be used for this purpose, although this technique requires maintaining a small supply of coins in each area where a pay telephone would be used in an emergency.

Ideally, for external communication, health care facilities should be equipped with two-way radio and the ability to communicate with the community emergency operations center and/or the local police and fire departments, as well as with the ambulance services. Ideally, for internal communications, all health care facilities should have a supply of functional walkie-talkie radio sets, continually maintained in working order, for two-way communication between vital nerve centers within the hospital.

The ultimate in effective disaster communication systems is the presence at the disaster site of a medical "on-scene controller," equipped with two-way radio communication (perhaps through on-scene ambulances) and capable of talking with the community emergency operations center and/or primary receiving health care facility. Such a system can best be organized through local and regional disaster councils. Use of amateur (RACES) and citizens' band (CB) networks should be considered, as well as such networks as Blue Cross teletype, where available.

1-3.5 Material Stockpiling. Contingency planning for disaster of necessity involves stockpiling of critical medical material or, as a minimum, knowledge of the type, location, and amount of such material that can readily be obtained in an emergency from local, regional, state, and federal sources. It will first be necessary to assess the medical resources currently available within the health care facility itself and within the local community as a whole. The latter job can most effectively be performed by the local disaster council, through the cooperation of local hospitals, nursing homes, clinics, and other outpatient facilities, retail pharmacies, wholesale drug suppliers, retail and wholesale surgical supply houses, ambulance services, and the local civil defense office. Knowing the location and amount of in-house and locally available medical resources, a given health care facility might then desire to stockpile such additional critical medical material as might be needed to effectively cope with the disaster situation.

The Bureau of Health Material, Emergency Health Services of the U.S. Public Health Service, will provide certain emergency support to larger facilities. These programs are now in the process of review within PHS. Certain larger hospitals can also qualify through state coordination as custodians of the packaged disaster hospital, a complete prepackaged 200-bed hospital with sufficient supplies and equipment to operate independently for a 30-day period. This packaged disaster hospital is intended primarily for use in a nuclear disaster but can be used in severe peacetime disasters; it may be set up as an independent facility, or any or all of the components in the package may be utilized to supplement material supplies in an existing hospital. All existing packaged disaster hospitals have been turned over to state health or civil defense agencies by the Division of Emergency Health Services of the U.S. Public Health Service. Prepackaging of "disaster kits" for use in the health care facility is advised. These would include administrative items (such as tags) and selected medical supplies.

The use and availability of packaged disaster hospitals varies from state to state. In many instances, they are not readily available or even in existance. Facilities should learn what is available in their areas.

The normal length of time that authorities having jurisdiction require health care facilities to maintain supplies for self-sufficiency is one week. When it is impractical to provide supplies for this length of time, a realistic alternative plan must be provided.

1-3.6 Security and Traffic Control. Disaster creates an expanded and often unique set of security and traffic control problems for a health care facility, compounding the difficulty of providing rapid and efficient medical care for mass casualties. Many health care facilities have no regular security forces, and even in the case of those that do, their numbers will often be inadequate to cope with the additional problems posed, even with the assistance of nonessential personnel from other facility departments. Through coordination with local law enforcement agencies and the office of civil defense in the disaster planning phase, assistance in this area can be assured in the event of actual disaster. In the small-scale disaster, local police can often provide the added assistance necessary for health care facility security and traffic control. In the large-scale disaster, military personnel can often be called in to assist. However, since there is no legal provision for request of military assistance by the individual police department or individual health care facility, military support of civil authority must be requested by the mayor of the city, the governor of the state, or an equivalent official. Invoking of martial rule (formerly called martial law) is also an act of governmental authority. However, it is an extremely inefficient and undesirable measure and is invoked only as a last resort in extreme situations. The extent of the security and traffic control problems for any given health care facility will depend upon its geographical location, physical arrangement, availability of visitor parking areas, number of entrances, etc.

Some facilities have no security forces because they have no need for them. Such facilities need to consider how security services can be quickly put into action in an emergency.

To minimize security requirements during disaster conditions, points of access and egress to buildings should be minimized. All staff and employees may be required to enter and leave the facility through easily controlled points and/or signs may be hung on doors directing people to active entrances and exits.

1-3.6.1 Visitor Control.   Visitors can be expected to increase in number with the severity of the disaster. The majority of these will have legitimate reasons for desiring to visit the health care facility, although curious onlookers may also seek entrance. Many casualties will be accompanied by friends and relatives, particularly in a large-scale disaster. These visitors will be anxious and concerned, and their feelings must be respected insofar as the situation will permit. However, they must not be allowed to disrupt the disaster functioning of the facility. The role of clergy must also be taken into consideration. Ideally, a visitor's reception center should be established away from the main facility itself, particularly in major disasters. The lobby of an adjoining nursing home, for example, is an ideal location for such a center. Volunteer personnel such as Red Cross or other helpers can be utilized as liaisons between the visitors and the health care facility itself, to determine whether particular patients have been admitted, to determine the condition of particular patients, to escort visitors to beds of critically ill or dying patients, etc. Normal visiting hours on the wards should be suspended, except in the case of patients in terminal condition, in which case visitors should be kept to a minimum (one or two) and should be escorted to the patient by volunteer personnel. The route taken by escorted visitors within the facility should be via stairs and back corridors, avoiding treatment areas, major access routes between critical areas, and elevators.

Health care facilities are better prepared to handle victims than they are to handle concerned families and friends of victims. A professional and efficient program for visitor control during the disaster will be significant in how the overall program is later perceived by the public. Identifying visitors with special badges, listing visitors' names in association with the patient they are inquiring about, and being prompt, courteous, and considerate in the handling of information and requests are all important factors in the visitor center.

It is a good practice to have a first aid cart at the visitor control center for treating visitors' medical problems resulting from the anxiety and shock of the emergency situation.

1-3.6.2 Reception of News Media.   Because of the intense public interest in disaster casualties, news media representatives must be given as much consideration as the situation will permit. However, news releases should be made only through a predesignated spokesman. Ideally, news media personnel should be provided with a reception area, such as the hospital library, with access to telephone communication and, if possible, an expediter who, though not permitted to act as spokesman for news releases, may provide other assistance to these individuals. News media personnel should not be allowed into the health care facility without proper identification. Cameras are generally not allowed. Use of broadcast media for alerting off-duty health care staff and for reassuring the public should be planned in advance with proper civil and media authorities.

All hospital personnel should be advised as to how media requests should be handled, especially during disaster implementation. Preplanning with media people can ease the trauma of having to deal for the first time with requests under trying circumstances.

1-3.6.3 Identification of Authorized Personnel. Visitor control creates the problem of distinguishing staff and employees from visitors, particularly in a large health care facility. Identification cards, preferably containing a photograph of the individual and of the type that can be attached to outside garments by an alligator clip, should be used for this purpose. Such cards should be issued to all facility personnel, including volunteer personnel who may be utilized in disaster functions, preferably at the time of employment, when joining the professional staff, or when accepted as regular volunteer personnel. Most hospitals now use such "security badges" on a day-to-day basis, but many nursing homes do not.

NOTE: Care must be taken to assure that identification cards are recalled whenever personnel terminate association with the health care facility.

Some consideration should be given to identifying critical staff who may be called in and may not have proper identification with them. Key medical personnel have been known to respond to facilities without necessary identification and have been denied entry. A phone contact to key areas to confirm identity can eliminate potential problems.

Members of the news media should be asked to wear some means of identification, such as the press card, on their outside garments so that they are readily identifiable by security guards controlling access to the facility or certain areas therein. Clergy also will frequently accompany casualties or arrive later for visitations and require some means of identification.

1-3.6.4 Vehicular Traffic Control. Arrangement for police assistance in vehicular traffic control into and on the facility premises should be made in the disaster planning period. Health care personnel, because of inexperience in traffic control and because their services are better used inside the facility, should not be used in external traffic control, except as a last resort. It will be necessary to direct ambulances and other vehicles carrying casualties to casualty-sorting areas or the emergency room entrance, to direct incoming and outgoing vehicles carrying supplies and equipment, to direct authorized personnel and visitors to proper entrances, to set up road blocks to keep unauthorized people off the facility premises, and to direct outgoing vehicular traffic. Traffic-flow charts indicating entrances to be used, evacuation routes to be followed, etc., should be prepared in the disaster planning phase and included in the Health Care Disaster Plan itself. Parking arrangements must not be overlooked. If a heliport is not already in use, one should be established on the grounds (or on the roof, if structurally suitable). (*See NFPA 418, Standard on Roof-top Heliport Construction and Protection.*)

If health care facility personnel are utilized for traffic control, basic instructions are essential. In addition, either orange traffic vests or some other suitable form of identification should be provided to signify their authority and to provide a measure of personal safety (i.e., they are more easily seen).

1-3.6.5 Internal Security and Traffic Control. Internal security and traffic control are best conducted by facility personnel, i.e., regular health care facility security forces, with reinforcements from the facility personnel reserve pool. However, these personnel may be inadequate in number to fully cope with the problems involved, so additional assistance from the local law enforcement agencies should be coordinated in the disaster planning phase. Upon activation of the Health Care Disaster Plan, security guards should be stationed at all unlocked entrances and exits. Entrance to the facility should be restricted to personnel bearing staff or employee identification cards and to casualties. Visitors and news media representatives should be directed or escorted to visitor and news media reception areas. Employees should be stationed at all elevators to control and direct elevator traffic; elevator usage should be allocated on a priority basis, with casualties, their attendants, and essential medical supplies receiving first priority. In the case of major access corridors between key areas of the facility, pedestrian traffic should be restricted to one side of the corridor, keeping one side of the corridor free for movement of casualties. Traffic flow charts for internal traffic should also be prepared in the planning phase, as is the case with external traffic control.

External disaster plans should always include a sequence for deactivation of the plan or for deactivation by functional unit as the casualty loads are treated and sent elsewhere. External traffic control should be the last function to be deactivated because the possibility of convergence may continue long after all casualties have been treated.

See 1-3.15, "Disaster Recovery Planning," which outlines some aspects to consider after the initial disaster has eased or been contained.

1-3.7 Special Aspects of Civil Disturbance. Large-scale civil disturbances in recent years have shown that health care facilities and their personnel are not immune to the direct effects of human violence in such disturbances. Hospitals in large urban areas must make special provisions in their disaster plans to assure the physical safety of their employees, particularly female employees, in transit from the hospital exit to and from a secure means of transportation to their homes. In extreme cases it may be necessary to house employees within the health care facility itself during such civil disturbances. Examples of attacks or sniping are extremely rare.

Another aspect of civil disturbances not to be overlooked in facility security planning is the possibility that a given health care facility may have to admit and treat large numbers of prisoners during such emergencies; however, security guards for such patients will normally be provided by the local police department.

Provisions for securing areas on lower floors which have windows, and may therefore be subject to items thrown from hostile crowds, should be included in the civil disturbance plan. Items such as heavy window screens or guards, and/or substantial drapes or window shades might be considered as reasonable precautions for those susceptible areas.

1-3.8 Special Aspects of Telephoned Bomb Threats. The disaster potential inherent in the telephoned bomb threat warrants inclusion of this disaster contingency in the Health Care Disaster Plan. Experience has shown that facility personnel must accompany police or military bomb demolition personnel in searching for the suspected bomb, since speed is of the essence and only individuals familiar with a given area can rapidly spot unfamiliar or suspicious objects in the area. This is particularly true in medical laboratory areas in which police are usually totally unfamiliar with the appearance of standard laboratory apparatus. The facility switchboard operator must be provided with a checklist to be kept available at all times, in order to obtain as much information as possible from the caller concerning location of the supposed bomb, time of detonation, and other essential data, which must be considered in deciding whether or not to evacuate all or part of the facility.

> Police and fire authorities vary considerably from locality to locality with regard to response to bomb threats. Knowing exactly what assistance local authorities provide will dictate the level of activity the health care facility will need to provide for them.

1-3.9 Special Aspects of Radioactive Contamination. Disaster planning must consider the possibility that radioactive fallout in the postnuclear attack period may require that health care staff and patients be sheltered. Shelter areas can be selected in existing structures, and should be planned for during design of new facilities or additions. Similarly, plans must also consider radiation dose control and decontamination of victims or staff personnel and public safety in connection with nuclear accidents or incidents such as reactor excursions. Wartime plans must consider the likely unavailability of power, water, or gas and mesh with the plans for coping with such utility failures in peacetime. Use of radiation-detection instruments must be covered. Specific guidance in designating and stocking with survival supplies those areas of the facility to be used as fallout shelters can be obtained from the local civil defense office.

> Radioactive contamination plans should consider both internal and external disasters. Transportation accidents have a high possibility of contaminating fire and police personnel responding to the accident.

1-3.10 Special Aspects of Hazardous Material. There are at least three major sources of concern with regard to nonradioactive hazardous materials. The first is the possibility of a large spill or venting of hazardous materials near the facility; this is especially likely near major rail or truck shipping routes, near pipelines, or near heavy manufacturing plants. Second, every facility contains within its boundaries varying amounts of such materials, especially in the laboratory and custodial areas. A spill of a highly volatile chemical can quickly contaminate an entire structure by way of the air ducts. Finally, contaminated patients can pose a risk to staff, though on a more localized basis. Usually removal of their clothing will reduce the risk materially. In any case, staff must be prepared to seek advice on unknown hazards. This type of advice is not usually available from poison centers, but rather from a central referral, such as CHEMTREC, through its WATS service (800-424-9300).

> During the revision for the 1984 edition of this Annex (Appendix D in NFPA 99-1984), this subject was added because of the growing problem created by the increasing use and shipment of hazardous materials (nonradioactive type). Action by health care facilities can range from localization and sealing off of contaminated areas or persons to complete evacuation of the facility. Thus, disaster plans need to consider both extremes.

1-3.11 Special Volcanic Eruption Protocol. While most of the direct effects of a volcanic eruption are covered in other protocols for internal disasters (fire, explosion, etc.) it is necessary to make special provisions for functioning in areas of heavy to moderate ashfall. This can be regarded as both an internal and an external disaster.

Volcanic "ash" is actually finely pulverized rock blown out of the volcano. Outside the area of direct damage, the ash varies from a fine powder to a coarse sand. Measures taken to exclude fallout from nuclear weapons (*see Section 1-3.9, "Special Aspects of Radioactive Contamination"*) can be effective in preventing entrance of ash into the facility buildings; the difference is that whereas outside traffic will be close to zero during fallout radiation conditions, people move about freely during and after ashfall. Ashfall presents four problems for health care facilities:

(1) People require cleanup (brushing, vacuuming) before entering the building.

(2) Electromechanical and automotive equipment and air-filtering systems require special care because of the highly abrasive and fine penetration nature of the ash.

(3) Increased flow of patients with respiratory complaints can be expected.

(4) Eye protection is required for people who must be out in the dust. (No contact lenses should be worn; goggles are suggested.) Dust masks are available. They are approved by the National Institute for Occupational Safety and Health (NIOSH), and are marked TC-21 plus other digits.

This section is a direct result of the 1980 eruption of Mount St. Helens in Washington. While this type of incident is more regional than other types of disasters listed above, it is included because the entire northwest part of the United States was affected, as well as a portion of Canada.

1-3.12 Evacuation and Relocation of Health Care Facility. Any Health Care Disaster Plan must consider the possibility of evacuation of the facility, as might be required because of severe structural damage in a hurricane, tornado, earthquake, or nuclear explosion. Total or partial temporary evacuation could be required in a fire, arson attempt, earthquake, telephoned bomb threat, or because of high radiation levels from fallout in the postnuclear attack period. In planning for evacuation, a variety of relocation sites must be selected, and the rationale for choice of each option incorporated into the plan for use at the time of implementation. The magnitude of the disaster will affect the choice, as will consideration of actual or potential damage to the facility itself. Experience has shown that planning for an execution of a total evacuation of staff and patients is both difficult and complex if loss of patients is to be precluded. Relocation site selections, their preparation, and regular relocation drills become of increasing importance. In localized disasters involving relatively small geographical areas, patients can be transferred to undamaged health care facilities in the vicinity. In a national disaster, such as nuclear warfare, the situation is not so simple; surviving staff and employees will be expected to relocate, with their nondischargeable patients, to a new site, such as a hotel or school, where they must be prepared to reestablish some degree of health care function and to accept an influx of additional patients as well. Federal civil preparedness plans also are tending to focus on major relocation prior to enemy attack. Some guidance is now in preparation by the Federal Emergency Management Agency. This agency addresses means of preparing for and carrying out such heroic measures as can require movement over long distances, local consolidation of patients who cannot move far with impunity, and arrangements for staffing the consolidation center, which presumably remains at higher risk of enemy action than the more remote facilities. Those health care facilities with access to packaged disaster hospitals must plan for reestablishment using such an asset.

Evacuation is more probable today in light of an increase in the types of activities that could prompt an order to evacuate a facility (e.g., more toxic chemicals are being produced and transported; incidence of arson has increased dramatically). In addition, natural events such as hurricanes, tornadoes, and volcanic eruptions cannot be ignored. Section 1-3.12 was expanded because of the incident at the Three Mile Island Nuclear Plant in Pennsylvania, and the eruption of Mount St. Helens. Hospitals had to be evacuated temporarily in both cases.

Most facilities require only an internal patient relocation plan due to the "defend-in-place" concept for health care facilities, whereby facilities are considered to be composed of many zones that can provide safe areas of refuge. Thus, patients can be relocated within facilities in most incidents. However, facilities also need to be prepared for outside relocation of patients should internal conditions or external events require it.

A well-organized relocation plan incorporates most components of an evacuation plan on a unit-by-unit or zone-by-zone basis as necessary. Should an evacuation be ordered, an additional requirement would be adequate care for patients once they have left the confines (and protection) of the facility. This would include shelter adjacent to the facility or transportation to another facility, inclusion of medical records and any vital supplies with each patient, and staff support for each patient.

1-3.13 Writing the Plan. The well-written Health Care Disaster Plan consists of a basic plan, annexes (by facility department), and disaster operating procedures (for all facility functions within each department). Disaster considerations should receive attention during basic planning (or new plant construction and modification). The basic plan should be written broadly, providing general but concise coverage of disaster responsibilities and procedures for each facility department and providing detailed responsibilities and procedures for those functions not normally a part of regular routines, e.g., operation of the disaster control center. Keyed to the basic plan, the departmental annexes of the plan then outline individual department responsibilities in greater detail. Finally, the disaster procedures for each function within each department are described in terms of actual instructions for individual staff members and employees. Facility disaster plans must be reviewed frequently for currency. Departmental reorganizations, even though seemingly minor, could have a serious impact upon the efficiency of the plan when implemented, as could seemingly minor staff changes, plus the more obvious effects of plant modification. All such changes must therefore be reflected in the Health Care Disaster Plan. Reorganizations or changes in mission of external agencies upon which the hospital may depend for mutual aid in disaster must also be reflected in the current plan. In order not to need to revise the plan daily, individuals should never be mentioned by name in the plan; rather, responsibilities and procedures should be written in terms of job title. The health care occupancy chapters of NFPA *101, Life Safety Code*, are relevant for review and rehearsals.

Figure 45   The plans for various types of disasters should be collated and kept in one folder. Several copies should be produced.

1-3.14 Rehearsing the Plan. Under current criteria of the Joint Commission on the Accreditation of Hospitals, Health Care Disaster Plans must be activated in an actual disaster exercise at least twice annually. Implementation of a facility's emergency preparedness program may be evidenced by documentation of a rehearsal or an actual disaster occurrence. In either case, it is recommended that the facility comply with current JCAH standards pertaining to emergency preparedness. (Note that compliance is mandatory for JCAH-accredited facilities. Refer to latest edition of JCAH's *Accreditation Manual for Hospitals* for details.) It is extremely important that the disaster exercise involve the entire facility and that it be made as realistic as possible. Several references in Section 1-7, "References," of this annex give useful guidance on planning for and conducting drills. The most valuable portion of the exercise is the postexercise critique, which should always result in subsequent modification of the plan to correct deficiencies and to increase efficiency when implemented.

Rehearsal of a disaster plan should be a realistic test of that plan. In preparing for the rehearsal, the following should be conducted: training, walk-through familiarizations, and discussions after the walk-through to resolve questions or problems.

Use of moulaged volunteer victims, who have been counseled on typical behavior for specific injury types, can provide a level of realism to which all levels or staff can relate. The concern is for persons who will be pressed into duty during the disaster but who have not dealt with the trauma of viewing, transporting, or attending to an injured victim. It is during the rehearsal that the possibility of not being able to perform should be discovered.

All parts of the plan should be tested, including media and visitors' functions as well as security and traffic control.

Non-JCAH accredited hospitals and other types of health care facilities should conduct disaster drills at least annually, unless enforcement authorities direct them to do otherwise.

1-3.15 Disaster Recovery Planning. As the stresses of the disaster begin to abate, there is often a tendency for staff to slip back into a "business as usual" mode. While restoral of predisaster effectiveness is always an objective, the wind-down must be managed as carefully as the buildup. In some cases, damage to the facility may dictate the sequence of events. In any case, the unusual location and distribution of patients, equipment, supplies, and staff will require proper guidance in order to accomplish a smooth transition to a more normal state. Only rarely will an "all-clear" signal be received from outside authorities; more often, management will note that, for example, the flood crest has passed, or all victims are accounted for, or that the fire is out. It is at this point that restoral and recovery measures must be thoughtfully initiated. As noted elsewhere, it is even possible that the recovery scheme (where damage to the facility has been significant) could provide the impetus for remodeling, redecorating, or even new construction.

This section was added in 1984 since a disaster plan must include not only actions to deal with a disaster while it is occurring, but also steps to take *after* the crisis stage has passed and a facility begins to return to a normative state of operation. Previous editions of NFPA 3M did not cover this latter aspect fully.

A very good article on recovery planning has been written by W. E. Rogers, Director of Risk Management at Conemaugh Valley Memorial Hospital, Johnstown, Pennsylvania ("Fire Recovery Planning in Health Care Institutions," *Fire Journal*, March, 1982). While it discusses only fire recovery planning, it can be applied to other types of disasters as well.

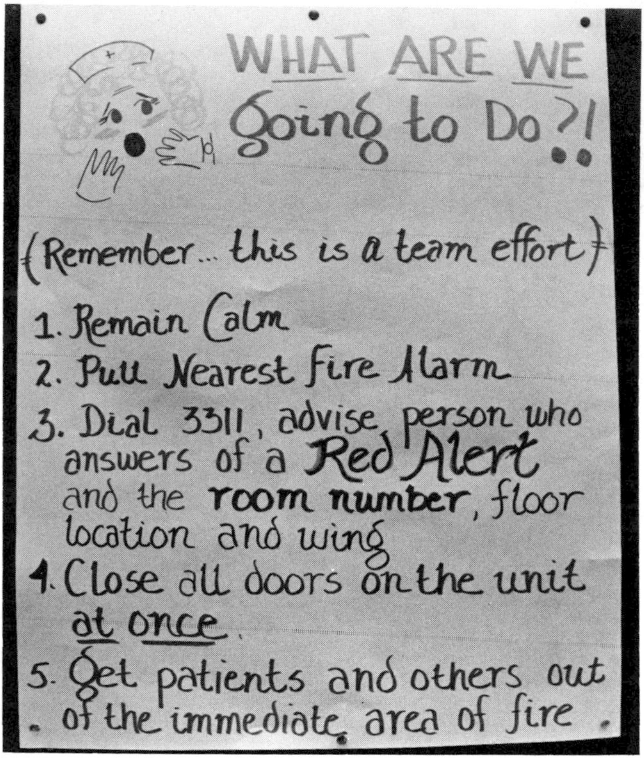

Figure 46 The responsibilities of all staff should be clear and related to their individual capabilities and normal responsibilities. Here, a sign posted near a nurses' station highlights the nursing staff's role in an emergency.

1-4 Responsibilities for Health Care Disaster Planning and Implementation.

1-4.1 Responsibilities of the Facility Administrator. The administrator is responsible for overall disaster planning within the facility, for activation of the plan in the event of a disaster, and for termination of disaster procedures under the plan, with return to normal functioning. The administrator is also responsible for the decision making in the disaster control center during disaster operations. He/she will often delegate some of these responsibilities, particularly those involved with disaster planning (which is normally delegated to a disaster planning chairman, who is often an assistant administrator in the case of larger facilities). The job of disaster planning chairman is rarely full-time. Since disasters can occur in the absence of the administrator, he/she must designate an alternate to activate, implement, and terminate the Health Care Disaster Plan in his/her absence. This alternate should be the senior administrative officer on duty or the senior nursing supervisor on duty at the time the disaster occurs. Only the administrator or his/her designated alternates should have the authority to activate or terminate the disaster plan.

1-4.2 Responsibilities of the Health Care Disaster Planning Chairman. Selection of the individual to fill this job is extremely important. Ideally, the chairman should have administrative and managerial experience, intimate familiarity with the facility and the community, and a personality enabling him or her to obtain active and enthusiastic cooperation from a large number of individuals for whom disaster planning often seems to be an irksome and unnecessary chore.

The chairman is responsible for writing and maintaining the currency of the Health Care Disaster Plan, for planning and executing facility disaster exercises, and for conducting postexercise critiques. He/she must work closely with the facility administrator, since the latter is responsible for all actions under the plan in the event of actual disaster. He/she must also maintain close liaison with his/her counterparts in other community agencies involved in disaster planning, and may represent the facility on the community disaster council. Ideally, the facility should also have a standing intrafacility disaster committee, composed of key professional staff and employees, to advise the chairman and administrator on key decisions to be incorporated into the Health Care Disaster Plan.

1-4.3 Responsibilities of the Triage Officer. This individual is responsible for establishing category of injury and priority of treatment for all incoming casualties in the mass casualty situation. Since in the majority of disasters casualties are primarily wounded or burned, this individual should be a surgeon, preferably with disaster or military field medical experience. In the planning phase, the triage officer, working with the disaster planning chairman and/or facility administrator, must select a triage area for use during disaster. This area should have ready access and egress for vehicular traffic and yet be conveniently close to the initial treatment area. In large facilities, the existing emergency room may suffice. In smaller facilities, other areas will need to be designated for such disaster use, and in major disasters, such as a nuclear disaster, a large area outside the facility will, in most instances, be required. The triage officer will also be responsible in the planning phase for developing a system of tagging casualties. These tags serve to identify patients; serve as a readily available temporary record of diagnosis, treatment, and vital signs; and serve as the source for preparing casualty rosters for the facility information desk. Commercially available multicopy tags may be purchased, although some facilities prefer to design their own. Such tags are normally prenumbered and designed to be rapidly but firmly attached to the patient's wrist. Plans should cover routing and filing of various copies of tags, as well as bed labeling. It is also extremely useful to have a communication link with the site of an external disaster, so that some selectivity can be exercised. Much triage can be done on site if competent people are available.

Depending on the nature of the emergency, considerable involvement of medical as well as surgical staff can be needed. This must be taken into account when developing the plan.

The sooner triage can be instituted, the higher the chances are of saving more victims.

1-5 Sample of Plan for External Disaster.

1-5.1 Validation of Information. Nature of disaster, location, and approximate number of anticipated casualties will be validated insofar as possible by the administrator or his/her alternate in authority. Such validation should be made through the community emergency operations center or equivalent (police department, sheriff's office, civil defense office).

1-5.2 Action of Administrator. Based on available information, the Health Care Disaster Plan will be activated, if deemed necessary, by the administrator or his/her alternate designated herein.

1-5.3 Disaster Control Center. The disaster control center will be activated to coordinate and direct all further activities under the Health Care Disaster Plan. This center will also function as the communications center for the facility for the duration of disaster functioning and, through advance planning, will be equipped with communications systems required for such purposes.

Development of the disaster must be closely monitored because many external events can spread to become internal disasters. These include rising waters, hazardous material spills, and nuclear contamination, for example. Any disaster that reaches a stage requiring evacuation of the facility automatically phases into the internal category.

1-5.4 Initiation of Specific Actions. The following actions under the Health Care Disaster Plan will be initiated simultaneously by the disaster control center.

1-5.4.1 Personnel Notification and Recall. Under a system to be described herein, the medical staff, key personnel, and other personnel needed will be notified and recalled as required. In order to relieve switchboard congestion, it is desirable to utilize a pyramidal system to recall individuals who are off duty or otherwise out of the facility. Under the pyramidal system, an individual who has been notified will notify two other individuals, who in turn will each notify two other individuals, and so on. A current copy of the notification and recall roster, with current home and on-call telephone numbers, will be maintained at the hospital switchboard at all times. In case the pyramidal system is to be utilized, each individual involved in the system must maintain a current copy of the roster at all times, in order that each may know whom they are to notify and the telephone numbers concerned. It is essential that key personnel rosters be kept current.

1-5.4.2 Activation of Disaster Functions. Each prime activity area, to be designated herein, will be alerted to activate disaster operations in that area, according to the Health Care Disaster Plan. These areas are:

(a) *Triage (Receiving and Sorting) Area.* Those personnel designated herein will report immediately to the preselected area and prepare to receive casualties. Rather detailed instructions in austere triage and patient routing will be required.

(b) *Treatment Areas.* Preselected maximum and minimum treatment areas will be activated, staffed, and prepared to initiate treatment of tagged casualties.

(c) *Central Supply.* Preassembled backup supplies for disaster treatment areas will be prepared, to be delivered immediately upon request from a treatment area that is running low on supplies. (It is assumed in this plan that adequate supplies to initiate treatment were prepositioned in the planning phase in those facility areas designated as maximum and minimum treatment areas for disaster functioning.) Packaged disaster hospital use must be covered.

(d) *Security and Traffic Control.* All personnel designated herein will report to prearranged duty stations at entrances and exits, elevators, and key areas to assume security guard duty. The facility control center will request assistance in external traffic control from the local police department; until such assistance arrives, or in the event such assistance cannot be forthcoming, facility personnel designated herein will report to preassigned duty stations external to the facility for vehicular and pedestrian traffic control.

(e) *Hospital Wards, Nursing Stations, Surgery, and Clinics.* Upon direction from the disaster control center, each ward officer will inventory patients on his ward, determine which patients can safely be discharged, and report to the control center the number of additional beds that could be made available on his ward through discharge of inpatients. Candidates for discharge include patients awaiting elective surgery, ambulatory patients previously admitted for diagnostic workup on the basis of convenience rather than necessity, etc. Upon direction from the disaster control center, such patients will be discharged from the facility. Upon direction from the control center to the department of surgery, all elective and nonemergency surgery will be suspended. Similarly, upon notification from the control center, all routine clinics will be closed.

(f) *Visitor, Clergy, and News Media Centers.* Upon notification to the information desk and the security guards at facility entrances and exits, routine visiting privileges and visiting hours will be suspended until the disaster control center deems it feasible to reinstitute normal visiting hours. Simultaneously, the visitor and news media centers will be activated and staffed as described herein. Volunteers will be recalled to assist in visitor control as required. Patients in terminal condition may receive visitors in limited numbers stated herein but they must be escorted to and from the patient.

(g) *Personnel Reserve Pool.* All staff personnel who can be spared from routine duties and do not have specific assignments under the Health Care Disaster Plan will report to the personnel reserve pool, located in a predesignated area. This center will function as a holding area for personnel to be utilized as litter bearers, wheelchair escorts, messengers, security forces, visitor escorts, etc.

(h) *Maintenance, Housekeeping, and Food Service.* These areas will be alerted and will assume disaster posture as required herein. On direction of the control center, the facility food service will suspend routine food service except for those inpatients on critical diets and will initiate disaster food service. The latter stresses speed, ease of preparation, and preparation of large quantities; it utilizes prepackaged convenience foods, stockpiled for such emergencies, and is served with throw-away plastic utensils and paper plates, which are also stockpiled for such emergencies.

(i) *Ancillary Clinical and Administrative Services.* Ancillary clinical services (laboratory, X-ray, blood bank, morgue) will assume disaster posture upon notification. Additional blood will be ordered from the central blood bank as deemed necessary by the anticipated number and type of casualties. The predesignated alternate morgue will be activated in order that it be prepared in the event that the number of fatalities exceeds the facilities of the regular morgue. (The male locker area on the ground floor of some hospitals can function adequately as an auxiliary morgue.) Facility social services, if any, will be activated since numbers of casualties who might not require hospitalization may have lost homes in the disaster; if a given facility does not have a social services department or if the magnitude of the disaster workload is such as to prove overwhelming for the staff of this department, assistance will be requested from the local Red Cross through the control center. A patient discharge and transfer center at a predesignated site will be activated as required by the control center. All casualties who, following treatment, are not to be admitted to the facility will be directed to this center. This center will also coordinate patient transfers to other health care facilities and will arrange transportation for such transfers. Arrangements must be made for managing decontamination of patients or staff carrying radioactive contamination.

(j) *Recovery.* Plans should reflect measures needed to restore the facility to predisaster operational capabilities. This may involve a simple repositioning of staff, equipment, and supplies, or it may require extensive cleanup and repair. It may also present an opportunity to evaluate long-range ideas concerning remodeling, paint change, etc. Fiscal aspects must be considered early, because of restoral costs and possible cash-flow losses associated with the disruption.

1-6 Sample of Plan for Internal Disaster.

1-6.1 Information on Disaster. The nature of the disaster, location within the health care facility, and actual or potential hazard to facility personnel and patients will be quickly assessed by the administrator or his/her alternate in authority. Even when fire is not involved, most local ordinances require that the fire department be immediately notified.

1-6.2 Action of Administrator. Based on this assessment, the Health Care Disaster Plan will be activated in part or in its entirety by the administrator or his/her designated alternate. Degree of structural damage will often be the major decision factor.

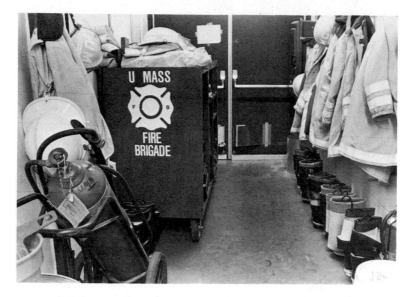

Figure 47 Responses to disasters will vary depending on a facility's capabilities. Some larger facilities can justify and support a fire brigade; however, a fire brigade is not a substitution for the fire department. (Pictured is a response cart containing various equipment. Mobile extinguisher is in foreground. Turnout coats and boots are ready on the right.)

1-6.3 Disaster Control Center. The disaster control center will be activated to coordinate and direct all further activities under the Health Care Disaster Plan, as described under the external disaster plan. (*See 1-5.4.*) The first function of the control center will be to determine whether patients and personnel should be removed from actual or threatened danger by partial or total evacuation of the facility, under an evacuation plan described herein. In localized disasters, the fire chief, upon arrival, will usually assume responsibility for evacuation decisions. In other cases, evacuation may be ordered by outside authorities.

1-6.4 Fire and/or Explosion Protocol (Including Arson Attempts). In the event that the health care facility need not be completely evacuated immediately, the following events will be simultaneously directed by the control center:

(a) notify fire department, if not already done;

(b) alert the facility fire brigade;

(c) confine the fire;

(d) fight the fire with the proper extinguishers and hose lines;

(e) rescue all persons in immediate danger;

(f) meet the fire department personnel and direct them to the scene;

(g) secure the area;

(h) control movement of all patients, staff, employees, and visitors;

(i) evacuate as required, either horizontally to an area behind smoke barriers or fire doors, or vertically by means of enclosed fire escape towers. Elevators are to be used only in critical situations where fire escape towers cannot be used.

(See references in Section 1-7 of this annex.)

Figure 48   All employees should know where fire extinguishers and fire hose cabinets are located. (In this facility, extinguishers are kept in fire hose cabinets.)

1-6.5 Severe Storm Protocol.   The warning system operated by the National Oceanic and Atmospheric Administration will, in most cases, provide adequate time to permit the health care facility to take certain precautions, and if disaster appears inevitable, to activate the Health Care Disaster Plan in advance of the disaster event. Precautions include the following:

(a) draw all shades and close all drapes as protection against shattering glass;

(b) lower all patient beds to the low position, wherever possible;

(c) place blankets on patients;

(d) close all doors and windows.

Studies by the U. S. Weather Bureau have resulted in the Bureau no longer recommending that windows on a particular side of a building be kept open during severe wind storms.

1-6.6 Fallout Shelter Protocol.   It is expected that a crisis period of variable duration will precede nuclear warfare and that the degree of crisis will progressively worsen. During this increasing crisis period the following actions will be taken:

(a) Discharge all inpatients who can safely be discharged.

(b) Admit only critically ill or injured patients for whom medical treatment is mandatory, and obstetric cases.

(c) Prepare those areas of the facility designated as fallout shelter areas, to assure that space and habitability is adequate, and that these areas are stocked with or have ready access to potable water and survival rations.

(d) Upon warning of imminent nuclear explosion threat or imminent fallout, evacuate patients and facility personnel to these fallout shelters. In the case of patients who cannot be moved at the required time to evacuate to shelter, e.g., certain patients in intensive care units, certain orthopedic patients, etc., provide them with the best available shelter on the site (i.e., position patient's bed so as to take advantage of whatever radiation shielding is available in the room).

(e) Wartime plans should not assume availability of utilities or refuse collection.

1-6.7 Evacuation Protocol. Evacuation may be partial or total. It may involve moving from one story to another, one lateral section or wing to another, or moving out of the structure. Even partial evacuations may involve all categories of patients; where these are people who would not routinely be moved, extraordinary measures may be required to support life. It is also necessary to assure movement of supplies in conjunction with any evacuation. Decisions to evacuate may be made as a result of internal problems or under menace of engulfing external threats. In all cases, the following considerations govern:

(a) Move to predesignated areas, whether in the facility, nearby, or in remote zones. Evacuation directives will normally indicate destinations.

(b) Assure movement of equipment and supplies to accompany or meet patients and staff in the new location.

(c) Execute predetermined staffing plans. Some staff will accompany patients; others will rendezvous in the new location. Maintenance of shifts is more complex than normal, especially when (1) some hard-to-move patients stay behind in the threatened location, and (2) staff may be separated from their own relocated families.

(d) Protection of patients and staff (during and after movement) against the threatening environment must be provided.

(e) Provisions of the fallout shelter protocol will be relevant in wartime or nuclear contamination situations.

(f) Planning must consider transportation arrangements.

1-6.8 VIP Admission Protocol. Admission of a VIP to a health care facility in an emergency creates two sets of problems, which may require partial activation of the Health Care Disaster Plan. These problems are:

1-6.8.1 Security. Provision of security forces in this situation will normally be a responsibility of the U. S. Secret Service or other governmental agency. However, activation of facility security forces may be required to prevent hordes of curious onlookers from entering facility work areas and interfering with routine facility functioning. Routine visiting privileges and routine visiting hours may need to be suspended in parts of the facility.

1-6.8.2 Reception of News Media. The news media reception center previously described will need to be activated. In this instance, additional communications to the news reception center will be required. Additional telephones and telephone lines can be installed on an emergency basis on request to the local telephone company. Such requests for additional telephone connections in the facility should, however, first be coordinated with the senior Secret Service officer or governmental representative accompanying the VIP.

1-6.9 Other Protocols as Deemed Desirable. In addition to the above, there should follow a number of additional protocols for internal disasters, to be determined by the geographical location of the individual health care facility, e.g., earthquake protocol, civil disturbance protocol, telephoned bomb threat protocol, hazardous material protocol, etc.

1-6.10 Recovery. Plans should reflect measures needed to restore the facility to predisaster operational capabilities. This may involve a simple repositioning of staff, equipment, and supplies, or it may require extensive cleanup and repair. It may also present an opportunity to evaluate long-range ideas concerning remodeling, paint change, etc. Fiscal aspects must be considered early because of restoral costs and possible cash-flow losses associated with the disruption.

1-6.11 Activation of Emergency Utility Resources. In the planning phase, backup utility resources will have been stockpiled and arrangements made for mutual aid when required. Such utilities include electrical power, water, and fuel. Through prior coordination with the local civil defense office or fire department, mobile generators and auxiliary pumps can be obtained in the internal disaster situation. Through these same sources arrangements could be made to supply water tank trucks. Obviously, such planning is in addition to routine planning, in which all health care facilities maintain emergency electrical power plants and, in those areas requiring central heating in winter, backup supplies of oil, coal, or gas. Priorities for use of available power (e.g., air circulation but not air conditioning) must be determined. Sanitation requirements can become overriding in prolonged disasters, and even an ordinary strike by garbage collectors can cause difficulties.

1-7 Informatory References and Bibliography to Annex 1.

1-7.1 NFPA Publications and Articles. National Fire Protection Association, Batterymarch Park, Quincy, MA 02269.

NFPA 49-1975, *Hazardous Chemicals Data*

NFPA *101*-1985, *Life Safety Code*

NFPA 418-1979, *Standard on Roof-top Heliport Construction and Protection*

Bahme, C. W. "Fire Officer's Guide to Disaster Control" (Pub. No. FSP-48), 1978

Rogers, W. E. Fire recovery planning in health care institutions. *Fire Journal*, March 1982, pp. 68-72

1-7.2 The following selected documents can be of assistance for planning purposes. They are available directly from the organization, unless otherwise noted.

1-7.2.1 Aerospace Industries Association, Vertical Lift Aircraft Council, 1725 DeSales Street, Washington, DC 20036.

Heliports-Helistops in the United States, Canada, Puerto Rico, 1968

1-7.2.2 American College of Surgeons, 55 East Erie Street, Chicago, IL 62704.

A Model of a Hospital Emergency Department, 1961

A Model Ordinance Regulating Ambulance Service, 1966

1-7.2.3 American Health Care Association, 1200 Fifteenth Street NW, Washington, DC 20005.

Fire Safety for Your Nursing Homes, 1978 (Cat. No. 901-00110)

1-7.2.4 American Hospital Association, 840 North Lake Shore Drive, Chicago, IL 60611.

Checklist for a Hospital Civil Disturbance Preparedness Program, 1968

Checklist for Hospital Disaster Planning (No. 4295), 1964

Emergency Services in the Hospital, 1966

Fire Safety Training in Health Care Institutions, 1975

Principles of Disaster Planning for Hospitals (AHA No. 2480), 1967

Readings in Disaster Planning for Hospitals (AHA No. 2540), 1966

1-7.2.5 American Medical Association, 535 North Dearborn Street, Chicago, IL 60610.

Emergency Department: A Handbook for the Medical Staff, 1966

1-7.2.6 American National Red Cross, National Headquarters, 17th & D Streets, NW, Washington, DC 20006.

Disaster Handbook for Physicians and Nurses (ARC 1640E), 1966

1-7.2.7 American Nurses' Association, 10 Columbus Circle, New York, NY 10019.

Emergency Health Preparedness and Your Nursing Service: An Action Program for Hospitals, Community Agencies, and Nursing Homes (Publication No. NS-11), 1968

1-7.2.8 Association of American Railroads, 1920 L St. NW, Washington, DC 20036.

Emergency Handling of Hazardous Materials in Surface Transportation

1-7.2.9 Dun-Donnelley Publishing Corp., 666 Fifth Avenue, New York, NY 10019.

Lynch, E. Guidelines to help you develop a master plan. *Fire Engineering*, 1976, p. 26

1-7.2.10 Federal Emergency Management Agency, Washington, DC 20472.

DPCA Attack Environmental Manual, 1973

1-7.2.11 International Association of Fire Chiefs, 1329 18th St., NW, Washington, DC 20036.

Disaster Planning Guidelines for Fire Chiefs (July, 1980)

1-7.2.12 National Council of Radiation Protection and Measurement, 7910 Woodmont Ave., Suite 1016, Washington, DC 20014.

Management of Persons Accidentally Contaminated with Radionuclides, April 1980 (Report No. 65)

1-7.2.13 Ohio State University, Disaster Research Center, Columbus, OH 43210.

Quarantelli, E. L. and Tierney, K. J., *Disaster Preparedness Planning*, 1979

1-7.2.14 Ohio State University, Instructional Materials Laboratory, 1885 Neil Avenue, Columbus, OH 43210.

Ohio Trade and Industrial Education Service, *Emergency Victim Care and Rescue Textbook for Squadmen*, 1968

1-7.2.15 Charles C. Thomas Publisher, 301-327 East Lawrence Avenue, Springfield, IL 60611.

Carl B. Young, Jr. *First Aid for Emergency Crews*, 1965

1-7.2.16   U.S. Department of Transportation (available from Superintendent of Documents, U.S. Government Printing Office, Washington, DC 20402).

Federal Highway Administration, *Highway Safety Program Manual: Emergency Medical Services*, Vol. 11, 1969

1-7.2.17   University of Iowa, Bureau of Police Science, Iowa City, IA 52240.

Lyle L. Shook and Richard L. Holcomb, eds., *Hospital-Based Ambulance Service*, 1968

1-7.2.19   Joint Commission on Accreditation of Hospitals, 875 N. Michigan Ave., Chicago, IL 60611.

Accreditation Manual for Hospitals

Long Term Care Standards Manual

Ambulatory Health Care Standards Manual

Hospice Standards Manual

Consolidated Manual for Child, Adolescent and Adult Psychiatric, Alcoholism, and Drug Abuse Facilities and Facilities Serving the Mentally Retarded/Developmentally Disabled

1-7.3   The following selected films and slide packages can be of assistance for planning purposes. Information on purchase and rental fees, if any, can be obtained directly from the organization listed. (All listings are films unless otherwise noted.)

This listing is neither exhaustive nor an endorsement by the Subcommittee responsible for this Annex. It merely represents examples of films and slide packages that Committee members were aware of at the time this Annex was reviewed. Audio/visual material is very useful in disaster planning.

1-7.3.1   National Fire Protection Association, Batterymarch Park, Quincy, MA 02269.

Evacuation of Medical Facilities (FL-59) (1982)

Hospital Fire, Osceola, MO, Dec. 3, 1974 (SL-26) (Slides)

1-7.3.2   Federal Emergency Management Agency, Office of Public Affairs, Washington, DC 20472.

Everglades and After (DDCP 55-285) (1979)

1-7.3.3   Abbott Laboratories, Audio/Visual Services, 565 Fifth Avenue, New York, NY 10017.

Disaster! Pre-Hospital Management of Mass Casualties

1-7.3.4   General Services Administration, National Audiovisual Center, Reference Section, Washington, DC 20409.

Flashover: Point of No Return

1-7.3.5   Brose Productions, Inc., 10850 Riverside Dr., N. Hollywood, CA 91602.

Bomb Threat! Plan, Don't Panic

1-7.3.6   Fire Prevention Through Films, Inc., P.O. Box 11, Newton Highlands, MA 02161.

Evacuation of Health Care Facilities

1-7.3.7   Pyramid, P.O. Box 1048, Santa Monica, CA 90406.

Hospitals Don't Burn Down

1-7.3.8   University of Illinois Medical Center, Circle Campus, Chicago, IL 60612.

Hospital Fire Safety (videotape)

ANNEX 2 THE SAFE USE OF HIGH-FREQUENCY ELECTRICITY IN HEALTH CARE FACILITIES

This annex is not a part of the requirements of this NFPA document but is included for information purposes only.

NOTE: Cross-references (of numbered paragraphs) refer to paragraphs within this annex unless otherwise noted.

Prologue

It has been recognized for many years that high-frequency electrosurgery can be a source of serious injury to both patients and personnel. For this reason, in the late 1960s, Dr. Carl W. Walter, Chairman of the then Commitee on Hospitals, appointed a Subcommittee to draft a document on the safe use of high-frequency devices. The result was a manual on the subject, adopted in 1970, designated NFPA 76CM, *Safe Use of High-Frequency Electrical Equipment in Hospitals*. It was upgraded to a recommended practice in 1975, and has remained as such since that time.

This recommended practice (Appendix E in the 1984 edition of NFPA 99; Annex 2 in this 1987 edition of NFPA 99) is a valuable guide to the safe use of this energy and equipment, and is highly recommended reading for anesthesiologists, anesthetists, operating room nurses, surgeons, and those who maintain and service this equipment. Since high-frequency electrosurgery is used so frequently in anesthetizing locations, readers should study this material in conjunction with Sections 12-4.1 and 13-4.1, "Anesthetizing Locations."

Although this annex contains recommendations and information, as opposed to requirements, users and manufacturers should note that these recommendations have generally been accepted as good practice for many years. While not intended to be incorporated into law, these recommendations have been referenced in litigation and have afforded valuable advice.

Finally, there is relatively little commentary on this Annex, as compared to other chapters in NFPA 99, because the text of this Annex incorporates a great deal of explanatory material (in keeping with the purpose of the document).

2-1 Introduction.

2-1.1 Purpose.   The purpose of this annex is to provide information and recommendations for the reduction of electrical and thermal hazards associated with the use of high-frequency electricity in health care facilities.

2-1.2 Scope.   This annex covers principles of design and use of electrical and electronic appliances generating high-frequency currents for medical treatment in hospitals, clinics, ambulatory care facilities, and dental offices, whether fixed or mobile.

While this annex covers many of the principles of design and use, it does not cover all of them. Emphasis is on those features that relate to fire hazards.

Exception No. 1: This annex does not cover communication equipment, resuscitation equipment (e.g., defibrillators), or physiological stimulators used for anesthesia, acupuncture, etc.

Exception No. 2: This annex does not cover experimental or research apparatus built to order, or under development, provided such apparatus is used under qualified supervision and provided the builder demonstrates to the authority having jurisdiction that the apparatus has a degree of safety equivalent to that described herein.

2-1.3 Frequency Range. For the purposes of this annex, *high-frequency* is intended to mean any electrical energy generated in the radio-frequency range from approximately 100 kHz to microwave frequencies.

2-1.4 Intended Use. This annex is intended for use by operating personnel practicing the electrical or the medical arts, as well as apparatus designers. It thus contains material of an informative nature as well as recommendations.

2-1.5 Responsibility of the Governing Body. It is the responsibility of the governing body of the health care facility to provide its staff, patients, and visitors with an environment that is reasonably safe from the shock and burn hazards associated with the use of high-frequency electricity. In order to discharge this obligation, the governing body is permitted to delegate appropriate authority to its medical staff, consultants, architects, engineers, and others. (*See Section 2-5 for further information.*)

2-1.6 Interpretations. The National Fire Protection Association does not approve, inspect, or certify any installation, procedure, equipment, or material. With respect to this annex, its role is limited solely to an advisory capacity. The acceptability of a particular piece of equipment, installation, or procedure is solely a matter between the health care facility and the authority having jurisdiction. However, in order to assist in the determination of such acceptability, the National Fire Protection Association has established interpretation procedures. These procedures are outlined in the NFPA *Regulations Governing Committee Projects.*

2-1.7 General Introduction. The flow of electric energy at conventional power frequencies is generally understood and predictable. As the frequency is increased to the radio-frequency range, i.e., above 100 kHz (100,000 cyc/sec), the electric current may not be restricted to obvious conductive paths, and consequently may have effects not generally appreciated.

High-frequency power-generating equipment can present a hazard to the patient or to the operator by the nature of its use, or by its electrical interference with other apparatus in contact with or implanted within the patient. Since the equipment usually requires direct connections to the patient, it can also present a current path through the body tissues for electrical faults occurring within it or in other equipment.

It should be kept in mind that this annex is intended for use by operating personnel practicing the electrical or the medical arts, as well as apparatus designers. Some of the comments may appear overly simple, since it was considered desirable to err on the side of clarity rather than conciseness.

Some statements in this annex concerning waveforms, frequency, etc., refer to specific designs of apparatus that are in common use. These are cited for illustrative purposes only. Other techniques for accomplishing the same medical purposes have been developed. This annex is not intended to assess the relative merits of any of these techniques, but rather to provide guidelines for the safe use of any type of high-frequency, power-generating, medical equipment.

The waveforms, energies, etc., commonly used were arrived at largely through experience. Research has been conducted on the mechanisms for therapeutic action, but it is not clear what would be an optimal design, if indeed there is an optimum. Therefore, technical descriptions have been kept general with the understanding that a variety of devices may achieve equivalent therapeutic results.

This annex indicates circumstances and procedures that can produce hazards during the use of high-frequency electrosurgical or diathermy equipment, and suggests protective measures against such hazards. This annex is concerned specifically with electrical effects and safety. The high-frequency power generated by these devices can interfere with the operation of other apparatus such as physiological monitors or pacemakers. The mechanisms of heat generation in body tissues by high-frequency energy must be understood and controlled to be effective therapeutically, while avoiding unwanted burning. The arc that is likely to occur when an energized high-frequency electrode contacts tissues can be an ignition source for flammable vapors and gases. Although referenced in this annex, full recommendations for safety from explosion hazards in the presence of flammable anesthetic agents are given in Section 12-4.1, "Anesthetizing Locations," of the requirement portion of this standard, and should be consulted for detailed specifications. Surgical effects of electrosurgery are described in Section 2-6 of this annex. A routine for the use of electrosurgical equipment is outlined in Section 2-7 of this annex. These sections are included because there is little available in the medical literature on the effective and safe use of these powerful electrical therapeutic instruments.

2-2 High-Frequency Equipment.

2-2.1 Types of Apparatus.

2-2.1.1 Electrosurgery.

2-2.1.1.1 General. Electrosurgical techniques utilize the heating effect of high-frequency current passing through tissues to desiccate, fulgurate, coagulate, or cut tissues. A very small active electrode concentrates the current with resulting rapid heating at the point of application. A larger dispersive electrode providing broad coupling with the skin is used to minimize the current density and heating at the other end of the body circuit.

2-2.1.1.2 Electrocoagulation and Fulguration. Coagulation and fulguration procedures generally employ a damped sine waveform or a train of low duty-cycle pulses. The frequency is in the 0.1 to 5 MHz (million cycles per second) region, but a wide spectrum of high frequencies also may be generated.

2-2.1.1.3 Electrocutting. High-frequency cutting of tissue is more effective with an un-damped sinusoidal current or pulse train. Most electrosurgical equipment provides a selection of coagulating current, cutting current, or a blended output.

2-2.1.1.4 Electrosurgical Oscillators. Electrosurgical oscillators operate in the general range of 0.5 to 5.0 MHz with average output power capabilities as high as 500 watts. The actual amount of power required depends on the type of electrode used, the modality (cutting or coagulating), the operative procedure, and the conditions surrounding the operating field. In open-air cutting or coagulating, the power will generally range from 50 to 100 watts. In a transurethral resection, higher power may be required because of the bypassing effect of the irrigating fluid around the electrode. An electrosurgical unit must have a relatively low output impedance (typically 100 to 1000 ohms) in order to match the tissue electrical load and to limit open-circuit peak voltage with its attendant danger of insulation failure of electrodes, surgical handles, etc.

NOTE: Most older instruments used a spark gap oscillator to generate highly damped radio-frequency sine waveforms, often modulated at 120 Hz, characterized by high peak voltages and low duty cycle, for coagulating purposes. Newer instruments use solid-state circuits to generate complex pulse trains with similar characteristics. Limited studies indicate that the frequency range is not very critical, but that the low duty cycle train is the key to the coagulating process. A continuous, unmodulated sine waveform or pulse train, delivering a high average power generated by a vacuum tube or solid state oscillator, is used for free cutting with little or no hemostasis. Higher-duty-cycle, moderately damped waveforms are used when a greater degree of hemostasis is desired while cutting. (*See Section 2-6 of this annex.*)

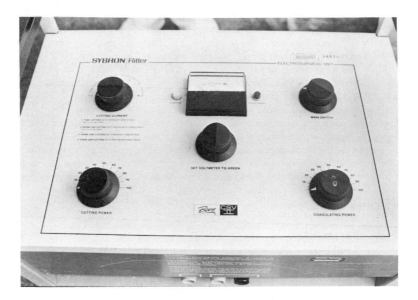

Figure 49 Operating panel of a typical electrosurgical unit.

The frequency used for electrosurgery is not critical. The range indicated, 0.1 to 5.0 MHz, is high enough that the frequency is well above the possibility of electrically stimulating nerve or muscle, but not so high that there is excessive radiation of power from leads or electrodes.

2-2.1.2 Electrocautery.

2-2.1.2.1 General. Electrocautery is a surgical technique that utilizes a heated electrode or glowing wire to conduct heat to the tissue. It usually uses power frequency (60 Hz) current at low voltage to heat the electrode and hence is not a high-frequency device. It is described here because of possible confusion in terminology. In electrocautery there is no intentional passage of current through the tissues. While the voltage and frequency are low, these are patient-connected devices using electrical power, and appropriate precautions should be used. (*See Chapter 7, "Electrical Equipment, Health Care Facilities" in the requirements portion of this document.*)

Hazards of patient-care-related electrical appliances are addressed in Chapter 7 of NFPA 99. Readers are urged to review that chapter.

2-2.1.2.2 Differences in Techniques. When the techniques or electrodes associated with electrocautery are used for electrosurgical procedures, the electrosurgical function may be interfered with and the patient endangered.

2-2.1.3 Neurosurgical Lesion Generator. Specialized instruments with lower power, 1 to 30 watts, are used in neurosurgery to make carefully delineated lesions in neural tissue. They employ continuous waveform radio-frequency power, and may use stereotactic instruments or neural signals for position control, and temperature measurement for size control. The temperature rise is limited to achieve tissue protein denaturation but not gross tissue destruction.

2-2.1.4 Radio-Frequency Diathermy.

2-2.1.4.1 General. Diathermy utilizes the heating effect of the passage of a high-frequency current or an electromagnetic field in body tissues. In contrast to electrosurgery, it applies a relatively even heat distribution within the tissue well below a temperature that would cause tissue destruction. Diathermy equipment operates at 27.12 MHz, with some older units at 13.56 MHz. These frequencies are assigned for this purpose by the Federal Communications Commission with rigid regulations regarding frequency control and harmonics or spurious radiation. (*See Section 2-9, "Informatory Referenced Publications and Articles," in this annex.*)

Radio-frequency fields may have undesirable effects on nonpatient populations and, thus, are regulated by safety rules generally based on ANSI Standard C95.1. These regulations are of concern with respect to exposure of the medical staff, visitors, etc. Patients for whom therapeutic effects are intended are, in general, exempt from these regulations. In addition to ANSI C95.1, a valuable source of information is NCRP Report No. 67, "Radio-Frequency Electromagnetic Fields," prepared by the National Council on Radiation Protection and Measurements, 7910 Woodmont Ave. NW, Washington, DC 20014.

2-2.1.4.2 Dielectric or Spaced-plate Diathermy. With spaced-plate applicators, heating is the result of alternating current in the tissues caused by the high potential difference between the electrodes. This alternating electric field permeates the interposed tissues, which act as a lossy dielectric between capacitor plates.

2-2.1.4.3 Inductive Diathermy. The high-frequency current of inductive diathermy is passed through a coil or coils to produce rapidly reversing magnetic fields through the tissue. Heating is caused by eddy currents set up by the alternating magnetic field.

2-2.1.5 Microwave Diathermy. Microwave energy is radiated from a reflector, usually parabolic, air-spaced from the tissue. The energy is "beamed" like light to the intended area. The depth of penetration and intensity of heating are determined by the spacing and energy output of the microwave source. The assigned medical frequency is 2450 MHz. Electromagnetic energy at this frequency has an appropriate combination of penetration and absorption in tissue.

2-2.1.6 Ultrasonic Diathermy. Ultrasonic energy in the high-frequency range (approximately 0.05 to 5 MHz) is also used for therapeutic heating, and for making lesions. It should be noted that the energy modality is mechanical and not electrical, and hence some of the hazards described herein do not apply. However, these are patient-connected devices employing substantial electrical power, and appropriate precautions must be used.

2-2.1.7 Hyperthermia. Heating, controlled in spatial distribution and temperature, may be applied to tumors as a therapeutic adjunct. Techniques similar to diathermy may be used, often with implanted antennas or coupling devices.

This is a recently developed technique and is included here for informational purposes. When more data on hazards associated with this technique are documented, guidance on mitigation will be added to this annex.

2-2.1.8 Medical Lasers. The spatial and frequency coherence properties of laser-generated radiation allow the localized deposition of large amounts of energy in tissue. This may be used for cutting, coagulation, or photochemoactivation. This apparatus per se is an electrical device, subject to the requirements of Chapter 7, "Electrical Equipment, Health Care Facilities," (in the requirements portion of this document), but the peculiar hazard is the result of the unusual optical properties of this radiation.

Light amplification by stimulated emission of radiation (laser) technology is well established; however, it has only been in the last few years that it has been applied in surgery. While not a high-frequency device as other types listed in Section 2-2.1, it does have some unique properties that present similar hazards. (*See 2-3.8.2 and commentary thereunder in this annex for further information and guidance.*)

Medical lasers use electromagnetic radiation in the infrared and visible spectrums. This is not usually considered high-frequency electricity in the radio-frequency sense of the term. However, in medical use, these devices apply thermal energy to tissue to cause cutting and coagulating analogous to electrosurgery.

Many of the cautions concerning thermal hazards of electrosurgery apply to lasers, e.g., burns in unintended places, ignition of drapes and flammable liquids. There are added hazards as well, because those laser devices that operate the invisible radiation spectrum can be reflected from surgical tools, etc., and injure attendant staff. Surgeons intending to use lasers must have special instructions in the use of this modality.

2-2.2 Properties of High-Frequency Circuits.

2-2.2.1 General. In low-frequency apparatus, the circuit elements are usually discrete components, physically obvious, interconnected by wires or other conductors. At higher frequencies, distributive elements and less obvious forms of coupling (capacitive, inductive, and radiative) become increasingly important. Since these properties may not be fully appreciated by personnel using high-frequency medical equipment, this section reviews some aspects of them.

2-2.2.2 Nonconductive Coupling.

2-2.2.2.1 Capacitive. Any two conductors separated by a dielectric constitute a capacitor through which alternating current will pass. This capacitor has a reactance that varies inversely with frequency. Thus, when a conductive material is placed near a conductor carrying high-frequency current, some of the high-frequency energy may be transferred to this material. This coupling may exist, for example, between an electrosurgical power cable and an adjacent input lead of an electrocardiograph. Similarly, a low-impedance ground path may be presented by the capacitance between an electrode lead and its grounded metal shield. Capacitive coupling exists at all frequencies but is relatively more significant at higher frequencies.

2-2.2.2.2 Inductive. Energy may also be transferred without an obvious interconnection by the magnetic field that surrounds all current paths. This effect is used in the familiar transformer, but may also produce coupling between two adventitiously placed adjacent wires. If a large conductor is placed in a magnetic field, the coupling may induce circulating current in the conductor. These "eddy currents" generate heat as would any other current in the conductor. Inductive coupling may be affected relatively little by shielding intended to inhibit capacitive coupling.

2-2.2.3 Skin Effect. Because of self-induced eddy currents, high-frequency current may be confined to the surface of metal conductors. This "skin effect" can cause a simple conductor to have a much higher effective impedance than it would have at low frequencies.

Skin effect should not be confused with the change of impedance of a patient's skin. Living tissue is a complex electrical system of ionic conductors and capacitors. The skin contact impedance shows a marked decrease at higher frequencies largely because of capacitive coupling through the poorly conductive outer skin layers.

2-2.2.4 Modulation and Detection. The high-frequency currents present in medical apparatus often have complex waveforms. The frequency and amplitude of the oscillations may vary. The peaks of successive oscillations form an "envelope" of the signal, or modulation. Thus a 1-MHz radio-frequency waveform may be modulated by a 120-Hz signal. When such a waveform passes through a nonlinear circuit element, other frequency waveforms are produced, including some at the modulating frequency (here 120 Hz). Since the contact between an electrode and tissue, and the tissue itself, contain nonlinear elements, low-frequency currents may be present when high-frequency currents pass through the body.

2-2.2.5 Electromagnetic Radiation.

2-2.2.5.1 General. In the radio-frequency region, energy is also propagated by direct radiation through air or other media. This is the basis of operation of radio communication and microwave diathermy, and can produce undesired effects with other high-frequency apparatus.

2-2.2.5.1.1 Long Wires and Antennas. At sufficiently high frequencies, a conductor such as a simple wire can become "electrically long" and constitute a complex circuit element. In free space this length is governed by the relation:

$$\lambda f = 300,$$

where λ is the wavelength, in meters, f is the frequency, in megahertz, and 300 is the velocity of light, in meters per microsecond. The velocity is less in other media. If the conductor is an appreciable fraction of a wavelength, it is no longer a simple resistive conductor. It may have a large impedance and may become an effective antenna. If the length approaches $\frac{1}{4}\lambda$ (or more) it may be part of the resonant output system of the apparatus.

2-2.2.5.2 Sources of High-Frequency Radiation.

(a) *Electrosurgical Equipment Radiation.* Such radiation derives from:

(1) The active cable.

(2) The dispersive return cable.

(3) Electrical power lines (minimized by filtering).

(4) Direct radiation from components, especially the spark gap and associated wiring (minimized by proper cabinet design).

(5) Radio-frequency current paths through the patient and from the patient to ground via alternative paths, such as capacitive coupling to the table.

Since the operating frequency is relatively low and the leads in the output circuit are electrically short, radiation from them is at a low level. Generally, interference with other equipment is caused by the conduction of high-frequency energy through common power lines or by capacitive and inductive coupling. It can be minimized by proper shielding and filtering.

(b) *Diathermy Equipment Radiation.* Such radiation derives from:

(1) Electromagnetic radiation from the applicators and their connecting cables. The amount of radiation is dependent on the treatment level and on the orientation of the drum or spaced plates and may be influenced by the placement of the leads.

(2) At 27.12 MHz, a quarter wavelength is 2.76 m (about 10.9 ft). The "ground" wire in the supply cable may be low impedance only at a low frequency, so that the cabinet of the diathermy acts as the "ground" plane for the unit and may under unusual conditions be at appreciable high-frequency voltage above power supply ground.

(3) A patient under treatment with spaced plates is in a strong electric field and is a conductor at some voltage above ground, as evidenced by the fact that he or she can receive a burn by touching a bare metal part of the cabinet. Since diathermy equipment is used to produce heat in tissues without direct contact with the body, the energy transferred must be by means of induction from resonant electrodes or applicators. This energy can be picked up by adjacent equipment, by remote monitoring systems, and by power lines, and can be difficult to control. Physical separation is the best solution since the signals attenuate rapidly with distance and interposed walls and building structures. The construction of shielded rooms may be necessary if the radiation problem is serious. The radiation from components and supply cable must be kept low to meet Federal Communications Commission requirements.

(c) *Microwave Therapy Radiation.* Such radiation is at extremely short wavelength. A quarter wavelength in tissue is about 3 cm (1.18 in.). The electrical properties of tissue at this frequency are complex and need to be investigated further.

The Subcommittee recognized the complexity of microwave therapy radiation and the need to investigate it further; therefore, only a limited statement was made.

The use of microwave radiation as a source of energy for hyperthermia for cancer therapy is expanding. This use requires attention to avoid unintended injury.

2-3 The Hazard.

2-3.1 Hazards Covered. This annex is concerned with the hazards that may exist during the use of high-frequency power equipment in the health care facility. The danger can be to the patient, the operating personnel, or to other equipment. Some of these problems are common to all electrical apparatus and are the subject of other manuals and codes. These are appropriately referenced. The following kinds of hazards are considered:

(a) Radio-frequency interference. (*See Section 2-3.2.*)

(b) High-frequency burns. (*See Section 2-3.3.*)

(c) Low-frequency electrical shock. (*See Section 2-3.4.*)

(d) Explosions and fire. (*See Section 2-3.5.*)

(e) Complications of the use of the apparatus. (*See Section 2-3.6.*)

(f) Direct current burns. (*See Section 2-3.7.*)

(g) Non-ionizing radiation burns and ignition. (*See Section 2-3.8.*)

2-3.2 Radio-Frequency Interference.

2-3.2.1 General. The high-frequency output of therapeutic equipment can propagate by radiation or other coupling through air, tissue, or current conductors, to affect the operation of other equipment, i.e., by distorting or obscuring displayed data, blocking normal operation, or causing damage through thermal or electrical breakdown. The extent of the effect will depend upon operating frequency, power level, intercoupling of circuits, distance, and the sensitivity and selectivity of the affected apparatus.

2-3.2.2 Equipment in Contact with Patient. High-frequency currents flowing through body tissues can be conducted directly to equipment having input electrodes on or in the patient, or can be capacitively or inductively coupled to implanted sensors, to affect their operation. The performance of implanted pacemakers can be disrupted, particularly those having sensing circuits. The pacemaker manufacturer's literature should be consulted before using high-frequency equipment on a patient with a pacemaker.

2-3.2.3 Equipment in Patient Area — No Direct Contact. Telemetering and similar equipment in the immediate vicinity of the patient may be affected by energy radiated from high-frequency sources. The degree of interference depends on the strength of the interfering radiation and on the sensitivity of the affected equipment to the interfering signal. Before utilizing new configurations of equipment, they should be checked to ensure that no unacceptable interference may occur.

2-3.2.4 Equipment in Remote Areas. Equipment in remote areas may be affected by radiated energy or by energy conducted through power lines. Intensive care areas adjacent to treatment or operating areas are examples. In extreme cases shielding may be necessary but spatial separation is usually adequate. If such interference occurs, the equipment should be modified or locations changed to reduce the interference to an acceptable level.

2-3.3 High-Frequency Burns.

2-3.3.1 Electrosurgical Equipment. When electricity flows in a conductor, heat is generated at a rate proportional to the product of the resistance and the square of the current. This thermal effect forms the basis of function for electrosurgical and dielectric diathermy equipment. In the case of electrosurgical equipment, the cutting electrode is made very small to produce a high current density and consequently a very rapid temperature rise at the point of contact with tissue. The high-frequency current is intended to flow through the patient to the dispersive electrode. However, when the resistance between the body and the dispersive electrode is excessive, significant current can flow via alternative paths. The dispersive electrode provides a large contact with skin to minimize the current density at that end of the patient circuit. The relative areas are indicated in Figure 2-3.3.1 (*see Section 2-6 of this annex*). If the dispersive electrode presents too

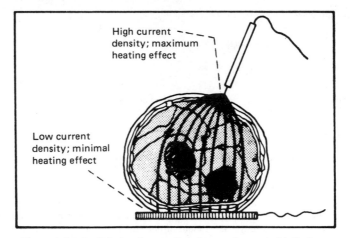

Figure 2-3.3.1   Relative Current Densities at Contact with Patient.

small a contact area, deep tissue burns may result not only at the dispersive electrode but also at other sites.

NOTE: The optimum characteristics and area of tissue contact for a dispersive electrode are matters of controversy. Factors pertinent to tissue injury include adequacy of gel, anatomic placement and orientation of the electrode, edge phenomena, and principles of fabrication (such as proprietary pregelled pads as opposed to metal foil or plate). Additional considerations are the manner or use of the ESU and the adequacy of skin perfusion (related to body temperature, circulatory integrity, and pressure points).

Thermal probes, monitoring electrodes, intravascular wires, or incidental contacts with metal furniture such as operating tables, IV poles, or instrument trays may provide better opportunities for return paths for current, particularly when the preferred path is inadequate.

Historical experience suggests that 1 cm^2 for each 1.5 watts of applied power appears to offer a generous margin of safety for most applications using gelled metal plates. Continuing research may establish confidence in the utilization of less generous contact areas in view of modern practices and equipment.

The subject of contact size of the dispersive electrode continues to be investigated. The issue becomes more complex as the number of devices connected to the patient increases (i.e., as the number of possible alternative paths for current to flow increases). Techniques such as thermography have been used to quantitatively study skin temperature rise at the dispersive electrode and other sites. These studies indicate that maximum heating takes place along the edges of the electrode, particularly the edge of the dispersive electrode closest to the active electrode.

2-3.3.1.1 Burns from Inadequate Dispersive Electrode Contact.   Inadequate contact with a dispersive electrode can result from:

(a) Electrode area too small for application.

(b) Electrode not in adequate contact with tissue.

(c) Electrode insulated from the skin by interposition of bedding, clothing, or other unintended material.

With the advent of a multitude of configurations and designs (e.g., pregelled, electrically conductive adhesive, capacitively coupled, and combinations), and since each type presents application requirements peculiar to its design, the manufacturers' instructions should be carefully read and followed.

Electrode paste reduces impedance of the contact, but it does not ensure good contact. Thus, care should be used when electrodes are first applied. They should also be checked periodically during long procedures.

A variety of pregelled electrodes are commercially available. However, their advantage of convenience may be nullified if they are opened and exposed to the air for too long before they are used; or, if by manufacturer error, insufficient gel has been provided; or, if by careless handling, the gel is removed.

Capacitively coupled electrodes do not use conductive gel. However, instructions must be followed carefully to ensure good electrical contact.

When electrosurgical equipment is brought into use after the start of an operating procedure and after the patient has been draped, extreme care is necessary in the placement and attachment of the dispersive electrode to be sure that proper contact is made directly with the skin and that there is no intervening insulating material. Electrode paste is useful to reduce the impedance of the contact between the electrode and the patient's skin. In a prolonged procedure, this should be checked periodically to ensure that the paste has not dried up.

It should be recognized that while a dispersive electrode may be making proper and sufficient contact with a patient at the beginning of an operation, conditions requiring repositioning of the patient may arise. This repositioning may reduce or completely eliminate contact with the electrode, and burns may result. Electrode placement must be checked whenever the patient is moved.

2-3.3.1.2 Burns from Uneven Electrode Contact. Pressure points caused by bony protuberances or irregularities in electrode surface can concentrate current flow with resulting excessive temperature rise. Loose skin overhanging the edges of the electrode, or areas pinched by sliding a plate beneath the patient without lifting the patient sufficiently contribute to the burn hazard. (*See Figure 2-3.3.1.2.*)

Heat is generated at the dispersive electrode contact, but it normally is carried away by the circulation of blood under the skin, so that the temperature rise is small. However, at pressure points or after prolonged pressure, the blood flow may be impeded, so that adequate cooling is not obtained. Skin and subcutaneous tissue blood flow may be altered by body temperature, anesthetic agents, and other drugs used during surgery. The effect may vary with the patient's age and clinical condition. The significance of these factors is not always fully understood.

2-3.3.1.3 Burns at Unintended Current Paths with Various Types of Electrosurgical Units.
Normally, the current from the active electrode flows through the patient to the dispersive electrode and then back to the generator via the dispersive cable as shown in Figure 2-3.3.1.3. If other paths are available, the current will divide among the several paths.

The effect of alternate paths will vary depending on the type of electrosurgical unit employed.

(a) *Electrosurgical Unit with a Grounded Dispersive Electrode and No Dispersive Cable Continuity Monitor.* Normally the high-frequency current will flow as shown in Figure 2-3.3.1.3. If the dispersive cable is broken and the unit is activated, then the current may flow through unintended ground paths as shown in Figures 2-3.3.1.3(a)(1) and (2).

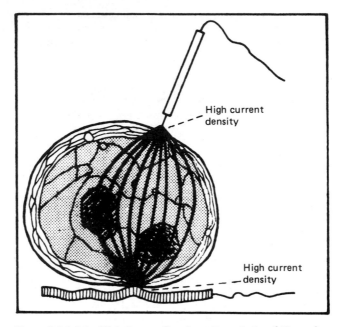

Figure 2-3.3.1.2   High Current Density at Irregularity of Electrode.

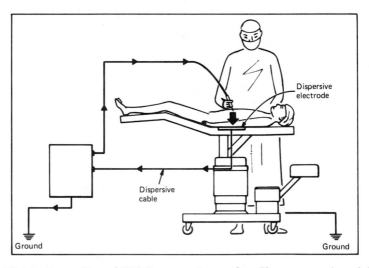

Figure 2-3.3.1.3   Correct Flow of High-Frequency Current from Electrosurgery through Tissue to Dispersive Electrode and Patient Cord back to Generator.

(b) *Electrosurgical Unit with a Grounded Dispersive Electrode and a Dispersive Cable Continuity Monitor.*   If an electrosurgical unit has a dispersive cable monitor, the break in the dispersive cable shown in Figure 2-3.3.1.3(a)(1) can be detected, and the machine inactivated.

(c) *Electrosurgical Unit with an RF Isolated Output Circuit (Floating Output).*   Because RF isolation is inherently imperfect, stray RF currents (leakage currents) can flow from the electrodes

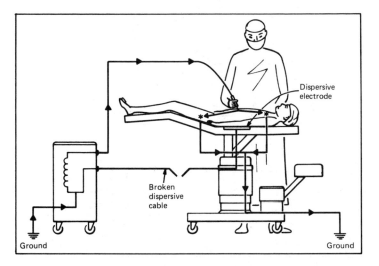

Figure 2-3.3.1.3(a)(1) Alternate Return Paths to Ground when Normal Return Path through Patient Cord is Broken.

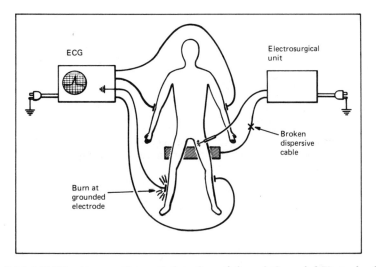

Figure 2-3.3.1.3(a)(2) Alternate Return Path to Ground through Grounded Electrode of ECG.

to any grounded conductor contacting the patient as shown in Figure 2-3.3.1.3(c). This stray RF current is greatest when the unit is activated with the active electrode not in contact with the patient.

Care should be taken not to activate these types of ESUs until the active electrode is about to contact the patient. Conversely, activation should be terminated as soon as possible after removing the active electrode.

2-3.3.1.4 Dispersive Cable Monitoring Circuits. The incorporation of a monitoring circuit will warn of a broken dispersive electrode cable. However, the monitoring circuit does not ensure

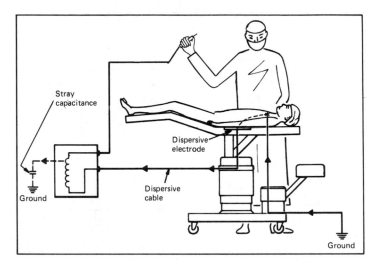

Figure 2-3.3.1.3(c)   Stray Current Flow from an RF Isolated Electrosurgical Unit.

that the dispersive electrode contact with the body is adequate, and may lead to a false sense of security on the part of the surgeon or his/her attendant.

To ensure alarm with broken cable but with alternate ground paths as shown in Figure 2-3.3.1.3(a)(1), the dispersive cable monitor should alarm if the series resistance [R in Figure 2-3.3.1.4(a)] exceeds 150 ohms.

NOTE: The monitoring current may produce interference on an ECG display.

If an electrosurgical unit has its dispersive cable connected as shown in Figure 2-3.3.1.4(b), with a capacitor between it and ground, then the dispersive cable monitor circuit will not respond to an alternate ground path.

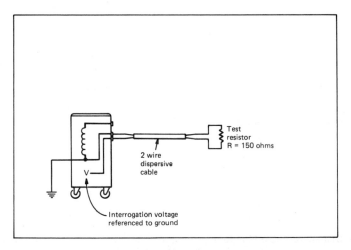

Figure 2-3.3.1.4(a)   Trip-Out Resistance R.

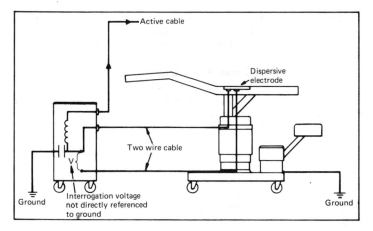

Figure 2-3.3.1.4(b)   Electrosurgical Unit with a DC Isolated Patient Plate.

Whether or not a monitoring circuit is provided, the method of attachment of the dispersive electrode should be such that the cable connector cannot be readily disconnected accidentally. A clip-on type of connection may be used only if it meets this criterion.

2-3.3.1.5 Other Causes of Burns at Unintended Current Paths.   These may be caused by:

(a) Other electrodes providing direct or capacitance-coupled ground returns. Needle electrodes are often used for ECG or other physiological monitoring procedures. The subcutaneous application of these needles provides good connection to the patient, but their small surfaces may produce high-current densities, especially if they are near the operating site. They should be used with great care when electrosurgery is employed. (*See Section 2-7 of this annex.*)

(b) Proximity of high-frequency leads to other wires, causing capacitive or inductive coupling, with resultant current in electrodes attached to the patient.

2-3.3.2 Diathermy.   Radio-frequency diathermy may induce currents that cause excessive heating in metal devices in the dielectric field (e.g., bone pins, dental fillings, metal sutures, implanted electrodes and leads), producing burns in the adjacent tissue and jeopardizing the tolerance of the metal in the tissues. The magnetic field of inductive diathermy may cause eddy currents that produce a similar effect in implanted metals.

2-3.4 Low-Frequency Shocks (60 Hz).

2-3.4.1 General.   Depending on the type of electrosurgical unit employed, the dispersive electrode may present a direct or low-impedance ground path for a fault current emanating from other equipment connected to the patient. These can be classified as:

(a) An electrosurgical unit with a grounded dispersive electrode which provides a direct path for low-frequency current.

(b) An RF grounded (low-frequency isolated) electrosurgical unit with capacitance between the electrodes and ground will provide isolation from low-frequency currents inversely proportional to the value of the capacitor (i.e., the smaller the capacitor, the better the low-frequency isolation).

2-3.4.2 Equipment Faults. Insulation failure or loose wiring in power-operated devices used for surgery, such as bone saws and dye injectors, or monitoring equipment such as an ECG can result in high voltage being applied to the patient through contact with the device.

2-3.4.3 Equipment Not Isolated from Power Lines. Low-voltage power sources of older design, which use an autotransformer, do not provide isolation from the main power lines. Contact of the patient with the frame or other exposed conductive surfaces of the device may apply full-line voltage to a grounded patient. This is often true of power sources for resectoscope lights, electrocautery units, stimulators, and other low-voltage devices commonly used in conjunction with electrosurgery, particularly in urology. Low-voltage equipment should not be used unless provided with an isolated power supply or used with an isolated power distribution system.

Isolated power systems may not be found in all anesthetizing locations. It should thus be made certain that older, lower-voltage power sources do indeed have an isolating transformer (not an autotransformer) if an anesthetizing location does not have an isolated power system.

2-3.4.4 Rectified Modulation. A peculiar hazard exists in electrosurgical equipment where the high-frequency energy is modulated at low frequencies, as in the coagulating mode. The contact between the active electrode and the tissue may demodulate the high-frequency current, generating power frequency components. If a low-impedance path is present through the apparatus and ground back to the patient, hazardous current levels may be generated. Thus, the application of what is believed to be solely high-frequency current may also be the application of dangerous low-frequency currents.

2-3.5 Explosion and Fire.

2-3.5.1 General. Since electrosurgery operates on the basis of tissue destruction by high-frequency arcs, it must be used with great caution when flammable anesthetic, disinfecting, or cleaning agents are employed. If the medical procedure requires the simultaneous use of electrosurgery and flammable agents, the responsible surgeon must be fully aware of the risks he or she is taking. (*See Section 12-4.1, "Anesthetizing Locations," in the requirements portion of this standard.*)

2-3.5.2 Explosions in Hollow Organs. The intestines, especially the colon, may contain flammable mixtures of hydrogen, hydrogen sulfide, methane, and oxygen. These gases are readily ignited and may burn explosively and disrupt organs. Hence, special precautions are necessary in surgery on the colon and paracolonic tissue. During laparoscopy, the abdominal cavity should be filled with a nonflammable gas, such as CO_2. When fulguration is done through a sigmoidoscope, an indwelling suction device is used to remove flammable gases. Explosive mixtures of hydrogen and oxygen form by electrolysis of electrolyte solutions used to distend the bladder during fulguration or resection. Isomolar solutions of crystalloids are used to avoid this complication.

In a large portion of the population of the United States, methane is a normal constituent of flatulent gas. It is prudent to assume it is present in all cases, and appropriate measures must be taken before the use of electrosurgery. Measures include evacuation, filling the colon with nonflammable gas, or clamping.

2-3.5.3 Explosions During Operations on Head, Neck, Oropharynx, and in Body Cavities. Flammable mixtures of anesthetic agents may persist in the exhaled air of patients for long periods, and such mixtures may persist in hollow viscera and body cavities. Electrosurgical equipment should not be used for operations on the head, neck, oropharynx, or body cavities during or following the administration of a flammable anesthetizing agent.

2-3.5.4 Ignition of Combustibles in Mouth or Oropharynx during Oxygen Administration.
A hot needle or blade can ignite combustibles such as dry sponges, lubricants on endotracheal tubes, or the endotracheal tube itself. In the presence of an oxygen-enriched atmosphere, a major conflagration can occur, resulting in severe burns to the mouth, oropharynx, or the respiratory tract. Wet sponges are employed when electrosurgery is contemplated in the mouth or oropharynx. It is necessary to exercise care to ensure that the blade, needle, or hot metal particles do not contact the endotracheal tube. It is not advisable to use lubricants in these circumstances. (*See NFPA 53M, Fire Hazards in Oxygen-Enriched Atmospheres, for details.*)

NOTE: Nitrous oxide will dissociate with heat to produce an oxygen-enriched atmosphere that readily supports combustion.

2-3.5.5 Fire from Flammable Germicides and Defatting Agents.
The vapors from flammable solutions of disinfecting agents, or fat solvents left on the skin or saturating the drapes, may persist for long periods and may be ignited by the arc that occurs when a high-frequency electrode contacts tissue. Nonflammable germicides or detergents should be used when the use of electrosurgery is contemplated.

2-3.6 Complications of Electrosurgery.

2-3.6.1 General.
Electrosurgery provides a method of cutting and hemostasis. It is an adjunct rather than a substitute for the scalpel, scissors, and hemostatic ligature. It always results in some tissue destruction and affects cells beyond the point of contact. Unless precautions are taken, electrosurgery may be followed by the complications of impaired tissue healing, enhanced risk of infection, surface burns, and explosion. It is effective in cutting muscle and in obtaining hemostasis of small or moderately sized blood vessels. It is also effective in excising and dissecting malignant lesions when primary healing is not important.

2-3.6.2 Tissue Damage.
Electrosurgery always destroys tissue. The damage extends radially from the needle or blade electrode. Too much power, especially damped sinusoidal coagulating currents, results in excessive destruction of tissue. When organs or tissues are isolated, as when on a stretched pedicel, current and heat concentrate in the pedicel and may destroy the circulation. Skin flaps and fascia may be overheated. Contact of the high-frequency electrode with instruments or retractors in the wound can result in accidental burns. Defective or extra-thin gloves may result in burns to the surgeon's fingers.

2-3.6.3 Special Electrosurgical Instruments.
Some surgical techniques require special instrumentation such as a resectoscope for transurethral resections or a laparoscope for tubal ligations. Since it is desired to keep the size of these instruments to a minimum, electrical distances are also minimal. To accomplish this, electrical insulation is used to provide isolation between various portions of these instruments. Complications during surgery may occur for the following reasons:

(a) the instrument has an insufficient amount of insulating material;

(b) the insulation has cracks;

(c) the instrument has a poor grade of insulating material;

(d) the insulation gets wet;

(e) more than normal power settings are required of the electrosurgical unit.

With all electrosurgical instruments the manufacturer's recommendations should be followed. (*See Section 2-7 in this annex.*)

These types of devices in particular, as well as those discussed in 2-3-6.4 below, should be carefully examined for signs of insulation breakdown before each use.

2-3.6.4 Use of Surgical Instruments to Deliver Electrosurgical Current. When electrosurgical current is intentionally delivered through a surgical instrument, insulation may be needed so that only the desired portion of the instrument is exposed. This will preclude undesired contact with the patient or operator.

2-3.7 Direct Current Burns. Some electrosurgical devices utilize low direct currents to interrogate the continuity of two leads in the dispersive electrode cable. The interruption of current may then be used to inhibit the operation of the machine. An alarm system is sometimes activated as well. (*See 2-3.3.1.4.*)

Where the dc voltage is referenced to ground, an inadvertent ground may provide a pathway for small direct currents to flow from the interrogation circuitry through the patient to ground.

The burns that may be produced due to the application of dc voltage are generally not thermal burns, as high-frequency ones are. Rather, they are electrochemical ones, caused by the production of caustic agents at the cathode site and chlorine gas at the anode.

The threshold level of voltage required to support electrolytic burning is close to 3 volts dc. The active electrolytic threshold depends in a complex way on many factors, some of which are electrode material, viscosity of electrolytic medium, and the chemical composition of electrolytic medium.

The amount of caustic and acidic products formed depends on the cumulative amount of current that flows through the electrolytic medium. The longer the current flows, the greater the quantity produced. Tissue fluids are converted chiefly to sodium and potassium hydroxides, and chlorine gas. Saline-soaked pads, jellies, etc., may be rendered caustic.

2-3.8 Nonionizing Radiation Burns and Ignition.

Although these subjects are beyond the scope of this annex, they are included to advise readers of hazards and standards related to these subjects.

2-3.8.1 Radio-Frequency Devices. In electrosurgery or diathermy it is intended to apply significant energy to the tissue of a patient for a desired therapeutic effect. However, the attendant staff may also be subjected to some level of radiant energy. While this hazard is usually insignificant, peculiar circumstances may warrant closer attention. The nature of radio-frequency hazard and recommended levels are addressed in ANSI standard C95.1, *Safety Levels of Electromagnetic Radiation with Respect to Personnel*.

2-3.8.2 Medical Laser Devices. Laser radiation does not present the same type of hazard as lower-frequency electromagnetic energy, nor does it have the ionizing effects of X rays and radioisotopes. However, the concentration of energy in a narrow beam is high enough to destroy tissue or to ignite combustible materials in its path. These issues are addressed in ANSI Z136.1, *Safe Use of Lasers*.

A relatively new entrant into the therapeutic and diagnostic medical appliances field is the laser system. These systems are now being utilized in various medical applications ranging from surgical instruments to pattern refractometer and teletherapy alignment scanning devices used for patient positioning.

The word "laser" is an acronym for Light Amplification by Stimulated Emission of Radiation. Laser systems differ in various ways: their names, active laser mediums, wavelengths generated, power outputs, operating modes, and clinical applications. The unique characteristics of the laser beam, those of being monochromatic and coherent, cause it to produce a very powerful beam. Hazards from the use of laser systems can be grouped as follows: optical radiation (hazards to the eye and skin), fire hazards (especially in an oxygen-enriched environment), chemical hazards, and RF emission hazards affecting other systems placed in close proximity to the laser system. Laser systems are classified into four control groups according to their output power and, thus, risk.

Electrical accidents (without injury), accidental shock of personnel working with lasers, and electrocutions and fires in operating rooms have been reported (*Safety With Lasers and Other Optical Sources*, David Sliney and Myron Wolbarsht, Plenum Press, New York, 1982; personal experiences and interviews by members of Subcommittee on High-Frequency Electricity). Thus, it is important to permit only trained professionals to use and maintain laser systems. The extremely high energies and voltages present in the power supplies of many lasers require institutions to establish and practice hazard-control policies and procedures. All precautionary labels and warning devices should be visible and operational, respectively.

Suggested safety measures for laser systems used in the operating theater should include the following:

1. An institutional Laser Safety Committee should be established to help set policies and procedures.

2. Before their first use, laser systems should be properly registered and calibrated.

3. Surgeons and other operating room (O.R.) personnel should be trained in, and thus be familiar with, the guidelines of laser radiation safety as outlined by respective state agencies.

4. Signs should be posted on O.R. door(s) indicating when lasers are in use in the room. No one should enter or exit an O.R. when a laser is actually being used.

5. O.R. personnel should be aware that the laser beam, though invisible for most systems, can ignite flammable or combustible materials; inflict third degree burns; and be reflected off shining metal or glass surfaces, causing severe eye injuries.

6. O.R. personnel should be aware that the visible He-Ne laser system aiming beam can also cause eye injuries.

7. Safety glasses are to be worn by *everyone* in the O.R. The glasses may be plastic or glass and should have sideguards.

8. The patient's eyes must be covered with moist eye pads.

9. A laser surgeon and his assistant must have attended a laser course prior to attempting laser surgery. In addition, the surgeon must have satisfied all the requirements for laser surgery privileges as set out by the Laser Safety Committee of the particular institution.

10. Lasers should not be used with or around alcohol preps and ether, or other flammable anesthetic gases.

11. Laser systems should be locked when not in use. Access keys should be kept by one person, preferably an O.R. nurse specifically in charge of the O.R. where the laser system is used.

12. An inhouse qualified person should be trained to troubleshoot minor problems with laser systems, e.g., problems involved with gas flow gauges, water temperature, mirror adjustments, miscroscope and the miscrosled, etc. The laser system must be maintained in accordance to the manufacturer guidelines and checked prior to *each* operation.

13. Ideally, only *one footpedal* should be used for a laser system.

14. During laser surgery, nonreflective or blackened retractors and other instruments are to be used since the laser beam may reflect off shiny instruments.

15. The laser system must be put on standby whenever the surgeon is performing a nonlaser maneuver (such as suturing, etc.). After all laser procedures are accomplished for an individual case, the laser system must be turned off *immediately* (the surgeon should provide the signal).

16. Flame-retardant drapes and surgical gowns must be used. In addition, the patient's skin that is not involved with surgery is to be protected, such as by saline-soaked gauze or towels.

17. The patient's breathing circuit and oxygen hoses should be well protected. One method used is covering them with aluminum foil and towels.

Site preparation for laser system installation is critical since most laser systems require special utilities. For example, electrical specifications may include a 3-phase, 208-VAC, 50-ampere service. Water requirements may include a minimum flow rate of 4 gal/min. at 50 psi, with an input temperature of not higher than 60°F and water conductivity of less than 100 micro ohms.

Since a loss of circulating water can cause system overheating problems, it is a good practice to connect the water pump to a circuit on the essential electrial system. This is especially important if the electrical power distribution for the laser system is supplied by a circuit on the essential electrical system. If the water pump is not on one of these circuits, the laser system would be operated without its needed cooling medium if the facility lost its normal power source. A sample site installation is pictured in Figure 50 on the next page.

In summary, practioners who use laser systems should be aware of two unique safety-related laser issues. One is that laser energy can travel over distances. The other is that the effect of laser radiation on tissue ranges from absorption, coagulation, and vaporization in the short term, to photochemical effect in the long term. As a result of these two factors, it is important for staff to control not only the area immediately around the laser instrument itself, but also the total environment where the system is being used. If both fire hazard and optical radiation are closely controlled, laser systems will provide the medical community with their benefits in an accident-free environment.

2-4 Equipment Safety Measures.

2-4.1 General.

2-4.1.1 Equipment Requirements. Special requirements for anesthetizing locations are discussed in Section 12-4.1, "Anesthetizing Locations," in the requirements portion of this standard. Additional considerations outlined in this section are primarily performance recommendations which may be implemented in the manner indicated or by other equivalent methods.

The general electrical safety requirements of Chapter 7, "Electrical Equipment," apply to high-frequency equipment. In particular, when not activated, such high-frequency equipment must meet the patient lead leakage current requirements. In large, high-power equipment, it may be difficult to meet the chassis

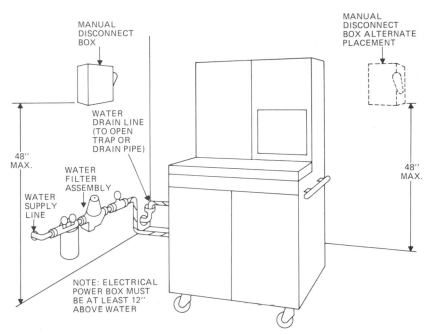

Figure 50   One type of installation for a laser system.

leakage current limits; as a result, isolation transformers, redundant grounds, or other special techniques may be necessary.

2-4.1.2 Applicability. These recommendations apply to the high-frequency equipment itself to reduce its potential as a source of radio-frequency interference, burns, shock, and explosion. Recommendations are also made relating to other associated electrical appliances to make them less susceptible to malfunction in the presence of the high-frequency apparatus.

2-4.2 High-Frequency Apparatus.

2-4.2.1 Input Power Circuits. Input power circuits may be provided with low-pass filters, electrostatically shielded isolation transformers, or other means for preventing the injection of high-frequency energy into the power lines. The use of a simple capacitive low-pass filter may introduce excessive line-to-ground leakage, which must be taken into account.

2-4.2.2 Output Circuits. High-frequency output circuits should be provided with isolation, high-pass filters, or other means to isolate these circuits from low-frequency voltages and rectified currents that may be produced in the patient circuit.

Exception: Specialized low-power equipment such as a neurosurgical lesion generator, where precise control is important, may have the return (dispersive) electrode directly connected to ground.

Isolated outputs are desirable practice for protection against 60-Hz electric shock. In some circumstances, however, the effective operation of devices individually or in combination may dictate connection, by the user, of a dispersive electrode to an equipment grounding conductor or to another grounding point. Such grounding will defeat any radio-frequency isolation existing in the electrosurgical unit.

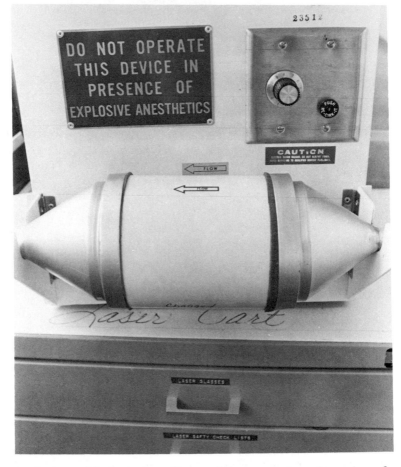

Figure 51   Device used for laser system. Note restriction to operations where only nonflammable inhalation anesthetics are used.

NOTE: In electrosurgery, low-frequency or faradic currents may result from a rectification phenomenon occurring between the active electrode and body tissue during arcing. These low-frequency currents may constitute an electric shock hazard to the patient, as discussed in Section 2-3.4.

While precise RF control can be achieved in several ways, direct connection to ground has many operational advantages. Since the devices identified in the exception are used only briefly during an operation, when the electrosurgical unit is not in use, the Committee considered this Exception acceptable.

2-4.2.3 Dispersive Cable Continuity Monitor.

2-4.2.3.1   In electrosurgical apparatus, a monitor circuit may be incorporated to indicate that the connection to the dispersive electrode is intact. This monitor should not utilize currents that could be a shock or burn hazard to the patient or that could interfere with other instruments.

2-4.2.3.2 It is preferable that the dispersive cable continuity monitor also indicate that the plate is in contact with the patient, but this should not result in increased hazard to the patient or surgeon.

2-4.2.3.3 There should be a suitable caution notice against defeat of the dispersive cable continuity-monitoring circuit. This could take the form of a label on the apparatus itself and explanatory material in the operating manual.

2-4.2.4 Foot Switches.

2-4.2.4.1 Electrically powered foot switches for use in flammable anesthetizing locations are to be explosionproof or approved as intrinsically safe, as required by Section 12-4.1, "Anesthetizing Locations," in the requirements portion of this standard.

2-4.2.4.2 All foot switches should be provided with features to prevent accidental operation to a degree consistent with the need for facility of operation.

2-4.2.5 Power-Supply Cord.

2-4.2.5.1 The power-supply cord for high-frequency equipment should incorporate a separate grounding conductor connected to the grounding contact in the attachment cap (plug).

2-4.2.5.2 Where a detachable power supply cord set is used, the design of the connectors at the instrument end should prevent accidental disconnection.

2-4.2.6 FCC Regulations.

2-4.2.6.1 Shortwave diathermy is to meet all requirements of Part 18, "Industrial, Scientific and Medical Service," of the *Rules and Regulations of the Federal Communications Commission. (See Section 2-9, "References," in this annex.)*

2-4.2.6.2 The power line filter must prevent the 13.56-MHz or 27.12-MHz energy from feeding back into the power line.

2-4.3 Protection of Associated Apparatus.

2-4.3.1 Input Power Circuits. The introduction of high-frequency energy into patient monitors or other apparatus by inductive coupling or radiation to the power supply cord, or by conduction on the power supply lines, should be minimized. Low-pass filters or shielding in the power input circuits of equipment may introduce excessive leakage paths from line to ground, in which case they should not be used.

2-4.3.2 Signal Input Circuits.

2-4.3.2.1 Low-pass filters may be incorporated in the signal input circuits of patient monitoring equipment to limit the flow of high-frequency currents from body electrodes to the equipment. Since the attenuation of the higher frequencies may be achieved by providing a low-impedance path to ground, such filters can increase the possibility of burns where small electrodes are used.

2-4.3.2.2 Isolation of input circuits from high-frequency signals may be accomplished by automatically disconnecting the input terminals when the high-frequency device is energized.

2-4.3.2.3 Short-circuiting of input terminals may be effective in protecting signal input circuits but care should be taken that a low-resistance path is not provided for the high-frequency currents.

2-4.3.3 Patient Monitoring Electrodes.

2-4.3.3.1 High-frequency current densities at a monitoring, electrode-to-skin interface can be reduced by the use of a large surfaced electrode. Needle electrodes normally should not be employed during an electrosurgical procedure, but if this mode of monitoring is judged necessary it should be done with extreme care.

2-4.3.3.2 In the application of inductive diathermy, remote placement of patient monitoring electrodes may eliminate high-frequency burns.

2-4.3.3.3 Where possible, all physiological monitoring circuits with conductive contacts of small surface area on or in the body should present a high impedance to the passage of high-frequency current between the contacts and ground.

2-4.3.4 Cardiac Pacemakers. Cardiac pacemakers, particularly external pacemakers of the demand type, may be susceptible to interference. Their input circuits require careful design to minimize these effects.

2-4.3.5 Low-Voltage Electrical Devices.

2-4.3.5.1 Low-voltage power sources for endoscopy illuminators and other devices should incorporate transformers with isolated secondary circuits so that there is no possibility of patient contact with the primary power source.

2-4.3.5.2 Exposed metal parts of line-operated low-voltage sources should be kept to a minimum. The chassis and exposed metal parts likely to become energized, if any, should be connected to ground through a third wire in the power supply cord or protected by double insulation when no grounding conductor is used. Low-voltage sources for devices that should have this protection include resectoscopes, stimulators, pumps, and photographic equipment. Small exposed surfaces not likely to come energized, particularly those that contact the patient, should not be grounded.

2-4.3.5.3 A particular problem exists with resectoscopes used in conjunction with electrosurgical apparatus for urological procedures. These devices often have small clearances and insulation resulting in capacitively coupled RF currents. Repeated use may damage the insulation and expose the operator and patient to high-frequency burns. These devices should be designed to withstand high RF voltages in addition to low voltages used for illumination.

The patient is not the only one who may receive a burn from either defective equipment or changes occurring in the active or dispersive electrode during an operation. The surgeon may be burned as well.

Care of the apparatus may be of particular concern because more operative procedures are being performed in walk-in clinics without full support from an operating room ancillary staff.

2-5 Administration and Maintenance.

2-5.1 Responsibility.

2-5.1.1 Administration. Responsibility for the maintenance of safe conditions surrounding the use of high-frequency equipment falls mutually upon the governing body of the health care facility, the administration, the physicians using the equipment, and all personnel concerned with the application of the equipment to the patient.

Given the litigious climate that exists in the United States today and the hazards surrounding the use of high-frequency equipment, everyone associated with its use shares the responsibility for its safe use. Burns and other problems allegedly associated with the use of high-frequency apparatus are some of the most common bases for liability litigation.

2-5.1.2 Medical Staff. It is important that the organized medical staff of the health care facility adopt regulations and practices with respect to the use of anesthetics and electrical devices in the presence of high-frequency energy, and jointly with the facility authorities set up requirements for training physicians, nurses, and other personnel who may be involved in the procurement, application, use, or maintenance of equipment used in conjunction with high-frequency equipment.

2-5.1.3 Qualifications for Use of Electrosurgery. No physician should attempt electrosurgery unless he or she is first adept with the scalpel and hemostat. Except for endoscopic surgery or when excising malignancy, sharp dissection provides safer surgery with more predictable wound healing.

The physician who chooses electrosurgery should know how to adjust the electrosurgical unit at his or her disposal. The physician is responsible for the proper placement of the dispersive electrode and the selection of the mode of attaching other electronic equipment to the patient.

2-5.2 Personnel, Training, and Clearance.

2-5.2.1 Qualifications for Use of High-Frequency Equipment. All personnel concerned with the application of high-frequency equipment, including surgeons, nurses, operating room technicians, and orderlies, should be fully cognizant of the potential hazards associated with its use, as outlined in Section 2-3 of this annex.

Surgical lasers, as an example, are inherently very hazardous if misused. Therefore, personnel must be specifically qualified in the use of these devices. As these devices are also sensitive to mechanical disturbances, such as misalignment of the aiming and power beams, ancillary staff must be instructed in their safe handling. As applicable, the recommendations contained in this section for electrosurgical devices apply to laser systems as well.

2-5.2.2 Instruction Manuals. A complete instruction manual for each model of apparatus should be conveniently available for reference at the location of use (*see 2-5.3.2*).

2-5.2.3 Operating Instructions on Apparatus. Information necessary for the safe use of the apparatus, in the form of condensed operating instructions, should be visibly and permanently displayed on, or attached to, the appliance itself.

2-5.2.4 Qualifications for Use of Monitoring Equipment in Presence of High-Frequency Currents. All personnel concerned with the application of monitoring or auxiliary apparatus that may be used in the same area as the high-frequency apparatus, or that may be in contact with the patient to whom high-frequency power is applied, should be fully cognizant of the hazards presented by that equipment in the presence of high-frequency energy.

2-5.3 Maintenance.

2-5.3.1 Periodic Maintenance. For the continued safe operation of high-frequency apparatus, a schedule of periodic preventive maintenance should be established. It is the responsibility of the health care facility to see that this program is effective. Because of the complex nature of this apparatus and associated electrical equipment, repairs should be made by qualified service personnel. Service may be provided by a competent internal engineering group, the manufacturer, or other reliable agency.

2-5.3.2 Instruction Manuals. Proper maintenance, as well as safe use, requires that the manufacturer provide operator's or user's manuals with all units. These manuals should include operating instructions, maintenance details, and calibration and testing procedures. The manuals should include:

(a) illustrations showing location of controls;

(b) explanation of the function of each control;

(c) illustrations of proper connection to the patient and to other equipment;

(d) step-by-step procedures for proper use of the apparatus;

(e) safety considerations in application and in servicing;

(f) effects of probable malfunction on safety;

(g) difficulties that might be encountered, and cautions to be observed, if the apparatus is used on a patient simultaneously with other electrical appliances;

(h) principles of operation;

(i) functional description of the circuitry;

(j) schematics, wiring diagrams, mechanical layouts, and parts list for the specific unit as shipped;

(k) power requirements, heat dissipation, weight, dimensions, output current, output voltage, and other pertinent data.

The instruction manual may be in two parts: one, primarily operating instructions, addressed to medical personnel; the other, detailed maintenance and repair instructions addressed to technical personnel, except that the separate maintenance manual should include essentially all the information included in the operating manual.

2-5.3.3 Physical Inspection.

2-5.3.3.1 Cables and Electrodes. Connectors, cables, and electrodes should be inspected for damage before each use of the apparatus.

2-5.3.3.2 Mechanical Damage. The apparatus should not be used if examination of the cabinet indicates that it has suffered mechanical damage. Dial markings should be clean and legible. At all times there should be evidence that the apparatus has been protected from liquid and electrolyte contamination.

2-5.3.3.3 Inspection. The governing body should provide training for user personnel and other appropriate personnel to detect externally evident damage. The apparatus should not be used if inspection of the cord, cabinet, switches, knobs, or dials discloses hazardous mechanical damage.

Specific procedures should be developed for reporting and repair of equipment found to be damaged.

2-5.3.4 Electrical Inspection.

2-5.3.4.1 Dispersive Cable Monitor. If the apparatus includes a continuity monitor for the dispersive cable, it should be checked for proper operation before each use of the apparatus.

2-5.3.4.2 Output Power. Provision for periodic measurement of the output power of the apparatus is essential. (*See Section 2-8 in this annex.*)

2-6 The Effects of Electrosurgery on Tissue.

2-6.1 Waveforms. High-frequency electricity applied to tissue through a suitable electrode results in an arc that produces three different effects: dehydration, coagulation, or dissolution (cutting). Pulsed sine waveforms [Figures 2-6.1(a) and 2-6.1(b)] with a low duty cycle are commonly used for dehydration and coagulation; for cutting, continuous undamped sine waveforms [(Figure 2-6.1(c)] are used. If additional hemostasis is required while cutting, modulated [Figure 2-6.1(d)] pulsed sine waveforms are used with a high duty cycle [Figures 2-6.1(e) and 2-6.1(f)]. Some instruments use other related waveforms.

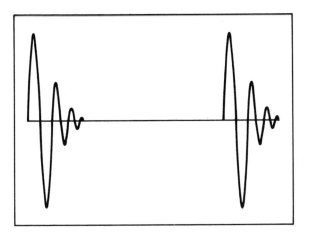

Figure 2-6.1(a)   Typical Spark-Gap Waveform with a Low Duty Cycle.

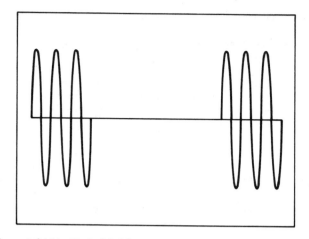

Figure 2-6.1(b)   Typical Solid-State Waveform with a Low Duty Cycle.

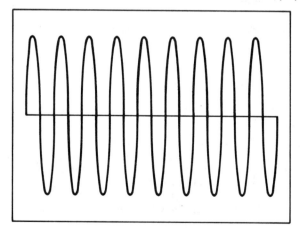

Figure 2-6.1(c)   Continuous Undamped Sine Waveform.

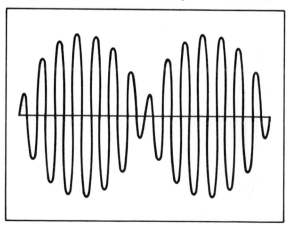

Figure 2-6.1(d)   120-Hz Modulated Sine Waveform also Referred to as a Fully Rectified Waveform.

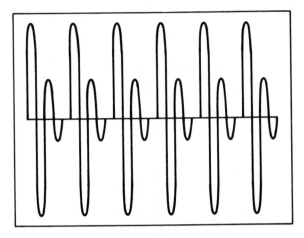

Figure 2-6.1(e)   Typical Spark-gap Waveform with a High Duty Cycle.

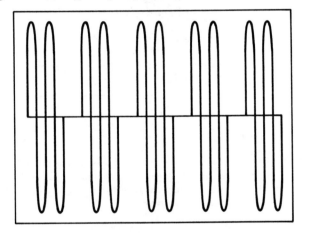

Figure 2-6.1(f)   Typical Solid-State Waveform with a High Duty Cycle.

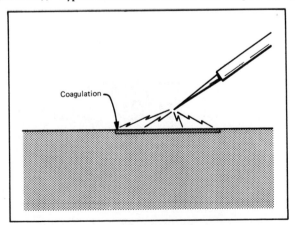

Figure 2-6.2   Fulguration.

2-6.2 Fulguration. This is a technique used for superficial dehydration or coagulation of the tissue. The electrode is held a short distance away and sparks jump to the tissue as shown in Figure 2-6.2 on previous page.

2-6.3 Desiccation. This is a technique used for dehydration and deliberate destruction of tissue. The electrode is placed in contact with the tissue and left in to char the tissue as shown in Figure 2-6.3.

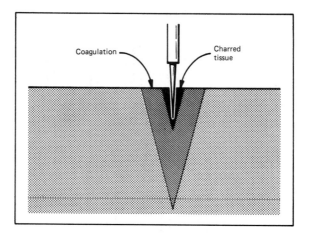

Figure 2-6.3   Desiccation.

2-6.4 Coagulation. This is the sealing of small blood vessels. The electrode is left in contact with the tissue for a period of time until a deep white coagulum is formed (Figure 2-6.4). Time is an important parameter for proper coagulation. Excessive power is of questionable advantage, since it may actually cause the tissue to dissolve.

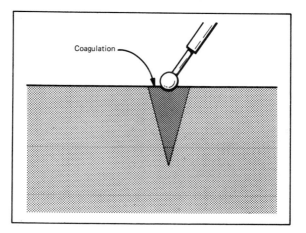

Figure 2-6.4   Coagulation.

2-6.5 Cutting. Dissolution (cutting) occurs when power is increased until arcing persists as the electrode is moved through the tissue. Dissolution of the molecular structure of tissue cells in the path of the arc makes it appear that the tissue is falling apart.

2-6.6 Hemostatic Cutting. Although the above effects of high-frequency current are quite different, they are interrelated. The success of electrosurgery results from an appropriate combination of the pulsed and continuous modes to achieve the desirable degree of cutting and hemostasis. Maximal hemostasis is generally accompanied by complete coagulation of tissue. The depth of coagulation is dependent upon the kind of tissue, the power, the waveforms, the type of electrode, and the cutting speed.

2-6.7 Procedures.

2-6.7.1 Cutting. When primary healing is desired, a small flat blade or needle electrode is used to cut with sufficient power to part tissues cleanly with little hemostasis of small vessels. A wire loop is also used to skive tissue; it is the electrode commonly used in the resectoscope. When cutting with the resectoscope more hemostasis is usually required, and a hemostatic cutting waveform may be required. The effect on tissue of electrosurgery is a function of waveform, time, and energy. Energy transfer and necrosis extend radially from the electrode. Greater power leads to greater energy release and wider areas of cell death. Hence, power should be maintained at the lowest level that achieves the desired results. A large dispersive electrode is essential.

2-6.7.2 Monoterminal Technique. Small or shallow surface growths are often desiccated with a monoterminal technique. A fine needle is inserted into the growth and current is applied for several seconds until a mild blanching of tissue occurs. When small lesions are to be destroyed the capacitance of the body suffices for coupling to ground, and the use of a dispersive electrode is unnecessary.

2-6.7.3 Bipolar Technique. Both conductors of the high-frequency electrical circuit are applied to the tissue by paired electrodes so that the energy is dissipated between and around them. Tissue destruction is restricted to a controllable volume. The depth is controlled by the distance to which the electrodes are inserted into the tissue; the breadth by the space between the two active electrodes. This modality is used for coagulation of larger lesions. Tissue destruction extends beyond the ends of the electrodes to about the same extent as is visible around the electrodes. Bipolar current is also used to coagulate blood vessels. The bleeder is grasped in the forceps and current is applied momentarily to congeal the vessel. A dispersive electrode need not be used with bipolar electrodes.

2-6.8 Spark-Gap versus Solid-State Coagulation. The principal clinical differences between spark-gap and solid-state coagulation lie in the ability of a spark-gap generator to develop higher peak powers, which results in a lower duty cycle for the same average power. This lower-duty-cycle waveform results in less cutting or dissolution in the coagulation mode. In addition, spark-gap generators are able to produce higher open-circuit voltages, which results in a better ability to fulgurate.

2-6.9 Demonstration of Effect on Tissue. The effects of the various modalities can be differentiated by holding a warm, moist, lean piece of beef in the hand while applying high-frequency current in various ways and strengths. The tester's body provides capacitance comparable to that of the patient at low powers. The meat should be placed on the dispersive electrode for higher power. The meat can be cut to reveal the extent of blanching that results from heating by the high-frequency current. Also, the amount of cutting in the coagulation mode between various units can be checked.

2-7 The Use of Electrosurgery.

2-7.1 Care in Electrosurgery.

2-7.2 General. This section is for the indoctrination of operating room nurses, aides, and technicians in the care and use of electrosurgical equipment.

2-7.3 Purpose and Scope. The indications for the use of high-frequency electrosurgery are described elsewhere in this annex. The purpose of this section is to promote safety for the patient and personnel and efficient operation of the unit. The steps detailed below for operating room personnel to follow for preparation, operation, and storage of the electrosurgical unit are designed to meet those ends.

2-7.4 Setting up the Electrosurgical Unit. The following procedures should be followed:

(a) Prior to the use of the electrosurgical unit, verify with anesthesia personnel the type of anesthetic to be used. Check Section 12-4.1, "Anesthetizing Locations," in the requirements portion of this standard, and the operating suite firesafety regulations as necessary.

(b) Prior to sterilization, inspect patient leads and fulgurating and coagulating tips for integrity and cleanliness and bits of tissue or carbon that would interfere with proper function. Test them for electrical continuity. Similarly, check when these leads and tips are removed from the sterile package by the instrument nurse.

(c) Make certain that the electrosurgical unit, together with its dispersive electrode and cable, foot switch and cable, and line cord, is free of dust and "operating room clean."

(d) Locate the electrosurgical unit on the operator's side of the table as far as possible from the anesthesia machine and monitoring equipment. Locate where the power cables, and the active electrode and dispersive electrode leads hang naturally and are not stretched across traffic lanes.

(e) Position the leads and electrodes for physiological monitoring equipment as far as possible from the active cable and active electrode when it is in use.

(f) Utilize as large a dispersive electrode as practical, commensurate with the site of the operation and position and size of the patient. Locate electrode as close as possible to the operative site. If a plate is used, exercise care so that the patient's skin is not traumatized or folded. Provide contact with as great an area of skin as is possible.

NOTE: If contact jelly is used on the dispersive electrode, use the correct type and spread uniformly over the electrode.

(g) Place the dispersive electrode against as large an area of soft tissue of the patient as practical. Avoid direct contact with bony prominences such as those of the scapula, sacrum, ilium, or patella. Check for continued contact during a long procedure, or when changes in patient's position are necessary.

With many medical procedures lasting several hours, checking becomes very important not only to avoid thermal burns, but to avoid chemical burns from the pooling of liquids, ischemic necrosis, and other effects that simulate thermal burns as well. It is common that other lesions are described as thermal burns.

(h) Attach the dispersive electrode securely to its cable, and check its mechanical and electrical integrity prior to preparing the operative site and draping the patient.

NOTE 1: On an electrosurgical unit with a dispersive cable continuity alarm and automatic cutoff switch, follow the manufacturer's directions for preoperative testing.

NOTE 2: On electrosurgical units without a continuity alarm, the hospital should provide an external means for periodically testing the integrity of the dispersive cable.

(i) Do not employ electrosurgery without use of the dispersive electrode, unless the operator specifically orders monoterminal or bipolar techniques and directs the omission of the dispersive electrode.

2-7.5 Operation of the Electrosurgical Unit.

2-7.5.1 It is important that personnel adjusting the electrosurgical unit during the operative procedure be aware that if the surgeon needs currents in excess of those usually required for a comparable procedure, a fault may have developed in the active electrode or dispersive electrode cables.

2-7.5.2 If a flammable anesthetic agent has been employed for induction of inhalation anesthesia, even if followed by a nonflammable agent for maintenance, the electrosurgical unit should not be used on the neck, nasopharynx, and adjacent areas.

2-7.6 Electrosurgery with the Resectoscope.
The resectoscope should be maintained in top working order by periodical inspection and factory service. Discard loop electrodes, sheaths, and cords that show breaks, holes, or other evidence of deterioration.

Safe, effective use of electrosurgery for transurethral resections requires:

(a) the prevention of injury to the patient;

(b) the prevention of injury to the user;

(c) minimizing electrical damage to equipment.

2-7.6.1 Patient Burns.
To minimize burns to the patient:

(a) make sure the conductive surface of the dispersive electrode is in good contact with the skin;

(b) do not make a large increase in power setting for an unexpected weak surgical effect;

(c) keep metal parts of the resectoscope from contact with the patient.

2-7.6.2 Operator Burns.
To minimize burns to the operator:

(a) Check to see that the control dials are set at the operator's minimum preferred settings.

(b) If the operator's hand touches some metal part of the resectoscope, as it often does, it should be with a firm, positive contact. Pinpoint contacts lead to burns even with low currents.

(c) Use only telescopes with fully insulated, nonmetal eyepieces.

(d) Avoid the use of eyeglasses with metal frames.

2-7.6.3 Telescope Use. To minimize damage to the telescope:

(a) Check to see that the loop is not bent. Guard against it touching or coming too close to the telescope.

(b) Avoid activating the electrosurgical unit when the electrode is not touching tissue.

(c) Use the minimum required power.

(d) Start each procedure with a new loop.

(e) Retract the telescope as far as possible to the point where the sheath is just visible under water to maximize the distance between the telescope and loop.

(f) Follow manufacturer's recommendations when using attached lenses.

2-7.7 Putaway and Storage. After using an electrosurgical unit:

(a) Clean cutting and fulgurating tips of all blood, debris, carbon, and tissue prior to storage.

If electrodes, tips, wires, etc., are sterilized after use, the manufacturer's recommendations should be followed to ensure that there is no mechanical or electrical damage, particularly so that insulation is not compromised.

(b) Clean all electrical contacts.

Dirt on contacts can increase their resistance. As a consequence, more power than normal will be necessary when the ESU is used. Since the resistance of dirty contacts may change with current flow, the operation of the device may become erratic.

(c) Coil lead cables neatly and store in appropriate locations.

(d) If the electrosurgical unit is stored other than in an operating room, select a dust-free location within the operating suite.

2-7.8 Repair of the Electrosurgical Unit.

2-7.8.1 The electrosurgical apparatus contains complex circuits which may develop malfunction after a period of operation. Prominently tag any item of electrosurgical equipment that is known or suspected to be defective and do not use again until it has been inspected and repaired by competent personnel.

2-8 Determination of Output Power.

2-8.1 Output Power. An approximate determination of output power of the electrosurgical device may be made using a radio-frequency ammeter of suitable range in series with a resistance. A simplified schema is shown in Figure 2-8.1. Maintain spacing and insulation appropriate to the high frequency and high voltage involved. The power, P, in watts may be calculated by:

$$P = I^2 \times 500$$

where I is the rms current in amperes.

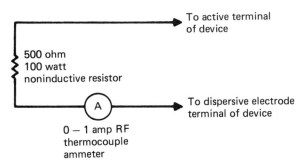

Figure 2-8.1   Simplified Apparatus to Measure Power Output of Electrosurgical Unit.

2-9 Informatory Referenced Publications and Articles in Annex 2.

2-9.1 NFPA Publication.   National Fire Protection Association, Batterymarch Park, Quincy, MA 02269.

NFPA 53M-1985, *Manual on Fire Hazards in Oxygen-Enriched Atmospheres*

2-9.2 ANSI Publications.   American National Standards Institute, 1930 Broadway, New York, NY 10018.

ANSI C95.1-1982, *Safety Levels of Electromagnetic Radiation with Respect to Personnel*

ANSI Z136.1-1980, *Safe Use of Lasers*

2-9.3 U.S. Government Publication.   *Federal Communications Commission Rules and Regulations*, Part 18, "Industrial Scientific, and Medical Service," can be purchased from the Superintendent of Documents, U.S. Government Printing Office, Washington, DC 20025.

2-9.4 Articles on the Subject of High-Frequency Electricity.

Battig, Charles G., M.D. Electrosurgical burn injuries and their prevention. *JAMA*, Vol. 204, No. 12, 17 June 1968.

Billin, A. G. *Electrosurgery in the Operating Room.* Ritter Company, Inc., 400 West Avenue, Rochester, NY 14611.

Conolly, W. B., Hunt, T. K. and Dunphy, J. E. The place of electrosurgery in abdominal operations. *Amer. J. of Surgery*, 118:422-426, (Sept.) 1969.

Dobbie, A. K. The electrical aspects of surgical diathermy. *Biomedical Engineering*, pp. 206-216, May 1969.

Fein, Richard L. Transurethral electrocautery procedures in patients with cardiac pacemakers. *JAMA*, Vol. 202, No. 2, pp. 101-103, 2 October 1967.

Hussey, John L., and Pois, Allen J. Bowel gas explosion. *Amer. J. of Surgery*, 120:103, 1970.

Kovacs, Richard, M.D. *Electrotherapy and Light Therapy,* 6th Edition, Lea and Febiger, Philadelphia, PA, 1950.

Leeming, M. N. Low voltage direct current burns. *JAMA*, 214:1681-1684, 1970.

Mitchell, J. P., and Lomb, G. N. *A Handbook of Surgical Diathermy.* John Wright and Sons Ltd., Bristol, 1966.

Cross-Reference to Previous Individual Documents

*Except Section 1-5, "Definitions," which became a part of Section 2-2 of NFPA 99.

Cross-Reference to Previous Individual Documents

Previous Individual Document	Location in NFPA 99-1984	Location in NFPA 99-1987
NFPA 56E-1982		
Chapter 1* General	Section 11-1	Deleted from NFPA 99, and made a separate document, designated NFPA 99B-1987, *Standard for Hypobaric Facilities*
Chapter 2 Construction and Equipment	Section 11-2	
Chapter 3 Administration and Maintenance	Section 11-3	
Appendix A Explanatory Notes	Appendix A-11	
Appendix B Referenced Publications	Chapter 12, Appendix B	
Appendix C Nature of Hazards	Appendix C-11-1	
Appendix D Suggested Fire Responses	Appendix C-11-2	
Appendix E Pressure Table	Appendix C-11-3	
NFPA 56F-1983		
Chapter 1 General	N/A	Sections 2-2, 4-1, 4-3 and 4-6.2.3
Chapter 2 Sources of Supply	N/A	Section 4-3.1
Chapter 3 Warning Systems	N/A	Sections 4-4.1.1 & 4-5.1
Chapter 4 Piping Systems	N/A	Section 4-4.1.2
Chapter 5 Installation & Testing of Piping Systems	N/A	Sections 4-4.1.4, 4-5.1 and 4-6.3
Chapter 6 Small Systems in Nonhospital-Based Facilities	N/A	Sections 2-2, 4-3, 4-4, 4-5, 4-6
Appendix A Explanatory Material	N/A	Appendix A-4
Appendix B Initial Testing	N/A	Appendix C-4.1
Appendix C Retesting & Maintenance	N/A	Appendix C-4.2
Appendix D Referenced Publications	N/A	Chapter 20 & Appendix B
NFPA 56G-1980		
Chapter 1* Introduction	Section 4-1	Section 13-4.1.1
Chapter 2 Nature of Hazards	Section 4-2	Sections 6-2.2 and 8-2
Chapter 3 Equipment	Section 4-3	Section 13-4.1.2
Chapter 4 Administration and Maintenance	Section 4-4	Sections 4-6 and 8-6
Appendix A Explanatory Statements	Appendix A-4	Appendix A-4
Appendix B Referenced Publications	Chapter 12, Appendix B	Chapter 20 & Appendix B
Appendix C Medical Gas Cylinder Table	Appendix C-4-1	Appendix C-13.1
Appendix D Test of Suggested Requirements	Appendix C-4-2	Appendix C-13.2
NFPA 56HM-1982		
Chapter 1 Introduction	Appendix F-1	Withdrawn entirely
Chapter 2 Scope	Appendix F-2	
Chapter 3 Definitions	Appendix F-3	
Chapter 4 Nature of Hazards	Appendix F-4	
Chapter 5 Equipment	Appendix F-5	
Chapter 6 Operation and Care of Equipment	Appendix F-6	
Appendix A Fire Response	Sub-Appendix F-A	
Appendix B Organizations	Sub-Appendix F-B	
Appendix C Glossary of Respiratory Therapy Terminology	Sub-Appendix F-C	
NFPA 56K-1980		
Chapter 1* Introduction	Section 6-1	Section 4-2.2
Chapter 2 Minimum Flow and Pressure Requirements	Section 6-2	Section 4-9.1
Chapter 3 System Components	Section 6-3	Sections 4-7 and 4-8
Chapter 4 Warning Systems	Section 6-4	Sections 4-8.1.1.5 and 4-8.1.1.6
Chapter 5 Installation of Piping System	Section 6-5	Sections 4-8 and 4-9
Chapter 6 Maintenance and System Protection	Section 6-6	Section 4-10
Appendix A Explanatory Statements	Appendix A-6	Appendix A-4-7 through A-4.10
Appendix B Examples	Appendix C-6-1	Appendix C-4.3
Appendix C Charts and Formulas	Appendix C-6-2	Appendix C-4.4
Appendix D Referenced Publications	Chapter 12, Appendix B	Chapter 20 & Appendix B
Appendix E Metric Conversion	Appendix C-6-3	Appendix C-4.5
Appendix F Derivation of Parameters	Appendix C-6-4	Appendix C-4.6

*Except Section 1-5, "Definitions," which became a part of Section 2-2 of NFPA 99.

Cross-Reference to Previous Individual Documents

Previous Individual Document	Location in NFPA 99-1984	Location in NFPA 99-1987
NFPA 76A-1977		
Chapter 1 General	Section 8-1	Sections 3-1 and 3-2.4
Chapter 2 Glossary	Section 2-2	Section 2-2
Chapter 3 General System Requirements	Section 8-2	Sections 3-3.2, 3-5.1.2, 3-5.2
Chapter 4 EES for Hospitals	Section 8-3	Section 12-3.3.2
Chapter 5 EES for Nursing Homes and Residential Custodial Care Facilities	Section 8-4	Section 13-3.3.2
Chapter 6 EES for Other Health Care Facilities	Section 8-5	Sections 14-3.3.2, 15-3.3.2, 16-3.3.2, 17-3.3.2, 18-3.3.2
Appendix A Typical Hospital Wiring	Appendix C-8-1	Appendix C-3.1
Appendix B Explanatory Statements	Appendix A-8	Appendix A-3
Appendix C Maintenance Guide	Appendix C-8-2	Appendix C-3.2
Appendix D Suggested Listing	Appendix C-8-3	Appendix C-3.3
NFPA 76B-1980		
Chapter 1 Introduction	Section 9-1	Sections 3-1, 3-2, 7-1, 7-2
Chapter 2 Glossary	Section 2-2	Section 2-2
Chapter 3 Electrical Power Systems	Section 9-2	Chapter 3
Chapter 4 Hospital Requirements for PCA Electrical Appliances	Section 9-3	Section 12-3.7.1
Chapter 5 Administration and Maintenance	Section 9-4	Section 7-6
Chapter 6 Requirements for Manufacture of PCA Electrical Appliances	Section 9-5	Section 9-2.1
Appendix A Explanatory Statements	Appendix A-9	Appendixes A-3, A-7, A-9
Appendix B Referenced Publications	Chapter 12, Appendix B	Chapter 20 & Appendix B
NFPA 76C-1980		
Chapter 1 Introduction	Appendix E-1	(Annex 2) 2-1
Chapter 2 High-Frequency Equipment	Appendix E-2	(Annex 2) 2-2
Chapter 3 The Hazard	Appendix E-3	(Annex 2) 2-3
Chapter 4 Equipment Safety Measures	Appendix E-4	(Annex 2) 2-4
Chapter 5 Administration and Maintenance	Appendix E-5	(Annex 2) 2-5
Appendix A Explanatory Statements	Sub-Appendix E-A	(Annex 2) N/A
Appendix B Effects of Electrosurgery	Sub-Appendix E-B	(Annex 2) 2-6
Appendix C Use of Electrosurgery	Sub-Appendix E-C	(Annex 2) 2-7
Appendix D Determination of Output Power	Sub-Appendix E-D	(Annex 2) 2-8
Appendix E Referenced Publications	Sub-Appendix E-E	(Annex 2) 2-9

INDEX